PHILOSOPHY NOW

PHILOSOPHY NOW:

AN INTRODUCTORY READER

THIRD EDITION

PAULA ROTHENBERG STRUHL
William Paterson College

KARSTEN J. STRUHL
College of New Rochelle
LaGuardia Community College

RANDOM HOUSE, NEW YORK

Third Edition

987654321

Copyright © 1972, 1975, 1980 by Random House, Inc.

Library of Congress Cataloging in Publication Data

Struhl, Paula Rothenberg, comp.
  Philosophy now.

  Includes bibliographical references and index.
  1. Philosophy—Collected works.   I. Struhl,
Karsten J., joint comp.   II. Title.
B21.S77   1980   100   79-27491
ISBN 0–394–32354–8

Cover design: Meryl Sussman Levavi

Manufactured in the United States of America

PERMISSIONS ACKNOWLEDGMENTS

Introduction and Chapter One from *An Incomplete Guide to the Future* by Willis W. Harman. Copyright © 1976, 1979 by Willis W. Harman. Reprinted by permission of W. W. Norton & Company, Inc. Originally published as part of *The Portable Stanford,* a series of volumes published by The Stanford Alumni Association, Stanford, California.

"The Great Transition," abridged from *The Meaning of the Twentieth Century* by Kenneth E. Boulding. Copyright © 1964 by Kenneth Ewart Boulding. Reprinted by permission of Harper & Row Publishers, Inc.

"The New Biology: What Price Relieving Man's Estate?" by Leon R. Kass, from *Science,* Vol. 174 (November 19, 1971), pp. 779–788. Copyright © 1971 by the American Association for the Advancement of Science. Reprinted by permission of the author and publisher.

PREFACE

The first edition of *Philosophy Now* appeared in 1971, and along with the revised edition, which appeared in 1975, it was a text for the 1970s. This third edition of *Philosophy Now* looks to the 1980s. Like its predecessors, this edition has grown out of the need in college classrooms for a text that combines a serious consideration of contemporary problems with substantial philosophical materials, both contemporary and traditional. It continues to reflect our belief that what makes material relevant is not so much when it was written as why and how it is read. But the students in our classrooms are different from those we found in them almost a decade ago, and their concerns, along with the concerns of our society in general, have undergone significant changes. This new edition of *Philosophy Now* attempts to reflect and clarify the new issues and the new directions that will characterize the 1980s. Like its predecessors, it has profited enormously from the suggestions and criticisms of countless teachers and students. We hope that each of them will find in this volume a text that is both useful and exciting, and we thank them for taking the time and trouble to help make it so.

PERSONAL ACKNOWLEDGMENTS

A number of friends were good enough to offer suggestions about the collection, and we want to thank each of them.

Paul Shensa bears initial responsibility for turning up the book, and Rick Kennedy, our first editor, continues to receive our thanks for the kind of very human concern he showed for us and the project.

This book, like all books, is the product of the labor of a large number of people. Without the hours spent by the people in the production, design, and permissions departments at Random House and without the work of the people on the editorial staff and those who did the clerical work, this volume could never have been produced. Our thanks go to: Jane Cullen, Acquisitions Editor; Deborah Connor, Manuscript Editor; Meryl Levavi, Art Director; and Della Mancuso, Production Manager.

In addition, we would like to express particular thanks to some of the people whose thoughtful comments on either the second edition of *Philosophy Now* or this manuscript were so helpful to us in preparing this third edition. Our thanks go to Professors: Jeffrey Berger, William F. Cooper, Byron Davidson, Jo-Ann Fuchs, Eli Hirsch, Donald Lewis, Willard M. Miller, Gerald H. Richards, and Neil Rossman.

Finally, Karsten would like to thank Jane Brotman for putting up with his moods, for sharing his struggles and allowing him to share hers, and most of all for being a good and loving friend.

CONTENTS

PHILOSOPHY NOW

INTRODUCTION: WHAT IS PHILOSOPHY?

Students who begin a course in history are prepared to memorize dates and names; students in the sciences expect to learn formulas, lists of bones, and kinds of rocks; students beginning a course in Spanish or French know that they must master a vocabulary and memorize conjugations. But what is it that philosophy demands?

An explanation or definition of philosophy can be offered from a number of perspectives. From one perspective, we might contrast the informal sense of *having* a philosophy with the formal sense of *doing* philosophy as a critical activity; that is, we could contrast philosophy as simply having a set of attitudes and beliefs that are often held uncritically with philosophy as the process of reflecting upon and criticizing our most deeply held beliefs and attitudes. It is this second sense of philosophy—where it becomes a process, a critical activity in which we engage—that will most directly concern us here. But note that the two senses cannot be treated entirely independent of each other, for if we did not have a philosophy in the informal, personal sense, then we could not do philosophy in the critical, reflective sense. On the other hand, *having* a philosophy is not sufficient for *doing* philosophy. There are skills of argumentation to be mastered, techniques of analysis to be employed, and a body of material to be synthesized. In addition, we must understand philosophy's relation to other disciplines and must become clear about what kinds of problems qualify as philosophy and what methods constitute the philosophical process.

TRADITIONAL BRANCHES OF PHILOSOPHY

Historically, philosophical concerns have been treated under the following broad categories: metaphysics, epistemology, value theory, and logic. *Metaphysics,* or the theory of reality, attempts to offer a comprehensive

1

account of all that exists. It is concerned with such problems as the relation of mind to matter, the nature of change, free will, the existence of God, and the belief in personal immortality.

Epistemology, or the theory of knowledge, attempts to discover the necessary limits of what can be known and the basic source (or sources) from which our knowledge of the world can be derived. Traditionally, most of those who have offered answers to these questions can be placed in one of two schools of thought—rationalism or empiricism. The rationalists hold that human reason alone can discover the basic principles of the universe. The empiricists claim that all knowledge is ultimately derived from sense experience, and thus, that our knowledge is necessarily limited to what can be experienced; any attempt to go beyond the bounds of experience is doomed to failure. It should be obvious that there is a necessary relation between metaphysics and epistemology. Our conception of reality depends upon our understanding of what can be known. Conversely, our theory of knowledge depends upon our understanding of ourselves as a part of reality.

The third main branch of philosophy concerns questions of values. It can be subdivided into *ethics,* which is concerned with the nature of the good life, right action, and moral obligation; *aesthetics,* or the theory of art and beauty; and *social and political philosophy,* which attempts to make and understand value judgments concerning society and the state and the individual's relation to them.

Finally, philosophy endeavors to understand the nature of correct thinking. It attempts to formulate precise patterns of sound reasoning, to distinguish between valid and invalid arguments, to show how certain premises entail certain conclusions, and so forth. Thus, the fourth main branch of philosophy, and the one that permeates the thinking of the other three branches, is *logic.* The ability to test arguments for logical consistency, to understand the logical consequences of certain assumptions, and the like are indispensable prerequisites for philosophical discussion.

PHILOSOPHY VERSUS SCIENCE AND RELIGION

Both science and philosophy trace their origin to the speculation by the ancient Greeks on the nature of the universe. For many centuries, thinkers did not make any serious attempt to distinguish between the two disciplines. Even Newton, Kepler, and Galileo were, in their time, referred to as "natural philosophers." Over the years, however, each of the individual sciences broke away and formulated its own special set of problems and procedures. Physics and chemistry, and not metaphysics, were to analyze the origin of the universe and the stuff of which nature was composed. Psychology has taken over much of what was once the material of epistemological theorizing, especially in such areas as memory, perception, and learning theory. More recently, the fields of political science, economics, and sociology have attempted to quantify their procedures and results and thus to transcend mere "theorizing" about government and society. From this perspective, it might seem that the role left to philosophy is little more than to serve as the repository of new sciences yet to emerge; that is, philosophy is left to function as a protoscience. When all the sciences have come into their own, philosophy will have died out.

Although we would agree that philosophy has had and will undoubtedly continue to have an important protoscientific function, it is not the case that this exhausts the unique role that philosophy performs. It has a continuing role in helping the already developed sciences to define their theoretical structures and to refine their procedures. Furthermore, inasmuch as each science works on a restricted range of problems, philosophy is needed to synthesize their individual conclusions into a comprehensive world view. The main point is that philosophical questions are always more comprehensive and fundamental than the questions asked in the sciences. Answers to scientific questions are to be settled by appealing to the evidence, but philosophical questions can never be settled entirely by such appeals. Philosophy may indeed reflect upon the evidence gained in the particular sciences (it always reflects on some evidence, if only the evidence of everyday experience), but it attempts to understand this evidence in a deeper way. Whereas the sciences accept certain facts as given, philosophy's concern is to analyze the way in which those facts are interpreted. Whereas each of the sciences accepts certain basic assumptions about the reality they examine and the utility of their procedures, philosophy questions the assumptions themselves.

It is this willingness to question our basic assumptions that distinguishes philosophy not only from science but also from religion. Religion often attempts to ask ultimate questions, but it does so within a framework of accepted assumptions about the existence of God and of God's relation to the universe. Philosophy cannot take these or any other assumptions for granted. Therefore, when philosophy turns its attention to religion, it assumes the role of an outsider and attempts to critically evaluate the theologian's frame of reference. For example, how to interpret what God told Moses is a theological question, but whether God exists is a philosophical one. This does not mean that theologians do not ask philosophical questions. Clearly they do—but when they do, they act as philosophers and not as theologians. In this respect they are like scientists who can alter their gaze and raise philosophical questions about matter, space and time, determinism, and the like. Just as the writings of Saint Thomas Aquinas are replete with philosophical analysis, so can much of the work of Albert Einstein properly be called philosophy of science.

Over the past several centuries, philosophers have repeatedly announced their intention of arriving at a presuppositionless knowledge—a way of knowing in which no prior commitment would precondition the conclusions that they draw. If such a program were ever fully realized,

philosophy would be clearly demarcated from religion and science. However, there are good reasons to believe that such a program is not possible. Conclusions always follow from certain premises, which themselves
can only be proved if they too follow from other premises. And so on.
The "ultimate" premises from which we begin will always remain un-
proved and, therefore, simply assumed. In the Middle Ages, the Church
provided some of these "ultimate" premises. Today, they are more often
furnished by science. This is another way of saying that while philosophy
can critically reflect on the basic assumptions of a given culture, it must
also begin from these same assumptions. Descartes notwithstanding, the
philosophical activity must always leave certain assumptions in the background while it proceeds to examine others. Thus, in our age—the age
of science—the distinction between philosophy and the sciences is relative, not absolute. To the extent that the assumptions and interpretations
of a scientific discipline are taken at face value and the problem posed
may be resolved by the weight of evidence, the inquiry is scientific. To
the extent that at least some of those assumptions and interpretations are
questioned and the problem posed is not to be resolved strictly by the
weight of the evidence, the enterprise is a philosophical one.

PHILOSOPHY AS CRITICAL INQUIRY

We are now in a position to focus more directly on a central feature of
the philosophical enterprise. It is that *philosophy is a radical critical inquiry into
the fundamental assumptions of any field of inquiry, including itself.* We are not
only able to have a philosophy of science and a philosophy of religion,
but also a philosophy of education, a philosophy of art (aesthetics), of
psychology, of mathematics, of language, and so forth. We can also apply
the critical focus of philosophy to any human concern. There can be a
philosophy of power, of sexuality, freedom, community, revolution—
even a philosophy of sports. Finally, philosophy can reflect upon itself;
that is, we can have a philosophy of philosophy. Philosophy can, then,
examine its own presuppositions, its own commitments. Even such fundamental commitments as those to rationality and truth can be examined
and perhaps challenged.

In all these activities, philosophical inquiry is necessarily radical in
two senses of the term. It is radical in a primary sense, because it attempts
to go "to the roots"—to clarify, question, and evaluate our root assumptions. It is also at least implicitly radical in a political sense; by examining
our basic assumptions, philosophy poses a challenge to the culture within
which those assumptions are rooted. This is most clearly the case when
philosophy asks questions concerning justice, freedom, and equality. But
even when philosophy casts its glance on problems that seem to be
removed from direct social and political concerns, it can permit us to see
the world differently, and hence, to act in a manner other than the one
that is commonly accepted. Philosophical questions never occur in isola-

tion. They are always rooted in the soil of a given culture and reflect back on the assumptions of that culture. Insofar as society's institutions exist through a set of common expectations and assumptions, philosophy is always potentially subversive of the status quo. It was not without cause that the Athenian citizenry condemned Socrates to death.

PHILOSOPHY AS DIALECTICAL

Thus far, our definition has tended to emphasize the kinds of questions philosophy asks. Now we need to understand it as a method. Because philosophy begins with questions about our fundamental assumptions, we must consider how it proceeds to answer those questions. If philosophical problems cannot be resolved exclusively by an appeal to the facts, how does philosophy resolve the problems it raises?

The basic method of all philosophical inquiry is dialectical. Philosophy proceeds through the dialectic of arguments. The term "dialectic," as we are using it here, refers strictly to a process of thinking that has its origins in the work of Plato. It should not be confused with the particular philosophical claim that the dialectical process occurring in thought mirrors the same process occurring in the material world. This latter thesis, held by many Marxists, is known as dialectical materialism. Although the thesis of dialectical materialism is an interesting metaphysical position in its own right, it need not concern us here.

The dialectic process is a dialogue between opposing positions. The dialogue may occur between two persons, or it may occur internally within the same person, in which case we can speak of it as an internal dialogue. In either case, what is important is not the person or persons who happen to hold the opposing positions but the development of thought through a clash of ideas.

Not all dialogue, and certainly not all thought, proceeds in this fashion. Dialogue between individuals may be essentially an emotional interaction. It may even be nonsensical, as in the plays of Becket, Ionesco, and Pinter. Certain phases of thought may consist wholly of a stream of free associations. Dialectical thinking is in sharp contrast to all these. It attempts to evolve a sustained pattern of argument in which the implications of opposing positions are drawn out and interact with each other. As the pattern unfolds, we may find that neither position has full claim to truth and that new considerations and alternatives begin to emerge. At each stage of the dialectic, we gain a deeper insight into the original problem, and this, we might say, brings us closer to the truth. But where do we stop? When have we solved the original philosophical problem? In an absolute sense, it is never fully solved, for there are always more questions to ask, more implications to be seen, more arguments to be challenged. Nonetheless, some tentative answers can be reached; at least certain answers will, in the course of careful argument and analysis, strike most of us as relatively satisfying, while other answers will appear untenable. How does this happen? What considerations can bear on even the tentative resolution of a philosophical problem? In the following, we suggest three general kinds of considerations.

(1) Analysis of concepts. Every philosophical problem involves certain key concepts. But the meanings of these concepts are not always clear. Sometimes problems arise because certain words are imported from one conceptual arena to another, without it being noted that there has been a change of meaning. In such cases, the solution to the problem requires that we relate the various key concepts to one another; in effect, that we attempt to construct a map of the conceptual terrain. For example, the term "freedom" has a number of uses, depending upon its context—it can refer to political freedom, psychological freedom, free will, and so on. Whether or not freedom (in the significant moral sense) is opposed to determinism is, at least in part, a problem for careful conceptual analysis. What is the legitimate range of uses of the terms "freedom," "determinism," and "moral responsibility," and what bearing do the meanings of these terms have on one another? (See section 3.)

The above approach assumes that there are some legitimate (meaningful) uses of the key terms in question. But, what if the concepts themselves are vacuous? For example, some philosophers have held that the claim that God exists is neither true nor false, because the sentence "God exists" is a meaningless utterance (see Antony Flew's "Theology and Falsification" in section 5). Of course, what is meaningful and what is meaningless is itself a philosophical problem.

(2) How well does the resolution of the philosophical problem accord with the totality of our experience? Sometimes, a solution that appears to be conceptually sound and that can account for much of our experience is found, upon more careful reflection, to be inadequate as an explanation of some other aspect of our experience. What do we do then? The temptation is to deny the experience and hold tight to the prior philosophical conclusion, but ultimately, to do this would be to undermine the philosophical enterprise. Dialectical thinking demands a continual reappraisal of even our most well-established theories, for the theory must be applicable to the whole of our experience and not merely to most of it. Of course, experience itself is never simply given as such but always presents itself through the lenses of some type of interpretation. Thus, there is a continual dialectical interplay between new experiences; the interpretation of those new experiences; and further reinterpretations, modifications, or, perhaps, even rejection of the philosophical theory in question. The question we must finally pose is not whether the dialectic can come to a final resting place (that would, indeed, be the death of the dialectic) but whether the last resolution of the problem is an advance over previous resolutions, and whether, at least for the time being, it helps us to link together the various aspects of our experience in a more satisfying manner. To take a previously used example, the problem of

freedom and determinism is not merely a problem for conceptual analysis but also a problem whose resolution demands that we reflect seriously and honestly on the *experience* of freedom in all relevant contexts. We need to examine the kinds of situations in which we experience having control over our actions and our self-development, as opposed to situations in which we experience ourselves being controlled by outside forces, or in which we can come to recognize that we have been under the control of outside forces. We need to arrive at a solution that can adequately account for the entire range of these experiences.

(3) Does the resolution of the philosophical problem provide a useful guide to practice? How well can the philosophical position at which we have arrived be translated into concrete action? What practical consequences follow from holding one philosophical position rather than another? Here, we may focus on the practical consequences for a variety of activities and practices: activities involved in daily living, scientific activity, and political practice. With respect to the last, we can ask what is the ideological function of the philosophical position under consideration? Which social groups does it support? What is its function in maintaining or subverting the existing social order? Which side of the political struggle is it on? Philosophical theories do not have to be directly concerned with political matters in order to have an ideological function. For example, philosophical claims about human nature, although often posited in a politically neutral manner, may turn out, on more careful analysis, to have important political implications (see section 1).

At this point in our discussion, the student who is beginning a course in philosophy may still wonder how concretely does one *do* philosophy? The only complete answer is that one only learns how to do philosophy by doing it. Philosophy is a skill, and like other skills, it requires practice and serious effort. The place to begin is at the beginning, with some interesting philosophical problem. The student will be called upon to read selected articles and to evaluate them critically. Critical evaluation includes not only understanding the author's claim but also focusing clearly on the author's reasons for that claim, considering whether and to what degree those reasons establish the validity of the author's position. The student should not be disappointed if he or she finds this difficult to do at first. Clarifying and evaluating the author's position will be one of the tasks of the ensuing class discussion. The class discussion should also attempt to locate the author's position within the context of the student's previous experience and concerns, and to relate the concerns of both author and student to the overall philosophical development of the course. In short, the student should become a full participant in the dialectic of the philosophical argument.

Finally, after careful reading and critical discussion, the student should be in a position to exhibit his or her philosophical development and skills in written form. Therefore, we will conclude these introductory remarks with some general guidelines that we hope will aid the beginning student in this task.

SOME RULES FOR WRITING A PHILOSOPHY PAPER

1. Philosophy takes positions and, using reasoning, argues for them. Be clear about which position you are defending and which you are opposing.
2. When challenging a philosophical position, be fair to it. Set up the position you oppose with the best possible arguments you can muster in favor of it before you begin to criticize it. Otherwise, you are merely setting up a straw man.
3. The criticism must be relevant to the position under consideration. Stay clear of informal fallacies (ad hominem, appeal to authority, appeal to ignorance, circular argument, genetic fallacy, and so on).
4. Be wary of emotional appeals. You may feel very strongly about the position you uphold or oppose, but the intensity of your feeling does not constitute an argument. Do not engage in long-winded emotional rants. They waste space and, we suspect, are generally used when you don't have a good argument.
5. Your argument should proceed in a logically coherent manner and ought to be at least formally valid (that is, assuming the premises are true, the conclusion should follow).
6. Make clear how your argument applies not only to the opposing position but to how it meets all standard objections.
7. Do not be afraid to state your position forcefully, but at the same time, recognize that you might need to admit certain qualifications and/or reservations.
8. Since philosophy demands close attention to the meaning of the concepts you use, be careful to draw the necessary conceptual distinctions. Make sure you do not use a term equivocally (using the same word to mean two different things within the same argument). Do not be satisfied with metaphors and explanations that "sort of make sense."
9. While sociological, historical, psychological, or literary examples may serve as illustrations of your position, they cannot, in and of themselves, settle philosophical disputes. Philosophical questions are decided not by how much empirical evidence you can bring forth but by whether you can properly interpret, analyze, systematize, and evaluate this evidence.
10. Philosophy requires an intellectual commitment to take nothing for granted—not one's most cherished values, not one's religious outlook, not one's trust in common sense and science, not one's politics. This does not mean that one has to give them up, but it does mean that they must all be examined with a critical eye. This is often a painful process. Nevertheless, it is one that is at the very heart of philosophical inquiry.

PART ONE

ON BEING HUMAN

SECTION ONE

THE NATURE OF HUMAN NATURE

Definition can be as inclusive or exclusive as we want it to be. If we define man as a creature who can fly, then we will have no problem demonstrating that he can. But the definition will have little application to creatures like ourselves.

Man, declared Aristotle, is a rational animal. Other definitions have vied for center stage: man is a language user, a symbolic animal, a toolmaker, the animal who laughs. But in all these definitions, an important philosophical consideration remains untapped. What we want to know is not merely how we differ from other animals, but what the possibilities are for becoming more human. We are concerned less with what we are than with what we could become. We want to know whether we can live together in peace and harmony, if we can enhance the human spirit, if we can avoid a nuclear holocaust. Can man create a new form of life, one that is more worth living? Or is there something so corrupt in human nature that we are doomed to repeat the terrors of the past and present?

These questions lead naturally to several others. First, what is the relation between human nature and society? Is there an immutable human nature that determines social forms—that makes brutality and suffering inevitable—or do social forms determine human nature? Second, does it make sense to explain human behavior in terms of human nature? In what sense is the category useful (or pernicious)? Is there even such a thing as human nature?

Now, let us go back and count the number of times the word "man" appears in these opening paragraphs. Is it surprising that there is no mention of "woman," or do we come to expect that discussions of human nature and humanity will emphasize the male of the species? But the term "man," after all, leaves out half of humanity. This is not merely a question of sexism in our language; it is a reflection of a fundamental social reality. Historically, human nature has been defined as man's nature. Woman, to be fully human, was supposed to aspire to the standards set by men. Thus, we might ask a third question: Is there a man's nature as distinguished from a woman's nature?

Thomas Hobbes
NATURAL MAN

Hobbes's Leviathan, *which first appeared in 1654, and from which this selection comes, was essentially an analysis of political authority. The title for his work was taken from the Old Testament, where the Leviathan was a magnificent crocodile who ruled the animal kingdom and whose scales were so tough that he could not be overthrown by those who, from pride—"the children of Pride"— had attempted to usurp his position. Hobbes, who had witnessed rebellion and civil war in England, was convinced that peace and order required a Leviathanlike state that was similarly impregnable to overthrow and that had absolute authority over its subjects.*

In this selection, Hobbes attempts to ground his political position in an analysis of human nature. Specifically, he argues that human beings are naturally competitive, aggressive, greedy, antisocial, and bellicose and that left to themselves they would be continuously at war with one another. He uses the device of positing a State of Nature, a time before the existence of society or government, so that he can argue for this view. If he had instead described human behavior as it exists within society, he would have been open to the challenge that such behavior is actually a product of society. In subjecting Hobbes's claim to critical scrutiny, one might ask whether his use of the "State of Nature" strengthens or weakens it.

Hobbes's position is often echoed by contemporary conservatives who argue that without "law and order," humanity's "baser" instincts will prevail. Society and the state are then perceived as being in opposition to an essentially "evil" human nature. According to this sentiment, human nature cannot be changed; the best we can do is to create laws by which people's natural greed and aggression can be controlled.

.   .   .

Nature hath made men so equal, in the faculties of the body and mind; as that, though there be found one man sometimes manifestly stronger in body or of quicker mind than another, yet when all is reckoned together, the difference between man and man is not so considerable, as that one man can thereupon claim to himself any benefit, to which another may not pretend as well as he. For as to the strength of body, the weakest has strength enough to kill the strongest, either by secret machination, or by confederacy with others that are in the same danger with himself.

And as to the faculties of the mind—setting aside the arts grounded upon words, and especially that skill of proceeding upon general and infallible rules, called science; which very few have, and but in few things;

as being not a native faculty, born with us; nor attained, as prudence, while we look after somewhat else—I find yet a greater equality amongst men, than that of strength. For prudence is but experience which equal time equally bestows on all men, in those things they equally apply themselves unto. That which may perhaps make such equality incredible, is but a vain conceit of one's own wisdom, which almost all men think they have in a greater degree than the vulgar; that is, than all men but themselves, and a few others, whom by fame, or for concurring with themselves, they approve. For such is the nature of men, that howsoever they may acknowledge many others to be more witty, or more eloquent, or more learned, yet they will hardly believe there be many so wise as themselves; for they see their own wit at hand, and other men's at a distance. But this proveth rather that men are in that point equal, than unequal. For there is not ordinarily a greater sign of the equal distribution of anything, than that every man is contented with his share.

From this equality of ability, ariseth equality of hope in the attaining of our ends. And therefore if any two men desire the same thing, which nevertheless they cannot both enjoy, they become enemies; and in the way to their end, which is principally their own conservation, and sometimes their delectation only, endeavor to destroy, or subdue one another. And from hence it comes to pass that where an invader hath no more to fear than another man's single power; if one plant, sow, build, or possess a convenient seat, others may probably be expected to come prepared with forces united, to dispossess and deprive him, not only of the fruit of his labor, but also of his life or liberty. And the invader again is in the like danger of another.

And from this diffidence of one another, there is no way for any man to secure himself so reasonable as anticipation; that is, by force or wiles to master the persons of all men he can, so long, till he see no other power great enough to endanger him: and this is no more than his own conservation requireth, and is generally allowed. Also because there be some, that taking pleasure in contemplating their own power in the acts of conquest, which they pursue farther than their security requires; if others, that otherwise would be glad to be at ease within modest bounds, should not by invasion increase their power, they would not be able, long time, by standing only on their defense, to subsist. And by consequence, such augmentation of dominion over men being necessary to a man's conservation, it ought to be allowed him.

Again, men have no pleasure, but on the contrary a great deal of grief, in keeping company, where there is no power able to overawe them all. For every man looketh that his companion should value him at the same rate he sets upon himself; and upon all signs of contempt, or undervaluing, naturally endeavors, as far as he dares (which amongst them that have no common power to keep them in quiet, is far enough to make them destroy each other), to extort a greater value from his contemners by damage, and from others by the example.

So that in the nature of man, we find three principal causes of quarrel. First, competition; second, diffidence; thirdly, glory.

The first maketh men invade for gain; the second, for safety; and the third, for reputation. The first use violence to make themselves masters of other men's persons, wives, children, and cattle; the second, to defend them; the third, for trifles, as a word, a smile, a different opinion, and any other sign of undervalue, either direct in their persons, or by reflection in their kindred, their friends, their nation, their profession, or their name.

Hereby it is manifest that during the time men live without a common power to keep them all in awe, they are in that condition which is called war; and such a war as is of every man against every man. For *war* consisteth not in battle only, or the act of fighting, but in a tract of time wherein the will to contend by battle is sufficiently known, and therefore the notion of *time* is to be considered in the nature of war, as it is in the nature of weather. For as the nature of foul weather lieth not in a shower or two of rain, but in an inclination thereto of many days together; so the nature of war consisteth not in actual fighting, but in the known disposition thereto, during all the time there is no assurance to the contrary. All other time is *peace*.

Whatsoever therefore is consequent to a time of war, where every man is enemy to every man; the same is consequent to the time, wherein men live without other security than what their own strength and their own invention shall furnish them withal. In such condition there is no place for industry, because the fruit thereof is uncertain: and consequently no culture of the earth; no navigation, nor use of the commodities that may be imported by sea; no commodious building; no instruments of moving, and removing, such things as require much force; no knowledge of the face of the earth; no account of time; no arts; no letters; no society; and which is worst of all, continual fear, and danger of violent death; and the life of man, solitary, poor, nasty, brutish, and short.

It may seem strange to some man that has not well weighed these things, that nature should thus dissociate, and render men apt to invade and destroy one another; and he may therefore, not trusting to this inference, made from the passions, desire perhaps to have the same confirmed by experience. Let him therefore consider with himself, when taking a journey, he arms himself and seeks to go well accompanied; when going to sleep, he locks his doors; when even in his house he locks his chests; and this when he knows there be laws, and public officers, armed, to revenge all injuries shall be done him: what opinion he has of his fellow-subjects, when he rides armed; of his fellow-citizens, when he locks his doors; and of his children, and servants, when he locks his chest. Does he not there as much accuse mankind by his actions, as I do by my words? But neither of us accuse man's nature in it. The desires, and other passions of man, are in themselves no sin. No more are the actions that proceed from those passions, till they know a law that forbids them: which till laws be made they cannot know; nor can any law be made, till they have agreed upon the person that shall make it.

It may peradventure be thought, there was never such a time nor condition of war as this; and I believe it was never generally so, over all the world: but there are many places where they live so now. For the savage people in many places of America, except the government of small families, the concord whereof dependeth on natural lust, have no government at all; and live at this day in that brutish manner, as I said before. Howsoever, it may be perceived what manner of life there would be, where there were no common power to fear; by the manner of life which men that have formerly lived under a peaceful government, use to degenerate into in a civil war.

But though there had never been any time wherein particular men were in a condition of war one against another; yet in all times, kings, and persons of sovereign authority, because of their independency, are in continual jealousies, and in the state and posture of gladiators; having their weapons pointing, and their eyes fixed on one another; that is, their forts, garrisons, and guns upon the frontiers of their kingdoms; and continual spies upon their neighbors; which is a posture of war. But because they uphold thereby the industry of their subjects, there does not follow from it that misery which accompanies the liberty of particular men.

To this war of every man against every man, this also is consequent: *that nothing can be unjust.* The notions of right and wrong, justice and injustice, have there no place. Where there is no common power, there is no law; where no law, no injustice. Force and fraud are in war the two cardinal virtues. Justice and injustice are none of the faculties neither of the body nor mind. If they were, they might be in a man that were alone in the world, as well as his senses and passions. They are qualities that relate to men in society, not in solitude. It is consequent also to the same condition, that there be no propriety, no dominion, no *mine* and *thine* distinct; but only that to be every man's, that he can get; and for so long as he can keep it. And thus much for the ill condition which man by mere nature is actually placed in; though with a possibility to come out of it, consisting partly in the passions, partly in his reason.

The passions that incline men to peace are fear of death, desire of such things as are necessary to commodious living, and a hope by their industry to obtain them. And reason suggesteth convenient articles of peace, upon which men may be drawn to agreement. These articles are they which otherwise are called the Laws of Nature whereof I shall speak more particularly in the two following chapters.

.   .   .

Arthur Koestler
MAN—ONE OF EVOLUTION'S MISTAKES?

Arthur Koestler begins this essay by pointing to the extraordinary success human beings have had in creating the technology to destroy themselves. The fact of this success, combined with the record of human cruelty and aggression that history offers, would seem to point to a natural tendency toward aggression in human beings. It is at this point that Koestler's analysis becomes intriguing, because although he is in essential agreement with Hobbes over how people behave (they are destructive and aggressive), Koestler locates the causes of such behavior not in an innate aggressiveness but in an opposite tendency.

Actually, Koestler offers several explanations for what he takes to be the uniquely destructive behavior of our species. The most interesting of these is the suggestion that it is our very unselfishness that is at the root of much of our destructive behavior. The flaw in our makeup lies in our need to identify with others, to commit ourselves unselfishly to some social group and to the ideals of that group. Thus, he argues, "the trouble with our species is not an overdose of self-asserting aggression, but an excess of self-transcending devotion."

In reading Koestler, we suggest that the reader ask whether he has answered the questions he set for himself. Does the tendency to identify with certain groups necessarily lead to destructiveness? Why do we identify with some groups rather than with others? Why do we not extend our identification to all of humanity? Why should the group itself be hostile and destructive rather than peaceful and creative?

The crisis of our time can be summed up in a single sentence. From the dawn of consciousness until the middle of our century man had to live with the prospect of his death as an individual; since Hiroshima, mankind as a whole has to live with the prospect of its extinction as a biological species.

This is a radically new prospect; but though the novelty of it will wear off, the prospect will not; it has become a basic and permanent feature of the human condition.

There are periods of incubation before a new idea takes hold of the mind; the Copernican doctrine which so radically downgraded man's status in the universe took nearly a century until it got a hold on European consciousness. The new downgrading of our species to the status of mortality is even more difficult to digest.

But there are signs that in a devious, roundabout way the process of mental assimilation has already started. It is as if the explosions had produced a kind of psychoactive fall-out, particularly in the younger generation, creating such bizarre phenomena as hippies, drop-outs, flower people and barefoot crusaders without a cross. They seem to be products of a kind of mental radiation sickness which causes an intense and distressing experience of meaninglessness, of an existential vacuum which the traditional values of their elders are unable to fill.

These symptoms will probably wear off. Already the word "Hiroshima" has become a historic cliché like the Boston Tea Party or the Storming of the Bastille. Sooner or later we shall return to a state of pseudo-normality. But there is no getting away from the fact that from now onward our species lives on borrowed time. It carries a time-bomb fastened round its neck. We shall have to listen to the sound of its ticking, now louder, now softer, now louder again, for decades and centuries to come, until it either blows up, or we succeed in de-fusing it.

Our concern is with the possibility of such a de-fusing operation. Obviously it requires more than disarmament conferences and appeals to sweet reasonableness. They have always fallen on deaf ears, for the simple reason that man is perhaps a sweet, but certainly not a reasonable being; nor are there any indications that he is in the process of becoming one. On the contrary, the evidence seems to indicate that at some point during the last explosive stages of the biological evolution of *homo sapiens* something has gone wrong; that there is a flaw, some subtle engineering mistake built into our native equipment which would account for the paranoid streak running through our history. This seems to me an unpleasant but plausible hypothesis, which I have developed at some length in a recent book.[1] Evolution has made countless mistakes; Sir Julian Huxley compared it to a maze with an enormous number of blind alleys. For every existing species hundreds must have perished in the past; the fossil record is a wastebasket of the Chief Designer's discarded hypotheses. To the biologist, it should appear by no means unlikely that *homo sapiens,* too, is the victim of some minute error in construction—perhaps in the circuitry of his nervous system—which makes him prone to delusions, and urges him towards self-destruction. But *homo sapiens* has also the unique resourcefulness to transcend biological evolution and to compensate for the shortcomings of his native equipment. He may even have the power to cure that congenitally disordered mental condition which played havoc with his past and now threatens him with extinction. Or, if he cannot cure it, at least to render it harmless.

The first step towards a possible therapy is a correct diagnosis. There have been countless diagnostic attempts, from the Hebrew prophets to contemporary ethologists, but none of them sounded very convincing, because none of them started from the premise that man is an aberrant species, suffering from a biological malfunction, a species-specific disorder of behavior which sets it apart from all other animal species—just as language, science and art sets it apart in a positive sense. The creativity and the pathology of man are two sides of the same medal, coined in the same evolutionary mint. I am going to propose a short list of some of the pathological symptoms reflected in the perverse history of our species,

---

[1] *The Ghost in the Machine* (London and New York, 1968).

and then pass from the symptoms to the presumed causative factors. The list of symptoms has five main headings.

First, at the very beginning of history, we find a striking phenomenon to which anthropologists seem to have paid too little attention: human sacrifice. It was a ubiquitous ritual which persisted from the prehistoric dawn to the peak of pre-Columbian civilizations, and in some parts of the world to the beginning of our century. From the Scandinavian Bog People to the South Sea Islanders, from the Etruscans to the pre-Columbian cultures, these practices arose independently in the most varied civilizations, as manifestations of a perverted logic to which the whole species was apparently prone. It is epitomized in one of the early chapters of Genesis, where Abraham prepares to cut the throat of his son out of sheer love of God. Instead of dismissing the subject as a sinister curiosity of the past, the universality and paranoid character of the ritual should be regarded as symptomatic.

The *second* symptom to be noted is the weakness of the inhibitory forces against the killing of con-specifics, which is virtually unique in the animal kingdom. As Konrad Lorenz[2] has recently emphasized, the predator's act of killing the prey should not be compared to murder, and not even be called aggressive because predator and prey always belong to different species—a hawk killing a field-mouse can hardly be accused of homicide. Competition and conflict between members of the same animal species are settled by ritualized combat or symbolic threat-behavior which ends with the flight or surrender gesture of one of the combatants, and hardly ever involves lethal injury. In man, however, this built-in inhibitory mechanism against killing con-specifics is notably ineffective.

This leads to the *third* symptom: intraspecific warfare in permanence, with its sub-varieties of mass persecution and genocide. The popular confusion between predatory and bellicose behavior tends to obscure the fact that the law of the jungle permits predation on other species, but forbids war within one's own; and that *homo sapiens* is the unique offender against this law (apart from some controversial warlike phenomena among rats and ants).

As the *fourth* symptom I would list the permanent, quasi-schizophrenic split between reason and emotion, between man's critical faculties and his irrational, affect-charged beliefs; I shall return to this point.

Lastly, there is the striking, symptomatic disparity between the growth-curves of technological achievement on the one hand and of ethical behavior on the other; or, to put it differently, between the powers of the intellect when applied to mastering the environment, and its impotence when applied to the conduct of human affairs. In the sixth century B.C. the Greeks embarked on the scientific adventure which, a few months ago, landed us on the moon. That surely is an impressive growth-curve. But the sixth century B.C. also saw the birth of Taoism, Confucianism and Buddhism; the twentieth of Stalinism, Hitlerism and Maoism. There is no

[2]K. Lorenz, *On Aggression* (London and New York, 1966).

discernible curve. We can control the motions of satellites orbiting the distant planets but cannot control the situation in Northern Ireland. Prometheus is reaching out for the stars with an empty grin on his face and a totem-symbol in his hand.

So far we have moved in the realm of facts. When we turn from *symptoms* to *causes*, we must have recourse to more or less speculative hypotheses. I shall mention five such hypotheses, which are interrelated, but pertain to different disciplines, namely, neurophysiology, anthropology, psychology, linguistics, and lastly eschatology.

The neurophysiological hypothesis is derived from the so-called Papez-MacLean theory of emotions. Though still controversial in some respects, it is supported by twenty years of experimental research, and has for quite some years attained textbook respectability. The theory is based on the structural and functional differences between the phylogenetically old and recent parts in the human brain which, when not in acute conflict, seem to lead a kind of agonized coexistence. Dr. MacLean has summed up this state of affairs in a technical paper, but in an unusually picturesque way:

> Man finds himself in the predicament that nature has endowed him essentially with three brains which, despite great differences in structure, must function together and communicate with one another. The oldest of these brains is basically reptilian. The second has been inherited from lower mammals, and the third is a late mammalian development, which . . . has made man peculiarly man. Speaking allegorically of these brains within a brain, we might imagine that when the psychiatrist bids the patient to lie on the couch, he is asking him to stretch out alongside a horse and a crocodile.[3]

Substitute for the individual patient humanity at large, for the clinical couch the stage of history, and you get a dramatized, but essentially truthful, picture. The reptilian and primitive mammalian brain together form the so-called limbic system which, for simplicity's sake, we may call the old brain, as opposed to the neocortex, the specifically human "thinking-cap" which contains the areas responsible for language, and abstract and symbolic thought. The neocortex of the hominids evolved in the last half-million years, from the middle Pleistocene onward, at an explosive speed, which as far as we know is unprecedented in the history of evolution. This brain explosion in the second half of the Pleistocene seems to have followed the type of exponential curve which has recently become so familiar to us—population explosion, knowledge explosion, etc.—and there may be more than a superficial analogy here, as both curves reflect the phenomenon of the acceleration of history on different levels. But explosions do not produce harmonious results. The result in this particular case seems to have been that the newly developing structures did not become properly integrated with the phylogenetically older ones—

an evolutionary blunder which provided rich opportunities for conflict. MacLean coined the term schizophysiology for this precarious state of affairs in our nervous system. He defines it as

> a dichotomy in the function of the phylogenetically old and new cortex that might account for differences between emotional and intellectual behaviour. While our intellectual functions are carried on in the newest and most highly developed part of the brain, our affective behaviour continues to be dominated by a relatively crude and primitive system, by archaic structures in the brain whose fundamental pattern has undergone but little change in the whole course of evolution, from mouse to man.[4]

To put it crudely: evolution has left a few screws loose somewhere between the neocortex and the hypothalamus. The hypothesis that this form of schizophysiology is built into our species could go a long way to explain symptoms Nos. 4 and 5. The delusional streak in our history, the prevalence of passionately held irrational beliefs, would at last become comprehensible and could be expressed in physiological terms. And any condition which can be expressed in physiological terms should ultimately be accessible to remedies.

My next two putative causes of man's predicament are the state of protracted dependence of the neonate on its parents, and the dependence of the earliest carnivorous hominids on the support of their hunting companions against prey faster and more powerful than themselves; a mutual dependence much stronger than that among other primate groups, out of which may have developed tribal solidarity and its later nefarious derivatives. Both factors may have contributed to the process of molding man into the loyal, affectionate and sociable creature which he is; the trouble is that they did it only too well and overshot the mark. The bonds forged by early helplessness and mutual dependence developed into various forms of bondsmanship within the family, clan or tribe. The helplessness of the human infant leaves its lifelong mark; it may be partly responsible for man's ready submission to authority wielded by individuals or groups, his quasi-hypnotic suggestibility by doctrines and commandments, his overwhelming urge to belong, to identify himself with tribe or nation, and, above all, with its system of beliefs. Brainwashing starts in the cradle. (Konrad Lorenz uses the analogy of imprinting, and puts the critical age of receptivity just after puberty. But there are two limitations to this analogy: the susceptibility for imprinting stretches in man from the cradle to the grave; and what he is imprinted with are mostly symbols.)

Now, historically speaking, for the vast majority of mankind, the belief system which they accepted, for which they were prepared to live or die, was not of their own choice, but imposed on them by the hazards of the social environment, just as their tribal or ethnic identity was deter-

[4]*American Journal of Medicine*, Vol. xxv, No. 4, October 1958.

mined by the hazards of birth. Critical reasoning played, if any, only a subordinate part in the process of accepting the imprint of a credo. If the tenets of the credo were too offensive to the critical faculties, schizophysiology provided the modus vivendi which permitted the hostile forces of faith and reason to coexist in a universe of doublethink—to use Orwell's term.

Thus one of the central features of the human predicament is this overwhelming capacity and need for identification with a social group and/or a system of beliefs which is indifferent to reason, indifferent to self-interest and even to the claims of self-preservation. Extreme manifestations of this *self-transcending tendency*—as one might call it—are the hypnotic rapport, a variety of trancelike or ecstatic states, the phenomena of individual and collective suggestibility which dominate life in primitive and not so primitive societies, culminating in mass hysteria in its overt and latent form. One need not march in a crowd to become a victim of crowd-mentality—the true believer is its captive all the time.

We are thus driven to the unfashionable and uncomfortable conclusion that the trouble with our species is not an overdose of self-asserting *aggression,* but an excess of self-transcending *devotion.* Even a cursory glance at history should convince one that individual crimes committed for selfish motives play a quite insignificant role in the human tragedy compared with the numbers massacred in unselfish love of one's tribe, nation, dynasty, church or ideology. The emphasis is on unselfish. Excepting a small minority of mercenary or sadistic disposition, wars are not fought for personal gain, but out of loyalty and devotion to king, country or cause.

Homicide committed for personal reasons is a statistical rarity in all cultures, including our own. Homicide for *un*selfish reasons, at the risk of one's own life, is the dominant phenomenon in history. Even the members of the Mafia feel compelled to rationalize their motives into an ideology, the Cosa Nostra, "our cause."

The theory that wars are caused by pent-up aggressive drives which can find no other outlet has no foundation either in history or in psychology. Anybody who has served in the ranks of an army can testify that aggressive feelings towards the so-called enemy hardly play a part in the dreary routine of waging war: boredom and discomfort, not hatred; homesickness, sex-starvation and longing for peace dominate the mind of the anonymous soldier. The invisible enemy is not an individual on whom aggression could focus; he is not a person but an abstract entity, a common denominator, a collective portrait. Soldiers fight the invisible, impersonal enemy either because they have no other choice, or out of loyalty to king and country, the true religion, the righteous cause. They are motivated not by aggression, but by *devotion.*

I am equally unconvinced by the fashionable theory that the phylogenetic origin of war is to be found in the so-called territorial imperative. The wars of man, with rare exceptions, were not fought for individual ownership of bits of space. The man who goes to war actually *leaves* the home which he is supposed to defend, and engages in combat hundreds or thousands of miles away from it; and what makes him fight is not the biological urge to defend his personal acreage of farmland or meadows, but—to say it once more—his loyalty to symbols and slogans derived from tribal lore, divine commandments or political ideologies. Wars are fought for words. They are motivated not by aggression, but by love.

We have seen on the screen the radiant love of the Führer on the faces of the Hitler Youth. We have seen the same expression on the faces of little Chinese boys reciting the words of the Chairman. They are transfixed with love like monks in ecstasy on religious paintings. The sound of the nation's anthem, the sight of its proud flag, makes you feel part of a wonderfully loving community.

Thus, in opposition to Lorenz, Ardrey and their followers, I would suggest that the trouble with our species is not an excess of aggression, but an excess of devotion. The fanatic is prepared to lay down his life for the object of his worship as the lover is prepared to die for his idol. He is equally prepared to kill anybody who represents a supposed threat to that idol. Here we come to a point of central importance. You watch a film version of the Moor of Venice. You fall in love with Desdemona and identify yourself with Othello (or the other way round); as a result the perfidious Iago makes your blood boil. Yet the psychological process which causes the boiling is quite different from facing a real opponent. You know that the people on the screen are merely actors or rather electronic projections—and anyway the whole situation is no personal concern of yours. The adrenaline in your bloodstream is not produced by a primary biological drive or hypothetical killer-instinct. Your hostility to Iago is a *vicarious* kind of aggressivity, devoid of self-interest and derived from a previous process of empathy and identification. This act of identification must come first; it is the *conditio sine qua non*, the trigger or catalyst of your dislike of Iago. In the same way, the savagery unleashed in primitive forms of warfare is also triggered by a previous act of identification with a social group, its rousing symbols and system of beliefs. It is a depersonalized, quite unselfish kind of savagery, generated by the group-mind, *which is largely indifferent, or even opposed, to the interests of the individuals who constitute the group.* Identification with the group always involves a sacrifice of the individual's critical faculties, and an enhancement of his emotional potential by a kind of group-resonance or positive feedback. Thus the mentality of the group is not the sum of individual minds; it has its own pattern and obeys its own rules which cannot be "reduced" to the rules which govern individual behavior. The individual is not a killer; the group is, and by identifying with it the individual is transformed into a killer. This is the infernal dialectics reflected in our history. The egotism of the group feeds on the altruism of its members; the savagery of the group feeds on the devotion of its members.

All this points to the conclusion that the predicament of man is not caused by the aggressivity of the individual, but by the dialectics of group-

formation; by man's irresistible urge to identify with the group and espouse its beliefs enthusiastically and uncritically. He has a peculiar
capacity—and need—to become emotionally committed to beliefs which
are impervious to reasoning, indifferent to self-interest and even to the
claims of self-preservation. Waddington has called man a belief-accepting
animal. He is as susceptible to being imprinted with slogans and symbols
as he is to infectious diseases. Thus one of the main pathogenic factors
is hyperdependence combined with suggestibility. If science could find a
way to make us immune against suggestibility, half the battle for survival
would be won. And this does not seem to be an impossible target.

The next item in this inventory of the possible causes of man's
predicament is language. Let me repeat: wars are fought for words. They
are man's most deadly weapon. The words of Adolf Hitler were more
effective agents of destruction than thermonuclear bombs. Long before
the printing press and the other mass media were invented, the fervent
words of the prophet Mohammed released an emotive chain-reaction,
whose blast shook the world from Central Asia to the Atlantic coast.
Without words there would be no poetry—and no war. Language is the
main source of our superiority over brother animal—and, in view of its
explosive potentials, the main threat to our survival.

Recent field-studies of Japanese monkeys have revealed that different tribes of a species may develop surprisingly different habits—one
might almost say, different cultures. Some tribes have taken to washing
bananas in the river before eating them, others have not. Sometimes
migrating groups of banana-washers meet nonwashers, and the two
groups watch each other's strange behavior with apparent bewilderment.
But unlike the inhabitants of Lilliput, who fought holy crusades over the
question whether eggs should be broken on the broad or pointed end,
the banana-washing monkeys do not go to war with the nonwashers,
because the poor creatures have no language which would enable them
to declare washing an ethical commandment and eating unwashed bananas a deadly heresy.

Obviously, the safest remedy for our ills would be to abolish language. But as a matter of fact, mankind did renounce language long ago
—if by language we mean a universal means of communication for the
whole species. Other species do possess a single system of communication by sign, sound or odor, which is understood by all its members.
Dolphins travel a lot, and when two strangers meet in the ocean they need
no interpreter. The Tower of Babel has remained a valid symbol. According to Margaret Mead, among the two million Aborigines in New Guinea,
750 different languages are spoken in 750 villages, which are at permanent war with one another. Our shrinking planet is split into several
thousand language-groups. Each language acts as a powerful cohesive
force within the group and as an equally powerful divisive force between
groups. Fleming detests Walloon, Maharati hates Gujerati, French Canadian despises Anglo-Saxon, differences in accent mark the boundary
between the upper and lower classes within the same nation.

Thus language appears to be one of the main reasons, perhaps *the* main reason, why the disruptive forces have always been stronger than the cohesive forces in our species. One might even ask whether the term "species" is applicable to man. I have mentioned that Lorenz attributed great importance to the instinct-taboo among animals against the killing of members of their own species; yet it may be argued that Greeks killing Barbarians, Moors killing Christian dogs did not perceive their victims as members of their own species. Aristotle expressly stated that "the slave is totally devoid of any faculty of reasoning"; the term "bar-bar-ous" is imitative of the alien's gibberish or the barking of a dog; honest Nazis believed that Jews were *Untermenschen*—not human but hominid. Men show a much greater variety in physique and behavior than any animal species (except for the domesticated products of selective breeding); and language, instead of counteracting intraspecific tensions and fratricidal tendencies, enhances their virulence. It is a grotesque paradox that we have communication satellites which can make a message visible and audible over the whole planet, but no planetwide language to make it also understandable. It seems even more odd that, except for a few stalwart Esperantists, neither Unesco nor any other international body has made a serious effort to promote a universal lingua franca—as the dolphins have.

The fifth and last pathogenic factor on my list is man's awareness of his mortality, the discovery of death. But one should rather say: its discovery by the intellect, and its rejection by instinct and emotion. We may assume that the inevitability of death was discovered, through inductive inference, by that newly acquired thinking-cap, the human neocortex; but the old brain won't have any of it; emotion rebels against the idea of personal nonexistence. This simultaneous acceptance and refusal of death reflects perhaps the deepest split in man's split mind; it saturated the air with ghosts and demons, invisible presences which at best were inscrutable, but mostly malevolent, and had to be appeased by human sacrifice, by holy wars and the burning of heretics. The paranoid delusions of eternal hell-fire are still with us. Paradise was always an exclusive club, but the gates of hell were open to all.

Yet once more we have to look at both sides of the medal: on one side religious art, architecture and music in the cathedral; on the other, the paranoid delusions of eternal hell-fire, the tortures of the living and the dead.

To sum up, I have listed five conspicuous symptoms of the pathology of man as reflected in the terrible mess we have made, and continue to make, of our history. I have mentioned the ubiquitous rites of sacrifice in the prehistoric dawn; the poverty of instinct-inhibition against the killing of con-specifics: intraspecific warfare in permanence; the schizoid split between rational thinking and irrational beliefs; and lastly the contrast between man's genius in mastering the environment and his moronic conduct of human affairs. It should be noted that each and all of these pathological phenomena are species-specific, that they are uniquely human, not found in any other animal species. It is only logical therefore that in the search for explanations we should concentrate our attention on those characteristics of man which are also exclusively human and not shared by other animals. Speaking in all humility, it seems to me of doubtful value to attempt a diagnosis of man entirely based on analogies with animal behavior—Pavlov's dogs, Skinner's rats, Lorenz's greylag geese, Morris's hairless apes. Such analogies are valid and useful as far as they go. But by the nature of things they cannot go far enough, because they stop short of those exclusively human characteristics—such as language—which are of necessity excluded from the analogy, although they are of decisive importance in determining the behavior of our species. There is no human arrogance involved in saying that dogs, rats, birds and apes do not have a neocortex which has evolved too fast for the good of its possessor; that they do not share the protracted helplessness of the human infant, nor the strong mutual dependence and esprit de corps of the ancestral hunters. Nor the dangerous privilege of using words to coin battle-cries; nor the inductive powers which make men frightened to death by death. These characteristics which I have mentioned as possible causative factors of the human predicament, are all specifically and exclusively human. They contribute to the uniqueness of man and the uniqueness of his tragedy. They combine in the double helix of guilt and anxiety which, like the genetic code, seems to be built into the human condition. They give indeed ample cause for anxiety regarding our future; but then, another unique gift of man is the power to make his anxiety work for him. He may even manage to de-fuse the time-bomb around his neck, once he has understood the mechanisms which make it tick. Biological evolution seems to have come to a standstill since the days of Cro-Magnon man; since we cannot expect in the foreseeable future a beneficial mutation to put things right, our only hope seems to be to supplant biological evolution by new, as yet undreamt of techniques. In my more optimistic moments my split brain suggests that this possibility may not be beyond our reach.

Barrows Dunham
THE MYTH OF HUMAN NATURE

If human nature can be changed, why do so many people cling to the myth that it cannot? In this selection, Barrows Dunham notes that the claim that human nature is unalterable seems always to be made with respect to just those issues that require significant social improvement. Focusing on the myth that human nature is incurably selfish, Dunham argues that what is at issue is not that people always act selfishly (surely there are many cases in which they do not) but that their selfishness occurs when the object of their desires cannot be obtained without causing injury to others. In other words, human desires are not themselves selfish, but people act selfishly when social conditions are such as to

*make them compete for the satisfaction of their desires. Thus, the myth that
human nature is inevitably selfish serves to obscure the role of the social
institutions that promote those conditions and to conceal from view those in
power who profit from those institutions. To hold that human nature is
unalterably selfish places the blame on our "nature" instead of placing it where
it properly belongs, on the exploiters and on the system of exploitation. In our
society, the myth of an unchangeable human nature functions as an apology for
the inequities of capitalism and serves as a dogmatic refusal to consider socialism
as an alternative.*

Concerning the world and all that is in it man has had many strange
opinions, but none more strange than those about himself. From time to
time he has been thought the victim of chance or of fate, the sport of gods
or of demons, the nursling of divinity or of nature, the "rubbish of an
Adam" or evolution's last and fairest animal. He has spun mythical
genealogies and embroidered those that were actual. He has mourned
lost Edens, golden ages, states of nature; and with equal conviction he
has awaited new heavens, new paradises, and new perfections. He has
explored the cosmos, and he has mastered the atom. He has seemed to
know everything except himself.

One reason is that knowledge is manifested in control. If a man
builds a bridge capable of sustaining all sorts of traffic, you will readily
believe that he understands engineering. But evidence of this sort, which
is the living testimony of practice, is singularly absent in social affairs. We
have already had occasion to observe that, however much men may control the physical universe, they exert far less conscious, planned control
over their relations with one another. In these, the most important of all
matters, men seem more ignorant than perhaps they really are.

This seeming ignorance can be found, also, in the anarchic state of
psychological theory. There is no single, reigning doctrine to which psychologists assent, as physicists do to the theory of relativity. On the
contrary, there are various doctrines which compete for acceptance.
Some of them, like the Freudian, hold that human behavior is decisively
conditioned by inborn impulses; others, like the Behaviorist, hold that it
is decisively conditioned by environmental influences. This welter of
opinion suggests that the science is still immature and that its assemblage
and analysis of data is very incomplete.

Immature as psychology may be, there is no reason to suppose that
it will not grow, or that successful generalizations about the data will
never be made. Further study will presumably reveal such generalizations, and an increasing stability in man's social relationships would undoubtedly speed the process. Meanwhile, one must look with some
caution upon all psychological theories, including, I suppose, the one I
shall present in this chapter.

The unsettled state of psychology, however, is favorable to the perpetuation of myths; and the myths, so long as they survive, retard the
progress of the science itself. Men who have their social conclusions

already in mind can borrow freely from what appears to be scientific data, there being no doctrine of sufficient authority to prevent such practices. Moreover, we are all of us men living among men, and our experiences of one another generate, almost unsolicited, certain convictions about human nature. That is to say, we are all of us amateur psychologists, and we bestow upon our views the sort of mystical accuracy which a believer in home remedies opposes to the advice of physicians.

In such a climate illusions multiply, and among them there is, I suppose, none more ubiquitous than the idea that "you can't change human nature." This ancient platitude might long ago have been relegated to a home for superannuated ideas, were it not so constantly useful. It has been voiced by a motley congregation of sinners and saints, rulers and slaves, philosophers, monks, theologians, psychiatrists, journalists, statesmen, and professors. Everyone has said it; many have believed it; few have understood it.

Its uses are multifarious. Is there poverty in the world? That's because men are naturally improvident. Are people unemployed? That's because men are naturally lazy. Are there wars? That's because men are naturally belligerent. Do men cheat, injure, and bankrupt one another in economic competition? That's because men naturally act on the profit motive. Have some men been slaves when others were slaveowners, or serfs when others were kings? That's because they were all born to be so, each in his kind.

Or again: Do we wish to prevent the development of criminals and to rehabilitate those already made? It's no use: you can't change human nature. Do we wish to enact justice and equality among races? It's no use: you can't change human nature. Do we wish to spread the enlightenment of science to all mankind? It's no use: you can't change human stupidity.

Or again, a much more cautious variant: Do we wish to extend the suffrage to millions now without it? Impossible: they must be educated first. Do we wish to abolish the several discriminations against Jews and Negroes? Impossible: people's "attitudes" must be changed first. Do we wish to make decisive improvements in the nature of society? Impossible: men's souls must first be changed, "materialism" giving way to "spirituality."

It may appear that the views in this last category assume the possibility of changing human nature. That appearance, however, is illusory, for the change which is assumed is completely divorced from the social milieu in which alone change can occur. It therefore becomes an abstract conception, floating agreeably in the minds of its possessors.

Take, for example, the disfranchisement of American Negroes. Our imaginary antagonist says that he is democratically fond of Negroes, but that he does not think they should vote until they have been educated. Very well, let us admire his democratic fondness. But the Negroes will not be adequately educated until they have adequate access to schools. They will not have adequate access to schools until there are adequate legislative appropriations. There will be no adequate legislative appropriations until legislators are elected who will really represent the disfranchised. Few such legislators will be elected until the disfranchised are allowed to vote. Thus our friend, in postponing the suffrage, postpones also the education which is supposed to qualify voters for the suffrage. The change he says he desires is one which he has rendered impossible, and cynics may surmise that he never really desired it.

It is easy enough to be an idealist so long as ideals are unrelated to action. Such men, when pressed with arguments or when confronted with the necessity of decision, will retreat into the assertion that there is no real change anyhow, that all we do is to tinker with externals. For the advocacy of impossible change is in fact the advocacy of no change at all. The third of our categories, then, reduces to the other two. These will repay study.

The opinions in the first category undertake to explain certain economic and political arrangements by asserting that men "naturally" act that way. This assertion is more than a simple statement of fact; it is an implicit justification. The point of view is what is hopefully called "realistic," and its holders may discourse largely, if not profoundly, upon the immutable laws which nature or nature's God have fixed in human affairs. The spectacle of planetary motion has always been watched with approval and indeed with awe. Transfer these feelings to a no less inevitable human motion, and you find that even the follies and brutalities of men begin to acquire a cosmic grandeur. The hard-headed realist (I use his own chosen title) gives rein to sentiment and surrenders himself happily to an invincible *status quo.*

The second group of opinions is very much like the first, except that it has abandoned ethics altogether. The proponents of these views disport themselves more blithely, being unencumbered by moral issues. Wars, they will agree, are certainly very bad, and so is starvation. But the question, they will say, is not what you want but what you can have; and, human nature being what it is, you must have wars and starvation. Equality is no doubt very admirable, but unluckily there is the "fact" that some people are inferior to others and cannot possibly be made equal with them.

Here we have the realist who would be an idealist if horse sense were not always neighing in his ear. He agrees fully with every principle found to be noble, by which agreement he assures you that his heart is in the right place, wherever that doubtful position may be determined to be. He does not entertain principles; they entertain him. He combines the pleasures of virtue with the comforts of inaction. One may imagine his happiness.

In all these varieties of opinion and temperament we can now detect a common purpose. That purpose is not the enlightenment of mankind through the radiance of a scientific fact. It is, on the contrary, the prevention of social change through the gloom of a disillusioning fiction. If men can be persuaded that between them and their hearts' desire lies an impassable barrier, they will (so it is thought) cease their struggles after improvement, and content themselves instead with such crumbs as circumstance vouchsafes them. Quieted by such a philosophy, they may work out their brief lives in the knowledge that toil, defeat, death, and all other disasters which beset them beset them naturally.

Now we can observe the bones on which this argument hangs its melancholy flesh. Human nature is said to be unalterable in certain respects, and these respects are such as to prevent any significant improvement in the condition of man. In other words, no matter how glamorous the prospects and persuasive the programs, men will go on acting in the old ways which have brought so much disaster. If such were really the case, then the only sensible thing to do would be to discard the programs and forget the prospects, even though the discarding and the forgetting mean an end to every human hope.

.   .   .

THE INCURABLE SELFISHNESS OF MAN

From Thrasymachus through Machiavelli down to their followers in the present day, a long line of dismal commentators has proclaimed this doctrine in accents of ill-concealed pleasure. Acceptance of it is supposed to be the essence of worldly wisdom and even, theologically speaking, a means of salvation. It seems odd that one should expect to enter heaven upon the assumption that one is a creature of hell; but, unless I misread the authorities, this is precisely what they assert.

At any rate, the term "selfishness" means what is sometimes called man's inhumanity to man, the sacrifice of other people's interests to one's own advantage. The extreme example of this is the form of organized violence which is war. Accordingly, we hear on all sides the assertion that war can never be abolished, because it has its source in the unchangeable nature of man. Let us look at a few expressions of this view:

> Man is a beast of prey. I shall say it again and again . . . Conflict is the original fact of life, is life itself, and not the most pitiful pacifist is able entirely to uproot the pleasure it gives his inmost soul.[1]

> It was in his [Dr. Charles W. Mayo's] opinion absurd to imagine that it would ever be possible to abolish war. War is part of our human inheritance and hence lies beyond our control.[2]

[1]Oswald Spengler: "The Return of the Caesars," *American Mercury,* Vol. 31, p. 137.
[2]John M. Fletcher: "Human Nature and World Peace," *Virginia Quarterly Review,* Vol. 20, p. 351. Mr. Fletcher takes the opposite view.

Nothing done at San Francisco will alter the essential nature of man—
in which are buried the complex causes of war.[3]

Mr. Baldwin proceeded to accept this "fact" with a stoicism worthy
of a military analyst:

The guiding star still shines; it cannot be attained in a century or two.
But it is nevertheless worth struggling forward, pushing on; it would be
worth the effort even if we knew the star was a mirage. Death is an accepted
part of life. Yet death is no cause for despair. The whole philosophy of man
is keyed to the conception of the ultimate triumph of life over death. Why,
then, despair because war recurs?

Why despair? Because in war one's friends get killed, one's children
get killed, and one gets killed oneself. Because everything one has built
may be destroyed. Because it is idiocy to fight one war for the sake of
fighting another later on. If human nature really does inevitably produce
war, let us accept the fact without surrounding it with this comfortless
nonsense.

One may take some encouragement from the fact that Mr. Baldwin
thinks it worth while to chase after mirages. In other words, he thinks that
some illusions are valuable for the entire human race. Now a man who
thinks that some illusions are valuable is a man who will be a little careless
of the distinction between illusion and reality. Perhaps, then, he is deceived about the connection between human nature and war. I think we
shall find that he certainly is, and that Herr Spengler (the converted Nazi)
and Dr. Mayo are deceived also.

I have said that war is an extreme case of man's inhumanity to man.
It is, therefore, a limit to a certain kind of behavior. If we can show that
this kind of behavior is not an essential part of human nature, then the
limiting case will not be an essential part of human nature either. For
example, extreme brilliance would be the limiting case of a burning light.
Then, if it can be shown that the light does not necessarily burn at
all, we can infer that the light does not necessarily have extreme brilliance.

Let us ask ourselves, then, whether everything that men do involves
loss and sacrifice for other people. There is no question that *some* of the
things men do are things which have this effect. But do *all* of them? The
answer is plainly, no. So far as one's personal relations with one's fellows
are concerned, the proportion of such acts is relatively small. On a social
scale the proportion is rather larger; but even here the division of labor,
which is a basic social fact, no matter how competitive the society may be,
is a sort of unconsciously co-operative behavior on behalf of the general
good. A society in which nobody ever did anything for the benefit of

[3]Hanson W. Baldwin: "San Francisco Outlook," *The New York Times,* May 21, 1945,
p. 10.

others would be one in which no division of labor could exist. It would, indeed, hardly be a society at all.

Well, then, we have established the fact that some of the things men do are things which benefit other people, although of course some of the things are not so. We can infer from this that behavior which benefits other people is at least as consistent with human nature as behavior which harms other people. This being true, it is plainly impossible to say that human nature is selfish in the sense that selfishness is present in all human actions.

Nevertheless, granting all this, it might still be true that selfishness exists in human nature side by side with social-mindedness, and that, as such, it is ineradicable. Expressed in concrete terms, such a view would mean that there are some things which men so profoundly need and desire that they will injure other people in order to get them. Apparently there are such things. But before you can predict that men will universally and inevitably commit these injuries for the sake of these gains, you must make one further and very important assumption: you must assume *that the gains are obtainable in no other way.* For if the gains are obtainable in some other way (by co-operation, for instance), what reason have you to suppose that men will not choose it? The only sufficient reason would be that human behavior is always selfish. But we have just established the falsity of that assertion. You have, therefore, no reason at all.

Suppose, now, it is said that all men have desires, that they seek to satisfy these desires, and that in this manner they constantly display an interest in themselves. Undoubtedly they do. No man has any desires except his own, and in satisfying them he may be said to display self-interest. But self-interest is not selfishness. Self-interest is the satisfaction of one's desires; selfishness is the satisfaction of one's desires at the expense of someone else. We may grant that self-interest is an essential part of human nature. I think, indeed, that it is. But we are still very far from being able to infer from this that selfishness is an essential part of human nature. We cannot possibly infer that it is so, unless we assume that all our desires are satisfied at cost to someone else. This concealed assumption, like the one previously discussed, is plainly false. We satisfy our desires in common with other people every day of our lives, and indeed the satisfaction of some of our desires *involves* the satisfaction of other people's. If this were not so, the institution of the meal, for example, would be wholly inconceivable.

Since we have now come to the question of desires, let us ask what it is that human beings may be said generally to want. If we set aside deceptive abstractions like "power," and if we attend to what may be called normal desires, as distinguished from manias and perversions (*i.e.* pathological states), we shall find that men chiefly want food, shelter, clothing, companionship, play, and sexual love. So far as one can tell from introspection into one's own behavior and from observation of other people's, both present and past, these desires are universal and basic. They are, furthermore, necessary conditions for the maintenance of the individual and of the race. It would make sense to say that human nature will always produce behavior in accordance with these desires.

But where is the "inevitable" selfishness? In themselves these desires certainly seem innocent, and at least two of them—companionship and sexual love—are social in their very essence. Upon so bland a substance how can the idea of human depravity be imposed? If such desires are in their own nature evil, then we shall be doing wrong every time we eat or play or put on a suit of clothes. Surely it is obvious that evil cannot exist in the desires themselves, but only in the way they are sometimes satisfied. The point of view which would consider these *desires* evil would be the point of view of a despot whose power is imperiled by the needs of common men. Indeed, it seems probable that precisely this is the social origin of the myth of human selfishness.

Let us recapitulate the argument. We have seen that not all, but only some, of men's acts involve injury to other people and thus merit the adjective "selfish." The selfishness of these acts, however, derives not from the desires which prompted them, but the conditions under which they are performed. But if human nature were inherently selfish, then it would have to be so under any and all conditions. It is so, however, only under some conditions. Human nature, therefore, is not inherently selfish. This argument is a *modus tollens* to the greater glory of the human race.

We can now return to the limiting case from which we started. If, as we see, there is nothing in human nature which necessitates men's injuring one another, then there is nothing in human nature which necessitates war. War can occur under certain conditions, but there is nothing in human nature which renders inevitable the existence of such conditions. As far as human nature is concerned, those conditions need not exist. I think, in fact, that human nature is such that men will one day render such conditions impossible. For, as things now stand, either men will render war impossible or war will render men impossible.

It is worth while to observe, also, that war is far more repugnant to human nature than consistent with it. If war were consistent with human nature in the same sense in which companionship, for example, is consistent with human nature, then war would be a state in which men felt free and at ease. Exactly the reverse, of course, is true. War is in fact so repugnant to normal human behavior that men have to be drafted into it, and all modern armies provide staffs of psychiatrists to care for the psychological ills which war engenders. Happiness is a good test of what conditions are in harmony with human nature, and by that test war must seem to be unnatural indeed.

One thing more remains to be said. The doctrine that human nature is incurably selfish is not just an assertion about a supposed fact; it is also a moral judgment of condemnation. Like other social myths, it contains a fusion (not to say, a confusion) of scientific and moral concepts. We are told not only that men are what they are, but that they are bad, too. Apparently, to see is to disapprove, to know is to condemn. We may wonder, perhaps, how creatures so dyed in villainy were ever able to conceive the moral standards by which they condemn themselves, how sinners so inveterate could ever have thought that they might be improved. But the moral judgment has certain social effects of its own, and these require examination.

If human nature is unalterably selfish, then to the extent that it is so, all men share an equal guilt. "In Adam's fall we sinned all." But if it is true as a fundamental fact that all men are equally guilty, then no man and no group of men can be singled out as especially iniquitous. Furthermore, there is a feeling that one sinner has no right to condemn another. From these conditions two social results follow:

(1) It becomes impossible to identify any one man or any one group of men as the source of social injustice and therefore as a menace to human welfare. Such a man or such a group of men can hide behind the alleged common and equal guilt of all, and thus escape condemnation. The exploiter and the profiteer and the colonial imperialist can say, "I'm only being human." In fact, that is exactly what they do say. The essence of Goering's defense at the Nuremberg trial was that he did exactly what anybody else would have done.

(2) It becomes impossible for any of us to claim the moral right to put an end to injustice. For if it is true that all men are equally sinners and that no sinner is entitled to condemn another, then none of us has the right to condemn profiteers and exploiters and imperialists. I well remember, during the Spanish Civil War, the assertions of the Reverend Mr. A. J. Muste that all nations had been guilty of aggression and that therefore no nation had the right to oppose German and Italian aggression in Spain. Such an argument is paralyzing. If we had taken it as our guide, we should simply have surrendered on high moral grounds to the Axis fascists.

Here, then, I think we have the true social reason for the doctrine of human selfishness. It exists because it has a special function to perform, not because it has any correspondence with fact. It exists because it conceals the men of power and their antisocial behavior. It exists because it robs us of the moral confidence necessary to attack them. It is, therefore, one of many ideological chains fastened upon mankind. Men may commit sins, but they can commit no sin so monstrous as believing themselves to be incurable.

· · ·

HUMAN NATURE AND SOCIAL CHANGE

Besides concealing the misdeeds of rulers, the doctrine that you can't change human nature has a larger purpose: defense of the existing social arrangements. Since these arrangements are, throughout most of the world, capitalist in character, the doctrine undertakes to show that, human nature being what it is, capitalism is the inevitable form of society. If by the term "capitalism" we understand a society in which the land and the means of production are owned and controlled by individual men, whose incentive is profit, then the opposite of such a society would be one in which the land and the means of production are owned and controlled by society, with the incentive, not of profit, but of the simple production of goods. Accordingly, the doctrine that you can't change human nature has, as part of its purpose, the task of showing that, human nature being what it is, socialism is impossible. Here are three examples:

> We believed that personal incentive and private initiative were fundamental to the continuity of progress, and that, whatever safeguards we might have to erect against a few lawless men and a few lawless enterprises, we must not destroy the dynamic that personal incentive and private initiative give to life and enterprise.[4]

> There are only two motives that make human beings work. One of them is the fear of punishment and the other is the hope of reward. Fear of punishment is what drives the slave to toil under the lash of a superior or boss. The hope of profit or reward is the incentive that inspires the efforts of freemen. If you destroy the incentive system, what they call the capitalistic system, the profit system, you destroy the initiative of the American people. Instead of freemen toiling under the glorious inspiration of the hope of reward, we all become the slaves of the state, driven to our tasks by fear of punishment.[5]

> The chief defect of the socialistic method has been clearly demonstrated by the experience of the last few years. It does not take into account human nature, it is therefore outside of reality, in that it will not recognize that the most powerful spring of human activities lies in individual self-interest and that therefore the elimination from the economic field of this interest results in complete paralysis.[6]

Very well. Suppose, now, that we ask the questions: Which is "outside of reality," the Italian Fascist State or the Union of Soviet Socialist Republics? In which is the paralysis complete? Events have dealt very sadly with Rocco's assertions. Indeed, the continuing existence of the Soviet Union is a source of deep perplexity, for by all the reasoning of the best economists it ought to have vanished long ago, as inconsistent with human nature. The theory can now be harmonized with the facts only upon the supposition that the Soviet Union is a capitalist state after all. This supposition is easy enough to test: take a hundred thousand

---

[4]Glenn Frank: "The Outlook for American Institutions," *Vital Speeches*, Vol. 4, p. 52.

[5]From the remarks of the Hon. John Rankin, in the *Congressional Record* for June 17, 1943, p. 5978. Shades of Jeremy Bentham and the "two sovereign masters"! The philosophy of a man who advocated universal suffrage has descended to a man who defends the poll tax.

[6]Alfredo Rocco: "The Political Doctrine of Fascism," a speech delivered at Perugia in 1925. It is reprinted entire in D. O. Wagner's *Social Reformers*, Macmillan, New York, 1939.

dollars with you into the Soviet Union, and see whether you will be permitted to build and equip a factory and to employ workmen. You will not get such permission, and that is exactly the difference between a socialist and a capitalist nation.

Instead of discussing the merits of the two systems, where they might have some reasonable arguments, opponents of the Soviet Union have for years encumbered themselves with the extraordinary paradox of believing socialism to be at one and the same time dangerous and on the verge of collapse. They have invoked the "defensive" aid of boycotts, treaties, and armed intervention against a nation which their own theory demonstrated to be powerless. The theory was internally consistent, for, if socialism were profoundly contrary to human nature, it could establish no industrial system, raise and equip no armies, and achieve no popular support. But the theory turned out to have no correspondence with fact.

What was wrong in the theory was the act of defining human nature narrowly in terms of behavior characteristic of one social system only. The mistake could readily have been avoided, without regard to socialist antipathies, simply by recognizing that human nature had at one time been consistent with feudalism, at an earlier time with chattel slavery, and at a still earlier time with various patriarchal arrangements. There need not even have been an appeal to history: an anthropological survey of societies existing in the contemporary world would have sufficed to show that human nature is consistent with manifold social systems. It may well be that human nature requires incentives, but profit-making is by no means the only one, and, in its strict interpretation, does not even exist for a large part of mankind.

If, then, man has lived under various social systems and has been recognizably the same human animal under them all, it follows that you cannot deduce from human nature what a given social system will be. You can, however, deduce from human nature the fact that there will be social change. For social change occurs precisely because men have universally the same basic needs, and when they find they cannot satisfy those needs within a given social system, they change to another. In the course of these changes men also transform themselves. The primitive warrior has long disappeared, and neither imitation nor cynical jest can reconstitute him in a modern society. The patriarch, the Greek gentleman, the Roman noble, are gone. The medieval knight lies buried with his battle-ax. With each have disappeared—and somewhat to the world's relief—not simply bone and sinew, but a whole way of acting. The modern man does not act as a freeman or slave in a small city-state, nor as a serf or feudal lord. He acts as one who is a citizen of a nation and is about to become a citizen of the world.

Thus, the essence of social man is change. Viewed historically, mankind will appear a vast and shifting multitude, with a lifetime not of seventy years, as individuals may be said to have, but of perhaps 500,000. Its collective history includes the most diverse cultures, civilizations, economic systems, religions, technologies, and philosophies. Among all these there have been manifold interactions, which have constantly transformed them. The Romans conquered the Greek world, only to have their own culture Hellenized. The modern colonization of Africa has imposed changes on the native peoples not always (or indeed often) to their advantage, but the natives may be said to have taken gentle revenge in the influence which their arts have had on European painting and sculpture. The recent vogue of Neo-Thomism shows how the philosophy of one economic system (feudalism) can be made to influence the thinking of another (capitalism).

There is no reason to suppose that the great process which is history will linger forever at its present stage. In our day, indeed, events have attained so formidable a tempo that a single lifetime, if one is lucky enough to prolong it sufficiently, will seem to contain more than there once appeared to be in history itself. The speed of events, however, is not altogether blinding. One can discern something of the direction and flow. One sees especially the common man, the "humble person" (as [one] essayist called him), moved by his very humanity, by the old unalterable need for food and shelter, into the acquisition of new skills, new knowledge, new modes of behavior by which his wants are now to be satisfied. One sees him discovering that when a more co-operative social behavior provides an ampler store, it is folly to persist in a jungle life of senseless competition. This transformation occurs not so much through the charm of abstract ideals as through the concrete needs of human nature and society. Human nature changes in some of its respects because it remains the same in others. The Old Adam is forever new because the New Adam is forever old.

Thus they are lost who placed their hope of personal dominion upon the changelessness of man. Perhaps, having now pursued them to the uttermost syllable, we may address them a final word:

The evil is not that you cannot change human nature. The evil is that human nature cannot change you.

Jean-Paul Sartre
MAN AS SELF-CREATOR

Jean-Paul Sartre is a contemporary French philosopher, playwright, and novelist who is probably the most famous spokesperson for the existentialist movement. The main thesis of Sartre's existentialism is that "existence precedes essence." This means that there is no objective human essence, that humanity does not have within itself any necessary function, God-given or otherwise. From this, it follows that there is nothing that a person necessarily is or has to be. What we are, individually, is the result of our past choices and actions, and each of us will be what we choose to be. Thus, each person must accept total responsibility for what he or she has become and will become. We cannot blame human nature,

*because there is no universal, unchangeable nature shared by all people. In the
course of living our lives, we create our nature.*

*It is important to recognize that although Sartre would agree with Dunham
that the human character is changeable, he would, in another respect, disagree
with him profoundly. For Sartre, "human nature" is not determined by society
any more than it is determined by instinct. Therefore, although changing certain
social conditions may be a good thing in itself, it cannot by itself transform the
human character. Conversely, if Sartre is correct, the pattern of human behavior
can be changed simply by each of us deciding to change it.*

My purpose here is to offer a defence of existentialism against several
reproaches that have been laid against it.

First, it has been reproached as an invitation to people to dwell in
quietism of despair. For if every way to a solution is barred, one would
have to regard any action in this world as entirely ineffective, and one
would arrive finally at a contemplative philosophy. Moreover, since contemplation is a luxury, this would be only another bourgeois philosophy.
This is, especially, the reproach made by the Communists.

From another quarter we are reproached for having underlined all
that is ignominious in the human situation, for depicting what is mean,
sordid or base to the neglect of certain things that possess charm and
beauty and belong to the brighter side of human nature: for example,
according to the Catholic critic, Mlle. Mercier, we forget how an infant
smiles. Both from this side and from the other we are also reproached
for leaving out of account the solidarity of mankind and considering man
in isolation. And this, say the Communists, is because we base our doctrine upon pure subjectivity—upon the Cartesian "I think": which is the
moment in which solitary man attains to himself; a position from which
it is impossible to regain solidarity with other men who exist outside of
the self. The *ego* cannot reach them through the *cogito.*

From the Christian side, we are reproached as people who deny the
reality and seriousness of human affairs. For since we ignore the commandments of God and all values prescribed as eternal, nothing remains
but what is strictly voluntary. Everyone can do what he likes, and will be
incapable, from such a point of view, of condemning either the point of
view or the action of anyone else.

It is to these various reproaches that I shall endeavour to reply
to-day; that is why I have entitled this brief exposition "Existentialism and
Humanism." Many may be surprised at the mention of humanism in this
connection, but we shall try to see in what sense we understand it. In any
case, we can begin by saying that existentialism, in our sense of the word,
is a doctrine that does render human life possible; a doctrine, also, which
affirms that every truth and every action implies both an environment and
a human subjectivity. The essential charge laid against us is, of course,
that of overemphasis upon the evil side of human life. I have lately been
told of a lady who, whenever she lets slip a vulgar expression in a moment
of nervousness, excuses herself by exclaiming, "I believe I am becoming

an existentialist." So it appears that ugliness is being identified with existentialism. That is why some people say we are "naturalistic," and if we are, it is strange to see how much we scandalise and horrify them, for no one seems to be much frightened or humiliated nowadays by what is properly called naturalism. Those who can quite well keep down a novel by Zola such as *La Terre* are sickened as soon as they read an existentialist novel. Those who appeal to the wisdom of the people—which is a sad wisdom—find ours sadder still. And yet, what could be more disillusioned than such sayings as "Charity begins at home" or "Promote a rogue and he'll sue you for damage, knock him down and he'll do you homage"?[1] We all know how many common sayings can be quoted to this effect, and they all mean much the same—that you must not oppose the powers-that-be; that you must not fight against superior force; must not meddle in matters that are above your station. Or that any action not in accordance with some tradition is mere romanticism; or that any undertaking which has not the support of proven experience is foredoomed to frustration; and that since experience has shown men to be invariably inclined to evil, there must be firm rules to restrain them, otherwise we shall have anarchy. It is, however, the people who are forever mouthing these dismal proverbs and, whenever they are told of some more or less repulsive action, say "How like human nature!"—it is these very people, always harping upon realism, who complain that existentialism is too gloomy a view of things. Indeed their excessive protests make me suspect that what is annoying them is not so much our pessimism, but, much more likely, our optimism. For at bottom, what is alarming in the doctrine that I am about to try to explain to you is—is it not?—that it confronts man with a possibility of choice. To verify this, let us review the whole question upon the strictly philosophic level. What, then, is this that we call existentialism?

Most of those who are making use of this word would be highly confused if required to explain its meaning. For since it has become fashionable, people cheerfully declare that this musician or that painter is "existentialist." A columnist in *Clartés* signs himself "The Existentialist," and, indeed, the word is now so loosely applied to so many things that it no longer means anything at all. It would appear that, for the lack of any novel doctrine such as that of surrealism, all those who are eager to join in the latest scandal or movement now seize upon this philosophy in which, however, they can find nothing to their purpose. For in truth this is of all teachings the least scandalous and the most austere: it is intended strictly for technicians and philosophers. All the same, it can easily be defined.

The question is only complicated because there are two kinds of existentialists. There are, on the one hand, the Christians, amongst whom I shall name Jaspers and Gabriel Marcel, both professed Catholics; and

[1] *Oignez vilain il vous plaindra, poignez vilain il vous oindra.*

on the other the existential atheists, amongst whom we must place Heidegger as well as the French existentialists and myself. What they have in common is simply the fact that they believe that *existence* comes before *essence*—or, if you will, that we must begin from the subjective. What exactly do we mean by that?

If one considers an article of manufacture—as, for example, a book or a paper-knife—one sees that it has been made by an artisan who had a conception of it; and he has paid attention, equally, to the conception of a paper-knife and to the pre-existent technique of production which is a part of that conception and is, at bottom, a formula. Thus the paper-knife is at the same time an article producible in a certain manner and one which, on the other hand, serves a definite purpose, for one cannot suppose that a man would produce a paper-knife without knowing what it was for. Let us say, then, of the paper-knife that its essence—that is to say the sum of the formulae and the qualities which made its production and its definition possible—precedes its existence. The presence of such-and-such a paper-knife or book is thus determined before my eyes. Here, then, we are viewing the world from a technical standpoint, and we can say that production precedes existence.

When we think of God as the creator, we are thinking of him, most of the time, as a supernal artisan. Whatever doctrine we may be considering, whether it be a doctrine like that of Descartes, or of Leibnitz himself, we always imply that the will follows, more or less, from the understanding or at least accompanies it, so that when God creates he knows precisely what he is creating. Thus, the conception of man in the mind of God is comparable to that of the paper-knife in the mind of the artisan: God makes man according to a procedure and a conception, exactly as the artisan manufactures a paper-knife, following a definition and a formula. Thus each individual man is the realisation of a certain conception which dwells in the divine understanding. In the philosophic atheism of the eighteenth century, the notion of God is suppressed, but not, for all that, the idea that essence is prior to existence; something of that idea we still find everywhere, in Diderot, in Voltaire and even in Kant. Man possesses a human nature; that "human nature," which is the conception of human being, is found in every man; which means that each man is a particular example of an universal conception, the conception of Man. In Kant, this universality goes so far that the wild man of the woods, man in the state of nature and the bourgeois are all contained in the same definition and have the same fundamental qualities. Here again, the essence of man precedes that historic existence which we confront in experience.

Atheistic existentialism, of which I am a representative, declares with greater consistency that if God does not exist there is at least one being whose existence comes before its essence, a being which exists before it can be defined by any conception of it. That being is man or, as Heidegger has it, the human reality. What do we mean by saying that existence precedes essence? We mean that man first of all exists, encounters himself, surges up in the world—and defines himself afterwards. If man as the existentialist sees him is not definable, it is because to begin with he is nothing. He will not be anything until later, and then he will be what he makes of himself. Thus, there is no human nature, because there is no God to have a conception of it. Man simply is. Not that he is simply what he conceives himself to be, but he is what he wills, and as he conceives himself after already existing—as he wills to be after that leap towards existence. Man is nothing else but that which he makes of himself. That is the first principle of existentialism. And this is what people call its "subjectivity," using the word as a reproach against us. But what do we mean to say by this, but that man is of a greater dignity than a stone or a table? For we mean to say that man primarily exists—that man is, before all else, something which propels itself towards a future and is aware that it is doing so. Man is, indeed, a project which possesses a subjective life, instead of being a kind of moss, or a fungus or a cauliflower. Before that projection of the self nothing exists; not even in the heaven of intelligence: man will only attain existence when he is what he purposes to be. Not, however, what he may wish to be. For what we usually understand by wishing or willing is a conscious decision taken—much more often than not—after we have made ourselves what we are. I may wish to join a party, to write a book or to marry—but in such a case what is usually called my will is probably a manifestation of a prior and more spontaneous decision. If, however, it is true that existence is prior to essence, man is reponsible for what he is. Thus, the first effect of existentialism is that it puts every man in possession of himself as he is, and places the entire responsibility for his existence squarely upon his own shoulders. And, when we say that man is responsible for himself, we do not mean that he is responsible only for his own individuality, but that he is responsible for all men. The word "subjectivism" is to be understood in two senses, and our adversaries play upon only one of them. Subjectivism means, on the one hand, the freedom of the individual subject and, on the other, that man cannot pass beyond human subjectivity. It is the latter which is the deeper meaning of existentialism. When we say that man chooses himself, we do mean that every one of us must choose himself; but by that we also mean that in choosing for himself he chooses for all men. For in effect, of all the actions a man may take in order to create himself as he wills to be, there is not one which is not creative, at the same time, of an image of man such as he believes he ought to be. To choose between this or that is at the same time to affirm the value of that which is chosen; for we are unable ever to choose the worse. What we choose is always the better; and nothing can be better for us unless it is better for all. If, moreover, existence precedes essence and we will to exist at the same time as we fashion our image, that image is valid for all and for the entire epoch in which we find ourselves. Our responsibility is thus much greater than we had supposed, for it concerns mankind as a whole. If I am a worker, for instance, I may choose to join a Christian rather than a

Communist trade union. And if, by that membership, I choose to signify that resignation is, after all, the attitude that best becomes a man, that man's kingdom is not upon this earth, I do not commit myself alone to that view. Resignation is my will for everyone, and my action is, in consequence, a commitment on behalf of all mankind. Or if, to take a more personal case, I decide to marry and to have children, even though this decision proceeds simply from my situation, from my passion or my desire, I am thereby committing not only myself, but humanity as a whole, to the practice of monogamy. I am thus responsible for myself and for all men, and I am creating a certain image of man as I would have him to be. In fashioning myself I fashion man.

This may enable us to understand what is meant by such terms—perhaps a little grandiloquent—as anguish, abandonment and despair. As you will soon see, it is very simple. First, what do we mean by anguish? The existentialist frankly states that man is in anguish. His meaning is as follows—When a man commits himself to anything, fully realising that he is not only choosing what he will be, but is thereby at the same time a legislator deciding for the whole of mankind—in such a moment a man cannot escape from the sense of complete and profound responsibility. There are many, indeed, who show no such anxiety. But we affirm that they are merely disguising their anguish or are in flight from it. Certainly, many people think that in what they are doing they commit no one but themselves to anything: and if you ask them, "What would happen if everyone did so?" they shrug their shoulders and reply, "Everyone does not do so." But in truth, one ought always to ask oneself what would happen if everyone did as one is doing; nor can one escape from that disturbing thought except by a kind of self-deception. The man who lies in self-excuse, by saying "Everyone will not do it" must be ill at ease in his conscience, for the act of lying implies the universal value which it denies. By its very disguise his anguish reveals itself. This is the anguish that Kierkegaard called "the anguish of Abraham." You know the story: An angel commanded Abraham to sacrifice his son: and obedience was obligatory, if it really was an angel who had appeared and said, "Thou, Abraham, shalt sacrifice thy son." But anyone in such a case would wonder, first, whether it was indeed an angel and secondly, whether I am really Abraham. Where are the proofs? A certain mad woman who suffered from hallucinations said that people were telephoning to her, and giving her orders. The doctor asked, "But who is it that speaks to you?" She replied: "He says it is God." And what, indeed, could prove to her that it was God? If an angel appears to me, what is the proof that it is an angel; or, if I hear voices, who can prove that they proceed from heaven and not from hell, or from my own subconsciousness or some pathological condition? Who can prove that they are really addressed to me?

Who, then, can prove that I am the proper person to impose, by my own choice, my conception of man upon mankind? I shall never find any proof whatever; there will be no sign to convince me of it. If a voice speaks to me, it is still I myself who must decide whether the voice is or is not that of an angel. If I regard a certain course of action as good, it is only I who choose to say that it is good and not bad. There is nothing to show that I am Abraham: nevertheless I also am obliged at every instant to perform actions which are examples. Everything happens to every man as though the whole human race had its eyes fixed upon what he is doing and regulated its conduct accordingly. So every man ought to say, "Am I really a man who has the right to act in such a manner that humanity regulates itself by what I do." If a man does not say that, he is dissembling his anguish. Clearly, the anguish with which we are concerned here is not one that could lead to quietism or inaction. It is anguish pure and simple, of the kind well known to all those who have borne responsibilities. When, for instance, a military leader takes upon himself the responsibility for an attack and sends a number of men to their death, he chooses to do it and at bottom he alone chooses. No doubt he acts under a higher command, but its orders, which are more general, require interpretation by him and upon that interpretation depends the life of ten, fourteen or twenty men. In making the decision, he cannot but feel a certain anguish. All leaders know that anguish. It does not prevent their acting, on the contrary it is the very condition of their action, for the action presupposes that there is a plurality of possibilities, and in choosing one of these, they realise that it has value only because it is chosen. Now it is anguish of that kind which existentialism describes, and moreover, as we shall see, makes explicit through direct responsibility towards other men who are concerned. Far from being a screen which could separate us from action, it is a condition of action itself.

And when we speak of "abandonment"—a favourite word of Heidegger—we only mean to say that God does not exist, and that it is necessary to draw the consequences of his absence right to the end. The existentialist is strongly opposed to a certain type of secular moralism which seeks to suppress God at the least possible expense. Towards 1880, when the French professors endeavoured to formulate a secular morality, they said something like this:—God is a useless and costly hypothesis, so we will do without it. However, if we are to have morality, a society and a law-abiding world, it is essential that certain values should be taken seriously; they must have an *à priori* existence ascribed to them. It must be considered obligatory *à priori* to be honest, not to lie, not to beat one's wife, to bring up children and so forth; so we are going to do a little work on this subject, which will enable us to show that these values exist all the same, inscribed in an intelligible heaven although, of course, there is no God. In other words—and this is, I believe, the purport of all that we in France call radicalism—nothing will be changed if God does not exist; we shall re-discover the same norms of honesty, progress and humanity, and we shall have disposed of God as an out-of-date hypothesis which will die away quietly of itself. The existentialist, on the contrary, finds it extremely embarrassing that God does not exist, for there disappears with him all possibility of finding values in an intelligible heaven. There can no longer be any good à *priori*, since there is no infinite and perfect consciousness to think it. It is nowhere written that "the good" exists, that one must be honest or must not lie, since we are now upon the plane where there are only men. Dostoievsky once wrote "If God did not exist, everything would be permitted"; and that, for existentialism, is the starting point. Everything is indeed permitted if God does not exist, and man is in consequence forlorn, for he cannot find anything to depend upon either within or outside himself. He discovers forthwith, that he is without excuse. For if indeed existence precedes essence, one will never be able to explain one's action by reference to a given and specific human nature; in other words, there is no determinism—man is free, man *is* freedom. Nor, on the other hand, if God does not exist, are we provided with any values or commands that could legitimise our behaviour. Thus we have neither behind us, nor before us in a luminous realm of values, any means of justification or excuse. We are left alone, without excuse. That is what I mean when I say that man is condemned to be free. Condemned, because he did not create himself, yet is nevertheless at liberty, and from the moment that he is thrown into this world he is responsible for every-thing he does. The existentialist does not believe in the power of passion. He will never regard a grand passion as a destructive torrent upon which a man is swept into certain actions as by fate, and which, therefore, is an excuse for them. He thinks that man is responsible for his passion. Nei-ther will an existentialist think that a man can find help through some sign being vouchsafed upon earth for his orientation; for he thinks that the man himself interprets the sign as he chooses. He thinks that every man, without any support or help whatever, is condemned at every instant to invent man. As Ponge has written in a very fine article, "Man is the future of man." That is exactly true. Only, if one took this to mean that the future is laid up in Heaven, that God knows what it is, it would be false, for then it would no longer even be a future. If, however, it means that, whatever man may now appear to be, there is a future to be fashioned, a virgin future that awaits him—then it is a true saying. But in the present one is forsaken.

As an example by which you may the better understand this state of abandonment, I will refer to the case of a pupil of mine, who sought me out in the following circumstances. His father was quarrelling with his mother and was also inclined to be a "collaborator"; his elder brother had been killed in the German offensive of 1940 and this young man, with a sentiment somewhat primitive but generous, burned to avenge him. His mother was living alone with him, deeply afflicted by the semi-treason of his father and by the death of her eldest son, and her one consolation was in this young man. But he, at this moment, had the choice between going to England to join the Free French Forces or of staying near his mother and helping her to live. He fully realised that his mother lived only for him and that his disappearance—or perhaps his death—would plunge her into despair. He also realised that, concretely and in fact, every action he performed on his mother's behalf would be sure of effect in the sense of aiding her to live, whereas anything he did in order to go and fight would be an ambiguous action which might vanish like water into sand and serve no purpose. For instance, to set out for England he would have to wait indefinitely in a Spanish camp on the way through Spain; or, on arriving in England or in Algiers he might be put into an office to fill up forms. Consequently, he found himself confronted by two very different modes of action; the one concrete, immediate, but directed towards only one individual; and the other an action addressed to an end infinitely greater, a national collectivity, but for that very reason ambiguous—and it might be frustrated on the way. At the same time, he was hesitating between two kinds of morality; on the one side the morality of sympathy, of personal devotion and, on the other side, a morality of wider scope but of more debatable validity. He had to choose between those two. What could help him to choose? Could the Christian doctrine? No. Christian doctrine says: Act with charity, love your neighbour, deny yourself for others, choose the way which is hardest, and so forth. But which is the harder road? To whom does one owe the more brotherly love, the patriot or the mother? Which is the more useful aim, the general one of fighting in and for the whole community, or the precise aim of helping one particular person to live? Who can give an answer to that à priori? No one. Nor is it given in any ethical scripture. The Kantian ethic says, Never regard another as a means, but always as an end. Very well; if I remain with my mother, I shall be regarding her as the end and not as a means: but by the same token I am in danger of treating as means those who are fighting on my behalf; and the converse is also true, that if I go to the aid of the combatants I shall be treating them as the end at the risk of treating my mother as a means.

If values are uncertain, if they are still too abstract to determine the particular, concrete case under consideration, nothing remains but to trust in our instincts. That is what this young man tried to do; and when I saw him he said, "In the end, it is feeling that counts; the direction in which it is really pushing me is the one I ought to choose. If I feel that I love my mother enough to sacrifice everything else for her—my will to be avenged, all my longings for action and adventure—then I stay with her. If, on the contrary, I feel that my love for her is not enough, I go." But how does one estimate the strength of a feeling? The value of his feeling for his mother was determined precisely by the fact that he was standing by her. I may say that I love a certain friend enough to sacrifice such or such a sum of money for him, but I cannot prove that unless I have done it. I may say, "I love my mother enough to remain with her," if actually I have remained with her. I can only estimate the strength of this affection if I have performed an action by which it is defined and ratified. But if I then appeal to this affection to justify my action, I find myself drawn into a vicious circle.

Moreover, as Gide has very well said, a sentiment which is play-acting and one which is vital are two things that are hardly distinguishable one from another. To decide that I love my mother by staying beside her, and to play a comedy the upshot of which is that I do so—these are nearly the same thing. In other words, feeling is formed by the deeds that one does; therefore I cannot consult it as a guide to action. And that is to say that I can neither seek within myself for an authentic impulse to action, nor can I expect, from some ethic, formulae that will enable me to act. You may say that the youth did, at least, go to a professor to ask for advice. But if you seek counsel—from a priest, for example—you have selected that priest; and at bottom you already knew, more or less, what he would advise. In other words, to choose an adviser is nevertheless to commit oneself by that choice. If you are a Christian, you will say, Consult a priest; but there are collaborationists, priests who are resisters and priests who wait for the tide to turn: which will you choose? Had this young man chosen a priest of the resistance, or one of the collaboration, he would have decided beforehand the kind of advice he was to receive. Similarly, in coming to me, he knew what advice I should give him, and I had but one reply to make. You are free, therefore choose—that is to say, invent. No rule of general morality can show you what you ought to do: no signs are vouchsafed in this world. The Catholics will reply, "Oh, but they are!" Very well; still, it is I myself, in every case, who have to interpret the signs. Whilst I was imprisoned, I made the acquaintance of a somewhat remarkable man, a Jesuit, who had become a member of that order in the following manner. In his life he had suffered a succession of rather severe setbacks. His father had died when he was a child, leaving him in poverty, and he had been awarded a free scholarship in a religious institution, where he had been made continually to feel that he was accepted for charity's sake, and, in consequence, he had been denied several of those distinctions and honours which gratify children. Later, about the age of eighteen, he came to grief in a sentimental affair; and finally, at twenty-two—this was a trifle in itself, but it was the last drop that overflowed his cup—he failed in his military examination. This young man, then, could regard himself as a total failure: it was a sign—but a sign of what? He might have taken refuge in bitterness or despair. But he took it—very cleverly for him—as a sign that he was not intended for secular successes, and that only the attainments of religion, those of sanctity and of faith, were accessible to him. He interpreted his record as a message from God, and became a member of the Order. Who can doubt but that this decision as to the meaning of the sign was his, and his alone? One could have drawn quite different conclusions from such a series of reverses—as, for example, that he had better become a carpenter or a revolutionary. For the decipherment of the sign, however, he bears the entire responsibility. That is what "abandonment" implies, that we ourselves decide our being. And with this abandonment goes anguish.

As for "despair," the meaning of this expression is extremely simple. It merely means that we limit ourselves to a reliance upon that which is within our wills, or within the sum of the probabilities which render our action feasible. Whenever one wills anything, there are always these elements of probability. If I am counting upon a visit from a friend, who may be coming by train or by tram, I presuppose that the train will arrive at the appointed time, or that the tram will not be derailed. I remain in the realm of possibilities; but one does not rely upon any possibilities beyond those that are strictly concerned in one's action. Beyond the point at which the possibilities under consideration cease to affect my action, I ought to disinterest myself. For there is no God and no prevenient design, which can adapt the world and all its possibilities to my will. When Descartes said, "Conquer yourself rather than the world," what he meant was, at bottom, the same—that we should act without hope.

Marxists, to whom I have said this, have answered: "Your action is limited, obviously, by your death; but you can rely upon the help of others. That is, you can count both upon what the others are doing to help you elsewhere, as in China and in Russia, and upon what they will do later, after your death, to take up your action and carry it forward to its final accomplishment which will be the revolution. Moreover you must rely upon this; not to do so is immoral." To this I rejoin, first, that I shall always count upon my comrades-in-arms in the struggle, in so far as they are committed, as I am, to a definite, common cause; and in the unity of a party or a group which I can more or less control—that is, in which I am enrolled as a militant and whose movements at every moment are known to me. In that respect, to rely upon the unity and the will of the party is exactly like my reckoning that the train will run to time or that the tram will not be derailed. But I cannot count upon men whom I do not know, I cannot base my confidence upon human goodness or upon man's interest in the good of society, seeing that man is free and that there is no human nature which I can take as foundational. I do not know whither the Russian revolution will lead. I can admire it and take it as an example in so far as it is evident, to-day, that the proletariat plays a part in Russia which it has attained in no other nation. But I cannot affirm that this will necessarily lead to the triumph of the proletariat: I must confine myself to what I can see. Nor can I be sure that comrades-in-arms will take up my work after my death and carry it to the maximum perfection, seeing that those men are free agents and will freely decide, to-morrow, what man is then to be. To-morrow, after my death, some men may decide to establish Fascism, and the others may be so cowardly or so slack as to let them do so. If so, Fascism will then be the truth of man, and so much the worse for us. In reality, things will be such as men have decided they shall be. Does that mean that I should abandon myself to quietism? No. First I ought to commit myself and then act my commitment, according to the time-honoured formula that "one need not hope in order to undertake one's work." Nor does this mean that I should not belong to a party, but only that I should be without illusion and that I should do what I can. For instance, if I ask myself "Will the social ideal as such, ever become a reality?" I cannot tell, I only know that whatever may be in my power to make it so, I shall do; beyond that, I can count upon nothing.

Quietism is the attitude of people who say, "let others do what I cannot do." The doctrine I am presenting before you is precisely the opposite of this, since it declares that there is no reality except in action. It goes further, indeed, and adds, "Man is nothing else but what he purposes, he exists only in so far as he realises himself, he is therefore nothing else but the sum of his actions, nothing else but what his life is." Hence we can well understand why some people are horrified by our teaching. For many have but one resource to sustain them in their misery, and that is to think, "Circumstances have been against me, I was worthy to be something much better than I have been. I admit I have never had a great love or a great friendship; but that is because I never met a man or a woman who was worthy of it; if I have not written any very good books, it is because I had not the leisure to do so; or, if I have had no children to whom I could devote myself it is because I did not find the man I could have lived with. So there remains within me a wide range of abilities, inclinations and potentialities, unused but perfectly viable, which endow me with a worthiness that could never be inferred from the mere history of my actions." But in reality and for the existentialist, there is no love apart from the deeds of love; no potentiality of love other than that which is manifested in loving; there is no genius other than that which is expressed in works of art. The genius of Proust is the totality of the works of Proust; the genius of Racine is the series of his tragedies, outside of which there is nothing. Why should we attribute to Racine the capacity to write yet another tragedy when that is precisely what he did not write? In life, a man commits himself, draws his own portrait and there is nothing but that portrait. No doubt this thought may seem comfortless to one who has not made a success of his life. On the other hand, it puts everyone in a position to understand that reality alone is reliable; that dreams, expectations and hopes serve to define a man only as deceptive dreams, abortive hopes, expectations unfulfilled; that is to say, they define him negatively, not positively. Nevertheless, when one says, "You are nothing else but what you live," it does not imply that an artist is to be judged solely by his works of art, for a thousand other things contribute no less to his definition as a man. What we mean to say is that a man is no other than a series of undertakings, that he is the sum, the organisation, the set of relations that constitute these undertakings.

.   .   .

You can see from these few reflections that nothing could be more unjust than the objections people raise against us. Existentialism is nothing else but an attempt to draw the full conclusions from a consistently atheistic position. Its intention is not in the least that of plunging men into despair. And if by despair one means—as the Christians do—any attitude of unbelief, the despair of the existentialists is something different. Existentialism is not atheist in the sense that it would exhaust itself in demonstrations of the non-existence of God. It declares, rather, that even if God existed that would make no difference from its point of view. Not that we believe God does exist, but we think that the real problem is not that of his existence; what man needs is to find himself again and to understand that nothing can save him from himself, not even a valid proof of the existence of God. In this sense existentialism is optimistic, it is a doctrine of action, and it is only by self-deception, by confusing their own despair with ours that Christians can describe us as without hope.

Simone de Beauvoir
THE SECOND SEX

Simone de Beauvoir is a well-known figure in the French existentialist movement. She has written several important philosophical works as well as novels, plays, and travel books. The Second Sex, *from which the following selection is taken, was first published in France in 1949. As one of the first major works to document women's biological, social, political, and sexual oppression, it anticipated the current women's liberation movement and has come to provide that movement with one of its most important theoretical works. In the following passages, de Beauvoir focuses on the special problem involved in defining "woman." While man is defined in his own terms, woman is defined by her role in man's world. The problem here is not only one of semantic asymmetry, but it also reflects a fundamental inequality between man and woman. (For further discussion of this problem, the reader should turn to three other articles reprinted in this book: Alice Rossi's "Sex Equality: The Beginnings of Ideology," page 409; Linda Phelps's "Female Sexual Alienation," page 440; and Ann Ferguson's "Androgyny as an Ideal for Human Development," page 447.)*

It is interesting to note that de Beauvoir does not attempt to deny the existence of a feminine character. She even allows that it is composed of many traits for which women are frequently criticized. However, she insists that such a feminine character (or nature) is conditioned by the social situation in which a woman finds herself, a situation in which the masculine universe is the frame of reference, and she is always the "other." With respect to this claim, the reader may want to compare Sartre's position with that of de Beauvoir. Is woman's character created by her free choice or by her situation? Is she responsible for her character, or is the blame to be placed on the patriarchal structure of our society? Perhaps we need a more complex theory of the relation between choice, the limitation of one's situation, and social conditioning. We should note, however, that de Beauvoir, in characterizing woman's resentment, writes: "A free individual blames only himself for his failures, he assumes responsibility for them; but everything happens to women through the agency of others, and therefore these others are responsible for her woes."

For a long time I have hestitated to write a book on woman. The subject is irritating, especially to women; and it is not new. Enough ink has been spilled in the quarreling over feminism, now practically over, and perhaps we should say no more about it. It is still talked about, however, for the voluminous nonsense uttered during the last century seems to have done little to illuminate the problem. After all, is there a problem? And if so, what is it? Are there women, really? Most assuredly the theory of the eternal feminine still has its adherents who will whisper in your ear: "Even in Russia women still are *women*"; and other erudite persons— sometimes the very same—say with a sigh: "Woman is losing her way, woman is lost." One wonders if women still exist, if they will always exist, whether or not it is desirable that they should, what place they occupy in this world, what their place should be. "What has become of women?" was asked recently in an ephemeral magazine.[1]

But first we must ask: what is a woman? *"Tota mulier in utero,"* says one, "woman is a womb." But in speaking of certain women, connois- seurs declare that they are not women, although they are equipped with a uterus like the rest. All agree in recognizing the fact that females exist in the human species; today as always they make up about one half of humanity. And yet we are told that femininity is in danger; we are ex- horted to be women, remain women, become women. It would appear, then, that every female human being is not necessarily a woman; to be so considered she must share in that mysterious and threatened reality known as femininity. Is this attribute something secreted by the ovaries? Or is it a Platonic essence, a product of the philosophic imagination? Is a rustling petticoat enough to bring it down to earth? Although some women try zealously to incarnate this essence, it is hardly patentable. It is frequently described in vague and dazzling terms that seem to have been borrowed from the vocabulary of the seers, and indeed in the times of St. Thomas it was considered an essence as certainly defined as the somniferous virtue of the poppy.

But conceptualism has lost ground. The biological and social sciences no longer admit the existence of unchangeably fixed entities that determine given characteristics, such as those ascribed to woman, the Jew, or the Negro. Science regards any characteristic as a reaction depen- dent in part upon a *situation.* If today femininity no longer exists, then it never existed. But does the word *woman,* then, have no specific content? This is stoutly affirmed by those who hold to the philosophy of the enlightenment, or rationalism, or nominalism; women, to them, are merely the human beings arbitrarily designated by the word *woman.* Many American women particularly are prepared to think that there is no longer any place for woman as such; if a backward individual still takes herself for a woman, her friends advise her to be psychoanalyzed and thus get rid of this obsession. In regard to a work, *Modern Woman: The Lost Sex,* which in other respects has its irritating features, Dorothy Parker has written: "I cannot be just to books which treat of woman as woman. . . . My idea is that all of us, men as well as women, should be regarded as human beings." But nominalism is a rather inadequate doctrine, and the

[1] *Franchise,* dead today.

antifeminists have had no trouble in showing that women simply *are not* men. Surely woman is, like man, a human being; but such a declaration is abstract. The fact is that every concrete human being is always a singular, separate individual. To decline to accept such notions as the eternal feminine, the black soul, the Jewish character, is not to deny that Jews, Negroes, women exist today—this denial does not represent a liberation for those concerned, but rather a flight from reality. Some years ago a well-known woman writer refused to permit her portrait to appear in a series of photographs especially devoted to women writers; she wished to be counted among the men. But in order to gain this privilege she made use of her husband's influence! Women who assert that they are men lay claim none the less to masculine consideration and respect. I recall also a young Trotskyite standing on a platform at a boisterous meeting and getting ready to use her fists, in spite of her evident fragility. She was denying her feminine weakness; but it was for love of a militant male whose equal she wished to be. The attitude of defiance of many American women proves that they are haunted by a sense of their femininity. In truth, to go for a walk with one's eyes open is enough to demonstrate that humanity is divided into two classes of individuals whose clothes, faces, bodies, smiles, gaits, interests, and occupations are manifestly different. Perhaps these differences are superficial, perhaps they are destined to disappear. What is certain is that right now they do most obviously exist.

If her functioning as a female is not enough to define woman, if we decline also to explain her through "the eternal feminine," and if nevertheless we admit, provisionally, that women do exist, then we must face the question: what is a woman?

To state the question is, to me, to suggest, at once, a preliminary answer. The fact that I ask it is in itself significant. A man would never get the notion of writing a book on the peculiar situation of the human male.[2] But if I wish to define myself, I must first of all say: "I am a woman"; on this truth must be based all further discussion. A man never begins by presenting himself as an individual of a certain sex; it goes without saying that he is a man. The terms *masculine* and *feminine* are used symmetrically only as a matter of form, as on legal papers. In actuality the relation of the two sexes is not quite like that of two electrical poles, for man represents both the positive and the neutral, as is indicated by the common use of *man* to designate human beings in general; whereas woman represents only the negative, defined by limiting criteria, without reciprocity. In the midst of an abstract discussion it is vexing to hear a man say: "You think thus and so because you are a woman"; but I know that my only defense is to reply: "I think thus and so because it is true," thereby removing my subjective self from the argument. It would be out

[2]The Kinsey Report [Alfred C. Kinsey and others: *Sexual Behavior in the Human Male* (W. B. Saunders Co., 1948)] is no exception, for it is limited to describing the sexual characteristics of American men, which is quite a different matter.

of the question to reply: "And you think the contrary because you are a man," for it is understood that the fact of being a man is no peculiarity. A man is in the right in being a man; it is the woman who is in the wrong. It amounts to this: just as for the ancients there was an absolute vertical with reference to which the oblique was defined, so there is an absolute human type, the masculine. Woman has ovaries, a uterus; these peculiarities imprison her in her subjectivity, circumscribe her within the limits of her own nature. It is often said that she thinks with her glands. Man superbly ignores the fact that his anatomy also includes glands, such as the testicles, and that they secrete hormones. He thinks of his body as a direct and normal connection with the world, which he believes he apprehends objectively, whereas he regards the body of woman as a hindrance, a prison, weighed down by everything peculiar to it. "The female is a female by virtue of a certain *lack* of qualities," said Aristotle; "we should regard the female nature as afflicted with a natural defectiveness." And St. Thomas for his part pronounced woman to be an "imperfect man," an "incidental" being. This is symbolized in Genesis where Eve is depicted as made from what Bossuet called "a supernumerary bone" of Adam.

Thus humanity is male and man defines woman not in herself but as relative to him; she is not regarded as an autonomous being. Michelet writes: "Woman, the relative being. . . ." And Benda is most positive in his *Rapport d'Uriel:* "The body of man makes sense in itself quite apart from that of woman, whereas the latter seems wanting in significance by itself. . . . Man can think of himself without woman. She cannot think of herself without man." And she is simply what man decrees; thus she is called "the sex," by which is meant that she appears essentially to the male as a sexual being. For him she is sex—absolute sex, no less. She is defined and differentiated with reference to man and not he with reference to her; she is the incidental, the inessential as opposed to the essential. He is the Subject, he is the Absolute—she is the Other.[3]

.   .   .

[3]E. Lévinas expresses this idea most explicitly in his essay *Temps et l'Autre.* "Is there not a case in which otherness, alterity [*altérité*], unquestionably marks the nature of a being, as its essence, an instance of otherness not consisting purely and simply in the opposition of two species of the same genus? I think that the feminine represents the contrary in its absolute sense, this contrariness being in no wise affected by any relation between it and its correlative and thus remaining absolutely other. Sex is not a certain specific difference . . . no more is the sexual difference a mere contradiction. . . . Nor does this difference lie in the duality of two complementary terms, for two complementary terms imply a preexisting whole. . . . Otherness reaches its full flowering in the feminine, a term of the same rank as consciousness but of opposite meaning."

I suppose that Lévinas does not forget that woman, too, is aware of her own consciousness, or ego. But it is striking that he deliberately takes a man's point of view, disregarding the reciprocity of subject and object. When he writes that woman is mystery, he implies that she is mystery for man. Thus his description, which is intended to be objective, is in fact an assertion of masculine privilege.

WOMAN'S SITUATION AND CHARACTER

We can now understand why there should be so many common features in the indictments drawn up against woman, from the Greeks to our times. Her condition has remained the same through superficial changes, and it is this condition that determines what is called the "character" of woman: she "revels in immanence," she is contrary, she is prudent and petty, she has no sense of fact or accuracy, she lacks morality, she is contemptibly utilitarian, she is false, theatrical, self-seeking, and so on. There is an element of truth in all this. But we must only note that the varieties of behavior reported are not dictated to woman by her hormones nor predetermined in the structure of the female brain: they are shaped as in a mold by her situation. In this perspective we shall endeavor to make a comprehensive survey of woman's situation. This will involve a certain amount of repetition, but it will enable us to apprehend the eternal feminine in the totality of her economic, social, and historical conditioning.

Sometimes the "feminine world" is contrasted with the masculine universe, but we must insist again that women have never constituted a closed and independent society; they form an integral part of the group, which is governed by males and in which they have a subordinate place. They are united only in a mechanical solidarity from the mere fact of their similarity, but they lack that organic solidarity on which every unified community is based; they are always compelled—at the time of the mysteries of Eleusis as today in clubs, salons, social-service institutes—to band together in order to establish a counter-universe, but they always set it up within the frame of the masculine universe. Hence the paradox of their situation: they belong at one and the same time to the male world and to a sphere in which that world is challenged; shut up in their world, surrounded by the other, they can settle down nowhere in peace. Their docility must always be matched by a refusal, their refusal by an acceptance. In this respect their attitude approaches that of the young girl, but it is more difficult to maintain, because for the adult woman it is not merely a matter of dreaming her life through symbols, but of living it out in actuality.

Woman herself recognizes that the world is masculine on the whole; those who fashioned it, ruled it, and still dominate it today are men. As for her, she does not consider herself responsible for it; it is understood that she is inferior and dependent; she has not learned the lessons of violence, she has never stood forth as subject before the other members of the group. Shut up in her flesh, her home, she sees herself as passive before these gods with human faces who set goals and establish values. In this sense there is truth in the saying that makes her the "eternal child." Workers, black slaves, colonial natives, have also been called grown-up children—as long as they were not feared; that meant that they were to accept without argument the verities and the laws laid down for them by other men. The lot of woman is a respectful obedience. She has no grasp, even in thought, on the reality around her. It is opaque to her eyes.

And it is true that she lacks the technical training that would permit her to dominate matter. As for her, it is not matter she comes to grips with, but life; and life cannot be mastered through the use of tools: one can only submit to its secret laws. The world does not seem to woman "an assemblage of implements" intermediate between her will and her goals, as Heidegger defines it; it is on the contrary something obstinately resistant, unconquerable; it is dominated by fatality and shot through with mysterious caprices. This mystery of a bloody strawberry that inside the mother is transformed into a human being is one no mathematics can express in an equation, no machine can hasten or delay; she feels the strength of a continuity that the most ingenious instruments are unable to divide or to multiply; she feels it in her body, swayed by the lunar rhythm and first ripened, then corrupted, by the years. Each day the kitchen also teaches her patience and passivity; here is alchemy; one must obey the fire, the water, wait for the sugar to melt, for the dough to rise, and also for the wash to dry, for the fruits to ripen on the shelf. Household activities come close to being technical operations, but they are too rudimentary, too monotonous, to prove to a woman the laws of mechanical causation. Besides, even here things are capricious; there are materials that will stand washing and others that will not, spots that can be removed and others that persist, objects that break all by themselves, dusts that spring up like plants.

Woman's mentality perpetuates that of agricultural civilizations which worshipped the magic powers of the land: she believes in magic. Her passive eroticism makes desire seem to her not will and aggression but an attraction akin to that which causes the divining rod to dip; the mere presence of her flesh swells and erects the male's sex; why should not hidden water make the hazel rod quiver? She feels that she is surrounded by waves, radiations, mystic fluids; she believes in telepathy, astrology, radiotherapy, mesmerism, theosophy, table-tipping, clairvoyants, faith healers; her religion is full of primitive superstition: wax candles, answered prayers; she believes the saints incarnate the ancient spirits of nature: this one protects travelers, that one women in labor, this other finds lost articles; and, of course, no prodigy can surprise her. Her attitude will be one of conjuration and prayer; to obtain a certain result, she will perform certain well-tested rites.

It is easy to see why woman clings to routine; time has for her no element of novelty, it is not a creative flow; because she is doomed to repetition, she sees in the future only a duplication of the past. If one knows the word and the formula, duration allies itself with the powers of fecundity—but this is itself subject to the rhythm of the months, the seasons; the cycle of each pregnancy, each flowering, exactly reproduces the one that preceded. In this play of cyclical phenomena the sole effect of time is a slow deterioration: it wears out furniture and clothes as it ruins the face; the reproductive powers are gradually destroyed by the passing of years. Thus woman puts no trust in this relentless force for destruction.

Not only is she ignorant of what constitutes a true action, capable of changing the face of the world, but she is lost in the midst of the world as if she were at the heart of an immense, vague nebula. She is not familiar with the use of masculine logic. Stendhal remarked that she could handle it as adroitly as a man if driven to it by necessity. But it is an instrument that she hardly has occasion to use. A syllogism is of no help in making a successful mayonnaise, nor in quieting a child in tears; masculine reasoning is quite inadequate to the reality with which she deals. And in the world of men, her thought, not flowing into any project, since she *does* nothing, is indistinguishable from daydreaming. She has no sense of factual truth, for lack of effectiveness; she never comes to grips with anything but words and mental pictures, and that is why the most contradictory assertions give her no uneasiness; she takes little trouble to elucidate the mysteries of a sphere that is in every way beyond her reach. She is content, for her purposes, with extremely vague conceptions, confusing parties, opinions, places, people, events; her head is filled with a strange jumble.

But, after all, to see things clearly is not her business, for she has been taught to accept masculine authority. So she gives up criticizing, investigating, judging for herself, and leaves all this to the superior caste. Therefore the masculine world seems to her a transcendent reality, an absolute. "Men make the gods," says Frazer, "women worship them." Men cannot kneel with complete conviction before the idols they have made; but when women encounter these mighty statues along the roads, they think they are not made with hands, and obediently bow down. In particular they like to have Order and Right embodied in a leader. In every Olympus there is a supreme god; the magic male essence must be concentrated in an archetype of which father, husband, lovers, are only faint reflections. It is rather satirical to say that their worship of this grand totem is of sexual nature; but it is true that in this worship they will fully satisfy their childhood dream of bowing the knee in resignation. In France generals like Boulanger, Pétain, and de Gaulle have always had the support of the women; and one recalls with what fluttering pens the lady journalists on the Communist paper *L'Humanité* formerly celebrated Tito and his splendid uniform. The general, the dictator—eagle-eyed, square-jawed—is the heavenly father demanded by all serious right-thinkers, the absolute guarantor of all values. Women's ineffectiveness and ignorance are what give rise to the respect accorded by them to heroes and to the laws of the masculine world; they accept them not through sound judgment but by an act of faith—and faith gets its fanatical power from the fact that it is not knowledge: it is blind, impassioned, obstinate, stupid; what it declares, it declares unconditionally, against reason, against history, against all denial.

This obstinate reverence can take one of two forms according to circumstances: it may be either the content of the law, or merely its empty form that woman passionately adheres to. If she belongs to the privileged elite that benefits from the established social order, she wants it to be unshakable and she is notably uncompromising in this desire. Man knows that he can develop different institutions, another ethic, a new legal code; aware of his ability to transcend what is, he regards history as a becoming. The most conservative man knows that some evolution is inevitable and realizes that he must adapt his action and his thinking to it; but as woman takes no part in history, she fails to understand its necessities; she is suspiciously doubtful of the future and wants to arrest the flow of time. If the idols set up by her father, her brothers, her husband, are being torn down, she can offer no way of repopulating the heavens; she rushes wildly to the defense of the old gods.

During the War of Secession no Southerners were more passionate in upholding slavery than the women. In England during the Boer War, in France during the Commune, it was the women who were most belligerently inflamed. They seek to compensate for their inactivity by the intensity of the sentiments they exhibit. With victory won, they rush like hyenas upon the fallen foe; in defeat, they bitterly reject any efforts at conciliation. Their ideas being merely attitudes, they support quite unconcernedly the most outdated causes: they can be legitimists in 1914, czarists in 1953. A man will sometimes smilingly encourage them, for it amuses him to see their fanatical reflections of ideas he expresses in more measured terms; but he may also find it irritating to have his ideas take on such a stupid, stubborn, aspect.

Woman assumes this indomitable attitude only in strongly integrated civilizations and social classes. More generally, she respects the law simply because it is the law, since her faith is blind; if the law changes, it retains its spell. In woman's eyes, might makes right because the rights she recognizes in men depend upon their power. Hence it is that when a society breaks down, women are the first to throw themselves at the feet of the conqueror. On the whole, they accept what is. One of their distinguishing traits is resignation. When the ruins of Pompeii were dug up, it was noticed that the incinerated bodies of the men were fixed in attitudes of rebellion, defying the heavens or trying to escape, while those of the women, bent double, were bowed down with their faces toward the earth. Women feel they are powerless against things: volcanoes, police, patrons, men. "Women are born to suffer," they say; "it's life—nothing can be done about it."

This resignation inspires the patience often admired in women. They can stand physical pain much better than men; they are capable of stoical courage when circumstances demand it; lacking the male's aggressive audacity, many women distinguish themselves by their calm tenacity in passive resistance. They face crises, poverty, misfortune, more energetically than their husbands; respecting duration, which no haste can overcome, they do not ration their time. When they apply their quiet persistence to an enterprise, they are sometimes startlingly successful. "Never underestimate the power of a woman." In a generous woman resignation takes the form of forbearance: she puts up with everything, she condemns no one, because she holds that neither people nor things can be other than they are. A proud woman can make a lofty virtue of resignation, as did the stoical Mme de Charrière. But it also engenders a sterile prudence; women are always trying to conserve, to adapt, to arrange, rather than to destroy and build anew; they prefer compromise and adjustment to revolution.

In the nineteenth century, women were one of the greatest obstacles in the way of the effort to free the workers: for one Flora Tristan, one Louise Michel, how many timid housewives begged their husbands not to take any chances! They were not only afraid of strikes, unemployment, and poverty: they feared that revolt might be a mistake. It is easy to understand that, if they must suffer, they preferred what was familiar to adventuring, for they could achieve a meager welfare more easily at home than in the streets.

Women's fate is bound up with that of perishable things; in losing them they lose all. Only a free subject, asserting himself as above and beyond the duration of things, can check all decay; this supreme recourse has been denied to woman. The real reason why she does not believe in a liberation is that she has never put the powers of liberty to a test; the world seems to her to be ruled by an obscure destiny against which it is presumptuous to rise in protest. She has not herself marked out those dangerous roads she is asked to follow, and so it is natural enough for her not to plunge into them with enthusiasm. Let the future be opened to her and she will no longer cling desperately to the past. When women are called upon for concrete action, when they recognize their interest in the designated goals, they are as bold and courageous as men.

Many of the faults for which women are reproached—mediocrity, laziness, frivolity, servility—simply express the fact that their horizon is closed. It is said that woman is sensual, she wallows in immanence; but she has first been shut up in it. The harem slave feels no morbid passion for rose preserves and perfumed baths: she has to kill time. When woman suffocates in a dull gynaeceum—brothel or middle-class home—she is bound to take refuge in comfort and well-being; besides that, if she eagerly seeks sexual pleasure, it is very often because she is deprived of it. Sexually unsatisfied, doomed to male crudeness, "condemned to masculine ugliness," she finds consolation in creamy sauces, heady wines, velvets, the caress of water, of sunshine, of a woman friend, of a young lover. If she seems to man so "physical" a creature, it is because her situation leads her to attach extreme importance to her animal nature. The call of the flesh is no louder in her than in the male, but she catches its least murmurs and amplifies them. Sexual pleasure, like rending pain, represents the stunning triumph of the immediate; in the violence of the instant, the future and the universe are denied; what lies outside the carnal flame is nothing; for the brief moment of this apotheosis, woman is no longer mutilated and frustrated. But, once again, she values these triumphs of immanence only because immanence is her lot.

Her frivolity has the same cause as her "sordid materialism"; she considers little things important for lack of any access to great things, and, furthermore, the futilities that fill her days are often of the most serious practical concern to her. She owes her charm and her opportunities to her dress and her beauty. She often appears to be lazy, indolent; but the occupations available to her are as empty as the pure passage of time. If she is a chatterer, a scribbler, it is to divert her idle hours: for impossible action, she substitutes words. The truth is that when a woman is engaged in an enterprise worthy of a human being, she is quite able to show herself as active, efficient, taciturn—and as ascetic—as a man.

She is accused of being servile; she is always ready, it is said, to lie down at her master's feet and kiss the hand that strikes her, and it is true that she is generally lacking in real pride. The counsel dispensed in columns of "advice to the lovelorn," to deceived wives and abandoned lovers, is full of the spirit of abject submission. Woman wears herself out in haughty scenes, and in the end gathers up the crumbs that the male cares to toss to her. But what can be done without masculine support by a woman for whom man is at once the sole means and the sole reason for living? She is bound to suffer every humiliation; a slave cannot have the sense of human dignity; it is enough if a slave gets out of it with a whole skin.

And finally, if woman is earthy, commonplace, basely utilitarian, it is because she is compelled to devote her existence to cooking and washing diapers—no way to acquire a sense of grandeur! It is her duty to assure the monotonous repetition of life in all its mindless factuality. It is natural for woman to repeat, to begin again without ever inventing, for time to seem to her to go round and round without ever leading anywhere. She is occupied without ever *doing* anything, and thus she identifies herself with what she *has*. This dependence on things, a consequence of the dependence in which men keep her, explains her frugality, her avarice. Her life is not directed toward ends: she is absorbed in producing or caring for things that are never more than means, such as food, clothing, and shelter. These things are inessential intermediaries between animal life and free existence. The sole value that appertains to the inessential means is utility; it is at the level of utility that the housekeeper lives, and she does not flatter herself that she is anything more than a person useful to her kindred.

But no existent can be satisfied with an inessential role, for that immediately makes means into ends—as may be observed, for example, in politicans—and the value of the means comes to seem an absolute value. Thus utility reigns in the housekeeper's heaven, above truth, beauty, liberty; and it is in this perspective that she envisages the entire universe. This is why she adopts the Aristotelian morality of the golden mean—that is, of mediocrity. How could one expect her to show audacity, ardor, disinterestedness, grandeur? These qualities appear only when a free being strikes forward through an open future, emerging far beyond all given actuality. Woman is shut up in a kitchen or in a boudoir, and astonishment is expressed that her horizon is limited. Her wings are clipped, and it is found deplorable that she cannot fly. Let but the future be opened to her, and she will no longer be compelled to linger in the present.

The same inconsistency is displayed when, after being enclosed within the limits of her ego or her household, she is reproached for her narcissism, her egotism, with all their train: vanity, touchiness, malice, and so on. She is deprived of all possibility of concrete communication with others; she does not experience either the appeal or the benefits of solidarity, since she is consecrated entirely to her own family, in isolation. She could hardly be expected, then, to transcend herself toward the general welfare. She stays obstinately within the one realm that is familiar to her, where she can control things and in the midst of which she enjoys a precarious sovereignty.

Lock the doors and close the shutters as she will, however, woman fails to find complete security in her home. It is surrounded by that masculine universe which she respects from afar, without daring to venture into it. And precisely because she is incapable of grasping it through technical skill, sound logic, and definite knowledge, she feels, like the child and the savage, that she is surrounded by dangerous mysteries. She projects her magical conception of reality into that male world; the course of events seems to her to be inevitable, and yet anything can happen; she does not clearly distinguish between the possible and the impossible and is ready to believe anything, no matter what. She listens to and spreads rumors and starts panics. Even when things are quiet, she feels anxious; lying half asleep at night, her rest is disturbed by the nightmare shapes that reality assumes; and thus for woman condemned to passivity, the inscrutable future is haunted by phantoms of war, revolution, famine, poverty; being unable to act, she worries. Her husband, her son, when undertaking an enterprise or facing an emergency, run their own risks; their plans, the regulations they follow, indicate a sure road through obscurity. But woman flounders in confusion and darkness; she gets used to it because she does nothing; in her imagination all possibilities have equal reality: the train may be derrailed, the operation may go wrong, the business may fail. What she is endeavoring to exorcize in her gloomy ruminations is the specter of her own powerlessness.

Her anxiety is the expression of her distrust of the world as given; if it seems threatening, ready to collapse, this is because she is unhappy in it. For most of the time she is not resigned to being resigned; she knows very well that she suffers as she does against her will: she is a woman without having been consulted in the matter. She dares not revolt; she submits unwillingly; her attitude is one of constant reproach. All those in whom women confide—doctors, priests, social workers—know that the usual tone is one of complaint. Among friends, woman groans over her own troubles, and they all complain in chorus about the injustice of fate, the world, and men in general.

A free individual blames only himself for his failures, he assumes responsibility for them; but everything happens to women through the agency of others, and therefore these others are responsible for her woes. Her mad despair spurns all remedies; it does not help matters to propose solutions to a woman bent on complaining: she finds none acceptable. She insists on living in her situation precisely as she does —that is, in a state of impotent rage. If some change is proposed she throws up her hands: "That's the last straw!" She knows that her trouble goes deeper than is indicated by the pretexts she advances for it, and she is aware that it will take more than some expedient to deliver her from it. She holds the entire world responsible because it has been made without her, and against her; she has been protesting against her condition since her adolescence, ever since her childhood. She has been promised compensations, she has been assured that if she would place her fortune in man's hands, it would be returned a hundredfold—and she feels she has been swindled. She puts the whole masculine universe under indictment. Resentment is the reverse side of dependence: when one gives all, one never receives enough in return.

Woman is obliged also, however, to regard the male universe with some respect; she would feel in danger without a roof over her head, if she were in total opposition; so she adopts the Manichaeist position—the clear separation of good and evil—which is also suggested by her experience as a housekeeper. The individual who acts considers himself, like others, as responsible for both evil and good, he knows that it is for him to define ends, to bring them to success; he becomes aware, in action, of the ambiguousness of all solutions; justice and injustice, gains and losses, are inextricably mixed. But anyone who is passive is out of the game and declines to pose ethical problems even in thought: the good *should* be realized, and if it is not, there must be some wrongdoing for which those to blame must be punished. Like the child, woman conceives good and evil in simple images, as coexisting, discrete entities; this Manichaeism of hers sets her mind at rest by doing away with the anxiety of making difficult choices. To decide between an evil and a lesser evil, between a present good and a greater good to come, to have to define for herself what is defeat and what is victory—all this involves terrible risks. For the Manichaeist, the good wheat is clearly distinct from the tares, and one has merely to remove the tares; dust stands self-condemned and cleanliness is complete absence of dirt; to clean house is to remove dirt and rubbish.

Thus woman thinks that "it is all the Jews' fault," or the Freemasons' or the Bolsheviks', or the government's; she is always *against* someone or something. Among those against Dreyfus the women were even more relentless than the men. They do not always know just where the evil principle may lie, but what they expect of a "good government" is to sweep it out as they sweep dust out of the house. For fervid de Gaullists, de Gaulle is the king of sweepers; they imagine him, feather duster and mop in hand, scrubbing and polishing to make France "nice and clean."

But these hopes are always for the uncertain future; in the meantime evil continues to corrode the good; and since she cannot get her hands on the Jews, the Freemasons, the Bolsheviks, the woman looks about for someone responsible against whom her indignation can find concrete expression. Her husband is the favorite victim. He embodies the masculine universe, through him male society has taken charge of her and swindled her. He bears the weight of the world, and if things go wrong, it is his fault. When he comes in at night, she complains to him about the children, the storekeepers, the cost of living, her rheumatism, the weather—and wants him to feel to blame. She often entertains special grievances against him; but he is guilty in the first place of being a man. He may very well have maladies and cares of his own—"that's different" —but he holds a privilege which she constantly feels as an injustice. It is a remarkable thing that the hostility she feels toward her husband or lover attaches her to him instead of alienating her from him. A man who has begun to detest wife or mistress tries to get away from her; but woman wants to have the man she hates close at hand so she can make him pay. Recrimination is not a way to get rid of her ills but to wallow in them; the wife's supreme consolation is to pose as a martyr. Life, men, have conquered her: she will turn defeat itself into victory. This explains why she will cheerfully abandon herself to frantic tears and scenes, as in her childhood.

Certainly woman's aptitude for facile tears comes largely from the fact that her life is built upon a foundation of impotent revolt; it is also doubtless true that physiologically she has less nervous control than man and that her education has taught her to let herself go more readily. This effect of education, or custom, is indeed evident, since in the past men like Benjamin Constant and Diderot, for instance, used to pour out floods of tears, and then men ceased weeping when it became unfashionable for them. But, above all, the fact is that woman is always prepared to take an attitude of frustration toward the world because she has never frankly accepted it. A man does accept the world; not even misfortune will change his attitude, he will face it, he will not let himself "give up"; whereas it takes only a little trouble to remind a woman of the hostility of the universe and the injustice of her lot. Then she hastily retires to her surest refuge: herself. These warm traces on her cheeks, these reddened eyes, what are they but the visible presence of her grief-stricken soul? Cool to her skin, scarcely salty on her tongue, tears are also a gentle if bitter caress; her face burns under the merciful flow. Tears are at once plaint and consolation, fever and cooling appeasement. Tears are woman's supreme alibi; sudden as a squall, loosed by fits and starts, typhoon, April shower, they make woman into a plaintive fountain, a stormy sky. Her eyes are blinded, misty; unseeing, they melt in rain; sightless, she returns to the passivity of natural things. One wants her conquered, but she founders in her defeat; she sinks like a stone, she drowns, she eludes the man who is contemplating her, powerless as before a cataract. He considers this performance unfair; but she considers the struggle unfair from the start, because no other effective weapon has been put in her hands. She is resorting once more to a magic conjuration. And the fact that her sobs infuriate the male is one more reason for sobbing.

Whenever tears are insufficient to express her revolt, she will make scenes of such incoherent violence as to abash a man still more. In some circles a husband may strike his wife actual blows; in others he declines to use violence precisely because he is the stronger and his fist is an effective weapon. But a woman, like a child, indulges in symbolic outbursts: she can throw herself on a man, beating and scratching, but it is only a gesture. Yet above all she is engaged in expressing, through the pantomime of the nervous crisis, the insubordination she is unable to carry out in actuality. There are other than physiological reasons for her susceptibility to convulsive manifestations: a convulsion is an interiorization of energy which, when directed outward into the environment, fails to act there on any object; it is an aimless discharge of all the negative forces set up by the situation. The mother rarely has nervous crises with her young children, because she can punish them, strike them; it is rather with her grown son, her husband, or her lover, over whom she has no real power, that woman gives way to her furious tantrums. Mme Tolstoy's hysterical scenes are significant; no doubt she did very wrong in never trying to understand her husband, and in the light of her diary she seems ungenerous, insensitive, and insincere, far from an engaging figure. But whether she was right or wrong in no way changes the horror of her situation. All her life she did nothing but bear up, amid constant reproaches, under marital embraces, maternities, solitude, and the mode of life imposed by her husband. When new decrees of Tolstoy's heightened the conflict, she was unarmed against his inimical will, which she opposed with all her powerless will, she burst out in theatrics of refusal—feigned suicides, feigned flights, feigned maladies, and the like—which were disagreeable to those about her and wearing for herself. It is hard to see that any other outcome was possible for her, since she had no positive reason to conceal her feelings of revolt, and no effective way of expressing them.

There is a way out that is open to the woman who has reached the end of her resistance—it is suicide. But it seems less often resorted to by women than by men. Here the statistics are very ambiguous. Successful suicides are much more common in men than in women, but attempts to end their lives are commoner in the latter. This may be so because women are more likely to be satisfied with play-acting: they *pretend* self-destruction more often than they really *want* it. It is also, in part, because the usual brutal methods are repellent: women almost never use cold steel or firearms. They are much more likely to drown themselves, like Ophelia, attesting the affinity of woman with water, where, in the still darkness, it seems that life might find passive dissolution. In general we see here again the ambiguity I have already signalized: what woman detests she does not honestly try to renounce. She plays at breaking off but in the end remains with the man who is the cause of her woes; she pretends to quit the life which hurts her, but it is relatively rare for her to succeed in killing herself. She has no taste for definitive solutions. She protests against man, against life, against her situation, but she does not make good her escape from them.

There are many aspects of feminine behavior that should be interpreted as forms of protest. We have seen that a woman often deceives her husband through defiance and not for pleasure; and she may be purposely careless and extravagant because he is methodical and economical. Misogynists who accuse woman of always being late think she lacks a sense of punctuality; but as we have seen, the fact is that she can adjust herself very well to the demands of time. When she is late, she has deliberately planned to be. Some coquettish women think they stimulate the man's desire in this way and make their presence the more highly appreciated; but in making the man wait a few minutes, the woman is above all protesting against that long wait: her life.

In a sense her whole existence is waiting, since she is confined in the limbo of immanence and contingence, and since her justification is always in the hands of others. She awaits the homage, the approval of men, she awaits love, she awaits the gratitude and praise of her husband or her lover. She awaits her support, which comes from man; whether she keeps the checkbook or merely gets a weekly or monthly allowance from her husband, it is necessary for him to have drawn his pay or obtained that raise if she is to be able to pay the grocer or buy a new dress. She waits for man to put in an appearance, since her economic dependence places her at his disposal; she is only one element in masculine life while man is her whole existence. The husband has his occupations outside the home, and the wife has to put up with his absence all day long; the lover —passionate as he may be—is the one who decides on their meetings and separations in accordance with his obligations. In bed, she awaits the male's desire, she awaits—sometimes anxiously—her own pleasure.

All she can do is arrive later at the rendezvous her lover has set, not be ready at the time designated by her husband; in that way she asserts the importance of her own occupations, she insists on her independence; and for the moment she becomes the essential subject to whose will the other passively submits. But these are timid attempts at revenge; however persistent she may be in keeping men waiting, she will never compensate for the interminable hours she has spent in watching and hoping, in awaiting the good pleasure of the male.

Woman is bound in a general way to contest foot by foot the rule of man, though recognizing his over-all supremacy and worshipping his idols. Hence that famous "contrariness" for which she has often been reproached. Having no independent domain, she cannot oppose positive truths and values of her own to those asserted and upheld by males; she can only deny them. Her negation is more or less thoroughgoing, according to the way respect and resentment are proportioned in her nature. But in fact she knows all the faults in the masculine system, and she has no hesitation in exposing them.

Women have no grasp on the world of men because their experience does not teach them to use logic and technique; inversely, masculine apparatus loses its power at the frontiers of the feminine realm. There is a whole region of human experience which the male deliberately chooses to ignore because he fails to *think* it: this experience woman *lives*. The engineer, so precise when he is laying out his diagrams, behaves at home like a minor god: a word, and behold, his meal is served, his shirts starched, his children quieted; procreation is an act as swift as the wave of Moses' wand; he sees nothing astounding in these miracles. The concept of the miracle is different from the idea of magic: it presents, in the midst of a world of rational causation, the radical discontinuity of an event without cause, against which the weapons of thought are shattered; whereas magical phenomena are unified by hidden forces the continuity of which can be accepted—without being understood—by a docile mind. The newborn child is miraculous to the paternal minor god, magical for the mother who has experienced its coming to term within her womb. The experience of the man is intelligible but interrupted by blanks; that of the woman is, within its own limits, mysterious and obscure but complete. This obscurity makes her weighty; in his relations with her, the male seems light: he has the lightness of dictators, generals, judges, bureaucrats, codes of law, and abstract principles. This is doubtless what a housekeeper meant when she said, shrugging her shoulders: "Men, they don't think!" Women say, also: "Men, they don't know, they don't know life." To the myth of the praying mantis, women contrast the symbol of the frivolous and obtrusive drone bee.

It is understandable, in this perspective, that woman takes exception to masculine logic. Not only is it inapplicable to her experience, but in his hands, as she knows, masculine reasoning becomes an underhand form of force; men's undebatable pronouncements are intended to confuse her. The intention is to put her in a dilemma: either you agree or you do not. Out of respect for the whole system of accepted principles she should agree; if she refuses, she rejects the entire system. But she cannot venture to go so far; she lacks the means to reconstruct society in different form. Still, she does not accept it as it is. Halfway between revolt and slavery, she resigns herself reluctantly to masculine authority. On each occasion he has to force her to accept the consequences of her halfhearted yielding. Man pursues that chimera, a companion half slave, half free: in yielding to him, he would have her yield to the convincingness of an argument, but she knows that he has himself chosen the premises on which his rigorous deductions depend. As long as she avoids questioning them, he will easily reduce her to silence; nevertheless he will not convince her, for she senses his arbitrariness. And so, annoyed, he will accuse her of being obstinate and illogical; but she refuses to play the game because she knows the dice are loaded.

·　　·　　·

Edward O. Wilson
HUMAN DECENCY IS ANIMAL

With the publication of his encyclopedic Sociobiology: A New Synthesis *in 1975, Edward O. Wilson, professor of zoology at Harvard University, announced the development of a new discipline. Wilson's earlier scientific work involved a study of the evolution of various insect societies. This new work was a far more ambitious project. In it, he attempted not merely to systematize previous studies on animal behavior and to compare the behavior of different animal species, but ultimately, to found an entirely new science that would investigate the biological basis of social behavior. Thus, with respect to the human species, sociobiology's task was to uncover the biological determinants of human social organization. Sociology was to be grounded, ultimately, in biology.*

The following article, which appeared in The New York Times Magazine *of October 12, 1975, is Wilson's attempt to make his theories more accessible to the general public. Among his claims are that altruism, while it takes different forms in different societies, is a genetically inherited trait that has developed through an evolutionary mechanism called* kin selection; *homosexuality is a naturally evolved characteristic that may have had an important function in hunter-gatherer societies; animal studies do not support the idea of a general aggressive drive but that, nonetheless, some amount of aggressive behavior is inherent in the human species; men are more aggressive and dominant than women; and it is natural for society to have a sexual division of labor (men hunt, women stay at home).*

During the American wars of this century, a large percentage of Congressional Medals of Honor were awarded to men who threw themselves on top of grenades to shield comrades, aided the rescue of others from battle sites at the price of certain death to themselves, or made other, often carefully considered but extraordinary, decisions that led to the same fatal end. Such altruistic suicide is the ultimate act of courage and emphatically deserves the country's highest honor. It is also only the extreme act that lies beyond the innumerable smaller performances of kindness and giving that bind societies together. One is tempted to leave the matter there, to accept altruism as simply the better side of human nature. Perhaps, to put the best possible construction on the matter, conscious altruism is a transcendental quality that distinguishes human beings from animals. Scientists are nevertheless not accustomed to declaring any phenomenon off limits, and recently there has been a renewed interest in analyzing such forms of social behavior in greater depth and as objectively as possible.

Much of the new effort falls within a discipline called sociobiology, which is defined as the systematic study of the biological basis of social behavior in every kind of organism, including man, and is being pieced together with contributions from biology, psychology and anthropology.

There is of course nothing new about analyzing social behavior, and even the word "sociobiology" has been around for some years. What is new is the way facts and ideas are being extracted from their traditional matrix of psychology and ethology (the natural history of animal behavior) and reassembled in compliance with the principles of genetics and ecology.

In sociobiology, there is a heavy emphasis on the comparison of societies of different kinds of animals and of man, not so much to draw analogies (these have often been dangerously misleading, as when aggression is compared directly in wolves and in human beings) but to devise and to test theories about the underlying hereditary basis of social behavior. With genetic evolution always in mind, sociobiologists search for the ways in which the myriad forms of social organization adapt particular species to the special opportunities and dangers encountered in their environment.

A case in point is altruism. I doubt if any higher animal, such as a hawk or a baboon, has ever deserved a Congressional Medal of Honor by the ennobling criteria used in our society. Yet minor altruism does occur frequently, in forms instantly understandable in human terms, and is bestowed not just on offspring but on other members of the species as well. Certain small birds, robins, thrushes and titmice, for example, warn others of the approach of a hawk. They crouch low and emit a distinctive thin, reedy whistle. Although the warning call has acoustic properties that make it difficult to locate in space, to whistle at all seems at the very least unselfish; the caller would be wiser not to betray its presence but rather to remain silent and let someone else fall victim.

When a dolphin is harpooned or otherwise seriously injured, the typical response of the remainder of the school is to desert the area immediately. But, sometimes, they crowd around the stricken animal and lift it to the surface, where it is able to continue breathing air. Packs of African wild dogs, the most social of all carnivorous mammals, are organized in part by a remarkable division of labor. During the denning season, some of the adults, usually led by a dominant male, are forced to leave the pups behind in order to hunt for antelopes and other prey. At least one adult, normally the mother of the litter, stays behind as a guard. When the hunters return, they regurgitate pieces of meat to all that stayed home. Even sick and crippled adults are benefited, and as a result they are able to survive longer than would be the case in less generous societies.

Other than man, chimpanzees may be the most altruistic of all mammals. Ordinarily, chimps are vegetarians, and during their relaxed foraging excursions they feed singly in the uncoordinated manner of other monkeys and apes. But, occasionally, the males hunt monkeys and young baboons for food. During these episodes, the entire mood of the troop shifts toward what can only be characterized as a manlike state. The males stalk and chase their victims in concert; they also gang up to repulse any of the victims' adult relatives which oppose them. When the hunters have dismembered the prey and are feasting, other chimps approach to beg for morsels. They touch the meat and the faces of the males, whimpering and *hoo*ing gently, and hold out their hands—palms up—in supplication. The meat eaters sometimes pull away in refusal or walk off. But, often, they permit the other animal to chew directly on the meat or to pull off small pieces with its hands. On several occasions, chimpanzees have actually been observed to tear off pieces and drop them into the outstretched hands of others—an act of generosity unknown in other monkeys and apes.

Adoption is also practiced by chimpanzees. Jane Goodall has observed three cases at the Gombe Stream National Park in Tanzania. All involved orphaned infants taken over by adult brothers and sisters. It is of considerable interest, for more theoretical reasons to be discussed shortly, that the altruistic behavior was displayed by the closest possible relatives rather than by experienced females with children of their own, females who might have supplied the orphans with milk and more adequate social protection.

In spite of a fair abundance of such examples among vertebrate creatures, it is only in the lower animals and in the social insects particularly, that we encounter altruistic suicide comparable to man's. A large percentage of the members of colonies of ants, bees and wasps are ready to defend their nests with insane charges against intruders. This is the reason that people move with circumspection around honeybee hives and yellowjacket burrows, but can afford to relax near the nests of solitary species such as sweat bees and mud daubers.

.   .   .

Honeybee workers have stings lined with reversed barbs like those on fishhooks. When a bee attacks an intruder at the hive, the sting catches in the skin; as the bee moves away, the sting remains embedded, pulling out the entire venom gland and much of the viscera with it. The bee soon dies, but its attack has been more effective than if it withdrew the sting intact. The reason is that the venom gland continues to leak poison into the wound, while a bananalike odor emanating from the base of the sting incites other members of the hive into launching Kamikaze attacks of their own at the same spot. From the point of view of the colony as a whole, the suicide of an individual accomplishes more than it loses. The total worker force consists of 20,000 to 80,000 members, all sisters born from eggs laid by the mother queen. Each bee has a natural life span of only about 50 days, at the end of which it dies of old age. So to give a life is only a little thing, with no genes being spilled in the process.

My favorite example among the social insects is provided by an African termite with the orotund, technical name *Globitermes sulfureus.*

Members of this species' soldier caste are quite literally walking bombs. Huge paired glands extend from their heads back through most of their bodies. When they attack ants and other enemies, they eject a yellow glandular secretion through their mouths; it congeals in the air and often fatally entangles both the soldiers and their antagonists. The spray appears to be powered by contractions of the muscles in the abdominal wall. Sometimes, the contractions become so violent that the abdomen and gland explode, spraying the defensive fluid in all directions.

Sharing a capacity for extreme sacrifice does not mean that the human mind and the "mind" of an insect (if such exists) work alike. But it does mean that the impulse need not be ruled divine or otherwise transcendental, and we are justified in seeking a more conventional biological explanation. One immediately encounters a basic problem connected with such an explanation: Fallen heroes don't have any more children. If self-sacrifice results in fewer descendants, the genes, or basic units of heredity, that allow heroes to be created can be expected to disappear gradually from the population. This is the result of the narrow mode of Darwinian natural selection: Because people who are governed by selfish genes prevail over those with altruistic genes, there should be a tendency over many generations for selfish genes to increase in number and for the human population as a whole to become less and less capable of responding in an altruistic manner.

How can altruism persist? In the case of the social insects, there is no doubt at all. Natural selection has been broadened to include a process called kin selection. The self-sacrificing termite soldier protects the rest of the colony, including the queen and king which are the soldier's parents. As a result, the soldier's more fertile brothers and sisters flourish, and it is *they* which multiply the altruistic genes that are shared with the soldier by close kinship. One's own genes are multiplied by the greater production of nephews and nieces. It is natural, then, to ask whether the capacity for altruism has also evolved in human beings through kin selection. In other words, do the emotions we feel, which on occasion in exceptional individuals climax in total self-sacrifice, stem ultimately from hereditary units that were implanted by the favoring of relatives during a period of hundreds or thousands of generations? This explanation gains some strength from the circumstance that during most of mankind's history the social unit was the immediate family and a tight network of other close relatives. Such exceptional cohesion, combined with a detailed awareness of kinship made possible by high intelligence, might explain why kin selection has been more forceful in human beings than in monkeys and other mammals.

To anticipate a common objection raised by many social scientists and others, let me grant at once that the intensity and form of altruistic acts are to a large extent culturally determined. Human social evolution is obviously more cultural than genetic. The point is that the underlying emotion, powerfully manifested in virtually all human societies, is what is considered to evolve through genes. This sociobiological hypothesis does not therefore account for differences among societies, but it could explain why human beings differ from other mammals and why, in one narrow aspect, they more closely resemble social insects.

In cases where sociobiological explanations can be tested and proved true, they will, at the very least, provide perspective and a new sense of philosophical ease about human nature. I believe that they will also have an ultimately moderating influence on social tensions. Consider the case of homosexuality. Homophiles are typically rejected in our society because of a narrow and unfair biological premise made about them: Their sexual preference does not produce children; therefore, they cannot be natural. To the extent that this view can be rationalized, it is just Darwinism in the old narrow sense: Homosexuality does not directly replicate .genes. But homosexuals *can* replicate genes by kin selection, provided they are sufficiently altruistic toward kin.

It is not inconceivable that in the early, hunter-gatherer period of human evolution, and perhaps even later, homosexuals regularly served as a partly sterile caste, enhancing the lives and reproductive success of their relatives by a more dedicated form of support than would have been possible if they produced children of their own. If such combinations of interrelated heterosexuals and homosexuals regularly left more descendants than similar groups of pure heterosexuals, the capacity for homosexual development would remain prominent in the population as a whole. And it has remained prominent in the great majority of human societies, to the consternation of anthropologists, biologists and others.

Supporting evidence for this new kin-selection hypothesis does not exist. In fact, it has not even been examined critically. But the fact that it is internally consistent and can be squared with the results of kin selection in other kinds of organisms should give us pause before labeling homosexuality an illness. I might add that if the hypothesis is correct, we can expect homosexuality to decline over many generations. The reason is that the extreme dispersal of family groups in modern industrial societies leaves fewer opportunities for preferred treatment of relatives. The labor of homosexuals is spread more evenly over the population at large, and the narrower form of Darwinian natural selection turns against the duplication of genes favoring this kind of altruism.

A peacemaking role of modern sociobiology also seems likely in the interpretation of aggression, the behavior at the opposite pole from altruism. To cite aggression as a form of social behavior is, in a way, contradictory; considered by itself, it is more accurately identified as antisocial behavior. But, when viewed in a social context, it seems to be one of the most important and widespread organizing techniques. Animals use it to stake out their own territories and to establish their rank in the pecking orders. And because members of one group often cooperate for the purpose of directing aggression at competitor groups, altruism and hostility have come to be opposite sides of the same coin.

Konrad Lorenz, in his celebrated book "On Aggression," argued that human beings share a general instinct for aggressive behavior with animals, and that this instinct must somehow be relieved, if only through competitive sport. Erich Fromm, in "The Anatomy of Human Destructiveness," took the still dimmer view that man's behavior is subject to a unique death instinct that often leads to pathological aggression beyond that encountered in animals. Both of these interpretations are essentially wrong. A close look at aggressive behavior in a variety of animal societies, many of which have been carefully studied only since the time Lorenz drew his conclusions, shows that aggression occurs in a myriad of forms and is subject to rapid evolution.

We commonly find one species of bird or mammal to be highly territorial, employing elaborate, aggressive displays and attacks, while a second, otherwise similar, species shows little or no territorial behavior. In short, the case for a pervasive aggressive instinct does not exist.

The reason for the lack of a general drive seems quite clear. Most kinds of aggressive behavior are perceived by biologists as particular responses to crowding in the environment. Animals use aggression to gain control over necessities—usually food or shelter—which are in short supply or likely to become short at some time during the life cycle. Many species seldom, if ever, run short of these necessities; rather, their numbers are controlled by predators, parasites or emigration. Such animals are characteristically pacific in their behavior toward one another.

Mankind, let me add at once, happens to be one of the aggressive species. But we are far from being the most aggressive. Recent studies of hyenas, lions and langur monkeys, to take three familiar species, have disclosed that under natural conditions these animals engage in lethal fighting, infanticide and even cannibalism at a rate far above that found in human beings. When a count is made of the number of murders committed per thousand individuals per year, human beings are well down the list of aggressive creatures, and I am fairly confident that this would still be the case even if our episodic wars were to be averaged in. Hyena packs even engage in deadly pitched battles that are virtually indistinguishable from primitive human warfare. Here is some action in the Ngorongoro Crater as described by Hans Kruuk of Oxford University:

"The two groups mixed with an uproar of calls, but within seconds the sides parted again and the Mungi hyenas ran away, briefly pursued by the Scratching Rock hyenas, who then returned to the carcass. About a dozen of the Scratching Rock hyenas, though, grabbed one of the Mungi males and bit him wherever they could—especially in the belly, the feet and the ears. The victim was completely covered by his attackers, who proceeded to maul him for about 10 minutes while their clan fellows were eating the wildebeest. The Mungi male was literally pulled apart, and when I later studied the injuries more closely, it appeared that his ears were bitten off and so were his feet and testicles, he was paralyzed by a spinal injury, had large gashes in the hind legs and belly, and subcutaneous hemorrhages all over. . . . The next morning, I found a hyena eating from the carcass and saw evidence that more had been there; about one-third of the internal organs and muscles had been eaten. Cannibals!

Alongside ants, which conduct assassinations, skirmishes and pitched battles as routine business, men are all but tranquil pacifists. Ant wars, incidentally, are especially easy to observe during the spring and summer in most towns and cities in the Eastern United States. Look for masses of small blackish brown ants struggling together on sidewalks or lawns. The combatants are members of rival colonies of the common pavement ant, *Tetramorium caespitum.* Thousands of individuals may be involved, and the battlefield typically occupies several square feet of the grassroots jungle.

Although some aggressive behavior in one form or another is characteristic of virtually all human societies (even the gentle !Kung Bushmen until recently had a murder rate comparable to that of Detroit and Houston), I know of no evidence that it constitutes a drive searching for an outlet. Certainly, the conduct of animals cannot be used as an argument for the widespread existence of such a drive.

In general, animals display a spectrum of possible actions, ranging from no response at all, through threats and feints, to an all-out attack; and they select the action that best fits the circumstances of each particular threat. A rhesus monkey, for example, signals a peaceful intention toward another troop member by averting its gaze or approaching with conciliatory lip-smacking. A low intensity of hostility is conveyed by an alert, level stare. The hard look you receive from a rhesus when you enter a laboratory or the primate building of a zoo is not simple curiosity—it is a threat.

From that point onward, the monkey conveys increasing levels of confidence and readiness to fight by adding new components one by one, or in combination: The mouth opens in an apparent expression of astonishment, the head bobs up and down, explosive *ho*'s! are uttered and the hands slap the ground. By the time the rhesus is performing all of these displays, and perhaps taking little forward lunges as well, it is prepared to fight. The ritualized performance, which up to this point served to demonstrate precisely the mood of the animal, may then give way to a shrieking, rough-and-tumble assault in which hands, feet and teeth are used as weapons. Higher levels of aggression are not exclusively directed at other monkeys.

Once, in the field, I had a large male monkey reach the hand-slapping stage three feet in front of me when I accidentally frightened an infant monkey which may or may not have been a part of the male's family. At that distance, the male looked like a small gorilla. My guide, Professor Stuart Altmann of the University of Chicago, wisely advised me to avert my gaze and to look as much as possible like a subordinate monkey.

Despite the fact that many kinds of animals are capable of a rich, graduated repertory of aggressive actions, and despite the fact that aggression is important in the organization of their societies, it is possible for individuals to go through a normal life, rearing offspring, with nothing more than occasional bouts of play-fighting and exchanges of lesser hostile displays. The key is the environment: Frequent intense display and escalated fighting are adaptive responses to certain kinds of social stress which a particular animal may or may not be fortunate enough to avoid during its lifetime. By the same token, we should not be surprised to find a few human cultures, such as the Hopi or the newly discovered Tasaday of Mindanao, in which aggressive interactions are minimal. In a word, the evidence from comparative studies of animal behavior cannot be used to justify extreme forms of aggression, bloody drama or violent competitive sports practiced by man.

This brings us to the topic which, in my experience, causes the most difficulty in discussions of human sociobiology: the relative importance of genetic vs. environmental factors in the shaping of behavioral traits. I am aware that the very notion of genes controlling behavior in human beings is scandalous to some scholars. They are quick to project the following political scenario: Genetic determinism will lead to support for the status quo and continued social injustice. Seldom is the equally plausible scenario considered: Environmentalism will lead to support for authoritarian mind control and worse injustice. Both sequences are highly unlikely, unless politicians or ideologically committed scientists are allowed to dictate the uses of science. Then anything goes.

That aside, concern over the implications of sociobiology usually proves to be due to a simple misunderstanding about the nature of heredity. Let me try to set the matter straight as briefly but fairly as possible. *What the genes prescribe is not necessarily a particular behavior but the capacity to develop certain behaviors and, more than that, the tendency to develop them in various specified environments.* Suppose that we could enumerate all conceivable behavior belonging to one category—say, all the possible kinds of aggressive responses—and for convenience label them by letters. In this imaginary example, there might be exactly 23 such responses, which we designate A through W. Human beings do not and cannot manifest all the behaviors; perhaps all societies in the world taken together employ A through P. Furthermore, they do not develop each of these with equal facility; there is a strong tendency under most possible conditions of child rearing for behaviors A through G to appear, and consequently H through P are encountered in very few cultures. It is this *pattern* of possibilities and probabilities that is inherited.

To make such a statement wholly meaningful, we must go on to compare human beings with other species. We note that hamadryas baboons can perhaps develop only F through J, with a strong bias toward F and G, while one kind of termite can show only A and another kind of termite only B. Which behavior a particular human being displays depends on the experience received within his own culture, but the total array of human possibilities, as opposed to baboon or termite possibilities, is inherited. It is the evolution of this pattern which sociobiology attempts to analyze.

We can be more specific about human patterns. It is possible to make a reasonable inference about the most primitive and general human social traits by combining two procedures. First, note is made of the most widespread qualities of hunter-gatherer societies. Although the behavior of the people is complex and intelligent, the way of life to which their cultures are adapted is primitive. The human species evolved with such an elementary economy for hundreds of thousands of years; thus, its innate pattern of social responses can be expected to have been principally shaped by this way of life. The second procedure is to compare the most widespread hunter-gatherer qualities with similar behavior displayed by the species of langurs, colobus, macaques, baboons, chimpanzees, gibbons and other Old World monkeys and apes that, together, comprise man's closest living relatives.

Where the same pattern of traits occurs in man—and in most or all of the primates—we conclude that it has been subject to relatively little evolution. Its possession by hunter-gatherers indicates (but does not prove) that the pattern was also possessed by man's immediate ancestors; the pattern also belongs to the class of behaviors least prone to change even in economically more advanced societies. On the other hand, when the behavior varies a great deal among the primate species, it is less likely to be resistant to change.

The list of basic human patterns that emerges from this screening technique is intriguing: (1) The number of intimate group members is variable but normally 100 or less; (2) some amount of aggressive and territorial behavior is basic, but its intensity is graduated and its particular forms cannot be predicted from one culture to another with precision; (3) adult males are more aggressive and are dominant over females; (4) the societies are to a large extent organized around prolonged maternal care and extended relationships between mothers and children; and (5) play, including at least mild forms of contest and mock-aggression, is keenly pursued and probably essential to normal development.

We must then add the qualities that are so distinctively ineluctably human that they can be safely classified as genetically based: the overwhelming drive of individuals to develop some form of a true, semantic language, the rigid avoidance of incest by taboo and the weaker but still strong tendency for sexually bonded women and men to divide their labor into specialized tasks.

In hunter-gatherer societies, men hunt and women stay at home. This strong bias persists in most agricultural and industrial societies and, on that ground alone, appears to have a genetic origin. No solid evidence exists as to when the division of labor appeared in man's ancestors or how resistant to change it might be during the continuing revolution for women's rights. My own guess is that the genetic bias is intense enough to cause a substantial division of labor even in the most free and most egalitarian of future societies.

As shown by research recently summarized in the book "The Psychology of Sex Differences," by Eleanor Emmons Maccoby and Carol Nagy Jacklin, boys consistently show more mathematical and less verbal ability than girls on the average, and they are more aggressive from the first hours of social play at age 2 to manhood. Thus, even with identical education and equal access to all professions, men are likely to continue to play a disproportionate role in political life, business and science. But that is only a guess and, even if correct, could not be used to argue for anything less than sex-blind admission and free personal choice.

Certainly, there are no a priori grounds for concluding that the males of a predatory species must be a specialized hunting class. In chimpanzees, males are the hunters; which may be suggestive in view of the fact that these apes are by a wide margin our closest living relatives. But, in lions, the females are the providers, typically working in groups with their cubs in tow. The stronger and largely parasitic males hold back from the chase, but rush in to claim first share of the meat when the kill has been made. Still another pattern is followed by wolves and African wild dogs: Adults of both sexes, which are very aggressive, cooperate in the hunt.

The moment has arrived to stress that there is a dangerous trap in sociobiology, one which can be avoided only by constant vigilance. The trap is the naturalistic fallacy of ethics, which uncritically concludes that what is, should be. The "what is" in human nature is to a large extent the heritage of a Pleistocene hunter-gatherer existence. When any genetic bias is demonstrated, it cannot be used to justify a continuing practice in present and future societies. Since most of us live in a radically new environment of our own making, the pursuit of such a practice would be bad biology; and like all bad biology, it would invite disaster. For example, the tendency under certain conditions to conduct warfare against competing groups might well be in our genes, having been advantageous to our Neolithic ancestors, but it could lead to global suicide now. To rear as many healthy children as possible was long the road to security; yet with the population of the world brimming over, it is now the way to environmental disaster.

Our primitive old genes will therefore have to carry the load of much more cultural change in the future. To an extent not yet known, we trust —we insist—that human nature can adapt to more encompassing forms of altruism and social justice. Genetic biases can be trespassed, passions averted or redirected, and ethics altered; and the human genius for making contracts can continue to be applied to achieve healthier and freer societies. Yet the mind is not infinitely malleable. Human sociobiology should be pursued and its findings weighed as the best means we have of tracing the evolutionary history of the mind. In the difficult journey ahead, during which our ultimate guide must be our deepest and, at present, least understood feelings, surely we cannot afford an ignorance of history.

Val Dusek
CRITIQUE OF SOCIOBIOLOGY

Edward O. Wilson's Sociobiology: A New Synthesis *and his more recent work,* On Human Nature, *have both generated considerable controversy. On the one hand, other self-proclaimed sociobiologists have followed his lead by arguing that much of human social behavior is biologically (genetically) determined and that many of our social institutions are a result of biological evolution. On the other hand, numerous critics have challenged sociobiology on both political and scientific grounds. Val Dusek, who teaches philosophy at the University of New Hampshire, is one of these critics. In the article that follows, he argues that Wilson's kin-selection model functions ideologically as a reflection of paternalistic capitalism and in defense of the nuclear family. He also argues that, in its more popular form, sociobiology does no more than present morality tales, under the guise of science. In addition, Dusek challenges the scientific status of Wilson's genetic determinism, arguing that we should substitute for it a theory of genetic possibilities.*

Since its appearance in 1975, Edward O. Wilson's *Sociobiology: A New Synthesis* has been the center of a huge controversy, which has been *both* scientific and political. The questions of scientific concern are the following: Is Wilson's attempt to explain human social structures on the basis of biology, especially on the basis of Darwinian evolutionary theory, a truly scientific theory? Is it based on fact? Is it testable by observation and experiment? Or is it merely a series of interesting stories and speculations about superficial similarities between human and animal societies? On the political level, is Wilson's human sociobiology a hardheaded description of the real biological limits to political and social reform, or is it an apology and justification for the oppression of women by men, of blacks by whites, and of poor by rich? After examining the theory and the arguments of its supporters and its defenders, I have come to the conclusion that, despite Wilson's undoubtedly valuable work in the study of insects, his work on human sociobiology is doubtfully scientific—often pseudoscientific—and that, politically, despite his consciously liberal beliefs and intentions, his theory has become popular precisely because it justifies the power structures that exist in contemporary society.

.   .   .

Wilson's work began with the study of insect societies. Insect behavior is programmed to a very high degree and is thus a prime example of the direct, very specific determination of behavior by the genetic program. Insect behavior is often extraordinarily rigid and stereotyped. The wasp, which buries its prey in a hole that it has dug, and which, when its captive prey is disturbed and removed, will go through the same sequence of behavior over and over again, is a case in point. The question is whether the explanation of behavior through specifically inherited determining factors can be extended from the rigid, programmed, specific behavior of wasps, ants, and bees, to the highly variable and culturally intertwined behavior of human beings. Wilson claims that even in the most complex human behavior there are genetically determined tendencies and limits, a claim that will be examined in detail later.

. . . At the core of sociobiological theory is the application of Darwin's biological theory of natural selection to animal and human behavior. Darwin's theory of natural selection involves characteristics that can vary and that, in any particular form, have a certain stability; and a process of selection by the environment, in which organisms bearing certain characteristics are eliminated. Thus, novel characteristics arise and perpetuate themselves to a great degree or to a small degree. Some of them survive, and others are eliminated through the process of selection. In the growth of an organism, and through interaction with the environment, the genes, sometimes apparently individually, but almost always in concert or in various combinations, produce the observable characteristics of the organism. Organisms that have certain characters reproduce themselves at a greater rate, or they live longer to reproduce themselves at the same rate for a greater period of time, or both. Those organisms that leave more offspring, which, in turn, reproduce themselves perpetuate their genetically based characteristics. This mechanism of variation, differential reproduction, and selection accounts for the characteristics that we find organisms to have today, and it also accounts for the way in which organisms and entire species have changed through time. This natural selection model can be used to account for behavioral characteristics of organisms only insofar as these characteristics are genetically determined.

A problem for this neo-Darwinian model of individual selection and survival through success in competition is the so-called altruistic behaviors of animals and humans. Altruistic behaviors involve the sacrifice made by an organism in an attempt to aid other organisms and at the expense of its own survival and/or reproduction. Social Darwinists in the latter part of the nineteenth century claimed that altruism went against Darwinian evolutionary theory and that only competitive and aggressive behaviors were biologically adaptive. The early social Darwinists used Darwin's theory to support the competition and aggression that existed in the late nineteenth-century American capitalist economy, in which ruthless competition and the success of the "robber barons" were characteristics. Some anarchists, such as Kropotkin, argued that altruism and mutual aid were just as much a feature of the biological world as competition, but such views were overwhelmed by those of others, who were attempting to defend unbridled competition on biological grounds. The sociobiologists do justify some competitive traits, such as entrepreneurship, deception, and spite, on biological grounds in a manner similar to the older social Darwinists, but they have added a new Darwinian explanation of altruism. This is the one truly novel theoretical contribution of sociobiology. Because sociobiologists leave a place for altruism, they claim that they are not conservative defenders of ruthless competition, like the old social Darwinists, and that their theory does not have direct political implications. I believe that this is false. Twentieth-century capitalism is characterized by the decline of unbridled competition and the rise of the paternalistic corporation and the welfare-warfare state, which plays a larger role in directing the economy. These institutions are still based on competition, but they demand larger areas of cooperation. I believe that the theory of the sociobiologists reflects this new paternalistic capitalism, just as the older theories of the social Darwinists reflected and justified the more competitive "free market" economy.

. . .

The sociobiologists' justification of altruism on the basis of individual selection is as follows: the unit of reproduction is not the group, or even the individual, but the *gene*. Genes can reproduce themselves in two ways. One is by means of ordinary sexual reproduction, which the original Darwinian theory dealt with. The other is by indirect reproduction—not by the passing on of one's own genes through mating, but by the aiding of a relative who shares a proportion of genes structurally similar to one's own. That is, if I save a brother or a sister who shares about half of "my" genes (that is, genes that are duplicates of my own), I am, in effect, reproducing half of "my" genes by helping a brother or sister to survive and reproduce. By saving a cousin, I am doing the same thing, but to a lesser extent, in that he or she shares only one-eighth of "my" genes. J. B. S. Haldane, who was a Marxist, as well as one of the leading biologists of our century, used to joke that he would lay down his life for two brothers or eight cousins. (Haldane's joke, by the way, shows that this idea was around several decades ago but did not get developed in great detail until the late sixties and seventies. He would probably be among the critics of the sociobiologists, who have developed his joke into a theory to explain all of human society.)

The sociobiologists' theory of individual selection as a basis for the survival of altruistic traits was first applied with greatest success to the social insects. The peculiar genetic arrangement of ants and bees (though not termites, which are an unexplained counterexample, even in Wilson's most solid territory) makes sister workers more closely related to their queen than they are to each other. They can reproduce "their" genes by aiding the queen to reproduce more effectively than if they themselves mated with drones and had offspring of their own. This ingenious application of selection for "altruism" among the social insects, in Wilson's field of specialty, led to the development and generalization of models for selection of altruistic traits in all sorts of much more complicated situations among other animals, including human beings. All sorts of ingenious, speculative, and sometimes perverse models of altruism selection were devised to explain everything from the nuclear family to pan-handling.

The kin-selection models, which are individualistic selection models for altruism, have been applied with wild abandon by sociobiologists to all sorts of phenomena in situations where experimental checks are absent or impossible and where simpler social explanations would do just as well (as in the case of panhandling). Why have they caught on so? Why did Haldane's joke become the basis of complicated biological theories and popularizations (in such publications as *Time* magazine) in the seventies? I believe that there are two reasons for this. One has to do with the questioning of the justice and authority of the large corporations, which has been occurring in the seventies; and the other has to do with the rise of the women's liberation movement in this decade, and with the resultant questioning of traditional sex roles and family arrangements.

The structure of the kin-selection models as individual selection models allows us to think about the biological world in terms with which we have become familiar through our economic reasoning as consumers. Wilson notes that we are all familiar with bloodlines and family trees and with economic calculations of costs and benefits from different lines of action. The kin-selection models combine these two familiar forms of thinking to calculate, "from the point of view of a gene," how much reproductive payoff we would get from helping various relatives to reproduce themselves. This kind of thinking allows us to view the biological world as if it were a marketplace, and genetic problems of evolution as if they were economic problems. This leads us to think of biological nature itself as a kind of economic marketplace. And if nature is a kind of economic marketplace, then our own capitalist markets, functioning as badly as they are—with inflation, energy shortages, Koreagate scandals, and the like—must be "natural." After all, they work like biological nature itself! But, what actually has been done here is that certain models have been borrowed from economics and applied to biology. Then, once we have come to believe in them sufficiently, we are led to take our economic theory for biological reality, and thus, to "see" that our economic system is justified by the workings of biological nature itself. But this is purely circular reasoning. We have speculatively applied economic models to biology and have then reapplied those same models to economics, which is where they came from originally, having forgotten that they were economic models to begin with. This is the same sort of thing that happened with Darwin's original theory. Both Darwin and his co-discoverer Wallace came up with the theory as a result of reading the economist Malthus. They applied Malthus's economic idea to biology, and the social Darwinists borrowed it back to apply it to the very society from which Malthus devised his original theory. But the social Darwinists could claim the prestige of a solid, natural science—biology—for their social and political theories.

.   .   .

The second cause, and one that is much more direct and obvious, for the scientific popularity of the kin-selection models is the concern with finding ways to defend the nuclear family against the new sex roles and new forms of sexual relations of men and women. The women's liberation movement; the demand for day-care centers for the children of working women; the growth of the commune movement in the early seventies, including groups in which children are reared collectively—all of these have threatened the nuclear family, in which husband works and wife stays home to perform the full-time job of rearing the children and keeping house. This nuclear family is still the ideal of television ads, but only a small fraction of households really correspond to it. The defense of this institution extends, with varying degrees of subtlety, from the New Right, with its campaign against the ERA and so on; through various social organizations and councils on "saving" the family; right up to the highest theoretical level—sociobiology. The kin-selection model "proves" that altruistic acts, if indeed they are the result of biological natural selection, would be most strongly selected for in the case of parents and children or brothers and sisters. Between uncles and aunts and nephews and nieces, or between cousins, in a society such as ours, altruistic acts would be biologically profitable, but much less so than they would be between members of the nuclear family. Altruistic acts between nonrelatives would have fewer advantages. There are models of reciprocal altruism that have been developed to explain altruism between nonrelatives, but their payoff (I use the monetary term advisedly) is generally much smaller than that between close relatives. Thus, sociobiology gives "biological" justification for the maintenance of the nuclear family and shows, or purports to show, why communal child rearing, day-care centers, and so on, are "biologically" unviable.

.   .   .

Around the core theory of sociobiology, that of kin selection, which we have already examined, are a series of successively vaguer and looser modes of theorizing. Much of sociobiology as a field, especially in the form in which it has been popularized in high school curricula, movies, and so on, takes the form of analogies between various human social behaviors and animal behaviors. Given a superficial similarity between a human social behavior and an animal behavior, it is claimed that the human behavior arose from the apparently similar animal behavior or that the human cultural institution arose by the same evolutionary mechanism by which the animal behavior arose. But, often, the comparisons are strained, superficial, and selective. The most obvious case of superficial analogy, which was pointed out by Lewontin in early criticisms of Wilson, is the presence of "castes" and "slaves" among ants. Ant castes involve highly deterministically-biologically inherited features of organisms, while human castes arise not from evolutionary differentiation but from conquest or religious incorporation. Ant slaves are members of a different species and are not bought and sold like human slaves. Wilson was apparently struck more by this than by other criticisms of his work, for in *On Human Nature,* he comes out bravely against slavery. Of course, opposition to slavery is quite consistent with a liberal defense of male dominance and corporate capitalism. In an article in *Psychology Today,* David Barash, one of the popularizers of sociobiology, discovers cuckoldry, prostitution, and a number of other "human" amatory institutions among the birds. But hummingbird "prostitution" does not involve any of the institutions or economics of human prostitution, nor is it related to marital institutions, as is human prostitution. David Barash, who is perhaps representative of the *Playboy* wing of sociobiology, uses his superficial analogies to justify various sorts of sexual libertinage, while Trivers, who contributed the reciprocal altruism model to sociobiology and who worked with Wilson at Harvard, and Dawkins, who wrote *The Selfish Gene*—a crude but lucid popularization of sociobiological theory— tend to use them to defend the flawed and conflict-ridden nuclear family. Barash thinks himself clever in his assertion, "Ironically, Mother Nature appears to be a sexist"[1]

Note that the sociobiologists *select* what animals to analogize with human societies and that they also *select* certain periods and versions of human societies on which to make their analogies. There are a great many, often mutually incompatible, animal behaviors in different species; and there are a great many different human social organizations in different parts of the world and at different times in human history. There are aggressive animals and peaceful animals; there are aggressive human societies and peaceful human societies. There are animal species in which males are physically dominant; and there are those in which females are physically dominant. But sociobiologists select a very small set from this diversity of human and animal traits, and they justify their *selected* human traits with their *selected* animal comparisons.

.   .   .

Much of the power and popularity of sociobiology comes not from the ingenious mathematical calculations of kin selection and reciprocal altruism but from the appeal to parallels of human nature to that of animals. Aesop's fables, animal myths, nursery rhymes, and many cartoon characters are examples of older and more primitive versions of the approach to moralizing through parables concerning animals. The sociobiologists often present the same sort of morality tales but with the appearance of more biological sophistication.

.   .   .

The sociobiologists also argue that race conflict and group conflict are "natural," on the basis of a speculative application of their kin-selec-

[1]David Barash, *Sociobiology and Human Behavior* (New York, John Wiley, 1976), 283.

tion models. Altruism, based supposedly on the "selfish gene" in its drive to reproduce itself, will be directed more toward close relatives than toward distant ones. Hence, altruism toward people who look like us, and hostility and aggression toward those who look different from us are justified biologically by the sociobiologists. Sociobiologists deny that they are racists, for they do not assert that whites are better than blacks; but they are *racialists,* who justify an account of history in terms of race struggle. However, it would be misleading to compare sociobiologists to the modern racist theorists who propose the inherited superiority of whites over blacks based on IQ, or to the nineteenth-century racist sociologists. But it is fair to compare them to the more academically "respectable" racialist theorists who contributed indirectly to racist tendencies.

The adaptive traits of the evolved human being and of human society, according to Wilson, are males dominant over females, aggression, territoriality, hostility to other races and ethnic groups, spite, and indoctrinability. Wilson does take "liberal" positions in opposing slavery, denying racial superiority, and defending homosexuality on speculative "biological" grounds. But the apologetic thrust of his theory can be seen in his choice of traits used for the weaving of his unproven evolutionary stories and speculations. Sociobiologists also choose their animal groups carefully, discussing only, or mainly, those that exhibit male dominance, deception, aggression, and so on. For instance, sociobiologists like to discuss the plains baboons, a group in which males dominate females, but they neglect to discuss the forest baboons, in which there are no male-dominance hierarchies.

Sociobiology expresses its defense of sexism and capitalist power relations on two levels. The more obvious level is in their selection of human traits, such as male aggressiveness and female passivity, or of "entrepreneurship" as an evolved human trait. But, at a deeper level, the very structure of the theory has capitalism and sexism built right into its logic. We have seen that the models of individual selection are quite clearly based on capitalist-market, economically-competitive economic models. Also, the account of the evolution of human traits emphasizes that males compete and struggle for females and that the only role of females is that of passively choosing the victor. Thus, the characteristics selected for are *male* characteristics, since it is the males, not the females, who compete. Females are merely passive receptacles for male genes. Indeed, Wilson claims that there is a biological propensity for males to occupy most posts of business, political, and intellectual leadership. As a "liberal," in his latest book, *On Human Nature,* he covers himself by noting that we *can* work to counteract the "natural" tendency. But the alternatives he mentions are: (1) the use of administrative and political constraint or pressure, which will lessen "freedom" in the society and (2) eugenics and genetic engineering. Thus, though Wilson claims that he has not argued for the inevitability of male dominance and for dominance by those selected for "entrepreneurship," the alternatives he offers are obviously not meant to be attractive. We are offered the choice between a free capitalist and sexist society or a managed society that: (1) restricts freedom and rights and (2) offers tendencies toward *Brave New World* biological programs. Wilson has offered a disguised and qualified version of the usual cold war alternatives.

But, even if Wilson's choice of the traits of "human nature" and of the animal behaviors that he uses for his analogies is biased, is there not, after all, a biological "human nature"? In answering this question, Wilson is more qualified and subtle than the earlier, cruder biological determinists. He does not emphasize specific, programmed behaviors (although, in the emotional realm, he sometimes comes close to this), but he emphasizes the "tendencies" and "limits" set by biology. But, even this apparently weaker version of biological determinism is open to considerable scientific and philosophical objections.

Wilson, attempting to emphasize the mildness of his views and the weakness of his biological determinism, guesses that human behavior is 10 percent biologically determined and 90 percent socially modulated. But the very idea that influences on behavior can be divided into percentages of influence in this way is surprisingly simpleminded for someone as well trained in evolutionary theory and as well read in animal behavior as Wilson.

One thing that the study of genetics and development in the last few decades has shown is that genes do not provide static, one-dimensional "tendencies" that can then be superficially and slightly modified for environmental influences. Also, genes do not operate in isolation. That is, most traits or characteristics are not the result of single genes but of the complex interaction of a number of individual genes. One of the differences between classical Mendelian genetics and the modern biochemical genetics, which has developed since the discovery of the structure of DNA, involves the complexity of the biochemical paths between the coded pattern of the DNA (the modern version of the "genes") and the expression of that code in the developed organism. This complexity, and the shift from the classical notion of gene as a hypothetical "factor," which is identified by the observable external trait (such as color, in Mendel's early work), to the chemical DNA-sequence mediated by numerous steps of biochemistry interacting with the biochemical products of other parts of the sequence, has led hardheaded philosophers of biology, such as David Hull, to question the simple "reduction" of classical genetics to biochemical genetics.

If simple chemical and physiological traits are often the outcome of this complex interaction, it is very likely that this is even more the case with behaviors that involve the coordination of many organs and physiological traits of the organism. And the very complex human traits that Wilson discusses, such as spite, homosexuality, or indoctrinability, are presumably even more complex, if indeed they are traits at all.

Furthermore, the same gene may, in one environment, be expressed by a characteristic that appears to a greater or lesser degree, depending on the increase or decrease of some environmental factor. But, it is also the case that a gene may cease to be expressed at all, or that it may express itself in a different way when that environmental factor rises above or falls below some threshold. If the gene ceases to express itself, then the expression of other genes may appear. As the environmental variable increases or decreases still further, yet *other* genes may express themselves in organisms nurtured in that environment. Even the most obvious and essential human trait (such as possessing hands) can fail to appear if the developing organism is exposed to subtle variations of the environment (such as the mother's taking of the drug thalidomide).

The sociobiologists tend to speak as if each gene or gene-complex controls a single, identifiable character and that there is a single "gene" for each obvious, observable characteristic. Sociobiologists also speak as if each gene or gene-complex constantly produces a single tendency to produce that character, which varies merely *quantitatively,* that is, merely becomes stronger or weaker as the environment varies. But this simpleminded, atomistic, linear conception of how genes work is misleading. There are no preexistent tendencies to express characteristics that are somehow sitting there behind the observable animal anatomy or behavior in different environments. The same gene or gene-complex may fail to show expression at all, or it may have entirely different expressions, depending on the environment of the growing organism.

An especially clear example that critics of sociobiology, such as Gould and Lewontin, have used is that of the human chin. There is no gene or gene-complex that operates directly to influence chin-length. A sociobiologist might talk as if the "strong chin" of Nelson Rockefeller or of the early Egyptian pharaohs was a genetic trait (here, to be neatly correlated with political rule). But it turns out that, when further analyzed by biologists, chin-length is not an evolutionary trait at all. The chin, so obvious to us common-sense observors of the human face, is a kind of evolutionary side-effect of the different rates of shrinking of two competing growth-fields of the skull. What we see as a "strong chin" is simply the result of the disparity of the rate of slowdown of these two unobvious growth rates that the student of human evolution has discovered. Indeed, if something so obvious a characteristic as chin-length turns out not to be an evolutionary trait, how much more complex and less obvious must be the interaction of the genetic traits that are necessary conditions for behavior.

Wilson's conception of "human nature" is in the form of an aggregate, or heap, of traits that preexist as determining "tendencies" or "predispositions." We now see that this conception of "human nature" is misleading on several levels. First, Wilson *selects* his characteristics for "human nature" on the basis of unrecognized biases. He emphasizes characteristics, such as aggressiveness, entrepreneurship, male dominance, and so on, which are the most obvious characteristics of humans living in male-dominated, capitalist-market, war-waging societies. He neglects or downplays those characteristics that humans show in tribes that are peaceful or are less male dominated than our own society. Second, Wilson assumes that these traits correlate in a one-to-one fashion with genes. The gene keeps pumping out the trait, and at best, the environment or learning fosters or dampens it to some degree. But the "traits" Wilson picks out, even if they *were* genuine universal characteristics of our common-sense description of humans, may not be what they appear to be, genetically or evolutionarily. Like the chin, they may be "obvious" characteristics to naive observation, but from the point of view of biology, they may be artifacts of the interaction of less obvious, more complex characteristics. Finally, genes in general, and in the complex traits involved in behavior, are most unlikely to produce static, preexisting determining tendencies that are merely expressed to quantitatively different degrees, depending on the environment. When the environment is varied ever so slightly, genes may produce widely differing traits, or no traits at all (as when the introduction of a tiny amount of thalidomide into the mother's physiology causes the baby to develop without hands).

An alternative to Wilson's genetic determinism, or even to his weaker genetic tendency theory, is the concept of genetic possibility. Genes open up possibilities. Those possibilities are not absolute determinants of individual traits, nor are they even preexisting tendencies to manifest some trait. They are merely possibilities that are played upon by the environment, both in the form of the chemical environment of the growing organism and in the form of the social environment of the behaving human organism.

Human beings (at least in environments not modified by some of the more unfortunate products of the chemical industry) have hands as a biologically based characteristic. But, what we do with those hands—what we build, what we raise to feed ourselves, what we create artistically—is not genetically determined. In the same way, the human capacity for language and the human need for sociality may well be genetically determined, but the variety of human languages and social structures shows that those capacities can be used in an enormous variety of ways. That human beings are dependent upon adult humans for a long period of time, in a way that baby insects or baby horses are not, is biologically determined; but what they learn or are taught during that relatively long period of dependency is not. The linguist Chomsky has claimed that to speak is just as natural for humans as swimming is for fish or flying is for birds. But Chomsky has also emphasized that the human capacity to speak involves the freedom to create an infinite variety of sentences through a simple, finite means. *What* we say, even if the capacity to speak has a genetic basis, is *not* biologically determined but is a product of the interaction of our creative capacity with our social environment. Similarly, it may be that the dependency of human infants upon adults is part of the "genetic" basis of human sociality. Given this sociality and the development of the human hand and brain, our forerunners may "naturally" have worked in social groups, allowing them to survive as members of a group, whereas, alone, they would have perished in confrontations with larger animals. As recent anthropologists, such as Washburn, have argued, the development of the prehensile hand for tool use may itself have led to the development of the enlarged brain. And tool use via the brain may have created further capacities for cooperation and language. But even though language, tool use, sociality, and hence, social labor are possibilities opened up to us by our biology, they do not determine the forms of society that may be developed on the basis of that biological capacity. As simple stone tools were creatively developed into complex technologies in different environments, and as humans used their language capacity to develop a variety of language systems, symbolism, and finally, science, the forms of society themselves changed vastly throughout history. Those forms of society supplied a variety of new environments in which humans made further changes and developments of technology and language. But these new developments and social and cultural evolution are no longer determined by biological evolution.

The vast variety of societies, technologies, languages, and ideas humans have developed are not "determined" by our genes. Wilson himself admits that the speed of recent social and cultural change is far too rapid to be accounted for by the much slower rate of change of biological evolution. The anatomy and physiology of modern humans is almost exactly the same as that which humans had during the last Ice Age. Our genetic makeup gives us the capacity for society and culture, but it does not at all determine the forms of that society and culture. Tens of thousands of years ago, once social change began to "take off," it proceeded ever more rapidly on its own and was not determined by biological evolution. Giant empires have risen and fallen in a few centuries (the Islamic conquests of Mohammed), in a few generations (the empire of Tamburlaine), or even in a decade (Nazi Germany), while biological evolution takes millennia. Wilson attempts to account for these sorts of phenomena by obviously *ad hoc* constructions such as "the multiplier effect," in which he simply *postulates* that small genetic changes can have huge effects.

Anthropologists have collected a wealth of data on the variety of social arrangements tribes of humans in different parts of the world have developed. Societies have been warlike and peaceful, male-ruled and female-ruled, capitalist and communist. Yet even this great variety of social arrangements is only a fragment of what might have been observed a few centuries ago, before anthropologists began to investigate, and before European exploration and the spread of European settlers and commodities destroyed numerous tribes—either through outright genocide or through social change affected by the new commodities—whose customs went unrecorded by their destroyers.

In short, both geographically and historically, we find a great variety of human customs, family structures, economies, and cultures, only a fraction of which anthropologists and historians have managed to record. Many tribes disappeared before anthropologists studied them, and recorded history deals, for the most part, with those societies that had writing and whose written records have survived for us to read and interpret.

Wilson's biological determinism, even in its weaker form, that of biological "propensities," to which sociobiologists retreat when faced by their critics, hardly does justice to the phenomena of human social history and development. The function of sociobiology can only be to narrow our conception of what human beings have been, what they are, and what they can be. It encourages the very provincial conception of "human nature" in terms of the characteristics of our industrial-capitalist, male-dominated society during the few centuries of its existence. And it unintentionally undermines what little cosmopolitan sense of human variety and tolerance of that variety that the researches of anthropologists and the growth of democracy have pointed up within that capitalist, male-dominated society.

Wilson and the sociobiologists are able scientists in their original fields of biological research, and they are often liberal in their intentions. But the doctrine of biological determinism, whether in its stronger or its weaker forms, only debilitates the sense of the openness of human cultural and intellectual development and the sense of possibility that encourages science and socially liberates human beings.

SECTION TWO

SELF
AND
SELF-IDENTITY

Could anything be more obvious than the statements that I am myself, and you are yourself? Why, then, do so many people continually ask, "Who am I?" and "What am I?" Why do philosophers, psychologists, poets, and novelists expend so much energy talking about the problem of the self. What exactly is the problem?

It is actually a number of interrelated problems. To begin with, there is the problem of how we come to know ourselves. Then, we can ask, what is this self that we come to know? Is it something present within us from the moment of birth? Or does it evolve through the process of interaction with others? Is it a single, unified entity that we grasp from within, or are there several such entities? Is the self simply a name for the totality of our sensations and thoughts?

We also need to ask why we are so concerned with "finding ourselves." What are we trying to find? It is often said that we are searching for our identity. But what is this self-identity? Is it simply a question of definition? Is there something already in existence that I can call my true identity? Or is self-identity something to be developed, something to be achieved? The articles in this section address all of these questions.

René Descartes
MEDITATIONS

The seventeenth century was a transitional age. The new scientific approach to reality developed by Kepler and Newton appeared to be in conflict with the traditional, religious world view. The scientific view held that the earth was not the center of the universe and that the movements of the physical universe could

86

be understood by the principles of mechanics, and the human body was itself subject to these same principles. God and the idea of the soul seemed no longer necessary for the explanation of things.

It was at this historical juncture that philosophy became truly critical. Through most of the Middle Ages, philosophy had been dominated by religious assumptions. Now, as the scientific world view was vying for center stage, would philosophy switch its allegiance and become the handmaiden of science? Better to take nothing for granted—neither the presuppositions of religion nor the presuppositions of science. How were we to know which view of reality was correct? Each world view claimed its own special route to knowledge, and the very foundations of knowledge were at issue.

René Descartes (1596–1650), often referred to as "the father of modern philosophy," rose to this challenge. He was educated as a Jesuit but had also absorbed most of the scientific knowledge of his day. He excelled in mathematics, and his philosophical method borrowed considerably from the form of proof used in geometry. In his most famous work, Meditations on First Philosophy, *from which the present selection is taken, Descartes declared that he would not accept anything as true unless it was demonstrated to be beyond doubt or, in the manner of geometry, could be derived from principles that were beyond doubt. Thus, Descartes begins his reflections with what may be called a methodological doubt; that is, a philosophical doubt of everything that can possibly (in the logical sense) be doubted, regardless of whether or not these things are really doubted in the ordinary course of daily living. As the following selection makes clear, this doubt extends not only to such things as the principles of science but even to the commonsense beliefs upon which the principles of science depend— that there exists a world external to me, that I have a body, that there are other persons. Even the basic "truths" of mathematics and geometry can be placed in doubt.*

However, Descartes argues that there is one thing that is absolutely certain. I cannot doubt the existence of the self that has these doubts. Thus, for Descartes, "I think, therefore I am" is the fundamental axiom from which all philosophy must begin. The "I" that thinks is defined simply as a thinking thing, and from this, it follows that the essential nature of the self is the mind, as distinct from the body.

CONCERNING THE THINGS OF WHICH WE MAY DOUBT

It is now several years since I first became aware how many false opinions I had from my childhood been admitting as true, and how doubtful was everything I have subsequently based on them. Accordingly I have ever since been convinced that if I am to establish anything firm and lasting in the sciences, I must once for all, and by a deliberate effort, rid myself of all those opinions to which I have hitherto given credence, starting entirely anew, and building from the foundations up. But as this enterprise was evidently one of great magnitude, I waited until I had attained an age so mature that I could no longer expect that I should at any later date be better able to execute my design. This is what has made me delay so long; and I should now be failing in my duty, were I to continue consuming in deliberation such time for action as still remains to me.

Today, then, as I have suitably freed my mind from all cares, and have secured for myself an assured leisure in peaceful solitude, I shall at last apply myself earnestly and freely to the general overthrow of all my former opinions. In doing so, it will not be necessary for me to show that they are one and all false; that is perhaps more than can be done. But since reason has already persuaded me that I ought to withhold belief no less carefully from things not entirely certain and indubitable than from those which appear to me manifestly false, I shall be justified in setting all of them aside, if in each case I can find any ground whatsoever for regarding them as dubitable. Nor in so doing shall I be investigating each belief separately—that, like inquiry into their falsity, would be an endless labor. The withdrawal of foundations involves the downfall of whatever rests on these foundations, and what I shall therefore begin by examining are the principles on which my former beliefs rested.

Whatever, up to the present, I have accepted as possessed of the highest truth and certainty I have learned either from the senses or through the senses. Now these senses I have sometimes found to be deceptive; and it is only prudent never to place complete confidence in that by which we have even once been deceived.

But, it may be said, although the senses sometimes deceive us regarding minute objects, or such as are at a great distance from us, there are yet many other things which, though known by way of sense, are too evident to be doubted; as, for instance, that I am in this place, seated by the fire, attired in a dressing-gown, having this paper in my hands, and other similar seeming certainties. Can I deny that these hands and this body are mine, save perhaps by comparing myself to those who are insane, and whose brains are so disturbed and clouded by dark bilious vapors that they persist in assuring us that they are kings, when in fact they are in extreme poverty; or that they are clothed in gold and purple when they are in fact destitute of any covering; or that their head is made of clay and their body of glass, or that they are pumpkins. They are mad; and I should be no less insane were I to follow examples so extravagant.

None the less I must bear in mind that I am a man, and am therefore in the habit of sleeping, and that what the insane represent to themselves in their waking moments I represent to myself, with other things even less probable, in my dreams. How often, indeed, have I dreamt of myself being in this place, dressed and seated by the fire, whilst all the time I was lying undressed in bed! At the present moment it certainly seems that in looking at this paper I do so with open eyes, that the head which I move is not asleep, that it is deliberately and of set purpose that I extend this hand, and that I am sensing the hand. The things which happen to the sleeper are not so clear nor so distinct as all of these are. I cannot, however, but remind myself that on many occasions I have in sleep been deceived by similar illusions; and on more careful study of them I see that there are no certain marks distinguishing waking from sleep; and I see this so manifestly that, lost in amazement, I am almost persuaded that I am now dreaming.

Let us, then, suppose ourselves to be asleep, and that all these particulars—namely, that we open our eyes, move the head, extend the hands—are false and illusory; and let us reflect that our hands perhaps, and the whole body, are not what we see them as being. Nevertheless we must at least agree that the things seen by us in sleep are as it were like painted images, and cannot have been formed save in the likeness of what is real and true. The types of things depicted, eyes, head, hands, etc.— these at least are not imaginary, but true and existent. For in truth when painters endeavor with all possible artifice to represent sirens and satyrs by forms the most fantastic and unusual, they cannot assign them natures which are entirely new, but only make a certain selection of limbs from different animals. Even should they excogitate something so novel that nothing similar has ever before been seen, and that their work represents to us a thing entirely fictitious and false, the colors used in depicting them cannot be similarly fictitious; they at least must truly exist. And by this same reasoning, even should those general things, viz., a body, eyes, a head, hands and such like, be imaginary, we are yet bound to admit that there are things simpler and more universal which are real existents and by the intermixture of which, as in the case of the colors, all the images of which we have any awareness, be they true and real or false and fantastic, are formed. To this class of things belong corporeal nature in general and its extension, the shape of extended things, their quantity or magnitude, and their number, as also the location in which they are, the time through which they endure, and other similar things.

This, perhaps, is why we not unreasonably conclude that physics, astronomy, medicine, and all other disciplines treating of composite things are of doubtful character, and that arithmetic, geometry, etc., treating only of the simplest and most general things and but little concerned as to whether or not they are actual existents, have a content that is certain and indubitable. For whether I am awake or dreaming, 2 and 3 are 5, a square has no more than four sides; and it does not seem possible that truths so evident can ever be suspected of falsity.

Yet even these truths can be questioned. That God exists, that He is all-powerful and has created me such as I am, has long been my settled opinion. How, then, do I know that He has not arranged that there be no Earth, no heavens, no extended thing, no shape, no magnitude, no location, while at the same time securing that all these things appear to me to exist precisely as they now do? Others, as I sometimes think, deceive themselves in the things which they believe they know best. How do I know that I am not myself deceived every time I add 2 and 3, or count the sides of a square, or judge of things yet simpler, if anything simpler can be suggested? But perhaps God has not been willing that I should be thus deceived, for He is said to be supremely good. If, however, it be repugnant to the goodness of God to have created me such that I am constantly subject to deception, it would also appear to be contrary to His goodness to permit me to be sometimes deceived, and that He does permit this is not in doubt.

There may be those who might prefer to deny the existence of a God so powerful, rather than to believe that all other things are uncertain. Let us, for the present, not oppose them; let us allow, in the manner of their view, that all which has been said regarding God is a fable. Even so we shall not have met and answered the doubts suggested above regarding the reliability of our mental faculties; instead we shall have given added force to them. For in whatever way it be supposed that I have come to be what I am, whether by fate or by chance, or by a continual succession and connection of things, or by some other means, since to be deceived and to err is an imperfection, the likelihood of my being so imperfect as to be the constant victim of deception will be increased in proportion as the power to which they assign my origin is lessened. To such argument I have assuredly nothing to reply; and thus at last I am constrained to confess that there is no one of all my former opinions which is not open to doubt, and this not merely owing to want of thought on my part, or through levity, but from cogent and maturely considered reasons: Henceforth, therefore, should I desire to discover something certain, I ought to refrain from assenting to these opinions no less scrupulously than in respect of what is manifestly false.

But it is not sufficient to have taken note of these conclusions; we must also be careful to keep them in mind. For long-established customary opinions perpetually recur in thought, long and familiar usage having given them the right to occupy my mind, even almost against my will, and to be masters of my belief. Nor shall I ever lose this habit of assenting to and of confiding in them, not at least so long as I consider them as in truth they are, namely, as opinions which, though in some fashion doubtful (as I have just shown), are still, none the less, highly probable and such as it is much more reasonable to believe than to deny. This is why I shall, as I think, be acting prudently if, taking a directly contrary line, I of set purpose employ every available device for the deceiving of myself, feigning that all these opinions are entirely false and imaginary. Then, in due course, having so balanced my old-time prejudices by this new prejudice that I cease to incline to one side more than to another, my judgment, no longer dominated by misleading usages, will not be hindered by them in the apprehension of things. In this course there can, I am convinced, be neither danger nor error. What I have under consideration is a question solely of knowledge, not of action, so that I cannot for the present be at fault as being over-ready to adopt a questioning attitude.

Accordingly I shall now suppose, not that a true God, who as such must be supremely good and the fountain of truth, but that some malignant genius exceedingly powerful and cunning has devoted all his powers in the deceiving of me; I shall suppose that the sky, the earth, colors, shapes, sounds and all external things are illusions and impostures of which this evil genius has availed himself for the abuse of my credulity; I shall consider myself as having no hands, no eyes, no flesh, no blood, nor any senses, but as falsely opining myself to possess all these things. Further, I shall obstinately persist in this way of thinking; and even if, while so doing, it may not be within my power to arrive at the knowledge of any truth, there is one thing I have it in me to do, viz., to suspend judgment, refusing assent to what is false. Thereby, thanks to this resolved firmness of mind, I shall be effectively guarding myself against being imposed upon by this deceiver, no matter how powerful or how craftily deceptive he may be.

This undertaking is, however, irksome and laborious, and a certain indolence drags me back into the course of my customary life. Just as a captive who has been enjoying in sleep an imaginary liberty, should he begin to suspect that his liberty is a dream, dreads awakening, and conspires with the agreeable illusions for the prolonging of the deception, so in similar fashion I gladly lapse back into my accustomed opinions. I dread to be wakened, in fear lest the wakefulness may have to be laboriously spent, not in the tranquilizing light of truth, but in the extreme darkness of the above-suggested questionings.

CONCERNING THE NATURE OF THE HUMAN MIND, AND HOW IT IS MORE EASILY KNOWN THAN THE BODY

So disquieting are the doubts in which yesterday's meditation has involved me that it is no longer in my power to forget them. Nor do I yet see how they are to be resolved. It is as if I had all of a sudden fallen into very deep water, and am so disconcerted that I can neither plant my feet securely on the bottom nor maintain myself by swimming on the surface. I shall however, brace myself for a great effort, entering anew on the path which I was yesterday exploring; that is, I shall proceed by setting aside all that admits even of the very slightest doubt, just as if I had convicted it of being absolutely false; and I shall persist in following this path, until I have come upon something certain, or, failing in that, until at least I know with certainty, that in the world there is nothing certain.

Archimedes, that he might displace the whole earth, required only that there might be some one point, fixed and immovable, to serve in leverage; so likewise I shall be entitled to entertain high hopes if I am fortunate enough to find some one thing that is certain and indubitable.

I am supposing, then, that all the things I see are false; that of all the happenings my memory has ever suggested to me, none has ever so existed; that I have no senses; that body, shape, extension, movement and location are but mental fictions. What is there, then, which can be esteemed true? Perhaps this only, that nothing whatsoever is certain.

But how do I know that there is not something different from all things I have thus far enumerated and in regard to which there is not the least occasion for doubt? Is there not some God, or other being by whatever name we call Him, who puts these thoughts into my mind? Yet why suppose such a being? May it not be that I am myself capable of being their author? Am I not myself at least a something? But already I have denied that I have a body and senses. This indeed raises awkward questions. But what is it that thereupon follows? Am I so dependent on the body and senses that without them I cannot exist? Having persuaded myself that outside me there is nothing, that there is no heaven, no Earth, that there are no minds, no bodies, am I thereby committed to the view that I also do not exist? By no means. If I am persuading myself of something, in so doing I assuredly do exist. But what if, unknown to me, there be some deceiver, very powerful and very cunning, who is constantly employing his ingenuity in deceiving me? Again, as before, without doubt, if he is deceiving me, I exist. Let him deceive me as much as he will, he can never cause me to be nothing so long as I shall be thinking that I am something. And thus, having reflected well, and carefully examined all things, we have finally to conclude that this declaration, *Ego sum, ego existo,* is necessarily true every time I propound it or mentally apprehend it.

But I do not yet know in any adequate manner what I am, I who am certain that I am; and I must be careful not to substitute some other thing in place of myself, and so go astray in this knowledge which I am holding to be the most certain and evident of all that is knowable by me. This is why I shall now meditate anew on what, prior to my venturing on these questionings, I believed myself to be. I shall withdraw those beliefs which can, even in the least degree, be invalidated by the reasons cited, in order that at length, of all my previous beliefs, there may remain only what is certain and undubitable.

What then did I formerly believe myself to be? Undoubtedly I thought myself to be a man. But what is a man? Shall I say a rational animal? No, for then I should have to inquire what is "animal," what "rational"; and thus from the one question I should be drawn on into several others yet more difficult. I have not, at present, the leisure for any subtle inquiries. Instead, I prefer to meditate on the thoughts which of themselves sprang up in my mind on my applying myself to the consideration of what I am, considerations suggested by my own proper nature. I thought that I possessed a face, hands, arms, and that whole structure to which I was giving the title "body," composed as it is of the limbs discernible in a corpse. In addition, I took notice that I was nourished, that I walked, that I sensed, that I thought, all of which actions I ascribed to the soul. But what the soul might be I did not stop to consider; or if I did, I imaged it as being something extremely rare and subtle, like a wind, a flame or an ether, and as diffused throughout my grosser parts.

As to the nature of "body," no doubts whatsoever disturbed me. I had, as I thought, quite distinct knowledge of it; and had I been called upon to explain the manner in which I then conceived it, I should have explained myself somewhat thus: by body I understand whatever can be determined by a certain shape, and comprised in a certain location, whatever so fills a certain space as to exclude from it every other body, whatever can be apprehended by touch, sight, hearing, taste or smell, and whatever can be moved in various ways, not indeed of itself but something foreign to it by which it is touched and impressed. For I nowise conceived the power of self-movement, of sensing or knowing, as pertaining to the nature of body: on the contrary I was somewhat astonished on finding in certain bodies faculties such as these.

But what am I now to say that I am, now that I am supposing that there exists a very powerful, and if I may so speak, malignant being, who employs all his powers and skill in deceiving me? Can I affirm that I possess any one of those things which I have been speaking of as pertaining to the nature of body? On stopping to consider them with closer attention, and on reviewing all of them, I find none of which I can say that it belongs to me; to enumerate them again would be idle and tedious. What then, of those things which I have been attributing not to body, but to the soul? What of nutrition or of walking? If it be that I have no body, it cannot be that I take nourishment or that I walk. Sensing? There can be no sensing in the absence of body; and besides I have seemed during sleep to apprehend things which, as I afterwards noted, had not been sensed. Thinking? Here I find what does belong to me: it alone cannot be separated from me. *I am, I exist.* This is certain. How often? As often as I think. For it might indeed be that if I entirely ceased to think, I should thereupon altogether cease to exist. I am not at present admitting anything which is not necessarily true; and, accurately speaking, I am therefore [taking myself to be] only a thinking thing, that is to say, a mind, an understanding or reason—terms the significance of which has hitherto been unknown to me. I am, then, a real thing, and really existent. What thing? I have said it, a thinking thing.

And what more am I? I look for aid to the imagination. [But how mistakenly!] I am not that assemblage of limbs we call the human body; I am not a subtle penetrating air distributed throughout all these members; I am not a wind, a fire, a vapor, a breath or anything at all that I can image. I am supposing all these things to be nothing. Yet I find, while so doing, that I am still assured that I am a something.

But may it not be that those very things which, not being known to me, I have been supposing non-existent, are not really different from the self that I know? As to that I cannot say, and am not now discussing it. I can judge only of things that are known to me. Having come to know that I exist, I am inquiring as to what I am, this I that I thus know to exist. Now quite certainly this knowledge, taken in the precise manner as above, is not dependent on things the existence of which is not yet known to me; consequently and still more evidently it does not depend on any of the things which are feigned by the imagination. Indeed this word *feigning* warns me of my error; for I should in truth be feigning were I to *image* myself to be a something; since imaging is in no respect distinguishable from the contemplating of the shape or image of a *corporeal* thing. Already I know with certainty that I exist, and that all these imaged things, and in general whatever relates to the nature of body, may possibly be dreams merely or deceptions. Accordingly, I see clearly that it is no more reasonable to say, "I will resort to my imagination in order to learn more distinctly what I am," than if I were to say, "I am awake and apprehend something that is real, true; but as I do not yet apprehend it sufficiently well, I will of express purpose go to sleep, that my dreams may represent it to me with greater truth and evidence." I know therefore that nothing of all I can comprehend by way of the imagination pertains to this knowledge I [already] have of myself, and that if the mind is to determine the nature of the self with perfect distinctness, I must be careful to restrain it, diverting it from all such imaginative modes of apprehension.

What then is it that I am? A thinking thing. What is a thinking thing? It is a thing that doubts, understands, affirms, denies, wills, abstains from willing, that also can be aware of images and sensations.

Assuredly if all these things pertain to me, I am indeed a something. And how could it be they should not pertain to me? Am I not that very being who doubts of almost everything, who none the less also apprehends certain things, who affirms that one thing only is true, while denying all the rest, who yet desires to know more, who is averse to being deceived, who images many things, sometimes even despite his will, and who likewise apprehends many things which seem to come by way of the senses? Even though I should be always dreaming, and though he who has created me employs all his ingenuity in deceiving me, is there any one of the above assertions which is not as true as that I am and that I exist? Any one of them which can be distinguished from my thinking? Any one of them which can be said to be separate from the self? So manifest is it that it is I who doubt, I who apprehend, I who desire, that there is here no need to add anything by way of rendering it more evident. It is no less certain that I can apprehend images. For although it may happen (as I have been supposing) that none of the things imaged are true, the imaging, *quâ* active power, is none the less really in me, as forming part of my thinking. Again, I am the being who senses, that is to say, who apprehends corporeal things, as if by the organs of sense, since I do in truth see light, hear noise, feel heat. These things, it will be said, are false, and I am only dreaming. Even so, it is none the less certain that it seems to me that I see, that I hear, and that I am warmed. This is what in me is rightly called sensing, and as used in this precise manner is nowise other than thinking.

.   .   .

David Hume
PERSONAL IDENTITY

As we have seen in the previous selection, Descartes held as beyond doubt the idea that there is an "I" that thinks. In the following selection, David Hume not only questions the certainty of this assertion but argues that there is no single entity of which we are conscious that we can call a self. In effect, Hume is arguing that Descartes's methodological doubt was not radical enough and that what Descartes took to be certain—the existence of the self—was not only questionable but false.

It is important to understand that Hume's analysis proceeds from the empiricist premise that every true idea must be derived from experience—from some concrete impression. From this, it follows that if we had an accurate idea of the self, it too would have to be derived from some impression. However, as Hume declares, we cannot upon reflection find any distinct impression that can be labeled a "self." "I never can catch myself," writes Hume, "without a perception, and never can observe anything but the perception." What we call the self is no single thing but merely "a bundle or collection of different perceptions, which succeed each other with an inconceivable rapidity, and are in a perpetual flux and movement."

There are some philosophers who imagine we are every moment intimately conscious of what we call our *self*; that we feel its existence and its continuance in existence; and are certain, beyond the evidence of a demonstration, both of its perfect identity and simplicity. The strongest sensation, the most violent passion, say they, instead of distracting us from this view, only fix it the more intensely and make us consider their influence on *self* either by their pain or pleasure. To attempt a further proof of this were to weaken its evidence; since no proof can be derived from any fact of which we are so intimately conscious; nor is there anything of which we can be certain if we doubt of this.

Unluckily all these positive assertions are contrary to that very experience which is pleaded for them; nor have we any idea of *self,* after the manner it is here explained. For from what impression could this idea be derived? This question it is impossible to answer without a manifest contradiction and absurdity; and yet it is a question which must necessarily be answered, if we would have the idea of self pass for clear and intelligible. It must be some one impression that gives rise to every real idea. But self or person is not any one impression, but that to which our several impressions and ideas are supposed to have a reference. If any impression gives rise to the idea of self, that impression must continue invariably the same, through the whole course of our lives; since self is supposed to exist after that manner. But there is no impression constant and invariable. Pain and pleasure, grief and joy, passions and sensations succeed each other, and never all exist at the same time. It cannot therefore be from any of these impressions, or from any other, that the idea of self is derived; and consequently there is no such idea.

But further, what must become of all our particular perceptions upon this hypothesis? All these are different, and distinguishable, and separable from each other, and may be separately considered, and may exist separately, and have no need of anything to support their existence. After what manner therefore do they belong to self, and how are they connected with it? For my part, when I enter most intimately into what I call *myself*, I always stumble on some particular perception or other, of heat or cold, light or shade, love or hatred, pain or pleasure. I never can catch *myself* at any time without a perception, and never can observe anything but the perception. When my perceptions are removed for any time, as by sound sleep, so long am I insensible of *myself*, and may truly be said not to exist. And were all my perceptions removed by death, and could I neither think, nor feel, nor see, nor love, nor hate, after the dissolution of my body, I should be entirely annihilated, nor do I conceive what is further requisite to make me a perfect nonentity. If any one, upon serious and unprejudiced reflection, thinks he has a different notion of *himself*, I must confess I can reason no longer with him. All I can allow him is, that he may be in the right as well as I, and that we are essentially different in this particular. He may, perhaps, perceive something simple and continued, which he calls *himself*; though I am certain there is no such principle in me.

But setting aside some metaphysicians of this kind, I may venture to affirm of the rest of mankind, that they are nothing but a bundle or collection of different perceptions, which succeed each other with an inconceivable rapidity, and are in a perpetual flux and movement. Our eyes cannot turn in their sockets without varying our perceptions. Our thought is still more variable than our sight; and all our other senses and faculties contribute to this change; nor is there any single power of the soul, which remains unalterably the same, perhaps for one moment. The mind is a kind of theatre, where several perceptions successively make their appearance; pass, repass, glide away, and mingle in an infinite variety of postures and situations. There is properly no *simplicity* in it at one time, nor *identity* in different, whatever natural propension we may have to imagine that simplicity and identity. The comparison of the theatre must not mislead us. They are the successive perceptions only, that constitute the mind; nor have we the most distant notion of the place where these scenes are represented, or of the materials of which it is composed.

What then gives us so great a propension to ascribe an identity to these successive perceptions, and to suppose ourselves possessed of an invariable and uninterrupted existence through the whole course of our lives? In order to answer this question we must distinguish betwixt personal identity, as it regards our thought or imagination, and as it regards our passions or the concern we take in ourselves. The first is our present subject; and to explain it perfectly we must take the matter pretty deep, and account for that identity, which we attribute to plants and animals; there being a great analogy betwixt it and the identity of a self or person.

We have a distinct idea of an object that remains invariable and uninterrupted through a supposed variation of time; and this idea we call that of *identity* or *sameness.* We have also a distinct idea of several different objects existing in succession, and connected together by a close relation; and this to an accurate view affords as perfect a notion of *diversity* as if there was no manner of relation among the objects. But though these two ideas of identity, and a succession of related objects, be in themselves perfectly distinct, and even contrary, yet it is certain that, in our common way of thinking, they are generally confounded with each other. That action of the imagination, by which we consider the uninterrupted and invariable object, and that by which we reflect on the succession of related objects, are almost the same to the feeling; nor is there much more effort of thought required in the latter case than in the former. The relation facilitates the transition of the mind from one object to another, and renders its passage as smooth as if it contemplated one continued object. This resemblance is the cause of the confusion and mistake, and makes us substitute the notion of identity, instead of that of related objects. However at one instant we may consider the related succession as variable or interrupted, we are sure the next to ascribe to it a perfect identity, and regard it as invariable and uninterrupted. Our propensity to this mistake is so great from the resemblance above mentioned, that we fall into it before we are aware; and though we incessantly correct ourselves by reflection, and return to a more accurate method of thinking, yet we cannot long sustain our philosophy, or take off this bias from the imagination. Our last resource is to yield to it, and boldly assert that these different related objects are in effect the same, however interrupted and variable. In order to justify to ourselves this absurdity, we often feign some new and unintelligible principle, that connects the objects together, and prevents their interruption or variation. Thus we feign the continued existence of the perceptions of our senses, to remove the interruption; and run into the notion of a *soul,* and *self,* and *substance,* to disguise the variation. But, we may further observe, that where we do not give rise to such a fiction, our propension to confound identity with relation is so great, that we are apt to imagine something unknown and mysterious,[1] connecting the parts, beside their relation; and this I take to be the case with regard to the identity we ascribe to plants and vegetables. And even when this does not take place, we still feel a propensity to confound these ideas, though we are not able fully to satisfy ourselves in that particular, nor find anything invariable and uninterrupted to justify our notion of identity.

[1]If the reader is desirous to see how a great genius may be influenced by these seemingly trivial principles of the imagination, as well as the mere vulgar, let him read my Lord Shaftesbury's reasonings concerning the uniting principle of the universe, and the identity of plants and animals. See his *Moralists,* or *Philosophical Rhapsody.*

Thus the controversy concerning identity is not merely a dispute of words. For when we attribute identity, in an improper sense, to variable or interrupted objects, our mistake is not confined to the expression, but is commonly attended with a fiction, either of something invariable and uninterrupted, or of something mysterious and inexplicable, or at least with a propensity to such fictions. What will suffice to prove this hypothesis to the satisfaction of every fair inquirer, is to show, from daily experience and observation, that the objects which are variable or interrupted, and yet are supposed to continue the same, are such only as consist of a succession of parts, connected together by resemblance, contiguity, or causation. For as such a succession answers evidently to our notion of diversity, it can only be by mistake we ascribe to it an identity; and as the relation of parts, which leads us into this mistake, is really nothing but a quality, which produces an association of ideas, and an easy transition of the imagination from one to another, it can only be from the resemblance, which this act of the mind bears to that by which we contemplate one continued object, that the error arises.

.   .   .

George Herbert Mead
THE SOCIAL SELF

Before his death in 1931, George Herbert Mead was not well known outside a small group of thinkers, later to be known as the Chicago School, who were centered around the University of Chicago. Although he had published articles and given numerous lectures, he had never published a definitive work. It was only after his death, with the publication of several volumes of his collected papers, that he came to be recognized as a towering figure in the development of pragmatism, very much on par with Charles Sanders Peirce, William James, and John Dewey. As a social psychologist, Mead was concerned with the relation of the individual's experience to the totality of his or her conduct and social interactions. He developed a theory that he termed "social behaviorism" and that he contrasted to the psychological behaviorism of John B. Watson. Watson had held that psychology should be concerned wholly with the correlation of an individual's overt behavior with external stimuli. Although agreeing with Watson that emphasis should be placed on behavior, Mead insisted that behavior should be understood in both individual and social terms (for him, they could not be entirely separate) and that consciousness has an important role to play in the process.

In the selection that follows, Mead develops his theory of individual self-consciousness. The self, he argues, is not immediately present at birth but develops in the process of social interaction. Specifically, the human organism develops a consciousness of self when it learns to respond to itself, to talk (inwardly) and reply to itself, as though it were another person. Thus, the self arises when the organism takes the attitude of other members of its social group toward itself. The self, then, is inherently a social process.

THE SELF AND THE ORGANISM

. . . The self has a character which is different from that of the physiological organism proper. The self is something which has a development; it is not initially there, at birth, but arises in the process of social experience and activity, that is, develops in the given individual as a result of his relations to that process as a whole and to other individuals within that process. The intelligence of the lower forms of animal life, like a great deal of human intelligence, does not involve a self. In our habitual actions, for example, in our moving about in a world that is simply there and to which we are so adjusted that no thinking is involved, there is a certain amount of sensuous experience such as persons have when they are just waking up, a bare thereness of the world. Such characters about us may exist in experience without taking their place in relationship to the self. One must, of course, under those conditions, distinguish between the experience that immediately takes place and our own organization of it into the experience of the self. One says upon analysis that a certain item had its place in his experience, in the experience of his self. We do inevitably tend at a certain level of sophistication to organize all experience into that of a self. We do so intimately identify our experiences, especially our affective experiences, with the self that it takes a moment's abstraction to realize that pain and pleasure can be there without being the experience of the self. Similarly, we normally organize our memories upon the string of our self. If we date things we always date them from the point of view of our past experiences. We frequently have memories that we cannot date, that we cannot place. A picture comes before us suddenly and we are at a loss to explain when that experience originally took place. We remember perfectly distinctly the picture, but we do not have it definitely placed, and until we can place it in terms of our past experience we are not satisfied. Nevertheless, I think it is obvious when one comes to consider it that the self is not necessarily involved in the life of the organism, nor involved in what we term our sensuous experience, that is, experience in a world about us for which we have habitual reactions.

We can distinguish very definitely between the self and the body. The body can be there and can operate in a very intelligent fashion without there being a self involved in the experience. The self has the characteristic that it is an object to itself, and that characteristic distinguishes it from other objects and from the body. It is perfectly true that the eye can see the foot, but it does not see the body as a whole. We cannot see our backs; we can feel certain portions of them, if we are agile, but we cannot get an experience of our whole body. There are, of course, experiences which are somewhat vague and difficult of location, but the bodily experiences are for us organized about a self. The foot and hand belong to the self. We can see our feet, especially if we look at them from the wrong end of an opera glass, as strange things which we have difficulty in recognizing as our own. The parts of the body are quite distinguishable from the self. We can lose parts of the body without any serious invasion of the self. The mere ability to experience different parts of the body is not different from the experience of a table. The table presents a different feel from what the hand does when one hand feels another, but it is an experience of something with which we come definitely into contact. The body does not experience itself as a whole, in the sense in which the self in some way enters into the experience of the self.

It is the characteristic of the self as an object to itself that I want to bring out. This characteristic is represented in the word "self," which is a reflexive, and indicates that which can be both subject and object. This type of object is essentially different from other objects, and in the past it has been distinguished as conscious, a term which indicates an experience with, an experience of, one's self. It was assumed that consciousness in some way carried this capacity of being an object to itself. In giving a behavioristic statement of consciousness we have to look for some sort of experience in which the physical organism can become an object to itself.[1]

When one is running to get away from someone who is chasing him, he is entirely occupied in this action, and his experience may be swallowed up in the objects about him, so that he has, at the time being, no consciousness of self at all. We must be, of course, very completely occupied to have that take place, but we can, I think, recognize that sort of a possible experience in which the self does not enter. We can, perhaps, get some light on that situation through those experiences in which in very intense action there appear in the experience of the individual, back of this intense action, memories and anticipations. Tolstoi as an officer in the war gives an account of having pictures of his past experience in the midst of his most intense action. There are also the pictures that flash into a person's mind when he is drowning. In such instances there is a contrast between an experience that is absolutely wound up in outside activity in which the self as an object does not enter, and an activity of memory and imagination in which the self is the principal object. The self is then entirely distinguishable from an organism that is surrounded by things and acts with reference to things, including parts of its own body. These latter may be objects like other objects, but they

[1]Man's behavior is such in his social group that he is able to become an object to himself, a fact which constitutes him a more advanced product of evolutionary development than are the lower animals. Fundamentally it is this social fact—and not his alleged possession of a soul or mind with which he, as an individual, has been mysteriously and supernaturally endowed, and with which the lower animals have not been endowed—that differentiates him from them.

are just objects out there in the field, and they do not involve a self that is an object to the organism. This is, I think, frequently overlooked. It is that fact which makes our anthropomorphic reconstructions of animal life so fallacious. How can an individual get outside himself (experientially) in such a way as to become an object to himself? This is the essential psychological problem of selfhood or of self-consciousness; and its solution is to be found by referring to the process of social conduct or activity in which the given person or individual is implicated. The apparatus of reason would not be complete unless it swept itself into its own analysis of the field of experience; or unless the individual brought himself into the same experiential field as that of the other individual selves in relation to whom he acts in any given social situation. Reason cannot become impersonal unless it takes an objective, non-affective attitude toward itself; otherwise we have just consciousness, not *self*-consciousness. And it is necessary to rational conduct that the individual should thus take an objective, impersonal attitude toward himself, that he should become an object to himself. For the individual organism is obviously an essential and important fact or constituent element of the empirical situation in which it acts; and without taking objective account of itself as such, it cannot act intelligently, or rationally.

The individual experiences himself as such, not directly, but only indirectly, from the particular standpoints of other individual members of the same social group, or from the generalized standpoint of the social group as a whole to which he belongs. For he enters his own experience as a self or individual, not directly or immediately, not by becoming a subject to himself, but only in so far as he first becomes an object to himself just as other individuals are objects to him or in his experience; and he becomes an object to himself only by taking the attitudes of other individuals toward himself within a social environment or context of experience and behavior in which both he and they are involved.

The importance of what we term "communication" lies in the fact that it provides a form of behavior in which the organism or the individual may become an object to himself. It is that sort of communication which we have been discussing—not communication in the sense of the cluck of the hen to the chickens, or the bark of a wolf to the pack, or the lowing of a cow, but communication in the sense of significant symbols, communication which is directed not only to others but also to the individual himself. So far as that type of communication is a part of behavior it at least introduces a self. Of course, one may hear without listening; one may see things that he does not realize; do things that he is not really aware of. But it is where one does respond to that which he addresses to another and where that response of his own becomes a part of his conduct, where he not only hears himself but responds to himself, talks and replies to himself as truly as the other person replies to him, that we have behavior in which the individuals become objects to themselves.

Such a self is not, I would say, primarily the physiological organism.

The physiological organism is essential to it, but we are at least able to think of a self without it. Persons who believe in immortality, or believe in ghosts, or in the possibility of the self leaving the body, assume a self which is quite distinguishable from the body. How successfully they can hold these conceptions is an open question, but we do, as a fact, separate the self and the organism. It is fair to say that the beginning of the self as an object, so far as we can see, is to be found in the experiences of people that lead to the conception of a "double." Primitive people assume that there is a double, located presumably in the diaphragm, that leaves the body temporarily in sleep and completely in death. It can be enticed out of the body of one's enemy and perhaps killed. It is represented in infancy by the imaginary playmates which children set up, and through which they come to control their experiences in their play.

The self, as that which can be an object to itself, is essentially a social structure, and it arises in social experience. After a self has arisen, it in a certain sense provides for itself its social experiences, and so we can conceive of an absolutely solitary self. But it is impossible to conceive of a self arising outside of social experience. When it has arisen we can think of a person in solitary confinement for the rest of his life, but who still has himself as a companion, and is able to think and to converse with himself as he had communicated with others. That process to which I have just referred, of responding to one's self as another responds to it, taking part in one's own conversation with others, being aware of what one is saying and using that awareness of what one is saying to determine what one is going to say thereafter—that is a process with which we are all familiar. We are continually following up our own address to other persons by an understanding of what we are saying, and using that understanding in the direction of our continued speech. We are finding out what we are going to say, what we are going to do, by saying and doing, and in the process we are continually controlling the process itself. In the conversation of gestures what we say calls out a certain response in another and that in turn changes our own action, so that we shift from what we started to do because of the reply the other makes. The conversation of gestures is the beginning of communication. The individual comes to carry on a conversation of gestures with himself. He says something, and that calls out a certain reply in himself which makes him change what he was going to say. One starts to say something, we will presume an unpleasant something, but when he starts to say it he realizes it is cruel. The effect on himself of what he is saying checks him; there is here a conversation of gestures between the individual and himself. We mean by significant speech that the action is one that affects the individual himself, and that the effect upon the individual himself is part of the intelligent carrying-out of the conversation with others. Now we, so to speak, amputate that social phase and dispense with it for the time being, so that one is talking to one's self as one would talk to another person.

This process of abstraction cannot be carried on indefinitely. One inevitably seeks an audience, has to pour himself out to somebody. In reflective intelligence one thinks to act, and to act solely so that this action remains a part of a social process. Thinking becomes preparatory to social action. The very process of thinking is, of course, simply an inner conversation that goes on, but it is a conversation of gestures which in its completion implies the expression of that which one thinks to an audience. One separates the significance of what he is saying to others from the actual speech and gets it ready before saying it. He thinks it out, and perhaps writes it in the form of a book; but it is still a part of social intercourse in which one is addressing other persons and at the same time addressing one's self, and in which one controls the address to other persons by the response made to one's own gesture. That the person should be responding to himself is necessary to the self, and it is this sort of social conduct which provides behavior within which that self appears. I know of no other form of behavior than the linguistic in which the individual is an object to himself, and, so far as I can see, the individual is not a self in the reflexive sense unless he is an object to himself. It is this fact that gives a critical importance to communication, since this is a type of behavior in which the individual does so respond to himself.

We realize in everyday conduct and experience that an individual does not mean a great deal of what he is doing and saying. We frequently say that such an individual is not himself. We come away from an interview with a realization that we have left out important things, that there are parts of the self that did not get into what was said. What determines the amount of the self that gets into communication is the social experience itself. Of course, a good deal of the self does not need to get expression. We carry on a whole series of different relationships to different people. We are one thing to one man and another thing to another. There are parts of the self which exist only for the self in relationship to itself. We divide ourselves up in all sorts of different selves with reference to our acquaintances. We discuss politics with one and religion with another. There are all sorts of different selves answering to all sorts of different social reactions. It is the social process itself that is responsible for the appearance of the self; it is not there as a self apart from this type of experience.

. . .

The unity and structure of the complete self reflects the unity and structure of the social process as a whole; and each of the elementary selves of which it is composed reflects the unity and structure of one of the various aspects of that process in which the individual is implicated. In other words, the various elementary selves which constitute, or are organized into, a complete self are the various aspects of the structure of that complete self answering to the various aspects of the structure of the social process as a whole; the structure of the complete self is thus a reflection of the complete social process. The organization and unification of a social group is identical with the organization and unification of any one of the selves arising within the social process in which that group is engaged, or which it is carrying on.[2]

.   .   .

THE SELF AND THE SUBJECTIVE

.   .   .

It has been the tendency of psychology to deal with the self as a more or less isolated and independent element, a sort of entity that could conceivably exist by itself. It is possible that there might be a single self in the universe if we start off by identifying the self with a certain feeling-consciousness. If we speak of this feeling as objective, then we can think of that self as existing by itself. We can think of a separate physical body existing by itself, we can assume that it has these feelings or conscious states in question, and so we can set up that sort of a self in thought as existing simply by itself.

Then there is another use of "consciousness" with which we have been particularly occupied, denoting that which we term thinking or reflective intelligence, a use of consciousness which always has, implicitly at least, the reference to an "I" in it. This use of consciousness has no necessary connection with the other; it is an entirely different conception. One usage has to do with a certain mechanism, a certain way in which an organism acts. If an organism is endowed with sense organs then there are objects in its environment, and among those objects will be parts of its own body.[3] It is true that if the organism did not have a retina and a central nervous system there would not be any objects of vision. For such objects to exist there have to be certain physiological conditions, but these objects are not in themselves necessarily related to a self. When we

[2]The unity of the mind is not identical with the unity of the self. The unity of the self is constituted by the unity of the entire relational pattern of social behavior and experience in which the individual is implicated, and which is reflected in the structure of the self; but many of the aspects or features of this entire pattern do not enter into consciousness, so that the unity of the mind is in a sense an abstraction from the more inclusive unity of the self.

[3]Our constructive selection of our environment is what we term "consciousness," in the first sense of the term. The organism does not project sensuous qualities—colors, for example—into the environment to which it responds; but it endows this environment with such qualities, in a sense similar to that in which an ox endows grass with the quality of being food, or in which—speaking more generally—the relation between biological organisms and certain environmental contents gives rise to food objects. If there were no organisms with particular sense organs there would be no environment, in the proper or usual sense of the term. An organism constructs (in the selective sense) its environment; and consciousness often refers to the character of the environment in so far as it is determined or constructively selected by our human organisms, and depends upon the relationship between the former (as thus selected or constructed) and the latter.

reach a self we reach a certain sort of conduct, a certain type of social process which involves the interaction of different individuals and yet implies individuals engaged in some sort of co-operative activity. In that process a self, as such, can arise.

. . .

We cannot identify the self with what is commonly called consciousness, that is, with the private or subjective thereness of the characters of objects.

There is, of course, a current distinction between consciousness and self-consciousness: consciousness answering to certain experiences such as those of pain or pleasure, self-consciousness referring to a recognition or appearance of a self as an object. It is, however, very generally assumed that these other conscious contents carry with them also a self-consciousness—that a pain is always somebody's pain, and that if there were not this reference to some individual it would not be pain. There is a very definite element of truth in this, but it is far from the whole story. The pain does have to belong to an individual; it has to be your pain if it is going to belong to you. Pain can belong to anybody, but if it did belong to everybody it would be comparatively unimportant. I suppose it is conceivable that under an anesthetic what takes place is the dissociation of experiences so that the suffering, so to speak, is no longer your suffering. We have illustrations of that, short of the anesthetic dissociation, in an experience of a disagreeable thing which loses its power over us because we give our attention to something else. If we can get, so to speak, outside of the thing, dissociating it from the eye that is regarding it, we may find that it has lost a great deal of its unendurable character. The unendurableness of pain is a reaction against it. If you can actually keep yourself from reacting against suffering you get rid of a certain content in the suffering itself. What takes place in effect is that it ceases to be your pain. You simply regard it objectively. Such is the point of view we are continually impressing on a person when he is apt to be swept away by emotion. In that case what we get rid of is not the offense itself, but the reaction against the offense. The objective character of the judge is that of a person who is neutral, who can simply stand outside of a situation and assess it. If we can get that judicial attitude in regard to the offenses of a person against ourselves, we reach the point where we do not resent them but understand them, we get the situation where to understand is to forgive. We remove much of experience outside of our own self by this attitude. The distinctive and natural attitude against another is a resentment of an offense, but we now have in a certain sense passed beyond that self and become a self with other attitudes. There is a certain technique, then, to which we subject ourselves in enduring suffering or any emotional situation, and which consists in partially separating one's self from the experience so that it is no longer the experience of the individual in question.

If, now, we could separate the experience entirely, so that we should not remember it, so that we should not have to take it up continually into the self from day to day, from moment to moment, then it would not exist any longer so far as we are concerned. If we had no memory which identifies experiences with the self, then they would certainly disappear so far as their relation to the self is concerned, and yet they might continue as sensuous or sensible experiences without being taken up into a self. That sort of a situation is presented in the pathological case of a multiple personality in which an individual loses the memory of a certain phase of his existence. Everything connected with that phase of his existence is gone and he becomes a different personality. The past has a reality whether in the experience or not, but here it is not identified with the self—it does not go to make up the self. We take an attitude of that sort, for example, with reference to others when a person has committed some sort of an offense which leads to a statement of the situation, an admission, and perhaps regret, and then is dropped. A person who forgives but does not forget is an unpleasant companion; what goes with forgiving is forgetting, getting rid of the memory of it.

There are many illustrations which can be brought up of the loose relationship of given contents to a self in defense of our recognition of them as having a certain value outside of the self. At the least, it must be granted that we can approach the point where something which we recognize as a content is less and less essential to the self, is held off from the present self, and no longer has the value for that self which it had for the former self. Extreme cases seem to support the view that a certain portion of such contents can be entirely cut off from the self. While in some sense it is there ready to appear under specific conditions, for the time being it is dissociated and does not get in above the threshold of our self-consciousness.

Self-consciousness, on the other hand, is definitely organized about the social individual, and that, as we have seen, is not simply because one is in a social group and affected by others and affects them, but because (and this is a point I have been emphasizing) his own experience as a self is one which he takes over from his action upon others. He becomes a self in so far as he can take the attitude of another and act toward himself as others act. In so far as the conversation of gestures can become part of conduct in the direction and control of experience, then a self can arise. It is the social process of influencing others in a social act and then taking the attitude of the others aroused by the stimulus, and then reacting in turn to this response, which constitutes a self.

Our bodies are parts of our environment; and it is possible for the individual to experience and be conscious of his body, and of bodily sensations, without being conscious or aware of himself—without, in other words, taking the attitude of the other toward himself. According to the social theory of consciousness, what we mean by consciousness is that peculiar character and aspect of the environment of individual human experience which is due to human society, a society of other individual selves who take the attitude of the other toward themselves. The physiological conception or theory of consciousness is by itself inadequate; it requires supplementation from the socio-psychological point of view. The taking or feeling of the attitude of the other toward yourself is what constitutes self-consciousness, and not mere organic sensations of which the individual is aware and which he experiences. Until the rise of his self-consciousness in the process of social experience, the individual experiences his body—its feelings and sensations—merely as an immediate part of his environment, not as his own, not in terms of self-consciousness. The self and self-consciousness have first to arise, and then these experiences can be identified peculiarly with the self, or appropriated by the self; to enter, so to speak, into this heritage of experience, the self has first to develop within the social process in which this heritage is involved.

.   .   .

Herbert Fingarette
KARMA, PSYCHOANALYSIS, AND THE INNER SELF

If, as George Herbert Mead suggests, self-consciousness develops out of the social process, it would follow that each of us incorporates many selves into our selves. In this next selection, Herbert Fingarette, a contemporary American philosopher, attempts to develop the idea that each self is, quite literally, a unity of many selves. This idea, he claims, has been developed, at least implicitly, in the Western world, through the theory of psychoanalysis; it has been more explicitly developed in the Eastern world, through the doctrine of karma.

Psychoanalysis recognizes that we live out many lives in fantasy (in play, in dreams, and in art) and that to do so is essential for human self-development. This process, Fingarette argues, is analogous to the literal living of many lives, which according to the Eastern doctrine of karma, actually occurs through the process of reincarnation.

.   .   .

Although familiar to the ancient Greek world, and stressed in Orphic, Pythagorean, and Platonic teachings, the most elaborate and sophisticated forms of karmic doctrine known to us are to be found in the Upanishadic and Buddhist texts. Avoiding the many specific differences among the sects, the general notion of reincarnation may be sketched along the following lines. My present life is only one of a set of lives. These lives are in certain respects entirely separate: their social, geographic, and physical characters may be quite unrelated to one another.

Yet they form an interdependent series by virtue of a peculiar continuity: *karma,* "action." This karmic continuity is a psychomoral one. In Christian terms: "Whatsoever a man soweth that shall he reap"—if not in this life, then in some other one.

.   .   .

Karmic law is not the edict of an All-Powerful Disciplinarian, not an expression of will accompanied by the threat of sanctions. It purports to be factual description: Somehow or other, things do eventually "balance out" in the moral realm; each moral action produces, eventually, its quite specific moral reaction. And our constant strivings are constantly producing new "karma" as well as bringing past karma to fruition; the weary round of births and deaths is perpetuated.

In the course of spiritual progress toward freedom from the round of births and rebirths one eventually achieves the power of remembering past lives. One then sees their connection with the present life. The ordinary person can neither remember nor understand: "And what happened to you in your mother's womb, all that you have quite forgotten."[1] The greater the spiritual progress, the greater the ability and the easier the task. Knowledge of one's former lives is one of the "five kinds of superknowledge."[2] In achieving this "superknowledge," one is concurrently achieving liberation from the karmic bonds. As in psychoanalysis, this knowledge is not the goal, but it is a distinctive ingredient in the achievement of freedom. Spiritual knowledge and spiritual freedom are born as one.

.   .   .

The notion that each Self has in some sense many selves is not elaborated systematically in any contemporary language in the West. But it is inherently congenial to the description of the human condition. It is as congenial a way of informal speaking for the psychoanalyst as it is for the novelist. For example when the distinguished psychoanalyst Lawrence Kubie talks informally about the human meaning of the psychotherapeutic experience, he says about one of his patients:

> With the elimination of certain of these inner blinders, it suddenly became clear that *a wholly different person was hidden* behind this façade of hostility and rage and hatred and meanness.[3] [Italics added]

In the very same paragraph, Kubie also reverts to the language of mythology. He describes the same woman as having behaved "like one of the

[1] *Saddharmapundarika,* V, 70, in *Buddhist Texts,* p. 125.
[2] *Ibid.,* V, 71, p. 125.
[3] Kubie, L. S., "The Neurosis Wears a Mask," in *Moments of Personal Discovery,* MacIver, R. M., ed., Harper & Bros., New York, 1952, p. 34.

ancient furies." This perfectly natural way of describing the situation in clear and universally understandable English has been for the most part preempted by the technical language. The technical language is useful, but for purposes other than those which concern us at the moment. The language of hidden selves, however, is not only perfectly clear and apt today, it was partly embodied in the once accepted doctrine of "possession," for millennia the nearest thing to a Western "psychological" language. The doctrines of possession by such alien, quasi persons as demons and of inspiration from within by the gods have a long history as antecedents and analogues of the concepts of regressive and sublimative eruptions of the unconscious.

There have been some fragmentary attempts at a more systematic use of such language even within the psychoanalytic stream of thought. Fritz Wittels[4] has remarked that psychoanalytic language would much more suggest the true state of things if we spoke less of having an Oedipus complex or introjecting father images and instead spoke of *being* Oedipus, of *being* father. What Wittels refers to here is, of course, the inner quality of the experience. After all, as Freud showed, in the life of the mind it is *psychic* reality which counts; the fantasy of introjecting father, of incorporating father into oneself, of becoming father is a psychic *reality.* The phrase "in fantasy" is a way of stressing that this experience is not a revelation of physical, physiological, or social reality. This emphasis is essential in some contexts, but in the present one we need to emphasize that "being father" *is* a psychic reality.

Within the Freudian tradition, the technical language which both most directly suggests and also strictly refers to these "many selves" is the language of "identification," "introjection," and of such special clinical phenomena as multiple personality ("a climax of multiple identifications"[5]) and hysterical identification.[6]

In psychoanalytic terms we can characterize the infantile aspects of the superego as consisting of "the internalized parental figures dressed in the variable garb of one's childhood mythology."[7] The ego, too, is from certain relevant vantage points "the precipitate of abandoned drive-objects, that is, of *identifications....*"[8]

What is more, the genuinely "personal" quality of these "sub-selves," especially when operating with some degree of autonomy, is particularly evident in situations where ego-control is for any reason lessened. Rapaport reports, for example:

    [4]Wittels, F., "Unconscious Phantoms in Neurosis," *Psychoanalytic Quarterly* 8:141–163 (1939).
    [5]Fenichel, O., *The Psychoanalytic Theory of Neurosis,* W. W. Norton & Co., 1945, p. 222.
    [6]Freud, S., *Group Psych.,* in *CPW*, XVIII, pp. 105–110.
    [7]Wexler, M., "The Structural Problem in Schizophrenia: The Role of the Internal Object," in *Psychotherapy with Schizophrenia,* Brody, E. B., and Redlich, F. C., eds., International Universities Press, New York, 1952, pp. 196–197.
    [8]Rapaport, D., *Organization and Pathology of Thought,* Columbia University Press, New York, 1951, p. 725.

In recording various thought formations of my own, ranging from those in hypnagogic to those in dream states, I obtained material suggesting that the closer the state approximates that of the dream, the more "me-ness" recedes ... though formations resembling those of multiple personality begin to occur.[9]

An example of this "many self" language from other than the Freudian standpoint is H. S. Sullivan's usage. He directs much attention to what he calls "self-dynamisms," each of which is, as the very language suggests, a self-like configuration of dispositions. Indeed, as soon as Sullivan lapses into more informal discussion, he drops the word "dynamism" and simply speaks of different selves, of different "me's" and "you's," of the various "persons," either real or illusory, who are involved in a specific interpersonal transaction.[10]

All of this is, of course, no secret to the literary artists of the West. Using neither the language of psychology nor of Eastern "metaphysics," they have known that, as Virginia Woolf's Mrs. Dalloway says, "our apparitions, the part of us which appears, are so momentary compared with the other, the unseen part of us, which spreads wide."[11]

By way of returning the compliment, psychoanalysts soon perceived a specific and related truth about art. According to Freud, the artist is one who not only perceives the truth about the many selves, his very art rests upon evoking them. To use Freud's own words:

In the realm of fiction we find the plurality of lives which we need. We die with the hero with whom we have identified ourselves; yet we survive him, and are ready to die again just as safely with another hero.[12]

This statement of Freud's expresses the important point that we can discriminate not merely other selves but also other *lives*, the lives lived through by these dynamic selves. Here Freud refers specifically to the living through (in fantasy) of other lives by means of literary techniques. It is this aspect of the matter in particular, the current and "vicarious" living through of many lives, to which we shall address ourselves in the pages to follow. And we may begin by noting that, although this participation in many lives is accounted for in the East within a religious or quasi-religious framework, in the modern West its institutionalized form has been that of the arts.

.   .   .

[9]*Ibid.*, p. 73.

[10]Sullivan, H. S., "Psychiatry: Introduction to the Study of Interpersonal Relations," in *A Study of Interpersonal Relations*, Mullahy, P., ed., Grove Press, New York, 1949, pp. 98–121.

[11]Woolf, V., *Mrs. Dalloway*, Harcourt, Brace & Co., New York, 1949, pp. 231–232.

[12]Freud, S., "Thoughts for the Times on War and Death," *op. cit.*, p. 291.

The vicarious living of other lives is not merely a desirable experience, it is essential. There can be no development into a *human* being without the incorporation into the total Self of a variety of lives and part-lives. The more these are fully lived, the more rich and deep a Self. Indeed, we know from psychoanalysis that we must live the lives of others around us as we perceive them (identification) in order to develop even that minimum unique blend of lives and part-lives which can establish us as individuals. Hence we may look with confidence to childhood as an area in which there must be institutionalized patterns of "fantasy" or "vicarious" living of lives.

It is now generally accepted that the play of children is not play in the trivial sense of that word. Indeed there is no trivial sense except as a reflection of our adult unawareness of what play is. Play is *playing-at.* It is the rehearsal of various roles and the practicing of these roles in a variety of situations. The very words "rehearsal" and "practicing" are misleading; they derive from the adult, retrospective view of the matter. From the standpoint of the child, play is the serious business of life. It is merely a life partly out of gear with his "official" self. Of course, the normal child can soon distinguish easily and quickly between what adults call "real life" and "play." The more psychological way of stating the matter is to say that the child acts out his fantasies and seriously tries, through the play-situation, to resolve conflicts in which these fantasies play a part. But he normally recognizes reasonably well which of these selves and lives are *defined* as real by the adults around him; and he learns to go along with their game—until finally he is quite unaware that it was *their* game, for it is now his, too.

The lives which the child lives through in play are not entirely distinct from one another. Situations, conflicts, and roles may be repeated, but the conflicts may be resolved either in a compulsively repetitive way or in different ways on different occasions. Sometimes the same "play" role and situation are carried on with continuity as in a "continued story." For months at a time, two girls will be rival queens of different planets. These lives and situations are evidently and at a glance (for the adult) closely related psychically. Though the nine-year-old girl may be queen of a planet in the distant future of space travel, this space-queen's problems are, to the observing adult, remarkably like those of the "English queen" of a month ago; and all these royal problems are, in turn, remarkably reminiscent of the child's present tensions and problems, the dynamic conflicts which dominate her present family life and "real" social life. There is a remarkable ability—which we tend to take for granted until we recall the case of the psychotic—to keep a variety of conscious and closely interrelated lives entirely unconfused.

Thus the child is daily, hourly "reincarnated"; not in the physical sense, but in the psychically, humanly important sense: the experienced reality of the moment is that of another person in another body in another life, yet a person whose destiny is strangely yet intimately connected with that of the young girl of today.

.   .   .

In dreams we live other lives both explicitly and implicitly. We openly appear in different times, places, and roles, while remaining recognizably ourself. We *implicitly* live still more lives. For, after all, the other persons in our dreams are *our* creatures; we live their lives for them. And this becomes evident to one who understands his dreams, whether he be Hindu, Buddhist, or psychoanalyzed Westerner.

"... the dreamer striving against his own wishes is like a combination of two persons, separate and yet somehow intimately united...."[13] Freud's words express the very essence of the reincarnation notion: a plurality of persons "separate and yet somehow intimately united." We need only remind ourselves that, taken collectively, our dream-world is a world infinitely rich in persons. In a dream we *are* sun-priests, gangsters, kings, warriors, lovers, haters, children, animals. Dream experience is not waking experience—but it is genuine experience, a part of our life, indeed of our most intimate life. Viewed in terms of its own inner life, the time-order of the dream experience is incommensurate with the time-order of the current waking life: our life as king or as slave is lived in a different time, a different place, a different world from our current waking life. One may be satisfied to locate the dream-life in past or future, or in some other region in the present world; or one may emphasize (as some reincarnationists have done) that these other lives are radically out of gear with the waking order of space-time and belong to different epochs or "cycles" of space and time. The role of the dream as profoundly revelatory of a reality is accepted in our oldest cultural wisdom. Aeschylus' Clytemnestra expresses the point succinctly:

> ... For the sense
> When shut in sleep hath then the spirit sight,
> But in the day the inward eye is blind.[14]

And we know the profound import of the dream in Biblical times and lands.

More apposite to the specific theme of dreams and reincarnation, however, is the attitude expressed in the Upanishads, the first Eastern texts to elaborate the reincarnation doctrine. Two notions in particular are conjoined in the Upanishadic references to the dream; both notions suggest the theses of this chapter. First, we are told that the dream experience is a creation of the inner Self; it is not contact as usual with the world it portrays, but a construction entirely of our own out of the

[13]Freud, S., *Gen. Intro.*, p. 195.
[14]Aeschylus, *The Furies*, Morshead, E. D. A., trans., in *Harvard Classics*, Vol. VIII, p. 119.

materials of our waking experience—it is the "play" of the inner Self. Second, discussion of the dream state is intimately related to discussions of the self as reincarnated, of the transcending of the everyday world of bondage, and of the "forms of death." The dream state is intermediate between the karmic world of birth-and-death and the "other" world which is the home of him who has become enlightened and free of karma.

.   .   .

Lord Raglan, in his study of death and rebirth,[15] argues that the dream could not be a basis for the belief in reincarnation since *any* sane man (in whatever culture) can distinguish between waking ("real") life and dream experiences. Of course it is precisely because of this obvious distinction that so many dreamers in human history have been led to suppose that their dream lives are *eruptions* of *other* lives into current life rather than elements within current life.

Having begun this discussion of the reality of dreams with the words of Freud, I shall conclude it with the words of a psychiatrist writing from the phenomenological standpoint. Medard Boss writes in his book on dream analysis that:

> We exist no less in dreams than we do in waking life. We "exist" in the sense that even in the dream we are always within a world, the reality of which we had best not deny too hastily.[16]

> ... man can realize his existence in dreams, just as in waking life, through the most varied relationships and attitudes.[17]

To summarize: the "living out" of fantasies, whether in play, art, or dream, is one major process which, I suggest, is an analogue to reincarnation. Through each of these experience forms we glimpse one transcending moral-psychic unity manifesting itself in a variety of discrete, phenomenal lives. The living of many lives enables the Self to work through, existentially and creatively, various moral tendencies potential in its nature. To "learn by experience" and eventually to profit by insight into these experiences: this is the way to spiritual progress and human freedom.

.   .   .

When Freud discovered the world of inner life and its remarkable degree of autonomy from the social and physical environment at any moment, he was forced to attribute to this nonlogical, nonphysical world

[15]Raglan, F. R., *Death and Rebirth,* Watts & Co., London, 1945.
[16]Boss, M., *The Analysis of Dreams,* Rider & Co., London, 1957, p. 85.
[17]*Ibid.,* p. 122.

a secondary kind of reality—it was "psychological," "subjective," "fantasy," unless reinterpreted in terms of some logical scheme tied to physical space-time events. At least this was his way of looking at it when theoretical and philosophical description was in question. In daily practice, Freud was precisely the man, as I have said, who systematically grasped the *reality* of this realm.

Freud was not alone. All of us in the West are so in bondage to the public, physical orientation that we can only allow ourselves to come to terms with the "inner" world (where it deviates from the physical) by indirection; we do so on various levels of awareness through art, play, or dream, conscious fantasy, neurosis, or psychosis. The limping metaphor "inner" serves to mark how we have crippled ourselves, cut ourselves off from the "outer" world, even in the language we use.

In those cultures which are not so fascinated by the public, the logical, and the physical, it is easier and more common to consider another mode of existence as reality. It is the world of the human being, the drama of men in their relations to each other and to nature, which plays the central role.

In such societies the physical-causal aspect of the world is as vague, shadowy, and crudely understood as is the dream-world in the West. In the modern West, the dream and the hallucination are still perceived by most persons as isolated, largely meaningless eruptions. For those who belong to nontechnological cultures, however, quite the reverse holds: it is the physical object—as physical—which, although recognized, is isolated, meaningless, unconnected with other events. No objects or events are firmly located in a clear structure of physical space-time and causality. Even when the rudiments of operating a Western machine are learned by someone from a nontechnological culture, the machine and its operation are still located by him in the larger structure of a world moved by persons and motives. He is, to the technician, a perversely superstitious and unteachable savage or peasant. In the nontechnological culture, the meaningful world, the real world, the world that binds together, is the highly elaborated and familiar world of human drama, of myth, ritual, dream, hallucination, and daily ritualized work. All these are bound in an essentially *dramatic* unity rather than a technological one.

It is a great discovery of the major civilizations that the person is a plurality-in-unity. The modern Westerner assigns the unity to the body (the reality) and assigns the multi-personal aspects of self, the appearances, to the mind, the psychic, the subjective. By contrast, the Easterner postulates a psychic-spiritual unity, and is quite at ease associating the multiplicity of many selves, the appearances, to a multiplicity of bodily lives. Thus, for each culture, what is familiar, sensitively elaborated, and fundamental is seen as the realm of unity; what is obscure, eccentric, and less important is seen as the realm of plurality, of appearances, illusion, maya, fantasy. East and West show an exact reversal of emphasis and conceptualization.

.   .   .

Erik H. Erikson
PSYCHOSOCIAL IDENTITY

Erik H. Erikson is a practicing psychoanalyst who has creatively attempted to go beyond the traditional limits of that field in his analysis of the developmental stages of human growth. For many years a senior staff member of the Austen Riggs Center, as well as the author of numerous books, including Identity, Youth, and Crisis, Childhood and Society, *and* Young Man Luther, *Erikson has consistently sought to integrate within psychoanalytic theory a social and historical perspective. Within this synthesis, the concept of* identity *plays a key role, for it refers not only to something that develops within the individual but also to a vital connection between the individual and the culture.*

In the selection reprinted here, Erikson discusses the formation of an individual's self-identity in adolescence as it emerges from the identifications in childhood and points out how this process is connected to the recognition of the community in which the individual lives. Erikson goes on to indicate how the formation of an individual's sense of identity is itself only one part of the "unfolding of the personality through phase-specific social crises." Thus, identity formation is only one stage in the development of the whole human life cycle.

In a number of writings (2, 3, 4, 5) I have been using the term *ego identity* to denote certain comprehensive gains which the individual, at the end of adolescence, must have derived from all of his pre-adult experience in order to be ready for the tasks of adulthood. My use of this term reflected the dilemma of a psychoanalyst who was led to a new concept not by theoretical preoccupation but rather through the expansion of his clinical awareness to other fields (social anthropology and comparative education) and through the expectation that such expansion would, in turn, profit clinical work. Recent clinical observations have, I feel, begun to bear out this expectation. . . .

First a word about the term identity. As far as I know Freud used it only once in a more than incidental way, and then with a psychosocial connotation. It was when he tried to formulate his link to Judaism, that he spoke of an "inner identity" which was not based on race or religion, but on a common readiness to live in opposition, and on a common freedom from prejudices which narrow the use of the intellect. Here, the term identity points to an individual's link with the unique values, fostered by a unique history, of his people. Yet, it also relates to the cornerstone of this individual's unique development: for the importance of the theme of "incorruptible observation at the price of professional isolation" played a central role in Freud's life (6). It is this identity of something in the individual's core with an essential aspect of a group's inner coherence which is under consideration here: for the young individual must learn to be most himself where he means most to others—those others, to be sure, who have come to mean most to him. The term identity expresses such a mutual relation in that it connotes both a persistent sameness within oneself (self-sameness) and a persistent sharing of some kind of essential character with others.

I can attempt to make the subject matter of identity more explicit only by approaching it from a variety of angles—biographic, pathographic, and theoretical; and by letting the term identity speak for itself in a number of connotations. At one time, then, it will appear to refer to a conscious *sense of individual identity;* at another to an unconscious striving for a *continuity of personal character;* at a third, as a criterion for the silent doings of *ego synthesis;* and, finally, as a maintenance of an inner *solidarity* with a group's ideals and identity. In some respects the term will appear to be colloquial and naïve; in another, vaguely related to existing concepts in psychoanalysis and sociology. If, after an attempt at clarifying this relation, the term itself will retain some ambiguity it will, so I hope, nevertheless have helped to delineate a significant problem, and a necessary point of view.

.   .   .

Adolescence is the last and the concluding stage of childhood. The adolescent process, however, is conclusively complete only when the individual has subordinated his childhood identifications to a new kind of identification, achieved in absorbing sociability and in competitive apprenticeship with and among his age-mates. These new identifications are no longer characterized by the playfulness of childhood and the experimental zest of youth: with dire urgency they force the young individual into choices and decisions which will, with increasing immediacy, lead to a more final self-definition, to irreversible role pattern, and thus to commitments "for life." The task to be performed here by the young person and by his society is formidable; it necessitates, in different individuals and in different societies, great variations in the duration, in the intensity, and in the ritualization of adolescence. Societies offer, as individuals require, more or less sanctioned intermediary periods between childhood and adulthood, institutionalized *psychosocial moratoria,* during which a lasting pattern of "inner identity" is scheduled for relative completion.

In postulating a "latency period" which precedes puberty, psychoanalysis has given recognition to some kind of *psychosexual moratorium* in human development—a period of delay which permits the future mate and parent first to "go to school" (i.e., to undergo whatever schooling is provided for in his technology) and to learn the technical and social rudiments of a work situation. It is not within the confines of the libido theory, however, to give adequate account of a second period of delay, namely, adolescence. Here the sexually matured individual is more or less retarded in his psychosexual capacity for intimacy and in the psychosocial readiness for parenthood. This period can be viewed as a *psychosocial moratorium* during which the individual through free role experimentation may find a niche in some section of his society, a niche which is firmly defined and yet seems to be uniquely made for him. In finding it the young adult gains an assured sense of inner continuity and social sameness which will bridge what he *was* as a child and what he is *about to become,* and will reconcile his *conception of himself* and his *community's recognition* of him.

If, in the following, we speak of the community's response to the young individual's need to be "recognized" by those around him, we mean something beyond a mere recognition of achievement; for it is of great relevance to the young individual's identity formation that he be responded to, and be given function and status as a person whose gradual growth and transformation make sense to those who begin to make sense to him. It has not been sufficiently recognized in psychoanalysis that such recognition provides an entirely indispensable support to the ego in the specific tasks of adolescing, which are: to maintain the most important ego defenses against the vastly growing intensity of impulses (now invested in a matured genital apparatus and a powerful muscle system); to learn to consolidate the most important "conflict-free" achievements in line with work opportunities; and to resynthesize all childhood identifications in some unique way, and yet in concordance with the roles offered by some wider section of society—be that section the neighborhood block, an anticipated occupational field, [or] an association of kindred minds.

.   .   .

Linguistically as well as psychologically, identity and identification have common roots. Is identity, then, the mere sum of earlier identifications, or is it merely an additional set of identifications?

The limited usefulness of the *mechanism of identification* becomes at once obvious if we consider the fact that none of the identifications of childhood (which in our patients stand out in such morbid elaboration and mutual contradiction) could, if merely added up, result in a functioning personality. True, we usually believe that the task of psychotherapy is the replacement of morbid and excessive identifications by more desirable ones. But as every cure attests, "more desirable" identifications, at the same time, tend to be quietly subordinated to a new, a unique Gestalt which is more than the sum of its parts. The fact is that identification as a mechanism is of limited usefulness. Children, at different stages of their development identify with those *part aspects* of people by which they themselves are most immediately affected, whether in reality or fantasy. Their identifications with parents, for example, center in certain overvalued and ill-understood body parts, capacities, and role appearances. These parts aspects, furthermore, are favored not because of their social acceptability (they often are everything but the parents' most adjusted attributes) but by the nature of infantile fantasy which only gradually gives way to a more realistic anticipation of social reality. The final identity, then, as fixed at the end of adolescence is superordinated to any single identification with individuals of the past: it includes all significant identifications, but it also alters them in order to make a unique and a reasonably coherent whole of them.

If we, roughly speaking, consider introjection-projection, identification, and identity formation to be the steps by which the ego grows in ever more mature interplay with the identities of the child's models, the following psychosocial schedule suggests itself:

The mechanisms of *introjection and projection* which prepare the basis for later identifications, depend for their relative integration on the satisfactory mutuality (3) between the *mothering adult(s) and the mothered child.* Only the experience of such mutuality provides a safe pole of self-feeling from which the child can reach out for the other pole: his first love "objects."

The fate of *childhood identifications,* in turn, depends on the child's satisfactory interaction with a trustworthy and meaningful hierarchy of roles as provided by the generations living together in some form of *family.*

Identity formation, finally, begins where the usefulness of identification ends. It arises from the selective repudiation and mutual assimilation of childhood identifications, and their absorption in a new configuration, which, in turn, is dependent on the process by which a *society* (often through subsocieties) *identifies the young individual,* recognizing him as somebody who had to become the way he is, and who, being the way he is, is taken for granted. The community, often not without some initial mistrust, gives such recognition with a (more or less institutionalized) display of surprise and pleasure in making the acquaintance of a newly emerging individual. For the community, in turn, feels "recognized" by the individual who cares to ask for recognition; it can, by the same token, feel deeply—and vengefully—rejected by the individual who does not seem to care.

While the end of adolescence thus is the stage of an overt identity *crisis,* identity *formation* neither begins nor ends with adolescence: it is a lifelong development largely unconscious to the individual and to his society. Its roots go back all the way to the first self-recognition: in the baby's earliest exchange of smiles there is something of a *self-realization coupled with a mutual recognition.*

All through childhood tentative crystallizations take place which make the individual feel and believe (to begin with the most conscious aspect of the matter) as if he approximately knew who he was—only to find that such self-certainty ever again falls prey to the *discontinuities of psychosocial development* (1). An example would be the discontinuity between the demands made in a given milieu on a little boy and those made on a "big boy" who, in turn, may well wonder why he was first made to believe that to be little is admirable, only to be forced to exchange this effortless status for the special obligations of one who is "big now." Such discontinuities can amount to a crisis and demand a decisive and strategic repatterning of action, and with it, to *compromises* which can be compensated for only by a consistently accruing sense of the social value of such increasing commitment. The cute or ferocious, or good small boy, who becomes a studious, or gentlemanly, or tough big boy must be able—and must be enabled—to combine both sets of values in recognized identity which permits him, in work and play, and in official and in intimate behavior to be (and to let others be) a big boy *and* a little boy.

The community supports such development to the extent to which it permits the child, at each step, to orient himself toward a complete *"life plan"* with a hierarchical order of roles as represented by individuals of different age grades. Family, neighborhood, and school provide contact and experimental identification with younger and older children and with young and old adults. A child, in the multiplicity of successive and tentative identifications, thus begins early to build up expectations of what it will be like to be older and what it will feel like to have been younger—expectations which become part of an identity as they are, step by step, verified in decisive experiences of psychosocial "fittedness."

. . .

It is the ego's function to integrate the psychosexual and psychosocial aspects on a given level of development, and, at the same time, to integrate the relation of newly added identity elements with those already in existence. For earlier crystallizations of identity can become subject to renewed conflict, when changes in the quality and quantity of drive, expansions in mental equipment, and new and often conflicting social demands all make previous adjustments appear insufficient, and, in fact, make previous opportunities and rewards suspect. Yet, such developmental and normative crises differ from imposed, traumatic, and neurotic crises in that the process of growth provides new energy as society offers new and specific opportunities (according to its dominant conception and institutionalization of the phases of life). From a genetic point of view, then, the process of identity formation emerges as an *evolving configuration* —a configuration which is gradually established by successive ego syntheses and resyntheses throughout childhood; it is a configuration gradually integrating *constitutional givens, idiosyncratic libidinal needs, favored capacities, significant identifications, effective defenses, successful sublimations, and consistent roles.*

The final assembly of all the converging identity elements at the end of childhood (and the abandonment of the divergent ones)[1] appears to be a formidable task: how can a stage as "abnormal" as adolescence be

---

[1]William James speaks of an abandonment of "the old alternative ego," and even of "the murdered self" (7).

trusted to accomplish it? Here it is not unnecessary to call to mind again that in spite of the similarity of adolescent "symptoms" and episodes to neurotic and psychotic symptoms and episodes, adolescence is not an affliction, but a *normative crisis,* i.e., a normal phase of increased conflict characterized by a seeming fluctuation in ego strength, and yet also by a high growth potential. Neurotic and psychotic crises are defined by a certain self-perpetuating propensity, by an increasing waste of defensive energy, and by a deepened psychosocial isolation; while normative crises are relatively more reversible, or, better, traversable, and are character- ized by an abundance of available energy which, to be sure, revives dormant anxiety and arouses new conflict, but also supports new and expanded ego functions in the searching and playful engagement of new opportunities and associations. What under prejudiced scrutiny may ap- pear to be the onset of a neurosis, often is but an aggravated crisis which might prove to be self-liquidating and, in fact, contributive to the process of identity formation.

.   .   .

Is the sense of identity conscious? At times, of course, it seems only too conscious. For between the double prongs of vital inner need and inexorable outer demand, the as yet experimenting individual may become the victim of a transitory extreme *identity consciousness* which is the common core of the many forms of "self-consciousness" typical for youth. Where the processes of identity formation are prolonged (a factor which can bring creative gain) such preoccupation with the "self-image" also prevails. We are thus most aware of our identity when we are just about to gain it and when we (with what motion pictures call "a double take") are somewhat surprised to make its acquaintance; or, again, when we are just about to enter a crisis and feel the encroachment of identity diffusion—a syndrome to be described presently.

An increasing sense of identity, on the other hand, is experienced preconsciously as a sense of psychosocial well-being. Its most obvious concomitants are a feeling of being at home in one's body, a sense of "knowing where one is going," and an inner assuredness of anticipated recognition from those who count. Such a sense of identity, however, is never gained nor maintained once and for all. Like a "good conscience," it is constantly lost and regained, although more lasting and more eco- nomical methods of maintenance and restoration are evolved and for- tified in late adolescence.

Like any aspect of well-being or for that matter, of ego synthesis, a sense of identity has a preconscious aspect which is available to aware- ness; it expresses itself in behavior which is observable with the naked eye; and it has unconscious concomitants which can be fathomed only by psychological tests and by the psychoanalytic procedure. I regret that, at this point, I can bring forward only a general claim which awaits detailed demonstration. The claim advanced here concerns a whole series of criteria of psychosocial health which find their specific elaboration and relative completion in stages of development preceding and following the identity crisis. This is condensed in Figure I.

Identity appears as only one concept within a wider conception of the human life cycle which envisages childhood as a *gradual unfolding of the personality through phase-specific psychosocial crises:* I have, on other occasions (3, 4), expressed this *epigenetic principle* by taking recourse to a diagram which, with its many empty boxes, at intervals may serve as a check on our attempts at detailing psychosocial development. (Such a diagram, however, can be recommended to the serious attention only of those who can take it *and* leave it.) The diagram (Figure I), at first, contained only the double-lined boxes along the descending diagonal (I,1—II,2—III,3 —IV,4—V,5—VI,6—VII,7—VIII,8) and, for the sake of initial orientation, the reader is requested to ignore all other entries for the moment. The *diagonal* shows the sequence of psychosocial crises. Each of these boxes is shared by a criterion of relative psychosocial health and the corresponding criterion of relative psychosocial ill-health: in "normal" development, the first must persistently outweigh (although it will never completely do away with) the second. The sequence of stages thus represents a successive development of the component parts of the psychosocial personality. Each part exists in some form (verticals) before the time when it becomes "phase-specific," i.e., when "its" psychosocial crisis is precipitated both by the individual's readiness and by society's pressure. But each component comes to ascendance and finds its more or less lasting solution at the conclusion of "its" stage. It is thus *systematically related* to all the others, and all depend on the proper development at the proper *time* of each; although individual make-up and the nature of society determine the rate of development of each of them, and thus the *ratio* of all of them. It is at the end of adolescence, then, that identity becomes phase-specific (V,5), i.e., must find a certain integration as a relatively conflict-free psychosocial arrangement—or remain defective or conflict-laden.

.   .   .

The word "psychosocial" so far has had to serve as an emergency bridge between the so-called "biological" formulations of psychoanalysis and newer ones which take the cultural environment into more systematic consideration.

The so-called basic *biological* orientation of psychoanalysis has gradually become a habitual kind of *pseudo biology,* and this especially in the conceptualization (or lack thereof) of man's "environment." In psychoanalytic writings the terms "outer world" or "environment" are often used to designate an uncharted area which is said to be outside merely because it fails to be inside—inside the individual's somatic skin, or inside his psychic systems, or inside his self in the widest sense. Such a vague and yet omnipresent "outerness" by necessity assumes a number of ideo-

	1.	2.	3.	4.	5.	6.	7.	8.
I. INFANCY	Trust vs. Mistrust				Unipolarity vs. Premature Self-Differentiation			
II. EARLY CHILDHOOD		Autonomy vs. Shame, Doubt			Bipolarity vs. Autism			
III. PLAY AGE			Initiative vs. Guilt		Play Identification vs. (Oedipal) Fantasy Identities			
IV. SCHOOL AGE				Industry vs. Inferiority	Work Identification vs. Identity Foreclosure			
V. ADOLESCENCE	Time Perspective vs. Time Diffusion	Self-Certainty vs. Identity Consciousness	Role Experimentation vs. Negative Identity	Anticipation of Achievement vs. Work Paralysis	Identity vs. Identity Diffusion	Sexual Identity vs. Bisexual Diffusion	Leadership Polarization vs. Authority Diffusion	Ideological Polarization vs. Diffusion of Ideals
VI. YOUNG ADULT					Solidarity vs. Social Isolation	Intimacy vs. Isolation		
VII. ADULTHOOD							Generativity vs. Self-Absorption	
VIII. MATURE AGE								Integrity vs. Disgust, Despair

Figure 1

logical connotations, and, in fact, assumes the character of a number of world images: sometimes "the outer world" is conceived of as reality's conspiracy against the infantile wish world; sometimes as the (indifferent or annoying) fact of the existence of other people; and then again as the (at least partially benevolent) presence of maternal care. But even in the recent admission of the significance of the "mother-child relationship," a stubborn tendency persists to treat the mother-child unit as a "biological" entity more or less isolated from its cultural surroundings which then, again, become an "environment" of vague supports or of blind pressures and mere "conventions." Thus, step for step, we are encumbered by the remnants of juxtapositions which were once necessary and fruitful enough: for it was important to establish the fact that moralistic and hypocritical social demands are apt to crush the adult and to exploit the child. It was important to conceptualize certain intrinsic antagonisms between the individual's and society's energy households. However, the implicit conclusion that an individual ego could exist against or without a specifically human "environment," i.e., social organization, is senseless; . . .

.   .   .

The specific kind of preadaptedness of the human infant (namely, the readiness to grow by predetermined steps through institutionalized psychosocial crises) calls not only for one basic environment, but for a whole chain of such successive environments. As the child "adapts" in spurts and stages, he has a claim, at any given stage reached, to the next "average expectable environment." In other words, the human environment must permit and safeguard a series of more or less discontinuous and yet culturally and psychologically consistent steps, each extending further along the radius of expanding life tasks. All of this makes man's so-called biological adaptation a matter of life cycles developing within their community's changing history. Consequently, a psychoanalytic sociology faces the task of conceptualizing man's environment as the persistent endeavor of the older and more adult egos to join in the organizational effort of providing an integrated series of average expectable environments for the young egos.

.   .   .

BIBLIOGRAPHY

1. Benedict, R. Continuities and discontinuities in cultural conditioning. *Psychiatry, 1*:161–167, 1938.
2. Erikson, E. H. Ego development and historical change. In *The Psychoanalytic Study of the Child, 2*:359–396. New York: International Universities Press, 1946.

3. Erikson, E. H. *Childhood and Society.* New York: W. W. Norton, 1950. London: Imago Publishing Co., 1951.
4. Erikson, E. H. Growth and crises of the "healthy personality." In *Symposium on the Healthy Personality,* Supplement II to the transactions of the fourth conference on *Problems of Infancy and Childhood,* ed. M. J. E. Senn. New York: Josiah Macy, Jr. Foundation, 1950.
5. Erikson, E. H. On the sense of inner identity. In *Health and Human Relations.* New York: The Blakiston Company, 1953.
6. Erikson, E. H. The dream specimen of psychoanalysis. *This Journal,* 2:5–56, 1954.
7. James, W. The will to believe. *New World,* 5, 1896.

Richard Schmitt
BECOMING MYSELF

With both Mead and Erikson, we have seen how self-identity is something that emerges through a process of development that is both individual and social. Richard Schmitt, who teaches philosophy at Brown University, distinguishes legal-moral identity from what he calls personal identity. *Lack of personal identity is one form of alienation—a condition much discussed and frequently deplored in our age. Alienation is overcome and personal identity achieved, Schmitt insists, only through personal efforts. Personal identity does not fall into our lap automatically but must be consciously created. Becoming a person in the fullest sense requires, among other things, adopting a clear social role; it is, nevertheless, quite clearly different from conformism that identifies personal identity and social role, because the emphasis for being a person is on choosing one's way of life and taking responsibility for it. Unlike the conformist, the genuine self chooses to carve out a world for him or herself and acquires the skills necessary to master it.*

When I was growing up, adult speech was often confusing to me. Particularly, when people said that someone "had not found" him or herself, I was unsure of what they meant. When I was in my teens, I was sometimes told to "be myself," usually in a critical tone of voice—but I had only the very vaguest idea of what that meant. As an adolescent I faced, so I was told, the task of becoming myself. I was very troubled by being expected to do something that I could not understand. I remember asking a few tentative questions but getting little satisfaction.

I never did make any headway with these questions of what it meant to be myself until much later, because I got stuck in the initial logical problem of how anybody could possibly be anything other than him or herself. If I was not myself, I must be somebody else. But that somebody else would have the same problems that I do, and adults would still scold him and tell him to be himself.

These were the years when change—physical, emotional, and intellectual—was the dominant experience. New emotions went hand in hand with new relationships, with new responsibilities, and hence, with successes and failures of new dimensions. I was changing, but it was *me* that was changing. Somewhere amid all this change, there was an "I," which remained the same, which I always was, however much I was different in other respects. I understood this simple, logical truth that whatever changes in certain respects must, at the same time, remain identical with itself.

Persons, of course, also have a legal identity that is unalterably theirs, whatever else they may do. As soon as they begin to work, young Americans acquire a Social Security number, which remains theirs as long as they live and survives them, in government records, long after they have died. Legal identities are an embarrassment to some. In detective thrillers, we read about criminals who have undergone painful surgery to alter their fingertips, because fingerprints can identify them without chance of error. But this only serves to conceal their legal identity; it does not change it. Their legal identity remains the same.

There is also an accompanying moral identity that all people have. Everyone is legally—within the statute of limitations—and morally responsible for their past actions. You can't act really badly at one time, and then, ten years later, say that you are a changed person and that, therefore, you can no longer be held responsible for what you did ten years ago. Even the sinner who has seen the error of his or her ways and has reformed—even to the point of becoming a saint—may be sure that he or she will not repeat past errors; but he or she cannot shed responsibility —and even guilt—for past misdeeds.

As an adolescent, I had difficulties understanding the advice to be myself, because I could not distinguish my logical, legal, and moral identity—with which we are all born and that survives us beyond the grave— from that other self, which I shall call the "personal self"—which some persons have and most do not. In fact, at least logically, someone can only lack a personal self if they are self-identical in these other ways. Thus, the first step in solving my childish confusion was to draw a distinction between myself as logically, legally, and morally self-identical, and myself as a person. The personal self is a much richer concept than these others. To have such a self, much more is required than logical, legal, or moral self-identity, and hence, there are many ways in which one can fall short of attaining such a personal self.

Are there examples of persons who are genuinely themselves? Let us not talk about Jesus, Buddha, or Albert Schweitzer; we do not know them, and they are too exceptional. But, on the other hand, alienation is a problem faced by everyone, not only by the exceptional. Everyone is, in their own way, struggling to become a person in the fullest sense. What does it mean to be a genuine person for ordinary people like you and me? Everyone has some image of what full self-identity is like. Who do you think of as being as close to being fully themselves as anybody you have ever met? I can recall two people like that.

The first was Levi, a woodsman in the Adirondacks. One summer I watched him build a monumental entrance arch to a summer camp out of the huge pines growing all around. The only tool he used was a two-headed axe, with which he felled, trimmed, and shaped the trees just as he wanted them. He handled that axe with almost magical precision. We talked some, but he was not much given to conversation; mostly, I just stood and watched him. He was a master at his craft and was at home in the woods, not only because he knew them but also because he was safe in them: he had the skills necessary to live well under those tall pines and by the sides of those many lakes. In short, he had mastered his world. Mastery is not domination, not the use of force, and not violation to get what one wants; but rather, mastery rests on the creation of a harmony with the world that is mastered—a harmony that flows from and that breeds a harmony of the soul.

The other person, a woman named Ann, whom I met in Maine a few summers later, had the same sort of mastery, but unlike Levi, she liked to talk and was not alone. I was young then, and married, but not happily. One day, my wife and I went canoeing, which I had never done before, and Ann drove us to the banks of the Penobscot River. She had lived her life with her eyes open, and she had learned a good deal. She could see, and she saw that my wife and I had launched our marriage as clumsily as we were launching our canoe. She gave us some hints about stashing the gear in the canoe and told us about her own life and marriage, without intruding upon or crowding us. She talked, without any anxiety, about reaching us, because she wanted to help, and she was not trying to meet any needs of her own in doing so. She was the master of her own life, and she knew what had made a good marriage for her. She also understood how little one person can learn from another, and she knew how to talk to others in such a way as to be helpful to them. She radiated a quiet assurance. In her own world, she knew what she was doing, and she was, therefore, completely at home in it. If she had felt exiled in her younger years, she was now at home. She was strong, and she knew it.

From those two people I learned much of what it means to be oneself. Both had chosen a way of life that seemed particularly suited to them. I don't know whether, at any time, they felt it necessary to make an explicit choice to become a woodsman or to live in a small town in Maine. But both had chosen to acquire the many skills it took to live well in their respective worlds. Ann had chosen to be married, and she was very serious about it and had given much thought to its difficulties and to their solutions. No doubt, she had fought out many of them. Thus, in becoming themselves, they had learned to face the dangers the world presented and had gained the calm confidence that so impressed me: little could occur for which they could not find remedies. They were free from the anxieties that torment the alienated; from the indecisiveness; from the sudden, panic-stricken question "What if . . .?" and from the constant reexamination of decisions, once they have been made, the ever-repeated "Perhaps I should have. . . ." They saw their environment with clear eyes, their vision unclouded by such anxieties or by their own unmet needs. Ann could, therefore, see the causes of my difficulties and address them helpfully.

To have a self, then, is to be someone in a world for which one has taken some degree of responsibility, by learning to master it, if not create it. It is to be a person who knows his or her strengths and who can stand calmly by his or her decisions, once they have been made. The lives of such people have content and meaning, because they stand for something. Typically, the alienated lack convictions and complain that the world no longer holds causes to which they can dedicate themselves. But the world, alone, is not at fault. Those who have a firm self-identity take firm stands, although more often than not, they do so unobtrusively and become demonstrative only when forced to do so.

While we are all born with logical, legal, and moral identities, our personal selves are only slowly developed. Every child must grow up to be an adult; every young person must grow into middle age; and every adult must ultimately confront declining powers and, eventually, death. This is, once again, universal human destiny that no one can escape. But the common experience we all share in the present age, which is expressed frequently in contemporary novels, plays, and books on sociology and psychology, attests to this fact: the attainment of a genuine self is virtually impossible in our society, and that of full selfhood is extremely rare. This is the insight we express by saying that we are alienated.

A few years ago, I was teaching a course on existentialism, in which the meaning of human life was one of the major topics. One of the students, Tom, came around occasionally to talk, ostensibly about the course, but really about the questions it raised about his own life. His life, he declared, was without meaning. Nothing he did or might do made the least bit of difference to him.

We began to talk. I asked some questions. What was it like for him to be in school? He was a freshman, and he was bored. A good deal of his talk about the meaninglessness of life was, more precisely, a reflection of his disenchantment with college. He had come, expecting to be excited, to find new worlds opening up to him, and instead, he was lonely and could barely get himself out of bed in the morning, or more accurately, around lunchtime. We talked some more. Why not quit school? His father would not hear of it, and that was that.

It seemed to me that, with that revelation, we had arrived at the center of his complaint: he did not particularly want to be in school; it had not really been his idea to begin with, and it certainly was not his decision to stay there. On the other hand, it also became clear that, regardless of his father's wishes, he had no clear idea of what he would like to do if he were not a student.

In this example, we see many of the symptoms of alienation from the self, and meaninglessness is by no means the most important among them. Central to Tom's experience was his sense that his life was not his own. This means that he did not like what he was doing; that he felt that he had no choice about whether or not to continue being where he was; and finally, that, if he had more freedom, he would not really know what to do with it. His immediate conflict pitted him against his father, who wanted him to go to college and then on to law school and into a successful career in law. He did not know whether or not that should be his course.

Lack of self presents itself here as a lack of a settled social role. His sense of insecurity sprang from his inability to decide who he wanted to be—a college graduate and lawyer, or someone else. Once that choice had been made, he would have found himself and would have been well on his way toward becoming a person in his own right.

Without doubt, the making of such occupational choices, as well as the corresponding decisions many young adults make about marriage and children, do provide a greatly strengthened sense of self. I can well remember the great sense of relief I felt when I finally emerged from graduate school— by that time almost thirty years old and having spent most of my life as a student. For the first time, I had some money of my own that was not earmarked for further education. More important, I had, for the first time, a clear identity of my own: I was a teacher; I had some authority by virtue of both my position and my expertise; and I even had some power over students, who were still in the condition I had labored under for so many years, that of being dependent on others—parents and school for money and teachers for instruction, help, and grades. While being a student is an identity of sorts, it lacks the central ingredient of a self, a certain degree of self-determination.

The decision to adopt a certain career, the first job, marriage, moving into one's first house—all of these are powerful experiences that help provide gains in self-identity. They are important stages in the process of becoming somebody, a person in one's own right who has a recognized position in the world and who is known by more than his or her legal identity. It is, therefore, not surprising that someone is said to have "found him or herself," or is said to have finally "discovered who he or she wants to be" when they have made career choices, taken a job, or settled in a nuclear relationship intended to last a long time. Self-identity is here defined implicitly as occupation, marital status, or social position.

. . .

But a definite identity requires more than just the creation of a settled way of life. Everything depends on how the person came to be settled, whether his or her permanence flowed from well-considered choices or from unthinking imitation. Was the present way of life embraced with open eyes, or was it a refuge from a threatening world or because of the anxiety of making independent life choices for which he or she must take responsibility?

Persons must, in time, decide many things about themselves if they are to have a genuine identity. But not all ways of settling these matters will succeed in creating a genuine self. Conformists create a sham identity, stuck together more or less haphazardly. Character and personality are not really theirs; it is something that they have put on, the way one puts on a suit of clothes, and that they can shed just as easily. Putting on a monkey suit does not make one a monkey. It takes more than a facade to make an identity. Social roles are important ingredients in one's identity, but only if they have been genuinely assimilated, not merely adopted as a front.

Without a settled character, a person has no identity. To be someone is to be a public person, in some respects, because one does certain things, and does them in certain ways. One can be counted on to take certain stands and to be visible in a variety of roles: identities exist in public space. Identity is one's own only to the extent that one has developed it oneself. My identity is genuine to the extent that it is mine, because I made it what it is.

Identities are therefore made, not found. One is not alienated because one has failed to find an identity. People never just fail to find themselves: they are prevented or prevent themselves from creating an identity for themselves. Identities do not lie around to be picked up as dimes off the sidewalk if you are looking for them and it is your lucky day; one makes oneself be a definite person only if conditions allow one that much space and creativity.

THE FREEDOM TO CHOOSE

Every day we make decisions. We decide what to order at a restaurant, what to wear, which movie to watch. Some decisions have more long-range consequences: deciding what courses to take next semester; what field of study to pursue as one's lifework; whether to marry, to join the army, to join a revolutionary movement. In each case, it may appear to us that we have chosen freely.

However, things are not always what they seem. Consider the case of individuals acting under posthypnotic suggestion; they may have been told that when given the option of choosing between the king of hearts and the ace of spades, they must choose the king of hearts. After watching them act on this suggestion, we ask them why they picked that card. Their answer may simply be "I felt like it." There is no question in their minds that they were free to decide, just as there may be no question in our minds that we are free to decide. The "feeling of freedom" is the same for each of us.

"But I haven't been hypnotized," we may say. "No one told me what to choose." Let us think about our choices again; about which career to pursue, for example. Was there no one who suggested it? And even if our choices cannot be traced to a straightforward suggestion by one or more persons, were there not some indirect suggestions? Were there not, at least, some factors of personal history that impelled us to make the choice? "No, I am genuinely free," we insist. But then, says the psychologist, we deny the possibility of a science of human behavior, for science must assume that everything has a cause, and if human behavior is caused, then free choice is an illusion. In short, the thesis of psychological determinism appears to be incompatible with human freedom.

Although some, like Skinner, seem perfectly content with such a conclusion, there are many others who find the denial of free choice deeply disturbing. (We have chosen the term "free choice" instead of the more common "free will" because the problem, as we are posing it, should not be confused with the attempt *to prove the existence of some special faculty called the "will.") Without free choice, there seems to be no room for morality, no merit or blame for human action, no human dignity. Furthermore, without free choice, our projects seem lifeless, and those inner struggles to change our life would be a cruel, cosmic hoax.*

In the selections that follow, we explore the metaphysical and moral status of the act of choosing.

B. F. Skinner
WALDEN TWO: FREEDOM AND THE HUMAN SCIENCES

Unquestionably, one of the foremost contemporary representatives of the behaviorist movement is the American psychologist B. F. Skinner. Behaviorism treats psychology as the science that studies the ways in which the human organism reacts to external conditions. It can be contrasted with introspective psychology, or with the psychoanalytic enterprise, which posits such intrapsychic entities as id, ego, superego, and the unconscious. For the behaviorist, human behavior can be adequately accounted for only in such terms as "stimulus," "response," "reinforcement," and "operant conditioning."

The key to Skinner's analysis is the concept of positive reinforcement, which involves the rewarding of certain kinds of behavior to increase their frequency. By using this technique, Skinner has taught pigeons to play table tennis.

The passages reprinted here are taken from Skinner's novel, Walden Two, *which is a description of Skinner's vision of a utopian society run by behaviorist psychologists. The citizens of this society are conditioned (by the use of positive reinforcement) to have desires and motives that make them behave as the psychologists in charge want them to. Skinner defends these practices through the voice of Frazier, the novel's protagonist and the creator of this psychological utopia. Frazier (Skinner) argues that since human behavior is determined in any case, it ought to be determined by those who are well instructed in the science of human behavior and concerned with the welfare of the individual and society. One of the interesting consequences of applying the technique of positive reinforcement is that the individual, though controlled, nonetheless feels free.*

.　　.　　.

"Mr. Castle," said Frazier very earnestly, "let me ask you a question. I warn you, it will be the most terrifying question of your life. *What would you do if you found yourself in possession of an effective science of behavior?* Suppose you suddenly found it possible to control the behavior of men as you wished. What would you do?"

"That's an assumption?"

"Take it as one if you like. *I* take it as a fact. And apparently you accept it as a fact too. I can hardly be as despotic as you claim unless I hold the key to an extensive practical control."

"What would I do?" said Castle thoughtfully. "I think I would dump your science of behavior in the ocean."

"And deny men all the help you could otherwise give them?"

"And give them the freedom they would otherwise lose forever!"

"How could you give them freedom?"

"By refusing to control them!"

"But you would only be leaving the control in other hands."

"Whose?"

"The charlatan, the demagogue, the salesman, the ward heeler, the bully, the cheat, the educator, the priest—all who are now in possession of the techniques of behavioral engineering."

"A pretty good share of the control would remain in the hands of the individual himself."

"That's an assumption, too, and it's your only hope. It's your only possible chance to avoid the implications of a science of behavior. If man is free, then a technology of behavior is impossible. But I'm asking you to consider the other case."

"Then my answer is that your assumption is contrary to fact and further consideration idle."

"And your accusations—?"

"—were in terms of intention, not of possible achievement."

Frazier sighed dramatically.

"It's a little late to be proving that a behavioral technology is well advanced. How can you deny it? Many of its methods and techniques are really as old as the hills. Look at their frightful misuse in the hands of the Nazis! And what about the techniques of the psychological clinic? What about education? Or religion? Or practical politics? Or advertising and salesmanship? Bring them all together and you have a sort of rule-of-thumb technology of vast power. No, Mr. Castle, the science is there for the asking. But its techniques and methods are in the wrong hands—they are used for personal aggrandizement in a competitive world or, in the case of the psychologist and educator, for futilely corrective purposes. My question is, have you the courage to take up and wield the science of behavior for the good of mankind? You answer that you would dump it in the ocean!"

"I'd want to take it out of the hands of the politicians and advertisers and salesmen, too."

"And the psychologists and educators? You see, Mr. Castle, you can't have that kind of cake. The fact is, we not only *can* control human behavior, we *must*. But who's to do it, and what's to be done?"

"So long as a trace of personal freedom survives, I'll stick to my position," said Castle, very much out of countenance.

"Isn't it time we talked about freedom?" I said. "We parted a day or so ago on an agreement to let the question of freedom ring. It's time to answer, don't you think?"

"My answer is simple enough," said Frazier. "I deny that freedom exists at all. I must deny it—or my program would be absurd. You can't have a science about a subject matter which hops capriciously about. Perhaps we can never *prove* that man isn't free; it's an assumption. But the increasing success of a science of behavior makes it more and more plausible."

"On the contrary, a simple personal experience makes it untenable," said Castle. "The experience of freedom. I *know* that I'm free."

"It must be quite consoling," said Frazier.

"And what's more—you do, too," said Castle hotly. "When you deny your own freedom for the sake of playing with a science of behavior, you're acting in plain bad faith. That's the only way I can explain it." He tried to recover himself and shrugged his shoulders. "At least you'll grant that you *feel* free."

"The 'feeling of freedom' should deceive no one," said Frazier. "Give me a concrete case."

"Well, right now," Castle said. He picked up a book of matches. "I'm free to hold or drop these matches."

"You will, of course, do one or the other," said Frazier. "Linguistically or logically there seem to be two possibilities, but I submit that there's only one in fact. The determining forces may be subtle but they are inexorable. I suggest that as an orderly person you will probably hold —ah! you drop them! Well, you see, that's all part of your behavior with respect to me. You couldn't resist the temptation to prove me wrong. It was all lawful. You had no choice. The deciding factor entered rather late, and naturally you couldn't foresee the result when you first held them up. There was no strong likelihood that you would act in either direction, and so you said you were free."

"That's entirely too glib," said Castle. "It's easy to argue lawfulness after the fact. But let's see you predict what I will do in advance. Then I'll agree there's law."

"I didn't say that behavior is always predictable, any more than the weather is always predictable. There are often too many factors to be taken into account. We can't measure them all accurately, and we couldn't perform the mathematical operations needed to make a prediction if we had the measurements. The legality is usually an assumption—but none the less important in judging the issue at hand."

"Take a case where there's no choice, then," said Castle. "Certainly a man in jail isn't free in the sense in which I am free now."

"Good! That's an excellent start. Let us classify the kinds of determiners of human behavior. One class, as you suggest, is physical restraint —handcuffs, iron bars, forcible coercion. There are ways in which we shape human behavior according to our wishes. They're crude, and they sacrifice the affection of the controllee, but they often work. Now, what other ways are there of limiting freedom?"

Frazier had adopted a professional tone and Castle refused to answer.

"The threat of force would be one," I said.

"Right. And here again we shan't encourage any loyalty on the part of the controllee. He has perhaps a shade more of the feeling of freedom, since he can always 'choose to act and accept the consequences,' but he doesn't feel exactly free. He knows his behavior is being coerced. Now what else?"

I had no answer.

"Force or the threat of force—I see no other possibility," said Castle after a moment.

"Precisely," said Frazier.

"But certainly a large part of my behavior has no connection with force at all. There's my freedom!" said Castle.

"I wasn't agreeing that there was no other possibility—merely that *you* could see no other. Not being a good behaviorist—or a good Christian, for that matter—you have no feeling for a tremendous power of a different sort."

"What's that?"

"I shall have to be technical," said Frazier. "But only for a moment. It's what the science of behavior calls 'reinforcement theory.' The things that can happen to us fall into three classes. To some things we are indifferent. Other things we like—we want them to happen, and we take steps to make them happen again. Still other things we don't like—we don't want them to happen and we take steps to get rid of them or keep them from happening again.

"*Now,*" Frazier continued earnestly, "if it's in our power to create any of the situations which a person likes or to remove any situation he doesn't like, we can control his behavior. When he behaves as we want him to behave, we simply create a situation he likes, or remove one he doesn't like. As a result, the probability that he will behave that way again goes up, which is what we want. Technically it's called 'positive reinforcement.'

"The old school made the amazing mistake of supposing that the reverse was true, that by removing a situation a person likes or setting up one he doesn't like—in other words by punishing him—it was possible to *reduce* the probability that he would behave in a given way again. That simply doesn't hold. It has been established beyond question. What is emerging at this critical stage in the evolution of society is a behavioral and cultural technology based on positive reinforcement alone. We are gradually discovering—at an untold cost in human suffering—that in the long run punishment doesn't reduce the probability that an act will occur. We have been so preoccupied with the contrary that we always take 'force' to mean punishment. We don't say we're using force when we send shiploads of food into a starving country, though we're displaying quite as much *power* as if we were sending troops and guns."

"I'm certainly not an advocate of force," said Castle. "But I can't agree that it's not effective."

"It's *temporarily* effective, that's the worst of it. That explains several thousand years of bloodshed. Even nature has been fooled. We 'instinctively' punish a person who doesn't behave as we like—we spank him if he's a child or strike him if he's a man. A nice distinction! The immediate effect of the blow teaches us to strike again. Retribution and revenge are the most natural things on earth. But in the long run the man we strike is no less likely to repeat his act."

"But he won't repeat it if we hit him hard enough," said Castle.

"He'll still *tend* to repeat it. He'll *want* to repeat it. We haven't really altered his potential behavior at all. That's the pity of it. If he doesn't repeat it in our presence, he will in the presence of someone else. Or it will be repeated in the disguise of a neurotic symptom. If we hit hard enough, we clear a little place for ourselves in the wilderness of civilization, but we make the rest of the wilderness still more terrible.

"Now, early forms of government are naturally based on punishment. It's the obvious technique when the physically strong control the weak. But we're in the throes of a great change to positive reinforcement—from a competitive society in which one man's reward is another man's punishment, to a cooperative society in which no one gains at the expense of anyone else.

"The change is slow and painful because the immediate, temporary effect of punishment overshadows the eventual advantage of positive reinforcement. We've all seen countless instances of the temporary effect of force, but clear evidence of the effect of not using force is rare. That's why I insist that Jesus, who was apparently the first to discover the power of refusing to punish, must have hit upon the principle by accident. He certainly had none of the experimental evidence which is available to us today, and I can't conceive that it was possible, no matter what the man's genius, to have discovered the principle from casual observation."

"A touch of revelation, perhaps?" said Castle.

"No, accident. Jesus discovered one principle because it had immediate consequences, and he got another thrown in for good measure."

I began to see light.

"You mean the principle of 'love your enemies'?" I said.

"Exactly! To 'do good to those who despitefully use you' has two unrelated consequences. You gain the peace of mind we talked about the other day. Let the stronger man push you around—at least you avoid the torture of your own rage. *That's* the immediate consequence. What an astonishing discovery it must have been to find that in the long run you could *control the stronger man* in the same way!"

"It's generous of you to give so much credit to your early colleague," said Castle, "but why are we still in the throes of so much misery? Twenty centuries should have been enough for one piece of behavioral engineering."

"The conditions which made the principle difficult to discover made it difficult to teach. The history of the Christian Church doesn't reveal many cases of doing good to one's enemies. To inoffensive heathens, perhaps, but not enemies. One must look outside the field of organized religion to find the principle in practice at all. Church governments are devotees of *power,* both temporal and bogus."

"But what has all this got to do with freedom?" I said hastily.

Frazier took time to reorganize his behavior. He looked steadily toward the window, against which the rain was beating heavily.

"Now that we *know* how positive reinforcement works and why negative doesn't," he said at last, "we can be more deliberate, and hence more successful, in our cultural design. We can achieve a sort of control under which the controlled, though they are following a code much more scrupulously than was ever the case under the old system, nevertheless *feel free.* They are doing what they want to do, not what they are forced to do. That's the source of the tremendous power of positive reinforcement—there's no restraint and no revolt. By a careful cultural design, we control not the final behavior, but the *inclination* to behave—the motives, the desires, the wishes.

"The curious thing is that in that case *the question of freedom never arises.* Mr. Castle was free to drop the matchbook in the sense that nothing was preventing him. If it had been securely bound to his hand he wouldn't have been free. Nor would he have been quite free if I'd covered him with a gun and threatened to shoot him if he let it fall. The question of freedom arises when there is restraint—either physical or psychological.

"But restraint is only one sort of control, and absence of restraint isn't freedom. It's not control that's lacking when one feels 'free,' but the objectionable control of force. Mr. Castle felt free to hold or drop the matches in the sense that he felt no restraint—no threat of punishment in taking either course of action. He neglected to examine his positive reasons for holding or letting go, in spite of the fact that these were more compelling in this instance than any threat of force.

"We have no vocabulary of freedom in dealing with what we want to do," Frazier went on. "The question never arises. When men strike for freedom, they strike against jails and the police, or the threat of them—against oppression. They never strike against forces which make them want to act the way they do. Yet, it seems to be understood that governments will operate only through force or the threat of force, and that all other principles of control will be left to education, religion, and commerce. If this continues to be the case, we may as well give up. A government can never create a free people with the techniques now allotted to it.

"The question is: Can men live in freedom and peace? And the answer is: Yes, if we can build a social structure which will satisfy the needs of everyone and in which everyone will want to observe the supporting code. But so far this has been achieved only in Walden Two. Your ruthless accusations to the contrary, Mr. Castle, this is the freest place on earth. And it is free precisely because we make no use of force or the threat of force. Every bit of our research, from the nursery through the psychological management of our adult membership, is directed toward that end—to exploit every alternative to forcible control. By skillful planning, by a wise choice of techniques we *increase* the feeling of freedom.

"It's not planning which infringes upon freedom, but planning which uses force. A sense of freedom was practically unknown in the planned society of Nazi Germany, because the planners made a fantastic use of force and the threat of force.

"No, Mr. Castle, when a science of behavior has once been achieved, there's no alternative to a planned society. We can't leave mankind to an accidental or biased control. But by using the principle of positive reinforcement—carefully avoiding force or the threat of force—we can preserve a personal sense of freedom."

Frazier threw himself back upon the bed and stared at the ceiling.

. . .

C. A. Campbell
IN DEFENSE OF FREE WILL

In the following essay, C. A. Campbell argues for what he terms the "Libertarian" position. This position not only takes the agent to be the sole cause of his or her action (the advocacy of this postulate alone Campbell terms the "Self-determinist" position) but also affirms that the agent can act against the influences of his or her heredity and environment. This, says Campbell, can occur in the situation of "moral temptation" in which the balance of desires impels us to do something that conflicts with what we believe to be right. In such a situation we can by "effort of will" act contrary to our desires; we can, in effect, act against the inclinations of our previously formed character. Were this not the case, argues Campbell, we could never be held morally responsible for our actions.

We should note that Campbell's libertarianism is a restricted one. In general, Campbell agrees with the determinist that the desires we have at any moment are the result of past environmental influences acting upon our hereditary nature and that we act in whatever way the balance of those desires should incline us. For Campbell, it is only in those situations where our desires conflict with what we take to be our moral obligations that we can act otherwise and, even then, only when our "effort of will" is strong enough to counter those desires.

With respect to Campbell's position, we urge the reader to consider several questions. Might not our appraisal of the nature of our moral obligations also be determined by past experience? Might not our ability to exert a sufficient "effort of will" to counter our desires be similarly determined? Finally, might not our very will to make the effort (of will) be itself determined by previous influences?

.   .   .

Let us begin by noting that the problem of free will gets its urgency for the ordinary educated man by reason of its close connection with the conception of moral responsibility. When we regard a man as morally responsible for an act, we regard him as a legitimate object of moral praise or blame in respect of it. But it seems plain that a man cannot be a legitimate object of moral praise or blame for an act unless in willing the act he is in some important sense a "free" agent. Evidently free will in some sense, therefore, is a pre-condition of moral responsibility. Without doubt it is the realization that any threat to freedom is thus a threat to moral responsibility—with all that that implies—combined with the knowledge that there are a variety of considerations, philosophic, scientific, and theological, tending to place freedom in jeopardy, that gives to the problem of free will its perennial and universal appeal. And it is therefore in close connection with the question of the conditions of moral responsibility that any discussion of the problem must proceed, if it is not to be academic in the worst sense of the term.

We raise the question at once, therefore, what are the conditions, in respect of freedom, which must attach to an act in order to make it a morally responsible act? It seems to me that the fundamental conditions are two. I shall state them with all possible brevity, for we have a long road to travel.

The first condition is the universally recognised one that the act must be *self*-caused, *self*-determined. But it is important to accept this condition in its full rigour. The agent must be not merely *a* cause but the *sole* cause of that for which he is deemed morally responsible. If entities other than the self have also a causal influence upon an act, then that act is not one for which we can say without qualification that the *self* is morally responsible. If in respect of it we hold the self responsible at all, it can only be for some feature of the act—assuming the possibility of disengaging such a feature—of which the self *is* the sole cause. I do not see how this conclusion can be evaded. But it has awkward implications which have led not a few people to abandon the notion of individual moral responsibility altogether.

This first condition, however, is quite clearly not sufficient. It is possible to conceive an act of which the agent is the sole cause, but which is at the same time an act *necessitated* by the agent's nature. Some philosophers have contended, for example, that the act of Divine creation is an act which issues necessarily from the Divine nature. In the case of such an act, where the agent could not do otherwise than he did, we must all agree, I think, that it would be inept to say that he *ought* to have done otherwise and is thus morally blameworthy, or *ought not* to have done otherwise and is thus morally praiseworthy. It is perfectly true that we do sometimes hold a person morally responsible for an act, even when we believe that he, being what he now is, virtually could not do otherwise. But underlying that judgment is always the assumption that the person has *come* to be what he now is in virtue of past acts of will in which he *was* confronted by real alternatives, by genuinely open possibilities: and, strictly speaking, it is in respect of these *past* acts of his that we praise or blame the agent *now*. For ultimate analysis, the agent's power of alternative action would seem to be an inexpugnable condition of his liability to moral praise or blame, i.e. of his moral responsibility.

We may lay down, therefore, that an act is a "free" act in the sense required for moral responsibility only if the agent *(a)* is the sole cause of the act; and *(b)* could exert his causality in alternative ways. And it may be pointed out in passing that the acceptance of condition *(b)* implies the recognition of the inadequacy for moral freedom of mere "self-determination." The doctrine called "Self-determinism" is often contrasted by its advocates with mere Determinism on the one hand and Indeterminism on the other, and pronounced to be the one true gospel. I must insist, however, that if "Self-determinism" rejects condition *(b)*, it cannot claim to be a doctrine of free will in the sense required to vindicate moral responsibility. The doctrine which demands, and asserts, the fulfilment of both conditions is the doctrine we call "Libertarianism." And it would in my opinion minister greatly to clarity if it were more widely recognized that for any doctrine which is not a species of Libertarianism to pose as a doctrine of "free will" is mere masquerade.

And now, the conditions of free will being defined in these general terms, we have to ask whether human beings are in fact capable of performing free acts; and if so, where precisely such acts are to be found. In order to prepare the way for an answer, it is desirable, I think, that we should get clear at once about the significance of a certain very familiar, but none the less formidable, criticism of free will which the Self-determinist as well as the Libertarian has to meet. This is the criticism which bases itself upon the facts of heredity on the one hand and of environment on the other. I may briefly summarize the criticism as follows.

Every historic self has an hereditary nature consisting of a group of inborn propensities, in range more or less common to the race, but specific to the individual in their respective strengths. With this equipment the self just *happens* to be born. Strictly speaking, it antedates the existence of the self proper, i.e. the existence of the self-conscious subject, and it is itself the effect of a series of causes leading back to indefinitely remote antiquity. It follows, therefore, that any of the self's choices that manifests the influence of his hereditary nature is not a choice of which *he*, the actual historic self, is the sole cause. The choice is determined, at least in part, by factors external to the self. The same thing holds good of "environment." Every self is born and bred in a particular physical and social environment, not of his own choosing, which plays upon him in innumerable ways encouraging this propensity, discouraging that, and so on. Clearly any of the self's choices that manifests the influence of environmental factors is likewise a choice which is determined, at least in part, by factors external to the self. But if we thus grant, as seems inevitable, that heredity and environment are external influences, where shall we find a choice in the whole history of a self that is not subject to external influence? Surely we must admit that every particular act of choice bears the marks of the agent's hereditary nature and environmental nurture; in which case a free act, in the sense of an act determined solely by the self, must be dismissed as a mere chimaera.

.   .   .

Let us proceed, then, by following up this clue. Let us ask, why do human beings so obstinately persist in believing that there is an indissoluble core of purely *self*-originated activity which even heredity and environment are powerless to affect? There can be little doubt, I think, of the answer in general terms. They do so, at bottom, because they feel certain of the existence of such activity from their immediate practical experience of themselves. Nor can there be in the end much doubt, I think, in what function of the self that activity is to be located. There seems to me to be one, and only one, function of the self with respect to which the agent can even pretend to have an assurance of that absolute self-origination which is here at issue. But to render precise the nature of that function is obviously of quite paramount importance: and we can do so, I think, only by way of a somewhat thorough analysis—which I now propose to attempt—of the experiential situation in which it occurs, viz., the situation of "moral temptation."

It is characteristic of that situation that in it I am aware of an end A which I believe to be morally right, and also of an end B, incompatible with A, towards which, in virtue of that system of conative dispositions which constitutes my "character" as so far formed, I entertain a strong desire. There may be, and perhaps must be, desiring elements in my nature which are directed to A also. But what gives to the situation its specific character as one of moral temptation is that the urge of our desiring nature towards the right end, A, is felt to be *relatively* weak. We are sure that if our desiring nature is permitted to issue directly in action, it is end B that we shall choose. That is what is meant by saying, as William James does, that end B is "in the line of least resistance" relatively to our conative dispositions. The expression is, of course, a metaphorical one, but it serves to describe, graphically enough, a situation of which we all have frequent experience, viz., where we recognize a specific end as that towards which the "set" of our desiring nature most strongly inclines us, and which we shall indubitably choose if no inhibiting factor intervenes.

But inhibiting factors, we should most of us say, *may* intervene: and that in two totally different ways which it is vital to distinguish clearly. The inhibiting factor may be of the nature of another desire (or aversion), which operates by changing the balance of the desiring situation. Though at one stage I desire B, which I believe to be wrong, more strongly than I desire A, which I believe to be right, it may happen that before action is taken I become aware of certain hitherto undiscerned consequences of A which I strongly desire, and the result may be that now not B but A presents itself to me as the end in the line of least resistance. Moral temptation is here overcome by the simple process of ceasing to be a moral temptation.

That is one way, and probably by far the commoner way, in which an inhibiting factor intervenes. But it is certainly not regarded by the self who is confronted by moral temptation as the *only* way. In such situations we all believe, rightly or wrongly, that even although B *continues* to be in the line of least resistance, even although, in other words, the situation remains one with the characteristic marks of moral temptation, we *can* nevertheless align ourselves with A. We can do so, we believe, because we have the power to introduce a new energy, to make what we call an "effort of will," whereby we are able to act contrary to the felt balance of mere desire, and to achieve the higher end despite the fact that it continues to be in the line of greater resistance relatively to our desiring nature. The self in practice believes that it has this power; and believes, moreover, that the decision rests solely with its self, here and now, whether this power be exerted or not.

Now the objective validity or otherwise of this belief is not at the moment in question. I am here merely pointing to its existence as a psychological fact. No amount of introspective analysis, so far as I can see, even tends to disprove that we do as a matter of fact believe, in situations of moral temptation, that it rests with our self absolutely to decide whether we exert the effort of will which will enable us to rise to duty, or whether we shall allow our desiring nature to take its course.

I have now to point out, further, how this act of moral decision, at least in the significance which it has for the agent himself, fulfills in full the two conditions which we found it necessary to lay down at the beginning for the kind of "free" act which moral responsibility presupposes.

For obviously it is, in the first place, an act which the agent believes he could perform in alternative ways. He believes that it is genuinely open to him to put forth effort—in varying degrees, if the situation admits of that—or withhold it altogether. And when he *has* decided—in whatever way—he remains convinced that these alternative courses were really open to him.

It is perhaps a little less obvious, but, I think, equally certain, that the agent believes the second condition to be fulfilled likewise, i.e. that the act of decision is determined *solely* by his self. It appears less obvious, because we all realize that formed character has a great deal to do with the choices that we make; and formed character is, without a doubt, partly dependent on the external factors of heredity and environment. But it is crucial here that we should not misunderstand the precise nature of the influence which formed character brings to bear upon the choices that constitute conduct. No one denies that it determines, at least largely, what things we desire, and again how greatly we desire them. It may thus fairly be said to determine the felt balance of desires in the situation of moral temptation. But all that that amounts to is that formed character prescribes the nature of the situation *within* which the act of moral decision takes place. It does not in the least follow that it has any influence whatsoever in determining the act of decision itself—the decision as to whether we shall exert effort or take the easy course of following the bent of our desiring nature: take, that is to say, the course which, in virtue of the determining influence of our character as so far formed, we feel to be in the line of least resistance.

When one appreciates this, one is perhaps better prepared to recognize the fact that the agent himself in the situation of moral temptation does not, and indeed could not, regard his formed character as having any influence whatever upon his act of decision as such. For the very nature of that decision, as it presents itself to him, is as to whether he will or will not permit his formed character to dictate his action. In other words, the agent distinguishes sharply between the self which makes the decision, and the self which, as formed character, determines not the decision but the situation within which the decision takes place. Rightly or wrongly, the agent believes that through his act of decision he can oppose and transcend his own formed character in the interest of duty. We are therefore obliged to say, I think, that the agent *cannot* regard his formed character as in any sense a determinant of the act of decision as such. The act is felt to be a genuinely creative act, originated by the self *ad hoc,* and by the self alone.

Here then, if my analysis is correct, in the function of moral decision in situations of moral temptation, we have an act of the self which at least *appears to the agent* to satisfy both of the conditions of freedom which we laid down at the beginning. The vital question now is, is this "appearance" true or false? Is the act of decision really what it appears to the agent to be, determined soley by the self, and capable of alternative forms of expression? If it is, then we have here a free act which serves as an adequate basis for moral responsibility. We shall be entitled to regard the agent as morally praiseworthy or morally blameworthy according as he decides to put forth effort or to let his desiring nature have its way. We shall be entitled, in short, to judge the agent as he most certainly judges himself in the situation of moral temptation. If, on the other hand, there is good reason to believe that the agent is the victim of illusion in supposing his act of decision to bear this character, then in my opinion the whole conception of moral responsibility must be jettisoned altogether. For it seems to me certain that there is no other function of the self that even looks as though it satisfied the required conditions of the free act.

Now in considering the claim to truth of this belief of our practical consciousness, we should begin by noting that the onus of proof rests upon the critic who rejects this belief. Until cogent evidence to the contrary is adduced, we are entitled to put our trust in a belief which is so deeply embedded in our experience as practical beings as to be, I venture to say, ineradicable from it. Anyone who doubts whether it is ineradicable may be invited to think himself imaginatively into a situation of moral temptation as we have above described it, and then to ask himself whether in that situation he finds it possible to *disbelieve* that his act of decision has the characteristics in question. I have no misgivings about the answer. It is possible to disbelieve only when we are thinking abstractly about the situation; not when we are living through it, either actually or in imagination. This fact certainly establishes a strong prima facie presumption in favour of the Libertarian position. Nevertheless I agree that we shall have to weigh carefully several criticisms of high authority before we can feel justified in asserting free will as an ultimate and unqualified truth.

Fortunately for our purpose, however, there are some lines of criticism which, although extremely influential in the recent past, may at the present time be legitimately ignored. We are not to-day confronted, for example, by any widely accepted system of metaphysic with implications directly hostile to free will. Only a decade or two ago one could hardly hope to gain a sympathetic hearing for a view which assigned an ultimate initiative to finite selves, unless one were prepared first to show reason for rejecting the dominant metaphysical doctrine that all things in the universe are the expression of a single Mind or Spirit. But the challenge so lately offered by monistic Idealism has in the present age little more significance than the challenge once offered by monistic Materialism.

Much the same thing holds good of the challenge from the side of physical science. Libertarianism is certainly inconsistent with a rigidly determinist theory of the physical world. It is idle to pretend that there can be open possibilities for psychical decision, while at the same time holding that the physical events in which such decisions manifest themselves are determined in accordance with irrevocable law. But whereas until a few years ago the weight of scientific authority was thrown overwhelmingly on the side of a universal determinism of physical phenomena, the situation has, as everybody knows, profoundly altered during the present century more especially since the advent of Planck's Quantum Theory and Heisenberg's Principle of Uncertainty. Very few scientists to-day would seek to impugn free will on the ground of any supposed implications of the aims or achievements of physical science. I am not myself, I should perhaps add in passing, disposed to rest any part of the case against a universal physical determinism upon these recent dramatic developments of physical science. In my view there never were in the established results of physical science cogent reasons for believing that the apparently universal determinism of inorganic processes holds good also of the processes of the human body. The only inference I here wish to draw from the trend of present-day science is that it removes from any *contemporary* urgency the problem of meeting one particular type of objection to free will. And it is with the contemporary situation that I am in this paper anxious to deal.

I may turn at once, therefore, to lines of argument which do still enjoy a wide currency among anti-Libertarians. And I shall begin with one which, though it is a simple matter to show its irrelevance to the Libertarian doctrine as I have stated it, is so extremely popular that it cannot safely be ignored.

The charge made is that the Libertarian view is incompatible with the *predictability* of human conduct. For we do make rough predictions of people's conduct, on the basis of what we know of their character, every day of our lives, and there can be no doubt that the practice, within certain limits, is amply justified by results. Indeed if it were not so, social life would be reduced to sheer chaos. The close relationship between character and conduct which prediction postulates really seems to be about as certain as anything can be. But the Libertarian view, it is urged, by ascribing to the self a mysterious power of decision uncontrolled by character, and capable of issuing in acts inconsistent with character, denies that continuity between character and conduct upon which prediction depends. If Libertarianism is true, prediction is impossible. But prediction *is* possible, therefore Libertarianism is untrue.

My answer is that the Libertarian view is perfectly compatible with prediction within certain limits, and that there is no empirical evidence at all that prediction is in fact possible beyond these limits. The following considerations will, I think, make the point abundantly clear.

(1) There is no question, on our view, of a free will that can will just anything at all. The range of possible choices is limited by the agent's character in every case; for nothing can be an object of possible choice which is not suggested by either the agent's desires or his moral ideals, and these depend on "character" for us just as much as for our opponents. We have, indeed explicitly recognized at an earlier stage that character determines the situation within which the act of moral decision takes place, although not the act of moral decision itself. This consideration obviously furnishes a broad basis for at least approximate predictions.

(2) There is *one* experiential situation, and *one only,* on our view, in which there is any possibility of the act of will not being in accordance with character; viz., the situation in which the course which formed character prescribes is a course in conflict with the agent's moral ideal: in other words, the situation of moral temptation. Now this is a situation of comparative rarity. Yet with respect to all other situations in life we are in full agreement with those who hold that conduct is the response of the agent's formed character to the given situation. Why should it not be so? There could be no reason, on our view any more than on another, for the

agent even to consider deviating from the course which his formed character prescribes and he most strongly desires, *unless* that course is believed by him to be incompatible with what is right.

(3) Even within that one situation which is relevant to free will, our view can still recognize a certain basis for prediction. In that situation our character as so far formed prescribes a course opposed to duty, and an effort of will is required if we are to deviate from that course. But of course we are all aware that a greater effort of will is required in proportion to the degree in which we have to transcend our formed character in order to will the right. Such action is, as we say, "harder." But if action is "harder" in proportion as it involves deviation from formed character, it seems reasonable to suppose that, on the whole, action will be of rarer occurrence in that same proportion: though perhaps we may not say that at any level of deviation it becomes flatly impossible. It follows that even with respect to situations of moral temptation we may usefully employ our knowledge of the agent's character as a clue to prediction. It will be a clue of limited, but of by no means negligible, value. It will warrant us in predicting, e.g., of a person who has become enslaved to alcohol, that he is unlikely, even if fully aware of the moral evil of such slavery, to be successful immediately and completely in throwing off its shackles. Predictions of this kind we all make often enough in practice. And there seems no reason at all why a Libertarian doctrine should wish to question their validity.

Now when these three considerations are borne in mind, it becomes quite clear that the doctrine we are defending is compatible with a very substantial measure of predictability indeed. And I submit that there is not a jot of empirical evidence that any larger measure than this obtains in fact.

Let us pass on then to consider a much more interesting and, I think, more plausible criticism. It is constantly objected against the Libertarian doctrine that it is fundamentally *unintelligible*. Libertarianism holds that the act of moral decision is the *self's* act, and yet insists at the same time that it is not influenced by any of those determinate features in the self's nature which go to constitute its "character." But, it is asked, do not these two propositions contradict one another? Surely a *self*-determination which is determination by something other than the self's *character* is a contradiction in terms? What meaning is there in the conception of a "self" in abstraction from its "character"? If you really wish to maintain, it is urged, that the act of decision is not determined by the self's character, you ought to admit frankly that it is not determined by the *self* at all. But in that case, of course, you will not be advocating a freedom which lends any kind of support to moral responsibility; indeed very much the reverse.

Now this criticism, and all of its kind, seem to me to be the product of a simple, but extraordinarily pervasive, error: the error of confining one's self to the categories of the external observer in dealing with the actions of human agents. Let me explain.

It is perfectly true that the standpoint of the external observer, which we are obliged to adopt in dealing with physical processes, does not furnish us with even a glimmering of a notion of what can be meant by an entity which acts causally and yet not through any of the determinate features of its character. So far as we confine ourselves to external observation, I agree that this notion must seem to us pure nonsense. But then we are *not* obliged to confine ourselves to external observation in dealing with the human agent. Here, though here alone, we have the inestimable advantage of being able to apprehend operations from the *inside,* from the standpoint of *living experience.* But if we do adopt this internal standpoint—surely a proper standpoint, and one which we should be only too glad to adopt if we could in the case of other entities—the situation is entirely changed. We find that we not merely can, but constantly do, attach meaning to a causation which is the self's causation but is yet not exercised by the self's character. We have seen as much already in our analysis of the situation of moral temptation. When confronted by such a situation, we saw, we are certain that it lies with our *self* to decide whether we shall let our character as so far formed dictate our action or whether we shall by effort oppose its dictates and rise to duty. We are certain, in other words, that the act is *not* determined by our *character,* while we remain equally certain that the act *is* determined by our *self.*

Or look, for a further illustration (since the point we have to make here is of the very first importance for the whole free will controversy), to the experience of effortful willing itself, where the act of decision has found expression in the will to rise to duty. In such an experience we are certain that it is our self which makes the effort. But we are equally certain that the effort does not flow from that system of conative dispositions which we call our formed character; for the very function that the effort has for us is to enable us to act against the "line of least resistance," i.e. to act in a way *contrary* to that to which our formed character inclines us.

I conclude, therefore, that those who find the Libertarian doctrine of the self's causality in moral decision inherently unintelligible find it so simply because they restrict themselves, quite arbitrarily, to an inadequate standpoint: a standpoint from which, indeed, a genuinely creative activity, if it existed, never *could* be apprehended.

It will be understood, of course, that it is no part of my purpose to deny that the act of moral decision is in *one* sense "unintelligible." If by the "intelligibility" of an act we mean that it is capable, at least in principle, of being inferred as a consequence of a given ground, then naturally my view is that the act in question is "*un*intelligible." But that, presumably, is not the meaning of "intelligibility" in the critic's mind when he says that the Libertarian holds an "unintelligible" doctrine. If it were all he meant, he would merely be pointing out that Libertarianism is not compatible with Determinism! And that tautologous pronouncement would hardly deserve the title of "criticism." Yet, strangely enough, not all of the critics seem to be quite clear on this matter. The Libertarian often has the experience of being challenged by the critic to tell him *why*, on his view, the agent now decides to put forth moral effort and now decides not to, with the obviously intended implication that if the Libertarian cannot say "why" he should give up his theory. Such critics apparently fail to see that if the Libertarian *could* say why he would already have given up his theory! Obviously to demand "intelligibility" in this sense is simply to prejudge the whole issue in favour of Determinism. The sense in which the critic is entitled to demand intelligibility of our doctrine is simply this; he may demand that the kind of action which our doctrine imputes to human selves should not be, for ultimate analysis, meaningless. And in that sense, as I have already argued, our doctrine is perfectly intelligible.

Let us suppose, then, that the Determinist, confronted by the plain evidence of our practical self-consciousness, now recognizes his obligation to give up the position that the Libertarian doctrine is without qualification "meaningless," and concedes that from the standpoint of our practical self-consciousness at any rate it is "meaningful." And let us ask what will be his next move. So far as I can see, his most likely move now will be to attack the value of that "internal" standpoint, contrasting it unfavourably, in respect of its claim to truth, with the rational, objective, standpoint of "pure philosophy." "I admit," he may tell us, "that there is begotten in the self, in the practical experience you refer to, a belief in a self-causality which is yet not a causality exercised through the self's character. But surely this must weigh but lightly in the balance against the proposition, which appeals to our reason with axiomatic certainty, that an act cannot be caused by a self if it has no ground in the determinate nature of that self. If the choice lies between either disbelieving that rational proposition, or dismissing the evidence of practical self-consciousness as illusion, it is the latter alternative which in my opinion any sane philosophy is bound to adopt."

But a very little reflection suffices to show that this position is in reality no improvement at all on that from which the critic has just fallen back. For it is evident that the proposition alleged to be axiomatic is axiomatic, at most, only to a reason which knows nothing of acts or events save as they present themselves to an external observer. It obviously is *not* axiomatic to a reason whose field of apprehension is broadened to include the data furnished by the direct experience of acting. In short, the proposition is axiomatic, at most, only to reason functioning *abstractly;* which most certainly cannot be identified with reason functioning *philosophically.*

What is required of the critic, of course, if he is to make good his case, is a reasoned justification of his cavalier attitude towards the testimony of practical self-consciousness. That is the primary desideratum. And the lack of it in the bulk of Determinist literature is in my opinion something of a scandal. Without it, the criticism we have just been examining is sheer dogmatism. It is, indeed, dogmatism of a peculiarly perverse kind. For the situation is, in effect, as follows. From our practical self-consciousness we gain a notion of a genuinely creative act—which might be defined as an act which nothing determines save the agent's doing of it. Of such a character is the act of moral decision as we experience it. But the critic says "No! This sort of thing cannot be. A person cannot without affront to reason be conceived to be the author of an act which bears, *ex hypothesi,* no intelligible relation to his character. A mere intuition of practical self-consciousness is the solitary prop of this fantastic notion, and surely that is quite incapable of bearing the weight that you would thrust upon it." Now observe the perversity! The critic says, excluding the evidence of practical self-consciousness, the notion makes nonsense. In other words, excluding the only evidence there ever *could* be for such a notion, the notion makes nonsense! For, of course, if there should be such a thing as creative activity, there is absolutely no other way save an intuition of practical self-consciousness in which we could become aware of it. Only from the inside, from the standpoint of the agent's living experience, can "activity" possibly be apprehended. So that what the critic is really doing is to condemn a notion as nonsensical on the ground that the only evidence for it is the only evidence there ever could be for it.

.   .   .

Moritz Schlick
FREEDOM AND RESPONSIBILITY

Moritz Schlick was born in Berlin in 1882 and was shot to death in 1936 by a graduate student to whom he had denied the doctoral degree. Schlick was a founding member of the Vienna Circle, a small group of philosophers that formed in Vienna in the early 1920s. The group formulated a philosophical position that has come to be known as "logical positivism." It maintains that philosophy's chief task is to determine the conditions under which statements can be meaningful, in effect, to clarify the meaning or to expose the lack of meaning of a variety of concepts. It was thus claimed that many of the problems posed by traditional metaphysics turn out, on careful analysis, to be pseudoproblems.

In the selection that follows, Schlick analyzes the problem of free will as a pseudoproblem. Let us recall that in the previous selection, Campbell defended free will on the grounds that without it we could never be held morally responsible for our actions. In other words, determinism is incompatible with human freedom and moral responsibility, and this, Campbell, as a libertarian, believes is surely a repugnant position. However, it is just this alleged incompatibility that Schlick challenges. The opposite of freedom is not determinism, he declares, but rather compulsion. As long as I can act as I desire, free from external compulsion, I have all the freedom I need to be considered morally responsible for my actions. Thus, the opposition "freedom versus determinism" is a pseudo-opposition.

Schlick's position is often called compatibilism, *or* reconciliationism, *because it takes freedom and moral responsibility to be compatible with determinism. It is also called "soft" determinism, as opposed to "hard" determinism, which accepts as a consequence of determinism the loss of freedom and moral responsibility. (Skinner's position might be taken as an example of hard determinism.)*

We might notice, then, that hard determinism and libertarianism both agree on one important premise: determinism entails the negation of freedom and moral responsibility. They disagree as to whether or not human actions are determined. In contrast, soft determinism opposes both libertarianism and hard determinism on their common premise and insists, instead, that determinism is fully compatible with freedom and moral responsibility.

WHEN IS A MAN RESPONSIBLE?[1]

1. The Pseudo-Problem of Freedom of the Will

With hesitation and reluctance I prepare to add this chapter to the discussion of ethical problems. For in it I must speak of a matter which, even at present, is thought to be a fundamental ethical question, but which got into ethics and has become a much discussed problem only because of a misunderstanding. This is the so-called problem of the freedom of the will. Moreover, this pseudo-problem has long since been settled by the efforts of certain sensible persons; and, above all, the state of affairs just described has been often disclosed—with exceptional clarity by Hume. Hence it is really one of the greatest scandals of philosophy that again and again so much paper and printer's ink is devoted to this matter, to say nothing of the expenditure of thought, which could have been applied to more important problems (assuming that it would have sufficed for these). Thus I should truly be ashamed to write a chapter on "freedom." In the chapter heading, the word "responsible"[1] indicates what concerns ethics, and designates the point at which misunderstanding arises. Therefore the concept of responsibility constitutes our theme, and if in the process of its clarification I also must speak of the concept of freedom I shall, of course, say only what others have already said better; consoling myself with the thought that in this way alone can anything be done to put an end at last to that scandal.

The main task of ethics . . . is to explain moral behavior. To explain means to refer back to laws: every science, including psychology, is possible only in so far as there are such laws to which the events can be

---

[1]The original title of this selection is "When Is a Man Responsible?" [Eds.]

referred. Since the assumption that *all* events are subject to universal laws is called the principle of causality, one can also say, "Every science presupposes the principle of causality." Therefore every explanation of human behavior must also assume the validity of causal laws; in this case the existence of psychological laws. . . . All of our experience strengthens us in the belief that this presupposition is realized, at least to the extent required for all purposes of practical life in intercourse with nature and human beings, and also for the most precise demands of technique. Whether, indeed, the principle of causality holds universally, whether, that is, *determinism* is true, we do not know; no one knows. But we do know that it is impossible to settle the dispute between determinism and inde-terminism by mere reflection and speculation, by the consideration of so many reasons for and so many reasons against (which collectively and individually are but pseudo-reasons). Such an attempt becomes especially ridiculous when one considers with what enormous expenditure and logical skill contemporary physics carefully approaches the question of whether causality can be maintained for the most minute intra-atomic events.

But the dispute concerning "freedom of the will" generally proceeds in such fashion that its advocates attempt to refute, and its opponents to prove, the validity of the causal principle, both using hackneyed argu-ments, and neither in the least abashed by the magnitude of the undertak-ing. . . .

Fortunately, it is not necessary to lay claim to a final solution of the causal problem in order to say what is necessary in ethics concerning responsibility; there is required only an analysis of the concept, the care-ful determination of the meaning which is in fact joined to the words "responsibility" and "freedom" as these are actually used. If men had made clear to themselves the sense of those propositions, which we use in everyday life, that pseudo-argument which lies at the root of the pseu-do-problem, and which recurs thousands of times within and outside of philosophical books, would never have arisen.

The argument runs as follows: "If determinism is true, if, that is, all events obey immutable laws, then my will too is always determined, by my innate character and my motives. Hence my decisions are necessary, not free. But if so, then I am not responsible for my acts, for I would be accountable for them only if I could do something about the way my decisions went; but I can do nothing about it, since they proceed with necessity from my character and the motives. And I have made neither, and have no power over them: the motives come from without, and my character is the necessary product of the innate tendencies and the exter-nal influences which have been effective during my lifetime. Thus deter-minism and moral responsiblity are incompatible. Moral responsibility presupposes freedom, that is, exemption from causality."

This process of reasoning rests upon a whole series of confusions, just as the links of a chain hang together. We must show these confusions to be such, and thus destroy them.

2. Two Meanings of the Word "Law"

It all begins with an erroneous interpretation of the meaning of "law." In practice this is understood as a rule by which the state prescribes certain behavior to its citizens. These rules often contradict the natural desires of the citizens (for if they did not do so, there would be no reason for making them), and are in fact not followed by many of them; while others obey, but under *compulsion*. The state does in fact compel its citizens by imposing certain sanctions (punishments) which serve to bring their desires into harmony with the prescribed laws.

In natural science, on the other hand, the word "law" means something quite different. The natural law is not a *pre*scription as to how something should behave, but a formula, a *de*scription of how something does in fact behave. The two forms of "laws" have only this in common: both tend to be expressed in *formulae*. Otherwise they have absolutely nothing to do with one another, and it is very blameworthy that the same word has been used for two such different things; but even more so that philosophers have allowed themselves to be led into serious errors by this usage. Since natural laws are only descriptions of what happens, there can be in regard to them no talk of "compulsion." The laws of celestial mechanics do not prescribe to the planets how they have to move, as though the planets would actually like to move quite otherwise, and are only forced by these burdensome laws of Kepler to move in orderly paths; no, these laws do not in any way "compel" the planets, but express only what in fact planets actually do.

If we apply this to volition, we are enlightened at once, even before the other confusions are discovered. When we say that a man's will "obeys psychological laws," these are not civic laws, which compel him to make certain decisions, or dictate desires to him, which he would in fact prefer not to have. They are laws of nature, merely expressing which desires he *actually has* under given conditions; they describe the nature of the will in the same manner as the astronomical laws describe the nature of planets. "Compulsion" occurs where man is prevented from realizing his natural desires. How could the rule according to which these natural desires arise itself be considered as "compulsion"?

3. Compulsion and Necessity

But this is the second confusion to which the first leads almost inevitably: after conceiving the laws of nature, anthropomorphically, as order imposed *nolens volens* upon the events, one adds to them the concept of "necessity." This word, derived from "need," also comes to us from practice, and is used there in the sense of inescapable compulsion. To apply the word with this meaning to natural laws is of course senseless, for the presupposition of an opposing desire is lacking; and it is then confused with something altogether different, which is actually an attribute of natural laws. That is, universality. It is of the essence of natural laws to be universally valid, for only when we have found a rule of events which holds without exception do we *call* the rule a law of nature. Thus when we say "a natural law holds necessarily" this has but one legitimate meaning: "It holds in *all* cases where it is applicable." It is again very deplorable that the word "necessary" has been applied to natural laws (or, what amounts to the same thing, with reference to causality), for it is quite superfluous, since the expression "universally valid" is available. Universal validity is something altogether different from "compulsion"; these concepts belong to spheres so remote from each other that once insight into the error has been gained one can no longer conceive the possibility of a confusion.

The confusion of two concepts always carries with it the confusion of their contradictory opposites. The opposite of the universal validity of a formula, of the existence of a law, is the nonexistence of a law, indeterminism, acausality; while the opposite of compulsion is what in practice everyone calls "freedom." Here emerges the nonsense, trailing through centuries, that freedom means "exemption from the causal principle," or "not subject to the laws of nature." Hence it is believed necessary to vindicate indeterminism in order to save human freedom.

4. Freedom and Indeterminism

This is quite mistaken. Ethics has, so to speak, no moral interest in the purely theoretical question of "determinism or indeterminism?," [but only a theoretical interest, namely: in so far as it seeks the laws of conduct, and can find them only to the extent that causality holds.] But the question of whether man is morally free (that is, has that freedom which, as we shall show, is the presupposition of moral responsibility) is altogether different from the problem of determinism. Hume was especially clear on this point. He indicated the inadmissible confusion of the concepts of "indeterminism" and "freedom"; but he retained, inappropriately, the word "freedom" for both, calling the one freedom of "the will," the other, genuine kind, "freedom of conduct." He showed that morality is interested only in the latter, and that such freedom, in general, is unquestionably to be attributed to mankind. And this is quite correct. Freedom means the opposite of compulsion; a man is *free* if he does not act under *compulsion,* and he is compelled or unfree when he is hindered from without in the realization of his natural desires. Hence he is unfree when he is locked up, or chained, or when someone forces him at the point of a gun to do what otherwise he would not do. This is quite clear, and everyone will admit that the everyday or legal notion of the lack of freedom is thus correctly interpreted, and that a man will be considered quite free and responsible if no such external compulsion is exerted upon him. There are certain cases which lie between these clearly described ones, as, say, when someone acts under the influence of alcohol or a narcotic. In such cases we consider the man to be more or less unfree, and hold him less accountable, because we rightly view the influence of the drug as "external," even though it is found within the body; it prevents him from making decisions in the manner peculiar to his nature. If he takes the narcotic of his own will, we make him completely responsible for *this* act and transfer a part of the responsibility to the consequences, making, as it were, an average or mean condemnation of the whole. In the case also of a person who is mentally ill we do not consider him free with respect to those acts in which the disease expresses itself, because we view the illness as a disturbing factor which hinders the normal functioning of his natural tendencies. We make not him but his disease responsible.

5. The Nature of Responsibility

But what does this really signify? What do we mean by this concept of responsibility which goes along with that of "freedom," and which plays such an important role in morality? It is easy to attain complete clarity in this matter; we need only carefully determine the manner in which the concept is used. What is the case in practice when we impute "responsibility" to a person? What is our aim in doing this? The judge has to discover who is responsible for a given act in order that he may *punish* him. We are inclined to be less concerned with the inquiry as to who deserves *reward* for an act, and we have no special officials for this; but of course the principle would be the same. But let us stick to punishment in order to make the idea clear. What is punishment, actually? The view still often expressed, that it is a natural *retaliation* for past wrong, ought no longer to be defended in cultivated society; for the opinion that an increase in sorrow can be "made good again" by further sorrow is altogether barbarous. Certainly the origin of punishment may lie in an impulse of retaliation or vengeance; but what is such an impulse except the instinctive desire to destroy the *cause* of the deed to be avenged, by the destruction of or injury to the malefactor? Punishment is concerned only with the institution of causes, of *motives* of conduct, and this alone is its meaning. Punishment is an educative measure, and as such is a means to the formation of motives, which are in part to prevent the wrongdoer from repeating the act (reformation) and in part to prevent others from committing a similar act (intimidation). Analogously, in the case of reward we are concerned with an incentive.

Hence the question regarding responsibility is the question: Who, in a given case, is to be punished? Who is to be considered the true wrongdoer? This problem is not identical with that regarding the original instigator of the act; for the great-grandparents of the man, from whom he inherited his character, might in the end be the cause, or the statesmen who are responsible for his social milieu, and so forth. But the "doer" is the one *upon whom the motive must have acted* in order, with certainty, to have prevented the act (or called it forth, as the case may be). Consideration of remote causes is of no help here, for in the first place their actual contribution cannot be determined, and in the second place they are generally out of reach. Rather, we must find the person in whom the decisive junction of causes lies. The question of who is responsible is the question concerning the *correct point of application of the motive*. And the important thing is that in this its meaning is completely exhausted; behind it there lurks no mysterious connection between transgression and requital, which is merely *indicated* by the described state of affairs. It is a matter only of knowing who is to be punished or rewarded, in order that punishment and reward function as such—be able to achieve their goal.

Thus, all the facts connected with the concepts of responsibility and imputation are at once made intelligible. We do not charge an insane person with responsibility, for the very reason that he offers no unified point for the application of a motive. It would be pointless to try to affect him by means of promises or threats, when his confused soul fails to respond to such influence because its normal mechanism is out of order. We do not try to give him motives, but try to heal him (metaphorically, we make his sickness responsible, and try to remove its causes). When a man is forced by threats to commit certain acts we do not blame him, but the one who held the pistol at his breast. The reason is clear: the act would have been prevented had we been able to restrain the person who threatened him; and this person is the one whom we must influence in order to prevent similar acts in the future.

6. The Consciousness of Responsibility

But much more important than the question of when a man is said to be responsible is that of when he *himself* feels responsible. Our whole treatment would be untenable if it gave no explanation of this. It is, then, a welcome confirmation of the view here developed that the subjective feeling of responsibility coincides with the objective judgment. It is a fact of experience that, in general, the person blamed or condemned is conscious of the fact that he was "rightly" taken to account—of course, under the supposition that no error has been made, that the assumed state of affairs actually occurred. What is this consciousness of having been the true doer of the act, the actual instigator? Evidently not merely that it was he who took the steps required for its performance; but there must be added the awareness that he did it "independently," "of his own initiative," or however it be expressed. This feeling is simply the consciousness of *freedom*, which is merely the knowledge of having acted of one's *own* desires. And "one's own desires" are those which have their origin in the regularity of one's character in a given situation, and are not imposed by an external power, as explained above. The absence of the external power expresses itself in the well-known feeling (usually considered characteristic of the consciousness of freedom) *that one could also have acted otherwise.* How this indubitable experience ever came to be an argument in favor of indeterminism is incomprehensible to me. It is of course obvious that I should have acted differently had I *willed* something else; but the feeling never says that I could also have willed something else, even though this is true, if, that is, other motives had been present. And it says even less that under *exactly the same* inner and outer conditions I could also have willed something else. How could such a feeling inform me of anything regarding the purely theoretical question of whether the principle of causality holds or not? Of course, after what has been said on the subject, I do not undertake to demonstrate the principle, but I do deny that from any such fact of consciousness the least follows regarding the principle's validity. This feeling is not the consciousness of the absence of a cause, but of something altogether different, namely, of *freedom,* which consists in the fact that I can act as I desire.

Thus the feeling of responsibility assumes that I acted freely, that my own desires impelled me; and if because of this feeling I willingly suffer blame for my behavior or reproach myself, and thereby admit that I might have acted otherwise, this means that other behavior was compatible with the laws of volition—of course, granted other motives. And I myself desire the existence of such motives and bear the pain (regret and sorrow) caused me by my behavior so that its repetition will be prevented. To blame oneself means just to apply motives of improvement to oneself, which is usually the task of the educator. But if, for example, one does something under the influence of torture, feelings of guilt and regret are absent, for one knows that according to the laws of volition no other behavior was possible—no matter what ideas, because of their feeling tones, might have functioned as motives. The important thing, always, is that the feeling of responsibility means the realization that one's self, one's own psychic processes constitute the point at which motives must be applied in order to govern the acts of one's body.

7. Causality as the Presupposition of Responsibility

We can speak of motives only in a causal context; thus it becomes clear how very much the concept of responsibility rests upon that of causation, that is, upon the regularity of volitional decisions. In fact if we should conceive of a decision as utterly without any cause (this would in all strictness be the indeterministic presupposition) then the act would be entirely a matter of *chance,* for chance is identical with the absence of a cause; there is no other opposite of causality. Could we under such conditions make the agent responsible? Certainly not. Imagine a man, always calm, peaceful and blameless, who suddenly falls upon and begins to beat a stranger. He is held and questioned regarding the motive of his action, to which he answers, in his opinion truthfully, as we assume: "There was no motive for my behavior. Try as I may I can discover no reason. My volition was without any cause—I desired to do so, and there is simply nothing else to be said about it." We should shake our heads and call him insane, because we have to believe that there was a cause, and lacking any other we must assume some mental disturbance as the only cause remaining; but certainly no one would hold him to be responsible. If decisions were causeless there would be no sense in trying to influence men; and we see at once that this is the reason why we could not bring such a man to account, but would always have only a shrug of the shoulders in answer to his behavior. One can easily determine that in practice we make an agent the more responsible the more motives we can find for his conduct. If a man guilty of an atrocity was an enemy of his victim, if previously he had shown violent tendencies, if some special circumstance angered him, then we impose severe punishment upon him; while the fewer the reasons to be found for an offense the less do we condemn the agent, but make "unlucky chance," a momentary aberration, or something of the sort, responsible. We do not find the causes of misconduct in his character, and therefore we do not try to influence it for the better: this and only this is the significance of the fact that we do not put the responsibility upon him. And he too feels this to be so, and says, "I cannot understand how such a thing could have happened to me."

In general we know very well how to discover the causes of conduct in the characters of our fellow men; and how to use this knowledge in the prediction of their future behavior, often with as much certainty as that with which we know that a lion and a rabbit will behave quite differently in the same situation. From all this it is evident that in practice no one thinks of questioning the principle of causality, that, thus, the attitude of the practical man offers no excuse to the metaphysician for confusing freedom from compulsion with the absence of a cause. If one makes clear to himself that a causeless happening is identical with a chance happening, and that, consequently, an indetermined will would destroy all responsibility, then every desire will cease which might be father to an indeterministic thought. No one can prove determinism, but it is certain that we assume its validity in all of our practical life, and that in particular we can apply the concept of responsibility to human conduct only in so far as the causal principle holds of volitional processes.

For a final clarification I bring together again a list of those concepts which tend, in the traditional treatment of the "problem of freedom," to be confused. In the place of the concepts on the left are put, mistakenly, those of the right, and those in the vertical order form a chain, so that sometimes the previous confusion is the cause of that which follows:

Natural Law.	Law of State.
Determinism (Causality).	Compulsion.
(Universal Validity).	(Necessity).
Indeterminism (Chance).	Freedom.
(No Cause).	(No Compulsion).

John Hospers
FREE WILL AND PSYCHOANALYSIS

In the preceding article, Schlick maintained that psychological laws are not to be thought of as compelling our actions but simply as describing the desires on the basis of which we act. Since, on Schlick's analysis, only behavior that is compelled is unfree, it follows that actions that are psychologically determined are nonetheless free in the morally relevant sense (the agent can be held morally responsible), so long as they are not subject to external compulsion. In the following article, John Hospers challenges Schlick's position on its own ground. By appealing to Freud's theory of unconscious motivation, Hospers argues that most, if not all, of our conscious desires and choices may be properly regarded as compelled (from the outside, so to speak) by unconscious forces and that, therefore, the individual is neither free nor morally responsible for his actions. In other words, actions that appear to be free because they are performed in the absence of external physical compulsion may still be psychologically compelled, and therefore, in a deeper sense, not free at all. Insofar as most of our actions are of this sort, it would follow that (unconscious) psychological determinism is incompatible with moral freedom.

Hospers does, however, make one qualification. Near the end of his article, he very briefly suggests another possible criteria for distinguishing between free and unfree acts—freedom is in inverse proportion to one's neuroticism—and therefore, freedom might be better thought of as admitting of degrees.

. . .

The free act is the uncompelled act, says Schlick, and controversies about causality and determinism have nothing to do with the case. When one asks whether an act done of necessity is free, the question is ambiguous: if "of necessity" means "by compulsion," then the answer is no; if, on the other hand, "of necessity" is a way of referring to "causal uniformity" in nature—the sense in which we may misleadingly speak of the laws of nature as "necessary" simply because there are no exceptions to them—then the answer is clearly yes; every act is an instance of some causal law (uniformity) or other, but this has nothing to do with its being free in the sense of uncompelled.

For Schlick, this is the end of the matter. Any attempt to discuss the matter futher simply betrays a failure to perceive the clarifying distinctions that Schlick has made.

> Freedom means the opposite of compulsion; a man is *free* if he does not act under *compulsion,* and he is compelled or unfree when he is hindered from without in the realization of his natural desires. Hence he is unfree when he is locked up, or chained, or when someone forces him at the point of a gun

to do what otherwise he would not do. This is quite clear, and everyone will admit that the everyday or legal notion of the lack of freedom is thus correctly interpreted, and that a man will be considered quite free ... if no such external compulsion is exerted upon him.[1]

This all seems clear enough. And yet if we ask whether it ends the matter, whether it states what we "really mean" by "free," many of us will feel qualms. We remember statements about human beings being pawns of their environment, victims of conditions beyond their control, the result of causal influences stemming from parents, etc., and we think, "Still, are we really free?" We do not want to say that the uniformity of nature itself binds us or renders us unfree; yet is there not something in what generations of wise men have said about man being fettered? Is there not something too facile, too sleight-of-hand, in Schlick's cutting of the Gordian knot?

It will be noticed that we have slipped from talking about acts as being free into talking about human beings as free. Both locutions are employed, I would say about 50–50. Sometimes an attempt is made to legislate definitely between the two: Stebbing, for instance, says that one must never call acts free, but only the doers of the acts.[2]

Let us pause over this for a moment. If it is we and not our acts that are to be called free, the most obvious reflection to make is that we are free to do some things and not free to do other things; we are free to lift our hands but not free to lift the moon. We cannot simply call ourselves free or unfree *in toto*; we must say at best that we are free in respect of certain actions only. G. E. Moore states the criterion as follows: we are free to do an act if we can do it *if* we want to; that which we can do if we want to is what we are free to do.[3] Some things certain people are free to do while others are not: most of us are free to move our legs, but paralytics are not; some of us are free to concentrate on philosophical reading matter for three hours at a stretch while others are not. In general, we could relate the two approaches by saying that a *person* is free *in respect of* a given action if he can do it if he wants to, and in this case his *act* is free.

Moore himself, however, has reservations that Schlick has not. He adds that there *is* a sense of "free" which fulfills the criterion he has just set forth; but that there may be *another* sense in which man cannot be said to be free in all the situations in which he could rightly be said to be so in the first sense.

And surely it is not necessary for me to multiply examples of the sort of thing we mean. In practice most of us would not call free many persons who behave voluntarily and even with calculation aforethought, and under no compulsion either of any obvious sort. A metropolitan newspaper

[1]Moritz Schlick, *The Problems of Ethics,* p. 150.
[2]L. Susan Stebbing, *Philosophy and the Physicists,* p. 242.
[3]G. E. Moore, *Ethics,* p. 205.

headlines an article with the words "Boy Killer Is Doomed Long Before He Is Born,"[4] and then goes on to describe how a twelve-year-old boy has just been sentenced to thirty years in Sing Sing for the murder of a girl; his family background includes records of drunkenness, divorce, social maladjustment, epilepsy, and paresis. He early displays a tendency to sadistic activity to hide an underlying masochism and "prove that he's a man"; being coddled by his mother only worsens this tendency, until, spurned by a girl in his attempt on her, he kills her—not simply in a fit of anger, but calculatingly, deliberately. Is he free in respect of his criminal act, or for that matter in most of the acts of his life? Surely to ask this question is to answer it in the negative. Perhaps I have taken an extreme case; but it is only to show the superficiality of the Schlick analysis the more clearly. Though not everyone has criminotic tendencies, everyone has been moulded by influences which in large measure at least determine his present behavior; he is literally the product of these influences, stemming from periods prior to his "years of discretion," giving him a host of character traits that he cannot change now even if he would. So obviously does what a man is depend upon how a man comes to be, that it is small wonder that philosophers and sages have considered man far indeed from being the master of his fate. It is not as if man's will were standing high and serene above the flux of events that have moulded him; it is itself caught up in this flux, itself carried along on the current. An act is free when it is determined by the man's character, say moralists; but when there was nothing the man could do to shape his character, and even the degree of will power available to him in shaping his habits and disciplining himself to overcome the influence of his early environment is a factor over which he has no control, what are we to say of this kind of "freedom"? Is it not rather like the freedom of the machine to stamp labels on cans when it has been devised for just that purpose? Some machines can do so more efficiently than others, but only because they have been better constructed.

It is not my purpose here to establish this thesis in general, but only in one specific respect which has received comparatively little attention, namely, the field referred to by psychiatrists as that of unconscious motivation. In what follows I shall restrict my attention to it because it illustrates as clearly as anything the points I wish to make.

Let me try to summarize very briefly the psychoanalytic doctrine on this point.[5] The conscious life of the human being, including the con-

[4] *New York Post,* Tuesday, May 18, 1948, p. 4.

[5] I am aware that the theory presented below is not accepted by all practicing psychoanalysts. Many non-Freudians would disagree with the conclusions presented below. But I do not believe that this fact affects my argument, as long as the concept of unconscious motivation is accepted. I am aware, too, that much of the language employed in the following descriptions is animistic and metaphorical; but as long as I am presenting a view I would prefer to "go the whole hog" and present it in its strongest possible light. The theory can in any case be made clearest by the use of such language, just as atomic theory can often be made clearest to students with the use of models.

scious decisions and volitions, is merely a mouthpiece for the unconscious—not directly for the enactment of unconscious drives, but of the
compromise between unconscious drives and unconscious reproaches.
There is a Big Three behind the scenes which the automaton called the
conscious personality carries out: the id, an "eternal gimme," presents
its wish and demands its immediate satisfaction; the super-ego says no to
the wish immediately upon presentation, and the unconscious ego, the
mediator between the two, tries to keep peace by means of compromise.[6]

To go into examples of the functioning of these three "bosses"
would be endless; psychoanalytic case books supply hundreds of them.
The important point for us to see in the present context is that it is the
unconscious that determines what the conscious impulse and the conscious action shall be. Hamlet, for example, had a strong Oedipus wish,
which was violently counteracted by super-ego reproaches; these early
wishes were vividly revived in an unusual adult situation in which his
uncle usurped the coveted position from Hamlet's father and won his
mother besides. This situation evoked strong strictures on the part of
Hamlet's super-ego, and it was this that was responsible for his notorious
delay in killing his uncle. A dozen times Hamlet could have killed
Claudius easily; but every time Hamlet "decided" not to: a free choice,
moralists would say—but no, listen to the super-ego: "What you feel such
hatred toward your uncle for, what you are plotting to kill him for, is
precisely the crime which you yourself desire to commit: to kill your
father and replace him in the affections of your mother. Your fate and
your uncle's are bound up together." This paralyzes Hamlet into inaction. Consciously all he knows is that he is unable to act; this conscious
inability he rationalizes, giving a different excuse each time.[7]

We have always been conscious of the fact that we are not masters
of our fate in every respect—that there are many things which we cannot
do, that nature is more powerful than we are, that we cannot disobey laws
without danger of reprisals, etc. Lately we have become more conscious,
too, though novelists and dramatists have always been fairly conscious of
it, that we are not free with respect to the emotions that we feel—whom
we love or hate, what types we admire, and the like. More lately still we
have been reminded that there are unconscious motivations for our basic
attractions and repulsions, our compulsive actions or inabilities to act.
But what is not welcome news is that our very acts of volition, and the
entire train of deliberations leading up to them, are but facades for the
expression of unconscious wishes, or rather, unconscious compromises
and defenses.

A man is faced by a choice: shall he kill another person or not?
Moralists would say, here is a free choice—the result of deliberation, an

---

[6]This view is very clearly developed in Edmund Bergler, *Divorce Won't Help,* especially
Chapter I.

[7]See *The Basic Writings of Sigmund Freud,* Modern Library Edition, p. 310. (In *The
Interpretation of Dreams.*) Cf. also the essay by Ernest Jones, " A Psycho-analytical Study of
Hamlet."

action consciously entered into. And yet, though the agent himself does not know it, and has no awareness of the forces that are at work within him, his choice is already determined for him: his conscious will is only an instrument, a slave, in the hands of a deep unconscious motivation which determines his action. If he has a great deal of what the analyst calls "free-floating guilt," he will not; but if the guilt is such as to demand immediate absorption in the form of self-damaging behavior, this accumulated guilt will have to be discharged in some criminal action. The man himself does not know what the inner clockwork is; he is like the hands on the clock, thinking they move freely over the face of the clock.

A woman has married and divorced several husbands. Now she is faced with a choice for the next marriage: shall she marry Mr. A, or Mr. B, or nobody at all? She may take considerable time to "decide" this question, and her decision may appear as a final triumph of her free will. Let us assume that A is a normal, well-adjusted, kind, and generous man, while B is a leech, an impostor, one who will become entangled constantly in quarrels with her. If she belongs to a certain classifiable psychological type, she will inevitably choose B, and she will do so even if her previous husbands have resembled B, so that one would think that she "had learned from experience." Consciously, she will of course "give the matter due consideration," etc., etc. To the psychoanalyst all this is irrelevant chaff in the wind—only a camouflage for the inner workings about which she knows nothing consciously. If she is of a certain kind of masochistic strain, as exhibited in her previous set of symptoms, she *must* choose B: her super-ego, always out to maximize the torment in the situation, seeing what dazzling possibilities for self-damaging behavior are promised by the choice of B, compels her to make the choice she does, and even to conceal the real basis of the choice behind an elaborate facade of rationalizations.

A man is addicted to gambling. In the service of his addiction he loses all his money, spends what belongs to his wife, even sells his property and neglects his children. For a time perhaps he stops; then, inevitably, he takes it up again, although he himself may think he chose to. The man does not know that he is a victim rather than an agent; or, if he sometimes senses that he is in the throes of something-he-knows-not-what, he will have no inkling of its character and will soon relapse into the illusion that he (his conscious self) is freely deciding the course of his own actions. What he does not know, of course, is that he is still taking out on his mother the original lesion to his infantile narcissism, getting back at her for her fancied refusal of his infantile wishes—and this by rejecting everything identified with her, namely education, discipline, logic, common sense, training. At the roulette wheel, almost alone among adult activities, chance—the opposite of all these things—rules supreme; and his addiction represents his continued and emphatic reiteration of his rejection of Mother and all she represents to his unconscious.

This pseudo-aggression of his is of course masochistic in its effects. In the long run he always loses; he can never quit while he is winning.

And far from playing in order to win, rather one can say that his losing is a *sine qua non* of his psychic equilibrium (as it was for example with Dostoyevsky): guilt demands punishment, and in the ego's "deal" with the super-ego the super-ego has granted satisfaction of infantile wishes in return for the self-damaging conditions obtaining. Winning would upset the neurotic equilibrium.[8]

A man has wash-compulsion. He must be constantly washing his hands—he uses up perhaps 400 towels a day. Asked why he does this, he says, "I need to, my hands are dirty"; and if it is pointed out to him that they are not really dirty, he says "They feel dirty anyway, I feel better when I wash them." So once again he washes them. He "freely decides" every time; he feels that he must wash them, he deliberates for a moment perhaps, but always ends by washing them. What he does not see, of course, is the invisible wires inside him pulling him inevitably to do the thing he does: the infantile id-wish concerns preoccupation with dirt, the super-ego charges him with this, and the terrified ego must respond, "No, I don't like dirt, see how clean I like to be, look how I wash my hands!"

Let us see what further "free acts" the same patient engages in (this is an actual case history): he is taken to a concentration camp, and given the worst of treatment by the Nazi guards. In the camp he no longer chooses to be clean, does not even try to be—on the contrary, his choice is now to wallow in filth as much as he can. All he is aware of now is a disinclination to be clean, and every time he must choose he chooses not to be. Behind the scenes, however, another drama is being enacted: the super-ego, perceiving that enough torment is being administered from the outside, can afford to cease pressing its charges in this quarter—the outside world is doing the torturing now, so the super-ego is relieved of the responsibility. Thus the ego is relieved of the agony of constantly making terrified replies in the form of washing to prove that the super-ego is wrong. The defense no longer being needed, the person slides back into what is his natural predilection anyway, for filth. This becomes too much even for the Nazi guards: they take hold of him one day, saying "We'll teach you how to be clean!" drag him into the snow, and pour bucket after bucket of icy water over him until he freezes to death. Such is the end-result of an original id-wish, caught in the machinations of a destroying super-ego.

Let us take, finally, a less colorful, more everyday example. A student at a university, possessing wealth, charm, and all that is usually considered essential to popularity, begins to develop the following personality-pattern: although well taught in the graces of social conversation, he always makes a *faux pas* somewhere, and always in the worst possible situation;

---

[8]See Edmund Bergler's article on the pathological gambler in *Diseases of the Nervous System* (1943). Also "Suppositions about the Mechanism of Criminosis," *Journal of Criminal Psychopathology* (1944) and "Clinical Contributions to the Psychogenesis of Alcohol Addiction," *Quarterly Journal of Studies on Alcohol,* 5:434 (1944).

to his friends he makes cutting remarks which hurt deeply—and always apparently aimed in such a way as to hurt the most: a remark that would not hurt A but would hurt B he invariably makes to B rather than to A, and so on. None of this is conscious. Ordinarily he is considerate of people, but he contrives always (unconsciously) to impose on just those friends who would resent it most, and at just the times when he should know that he should not impose: at 3 o'clock in the morning, without forewarning, he phones a friend in a near-by city demanding to stay at his apartment for the weekend; naturally the friend is offended, but the person himself is not aware that he has provoked the grievance ("common sense" suffers a temporary eclipse when the neurotic pattern sets in, and one's intelligence, far from being of help in such a situation, is used in the interest of the neurosis), and when the friend is cool to him the next time they meet, he wonders why and feels unjustly treated. Aggressive behavior on his part invites resentment and aggression in turn, but all that he consciously sees is the other's behavior toward him—and he considers himself the innocent victim of an unjustified "persecution."

Each of these choices is, from the moralist's point of view, free: he chose to phone his friend at 3 a.m.; he chose to make the cutting remark that he did, etc. What he does not know is that an ineradicable masochistic pattern has set in. His unconscious is far more shrewd and clever than is his conscious intellect; it sees with uncanny accuracy just what kind of behavior will damage him most, and unerringly forces him into that behavior. Consciously, the student "doesn't know why he did it"—he gives different "reasons" at different times, but they are all, once again, rationalizations cloaking the unconscious mechanism which propels him willy-nilly into actions that his "common sense" eschews.

The more of this sort of thing you see, the more you can see what the psychoanalyst means when he talks about "the illusion of free-will." And the more of a psychiatrist you become, the more you are overcome with a sense of what an illusion this precious free-will really is. In some kinds of cases most of us can see it already: it takes no psychiatrist to look at the epileptic and sigh with sadness at the thought that soon this person before you will be as one possessed, not the same thoughtful intelligent person you knew. But people are not aware of this in other contexts, for example when they express surprise at how a person whom they have been so good to could treat them so badly. Let us suppose that you help a person financially or morally or in some other way, so that he is in your debt; suppose further that he is one of the many neurotics who unconsciously identify kindness with weakness and aggression with strength, then he will unconsciously take your kindness to him as weakness and use it as the occasion for enacting some aggression against you. He can't help it, he may regret it himself later; still, he will be driven to do it. If we gain a little knowledge of psychiatry, we can look at him with pity, that a person otherwise so worthy should be so unreliable—but we will exercise realism too and be aware that there are some types of people that you cannot be good to in "free" acts of their conscious volition, they will use your own goodness against you.

Sometimes the persons themselves will become dimly aware that "something behind the scenes" is determining their behavior. The divorcee will sometimes view herself with detachment, as if she were some machine (and indeed the psychoanalyst does call her a "repeating-machine"): "I know I'm caught in a net, that I'll fall in love with this guy and marry him and the whole ridiculous merry-go-round will start all over again."

We talk about free will, and we say, yes, the person is free to do so-and-so if he can do so *if* he wants to—and we forget that his wanting to is itself caught up in the stream of determinism, that unconscious forces drive him into the wanting or not wanting to do the thing in question. The idea of the puppet whose motions are manipulated from behind by invisible wires, or better still, by springs inside, is no mere figure of speech. The analogy is a telling one at almost every point.

And the pity of it is that it all started so early, before we knew what was happening. The personality-structure is inelastic after the age of five, and comparatively so in most cases after the age of three. Whether one acquires a neurosis or not is determined by that age—and just as involuntarily as if it had been a curse of God. If, for example, a masochistic pattern was set up, under pressure of hyper-narcissism combined with real or fancied infantile deprivation, then the masochistic snowball was on its course downhill long before we or anybody else knew what was happening, and long before anyone could do anything about it. To speak of human beings as "puppets" in such a context is no mere metaphor, but a stark rendering of a literal fact: only the psychiatrist knows what puppets people really are; and it is no wonder that the protestations of philosophers that "the act which is the result of a volition, a deliberation, a conscious decision, is free" leave these persons, to speak mildly, somewhat cold.

.   .   .

Now, what of the notion of responsibility? What happens to it on our analysis?

Let us begin with an example, not a fictitious one. A woman and her two-year-old baby are riding on a train to Montreal in mid-winter. The child is ill. The woman wants badly to get to her destination. She is, unknown to herself, the victim of a neurotic conflict whose nature is irrelevant here except for the fact that it forces her to behave aggressively toward the child, partly to spite her husband whom she despises and who loves the child, but chiefly to ward off super-ego charges of masochistic attachment. Consciously she loves the child, and when she says this she says it sincerely, but she must behave aggressively toward it nevertheless, just as many children love their mothers but are nasty to them most of the time in neurotic pseudo-aggression. The child becomes more ill as the train approaches Montreal; the heating system of the train is not working, and the conductor advises the woman to get off the train at the next town and get the child to a hospital at once. The woman says no, she must get to Montreal. Shortly afterward, the child's condition worsens, and the mother does all she can to keep it alive without, however, leaving the train, for she declares that it is absolutely necessary that she reach her destination. But before she gets there the child is dead. After that, of course, the mother grieves, blames herself, weeps hysterically, and joins the church to gain surcease from the guilt that constantly overwhelms her when she thinks of how her aggressive behavior has killed her child.

Was she responsible for her deed? In ordinary life, after making a mistake, we say, "Chalk it up to experience." Here we say, "Chalk it up to the neurosis." No, she is not responsible. She could not help it if her neurosis forced her to act this way—she didn't even know what was going on behind the scenes, she merely acted out the part assigned to her. This is far more true than is generally realized: criminal actions in general are not actions for which their agents are responsible; the agents are passive, not active—they are victims of a neurotic conflict. Their very hyperactivity is unconsciously determined.

To say this is, of course, not to say that we should not punish criminals. Clearly, for our own protection, we must remove them from our midst so that they can no longer molest and endanger organized society. And, of course, if we use the word "responsible" in such a way that justly to hold someone responsible for a deed is by definition identical with being justified in punishing him, then we can and do hold people responsible. But this is like the sense of "free" in which free acts are voluntary ones. It does not go deep enough. In a deeper sense we cannot hold the person responsible: we may hold his neurosis responsible, but he is not responsible for his neurosis, particularly since the age at which its onset was inevitable was an age before he could even speak.

The neurosis is responsible—but isn't the neurosis a part of *him*? We have been speaking all the time as if the person and his unconscious were two separate beings; but isn't he one personality, including conscious and unconscious departments together?

I do not wish to deny this. But it hardly helps us here; for what people want when they talk about freedom, and what they hold to when they champion it, is the idea that the *conscious* will is the master of their destiny. "I am the master of my fate, I am the captain of my soul"—and they surely mean their conscious selves, the self that they can recognize and search and introspect. Between an unconscious that willy-nilly determines your actions, and an external force which pushes you, there is little if anything to choose. The unconscious is just *as if* it were an outside force; and indeed, psychiatrists will assert that the inner Hitler can torment you far more than any external Hitler can. Thus the kind of freedom that people want, the only kind they will settle for, is precisely the kind that psychiatry says that they cannot have.

Heretofore it was pretty generally thought that, while we could not rightly blame a person for the color of his eyes or the morality of his parents, or even for what he did at the age of three, or to a large extent what impulses he had and whom he fell in love with, one *could* do so for other of his adult activities, particularly the acts he performed voluntarily and with premeditation. Later this attitude was shaken. Many voluntary acts came to be recognized, at least in some circles, as compelled by the unconscious. Some philosophers recognized this too—Ayer[9] talks about the kleptomaniac being unfree, and about a person being unfree when another person exerts a habitual ascendancy over his personality. But this is as far as he goes. The usual examples, such as the kleptomaniac and the schizophrenic, apparently satisfy most philosophers, and with these exceptions removed, the rest of mankind is permitted to wander in the vast and alluring fields of freedom and responsibility. So far, the inroads upon freedom left the vast majority of humanity untouched; they began to hit home when psychiatrists began to realize, though philosophers did not, that the domination of the conscious by the unconscious extended, not merely to a few exceptional individuals, but to all human beings, that the "big three behind the scenes" are not respecters of persons, and dominate us all, even including that *sanctum sanctorum* of freedom, our conscious will. To be sure, the domination in the case of "normal" individuals is somewhat more benevolent than the tyranny and despotism exercised in neurotic cases, and therefore the former have evoked less comment; but the principle remains in all cases the same: the unconscious is the master of every fate and the captain of every soul.

We speak of a machine turning out good products most of the time but every once in a while it turns out a "lemon." We do not, of course, hold the product responsible for this, but the machine, and via the machine, its maker. Is it silly to extend to inanimate objects the idea of responsibility? Of course. But is it any less silly to employ the notion in speaking of human creatures? Are not the two kinds of cases analogous in countless important ways? Occasionally a child turns out badly too, even when his environment and training are the same as that of his brothers and sisters who turn out "all right." He is the "bad penny." His acts of rebellion against parental discipline in adult life (such as the case of the gambler, already cited) are traceable to early experience of real or fancied denial of infantile wishes. Sometimes the denial has been real, though many denials are absolutely necessary if the child is to grow up to observe the common decencies of civilized life; sometimes, if the child has an unusual quantity of narcissism, every event that occurs is interpreted by him as a denial of his wishes, and nothing a parent could do, even granting every humanly possible wish, would help. In any event, the later neurosis can be attributed to this. Can the person himself be held responsible? Hardly. If he engages in activities which are a menace to society, he must be put into prison, of course, but responsibility is an-

[9]A. J. Ayer, "Freedom and Necessity," *Polemic* (September–October 1946), pp. 40–43.

other matter. The time when the events occurred which rendered his neurotic behavior inevitable was a time long before he was capable of thought and decision. As an adult, he is a victim of a world he never made —only this world is inside him.

What about the children who turn out "all right"? All we can say is that "it's just lucky for them" that what happened to their unfortunate brother didn't happen to them; *through no virtue of their own* they are not doomed to the life of unconscious guilt, expiation, conscious depression, terrified ego-gestures for the appeasement of a tyrannical super-ego that he is. The machine turned them out with a minimum of damage. But if the brother cannot be blamed for his evils, neither can they be praised for their good. It will take society a long time to come round to this attitude. We do not blame people for the color of their eyes, but we have not attained the same attitude toward their socially significant activities.

We all agree that machines turn out "lemons," we all agree that nature turns out misfits in the realm of biology: the blind, the crippled, the diseased; but we hesitate to include the realm of the personality, for here, it seems, is the last retreat of our dignity as human beings. Our ego can endure anything but this; this island at least must remain above the encroaching flood. But may not precisely the same analysis be made here also? Nature turns out psychological "lemons" too, in far greater quantities than any other kind; and indeed all of us are "lemons" in some respect or other, the difference being one of degree. Some of us are lucky enough not to have a gambling-neurosis or criminotic tendencies or masochistic mother-attachment or overdimensional repetition-compulsion to make our lives miserable, but most of our actions, those usually considered the most important, are unconsciously dominated just the same. And, if a neurosis may be likened to a curse of God, let those of us, the elect, who are enabled to enjoy a measure of life's happiness without the hell-fire of neurotic guilt, take this, not as our own achievement, but simply for what it is—a gift of God.

Let us, however, quit metaphysics and put the situation schematically in the form of a deductive argument.

1. An occurrence over which we had no control is something we cannot be held responsible for.

2. Events E, occurring during our babyhood, were events over which we had no control.

3. Therefore events E were events which we cannot be held responsible for.

4. But if there is something we cannot be held responsible for, neither can we be held responsible for something that inevitably results from it.

5. Events E have as inevitable consequence Neurosis N, which in turn has as inevitable consequence Behavior B.

6. Since N is the inevitable consequence of E and B is the inevitable consequence of N, B is the inevitable consequence of E.

7. Hence, not being responsible for E, we cannot be responsible for B.

In Samuel Butler's Utopian satire *Erewhon* there occurs the following passage, in which a judge is passing sentence on a prisoner:

> It is all very well for you to say that you came of unhealthy parents, and had a severe accident in your childhood which permanently undermined your constitution; excuses such as these are the ordinary refuge of the criminal; but they cannot for one moment be listened to by the ear of justice. I am not here to enter upon curious metaphysical questions as to the origin of this or that—questions to which there would be no end were there introduction once tolerated, and which would result in throwing the only guilt on the tissues of the primordial cell, or on the elementary gases. There is no question of how you came to be wicked, but only this—namely, are you wicked or not? This has been decided in the affirmative, neither can I hesitate for a single moment to say that it has been decided justly. You are a bad and dangerous person, and stand branded in the eyes of your fellow countrymen with one of the most heinous known offenses.[10]

As moralists read this passage, they may perhaps nod with approval. But the joke is on them. The sting comes when we realize what the crime is for which the prisoner is being sentenced: namely, consumption. The defendant is reminded that during the previous year he was sentenced for aggravated bronchitis, and is warned that he should profit from experience in the future. Butler is employing here his familiar method of presenting some human tendency (in this case, holding people responsible for what isn't their fault) to a ridiculous extreme and thereby reducing it to absurdity. How soon will mankind appreciate the keen edge of Butler's bitter irony? How long will they continue to read such a passage, but fail to smile, or yet to wince?

.   .   .

Can human beings, in the light of psychiatric knowledge, be called "free" in any respect at all?

.   .   .

If we asked the psychoanalysts for their opinion on this, they would doubtless reply somewhat as follows. They would say that they were not accustomed to using the term "free" at all, but that if they had to suggest a criterion for distinguishing the free from the unfree, they would say that a person's freedom occurs in inverse proportion to his neuroticism; the more he is compelled in his behavior by a *malevolent* unconscious, the less free he is. We speak of degrees of freedom—and the psychologically

[10]Samuel Butler, *Erewhon* (Modern Library edition), p. 107.

normal and well-adjusted individual is comparatively the freest, even though most of his behavior is determined by his unconscious.

But suppose it is the determination of his behavior by his unconscious, no matter what kind, that we balk at? We may then say that a man is free only to the extent that his behavior is *not* unconsciously motivated at all. If this be our criterion, most of our behavior could not be called free: everything, including both impulses and volitions, having to do with our basic attitudes toward life, the general tenor of our tastes, whether we become philosophers or artists or business men, our whole affective life including our preferences for blondes or brunettes, active or passive, older or younger, has its inevitable basis in the unconscious. Only those comparatively vanilla-flavored aspects of life—such as our behavior toward people who don't really matter to us—are exempted from this rule.

These, I think, are the two principal criteria for distinguishing freedom from the lack of it which we might set up on the basis of psychoanalytic knowledge. Conceivably we might set up others. In every case, of course, it remains trivially true that "it all depends on how we choose to use the word." The facts are what they are, regardless of how we choose to label them. But if we choose to label facts in a way which is out of accordance with people's deep-seated and traditional methods of labeling them, as we would be doing if we labeled "free" human actions which we know as much about as we now do through modern psychiatry, then we shall only be manipulating words to mislead our fellow creatures.

Nancy Holmstrom
FIRMING UP SOFT DETERMINISM

We have now been introduced to two forms of psychological determinism—behaviorism and psychoanalytic theory—and it has been argued with respect to each (by Skinner and Hospers, respectively) that all, or at least most, human action is ultimately unfree. The problem of freedom is not only, as Schlick would have it, the problem of external compulsion, but it is also that of internal (psychological) constraints. If human actions are motivated by desires, which are themselves determined by forces over which we have no control, then, even in the absence of external constraints, they cannot be considered free actions. Thus, a serious analysis of the ultimate sources of our actions reveals that determinism and freedom are incompatible. It would seem, then, that the program of soft determinism—to reconcile determinism and freedom—cannot be carried through.

In the following article, Nancy Holmstrom, who teaches philosophy at Rutgers University, attempts to "firm up" soft determinism by having it take into account the problem of how our beliefs and desires are determined. She recognizes that at the heart of the question of freedom is not only being able to act on our beliefs and desires but also having control over those beliefs and desires. In other words, soft determinism, in order to make good its compatibilist claim, must show how people can have control over the sources of their actions; that is, how people can have control over the sources of the beliefs and desires that motivate them to act.

In the course of her analysis, Holmstrom indicates how a free action can be distinguished from an action performed as a result of brainwashing, subliminal advertising, and other forms of conditioning in which one's desires are acquired through coercion. The upshot of her analysis ties the question of human freedom in the general sense to social and political freedom, for only if people have control over the social conditions under which they live can they have significant control over the sources of their desires and beliefs and, hence, over their actions.

I

An important position on the question of freedom and determinism holds that determinism and predictability *per se* constitute no threat to the freedom and responsibility of an agent. What matters, according to this view, called soft determinism, is the basis on which the prediction is made or the nature of the conditions such that given those conditions, the agent will do what he/she does.[1] When the agent does what he does because of his beliefs and desires[2] to do it, then what the agent does is "up to him"; the causal chain goes through the person or the self, as it were. In such cases the agent can be said to be the cause of the action. Such actions are free. On the other hand, when the causes of an action, or, more generally, of what a person does, are not his/her beliefs and desires to do that action, then what happens is not "up to him" and the action is not free. However, it may not be compelled either. It is where the action is in contradiction to what the agent wants that the act can be said to be compelled. The agent is not responsible for the action because the action occurs in spite of him.

Among the objections that have been raised to this account of the distinction between free and unfree acts is that it provides an insufficient account of what it is for an agent to do an act freely. The problem is the

[1]Representative of contemporary approaches but somewhat different and less adequate in my opinion than the version I present are Moritz Schlick's "When Is a Man Responsible?" and R. E. Hobart's "Free Will as Involving Determinism and Inconceivable Without It" in *Free Will and Determinism*, ed. by Bernard Berofsky (N.Y.: Harper and Row, 1966). Earlier versions are found in J. S. Mill, *An Examination of Sir William Hamilton's Philosophy* (London: Longmans Green and Co., Ltd., 1872) and David Hume's "Of Liberty and Necessity" in *An Inquiry Concerning Human Understanding* (Los Angeles: Henry Regnery Co., 1956).

[2]I intend "beliefs" and "desires" to cover all mental sources of action whatever exactly these are. I will not consider the question of the differences between these ostensible causes, (intentions, motives, wants, etc.), and their mutual relations, as this is a very involved issue and not crucial to my arguments. I use the word "desire" rather than "want" because there is one very weak sense of "want" in which I want to do everything I do intentionally. When I do use "want" it should be understood in the stronger sense in which it is equivalent to "desire."

source of the sources of one's allegedly free actions, i.e., the sources of one's beliefs and desires. Many philosophers have felt that if an agent's beliefs and desires are themselves determined, then actions proceeding from them must be as unfree as actions that are not caused by the agent's beliefs and desires. For example, Richard Taylor bids us to suppose that:

> while my behavior is entirely in accordance with my own volitions, and thus "free" in terms of the conception of freedom we are examining, my volitions themselves are caused. To make this graphic, we can suppose that an ingenious physiologist can induce in me any volition he pleases, simply by pushing various buttons on an instrument to which, let us suppose, I am attached by numerous wires. All the volitions I have in that situation, are, accordingly, precisely the ones he gives me. . . . This is the description of a man who is acting in accordance with his inner volitions, a man whose body is unimpeded and unconstrained in its motions, these motions being the effects of those inner states. It is hardly the description of a free and responsible agent. It is the perfect description of a puppet.[3]

The same point can be made by examples of beliefs and desires acquired by brainwashing, hypnosis, subliminal advertising, etc. If a person acts because of beliefs and desires acquired in such ways, the action is clearly not free even though the action was done because of the agent's beliefs and desires. This shows that it is not the case that an act is free just because it is caused by the beliefs and desires of the agent to do the act. The standard soft determinist position is inadequate as it stands.

One way of dealing with the objection might be to distinguish freedom of action and freedom of will and to maintain that the act was free but the will was not.[4] However, I think such examples show that these concepts cannot be so easily separated. Because the "will" is unfree in such cases, we would not call the act free. Taylor thinks this point applies much more generally than just to these sorts of examples and concludes that the standard conception of determinism cannot apply to a free act. He introduces, instead, a special notion of "agent causality."[5] I prefer to explore a response to the above objection that remains within the standard compatibilist framework.

I think that the objection I raised to soft determinism shows that soft determinists have too limited a notion of what is required for an agent to be the source of his/her actions. All that they require is that the agent do what he or she pleases. They ignore the question of whether the agent has control over the sources of the actions, his/her desires and beliefs. Taylor inferred that if the desires causing an action are themselves caused then the action is not free. This does not follow. Just because some causes of desires and beliefs, such as brainwashing, make actions resulting from

---

[3]Taylor, Richard, *Metaphysics* (Englewood Cliffs, N.J.: Prentice Hall, Inc., 1963), p. 45.

[4]Harry Frankfurt seems to do this, although it is not entirely clear what he would say about this sort of example, in "Freedom of Will and the Concept of a Person," *Journal of Philosophy,* Vol. LXVIII, No. 1, January 14, 1971.

[5]Taylor, Richard, *Action and Purpose* (Englewood Cliffs, N.J.: Prentice Hall, Inc., 1966).

them unfree, it does not follow that any cause of desires and beliefs has the same implications for the freedom of actions resulting from them.

Since the notion of having control is at the heart of the notion of freedom for me,[6] let me stop to clarify the concept briefly. If I have control over x then x depends on what I do or do not do. I am an important part of the causal process producing x, such that if I did something different x would be different. Moreover, I must be conscious of x's dependence on me in order for x to be under my control. Whether some insect lives or not depends on whether or not I step on him as I walk down the street. But if I do not know he is there his life is not under my control. So for x to be under my control what I do or do not do must be an important part of the cause of x and I must know this. X therefore must depend on what I want or on my "will" in order for x to be under my control. Now since one can make more or less of a difference, be more or less important a part of the causal process, it therefore follows that one can have more or less control over something. The more control a person has the freer that person is. Clearly, then, a person is not simply free or unfree. Nor is every action simply free or unfree. Rather, there is a continuum between free and unfree with many or most acts lying somewhere in between. When I say that an act is free what I mean is that the act falls on the free side of the continuum. Or, since there is no line in the middle of a continuum, it might be clearer to say that a free act falls in the direction of the free end of the continuum. Acts are more or less free according to how close they are to the free end of the continuum.[7]

What I want to argue in this paper is that people can have differing amounts of control over what they desire and what they believe. People can be more or less important a part of the causal process leading to their having the desires and beliefs that they do. Our discussion thus far shows that only if they have control over their beliefs and desires do they really have control over their actions. The key question, then, is whether this idea of having control over one's beliefs and desires makes any sense and whether in fact we do have such control. Many people would probably say that while what we do is often up to us, what we believe and desire depends on factors completely beyond our control. Speaking generally, it depends on the way the world is; more specifically, it depends on our biological and psychological natures, the society in which we live, and our particular portion of it (i.e., our class, race, ethnic group, etc.). Others would object that it makes no sense to separate the person or self from his/her desires and beliefs, and hence makes no sense to talk of the

---

[6]If there are other conceptions of freedom in which control is not central then I am simply not interested in them and what I say may not apply to these other senses.

[7]It should be clear that I am using "free" and "unfree" (or "compelled") as contraries and not contradictories. Many acts we do every day, such as putting on our shoes, cannot sensibly be said to be either free or unfree. They belong in the middle of the continuum or—better perhaps—not on the continuum at all. Of other acts, it makes good sense to ask whether they are free or unfree, it is the answer that is complicated and which would place them somewhere in the middle of the continuum.

person having control over his/her desires and beliefs, and hence makes no sense to talk of the person having control over his/her desires and beliefs. My major purpose in this paper will be to give substance to the idea that people can have control over the sources of their actions, that is, have control over their desires and beliefs.

If an agent can be said to be the source of his/her beliefs and desires, then it makes no sense to say that the agent is a self-determining being. This is a concept that many have taken to be at the heart of freedom, whether they be determinists, indeterminists or hold to the idea of "agent causality."[8] If we can give substance to this notion of a person having control over his desires and beliefs, we will have given substance to the notion of a self-determining being.

II

Before turning directly to the central task, I wish to raise another sort of counterexample to soft determinism. Some acts that are done because of the agent's desires and beliefs to do them are nevertheless unfree, but for reasons other than the sources of those desires and beliefs. However, we will see that these counterexamples do not challenge the fundamental thrust of soft determinism because the examples are all such that we have reason to say that the actions in the examples are not truly self-determined.

A heroin addict steals some money and uses it to buy heroin which he then takes. It might be said that all three acts (stealing, buying the drug and taking it) are done because of the addict's desire to achieve a certain state and the belief that these are ways of achieving it. If we imagine that this addict does not want to be an addict,[9] as is the case with most addicts, then these acts of his are crucially different from most acts done because of the agent's beliefs and desires. While the addict wants the heroin he also wants to not take the drug. Moreover, he wants a great number of things which he believes to be incompatible with taking the drug, e.g., health, self-respect, an ordinary life, etc. These contrary desires, values and beliefs are greater in number and also are part of an integrated whole. The desire to take the drug is not part of such an integrated whole, but nevertheless it outweighs all these contrary desires and beliefs. A kleptomaniac's desire to steal would probably be similar. Most actions done because of the agent's desires are not in conflict with a greater number of his/her integrated desires and beliefs. I think it is this factor which leads compatibilists to reject such cases as not really counterexamples to their analysis of a free act as one resulting from the wants of the

[8]"The principle of free will says: 'I produce my volitions. Determinism says: My volitions are produced by me.' Determinism is free will expressed in the passive voice." R. E. Hobart, *op. cit.*, p. 71.

[9]If, on the other hand, we suppose that the addict does not mind being an addict, then none of the following holds.

agent. An act resulting from such a conflict does not seem to proceed from the self as a free act must; it occurs in spite of the person. Moritz Schlick says "We rightly consider the man to be more or less unfree, and hold him less responsible, because we rightly view the influence of the drug as "external" even though it is found within the body; it prevents him from making decisions in the manner peculiar to his nature."[10] This integrated set of desires, beliefs and values might be said to constitute the person's nature or self as it is at that time.[11] Acts proceeding from desires that are external to this and yet dominant would seem to be unfree. There are certain exceptions to this, however, which we will discover as we progress.

III

I wish at this point to introduce the notion of a second order volition as discussed by Harry Frankfurt in "Free Will and the Concept of a Person."[12] Someone has a volition of the second order when he wants to have a certain desire and, moreover, wants that desire to be his effective desire, i.e., his will, in Frankfurt's terminology. The addict in our example may simply suffer from a conflict between the desire to take the drug and a number of contradictory or incompatible desires. However, he may, further, want that the latter desires be his effective desires. If so, then the addict's desire to take the drug is in conflict not only with a greater number of integrated desires and beliefs, but with a second order volition as well. Yet it still determines the addict's actions. By being in conflict with the will he wants to have, it is in conflict with the want with which he has thereby identified himself. Hence, when this desire determines action, the action is in sharp contrast to most acts done because of the agent's beliefs and desires. Instead of being an act that depends on the agent, that is "up to him," it happens against his will. This provides further grounds for saying that the act does not proceed from the self. Quite aside from the nature of the desire that is in conflict with the second order volition in our example (i.e., the desire to take heroin), it would seem plausible to take as a sufficient condition for making an act unfree that it proceed from beliefs and desires that are in conflict with a second order volition. A necessary condition, then, of a free act is that it proceed

[10]*Op. cit.*, p. 59.

[11]It might be questioned whether the addict really does have such an integrated set at the time he/she is intent on procuring the heroin. (Alastair Hannay raised this question.) I think that when we ascribe wants or beliefs to a person we are talking of dispositions that a person has over some longish time period (the precise duration of which I could not say). So their having certain beliefs and desires is not contradicted by their behaving inconsistently with them on some occasion. If one prefers to say that they do not have these beliefs and desires when their behavior is inconsistent with them, then we could talk about the self as consisting of the integrated set of beliefs and desires that exist over some longish period of time, the precise duration of which it would be impossible to set.

[12]*Op. cit.*

from desires and beliefs that are consistent with second order volitions. This should be seen as a development of the compatibilist account of a free act as one caused by the self, specifically the agent's beliefs and desires.

IV

Consistency with an integrated set of beliefs and desires and with second order volitions is not sufficient for an act to be free. We saw at the outset that the source of the beliefs and desires causing an act is relevant to the freedom of that act. The sorts of examples which first showed us that the soft determinist position was unsatisfactory as thus far presented were examples of acts done because of beliefs and desires that seemed in some way to have been forced upon the agent. Whether the person acquired beliefs and desires (volitions or the reasons for doing what he/she does) by being hooked up to a machine someone else controls, or by being brainwashed or exposed to subliminal advertising, the following is true. The beliefs and desires were acquired by measures taken by others in order to induce them, which measures were taken either explicitly against the person's will (brainwashing), and/or without his/her knowledge (subliminal advertising). (Taylor's case could be either.) Being ignorant of the measures taken to induce the beliefs and desires, the person is as much lacking in control over them as if they were taken explicitly against his/her will. In both cases the person, as an active determining being, is irrelevant to what happens. He/she has no control, and—more importantly—no possibility of control over the beliefs and desires he/she acquires. Actions done because of beliefs and desires acquired under such conditions are not free.

Now is it really necessary that a person's beliefs and desires be caused by other people in order for it to be the case that they were forced upon him/her? Although it was true of our original examples, I do not think it is a necessary condition. While it may sound odd to say they were the result of force or coercion where no persons were the cause, it can certainly be said that the desires were not acquired freely, or even that they were acquired under coercive conditions. The issue about causation of beliefs and desires that is crucial to the freedom of acts resulting from them is whether the person enters into the causal process as an active determinant. If the person does not, then the beliefs and desires were not acquired freely, and acts resulting from them are not free because not self-determined. If, on the contrary, the beliefs and desires are opposed to the person's desires, first or second order, then acts resulting from them are unfree or compelled. All this can be true even though the causes of the beliefs and desires were not measures taken by others to induce them. Suppose that a person lives under conditions of economic scarcity, which entails that not everyone will get what he/she needs and wants. A consequence of a person getting enough for himself and his family is that others will not have enough. A person in these conditions might, partly as a survival mechanism, come to desire that others not have enough—and might act on this desire. If this occurred, it seems to me that such an act would be an unfree one (although perhaps not at the very end of the continuum). If the person did not want to want that others not have enough, if in fact he/she wanted not to want this, then the desire would conflict with a second order volition. Acts resulting from such desires are unfree. However, in the absence of a conflicting or reinforcing second order volition, I would still wish to put the act on the unfree end of the continuum because the desires causing the act were produced under coercive conditions. The conditions were coercive because the person had no control over them, their existence was contrary to his/her desires, and his/her personality and character had little or no effect on their influence. Remove economic scarcity and the desire would be removed (although perhaps not immediately). Similar examples could be given of beliefs and desires caused by particular social systems and particular institutions within a social system.

V

Let us examine in some greater detail the conditions I have given under which desires could be said to have been acquired unfreely or coercively. It might be thought that my conditions apply too widely and would make too many desires turn out to have been unfreely acquired. For example, suppose a person has a strong desire to hear Bach because her parents regularly played Bach records in order to induce that desire. Her desire was acquired because of her parents' efforts to induce the desire. Their efforts consisted of intensively exposing her to the object they wished her to desire. If my conditions apply to such cases then her going to a concert as an adult because she wants to hear Bach played would be unfree—and this is an unattractive conclusion. However, my conditions do not lead to this conclusion, because the conditions I set are not met in the example. The child was not unaware of the causes of her later desire, which is what my condition requires; in fact it was by being aware of the music that was regularly played that she came to desire to hear it. Conceivably, but improbably, she was unaware that hearing the music was the cause of her later desire or that her parents regularly played it in order to produce that desire in her. However, these are different conditions [from] the one I gave. In general, where the measures taken to induce a desire simply amount to exposing a person to the object of the hoped-for desire, this does not meet my conditions, because the person cannot be unaware of the causes of the desire (although he/she may be unaware that they are the causes).[13]

[13]A desire acquired merely by exposure to the object or experience will not be a free desire if it meets other criteria for unfree desires. An example of such a desire might be the desire for heroin. The need for this qualification was pointed out to me by Gary Young.

I am inclined to think that my conditions as they stand thus far are in need of revision in the other direction, that is, to make them apply more widely. Suppose that what was done to induce the desire was not mere exposure to the object, but rather conditioning. If they had conditioned her, the parents would have accompanied the playing of the music with pleasurable stimuli and they would have negatively reinforced any expressions of negative feelings toward the music. If this had been done, the desire would be the result of more than the interrelation of the person and the object of the desire, as is the case when the desire for something comes into being because of exposure to it. A desire that is the result of conditioning is the result of pleasures and pains that accompany the object, but are external to the person, the object and the relation between them. When a person acquires desires and aversions for things because of pleasures and pains that are intrinsic to those things, such as the pleasures of eating good food, the pains of overeating, then those desires and aversions are freely acquired. Where the pleasures and pains are external, the *person* (i.e., his/her personality, reasoning capacities, etc.), is bypassed in the process. This should make the process coercive. However, as my conditions stand they do not give this result. The person could be aware of the elements of the conditioning process (the music, the accompanying pleasures and pains), though unaware of the connexions between them, the purposes behind them and their effect. She was aware of the measures taken and, therefore, if it were not explicitly against her will, the conditioning would not be coercive according to what I have said about coercion thus far. I take this to indicate that something more must be said.

In the hopes of working out how conditioning differs from mere exposure, let us go back to the example of the person who acquired a desire to hear the music of Bach because of repeated exposure to his music as a child. Whether the exposure was the deliberate work of others, as in our example, or not, acquisition of a desire through exposure differs from clearly coercive ways of acquiring desires. When people acquire a desire through being acquainted with the object or experience, they have the possibility of coming to have that desire or not. Whether they do or not will depend on facts about them: their aptitudes, beliefs, personality, other desires, etc. Where this is the case they can be said to have control, or at least the possibility of control, over the desires they acquire. Where, on the other hand, the causes of their beliefs and desires would exist and would effectively operate regardless of the fact that their personality, character, other beliefs and desires are opposed to these causes, then they obviously have no chance of controlling what beliefs and desires they come to have.

We can distinguish, then, between cases where people can have control over their beliefs and desires and those where they cannot. Knowledge is necessary in order that a person have this possibility of control. In the account I gave of when a person could be said to have freely acquired his/her desires I only required that the person have knowledge of the causes (and also that they not be against the person's will), in order that the causes not be coercive. Oftentimes, however, one needs to have more than simple knowledge of the causes. Conditioning is a case where the person being conditioned might know the causes, that is, might know the elements of the causal process, but might not know their interconnections or the purposes behind them. The person is acquainted with the causes but unaware that they are the causes or how and why they operate. If conditioning would operate regardless of whether a person knew the latter, then it is a causal process that the person cannot have any control over. Hence it is coercive.

Sometimes the efficacy of causal conditions depends on people's ignorance of them, that they are or may be causes, and how and why they operate. In such cases, people's ignorance of these facts would deprive them of whatever control knowledge might give them. People are less free to the extent that they operate on unconscious motives. Successful psychoanalysis can increase the patient's control and therefore freedom, by making conscious things that had hithertofore been unconscious. Sometimes just knowing the purposes behind potential causes (e.g., that it is designed to convince you, scare you, buy you off, or get you to buy something), can make a difference to whether those purposes are realized. Without the knowledge, one's attitudes towards these purposes cannot come into play and one cannot exercise any control over them. If the efficacy of the causes depends on one's ignorance of such facts about the causes, then the causes are coercive. It is where knowledge about the causes would have made a difference that ignorance makes the causes coercive. Causes of beliefs and desires are coercive where they operate contrary to the person's other beliefs, desires, character and personality. This is so when the causes are explicitly against the person's will, or unknown to the person, or when they depend for their efficacy on the person's ignorance of certain facts about them. According to these conditions, conditioning would usually be coercive, which, I think, is as it should be.

Suppose one came to know that one was being conditioned and the knowledge made no difference to the efficacy of the causes. Is this a coercive way of acquiring desires? The answer depends on whether the conditioning process was against the person's will. If the causes operate against his/her will then they are coercive. On the other hand, suppose they are not operating against the person's will; in other words, suppose a person voluntarily chooses to be conditioned. A person might deliberately expose himself to conditions which will cause him to have (or not have) certain desires, e.g., not to smoke. Once he puts himself into the situation, the causes operate independent of his other beliefs and desires, personality, etc. His new effective desire not to smoke will be the result of conditioning, and we have said that conditioning is a form of coercion. However, I think that the circumstances of this kind of case make a significant difference. The person's self does enter into the causal process as an active determinant, whereas in most cases of conditioning this is not so. The person in our example who voluntarily has himself conditioned has a second order volition not to smoke, which is in conflict with his or her volition to smoke. If the second order volition were sufficiently strong to outweigh the first order volition by itself, then the new effective desire would be acquired in a completely free manner. However, it is not sufficiently strong to do this by itself. Causes that are independent of the person are necessary to change his desire. However, these other causes come into play only because of his second order volition. He had himself conditioned because he has a desire not to desire to smoke. So I think we can say that the cause of his new effective desire not to smoke is his second order volition. The new desire is not the result of coercion; it does spring from the self. However, it does not only spring from the self. It was not acquired in as free a manner as if the second order volition was sufficient by itself to cause it, but I would still put it towards the free end of the continuum.

What we have come up with is what we started with and that is, that to the extent that the causes of one's actions are themselves caused by things over which people have no control (even with knowledge of them), to that extent one's actions are unfree. What I have tried to do is to make sense of the idea of having control over one's desires. In order to say that one has control over one's desires it is necessary that what we identify as the self determines what one desires and what desires one acts on. To put together the criteria elaborated thus far: in order for actions caused by desire to be free, these desires must first of all not have been coercively acquired. What this means has been explained. Knowledge was seen to be a key factor. Secondly, they must not be contrary to the person's second order volitions. This second condition implies that the person has second order volitions. We will not be able to say that these desires are the desires the person wants to have unless a) he/she has second order volitions and unless b) these volitions outweigh first order volitions in the case of a conflict. Thirdly, the desire must be in harmony with an integrated set of desires and beliefs—hence one's self at that given time. This third requirement must be qualified. A desire causing a free action may be inconsistent with this integrated set if the set does not meet one of the necessary conditions and the desire fulfills both the conditions. If the set was coercively acquired and the conflicting desire was not, or if the conflicting desire is supported by a second order volition and the set is not, then an action caused by the conflicting desire would be free. Any person missing second order volitions is missing an important kind of control over his/her actions, and hence an important dimension of freedom.[14] That is why an action that proceeds from a

[14]What Frankfurt says is somewhat different. According to him, such a being would not be a person because having second order volitions is essential to being a person in his sense; a being without them is a wanton. We also differ in that I connect freedom of will and freedom of action whereas he separates them, and thirdly, in that I give a sense to the idea of controlling one's desires (freedom of will) independent of the idea of second order volitions.

conflicting desire which is supported by a second order volition is freer than one that proceeded from the integrated set, where there are no effective second order volitions. This sort of situation could lead to a revision of the set—a restructuring of the self. However, lacking an integrated set which is responsible for his/her actions, the person is divided, and it is less possible for that person to be a self-determining being. Therefore, the person is most free when there is an integrated set which is in accordance with his/her second order volitions. Then we can say that this is a self-determining person.[15]

. . .

VII

As a prelude to concluding, I wish to consider the implications of my general and abstract analysis to the concrete question of just how free most people are today. We shall see that although my view implies that people can be free, though determined, it is also an implication of my view that most people are quite unfree today. The answer to this question of how free people are is not one that applies to all people just in virtue of their being human, but rather depends on who the people are and where and when they are living. It turns out, then, on my view, that human freedom is closely tied to social and political freedom and is not a distinct metaphysical question. (In considering this part of the philosophical question we are inevitably drawn into empirical issues, including political ones, so my own opinion on these matters will certainly intrude.)

Desires arise in us because of a whole complex set of conditions which affect one another. (Neither they nor their influence can actually be separated so the following remarks are unavoidably artificial.) These determining conditions include physical and psychological conditions, which to some extent we share with others, but which also differ from person to person. People today are capable of some but not much control over these conditions. Greater knowledge, aided by money, gives a person greater possibilities of control, but there are still very definite limits which no one today is capable of transcending. Greater knowledge will give greater possibilities of human control, but it is probable that there will always be limits that one cannot transcend. What is possible is for a person to exercise some control over the form of the desires these condi-

---

[15]It may be worth pointing out that all of my criteria allow for the possibility that two people could perform the same act for the same reasons but one does it freely, the other unfreely. I do not see this as an objection of my account. (Paul Teller raised it as an objection.) All accounts of freedom allow the possibility of the same act (type) performed by one person being free and by another person being unfree. The act's (un)freedom depends on facts about its cause. Incompatibilists would say it depends on whether it's caused; compatibilists would say it depends on what the cause is. Since my account goes beyond the act, and its causes or lack thereof, to the causes of the causes of the act, it makes sense that the (un)freedom of the act would depend on facts about the causes of the causes.

tions tend to produce, and also over whether and how these desires are acted upon.

How much control a person can exercise over the social and political conditions causing his/her desires depends on the particular social system in which the person lives, and also the place that the person occupies in the system. Some changes are possible in the latter in most societies but usually quite little. In any case, it is only within the framework allowed by that system and it is not possible within the framework of *any* present society for *most* people to change their positions within that framework. As for the framework itself, one cannot change the time in which one lives, and since what social systems are possible depends on the time and place, there is a certain inevitable limitation. However, there are many fewer inevitable limitations on the degree of control one can exercise over social causes than over physical causes—in the future, but also in the present. Given the limitations of time and place, there is great potential today for people to collectively control the social conditions under which they live, and hence the beliefs and desires these conditions tend to produce, even if there are some conditions they still would not be able to control. However, with some notable exceptions, the ability to control the social conditions in which one lives is only potential today, not actual. This is partially because people do not realize they have this ability.[16] This lack of realization is strongly supported, of course, by the social system in which they live and by those who do control it. There is, again, the possibility of exercising some control over the form of the desires likely to be produced by these conditions, and also over whether and how these desires are acted upon. However, so long as one does not control the social causes of one's beliefs and desires, one does not have much chance of controlling the actual beliefs and desires one comes to have.

Leaving aside the nature of the influence, what is necessary in order to be able to exercise control over the influences acting upon one, is to be a certain kind of person, as well as to have knowledge and the cooperation of others. A person who is critical and discriminating and sees him/herself as actively shaping the world, history and also him/herself, is capable of doing just that—not alone, but in cooperation with others. There are, of course, varying conditions where people may be more or less aware and/or more or less able not to be passive products. However, it seems that most people today are quite uncritical and undiscriminating and lack this self-conception. Many feel themselves to be more like passive products of history and their own particular environment—and their environment makes them feel that way. However, in the course of struggle against the oppressive aspects of their environment, they can come to realize their potential to bring the world under their conscious collective control. The realization of this is a first step towards changing the

---

[16]This is the phenomenon of fetishism that Marx discusses. "Such conditions are . . . independent of individuals and appear, although they are created by society, to be the same as natural conditions, i.e., uncontrollable by the individual." *The Grundrisse—Karl Marx,* edited by David McLellan (New York, Harper and Row, 1971), p. 72.

framework that keeps them without control. This capacity to change the world and consequently their own nature is unique to human beings. It gives them the potential of being free in the fullest sense that is possible in a deterministic world.[17]

Jean-Paul Sartre
FREEDOM AND ACTION

Perhaps the most radical view of human freedom held by any philosopher is the one offered by the existentialist Jean-Paul Sartre. The absolute freedom and corresponding absolute responsibility ascribed to human beings by Sartre is, for him, one of the main factors defining the human condition. According to Sartre, there is only one freedom we do not have—the freedom not to choose. We are, as he puts it, condemned to be free. Our responsibility for our choices is comprehensive, and there is no way to avoid it. This aspect of Sartre's position is expressed in the selection reprinted in this book on pages 36–48. The selection that we are now going to consider comes from his major work, Being and Nothingness, *and is an attempt to analyze the nature of choice and to demonstrate how it can be that our choices are always ultimately free.*

Sartre's position rests on his claim about how motives are formed. Our actions, he acknowledges, are determined in the sense that they have motives. But, Sartre maintains, it is human consciousness that freely creates these motives. Our choices are free, not in the sense that they are unconnected to motives, but insofar as consciousness has the power to withdraw itself from what is at any moment, to recognize that something is lacking in the present state of affairs, and thus, to present this "negation" as a motive for action. This "nihilating" power of consciousness has a double layer: it posits a desired (ideal) state of affairs as not now existing; *and it recognizes that the present situation is not yet this ideal state of affairs. Since, according to this view, it is the absence of something rather than its presence that motivates us, no existing state of affairs can be said to cause my actions. This does not mean that my choices are arbitrary and that they have no relation to my character or to my past experience; for, each individual choice is part of an ensemble of choices, of an "organic totality of the projects which I am." And this ensemble, this totality, must, in turn, be referred to my original project of being what I am. Yet, this original project is itself a choice that relates my consciousness to my body and both my body and my*

---

[17]This perspective is similar to that expressed by Marx in *Capital* where he says, "The freedom in this field [i.e., the realm of necessity] cannot consist of anything else but the fact that socialized man, the associated producers, regulate their interchange with nature rationally, bring it under their human control, instead of being ruled by it as by some blind power; that they accomplish their task with the least expenditure of energy and under conditions most adequate to their human nature and most worthy of it. But it always remains a realm of necessity. Beyond it begins that development of human power, which is its own end, the true realm of freedom, which, however, can flourish only upon that realm of necessity as its basis." *Capital,* Vol. III, English translation, p. 820.

consciousness to the world and other persons. It is the basic choice of my
"being-in-the-world." Thus, I am ultimately free to reconstitute myself.

The reader may find Sartre's special philosophical vocabulary (borrowed
from Hegel and the phenomenological tradition) difficult to follow. At the risk of
some oversimplification, we suggest that "for-itself" be translated as the power of
consciousness (or the power that is consciousness) to act upon the world as
given. What is there to be acted upon is the "in-itself." The very term "for-itself"
refers to Sartre's contention that consciousness is not a thing (hence, a "no-
thing," or a "nothingness"—the antipode of Being) and that it therefore
cannot exist in the world "in-itself" but exists only for itself as consciousness.
The relation of "Being" and "Nothingness" is best stated in the reverse, as the
relation of the "for-itself" to the "in-itself," as the relation of consciousness to
the world by which it constitutes its "being-in-the-world."

FREEDOM: THE FIRST CONDITION OF ACTION

It is strange that philosophers have been able to argue endlessly about
determinism and free will, to cite examples in favor of one or the other
thesis without ever attempting first to make explicit the structures contained in the very idea of *action.* The concept of an act contains, in fact,
numerous subordinate notions which we shall have to organize and arrange in a hierarchy: to act is to modify the *shape* of the world; it is to
arrange means in view of an end; it is to produce an organized instrumental complex such that by a series of concatenations and connections the
modification effected on one of the links causes modifications throughout
the whole series and finally produces an anticipated result. But this is not
what is important for us here. We should observe first that an action is
on principle *intentional.* The careless smoker who has through negligence
caused the explosion of a powder magazine has not *acted.* On the other
hand the worker who is charged with dynamiting a quarry and who obeys
the given orders has acted when he has produced the expected explosion;
he knew what he was doing or, if you prefer, he intentionally realized a
conscious project.

This does not mean, of course, that one must foresee all the consequences of his act. The emperor Constantine when he established himself
at Byzantium, did not foresee that he would create a center of Greek
culture and language, the appearance of which would ultimately provoke
a schism in the Christian Church and which would contribute to weakening the Roman Empire. Yet he performed an act just in so far as he
realized his project of creating a new residence for emperors in the
Orient. Equating the result with the intention is here sufficient for us to
be able to speak of action. But if this is the case, we establish that the
action necessarily implies as its condition the recognition of a "desideratum"; that is, of an objective lack or again of a *négatité. The intention* of
providing a rival for Rome can come to Constantine only through the

apprehension of an objective lack: Rome lacks a counterweight; to this still profoundly pagan city ought to be opposed a Christian city which at the moment is *missing.* Creating Constantinople is understood as an *act* only if first the conception of a new city has preceded the action itself or at least if this conception serves as an organizing theme for all later steps. But this conception can not be the pure representation of the city as *possible.* It apprehends the city in its essential characteristic, which is to be a *desirable* and not yet realized possible.

This means that from the moment of the first conception of the act, consciousness has been able to withdraw itself from the full world of which it is consciousness and to leave the level of being in order frankly to approach that of non-being. Consciousness in so far as it is considered exclusively in its being, is perpetually referred from being to being and can not find in being any motive for revealing non-being. The imperial system with Rome as its capital functions positively and in a certain real way which can be easily discovered. Will someone say that the taxes are collected badly, that Rome is not secure from invasions, that it does not have the geographical location which is suitable for the capital of a Mediterranean empire which is threatened by barbarians, that its corrupt morals make the spread of Christian religion difficult? How can anyone fail to see that all these considerations are *negative;* that is, that they aim at what is not, not at what is. To say that sixty per cent of the anticipated taxes have been collected can pass, if need be for a positive appreciation of the situation *such as it is.* To say that they are *badly* collected is to consider the situation across a situation which is posited as an absolute end but which precisely is *not.* To say that the corrupt morals at Rome hinder the spread of Christianity is not to consider this diffusion for what it is; that is, for a propagation at a rate which the reports of the clergy can enable us to determine. It is to posit the diffusion in itself as insufficient; that is, as suffering from a secret nothingness. But it appears as such only if it is surpassed toward a limiting-situation posited *a priori* as a value (for example, toward a certain rate of religious conversions, toward a certain mass morality). This limiting-situation can not be conceived in terms of the simple consideration of the real state of things; for the most beautiful girl in the world can offer only what she *has,* and in the same way the most miserable situation can by itself be designated only as it *is* without any reference to an ideal nothingness.

In so far as man is immersed in the historical situation, he does not even succeed in conceiving of the failures and lacks in a political organization or determined economy; this is not, as is stupidly said, because he "is accustomed to it," but because he apprehends it in its plenitude of being and because he can not even imagine that he can exist in it otherwise. For it is necessary here to reverse common opinion and on the basis of what it is not, to acknowledge the harshness of a situation or the sufferings which it imposes, both of which are motives for conceiving of another state of affairs in which things would be better for everybody. It is on the day that we can conceive of a different state of affairs that a new light falls on our troubles and our suffering and that we *decide* that these are unbearable. A worker in 1830 is capable of revolting if his salary is lowered, for he easily conceives of a situation in which his wretched standard of living would be not as low as the one which is about to be imposed on him. But he does not represent his sufferings to himself as unbearable; he adapts himself to them not through resignation but because he lacks the education and reflection necessary for him to conceive of a social state in which these sufferings would not exist. Consequently *he does not act.* Masters of Lyon following a riot, the workers at Croix-Rousse do not know what to do with their victory; they return home bewildered, and the regular army has no trouble in overcoming them. Their misfortunes do not appear to them "habitual" but rather *natural;* they *are,* that is all, and they constitute the worker's condition. They are not detached; they are not seen in the clear light of day, and consequently they are integrated by the worker with his being. He suffers without considering his suffering and without conferring value upon it. To suffer and to *be* are one and the same for him. His suffering is the pure affective tenor of his non-positional consciousness, but he does not *contemplate* it. Therefore this suffering can not be in itself a *motive*[1] for his acts. Quite the contrary, it is after he has formed the project of changing the situation that it will appear intolerable to him. This means that he will have had to give himself room, to withdraw in relation to it, and will have to have effected a double nihilation: on the one hand, he must posit an ideal state of affairs as a pure *present* nothingness; on the other hand, he must posit the actual situation as nothingness in relation to this state of affairs. He will have to conceive of a happiness attached to his class as a pure possible —that is, presently as a certain nothingness—and on the other hand, he will return to the present situation in order to illuminate it in the light of this nothingness and in order to nihilate it in turn by declaring: "I *am not* happy."

Two important consequences result. (1) No factual state whatever it may be (the political and economic structure of society, the psychological "state," *etc.*) is capable by itself of motivating any act whatsoever. For an act is a projection of the for-itself toward what is not, and what is can in no way determine by itself what is not. (2) No factual state can determine consciousness to apprehend it as a *négatité* or as a lack. Better yet no factual state can determine consciousness to define it and to circumscribe it since, as we have seen, Spinoza's statement, "Omnis determinatio est negatio," remains profoundly true. Now every action has for its express condition not only the discovery of a state of affairs as "lacking in—," *i.e.,* as a *négatité*—but also, and before all else, the constitution of the state

---

[1]In [these passages] Sartre makes a sharp distinction between *motif* and *mobile.* The English word "motive" expresses sufficiently adequately the French *mobile,* which refers to an inner subjective fact or attitude. For *motif* there is no true equivalent. Since it refers to an external fact or situation, I am translating it by "cause." The reader must remember, however, that this carries with it no idea of determinism. Sartre emphatically denies the existence of any cause in the usual deterministic sense. Tr.

of things under consideration into an isolated system. There *is* a factual state—satisfying or not—only by means of the nihilating power of the for-itself. But this power of nihilation can not be limited to realizing a simple *withdrawl* in relation to the world. In fact in so far as consciousness is "invested" by being, in so far as it simply suffers what is, it must be included in being. It is the organized form—worker-finding-his-suffering-natural—which must be surmounted and denied in order for it to be able to form the object of a revealing contemplation. This means evidently that it is by a pure wrenching away from himself and the world that the worker can posit his suffering as unbearable suffering and consequently can *make of it the motive* for his revolutionary action. This implies for consciousness the permanent possibility of effecting a rupture with its own past, of wrenching itself away from its past so as to be able to consider it in the light of a non-being and so as to be able to confer on it the meaning which *it has* in terms of the project of a meaning which it *does not have*. Under no circumstances can the past in any way by itself produce *an act;* that is, the positing of an end which turns back upon itself so as to illuminate it. This is what Hegel caught sight of when he wrote that "the mind is the negative," although he seems not to have remembered this when he came to presenting his own theory of action and of freedom. In fact as soon as one attributes to consciousness this negative power with respect to the world and itself, as soon as the nihilation forms an integral part of the *positing* of an end, we must recognize that the indispensable and fundamental condition of all action is the freedom of the acting being.

Thus at the outset we can see what is lacking in those tedious discussions between determinists and the proponents of free will. The latter are concerned to find cases of decision for which there exists no prior cause, or deliberations concerning two opposed acts which are equally possible and possess causes (and motives) of exactly the same weight. To which the determinists may easily reply that there is no action without a *cause* and that the most insignificant gesture (raising the right hand rather than the left hand, *etc.*) refers to causes and motives which confer its meaning upon it. Indeed the case could not be otherwise since every action must be *intentional;* each action must, in fact, have an end, and the end in turn is referred to a cause. Such indeed is the unity of the three temporal ekstases; the end or temporalization of my future implies a cause (or motive); that is, it points toward my past, and the present is the upsurge of the act. To speak of an act without a cause is to speak of an act which would lack the intentional structure of every act; and the proponents of free will by searching for it on the level of the act which is in the process of being performed can only end up by rendering the act absurd. But the determinists in turn are weighting the scale by stopping their investigation with the mere designation of the cause and motive. The essential question in fact lies beyond the complex organization "cause-intention-act-end"; indeed we ought to ask how a cause (or motive) can be constituted as such.

Now we have just seen that if there is no act without a cause, this is not in the sense that we can say that there is no phenomenon without a cause. In order to be a *cause,* the *cause* must be *experienced* as such. Of course this does not mean that it is to be thematically conceived and made explicit as in the case of deliberation. But at the very least it means that the for-itself must confer on it its value as cause or motive. And, as we have seen, this constitution of the cause as such can not refer to another real and positive existence; that is, to a prior cause. For otherwise the very nature of the act as engaged intentionally in non-being would disappear. The motive is understood only by the end; that is, by the non-existent. It is therefore in itself a *négatité.* If I accept a niggardly salary it is doubt-less because of fear; and fear is a motive. But it is *fear of dying from starvation;* that is, this fear has meaning only outside itself in an end ideally posited, which is the preservation of a life which I apprehend as "in danger." And this fear is understood in turn only in relation to the *value which I* implicitly give to this life; that is, it is referred to that hierarchal system of ideal objects which are values. Thus the motive makes itself understood as what is by means of the ensemble of beings which "are not," by ideal existences, and by the future. Just as the future turns back upon the present and the past in order to elucidate them, so it is the ensemble of my projects which turns back in order to confer upon the *motive* its structure as a motive. It is only because I escape the in-itself by nihilating myself toward my possibilities that this in-itself can take on value as cause or motive. Causes and motives have meaning only inside a projected ensemble which is precisely an ensemble of non-existents. And this ensemble is ultimately myself as transcendence; it is Me in so far as I have to be myself outside of myself.

If we recall the principle which we established earlier—namely that it is the apprehension of a revolution as possible which gives to the workman's suffering its value as a motive—we must thereby conclude that it is by fleeing a situation toward our possibility of changing it that we organize this situation into complexes of causes and motives. The nihila-tion by which we achieve a withdrawal in relation to the situation is the same as the ekstasis by which we project ourselves toward a modification of this situation. The result is that it is in fact impossible to find an act without a motive but that this does not mean that we must conclude that the motive causes the act; the motive is an integral part of the act. For as the resolute project toward a change is not distinct from the act, the motive, the act, and the end are all constituted in a single upsurge. Each of these three structures claims the two others as its meaning. But the organized totality of the three is no longer explained by any particular structure, and its upsurge as the pure temporalizing nihilation of the in-itself is one with freedom. It is the act which decides its ends and its motives, and the act is the expression of freedom.

.   .   .

By the same token freedom appears as an unanalyzable totality; causes, motives, and ends, as well as the mode of apprehending causes, motives, and ends, are organized in a unity within the compass of this freedom and must be understood in terms of it. Does this mean that one must view freedom as a series of capricious jerks comparable to the Epicurean clinamen? Am I free to wish anything whatsoever at any moment whatsoever? And must I at each instant when I wish to explain this or that project encounter the irrationality of a free and contingent choice? Inasmuch as it has seemed that the recognition of freedom had as its consequence these dangerous conceptions which are completely contradictory to experience, worthy thinkers have turned away from a belief in freedom. One could even state that determinism—if one were careful not to confuse it with fatalism—is "more human" than the theory of free will. In fact while determinism throws into relief the strict conditioning of our acts, it does at least give the *reason* for each of them. And if it is strictly limited to the psychic, if it gives up looking for a conditioning in the ensemble of the universe, it shows that the reason for our acts is in ourselves: we act as we are, and our acts contribute to making us.

. . .

Thus we do not intend here to speak of anything arbitrary or capricious. An existent which as consciousness is necessarily separated from all others because they are in connection with it only to the extent that they are *for it,* an existent which decides its past in the form of a tradition in the light of its future instead of allowing it purely and simply to determine its present, an existent which makes known to itself what it is by means of *something other than it* (that is, by an end which it is not and which it projects from the other side of the world)—this is what we call a free existent. This does not mean that I am free to get up or to sit down, to enter or to go out, to flee or to face danger—if one means by freedom here a pure capricious, unlawful, gratuitous, and incomprehensible contingency. To be sure, each one of my acts, even the most trivial, is entirely free in the sense which we have just defined; but this does not mean that my act can be anything *whatsoever* or even that it is *unforeseeable.* Someone, nevertheless may object and ask how if my act can be understood *neither* in terms of the state of the world *nor* in terms of the ensemble of my past taken as an irremediable thing, it could possibly be anything but gratuitous. Let us look more closely.

Common opinion does not hold that to be free means only to choose oneself. A choice is said to be free if it is such that it could have been other than what it is. I start out on a hike with friends. At the end of several hours of walking my fatigue increases and finally becomes very painful. At first I resist and then suddenly I let myself go, I give up, I throw my knapsack down on the side of the road and let myself fall down beside it. Someone will reproach me for my act and will mean thereby that I was free—that is, not only was my act not determined by any thing or person, but also I could have succeeded in resisting my fatigue longer, I could have done as my companions did and reached the resting place before relaxing. I shall defend myself by saying that I was *too tired.* Who is right? Or rather is the debate not based on incorrect premises? There is no doubt that I could have done otherwise, but that is not the problem. It ought to be formulated rather like this: could I have done otherwise without perceptibly modifying the organic totality of the projects which I am; or is the fact of resisting my fatigue such that instead of remaining a purely local and accidental modification of my behavior, it could be effected only by means of a radical transformation of my being-in-the-world—a transformation, moreover, which is *possible?* In other words: I could have done otherwise. Agreed. But *at what price?*

We are going to reply to this question by first presenting a *theoretical* description which will enable us to grasp the principle of our theses. We shall see subsequently whether the concrete reality is not shown to be more complex and whether without contradicting the results of our theoretical inquiry, it will not lead us to enrich them and make them more flexible.

Let us note first that the fatigue by itself could not provoke my decision. As we saw with respect to physical pain, fatigue is only the way in which I exist my body. It is not at first the object of a positional consciousness, but it is the very facticity of my consciousness. If then I hike across the country, what is revealed to me is the surrounding world; this is the object of my consciousness, and this is what I transcend toward possibilities which are my own—those, for example, of arriving this evening at the place which I have set for myself in advance. Yet to the extent that I apprehend this countryside with my eyes which unfold distances, my legs which climb the hills and consequently cause new sights and new obstacles to appear and disappear, with my back which carries the knapsack—to this extent I have a non-positional consciousness (of) this body which rules my relations with the world and which signifies my engagement in the world, in the form of fatigue. Objectively and in correlation with this non-thetic consciousness the roads are revealed as interminable, the slopes as *steeper,* the sun as more burning, *etc.* But I do not yet *think* of my fatigue; I apprehend it as the quasi-object of my reflection. Nevertheless there comes a moment when I do seek to consider my fatigue and to recover it. We really ought to provide an interpretation for this same intention; however, let us take it for what it is. It is not at all a contemplative apprehension of my fatigue; rather, as we saw with respect to pain, I *suffer* my fatigue. That is, a reflective consciousness is directed upon my fatigue in order to live it and to confer on it a value and a practical relation to myself. It is only on this plane that the fatigue will appear to me as bearable or intolerable. It will never be anything in itself, but it is the reflective for-itself which rising up suffers the fatigue as intolerable.

Here is posited the essential question: my companions are in good health—like me; they have had practically the same training as I so that although it is not possible to *compare* psychic events which occur in different subjectives, I usually conclude—and witnesses after an objective consideration of our bodies-for-others conclude—that they are for all practical purposes "as fatigued as I am." How does it happen therefore that they suffer their fatigue differently? Someone will say that the difference stems from the fact that I am a "sissy" and that the others are not. But although this evaluation undeniably has a practical bearing on the case and although one could take this into account when there arose a question of deciding whether or not it would be a good idea to take me on another expedition, such an evaluation can not satisfy us here. We have seen that to be ambitious is to project conquering a throne or honors; it is not a *given* which would incite one to conquest; it is this conquest itself. Similarly to be a "sissy" can not be a factual given and is only a name given to the way in which I suffer my fatigue. If therefore I wish to understand under what conditions I can suffer a fatigue as unbearable, it will not help to address oneself to so-called factual givens, which are revealed as being only a choice; it is necessary to attempt to examine this choice itself and to see whether it is not explained within the perspective of a larger choice in which it would be integrated as a secondary structure. If I question one of my companions, he will explain to me that he is fatigued, of course, but that he *loves* his fatigue; he gives himself up to it as to a bath; it appears to him in some way as the privileged instrument for discovering the world which surrounds him, for adapting himself to the rocky roughness of the paths, for discovering the "mountainous" quality of the slopes. In the same way it is this light sunburn on the back of his neck and this slight ringing in his ears which will enable him to realize a direct contact with the sun. Finally the feeling of effort is for him that of fatigue overcome. But as his fatigue is nothing but the passion which he endures so that the dust of the highways, the burning of the sun, the roughness of the roads may exist to the fullest, his effort (*i.e.,* this sweet familiarity with a fatigue which he loves, to which he abandons himself and which nevertheless he himself directs) is given as a way of appropriating the mountain, of suffering it to the end and being victor over it. . . . Thus my companion's fatigue is lived in a vaster project of a trusting abandon to nature, of a passion consented to in order that it may exist at full strength, and at the same time the project of sweet mastery and appropriation. It is only through this project that the fatigue will be able to be understood and that it will have meaning for him.

But this meaning and this vaster, more profound project are still by themselves *unselbständig*. They are not sufficient. For they precisely presuppose a particular relation of my companion to his body, on the one hand, and to things, on the other. It is easy to see, indeed, that there are as many ways of existing one's body as there are For-itselfs although naturally certain original structures are invariable and in each For-itself constitute human-reality. We shall be concerned elsewhere with what is incorrectly called the relation of the individual to space and to the conditions of a universal truth. For the moment we can conceive in connection with thousands of meaningful events that there is, for example, a certain type of flight before facticity, a flight which consists precisely in abandoning oneself to this facticity; that is, in short, in trustingly reassuming it and loving it in order to try to recover it. This original project of recovery is therefore a certain choice which the For-itself makes of itself in the presence of the problem of being. Its project remains a nihilation, but this nihilation turns back upon the in-itself which it nihilates and expresses itself by a particular valorization of facticity. This is expressed especially by the thousands of behavior patterns called *abandon*. To abandon oneself to fatigue, to warmth, to hunger, to thirst, to let oneself fall back upon a chair or a bed with sensual pleasure, to relax, to attempt to let oneself be drunk in by one's own body, not now beneath the eyes of others as in masochism but in the original solitude of the For-itself—none of these types of behavior can ever be confined to itself. We perceive this clearly since in another person they irritate or attract. Their condition is an initial project of the recovery of the body; that is, an attempt at a solution of the problem of the absolute (of the in-itself-for-itself).

This initial form can itself be limited to a profound acceptance of facticity; the project of "making oneself body" will mean then a happy abandon to a thousand little passing gluttonies, to a thousand little desires, a thousand little weaknesses. One may recall from Joyce's *Ulysses* Mr. Bloom satisfying his natural needs and inhaling with favor "the intimate odor rising from beneath him." But it is also possible (and this is the case with my companion) that by means of the body and by compliance to the body, the For-itself seeks to recover the totality of the nonconscious—that is, the whole universe as the ensemble of material *things*. In this case the desired synthesis of the in-itself with the for-itself will be the quasi pantheistic synthesis of the totality of the in-itself with the for-itself which recovers it. Here the body is the instrument of the synthesis; it loses itself in fatigue, for example, in order that this in-itself may exist to the fullest. And since it is the body which the for-itself exists as its own, this passion of the body coincides for the for-itself with the project of "making the in-itself exist." The ensemble of this attitude—which is that of one of my companions—can be expressed by the dim feeling of a kind of mission: he is going on this expedition because the mountain which he is going to climb and the forests which he is going to cross *exist;* his mission is to be the one by whom their meaning will be made manifest. Therefore he attempts to be the one who founds them in their very existence.

. . . it is evident following our analysis that the way in which my companion *suffers* his fatigue necessarily demands—if we are to understand it—that we undertake a regressive analysis which will lead us back to an initial project. Is this project we have outlined finally *selbständig?* Certainly—and it can be easily proved to be so. In fact by going further and further back we have reached the original relation which the for-itself chooses with its facticity and with the world. But this original relation is nothing other than the for-itself's being-in-the-world inasmuch as this

being-in-the-world is a choice—that is, we have reached the original type
of nihilation by which the for-itself has to be its own nothingness. No
interpretation of this can be attempted, for it would implicitly suppose
the being-in-the-world of the for-itself just as all the demonstrations
attempted by Euclid's Postulate implicitly suppose the adoption of this
postulate.

Therefore if I apply this same method to interpret the way in which
I suffer my fatigue, I shall first apprehend in myself a distrust of my body
—for example, a way of wishing not "to have anything to do with it,"
wanting not to take it into account, which is simply one of numerous
possible modes in which I can *exist my body*. I shall easily discover an
analogous distrust with respect to the in-itself and, for example, an original project for recovering the in-itself which I nihilate *through the intermedi-*
acy of others, which project in turn refers me to one of the initial projects
which we enumerated in our preceding discussion. Hence my fatigue
instead of being suffered "flexibly" will be grasped "sternly" as an impor-
tunate phenomenon which I want to get rid of—and this simply because
it incarnates my body and my brute contingency in the midst of the world
at a time when my project is to preserve my body and my presence in the
world by means of the looks of others. I am referred to myself as well as
to my original project; that is, to my being-in-the-world in so far as this
being is a choice.

·   ·   ·

SECTION FOUR

THE GOOD LIFE

There are few people who would not say that what they want most in life is happiness, but if we question them further and ask them what happiness consists of, we would probably find little agreement and much confusion over its nature. For centuries, philosophers have inquired into the nature of the good life and in this way have tried to understand what would constitute happiness for men and women. Their answers have been diverse: some point to physical comfort and pleasures; others emphasize the need for human beings to develop their "rational" or intellectual capacities; still others think the way to happiness lies in resigning oneself to the way things are.

Most recently, questions about the good life have taken on a new dimension. This is because the United States and many other Western countries have reached such an advanced stage of industrialization that they now have the capacity to fulfill virtually all people's basic biological needs for food and shelter and have begun to concentrate much of their energies on techniques that create new needs in people—needs for electric combs, deodorant sprays, a vast array of cosmetic products, and other such previously unimagined (and unnecessary) material possessions. Advertising assures us that the good life consists of possessing as many shiny new gadgets, as many pairs of shoes and sunglasses, as we possibly can. While many people would agree that a certain level of material well-being is necessary to enable a person to live the good life, the question that contemporary society prods us to ask is whether happiness can really consist of fulfilling all the needs that have been produced in us by the propagandists for advanced industrial capitalism. Are some needs "true" and others "false"? As automation creates more and more leisure time, and the corporations besiege us with more and more material objects that, we are assured, will render us happy, satisfied, beautiful, clever, handsome, sexy, and accomplished, the timeless philosophical question about the nature of human happiness takes on a new urgency.

Aristotle
THE RATIONAL LIFE

Aristotle offers a teleological analysis of the good life. He begins by asking what the particular aim or end of the human being is, and having defined it in terms of the human being's rational nature, goes on to argue that the most appropriate life is the one directed to developing that nature. According to Aristotle, this emphasis on reason is to be achieved both through the direct development of people's capacities for intellectual contemplation, and secondarily, by a striving to keep one's physical desires under control, so that one learns to practice moderation in all things. It is interesting to note that Aristotle, along with his teacher Plato, was one of the first major thinkers to distinguish between people's mental and physical capacities, and in so doing, to downgrade the body and its needs while elevating the mind. This way of viewing the human being persists throughout the history of Western philosophy and plays an important role in the thought of René Descartes, whose analysis of the relation between mind and body and the role of each in defining the human being is included in Section 2 of this book. It also persists in our attitudes toward sexuality; for a discussion of this problem the reader should consult the essay by Alan Watts in Section 10.

BOOK I

(1) Every art and every inquiry, and similarly every action and pursuit, is thought to aim at some good; and for this reason the good has rightly been declared to be that at which all things aim. But a certain difference is found among ends; some are activities, others are products apart from the activities that produce them. Where there are ends apart from the actions, it is the nature of the products to be better than the activities. Now, as there are many actions, arts, and sciences, their ends also are many; the end of the medical art is health, that of shipbuilding a vessel, that of strategy victory, that of economics wealth. But where such arts fall under a single capacity—as bridle-making and the other arts concerned with the equipment of horses fall under the art of riding, and this and every military action under strategy, in the same way other arts fall under yet others—in all of these the ends of the master arts are to be preferred to all the subordinate ends; for it is for the sake of the former that the latter are pursued. It makes no difference whether the activities themselves are the ends of the actions, or something else apart from the activities, as in the case of the sciences just mentioned.

. . .

(4) Let us resume our inquiry and state, in view of the fact that all knowledge and every pursuit aims at some good, what it is that we say political science aims at and what is the highest of all goods achievable

by action. Verbally there is very general agreement; for both the general run of men and people of superior refinement say that it is happiness, and identify living well and doing well with being happy; but with regard to what happiness is they differ, and the many do not give the same account as the wise. For the former think it is some plain and obvious thing, like pleasure, wealth, or honour; they differ, however, from one another—and often even the same man identifies it with different things, with health when he is ill, with wealth when he is poor; but, conscious of their ignorance, they admire those who proclaim some great ideal that is above their comprehension. Now some thought that apart from these many goods there is another which is self-subsistent and causes the goodness of all these as well. To examine all the opinions that have been held were perhaps somewhat fruitless; enough to examine those that are most prevalent or that seem to be arguable.

Let us not fail to notice, however, that there is a difference between arguments from and those to the first principles. For Plato, too, was right in raising this question and asking, as he used to do, "are we on the way from or to the first principles?" There is a difference, as there is in a race-course between the course from the judges to the turning-point and the way back. For, while we must begin with what is known, things are objects of knowledge in two senses—some to us, some without qualification. Presumably, then, *we* must begin with things known to *us*. Hence any one who is to listen intelligently to lectures about what is noble and just and, generally, about the subjects of political science must have been brought up in good habits. For the fact is the starting-point, and if this is sufficiently plain to him, he will not at the start need the reason as well; and the man who has been well brought up has or can easily get starting-points. And as for him who neither has nor can get them, let him hear the words of Hesiod:

> Far best is he who knows all things himself;
> Good, he that hearkens when men counsel right;
> But he who neither knows, nor lays to heart
> Another's wisdom, is a useless wight.

(5) Let us, however, resume our discussion from the point at which we digressed. To judge from the lives that men lead, most men, and men of the most vulgar type, seem (not without some ground) to identify the good, or happiness, with pleasure; which is the reason why they love the life of enjoyment. For there are, we may say, three prominent types of life —that just mentioned, the political, and thirdly the contemplative life. Now the mass of mankind are evidently quite slavish in their tastes, preferring a life suitable to beasts, but they get some ground for their view from the fact that many of those in high places share the tastes of Sardanapalus. A consideration of the prominent types of life shows that people of superior refinement and of active disposition identify happiness with honour; for this is, roughly speaking, the end of the political

life. But it seems too superficial to be what we are looking for, since it is thought to depend on those who bestow honour rather than on him who receives it, but the good we divine to be something proper to a man and not easily taken from him. Further, men seem to pursue honour in order that they may be assured of their goodness; at least it is by men of practical wisdom that they seek to be honoured, and among those who know them, and on the ground of their virtue; clearly, then, according to them, at any rate, virtue is better. And perhaps one might even suppose this to be, rather than honour, the end of the political life. But even this appears somewhat incomplete; for possession of virtue seems actually compatible with being asleep, or with lifelong inactivity, and, further, with the greatest sufferings and misfortunes; but a man who was living so no one would call happy, unless he were maintaining a thesis at all costs. But enough of this; for the subject has been sufficiently treated even in the current discussions. Third comes the contemplative life, which we shall consider later.

.   .   .

(7) Let us again return to the good we are seeking, and ask what it can be. It seems different in different actions and arts; it is different in medicine, in strategy, and in the other arts likewise. What then is the good of each? Surely that for whose sake everything else is done. In medicine this is health, in strategy victory, in architecture a house, in any other sphere something else, and in every action and pursuit the end; for it is for the sake of this that all men do whatever else they do. Therefore, if there is an end for all that we do, this will be the good achievable by action, and if there are more than one, these will be the goods achievable by action.

So the argument has by a different course reached the same point; but we must try to state this even more clearly. Since there are evidently more than one end, and we choose some of these (e.g. wealth, flutes, and in general instruments) for the sake of something else, clearly not all ends are final ends; but the chief good is evidently something final. Therefore, if there is only one final end, this will be what we are seeking, and if there are more than one, the most final of these will be what we are seeking. Now we call that which is in itself worthy of pursuit more final than that which is worthy of pursuit for the sake of something else, and that which is never desirable for the sake of something else more final than the things that are desirable both in themselves and for the sake of that other thing, and therefore we call final without qualification that which is always desirable in itself and never for the sake of something else.

Now such a thing happiness, above all else, is held to be; for this we choose always for itself and never for the sake of something else, but honour, pleasure, reason, and every virtue we choose indeed for them-selves (for if nothing resulted from them we should still choose each of them), but we choose them also for the sake of happiness, judging that by means of them we shall be happy. Happiness, on the other hand, no one chooses for the sake of these, nor, in general, for anything other than itself.

From the point of view of self-sufficiency the same result seems to follow; for the final good is thought to be self-sufficient. Now by self-sufficient we do not mean that which is sufficient for a man by himself, for one who lives a solitary life, but also for parents, children, wife, and in general for his friends and fellow citizens, since man is born for citizenship. But some limit must be set to this; for if we extend our requirement to ancestors and descendants and friends' friends we are in for an infinite series. Let us examine this question, however, on another occasion; the self-sufficient we now define as that which when isolated makes life desirable and lacking in nothing; and such we think happiness to be; and further we think it most desirable of all things, without being counted as one good thing among others—if it were so counted it would clearly be made more desirable by the addition of even the least of goods; for that which is added becomes an excess of goods, and of goods the greater is always more desirable. Happiness, then, is something final and self-sufficient, and is the end of action.

Presumably, however, to say that happiness is the chief good seems a platitude, and a clearer account of what it is is still desired. This might perhaps be given, if we could first ascertain the function of man. For just as for a flute-player, a sculptor, or any artist, and, in general, for all things that have a function or activity, the good and the "well" is thought to reside in the function, so would it seem to be for man, if he has a function. Have the carpenter, then, and the tanner certain functions or activities, and has man none? Is he born without a function? Or as eye, hand, foot, and in general each of the parts evidently has a function, may one lay it down that man similarly has a function apart from all these? What then can this be? Life seems to be common even to plants, but we are seeking what is peculiar to man. Let us exclude, therefore, the life of nutrition and growth. Next there would be a life of perception, but *it* also seems to be common even to the horse, the ox, and every animal. There remains, then, an active life of the element that has a rational principle; of this, one part has such a principle in the sense of being obedient to one, the other in the sense of possessing one and exercising thought. And, as "life of the rational element" also has two meanings, we must state that life in the sense of activity is what we mean; for this seems to be the more proper sense of the term. Now if the function of man is an activity of soul which follows or implies a rational principle, and if we say "a so-and-so" and "a good so-and-so" have a function which is the same in kind, e.g. a lyre-player and a good lyre-player, and so without qualification in all cases, eminence in respect of goodness being added to the name of the function (for the function of a lyre-player is to play the lyre, and that of a good lyre-player is to do so well): if this is the case, [and we state the function of man to be a certain kind of life, and this to be an activity or actions of the soul implying a rational principle, and the function of a good man to be the good and noble performance of these, and if any action is well performed when it is performed in accordance with the appropriate excellence: if this is the case] human good turns out to be activity of soul in accordance with virtue, and if there are more than one virtue, in accordance with the best and most complete.

But we must add "in a complete life." For one swallow does not make a summer, nor does one day; and so too one day, or a short time, does not make a man blessed and happy.

BOOK II

(1) Virtue, then, being of two kinds, intellectual and moral, intellectual virtue in the main owes both its birth and its growth to teaching (for which reason it requires experience and time), while moral virtue comes about as a result of habit, whence also its name *ethike* is one that is formed by a slight variation from the word *ethos* (habit). From this it is also plain that none of the moral virtues arises in us by nature; for nothing that exists by nature can form a habit contrary to its nature. For instance the stone which by nature moves downwards cannot be habituated to move upwards, not even if one tries to train it by throwing it up ten thousand times; nor can fire be habituated to move downwards, nor can anything else that by nature behaves in one way be trained to behave in another. Neither by nature, then, nor contrary to nature do the virtues arise in us; rather we are adapted by nature to receive them, and are made perfect by habit.

Again, of all the things that come to us by nature we first acquire the potentiality and later exhibit the activity (this is plain in the case of the senses; for it was not by often seeing or often hearing that we got these senses, but on the contrary we had them before we used them, and did not come to have them by using them); but the virtues we get by first exercising them, as also happens in the case of the arts as well. For the things we have to learn before we can do them, we learn by doing them, e.g. men become builders by building and lyre-players by playing the lyre; so too we become just by doing just acts, temperate by doing temperate acts, brave by doing brave acts.

This is confirmed by what happens in states; for legislators make the citizens good by forming habits in them, and this is the wish of every legislator, and those who do not effect it miss their mark, and it is in this that a good constitution differs from a bad one.

Again, it is from the same causes and by the same means that every virtue is both produced and destroyed, and similarly every art; for it is from playing the lyre that both good and bad lyre-players are produced. And the corresponding statement is true of builders and of all the rest;

men will be good or bad builders as a result of building well or badly. For if this were not so, there would have been no need of a teacher, but all men would have been born good or bad at their craft. This, then, is the case with the virtues also; by doing the acts that we do in our transactions with other men we become just or unjust, and by doing the acts that we do in the presence of danger, and being habituated to feel fear or confidence, we become brave or cowardly. The same is true of appetites and feelings of anger; some men become temperate and good-tempered, others self-indulgent and irascible, by behaving in one way or the other in the appropriate circumstances. Thus, in one word, states of character arise out of like activities. This is why the activities we exhibit must be of a certain kind; it is because the states of character correspond to the differences between these. It makes no small difference, then, whether we form habits of one kind or of another from our very youth; it makes a very great difference, or rather *all* the difference.

(2) Since, then, the present inquiry does not aim at theoretical knowledge like the others (for we are inquiring not in order to know what virtue is, but in order to become good, since otherwise our inquiry would have been of no use), we must examine the nature of actions, namely how we ought to do them; for these determine also the nature of the states of character that are produced, as we have said. Now, that we must act according to the right is a common principle and must be assumed. . . . But this must be agreed upon beforehand, that the whole account of matters of conduct must be given in outline and not precisely, . . . the accounts we demand must be in accordance with the subject-matter; matters concerned with conduct and questions of what is good for us have no fixity, any more than matters of health. The general account being of this nature, the account of particular cases is yet more lacking in exactness; for they do not fall under any art or precept but the agents themselves must in each case consider what is appropriate to the occasion, as happens also in the art of medicine or of navigation.

But though our present account is of this nature we must give what help we can. First, then, let us consider this, that it is the nature of such things to be destroyed by defect and excess, as we see in the case of strength and of health (for to gain light on things imperceptible we must use the evidence of sensible things); both excessive and defective exercise destroys the strength, and similarly drink or food which is above or below a certain amount destroys the health, while that which is proportionate both produces and increases and preserves it. So too is it, then, in the case of temperance and courage and the other virtues. For the man who flies from and fears everything and does not stand his ground against anything becomes a coward, and the man who fears nothing at all but goes to meet every danger becomes rash; and similarly the man who indulges in every pleasure and abstains from none becomes self-indulgent, while the man who shuns every pleasure, as boors do, becomes in a way insensible; temperance and courage, then, are destroyed by excess and defect, and preserved by the mean.

But not only are the sources and causes of their origination and growth the same as those of their destruction, but also the sphere of their actualization will be the same; for this is also true of the things which are more evident to sense, e.g. of strength; it is produced by taking much food and undergoing much exertion, and it is the strong man that will be most able to do these things. So too is it with the virtues; by abstaining from pleasures we become temperate, and it is when we have become so that we are most able to abstain from them; and similarly too in the case of courage; for by being habituated to despise things that are terrible and to stand our ground against them we become brave, and it is when we have become so that we shall be most able to stand our ground against them.

(3) We must take as a sign of states of character the pleasure or pain that ensues on acts; for the man who abstains from bodily pleasures and delights in this very fact is temperate, while the man who is annoyed at it is self-indulgent, and he who stands his ground against things that are terrible and delights in this or at least is not pained is brave, while the man who is pained is a coward. For moral excellence is concerned with pleasures and pains; it is on account of the pleasure that we do bad things, and on account of the pain that we abstain from noble ones. Hence we ought to have been brought up in a particular way from our very youth, as Plato says, so as both to delight in and to be pained by the things that we ought; for this is the right education.

Again, if the virtues are concerned with actions and passions, and every passion and every action is accompanied by pleasure and pain, for this reason also virtue will be concerned with pleasures and pains. This is indicated also by the fact that punishment is inflicted by these means; for it is a kind of cure, and it is the nature of cures to be effected by contraries.

Again, as we said but lately, every state of soul has a nature relative to and concerned with the kind of things by which it tends to be made worse or better; but it is by reason of pleasures and pains that men become bad, by pursuing and avoiding these—either the pleasures and pains they ought not or when they ought not or as they ought not, or by going wrong in one of the other similar ways that may be distinguished. Hence men even define the virtues as certain states of impassivity and rest; not well, however, because they speak absolutely, and do not say "as one ought" and "as one ought not" and "when one ought or ought not," and the other things that may be added. We assume, then, that this kind of excellence tends to do what is best with regard to pleasures and pains, and vice does the contrary.

The following facts also may show us that virtue and vice are concerned with these same things. There being three objects of choice and three of avoidance, the noble, the advantageous, the pleasant, and their contraries, the base, the injurious, the painful, about all of these the good man tends to go right and the bad man to go wrong, and especially about pleasure; for this is common to the animals, and also it accompanies all objects of choice; for even the noble and the advantageous appear pleasant.

Again, it has grown up with us all from our infancy; this is why it is difficult to rub off this passion, engrained as it is in our life. And we measure even our actions, some of us more and others less, by the rule of pleasure and pain. For this reason, then, our whole inquiry must be about these; for to feel delight and pain rightly or wrongly has no small effect on our actions.

Again, it is harder to fight with pleasure than with anger, to use Heraclitus' phrase, but both art and virtue are always concerned with what is harder; for even the good is better when it is harder. Therefore for this reason also the whole concern both of virtue and of political science is with pleasures and pains; for the man who uses these well will be good, he who uses them badly bad.

That virtue, then, is concerned with pleasures and pains, and that by the acts from which it arises it is both increased and, if they are done differently, destroyed, and that the acts from which it arose are those in which it actualizes itself—let this be taken as said.

(4) The question might be asked, what we mean by saying that we must become just by doing just acts, and temperate by doing temperate acts; for if men do just and temperate acts, they are already just and temperate, exactly as, if they do what is in accordance with the laws of grammar and of music, they are grammarians and musicians.

Or is this not true even of the arts? It is possible to do something that is in accordance with the laws of grammar, either by chance or at the suggestion of another. A man will be a grammarian, then, only when he has both done something grammatical and done it grammatically; and this means doing it in accordance with the grammatical knowledge in himself.

Again, the case of the arts and that of the virtues are not similar; for the products of the arts have their goodness in themselves, so that it is enough that they should have a certain character, but if the acts that are in accordance with the virtues have themselves a certain character it does not follow that they are done justly or temperately. The agent also must be in a certain condition when he does them; in the first place he must have knowledge, secondly he must choose the acts, and choose them for their own sakes, and thirdly his action must proceed from a firm and unchangeable character. These are not reckoned in as conditions of the possession of the arts, except the bare knowledge; but as a condition of the possession of the virtues knowledge has little or no weight, while the other conditions count not for a little but for everything, i.e. the very conditions which result from often doing just and temperate acts.

Actions, then, are called just and temperate when they are such as the just or the temperate man would do; but it is not the man who does these that is just and temperate, but the man who also does them as just and temperate men do them. It is well said, then, that it is by doing just acts that the just man is produced, and by doing temperate acts the temperate man; without doing these no one would have even a prospect of becoming good.

But most people do not do these, but take refuge in theory and think they are being philosophers and will become good in this way, behaving somewhat like patients who listen attentively to their doctors, but do none of the things they are ordered to do. As the latter will not be made well in body by such a course of treatment, the former will not be made well in soul by such a course of philosophy.

. . .

(6) Now that we have spoken of the virtues, the forms of friendship, and the varieties of pleasure, what remains is to discuss in outline the nature of happiness, since this is what we state the end of human nature to be. Our discussion will be the more concise if we first sum up what we have said already. We said, then, that it is not a disposition; for if it were it might belong to some one who was asleep throughout his life, living the life of a plant, or, again, to some one who was suffering the greatest misfortunes. If these implications are unacceptable, and we must rather class happiness as an activity, as we have said before, and if some activities are necessary, and desirable for the sake of something else, while others are so in themselves, evidently happiness must be placed among those desirable in themselves, not among those desirable for the sake of something else; for happiness does not lack anything, but is self-sufficient. Now those activities are desirable in themselves from which nothing is sought beyond the activity. And of this nature virtuous actions are thought to be; for to do noble and good deeds is a thing desirable for its own sake.

Pleasant amusements also are thought to be of this nature; we choose them not for the sake of other things; for we are injured rather than benefited by them, since we are led to neglect our bodies and our property. But most of the people who are deemed happy take refuge in such pastimes, which is the reason why those who are readywitted at them are highly esteemed at the courts of tyrants; they make themselves pleasant companions in the tyrants' favourite pursuits, and that is the sort of man they want. Now these things are thought to be of the nature of happiness because people in despotic positions spend their leisure in them, but perhaps such people prove nothing; for virtue and reason, from which good activities flow, do not depend on despotic position; nor, if these people, who have never tasted pure and generous pleasure, take refuge in the bodily pleasures, should these for that reason be thought more desirable; for boys, too, think the things that are valued among themselves are the best. It is to be expected, then, that, as different things seem valuable to boys and to men, so they should to bad men and to good. Now, as we have often maintained, those things are both valuable and pleasant which are such to the good man; and to each man the activity in accordance with his own disposition is most desirable, and, therefore, to the good man that which is in accordance with virtue. Happiness, therefore, does not lie in amusement; it would, indeed, be strange if the end were amusement, and one were to take trouble and suffer hardship all one's life in order to amuse oneself. For, in a word, everything that we choose we choose for the sake of something else—except happiness, which is an end. Now to exert oneself and work for the sake of amusement seems silly and utterly childish. But to amuse oneself in order that one may exert oneself, as Anacharsis puts it, seems right; for amusement is a sort of relaxation, and we need relaxation because we cannot work continuously. Relaxation, then, is not an end; for it is taken for the sake of activity.

The happy life is thought to be virtuous; now a virtuous life requires exertion, and does not consist in amusement. And we say that serious things are better than laughable things and those connected with amusement, and that the activity of the better of any two things—whether it be two elements of our being or two men—is the more serious; but the activity of the better is *ipso facto* superior and more of the nature of happiness. And any chance person—even a slave—can enjoy the bodily pleasures no less than the best man; but no one assigns to a slave a share in happiness—unless he assigns to him also a share in human life. For happiness does not lie in such occupations, but, as we have said before, in virtuous activities.

(7) If happiness is activity in accordance with virtue, it is reasonable that it should be in accordance with the highest virtue; and this will be that of the best thing in us. Whether it be reason or something else that is this element which is thought to be our natural ruler and guide and to take thought of things noble and divine, whether it be itself also divine or only the most divine element in us, the activity of this in accordance with its proper virtue will be perfect happiness. That this activity is contemplative we have already said.

Now this would seem to be in agreement both with what we said before and with the truth. For, firstly, this activity is the best (since not only is reason the best thing in us, but the objects of reason are the best of knowable objects); and, secondly, it is the most continuous, since we can contemplate truth more continuously than we can *do* anything. And we think happiness has pleasure mingled with it, but the activity of philosophic wisdom is admittedly the pleasantest of virtuous activities; at all events the pursuit of it is thought to offer pleasures marvellous for their purity and their enduringness, and it is to be expected that those who know will pass their time more pleasantly than those who inquire. And the self-sufficiency that is spoken of must belong most to the contemplative activity. For while a philosopher, as well as a just man or one possessing any other virtue, needs the necessaries of life, when they are sufficiently equipped with things of that sort the just man needs people towards whom and with whom he shall act justly, and the temperate man, the brave man, and each of the others is in the same case, but the philosopher, even when by himself, can contemplate truth, and the better the

wiser he is; he can perhaps do so better if he has fellow-workers, but still
he is the most self-sufficient. And this activity alone would seem to be
loved for its own sake; for nothing arises from it apart from the contemplating, while from practical activities we gain more or less apart from the
action. And happiness is thought to depend on leisure; for we are busy
that we may have leisure, and make war that we may live in peace. Now
the activity of the practical virtues is exhibited in political or military
affairs, but the actions concerned with these seem to be unleisurely.
Warlike actions are completely so (for no one chooses to be at war, or
provokes war, for the sake of being at war; any one would seem absolutely
murderous if he were to make enemies of his friends in order to bring
about battle and slaughter); but the action of the statesman is also unleisurely, and—apart from the political action itself—aims at despotic power
and honours, or at all events happiness, for him and his fellow citizens
—a happiness different from political action, and evidently sought as
being different. So if among virtuous actions political and military actions
are distinguished by nobility and greatness, and these are unleisurely and
aim at an end and are not desirable for their own sake, but the activity
of reason, which is contemplative, seems both to be superior in serious
worth and to aim at no end beyond itself, and to have its pleasure proper
to itself (and this augments the activity), and the self-sufficiency, leisureli-
ness, unweariedness (so far as this is possible for man), and all the other
attributes ascribed to the supremely happy man are evidently those connected with this activity, it follows that this will be the complete happiness
of man, if it be allowed a complete term of life (for none of the attributes
of happiness is *in*complete).

But such a life would be too high for man; for it is not in so far as
he is man that he will live so, but in so far as something divine is present
in him; and by so much as this is superior to our composite nature is its
activity superior to that which is the exercise of the other kind of virtue.
If reason is divine, then, in comparison with man, the life according to
it is divine in comparison with human life. But we must not follow those
who advise us, being men, to think of human things, and, being mortal,
of mortal things, but must, so far as we can, make ourselves immortal, and
strain every nerve to live in accordance with the best thing in us; for even
if it be small in bulk, much more does it in power and worth surpass
everything. This would seem, too, to be each man himself, since it is the
authoritative and better part of him. It would be strange, then, if he were
to choose not the life of his self but that of something else. And what we
said before will apply now; that which is proper to each thing is by nature
best and most pleasant for each thing; for man, therefore, the life according to reason is best and pleasantest, since reason more than anything
else *is* man. This life therefore is also the happiest.

(8) But in a secondary degree the life in accordance with the other
kind of virtue is happy; for the activities in accordance with this befit our

human estate. Just and brave acts, and other virtuous acts, we do in relation to each other, observing our respective duties with regard to contracts and services and all manner of actions and with regard to passions; and all of these seem to be typically human. Some of them seem even to arise from the body, and virtue of character to be in many ways bound up with the passions. Practical wisdom, too, is linked to virtue of character, and this to practical wisdom, since the principles of practical wisdom are in accordance with the moral virtues and rightness in morals is in accordance with practical wisdom. Being connected with the passions also, the moral virtues must belong to our composite nature; and the virtues of our composite nature are human; so, therefore, are the life and the happiness which correspond to these. The excellence of the reason is a thing apart; we must be content to say this much about it, for to describe it precisely is a task greater than our purpose requires. It would seem, however, also to need external equipment but little, or less than moral virtue does. Grant that both need the necessaries, and do so equally, even if the statesman's work is the more concerned with the body and things of that sort; for there will be little difference there; but in what they need for the exercise of their activities there will be much difference. The liberal man will need money for the doing of his liberal deeds, and the just man too will need it for the returning of services (for wishes are hard to discern, and even people who are not just pretend to wish to act justly); and the brave man will need power if he is to accomplish any of the acts that correspond to his virtue, and the temperate man will need opportunity; for how else is either he or any of the others to be recognized? It is debated, too, whether the will or the deed is more essential to virtue, which is assumed to involve both; it is surely clear that its perfection involves both; but for deeds many things are needed, and more, the greater and nobler the deeds are. But the man who is contemplating the truth needs no such thing, at least with a view to the exercise of his activity; indeed they are, one may say, even hindrances, at all events to his contemplation; but in so far as he is a man and lives with a number of people, he chooses to do virtuous acts; he will therefore need such aids to living a human life.

But that perfect happiness is a contemplative activity will appear from the following consideration as well. We assume the gods to be above all other beings blessed and happy; but what sort of actions must we assign to them? Acts of justice? Will not the gods seem absurd if they make contracts and return deposits, and so on? Acts of a brave man, then, confronting dangers and running risks because it is noble to do so? Or liberal acts? To whom will they give? It will be strange if they are really to have money or anything of the kind. And what would their temperate acts be? Is not such praise tasteless, since they have no bad appetites? If we were to run through them all, the circumstances of action would be found trivial and unworthy of gods. Still, every one supposes that they *live* and therefore that they are active; we cannot suppose them to sleep like Endymion. Now if you take away from a living being action, and still more production, what is left but contemplation? Therefore the activity of God, which surpasses all others in blessedness, must be contemplative; and of human activities, therefore, that which is most akin to this must be most of the nature of happiness.

This is indicated, too, by the fact that the other animals have no share in happiness, being completely deprived of such activity. For while the whole life of the gods is blessed, and that of men too in so far as some likeness of such activity belongs to them, none of the other animals is happy, since they in no way share in contemplation. Happiness extends, then, just so far as contemplation does, and those to whom contemplation more fully belongs are more truly happy, not as a mere concomitant but in virtue of the contemplation; for this is in itself precious. Happiness, therefore, must be some form of contemplation.

But, being a man, one will also need external prosperity; for our nature is not self-sufficient for the purpose of contemplation, but our body also must be healthy and must have food and other attention. Still, we must not think that the man who is to be happy will need many things or great things, merely because he cannot be supremely happy without external goods; for self-sufficiency and action do not involve excess, and we can do noble acts without ruling earth and sea; for even with moderate advantages one can act virtuously (this is manifest enough; for private persons are thought to do worthy acts no less than despots—indeed even more); and it is enough that we should have so much as that; for the life of the man who is active in accordance with virtue will be happy. Solon, too, was perhaps sketching well the happy man when he described him as moderately furnished with externals but as having done (as Solon thought) the noblest acts, and lived temperately; for one can with but moderate possessions do what one ought. Anaxagoras also seems to have supposed the happy man not to be rich nor a despot, when he said that he would not be surprised if the happy man were to seem to most people a strange person; for they judge by externals, since these are all they perceive. The opinions of the wise seem, then, to harmonize with our arguments. But while even such things carry some conviction, the truth in practical matters is discerned from the facts of life; for these are the decisive factor. We must therefore survey what we have already said, bringing it to the test of the facts of life, and if it harmonizes with the facts we must accept it, but if it clashes with them we must suppose it to be mere theory. Now he who exercises his reason and cultivates it seems to be both in the best state of mind and most dear to the gods. For if the gods have any care for human affairs, as they are thought to have, it would be reasonable both that they should delight in that which was best and most akin to them (i.e. reason) and that they should reward those who love and honour this most, as caring for the things that are dear to them and acting both rightly and nobly. And that all these attributes belong most of all to the philosopher is manifest. He, therefore, is the dearest to the gods. And he who is that will presumably be also the happiest; so that in this way too the philosopher will more than any other be happy.

.   .   .

Epictetus
STOICISM

Epictetus was born in Asia Minor in about the middle of the first century A.D.
He was sold into slavery as a child, later gained his freedom, and taught
philosophy in Rome and on the Greek mainland. Stoicism, the philosophy he
represents, was very much a response to the social upheaval of the times.
Essentially a philosophy for the upper classes, Stoicism instructed those who had
seen the decline of the Greek polis and were now part of the vast and impersonal
Hellenic and Roman empires that the best course was to learn to resign
themselves to what could not be changed. Tempered expectations and acceptance
of the unalterable would lead to a reasonably happy life, happy not in the sense
of experiencing great pleasure but in the sense of being protected from great pain
and unhappiness. In its urgings to seek to change desires rather than to alter the
world, Stoicism provides us with a good example of one of the principle functions
of ethics over the centuries, that of supporting the status quo by urging people to
accept their society as it is.

(1) Of things some are in our power, and others are not. In our power are opinion, movement toward a thing, desire, aversion (turning from a thing), and, in a word, whatever are our own acts; not in our power are the body, property, reputation, offices (magisterial power), and, in a word, whatever are not our own acts. And the things in our power are by nature free, not subject to restraint nor hindrance; but the things not in our power are weak, slavish, subject to restraint, in the power of others. Remember then that if you think the things which are by nature slavish to be free, and the things which are in the power of others to be your own, you will be hindered, you will lament, you will be disturbed, you will blame both gods and men; but if you think that only which is your own to be your own, and if you think that what is another's, as it really is, belongs to another, no man will ever compel you, no man will hinder you, you will never blame any man, you will accuse no man, you will do nothing involuntarily (against your will), no man will harm you, you will have no enemy, for you will not suffer any harm.

If then you aim at such high matters, remember that you must not attempt to lay hold of them with a small effort; but you must give up some things entirely, and postpone others for the present. But if you wish for these things also—power and wealth—perhaps you will not gain even these because you aim also at the former; certainly you will fail in those things through which alone happiness and freedom are secured. Straightway then practice saying to every harsh appearance, "You are an appearance, and in no manner what you appear to be." Then examine it by the rules which you possess, and by this first and chiefly, whether it relates to the things which are in our power or to the things which are not in our power: and if it relates to anything which is not in our power, be ready to say that it does not concern you.

(2) Remember that desire contains in it the hope of obtaining that which you desire; and the hope in aversion is that you will not fall into that which you attempt to avoid. He who fails in his desire is unfortunate; and he who falls into that which he would avoid, is unhappy. If then you attempt to avoid only the things contrary to nature which are within your power, you will not be involved in any of the things which you would avoid. But if you attempt to avoid disease or death or poverty, you will be unhappy. Take away then aversion from all things which are not in our power, and transfer it to the things contrary to nature which are in our power. But destroy desire completely for the present. If you desire anything which is not in our power, you must be unfortunate; things in our power which it would be good to desire are within your reach. But employ only the impulses of moving toward an object and retiring from it, and these indeed only slightly and with exceptions and with remission.

(3) In everything which pleases the soul, or supplies a want, or is loved, remember to add this: "What is its nature?" If you love an earthen vessel, say it is an earthen vessel which you love; when it has been broken, you will not be disturbed. If you are kissing your child or wife, say that it is a human being whom you are kissing; if the wife or child dies, you will not be disturbed.

(4) When you are going to take in hand any act, remind yourself what kind of an act it is. If you are going to bathe, place before yourself what happens in the bath: some splashing the water, others pushing against one another, others abusing one another, and some stealing. You will undertake the matter with more safety if you say to yourself, "I now intend to bathe, and to maintain my will in a manner conformable to nature." And so you will do in every act. If any hindrance to bathing shall happen, let this thought be ready: "It was not this only that I intended, but I intended also to maintain my will in a way conformable to nature; but I shall not maintain it so, if I am vexed at what happens."

(5) Men are disturbed not by the things which happen, but by the opinions about the things: for example, death is nothing terrible, for if it were, it would have seemed so to Socrates. The opinion that death is terrible is the terrible thing. When then we are impeded or disturbed or grieved, let us never blame others, but ourselves, that is, our opinions. It is the act of an ill-instructed man to blame others for his own bad condition; it is the act of one who has begun to be instructed, to lay the blame on himself; and of one whose instruction is completed, neither to blame another nor himself.

(6) Be not elated at any excellence which belongs to another. If a horse when he is elated should say, "I am beautiful," one might endure it. But when you are elated and say, "I have a beautiful horse," you must know that the horse is the cause of your elation. What then is your own? The use of appearances. Consequently when in the use of appearances you are conformable to nature, then be elated, for then you will be elated at something good which is your own.

(7) As on a voyage when the vessel has reached a port, if you go out to get water, it is an amusement by the way to pick up a shellfish or some bulb, but your thoughts ought to be directed to the ship, and you ought to be constantly watching if the captain should call, and then you must throw away all those things, that you may not be bound and pitched into the ship like sheep; so in life also, if there be given to you instead of a little bulb and a shell a wife and child, there will be nothing to prevent you from taking them. But if the captain should call, run to the ship, and leave all those things without looking back. But if you are old, do not even go far from the ship, lest when you are called you fail to appear.

(8) Seek not that the things which happen should happen as you wish; but wish the things which happen to be as they are, and you will have a tranquil flow of life.

(9) Disease is an impediment to the body, but not to the will, unless the will itself chooses. Lameness is an impediment to the leg, but not to the will. Say this on the occasion of everything that happens; you will find it an impediment to something else, but not to yourself.

(10) On the occasion of every accidental event that befalls you, remember to turn to yourself and inquire what power you have for dealing with it. If you see a fair man or a fair woman, you will find that the power to resist is continence. If trouble be presented to you, you will find that it is endurance. If it be abusive words, you will find it to be patience. And if you have been thus formed to the proper habit, the appearances will not carry you along with them.

(11) Never say about anything, "I have lost it," but say "I have restored it." Is your child dead? It has been restored. Is your wife dead? She has been restored. Has your estate been taken from you? Has not this also been restored? "But he who has taken it from me is a bad man." But what is it to you by whose hands the giver demanded it back? So long as he may allow you, take care of it as a thing which belongs to another, as travelers do with their inn.

(12) If you intend to improve, throw away such thoughts as these: "If I neglect my affairs, I shall not have the means of living: unless I chastise my son, he will be bad." For it is better to die of hunger and so to be released from grief and fear than to live in abundance with perturbation; and it is better for your son to be bad than for you to be unhappy. Begin then from little things. Is the oil spilled? Is a little wine stolen? Say: this is the price of freedom from perturbation; this is the price of tranquility, nothing is got for nothing. And when you call your slave, consider that it is possible that he does not hear; and if he does hear, that he will do nothing which you wish. But matters are not so well with him that it should be in his power to give you peace of mind.

(13) If you would improve, submit to being considered a simpleton and foolish with respect to externals. Wish to be considered to know nothing: and if you shall seem to some to be a person of importance, distrust yourself. For you should know that it is not easy both to keep your will in a condition conformable to nature and to secure external things. If a man is careful about the one, he must needs neglect the other.

(14) If you would have your children and your wife and your friends live forever, you are silly; for you would have the things which are not in your power to be in your power, and the things which belong to others to be yours. So if you would have your slave to be free from faults, you are a fool; for you would have badness not to be badness, but something else. But if you wish not to fail in your desires, that you are able to do. Practice what you are able to do. He is the master of every man who has the power over the things which another person wishes or does not wish, the power to confer them on him or to take them away. Whoever then wishes to be free, let him neither wish for anything nor avoid anything which depends on others. If he does not observe this rule, he must be a slave.

(15) Remember that in life you ought to behave as at a banquet. Suppose that something is carried round and is opposite to you. Stretch out your hand and take a portion with decency. Suppose that it passes by you. Do not detain it. Suppose that it is not yet come to you. Do not send your desire forward to it, but wait till it is opposite you. Do so with respect to children, with respect to a wife, with respect to magisterial offices, with respect to wealth, and you will be some time a worthy partner of the banquets of the gods. But if you take none of the things which are set before you, and even despise them, then you will be not only a fellow-banqueter with the gods, but also a partner with them in power. For by acting so Diogenes and Heraclitus and those like them were deservedly divine, and were so called.

(16) When you see a person weeping in sorrow for a child gone abroad or dead, or for loss of his property, take care that the appearances do not carry you away, as if he were suffering in external things. Make a distinction in your own mind and say, "It is not what happened that afflicts this man, but it is the opinion about this thing which afflicts the man." So far as words, then, do not be unwilling to show him sympathy, and even to lament with him. But take care that you do not lament in your inner being also.

(17) Remember that you are an actor in a play of such a kind as the author may choose; if short, of a short one; if long, of a long one. If he wishes you to act the part of a poor man, see that you act the part naturally; if the part of a lame man, of a magistrate, of a private person, do the same. For this is your duty: to act well the part that is given to you; but to select the part, belongs to another.

(18) When a raven has croaked inauspiciously, let not the appear-

ance carry you away, but straightway make a distinction in your mind and say, "None of these portents signifies to me, but either to my poor body, or to my small property, or to my reputation, or to my children or to my wife. But to me all omens are auspicious if I choose. For whatever results, it is in my power to derive benefit from it."

(19) You can be invincible if you enter into no contest in which it is not in your power to conquer. Take care, then, when you observe a man honored before others or possessed of great power or highly esteemed for any reason, not to suppose him happy, and be not carried away by the appearance. For if the nature of the good is in our power, neither envy nor jealousy will have a place in us. But you yourself will not wish to be a general or senator or consul, but a free man. There is only one way to this: to despise the things which are not in our power.

(20) Remember that it is not he who reviles or strikes you who insults you, but your opinion that these things are insulting. When then a man irritates you, you must know that it is your own opinion which has irritated you. Therefore try especially not to be carried away by the appearance. For if you once gain time and delay, you will more easily master yourself.

(21) Let death and exile and every other thing which appears dreadful be daily before your eyes, but most of all death; you will never think of anything mean nor will you desire anything extravagantly.

. . .

Jeremy Bentham
THE PRINCIPLE OF UTILITY

Jeremy Bentham's utilitarianism provides us with a straightforward definition of happiness in terms of pleasure. In sharp contrast to Aristotle, Bentham draws no distinctions between pleasures of the mind and pleasures of the body but argues that all pleasures have equal value in the calculation of happiness. This view provoked considerable outrage from the intellectual community of the day, as many recalled Aristotle's argument that if mental pleasure is worth no more than physical pleasure, a slave would be as capable of achieving happiness as a free man or a philosopher. To some, this possibility was inconceivable, and in itself, disproved Bentham's thesis.

Shortly after Bentham, John Stuart Mill revised utilitarianism considerably, reintroducing Aristotle's emphasis on the rational side of the human being and insisting that the so-called higher, or intellectual, pleasures are more valuable than the lower, or physical, pleasures. In the struggle over the utilitarian definition of happiness, we see a reflection of the political struggle between the entrenched aristocracy, which insisted upon equating capacity to rule with noble birth, and the emerging democratic bourgeoisie, which had acquired economic power and now wished to complement their material well-being with political prerogatives.

OF THE PRINCIPLE OF UTILITY

Nature has placed mankind under the governance of two sovereign masters, *pain* and *pleasure*. It is for them alone to point out what we ought to do, as well as to determine what we shall do. On the one hand the standard of right and wrong, on the other the chain of causes and effects, are fastened to their throne. They govern us in all we do, in all we say, in all we think: every effort we can make to throw off our subjection, will serve but to demonstrate and confirm it. In words a man may pretend to abjure their empire, but in reality he will remain subject to it all the while. The *principle of utility* recognizes this subjection, and assumes it for the foundation of that system, the object of which is to rear the fabric of felicity by the hands of reason and of law. Systems which attempt to question it deal in sounds instead of sense, in caprice instead of reason, in darkness instead of light.

But enough of metaphor and declamation: it is not by such means that moral science is to be improved.

ii. The principle of utility is the foundation of the present work: it will be proper therefore at the outset to give an explicit and determinate account of what is meant by it. By the principle of utility is meant that principle which approves or disapproves of every action whatsoever, according to the tendency which it appears to have to augment or diminish the happiness of the party whose interest is in question: or, what is the same thing in other words, to promote or to oppose that happiness. I say of every action whatsoever; and therefore not only of every action of a private individual, but of every measure of government.

iii. By utility is meant that property in any object, whereby it tends to produce benefit, advantage, pleasure, good, or happiness (all this in the present case comes to the same thing), or (what comes again to the same thing) to prevent the happening of mischief, pain, evil, or unhappiness to the party whose interest is considered: if that party be the community in general, then the happiness of the community; if a particular individual, then the happiness of that individual.

iv. The interest of the community is one of the most general expressions that can occur in the phraseology of morals: no wonder that the meaning of it is often lost. When it has a meaning, it is this. The community is a fictitious *body,* composed of the individual persons who are considered as constituting as it were its *members.* The interest of the community then is—what? The sum of the interest of the several members who compose it.

v. It is in vain to talk of the interest of the community, without understanding what is the interest of the individual. A thing is said to promote the interest, or to be *for* the interest, of an individual, when it tends to add to the sum total of his pleasures; or, what comes to the same thing, to diminish the sum total of his pains.

vi. An action then may be said to be conformable to the principle of utility, or, for shortness sake, to utility (meaning with respect to the community at large), when the tendency it has to augment the happiness of the community is greater than any it has to diminish it.

vii. A measure of government (which is but a particular kind of action, performed by a particular person or persons) may be said to be conformable to or dictated by the principle of utility, when in like manner the tendency which it has to augment the happiness of the community is greater than any which it has to diminish it.

viii. When an action, or in particular a measure of government, is supposed by a man to be conformable to the principle of utility, it may be convenient, for the purposes of discourse, to imagine a kind of law or dictate, called a law or dictate of utility; and to speak of the action in question, as being conformable to such law or dictate.

ix. A man may be said to be a partisan of the principle of utility, when the approbation or disapprobation he annexes to any action, or to any measure, is determined by and proportioned to the tendency which he conceives it to have to augment or to diminish the happiness of the community; or in other words, to its conformity or unconformity to the laws or dictates of utility.

x. Of an action that is conformable to the principle of utility, one may always say either that it is one that ought to be done, or at least that it is not one that ought not to be done. One may say also that it is right it should be done—at least that it is not wrong it should be done; that it is a right action—at least that it is not a wrong action. When thus interpreted, the words *ought,* and *right* and *wrong,* and others of that stamp, have a meaning: when otherwise, they have none.

xi. Has the rectitude of this principle been ever formally contested? It should seem that it had, by those who have not known what they have been meaning. Is it susceptible of any direct proof? It should seem not; for that which is used to prove everything else, cannot itself be proved: a chain of proofs must have their commencement somewhere. To give such proof is as impossible as it is needless.

xii. Not that there is or ever has been that human creature breathing, however stupid or preverse, who has not on many, perhaps on most occasions of his life, deferred to it. By the natural constitution of the human frame, on most occasions of their lives men in general embrace this principle, without thinking of it: if not for the ordering of their own actions, yet for the trying of their own actions, as well as of those of other men. There have been, at the same time, not many perhaps even of the most intelligent, who have been disposed to embrace it purely and without reserve. There are even few who have not taken some occasion or other to quarrel with it, either on account of their not understanding always how to apply it, or on account of some prejudice or other which they were afraid to examine into, or could not bear to part with. For such is the stuff that man is made of: in principle and in practice, in a right track and in a wrong one, the rarest of all human qualities is consistency.

xiii. When a man attempts to combat the principle of utility, it is with reasons drawn, without his being aware of it, from that very principle itself. His arguments, if they prove anything, prove not that the principle is *wrong,* but that, according to the applications he supposes to be made of it, it is *misapplied.* Is it possible for a man to move the earth? Yes; but he must first find out another earth to stand upon.

xiv. To disprove the propriety of it by arguments is impossible; but, from the causes that have been mentioned, or from some confused or partial view of it, a man may happen to be disposed not to relish it. Where this is the case, if he thinks the settling of his opinions on such a subject worth the trouble, let him take the following steps, and at length, perhaps, he may come to reconcile himself to it.

(1) Let him settle with himself whether he would wish to discard this principle altogether; if so, let him consider what it is that all his reasonings (in matters of politics especially) can amount to?

(2) If he would, let him settle with himself whether he would judge and act without any principle, or whether there is any other he would judge and act by?

(3) If there be, let him examine and satisfy himself whether the principle he thinks he has found is really any separate intelligible principle; or whether it be not a mere principle in words, a kind of phrase, which at bottom expresses neither more nor less than the mere averment of his own unfounded sentiments—that is, what in another person he might be apt to call caprice?

(4) If he is inclined to think that his own approbation or disapprobation annexed to the idea of an act, without any regard to its consequences, is a sufficient foundation for him to judge and act upon, let him ask himself whether his sentiment is to be a standard of right and wrong with respect to every other man, or whether every man's sentiment has the same privilege of being a standard to itself?

(5) In the first case, let him ask himself whether his principle is not despotical, and hostile to all the rest of [the] human race.

(6) In the second case, whether it is not anarchial, and whether at this rate there are not as many different standards of right and wrong as there are men? and whether even to the same man, the same thing which is right today, may not (without the least change in its nature) be wrong tomorrow? and whether the same thing is not right and wrong in the same place at the same time? and in either case, whether all argument is not at an end? and whether, when two men have said, "I like this," and "I don't like it," they can (upon such a principle) have anything more to say?

(7) If he should have said to himself, No: for that the sentiment which he proposes as a standard must be grounded on reflection, let him say on what particulars the reflection is to turn? If on particulars having relation to the utility of the act, then let him say whether this is not

deserting his own principle, and borrowing assistance from that very one in opposition to which he sets it up; or if not on those particulars, on what other particulars?

(8) If he should be for compounding the matter, and adopting his own principle in part, and the principle of utility in part, let him say how far he will adopt it?

(9) When he has settled with himself where he will stop, then let him ask himself how he justifies to himself the adopting it so far? and why he will not adopt it any farther?

(10) Admitting any other principle than the principle of utility to be a right principle, a principle that it is right for a man to pursue; admitting (what is not true) that the word 'right' can have a meaning without reference to utility, let him say whether there is any such thing as a *motive* that a man can have to pursue the dictates of it: if there is, let him say what that motive is, and how it is to be distinguished from those which enforce the dictates of utility; if not, then lastly let him say what it is this other principle can be good for?

VALUE OF A LOT OF PLEASURE OR PAIN, HOW TO BE MEASURED

Pleasures then, and the avoidance of pains, are the *ends* which the legislator has in view: it behooves him therefore to understand their *value*. Pleasures and pains are the *instruments* he has to work with: it behooves him therefore to understand their force, which is again, in other words, their value.

ii. To a person considered *by himself,* the value of a pleasure or pain considered *by itself,* will be greater or less according to the four following circumstances:

1. Its *intensity.*
2. Its *duration.*
3. Its *certainty* or *uncertainty.*
4. Its *propinquity* or *remoteness.*

iii. These are the circumstances which are to be considered in estimating a pleasure or a pain considered each of them by itself. But when the value of any pleasure or pain is considered for the purpose of estimating the tendency of any *act* by which it is produced, there are two other circumstances to be taken into the account. These are:

5. Its *fecundity,* or the chance it has of being followed by sensations of the *same* kind: that is, pleasures, if it be a pleasure; pains, if it be a pain.
6. Its *purity,* or the chance it has of *not* being followed by sensations of the *opposite* kind: that is, pains, if it be a pleasure; pleasures, if it be a pain.

These two last, however, are in strictness scarcely to be deemed properties of the pleasure or the pain itself; they are not, therefore, in strictness to be taken into the account of the value of that pleasure or that pain. They are in strictness to be deemed properties only of the act, or other event, by which such pleasure or pain has been produced; and accordingly are only to be taken into the account of the tendency of such act or such event.

iv. To a *number* of persons, with reference to each of whom the value of a pleasure or a pain is considered, it will be greater or less, according to seven circumstances: to wit, the six preceding ones; viz.,

1. Its *intensity.*
2. Its *duration.*
3. Its *certainty* or *uncertainty.*
4. Its *propinquity* or *remoteness.*
5. Its *fecundity.*
6. Its *purity.*

And one other; to wit:

7. Its *extent*; that is, the number of persons to whom it *extends,* or (in other words) who are affected by it.

v. To take an exact account then of the general tendency of any act by which the interests of a community are affected, proceed as follows. Begin with any one person of those whose interests seem most immediately to be affected by it, and take an account:

1. Of the value of each distinguishable *pleasure* which appears to be produced by it in the *first* instance.
2. Of the value of each *pain* which appears to be produced by it in the *first* instance.
3. Of the value of each pleasure which appears to be produced by it *after* the first. This constitutes the *fecundity* of the first *pleasure* and the *impurity* of the first *pain.*
4. Of the value of each *pain* which appears to be produced by it after the first. This constitutes the *fecundity* of the first *pain,* and the *impurity* of the first *pleasure.*
5. Sum up all the values of all the *pleasures* on the one side, and those of all the pains on the other. The balance, if it be on the side of pleasure, will give the *good* tendency of the act upon the whole, with respect to the interests of that *individual* person; if on the side of pain, the *bad* tendency of it upon the whole.
6. Take an account of the *number* of persons whose interests appear to be concerned, and repeat the above process with respect to each. *Sum up* the numbers expressive of the degrees of *good* tendency which the act has, with respect to each individual in regard to whom the tendency of it is *good* upon the whole; do this again with respect to each

individual in regard to whom the tendency of it is *bad* upon the whole. Take the *balance*; which, if on the side of *pleasure,* will give the general *good tendency* of the act, with respect to the total number of community of individuals concerned; if on the side of pain, the general *evil tendency,* with respect to the same community.

vi. It is not to be expected that this process should be strictly pursued previously to every moral judgment, or to every legislative or judicial operation. It may, however, be always kept in view; and as near as the process actually pursued on these occasions approaches to it, so near will such process approach to the character of an exact one.

vii. The same process is alike applicable to pleasure and pain, in whatever shape they appear, and by whatever denomination they are distinguished: to pleasure, whether it be called *good* (which is properly the cause or instrument of pleasure), or *profit* (which is distant pleasure, or the cause or instrument of distant pleasure), or *convenience,* or *advantage, benefit, emolument, happiness,* and so forth; to pain, whether it be called *evil* (which corresponds to *good*), or *mischief,* or *inconvenience,* or *disadvantage,* or *loss,* or *unhappiness,* and so forth.

viii. Nor is this a novel and unwarranted, any more than it is a useless theory. In all this there is nothing but what the practice of mankind, wheresoever they have a clear view of their own interest, is perfectly conformable to. An article of property, an estate in land, for instance, is valuable, on what account? On account of the pleasures of all kinds which it enables a man to produce, and (what comes to the same thing) the pains of all kinds which it enables him to avert. But the value of such an article of property is universally understood to rise or fall according to the length or shortness of the time which a man has in it: the certainty or uncertainty of its coming into possession, and the nearness or remoteness of the time at which, if at all, it is to come into possession. As to the *intensity* of the pleasures which a man may derive from it, this is never thought of, because it depends upon the use which each particular person may come to make of it; which cannot be estimated till the particular pleasures he may come to derive from it, or the particular pains he may come to exclude by means of it, are brought to view. For the same reason, neither does he think of the *fecundity* or *purity* of those pleasures.

.   .   .

Erich Fromm
HUMANIZED CONSUMPTION

Erich Fromm, a prominent psychoanalyst and author of innumerable books, including The Sane Society *and* Escape from Freedom, *asks us to look at the way in which contemporary society has encouraged us to equate happiness with unbridled material consumption, and he suggests that it may be time to start distinguishing between those human needs that are life-furthering and those that are life-hindering. In effect, Fromm is asking whether there can be an objective rather than a merely subjective criterion for happiness. According to this view, people may feel happy and free without being either.*

.   .   .

The aim of the activation of man in the technological society requires another step as important and as difficult as replacement of the alienated bureaucratic structure by methods of humanist management. . . . I want to ask the reader to take the following proposals only as illustrations of desirable possibilities, not as definite aims and methods.

Up to the present, our industrial system has followed the principle that anything man wants or desires is to be accepted indiscriminately, and that if possible society should satisfy all of man's desires. We make a few exceptions to this principle, for instance, certain laws which restrict or even forbid the use of liquor regardless of a person's desire to drink as much as he likes; stronger ones against the taking of drugs, where even the possession of drugs like marijuana (the degree of whose harmfulness is still under debate) is penalized severely; we also restrict the sale and exhibition of so-called pornography. Furthermore, our laws forbid the sale of harmful food under the Food and Drug Act. In these areas, there is general consensus, crystallized in state and federal laws, that there are desires which are harmful to man and which should not be fulfilled in spite of the fact that a person craves the satisfaction of these desires. While one can argue that so-called pornography does not constitute a real threat and, furthermore, that the *hidden* lasciviousness of our adver-tisements are at least as effective in arousing sexual cupidity as straight pornography would be, the principle is recognized that there are limits to the freedom of the satisfaction of subjective desires. Yet these restric-tions are essentially based on only two principles: the concern for bodily harm, and the vestigial remnants of the Puritan morality. It is time we began to examine the whole problem of subjective needs and whether their *existence* is a sufficiently valid reason for their fulfillment; to question and examine the generally accepted principle of satisfying all needs—while never asking about their origins or effects.

In trying to find adequate solutions, we meet with two powerful obstacles. First, the interests of industry, whose imagination is fired by too many alienated men who cannot think of products which would help to make a human being more active rather than more passive. Besides this, industry knows that by advertising it can create needs and cravings which can be calculated in advance, so that there is little risk in losing profit if one continues the safe method of creating needs and selling the products which satisfy them.

The other difficulty lies in a certain concept of freedom which gains ever-increasing importance. The most important freedom in the nineteenth century was the freedom to use and invest property in any form which promised profit. Since managers of enterprises were at the same time the owners, their own acquisitive motivations made them emphasize this freedom of the use and investment of capital. In the middle of the twentieth century, most Americans do not own much property—even though there are a relatively large number of people who own large fortunes. The average American is employed and he is satisfied with relatively small savings, in cash, stocks, bonds, or life insurance. For him, the freedom of investment of capital is a relatively minor issue; and even for most people who are able to buy stocks, this is a form of gambling in which they are counseled by investment advisers or simply trust the mutual investment funds. But the real feeling of freedom today lies in another sphere, that of consumption. In this sphere, everybody except those who live a substandard existence experiences the *freedom of the consumer.*

Here is an individual who is powerless to have any influence— beyond a marginal one—on the affairs of the state or the enterprise in which he is employed. He has a boss, and his boss has a boss, and the boss of his boss has a boss, and there are very few individuals left who do not have a boss and do not obey the program of the managerial machine—of which they are a part. But what power does he have as a consumer? There are dozens of brands of cigarettes, toothpastes, soaps, deodorants, radios, television sets, movie and television programs, etc., etc. And they all woo his favor. They are all there "for his pleasure." He is free to favor the one against the other and he forgets that essentially there are no differences. This freedom to give his favors to his favorite commodity creates a sense of potency. The man who is impotent humanely becomes potent—as a buyer and consumer. Can one make any attempt to restrict this sense of potency by restricting the freedom of choice in consumption? It seems reasonable to assume one can do so only under one condition, and that is that the whole climate of society changes and permits man to be more active and interested in his individual and social affairs, and hence less in need of that fake freedom to be the king in the supermarket.[1]

The attempt to question the pattern of unlimited consumption meets with another difficulty. Compulsive consumption compensates for anxiety. . . . The need for this type of consumption stems from the sense of inner emptiness, hopelessness, confusion, and tension. By "taking in" articles of consumption, the individual reassures himself that "he is," as it were. If consumption were to be reduced, a good deal of anxiety would become manifest. The resistance against the possible arousal of anxiety would result in an unwillingness to reduce consumption.

---

[1]A similar feeling of power exists in the voter who can choose from among the several candidates who woo his favor, or in the film-star fan who senses his power because he can make or break his idol.

The most telling example of this mechanism is to be found in the public's attitude toward cigarette consumption. In spite of the well-known dangers to health, the majority go on consuming cigarettes. Is it because they would rather take a chance of earlier death than forgo the pleasure? An analysis of the attitude of smokers shows that this is largely a rationalization. Cigarette consumption allays hidden anxiety and tension, and people would rather risk their health than be confronted with their anxiety. Yet, once the quality of the process of living becomes more important than it is now, many people will stop smoking or overconsuming, not for the sake of their physical health but because only when they face their anxieties can they find ways to more productive living. (In passing—most urges for pleasure, if they are compulsive, including sex, are not caused by the wish for pleasure but by the wish for avoidance of anxiety.)

The problem of limits to consumption is so difficult to assess because, even in the affluent society of the United States, not all unquestionably legitimate needs are fulfilled. This holds true for at least 40 percent of the population. How can we even think of reduced consumption when the optimum consumption level has not been reached? The answer to this question must be guided by two considerations: first, that in the affluent sector we have already reached the point of harmful consumption; second, that the aim of ever-increasing consumption creates, even before the optimal consumption level is reached, an attitude of greed in which one wishes not only to have one's legitimate needs fulfilled but dreams of a never-ending increase in desires and satisfactions. In other words, the idea of the limitless rise of the production and consumption curve greatly contributes to the development of passivity and greed in the individual, even before peak consumption is reached.

In spite of these considerations, I believe that the transformation of our society into one which serves life must change the consumption and thereby change, indirectly, the production pattern of present industrial society. Such a change would obviously come not as a result of bureaucratic orders but of studies, information, discussion, and decision making on the part of the population, educated to become aware of the problem of the difference between life-furthering and life-hindering kinds of needs.

The first step in this direction would be studies which, to my knowledge, have never been seriously made, studies that would try to distinguish between these two kinds of needs. A group of psychologists, sociologists, economists, and representatives of the consuming public could undertake a study of those needs which are "humane," in the sense that they serve man's growth and joy, and those synthetic needs suggested by industry and its propaganda in order to find an outlet for profitable investment. As in so many other problems, the question is not so much the difficulty in determining the difference between these two types of needs and certain intermediate types but rather the raising of an extremely important question which can be brought up only if the social scientists begin to be concerned with man instead of the alleged smooth functioning of our society or their function as its apologists.

One general consideration may be introduced at this point concerning the concept of happiness. The term "happiness" has a long history, and this is not the place to go into the meaning of this concept from its derivation from Greek hedonism to its contemporary usage. It may suffice to say that what most people experience as happiness today is really a state of full satisfaction of their desires regardless of their quality; if it is conceived in this sense, it loses the important qualifications which Greek philosophy gave it, namely, that happiness is not a state of fulfillment of purely subjective needs but of those needs which have an objective validity in terms of the total existence of man and his potentialities. We would do better to think of joy and intense aliveness instead of happiness. The sensitive person, not only in an irrational society but also in the best of all societies, cannot help being deeply saddened by the inevitable tragedies of life. Both joy and sadness are unavoidable experiences for the sensitive and alive person. Happiness in its present meaning usually implies a superficial, contented state of satiation, rather than that condition accompanying the fullness of human experience; "happiness" may be said to be the alienated form of joy.

How can such a change in the consumption and production pattern occur? To begin with, it is feasible that many individuals experiment with changes in this consumption pattern. To some extent this has already been done in small groups. The point here is not asceticism or poverty, but life-affirming as against life-denying consumption. This distinction can be made only on the basis of awareness of what life is, what activeness is, what is stimulating, and what their opposites are. A dress, an object of art, a house may be in the one or in the other categories. The dress which follows the fashion presented by the profit interests of the dressmakers and their public relations staffs is quite different from the dress which is beautiful or attractive and the result of personal choice and taste. A number of dressmakers might choose to sell their products to women who prefer to wear what they like rather than what is forced upon them. The same holds true of art objects, and all kinds of aesthetic enjoyment. If they lose their function as either status symbols or capital investments, the sense for the beautiful will have a chance for a new development. The unnecessary, or merely laziness-promoting, would be out. The private automobile, if it became a useful vehicle for transportation and not a status symbol, would change in significance. Certainly there would be no reason to buy a new car every two years, and industry would find itself forced to make some drastic changes in production. To put it in a nutshell: up to now the consumer has permitted and even invited industry to brainwash or control him. The consumer has a chance of becoming aware of his power over industry by turning around and forcing industry to produce what he wants or suffer considerable losses by producing what he rejects. The *revolution of the consumer* against the domination by industry has yet to come. It is perfectly feasible and its consequences far-reaching, unless industry takes control of the state and enforces its right to manipulate the consumer.

•   •   •

CARL ROGERS
ON BECOMING A PERSON

Carl Rogers is a well-known practicing psychotherapist who has made major contributions to the theory and practice of client-centered psychotherapy. In the following essay, he offers an account of the good life that focuses on the openness of the human being who freely explores his or her world. For Rogers, living the good life is a matter of adopting a certain kind of attitude toward experience.

My views regarding the meaning of the good life are largely based upon my experience in working with people in the very close and intimate relationship which is called psychotherapy. These views thus have an empirical or experiential foundation, as contrasted perhaps with a scholarly or philosophical foundation. I have learned what the good life seems to be by observing and participating in the struggle of disturbed and troubled people to achieve that life.

I should make it clear from the outset that this experience I have gained comes from the vantage point of a particular orientation to psychotherapy which has developed over the years. Quite possibly all psychotherapy is basically similar, but since I am less sure of that than I once was, I wish to make it clear that my therapeutic experience has been along the lines that seem to me most effective, the type of therapy termed "client-centered."

Let me attempt to give a very brief description of what this therapy would be like if it were in every respect optimal, since I feel I have learned most about the good life from therapeutic experiences in which a great deal of movement occurred. If the therapy were optimal, intensive as well as extensive, then it would mean that the therapist has been able to enter into an intensely personal and subjective relationship with the client— relating not as a scientist to an object of study, not as a physician expecting to diagnose and cure, but as a person to a person. It would mean that the therapist feels this client to be a person of unconditional self-worth: of value no matter what his condition, his behavior, or his feelings. It would mean that the therapist is genuine, hiding behind no defensive façade, but meeting the client with the feelings which organically he is experiencing. It would mean that the therapist is able to let himself go in understanding this client; that no inner barriers keep him from sensing what it feels like to be the client at each moment of the relationship; and that he can convey something of his empathic understanding to the client. It means that the therapist has been comfortable in entering this relationship fully, without knowing cognitively where it will lead, satisfied with providing a climate which will permit the client the utmost freedom to become himself.

For the client, this optimal therapy would mean an exploration of increasingly strange and unknown and dangerous feelings in himself, the exploration proving possible only because he is gradually realizing that he is accepted unconditionally. Thus he becomes acquainted with elements of his experience which have in the past been denied to awareness as too threatening, too damaging to the structure of the self. He finds himself experiencing these feelings fully, completely, in the relationship, so that for the moment he *is* his fear, or his anger, or his tenderness, or his strength. And as he lives these widely varied feelings, in all their degrees of intensity, he discovers that he has experienced *himself,* that he *is* all these feelings. He finds his behavior changing in constructive fashion in accordance with his newly experienced self. He approaches the realization that he no longer needs to fear what experience may hold, but can welcome it freely as a part of his changing and developing self.

This is a thumbnail sketch of what client-centered therapy comes close to, when it is at its optimum. I give it here simply as a brief picture of the context in which I have found my views of the good life.

A Negative Observation

As I have tried to live understandingly in the experiences of my clients, I have gradually come to one negative conclusion about the good life. It seems to me that the good life is not any fixed state. It is not, in my estimation, a state of virtue, or contentment, or nirvana, or happiness. It is not a condition in which the individual is adjusted, or fulfilled, or actualized. To use psychological terms, it is not a state of drive-reduction, or tension-reduction, or homeostasis.

I believe that all of these terms have been used in ways which imply that if one or several of these states is achieved, then the goal of life has been achieved. Certainly, for many people happiness, or adjustment, are seen as states of being which are synonymous with the good life. And social scientists have frequently spoken of the reduction of tension, or the achievement of homeostasis or equilibrium as if these states constituted the goal of the process of living.

So it is with a certain amount of surprise and concern that I realize that my experience supports none of these definitions. If I focus on the experience of those individuals who seem to have evidenced the greatest degree of movement during the therapeutic relationship, and who, in the years following this relationship, appear to have made and to be making real progress toward the good life, then it seems to me that they are not adequately described at all by any of these terms which refer to fixed states of being. I believe they would consider themselves insulted if they were described as "adjusted," and they would regard it as false if they were described as "happy" or "contented," or even "actualized." As I have known them I would regard it as most inaccurate to say that all their drive tensions have been reduced, or that they are in a state of homeostasis. So I am forced to ask myself whether there is any way in which I can generalize about their situation, any definition which I can give of the good life which would seem to fit the facts as I have observed them. I find this not at all easy, and what follows is stated very tentatively.

A Positive Observation

If I attempt to capture in a few words what seems to me to be true of these people, I believe it will come out something like this:

The good life is a *process,* not a state of being.

It is a direction, not a destination.

The direction which constitutes the good life is that which is selected by the total organism, when there is psychological freedom to move in *any* direction.

This organismically selected direction seems to have certain discernible general qualities which appear to be the same in a wide variety of unique individuals.

So I can integrate these statements into a definition which can at least serve as a basis for consideration and discussion. The good life, from the point of view of my experience, is the process of movement in a direction which the human organism selects when it is inwardly free to move in any direction, and the general qualities of this selected direction appear to have a certain universality.

THE CHARACTERISTICS OF THE PROCESS

Let me now try to specify what appear to be the characteristic qualities of this process of movement, as they crop up in person after person in therapy.

An Increasing Openness to Experience

In the first place, the process seems to involve an increasing openness to experience. This phrase has come to have more and more meaning for me. It is the polar opposite of defensiveness. Defensiveness I have described in the past as being the organism's response to experiences which are perceived or anticipated as threatening, as incongruent with the individual's existing picture of himself, or of himself in relationship to the world. These threatening experiences are temporarily rendered harmless by being distorted in awareness, or being denied to awareness. I quite literally cannot see, with accuracy, those experiences, feelings, reactions in myself which are significantly at variance with the picture of myself which I already possess. A large part of the process of therapy is the continuing discovery by the client that he is experiencing feelings and attitudes which heretofore he has not been able to be aware of, which he has not been able to "own" as being a part of himself.

If a person could be fully open to his experience, however, every stimulus—whether originating within the organism or in the environment—would be freely relayed through the nervous system without being distorted by any defensive mechanism. There would be no need of the mechanism of "subception" whereby the organism is forewarned of any experience threatening to the self. On the contrary, whether the stimulus was the impact of a configuration of form, color, or sound in the environment on the sensory nerves, or a memory trace from the past, or a visceral sensation of fear or pleasure or disgust, the person would be "living" it, would have it completely available to awareness.

Thus, one aspect of this process which I am naming "the good life" appears to be a movement away from the pole of defensiveness toward the pole of openness to experience. The individual is becoming more able to listen to himself, to experience what is going on within himself. He is more open to his feelings of fear and discouragement and pain. He is also more open to his feelings of courage, and tenderness, and awe. He is free to live his feelings subjectively, as they exist in him, and also free to be aware of these feelings. He is more able fully to live the experiences of his organism rather than shutting them out of awareness.

Increasingly Existential Living

A second characteristic of the process which for me is the good life, is that it involves an increasing tendency to live fully in each moment. This is a thought which can easily be misunderstood, and which is perhaps somewhat vague in my own thinking. Let me try to explain what I mean.

I believe it would be evident that for the person who was fully open to his new experience, completely without defensiveness, each moment would be new. The complex configuration of inner and outer stimuli which exists in this moment has never existed before in just this fashion. Consequently such a person would realize that "What I will be in the next moment, and what I will do, grows out of that moment, and cannot be predicted in advance either by me or by others." Not infrequently we find clients expressing exactly this sort of feeling.

One way of expressing the fluidity which is present in such existential living is to say that the self and personality emerge *from* experience, rather than experience being translated or twisted to fit preconceived self-structure. It means that one becomes a participant in and an observer of the ongoing process of organismic experience, rather than being in control of it.

Such living in the moment means an absence of rigidity, of tight organization, of the imposition of structure on experience. It means instead a maximum of adaptability, a discovery of structure *in* experience, a flowing, changing organization of self and personality.

It is this tendency toward existential living which appears to me very evident in people who are involved in the process of the good life. One might almost say that it is the most essential quality of it. It involves discovering the structure of experience in the process of living the experience. Most of us, on the other hand, bring a preformed structure and evaluation to our experience and never relinquish it, but cram and twist the experience to fit our preconceptions, annoyed at the fluid qualities which make it so unruly in fitting our carefully constructed pigeonholes. To open one's spirit to what is going on *now*, and to discover in that present process whatever structure it appears to have—this to me is one of the qualities of the good life, the mature life, as I see clients approach it.

An Increasing Trust in His Organism

Still another characteristic of the person who is living the process of the good life appears to be an increasing trust in his organism as a means of arriving at the most satisfying behavior in each existential situation. Again let me try to explain what I mean.

In choosing what course of action to take in any situation, many people rely upon guiding principles, upon a code of action laid down by some group or institution, upon the judgment of others (from wife and friends to Emily Post), or upon the way they have behaved in some similar past situation. Yet as I observe the clients whose experiences in living have taught me so much, I find that increasingly such individuals are able to trust their total organismic reaction to a new situation because they discover to an ever-increasing degree that if they are open to their experience, doing what "feels right" proves to be a competent and trustworthy guide to behavior which is truly satisfying.

As I try to understand the reason for this, I find myself following this line of thought. The person who is fully open to his experience would have access to all of the available data in the situation, on which to base his behavior; the social demands, his own complex and possibly conflicting needs, his memories of similar situations, his perception of the uniqueness of this situation, etc., etc. The data would be very complex indeed. But he could permit his total organism, his consciousness participating, to consider each stimulus, need, and demand, its relative intensity and importance, and out of this complex weighing and balancing, discover that course of action which would come closest to satisfying all his needs in the situation. An analogy which might come close to a description would be to compare this person to a giant electronic computing machine. Since he is open to his experience, all of the data from his sense impressions, from his memory, from previous learning, from his visceral and internal states, is fed into the machine. The machine takes all of these multitudinous pulls and forces which are fed in as data, and quickly computes the course of action which would be the most economical vector of need satisfaction in this existential situation. This is the behavior of our hypothetical person.

The defects which in most of us make this process untrustworthy are the inclusion of information which does *not* belong to this present situation, or the exclusion of information which *does*. It is when memories and previous learnings are fed into the computations as if they were *this* reality, and not memories and learnings, that erroneous behavioral answers arise. Or when certain threatening experiences are inhibited from awareness, and hence are withheld from the computation or fed into it in distorted form, this too produces error. But our hypothetical person would find his organism thoroughly trustworthy, because all of the available data would be used, and it would be present in accurate rather than distorted form. Hence his behavior would come as close as possible to satisfying all his needs—for enhancement, for affiliation with others, and the like.

In this weighing, balancing, and computation, his organism would not by any means be infallible. It would always give the best possible answer for the available data, but sometimes data would be missing. Because of the element of openness to experience, however, any errors, any following of behavior which was not satisfying, would be quickly corrected. The computations, as it were, would always be in process of being corrected, because they would be continually checked in behavior.

Perhaps you will not like my analogy of an electronic computing machine. Let me return to the clients I know. As they become more open to all of their experiences, they find it increasingly possible to trust their reactions. If they "feel like" expressing anger they do so and find that this comes out satisfactorily, because they are equally alive to all of their other desires for affection, affiliation, and relationship. They are surprised at their own intuitive skill in finding behavioral solutions to complex and troubling human relationships. It is only afterward that they realize how surprisingly trustworthy their inner reactions have been in bringing about satisfactory behavior.

The Process of Functioning More Fully

I should like to draw together these three threads describing the process of the good life into a more coherent picture. It appears that the person who is psychologically free moves in the direction of becoming a more fully functioning person. He is more able to live fully in and with each and all of his feelings and reactions. He makes increasing use of all his organic equipment to sense, as accurately as possible, the existential situation within and without. He makes use of all of the information his nervous system can thus supply, using it in awareness, but recognizing that his total organism may be, and often is, wiser than his awareness. He is more able to permit his total organism to function freely in all its complexity in selecting, from the multitude of possibilities, that behavior which in this moment of time will be most generally and genuinely satisfying. He is able to put more trust in his organism in this functioning, not because it is infallible, but because he can be fully open to the consequences of each of his actions and correct them if they prove to be less than satisfying.

He is more able to experience all of his feelings, and is less afraid of any of his feelings; he is his own sifter of evidence, and is more open to evidence from all sources; he is completely engaged in the process of being and becoming himself, and thus discovers that he is soundly and realistically social; he lives more completely in this moment, but learns that this is the soundest living for all time. He is becoming a more fully functioning organism, and because of the awareness of himself which flows freely in and through his experience, he is becoming a more fully functioning person.

SOME IMPLICATIONS

Any view of what constitutes the good life carries with it many implications, and the view I have presented is no exception. I hope that these implications may be food for thought. There are two or three of these about which I would like to comment.

A New Perspective on Freedom vs. Determinism

The first of these implications may not immediately be evident. It has to do with the age-old issue of "free will." Let me endeavor to spell out the way in which this issue now appears to me in a new light.

For some time I have been perplexed over the living paradox which exists in psychotherapy between freedom and determinism. In the therapeutic relationship some of the most compelling subjective experiences are those in which the client feels within himself the power of naked choice. He is *free*—to become himself or to hide behind a façade; to move forward or to retrogress; to behave in ways which are destructive of self and others, or in ways which are enhancing; quite literally free to live or die, in both the physiological and psychological meaning of those terms. Yet as we enter this field of psychotherapy with objective research methods, we are, like any other scientist, committed to a complete determinism. From this point of view every thought, feeling, and action of the client is determined by what preceded it. There can be no such thing as freedom. The dilemma I am trying to describe is no different than that found in other fields—it is simply brought to sharper focus, and appears more insoluble.

This dilemma can be seen in a fresh perspective, however, when we consider it in terms of the definition I have given of the fully functioning person. We could say that in the optimum of therapy the person rightfully experiences the most complete and absolute freedom. He wills or chooses to follow the course of action which is the most economical vector in relationship to all the internal and external stimuli, because it is that behavior which will be most deeply satisfying. But this is the same course of action which from another vantage point may be said to be determined by all the factors in the existential situation. Let us contrast this with the picture of the person who is defensively organized. He wills or chooses to follow a given course of action, but finds that he *cannot* behave in the fashion that he chooses. He is determined by the factors in the existential situation, but these factors include his defensiveness, his denial or distortion of some of the relevant data. Hence it is certain that his behavior will be less than fully satisfying. His behavior is determined, but he is not free to make an effective choice. The fully functioning person, on the other hand, not only experiences, but utilizes, the most absolute freedom when he spontaneously, freely, and voluntarily chooses and wills that which is also absolutely determined.

I am not so naive as to suppose that this fully resolves the issue between subjective and objective, between freedom and necessity. Nevertheless it has meaning for me that the more the person is living the good life, the more he will experience a freedom of choice, and the more his choices will be effectively implemented in his behavior.

Creativity as an Element of the Good Life

I believe it will be clear that a person who is involved in the directional process which I have termed "the good life" is a creative person. With his sensitive openness to his world, his trust of his own ability to form new relationships with his environment, he would be the type of person from whom creative products and creative living emerge. He would not necessarily be "adjusted" to his culture, and he would almost certainly not be a conformist. But at any time and in any culture he would live constructively, in as much harmony with his culture as a balanced satisfaction of needs demanded. In some cultural situations he might in some ways be very unhappy, but he would continue to move toward becoming himself, and to behave in such a way as to provide the maximum satisfaction of his deepest needs.

Such a person would, I believe, be recognized by the student of evolution as the type most likely to adapt and survive under changing environmental conditions. He would be able creatively to make sound adjustments to new as well as old conditions. He would be a fit vanguard of human evolution.

Basic Trustworthiness of Human Nature

It will be evident that another implication of the view I have been presenting is that the basic nature of the human being, when functioning freely, is constructive and trustworthy. For me this is an inescapable conclusion from a quarter-century of experience in psychotherapy. When we are able to free the individual from defensiveness, so that he is open to the wide range of his own needs, as well as the wide range of environmental and social demands, his reactions may be trusted to be positive, forward-moving, constructive. We do not need to ask who will socialize him, for one of his own deepest needs is for affiliation and communication with others. As he becomes more fully himself, he will become more realistically socialized. We do not need to ask who will control his aggressive impulses; for as he becomes more open to all of his impulses, his need to be liked by others and his tendency to give affection will be as strong as his impulses to strike out or to seize for himself. He will be aggressive in situations in which aggression is realistically appropriate, but there will be no runaway need for aggression. His total behavior, in these and other areas, as he moves toward being open to all his experience, will be more balanced and realistic, behavior which is appropriate to the survival and enhancement of a highly social animal.

I have little sympathy with the rather prevalent concept that man is basically irrational, and that his impulses, if not controlled, will lead to destruction of others and self. Man's behavior is exquisitely rational, moving with subtle and ordered complexity toward the goals his organism is endeavoring to achieve. The tragedy for most of us is that our defenses keep us from being aware of this rationality, so that consciously we are moving in one direction, while organismically we are moving in another. But in our person who is living the process of the good life, there would be a decreasing number of such barriers, and he would be increasingly a participant in the rationality of his organism. The only control of impulses which would exist, or which would prove necessary, is the natural and internal balancing of one need against another, and the discovery of behaviors which follow the vector most closely approximating the satisfaction of all needs. The experience of extreme satisfaction of one need (for aggression, or sex, etc.) in such a way as to do violence to the satisfaction of other needs (for companionship, tender relationship, etc.) —an experience very common in the defensively organized person— would be greatly decreased. He would participate in the vastly complex self-regulatory activities of his organism—the psychological as well as physiological thermostatic controls—in such a fashion as to live in increasing harmony with himself and with others.

The Greater Richness of Life

One last implication I should like to mention is that this process of living in the good life involves a wider range, a greater richness, than the constricted living in which most of us find ourselves. To be a part of this process means that one is involved in the frequently frightening and frequently satisfying experience of a more sensitive living, with greater range, greater variety, greater richness. It seems to me that clients who have moved significantly in therapy live more intimately with their feelings of pain, but also more vividly with their feelings of ecstasy; that anger is more clearly felt, but so also is love; that fear is an experience they know more deeply, but so is courage. And the reason they can thus live fully in a wider range is that they have this underlying confidence in themselves as trustworthy instruments for encountering life.

I believe it will have become evident why, for me, adjectives such as happy, contented, blissful, enjoyable, do not seem quite appropriate to any general description of this process I have called the good life, even though the person in this process would experience each one of these feelings at appropriate times. But the adjectives which seem more generally fitting are adjectives such as enriching, exciting, rewarding, challenging, meaningful. This process of the good life is not, I am convinced, a life for the faint-hearted. It involves the stretching and growing of becoming more and more of one's potentialities. It involves the courage to be. It means launching oneself fully into the stream of life. Yet the deeply exciting thing about human beings is that when the individual is inwardly free, he chooses as the good life this process of becoming.

SECTION FIVE

THE RELIGIOUS LIFE

Before Galileo looked through his telescope, few people doubted that the earth was at the center of the universe—placed there by a powerful and loving God who arranged all things to further the existence of the human race. Explanations took the form of teleological accounts, accounts that explained natural phenomena in terms of the ends they accomplished for human life; thus, the question "Why does rain fall?" required no explanation in terms of antecedent conditions; it was transparently clear that "Rain falls to nourish our crops." Suddenly all that changed. The earth was found to be one of a number of planets revolving around the sun, and for this and other reasons, God's unquestioned presence and efficacy were cast into doubt. It was at this point that considerable attention began to be focused on attempts to prove the existence of God and on attempts to challenge that existence. In the section that follows, we shall consider a number of different approaches to the question of God's existence, and we shall examine ways in which human beings have attempted to make their experience of reality more meaningful and/or less frightening.

In a consideration of the attempts to prove God's existence, it may be helpful to keep in mind that it is only when a generally held system of beliefs breaks down that people feel the need to justify it. For example, the Bible does not attempt to prove the existence of God—it assumes it. The world of experience is interpreted through religious categories. The rose and the thorn are God's handiwork. Love is the spirit of God within us. At one time, to question those categories meant to question experience itself.

But contemporary human beings see through the categories of science. Thus, a chair is not merely a chair, but a bundle of atoms; water not merely water, but H_2O. Science brings us an understanding of natural phenomena in causal terms and reveals regularities within nature. The world becomes intelligible through science, and there is less of a need to posit the existence of an omnipotent being in order to make our experience understandable.

232

A. C. Ewing
PROOFS OF GOD'S EXISTENCE

In the following selection, A. C. Ewing considers several major forms of proof of God's existence. Although unconvinced by the ontological proof, Ewing finds some merit in the argument from first cause (the cosmological argument) and is most persuaded by the teleological argument. Like many of us, Ewing seeks a comprehensive understanding of the nature of the universe as we experience it; he claims that God's existence is a satisfying way to develop such an understanding. A question that might well be asked of Ewing is whether we really offer any more of an explanation of the universe when we say "God caused it to be as it is" than if we say "Science can explain all natural phenomena" or even "I don't know what caused it."

. . . By "God" I shall understand in this chapter a supreme mind regarded as either omnipotent or at least more powerful than anything else and supremely good and wise. It is not within the scope of a purely philosophical work to discuss the claims of revelation on which belief in God and his attributes has so often been based, but philosophers have also formulated a great number of *arguments* for the existence of God.

THE ONTOLOGICAL ARGUMENT

To start with the most dubious and least valuable of these, the *ontological* argument claims to prove the existence of God by a mere consideration of our idea of him. God is defined as the most perfect being or as a being containing all positive attributes.[1] It is then argued that existence is a "perfection" or a positive attribute, and that therefore, if we are to avoid contradicting ourselves, we must grant the existence of God. The most important of the objections to the argument is to the effect that existence is not a "perfection" or an attribute. To say that something exists is to assert a proposition of a very different kind from what we assert when we ascribe any ordinary attribute to a thing. It is not to increase the concept of the thing by adding a new characteristic, but merely to affirm that the concept is realized in fact. This is one of the cases where we are apt to be misled by language. Because "cats exist" and "cats sleep," or "cats are existent" and "cats are carnivorous," are sentences of the same grammatical form, people are liable to suppose that they also express the same form of proposition, but this is not the case. To say that cats are carnivorous is to ascribe an additional quality to beings already presupposed as

---

[1]"Positive" (1) enables us to exclude evil attributes on the ground that they are negative, (2) implies the infinity of God, for there would be an element of negativity in him if he possessed any attribute in any limited degree, i. e. superior degrees would be denied of him.

existing; to say that cats are existent is to say that propositions ascribing to something the properties which constitute the definition of a cat are sometimes true. The distinction is still more obvious in the negative case. If "dragons are not existent animals" were a proposition of the same form as "lions are not herbivorous animals," to say that dragons are not existent would already be to presuppose their existence. A lion has to exist in order to have the negative property of not being herbivorous, but in order to be non-existent a dragon need not first exist.[2] "Dragons are non-existent" means that nothing has the properties commonly implied by the word "dragon."

It has sometimes been said that "the ontological proof" is just an imperfect formulation of a principle which no one can help admitting and which is a necessary presupposition of all knowledge. This is the principle that what we really must think must be true of reality. ("Must" here is the logical, not the psychological must.) If we did not assume this principle, we should never be entitled to accept something as a fact because it satisfied our best intellectual criteria, and therefore we should have no ground for asserting anything at all. Even experience would not help us, since any proposition contradicting experience might well be true if the law of contradiction were not assumed to be objectively valid. This, however, is so very different from what the ontological proof as formulated by its older exponents says that it should not be called by the same name. And in any case the principle that what we must think must be true of reality could only be used to establish the existence of God if we already had reached the conclusion that we must think this, i. e. had already justified the view that God exists (or seen it to be self-evident).

THE FIRST CAUSE ARGUMENT

The *cosmological* or first cause argument is of greater importance. The greatest thinker of the Middle Ages, St. Thomas Aquinas (*circa* 1225–74), while rejecting the ontological argument, made the cosmological the main intellectual basis of his own theism, and in this respect he has been followed by Roman Catholic orthodoxy. To this day it is often regarded in such circles as proving with mathematical certainty the existence of God. It has, however, also played a very large part in Protestant thought; and an argument accepted in different forms by such varied philosophers of the highest eminence as Aristotle, St. Thomas, Descartes, Locke, Leibniz, and many modern thinkers certainly ought not to be despised. The argument is briefly to the effect that we require a reason to account for the world and this ultimate reason must be of such a kind as itself not to require a further reason to account for it. It is then argued that God is

[2]We can of course say that dragons are not herbivorous if we are merely making a statement about the content of fictitious stories of dragons.

the only kind of being who could be conceived as self-sufficient and so as not requiring a cause beyond himself but being his own reason. The argument has an appeal because we are inclined to demand a reason for things, and the notion of a first cause is the only alternative to the notion of an infinite regress, which is very difficult and seems even self-contradictory. Further, if any being is to be conceived as necessarily existing and so not needing a cause outside itself, it is most plausible to conceive God as occupying this position. But the argument certainly makes assumptions which may be questioned. It assumes the principle of causation in a form in which the cause is held to give a reason for the effect, a doctrine with which I have sympathy but which would probably be rejected by the majority of modern philosophers outside the Roman Catholic Church. Further, it may be doubted whether we can apply to the world as a whole the causal principle which is valid within the world; and if we say that the causal principle thus applied is only analogous to the latter the argument is weakened. Finally, and this I think the most serious point, it is exceedingly difficult to see how anything could be its own reason. To be this it would seem that it must exist necessarily *a priori*. Now we can well see how it can be necessary *a priori* that something, p, should be true if something else, q, is, or again how it can be necessary *a priori* that something self-contradictory should not exist, but it is quite another matter to see how it could be *a priori* necessary in the logical sense that something should positively exist. What contradiction could there be in its not existing?[3] In the mere blank of non-existence there can be nothing to contradict. I do not say that it can be seen to be absolutely impossible that a being could be its own logical reason, but I at least have not the faintest notion how this could be. The advocates of the cosmological proof might, however, contend that God was necessary in some non-logical sense, which is somewhat less unplausible though still quite incomprehensible to us.

Can the cosmological argument, clearly invalid as a complete proof, be stated in a form which retains some probability value? It may still be argued that the world will at least be more rational if it is as the theist pictures it than if it is not, and that it is more reasonable to suppose that the world is rational than to suppose that it is irrational. Even the latter point would be contradicted by many modern thinkers, but though we cannot prove the view they reject to be true, we should at least note that it is the view which is presupposed by science, often unconsciously, in its own sphere. For . . . practically no scientific propositions can be established by strict demonstration and/or observation alone. Science could not advance at all if it did not assume some criterion beyond experience and the laws of logic and mathematics. What is this criterion? It seems to be coherence in a rational system. We have rejected the view that this is the only criterion, but it is certainly one criterion of truth. For of two

---

[3]It is one of the objections to the ontological proof that it claims to find a contradiction in God not existing.

hypotheses equally in accord with the empirical facts, scientists will always prefer the one which makes the unvierse more of a rational system to the one which does not. Science does this even though neither hypothesis is capable of rationalizing the universe completely or even of giving a complete ultimate explanation of the phenomena in question. It is sufficient that the hypothesis adopted brings us a step nearer to the ideal of a fully coherent, rationally explicable world. Now theism cannot indeed completely rationalize the universe till it can show how God can be his own cause, or how it is that he does not need a cause, and till it can also overcome the problem of evil completely, but it does come nearer to rationalizing it than does any other view. The usual modern philosophical views opposed to theism do not try to give any rational explanation of the world at all, but just take it as a brute fact not to be explained, and it must certainly be admitted that we come at least nearer to a rational explanation if we regard the course of the world as determined by purpose and value than if we do not. So it may be argued that according to the scientific principle that we should accept the hypothesis which brings the universe nearest to a coherent rational system theism should be accepted by us. The strong point of the cosmological argument is that after all it does remain incredible that the physical universe should just have happened, even if it be reduced to the juxtaposition of some trillions of electrons. It calls out for some further explanation of some kind.

THE ARGUMENT FROM DESIGN

The *teleological argument* or the *argument from design* is the argument from the adaptation of the living bodies of organisms to their ends and the ends of their species. This is certainly very wonderful: there are thousands of millions of cells in our brain knit together in a system which works; twenty or thirty different muscles are involved even in such a simple act as a squeeze; directly a wound is inflicted or germs enter an animal's body all sorts of protective mechanisms are set up, different cells are so cunningly arranged that, if we cut off the tail of one of the lower animals, a new one is grown, and the very same cells can develop according to what is needed into a tail or into a leg. Such intricate arrangements seem to require an intelligent purposing mind to explain them. It may be objected that, even if such an argument shows wisdom in God, it does not show goodness and is therefore of little value. The reply may be made that it is incredible that a mind who is so much superior to us in intelligence as to have designed the whole universe should not be at least as good as the best men and should not, to put it at its lowest, care for his offspring at least as well as a decent human father and much more wisely because of his superior knowledge and intellect. Still it must be admitted that the argument could not at its best establish all that the theist would ordinarily wish to establish. It might show that the designer was very powerful, but it could not show him to be omnipotent or even to have created the world as opposed to manufacturing it out of given material; it might make it probable that he was as good, but it could not possibly prove him perfect. And of course the more unpleasant features of the struggle for existence in nature are far from supporting the hypothesis of a good God.

But does the argument justify any conclusion at all? It has been objected that it does not on the following ground. It is an argument from analogy, it is said, to this effect: animal bodies are like machines, a machine has a designer, therefore animal bodies have a designer. But the strength of an argument from analogy depends on the likeness between what is compared. Now animal bodies are really not very like machines, and God is certainly not very like a man. Therefore the argument from analogy based on our experience of men designing machines has not enough strength to give much probability to its conclusion. This criticism, I think, would be valid if the argument from design were really in the main an argument from analogy, but I do not think it is. The force of the argument lies not in the analogy, but in the extraordinary intricacy with which the details of a living body are adapted to serve its own interests, an intricacy far too great to be regarded as merely a coincidence. Suppose we saw pebbles on the shore arranged in such a way as to make an elaborate machine. It is theoretically possible that they might have come to occupy such positions by mere chance, but it is fantastically unlikely, and we should feel no hesitation in jumping to the conclusion that they had been thus deposited not by the tide but by some intelligent agent. Yet the body of the simplest living creature is a more complex machine than the most complex ever devised by a human engineer.

Before the theory of evolution was accepted the only reply to this argument was to say that in an infinite time there is room for an infinite number of possible combinations, and therefore it is not, even apart from a designing mind, improbable that there should be worlds or stages in the development of worlds which display great apparent purposiveness. If a monkey played with a typewriter at random, it is most unlikely that it would produce an intelligible book; but granted a sufficient number of billions of years to live and keep playing, the creature would probably eventually produce quite by accident a great number. For the number of possible combinations of twenty-six letters in successions of words is finite, though enormously large, and therefore given a sufficiently long time it is actually probable that any particular one would be reached. This may easily be applied to the occurrence of adaptations in nature. Out of all the possible combinations of things very few would display marked adaptation; but if the number of ingredients of the universe is finite the number of their combinations is also finite, and therefore it is only probable that, given an infinite time, some worlds or some stages in a world process should appear highly purposeful, though they are only the result of a chance combination of atoms. The plausibility of this reply is diminished when we reflect what our attitude would be to somebody who, when playing bridge, had thirteen spades in his hand several times running—according to the laws of probability an enormously less improbable coincidence than would be an unpurposed universe with so much design unaccounted for—and then used such an argument to meet the charge of cheating. Our attitude to his reply would surely hardly be changed even if we believed that people had been playing bridge for an infinite time. If only we were satisfied that matter had existed and gone on changing for ever, would we conclude that the existence of leaves or pebbles on the ground in such positions as to make an intelligible book no longer provided evidence making it probable that somebody had deliberately arranged them? Surely not. And, if not, why should the supposition that matter had gone on changing for ever really upset the argument from design? Of course the appearance of design *may be* fortuitous; the argument from design never claims to give certainty but only probability. But, granted the universe as we have it, is it not a much less improbable hypothesis that it should really have been designed than that it should constitute one of the fantastically rare stages which showed design in an infinite series of chance universes? Further, that matter has been changing for an infinite time is a gratuitous assumption and one not favoured by modern science.[4]

But now the theory of evolution claims to give an alternative explanation of the adaptation of organisms that removes the improbability of which we have complained. Once granted the existence of some organisms their offspring would not all be exactly similar. Some would necessarily be somewhat better equipped than others for surviving and producing offspring in their turn, and their characteristics would therefore tend to be more widely transmitted. When we take vast numbers into account, this will mean that a larger and larger proportion of the species will have had relatively favourable variations transmitted to them by their parents, while unfavourable variations will tend to die out. Thus from small beginnings accumulated all the extraordinarily elaborate mechanism which now serves the purpose of living creatures.

There can be no question for a properly informed person of denying the evolution theory, but only of considering whether it is adequate by itself to explain the striking appearance of design. If it is not, it may perfectly well be combined with the metaphysical hypothesis that a mind has designed and controls the universe. Evolution will then be just the way in which God's design works out. Now in reply to the purely evolutionary explanation it has been said that for evolution to get started at

[4]Strictly speaking, what is required by those who put forward the objection in question to the argument from design is not necessarily that matter should have been changing for an infinite time but only for a sufficiently long, though finite, time. But the length of time allowed by modern science for the development of the earth and indeed for that of the whole universe does not in the faintest degree approach what would be needed to make the appearance of organized beings as a result of mere random combinations of atoms anything less than monstrously improbable.

all some organisms must have already appeared. Otherwise the production of offspring and their survival or death in the struggle for existence would not have come into question at all. But even the simplest living organism is a machine very much more complex than a motor car. Therefore, if it would be absurd to suppose inorganic matter coming together fortuitously of itself to form a motor car, it would be even more absurd to suppose it thus coming together to form an organism, so without design the evolutionary process would never get started at all. Nor, even granting that this miracle had occurred, could the evolutionists claim that they had been altogether successful in removing the antecedent improbability of such an extensive adaptation as is in fact shown by experience. It has been urged that, since we may go wrong in a vast number of ways for one in which we may go right, the probability of favourable variations is very much less than that of unfavourable; that in order to produce the effect on survival required a variation would have to be large, but if it were large it would usually lessen rather than increase the chance of survival, unless balanced by other variations the occurrence of which simultaneously with the first would be much more improbable still; and that the odds are very great against either a large number of animals in a species having the variations together by chance or their spreading from a single animal through the species by natural selection. The arguments suggest that, so to speak, to weight the chances we require a purpose, which we should not need, however, to think of as intervening at odd moments but as controlling the whole process. The establishment of the evolution theory no doubt lessens the great improbability of the adaptations having occurred without this, but the original improbability is so vast as to be able to survive a great deal of lessening, and it does not remove it.

Some thinkers would regard it as adequate to postulate an unconscious purpose to explain design, but it is extraordinarily difficult to see what such a thing as an unconscious purpose could be. In one sense indeed I can understand such a phrase. "Unconscious" might mean "unintrospected" or "unintrospectible," and then the purpose would be one which occurred in a mind that did think on the matter but did not self-consciously notice its thinking. But this sense will not do here, for it already presupposes a mind. To talk of a purpose which is not present in any mind at all seems to me as unintelligible as it would be to talk of rectangles which had no extension. The argument from design has therefore to my mind considerable, though not, by itself at least, conclusive force. It is also strange that there should be so much beauty in the world, that there should have resulted from an unconscious unintelligent world beings who could form the theory that the world was due to chance or frame moral ideals in the light of which they could condemn it. It might be suggested that a mind designed the organic without designing the inorganic, but the connection between organic and inorganic and the unity of the world in general are too close to make this a plausible view.

The counter argument from evil is of course formidable, but I shall defer discussion of it, as it is rather an argument against theism in general than a specific objection to the argument from design. I must, however, make two remarks here. First, it is almost a commonplace that the very large amount of apparent waste in nature is a strong prima facie argument against the world having been designed by a good and wise being. But is there really much "wasted"? A herring may produce hundreds of thousands or millions of eggs for one fish that arrives at maturity, but most of the eggs which come to grief serve as food for other animals. We do not look on the eggs we eat at breakfast, when we can get them, as "wasted," though the hen might well do so. It is certainly very strange that a good God should have designed a world in which the living beings can only maintain their life by devouring each other, but this is part of the general problem of evil and not a specific problem of waste in nature. Secondly, the occurrence of elaborate adaptations to ends is a very much stronger argument for the presence of an intelligence than its apparent absence in a good many instances is against it. A dog would see no purpose whatever in my present activity, but he would not therefore have adequate grounds for concluding that I had no intelligence. If there is a God, it is only to be expected *a priori* that in regard to a great deal of his work we should be in the same position as the dog is in regard to ours, and therefore the fact that we are in this position is no argument that there is no God. The occurrence of events requiring intelligence to explain them is positive evidence for the presence of intelligence, but the absence of results we think worth while in particular cases is very slight evidence indeed on the other side where we are debating the existence of a being whose intelligence, if he exists, we must in any case assume to be as much above ours as that of the maker of the whole world would have to be. The existence of positive evil of course presents a greater difficulty to the theist.

.   .   .

Antony Flew
THEOLOGY AND FALSIFICATION

Antony Flew is a contemporary British philosopher who challenges the meaningfulness of all claims made about God. He asks not whether they are true but whether they are even intelligible, and in this way, he undercuts all the standard arguments that have been used to prove God's existence. Sometimes, when we talk about whether something is meaningful, we are asking whether it is important to us or significant for our lives. Bear in mind that when Flew claims that utterances about God are not meaningful, he is denying them cognitive status, not talking about whether they fulfill certain psychological needs; he is making a claim about the utterances themselves and suggesting that most are gibberish.

Let us begin with a parable. It is a parable developed from a tale told by John Wisdom in his haunting and revelatory article "Gods."[1] Once upon a time two explorers came upon a clearing in the jungle. In the clearing were growing many flowers and many weeds. One explorer says, "Some gardener must tend this plot." The other disagrees, "There is no gardener." So they pitch their tents and set a watch. No gardener is ever seen. "But perhaps he is an invisible gardener." So they set up a barbed-wire fence. They electrify it. They patrol with bloodhounds. (For they remember how H. G. Wells's *The Invisible Man* could be both smelt and touched though he could not be seen.) But no shrieks ever suggest that some intruder has received a shock. No movements of the wire ever betray an invisible climber. The bloodhounds never give cry. Yet still the Believer is not convinced. "But there is a gardener, invisible, intangible, insensible to electric shocks, a gardener who has no scent and makes no sound, a gardener who comes secretly to look after the garden which he loves." At last the Sceptic despairs, "But what remains of your original assertion? Just how does what you call an invisible, intangible, eternally elusive gardener differ from an imaginary gardener or even from no gardener at all?"

In this parable we can see how what starts as an assertion, that something exists or that there is some analogy between certain complexes of phenomena, may be reduced step by step to an altogether different status, to an expression perhaps of a "picture preference."[2] The Sceptic says there is no gardener. The Believer says there is a gardener (but invisible, etc.). One man talks about sexual behaviour. Another man prefers to talk of Aphrodite (but knows that there is not really a superhuman person additional to, and somehow responsible for, all sexual phenomena). The process of qualification may be checked at any point before the original assertion is completely withdrawn and something of that first assertion will remain (Tautology). Mr. Wells's invisible man could not, admittedly, be seen, but in all other respects he was a man like the rest of us. But though the process of qualification may be, and of course usually is, checked in time, it is not always judiciously so halted. Someone may dissipate his assertion completely without noticing that he has done so. A fine brash hypothesis may thus be killed by inches, the death by a thousand qualifications.

And in this, it seems to me, lies the peculiar danger, the endemic evil, of theological utterance. Take such utterances as "God has a plan," "God created the world," "God loves us as a father loves his children." They look at first sight very much like assertions, vast cosmological assertions. Of course, this is no sure sign that they either are, or are intended to be, assertions. But let us confine ourselves to the cases where those

---

[1]*P.A.S.*, 1944–5, reprinted as Ch.X of *Logic and Language*, Vol. I (Blackwell, 1951), and in his *Philosophy and Psychoanalysis* (Blackwell, 1953).

[2]Cf. J. Wisdom, "Other Minds," *Mind*, 1940; reprinted in his *Other Minds* (Blackwell, 1952).

who utter such sentences intend them to express assertions. (Merely remarking parenthetically that those who intend or interpret such utterances as crypto-commands, expressions of wishes, disguised ejaculations, concealed ethics, or as anything else but assertions, are unlikely to succeed in making them either properly orthodox or practically effective.)

Now to assert that such and such is the case is necessarily equivalent to denying that such and such is not the case. Suppose then that we are in doubt as to what someone who gives vent to an utterance is asserting, or suppose that, more radically, we are sceptical as to whether he is really asserting anything at all, one way of trying to understand (or perhaps it will be to expose) his utterance is to attempt to find what he would regard as counting against, or as being incompatible with, its truth. For if the utterance is indeed an assertion, it will necessarily be equivalent to a denial of the negation of that assertion. And anything which would count against the assertion, or which would induce the speaker to withdraw it and to admit that it had been mistaken, must be part of (or the whole of) the meaning of the negation of that assertion. And to know the meaning of the negation of an assertion, is as near as makes no matter, to know the meaning of that assertion. And if there is nothing which a putative assertion denies then there is nothing which it asserts either: and so it is not really as assertion. When the Sceptic in the parable asked the Believer, "Just how does what you call an invisible, intangible, eternally elusive gardener differ from an imaginary gardener or even from no gardener at all?" he was suggesting that the Believer's earlier statement had been so eroded by qualification that it was no longer an assertion at all.

Now it often seems to people who are not religious as if there was no conceivable event or series of events the occurrence of which would be admitted by sophisticated religious people to be a sufficient reason for conceding "There wasn't a God after all" or "God does not really love us then." Someone tells us that God loves us as a father loves his children. We are reassured. But then we see a child dying of inoperable cancer of the throat. His earthly father is driven frantic in his efforts to help, but his Heavenly Father reveals no obvious sign of concern. Some qualification is made—God's love is "not a merely human love" or it is "an inscrutable love," perhaps—and we realize that such sufferings are quite compatible with the truth of the assertion that "God loves us as a father (but, of course, . . .)." We are reassured again. But then perhaps we ask: what is this assurance of God's (appropriately qualified) love worth, what is this apparent guarantee really a guarantee against? Just what would have to happen not merely (morally and wrongly) to tempt but also (logically and rightly) to entitle us to say "God does not love us" or even "God does not exist"? I therefore put [forward] the simple central question, "What would have to occur or to have occurred to constitute for you a disproof of the love of, or of the existence of, God?"

Sigmund Freud
A PHILOSOPHY OF LIFE

Contrary to seeing religious commitment as a proof of God's existence, Sigmund Freud sought to explain it in terms of certain emotional needs that human beings have, which are first satisfied by their relationship with their earthly parents and then transferred to a hypothetical "God the Father." In the following essay, Freud claims that religion is an attempt to fulfill very real human needs but is doomed to failure because it simply cannot provide as ultimately satisfying an account of reality as can science. His conclusion is that religion is a kind of cultural neurosis that must be transcended as civilization moves from infancy to childhood. As science is able to take over more and more of the functions once performed by religion, science replaces religion as the basic perspective from which to view reality.

. . .

If we are to give an account of the grandiose nature of religion, we must bear in mind what it undertakes to do for human beings. It gives them information about the origin and coming into existence of the universe, it assures them of its protection and of ultimate happiness in the ups and downs of life and it directs their thoughts and actions by precepts which it lays down with its whole authority. Thus it fulfills three functions. With the first of them it satisfies the human thirst for knowledge; it does the same thing that science attempts to do with *its* means, and at that point enters into rivalry with it. It is to its second function that it no doubt owes the greatest part of its influence. Science can be no match for it when it soothes the fear that men feel of the dangers and vicissitudes of life, when it assures them of a happy ending and offers them comfort in unhappiness. It is true that science can teach us how to avoid certain dangers and that there are some sufferings which it can successfully combat; it would be most unjust to deny that it is a powerful helper to men; but there are many situations in which it must leave a man to his suffering and can only advise him to submit to it. In its third function, in which it issues precepts and lays down prohibitions and restrictions, religion is furthest away from science. For science is content to investigate and to establish facts, though it is true that from its applications rules and advice are derived on the conduct of life. In some circumstances these are the same as those offered by religion, but, when this is so, the reasons for them are different.

The convergence between these three aspects of religion is not entirely clear. What has an explanation of the origin of the universe to do with the inculcation of certain particular ethical precepts? The assurances of protection and happiness are more intimately linked with the ethical requirements. They are the reward for fulfilling these commands; only those who obey them may count upon these benefits, punishment awaits the disobedient. Incidentally, something similar is true of science. Those who disregard its lessons, so it tells us, expose themselves to injury.

The remarkable combination in religion of instruction, consolation and requirements can only be understood if it is subjected to a genetic analysis. This may be approached from the most striking point of the aggregate, from its instruction on the origin of the universe; for why, we may ask, should a cosmogony be a regular component of religious systems? The doctrine is, then, that the universe was created by a being resembling a man, but magnified in every respect, in power, wisdom, and the strength of his passions—an idealized super-man. Animals as creators of the universe point to the influence of totemism, upon which we shall have a few words at least to say presently. It is an interesting fact that this creator is always only a single being, even when there are believed to be many gods. It is interesting, too, that the creator is usually a man, though there is far from being a lack of indications of female deities; and some mythologies actually make the creation begin with a male god getting rid of a female deity, who is degraded into being a monster. Here the most interesting problems of detail open out; but we must hurry on. Our further path is made easy to recognize, for this god-creator is undisguisedly called "father." Psychoanalysis infers that he really is the father, with all the magnificence in which he once appeared to the small child. A religious man pictures the creation of the universe just as he pictures his own origin.

This being so, it is easy to explain how it is that consoling assurances and strict ethical demands are combined with a cosmogony. For the same person to whom the child owed his existence, the father (or more correctly, no doubt, the parental agency compounded of the father and mother), also protected and watched over him in his feeble and helpless state, exposed as he was to all the dangers lying in wait in the external world; under his father's protection he felt safe. When a human being has himself grown up, he knows, to be sure, that he is in possession of greater strength, but his insight into the perils of life has also grown greater, and he rightly concludes that fundamentally he still remains just as helpless and unprotected as he was in his childhood, that faced by the world he is still a child. Even now, therefore, he cannot do without the protection which he enjoyed as a child. But he has long since recognized, too, that his father is a being of narrowly restricted power, and not equipped with every excellence. He therefore harks back to the mnemic image of the father whom in his childhood he so greatly overvalued. He exalts the image into a deity and makes it into something contemporary and real. The effective strength of the mnemic image and the persistence of his need for protection jointly sustain his belief in God.

The third main item in the religious programme, the ethical demand, also fits into this childhood situation with ease. I may remind you of Kant's famous pronouncement in which he names, in a single breath, the starry heavens and the moral law within us. . . . However strange this juxtaposition may sound—for what have the heavenly bodies to do with the question of whether one human creature loves another or kills him? —it nevertheless touches on a great psychological truth. The same father (or parental agency) which gave the child life and guarded him against its perils, taught him as well what he might do and what he must leave undone, instructed him that he must adapt himself to certain restrictions on his instinctual wishes, and made him understand what regard he was expected to have for his parents and brothers and sisters, if he wanted to become a tolerated and welcome member of the family circle and later on of larger associations. The child is brought up to a knowledge of his social duties by a system of loving rewards and punishments, he is taught that his security in life depends on his parents (and afterwards other people) loving him and on their being able to believe that he loves them. All these relations are afterwards introduced by men unaltered into their religion. Their parents' prohibitions and demands persist within them as a moral conscience. With the help of this same system of rewards and punishments, God rules the world of men. The amount of protection and happy satisfaction assigned to an individual depends on his fulfillment of the ethical demands; his love of God and his consciousness of being loved by God are the foundations of the security with which he is armed against the dangers of the external world and of his human environment. Finally, in prayer he has assured himself a direct influence on the divine will and with it a share in the divine omnipotence.

I feel sure that while you have been listening to me you have been bothered by a number of questions which you would be glad to hear answered. I cannot undertake to do so here and now, but I feel confident that none of these detailed enquiries would upset our thesis that the religious *Weltanschauung* is determined by the situation of our childhood. That being so, it is all the more remarkable that, in spite of its infantile nature, it nevertheless has a precursor. There is no doubt that there was a time without religion, without gods. This is known as the stage of animism. At that time, too, the world was peopled with spiritual beings resembling men—we call them demons. All the objects in the external world were their habitation, or perhaps were identical with them; but there was no superior power which had created them all and afterwards ruled them and to which one could turn for protection and help. The demons of animism were for the most part hostile in their attitude to human beings, but it appears that human beings had more self-confidence then than later on. They were certainly in a constant state of the most acute fear of these evil spirits; but they defended themselves against them by certain actions to which they ascribed the power to drive them away. Nor apart from this did they regard themselves as defenceless. If they desired something from Nature—if they wished for rain, for instance —they did not direct a prayer to the weather-god, but they performed a magical act which they expected to influence Nature directly: they themselves did something which resembled rain. In their struggle against the powers of the world around them their first weapon was *magic,* the earliest fore-runner of the technology of to-day. Their reliance on magic was, as we suppose, derived from their overvaluation of their own intellectual operations, from their belief in the "omnipotence of thoughts," which, incidentally, we come upon again in our obsessional neurotic patients. We may suppose that human beings at that period were particularly proud of their acquisitions in the way of language, which must have been accompanied by a great facilitation of thinking. They attributed magical power to words. This feature was later taken over by religion. "And God said 'Let there be light!' and there was light." Moreover the fact of their magical actions shows that animistic men did not simply rely on the power of their wishes. They expected results, rather, from the performance of an action which would induce Nature to imitate it. If they wanted rain, they themselves poured out water; if they wanted to encourage the earth to be fruitful, they demonstrated a dramatic performance of sexual inter-course to it in the fields.

You know how hard it is for anything to die away when once it has achieved psychical expression. So you will not be surprised to hear that many of the utterances of animism have persisted to this day, for the most part as what we call superstition, alongside of and behind religion. But more than this, you will scarcely be able to reject a judgment that the philosophy of today has retained some essential features of the animistic mode of thought—the overvaluation of the magic of words and the belief that the real events in the world take the course which our thinking seeks to impose on them. It would seem, it is true, to be an animism without magical actions. On the other hand, we may suppose that even in those days there were ethics of some sort, precepts upon the mutual relations of men; but nothing suggests that they had any intimate connection with animistic beliefs. They were probably the direct expression of men's relative powers and of their practical needs.

It would be well worth knowing what brought about the transition from animism to religion, but you may imagine the obscurity which to-day still veils these primaeval ages of the evolution of the human spirit. It appears to be a fact that the first form assumed by religion was the remarkable phenomenon of totemism, the worship of animals, in whose train the first ethical commandments, the taboos, made their appearance. In a volume called *Totem and Taboo* [1912–13], I once elaborated a notion which traced this transformation back to a revolution in the circum-stances of the human family. The main achievement of religion as com-pared with animism lies in the psychical binding of the fear of demons. Nevertheless a vestige of this primaeval age, the Evil Spirit, has kept a place in the religious system.

This being the prehistory of the religious *Weltanschauung,* let us turn now to what has happened since then and to what is still going on before our eyes. The scientific spirit, strengthened by the observation of natural processes, has begun, in the course of time, to treat religion as a human affair and to submit it to a critical examination. Religion was not able to stand up to this. What first gave rise to suspicion and scepticism were its tales of miracles, for they contradicted everything that had been taught by sober observation and betrayed too clearly the influence of the activity of the human imagination. After this its doctrines explaining the origin of the universe met with rejection, for they gave evidence of an ignorance which bore the stamp of ancient times and to which, thanks to their increased familiarity with the laws of nature, people knew they were superior. The idea that the universe came into existence through acts of copulation or creation analogous to the origin of individual people had ceased to be the most obvious and self-evident hypothesis since the distinction between animate creatures with a mind and an inanimate Nature had impressed itself on human thought—a distinction which made it impossible to retain belief in the original animism. Nor must we overlook the influence of the comparative study of different religious systems and the impression of their mutual exclusiveness and intolerance.

Strengthened by these preliminary exercises, the scientific spirit gained enough courage at last to venture on an examination of the most important and emotionally valuable elements of the religious *Weltanschauung.* People may always have seen, though it was long before they dared to say so openly, that the pronouncements of religion promising men protection and happiness if they would only fulfill certain ethical requirements had also shown themselves unworthy of belief. It seems not to be the case that there is a Power in the universe which watches over the well-being of individuals with parental care and brings all their affairs to a happy ending. On the contrary, the destinies of mankind can be brought into harmony neither with the hypothesis of a Universal Benevolence nor with the partly contradictory one of a Universal Justice. Earthquakes, tidal waves, conflagrations, make no distinction between the virtuous and pious and the scoundrel or unbeliever. Even where what is in question is not inanimate Nature but where an individual's fate depends on his relations to other people, it is by no means the rule that virtue is rewarded and that evil finds its punishment. Often enough the violent, cunning or ruthless man seizes the envied good things of the world and the pious man goes away empty. Obscure, unfeeling and unloving powers determine men's fate: the system of rewards and punishments which religion ascribes to the government of the universe seems not to exist. Here once again is a reason for dropping a portion of the animistic theory which had been rescued from animism by religion.

The last contribution to the criticism of the religious *Weltanschauung* was effected by psycho-analysis, by showing how religion originated from the helplessness of children and by tracing its contents to the survival into maturity of the wishes and needs of childhood. This did not precisely mean a contradiction of religion, but it was nevertheless a necessary rounding-off of our knowledge about it, and in one respect at least it was a contradiction, for religion itself lays claim to a divine origin. And, to be sure, it is not wrong in this, provided that our interpretation of God is accepted.

In summary, therefore, the judgment of science on the religious *Weltanschauung* is this. While the different religions wrangle with one another as to which of them is in possession of the truth, our view is that the question of the truth of religious beliefs may be left altogether on one side. Religion is an attempt to master the sensory world in which we are situated by means of the wishful world which we have developed within us as a result of biological and psychological necessities. But religion cannot achieve this. Its doctrines bear the imprint of the times in which they arose, the ignorant times of the childhood of humanity. Its consolations deserve no trust. Experience teaches us that the world is no nursery. The ethical demands on which religion seeks to lay stress need, rather, to be given another basis; for they are indispensable to human society and it is dangerous to link obedience to them with religious faith. If we attempt to assign the place of religion in the evolution of mankind, it appears not as a permanent acquisition but as a counterpart to the neurosis which individual civilized men have to go through in their passage from childhood to maturity.

You are of course free to criticize this description of mine; I will even go halfway to meet you on this. What I told you about the gradual crumbling away of the religious *Weltanschauung* was certainly incomplete in its abbreviated form. The order of the different processes was not given quite correctly; the co-operation of various forces in the awakening of the scientific spirit was not followed out. I also left out of account the alterations which took place in the religious *Weltanschauung* itself during the period of its undisputed sway and afterwards under the influence of growing criticism. Finally, I restricted my remarks, strictly speaking, to one single form taken by religion, that of the Western peoples. I constructed an anatomical model, so to speak, for the purpose of a hurried demonstration which was to be as impressive as possible. Let us leave on one side the question of whether my knowledge would in any case have been sufficient to do the thing better and more completely. I am aware that you can find everything I said to you said better elsewhere. Nothing in it is new. But let me express a conviction that the most careful working-over of the material of the problems of religion would not shake our conclusions.

The struggle of the scientific spirit against the religious *Weltanschauung* is, as you know, not at an end: it is still going on to-day under our eyes. Though as a rule psycho-analysis makes little use of the weapon of controversy, I will not hold back from looking into this dispute. In doing so I may perhaps throw some further light on our attitude to *Weltanschauungen*. You will see how easily some of the arguments brought forward by the supporters of religion can be answered, though it is true that others may evade refutation.

The first objection we meet with is to the effect that it is an impertinence of the part of science to make religion a subject for its investiga-
tions, for religion is something sublime, superior to any operation of the
human intellect, something which may not be approached with hair-
splitting criticisms. In other words, science is not qualified to judge religion: it is quite serviceable and estimable otherwise, so long as it keeps
to its own sphere. But religion is not its sphere, and it has no business
there. If we do not let ourselves be put off by this brusque repulse and
enquire further what is the basis of this claim to a position exceptional
among all human concerns, the reply we receive (if we are thought worthy
of any reply) is that religion cannot be measured by human measurements, for it is of divine origin and was given us as a revelation by a Spirit
which the human spirit cannot comprehend. One would have thought
that there was nothing easier than the refutation of this argument: it is
a clear case of *petito principii,* of "begging the question"—I know of no
good German equivalent expression. The actual question raised is
whether there *is* a divine spirit and a revelation by it; and the matter is
certainly not decided by saying that this question cannot be asked, since
the deity may not be put in question. The position here is what it occasionally is during the work of analysis. If a usually sensible patient rejects
some particular suggestion on specially foolish grounds, this logical
weakness is evidence of the existence of a specially strong motive for the
denial—a motive which can only be of an affective nature, an emotional
tie.

We may also be given another answer, in which a motive of this kind
is openly admitted: religion may not be critically examined because it is
the highest, most precious, and most sublime thing that the human spirit
has produced, because it gives expression to the deepest feelings and
alone makes the world tolerable and life worthy of men. We need not
reply by disputing this estimate of religion but by drawing attention to
another matter. What we do is to emphasize the fact that what is in
question is not in the least an invasion of the field of religion by the
scientific spirit, but on the contrary an invasion by religion of the sphere
of scientific thought. Whatever may be the value and importance of religion, it has no right in any way to restrict thought—no right, therefore,
to exclude itself from having thought applied to it.

Scientific thinking does not differ in its nature from the normal
activity of thought, which all of us, believers and unbelievers, employ in
looking after our affairs in ordinary life. It has only developed certain
features: it takes an interest in things even if they have no immediate,
tangible use; it is concerned carefully to avoid individual factors and
affective influences; it examines more strictly the trustworthiness of the
sense-perceptions on which it bases its conclusions; it provides itself with
new perceptions which cannot be obtained by everyday means and it
isolates the determinants of these new experiences in experiments which
are deliberately varied. Its endeavour is to arrive at correspondence with
reality—that is to say, with what exists outside us and independently of

us and, as experience has taught us, is decisive for the fulfillment or disappointment of our wishes. This correspondence with the real external world we call "truth." It remains the aim of scientific work even if we leave the practical value of that work out of account. When, therefore, religion asserts that it can take the place of science, that, because it is beneficent and elevating, it must also be true, that is in fact an invasion which must be repulsed in the most general interest. It is asking a great deal of a person who has learnt to conduct his ordinary affairs in accordance with the rules of experience and with a regard to reality, to suggest that he shall hand over the care of what are precisely his most intimate interests to an agency which claims as its privilege freedom from the precepts of rational thinking. And as regards the protection which religion promises its believers, I think none of us would be so much as prepared to enter a motor-car if its driver announced that he drove, unperturbed by traffic regulations, in accordance with the impulses of his soaring imagination.

The prohibition against thought issued by religion to assist in its self-preservation is also far from being free from danger either for the individual or for human society. Analytic experience has taught us that a prohibition like this, even if it is originally limited to a particular field, tends to widen out and thereafter to become the cause of severe inhibitions in the subject's conduct of life. This result may be observed, too, in the female sex, following from their being forbidden to have anything to do with their sexuality even in thought. Biography is able to point to the damage done by the religious inhibition of thought in the life stories of nearly all eminent individuals in the past. On the other hand intellect —or let us call it by the name that is familiar to us, reason—is among the powers which we may most expect to exercise a unifying influence on men —on men who are held together with such difficulty and whom it is therefore scarcely possible to rule. It may be imagined how impossible human society would be, merely if everyone had his own mutiplication table and his own private units of length and weight. Our best hope for the future is that intellect—the scientific spirit, reason—may in process of time establish a dictatorship in the mental life of man. The nature of reason is a guarantee that afterwards it will not fail to give man's emotional impulses and what is determined by them the position they deserve. But the common compulsion exercised by such a dominance of reason will prove to be the strongest uniting bond among men and lead the way to further unions. Whatever, like religion's prohibition against thought, opposes such a development, is a danger for the future of mankind.

It may then be asked why religion does not put an end to this dispute which is so hopeless for it by frankly declaring: "It is a fact that I cannot give you what is commonly called 'truth'; if you want that, you must keep to science. But what I have to offer you is something incomparably more beautiful, more consoling and more uplifting than anything you could get from science. And because of that, I say to you that it is true in another, higher sense." It is easy to find the answer to this. Religion cannot make this admission because it would involve its forfeiting all its influence on the mass of mankind. The ordinary man only knows one kind of truth, in the ordinary sense of the word. He cannot imagine what a higher or a highest truth may be. Truth seems to him no more capable of comparative degrees than death; and he cannot join in the leap from the beautiful to the true. Perhaps you will think as I do that he is right in this.

So the struggle is not at an end. The supporters of the religious *Weltanschauung* act upon the ancient dictum: the best defence is attack. "What," they ask, "is this science which presumes to disparage our religion—our religion which has brought salvation and consolation to millions of people over many thousands of years? What has it accomplished so far? What can we expect from it in the future? On its own admission it is incapable of bringing consolation and exaltation. Let us leave them on one side then, though that is no light renunciation. But what about its theories? Can it tell us how the universe came about and what fate lies before it? Can it even draw us a coherent picture of the universe, or show us where we are to look for the unexplained phenomena of life or how the forces of the mind are able to act upon inert matter? If it could do this we should not refuse it our respect. But none of these, no problem of this kind, has been solved by it hitherto. It gives us fragments of alleged discovery, which it cannot bring into harmony with one another; it collects observations of uniformities in the course of events which it dignifies with the name of laws and submits to its risky interpretations. And consider the small degree of certainty which it attaches to its findings! Everything it teaches is only provisionally true: what is praised to-day as the highest wisdom will be rejected to-morrow and replaced by something else, though once more only tentatively. The latest error is then described as the truth. And for this truth we are to sacrifice our highest good!"

I expect, Ladies and Gentlemen, that, in so far as you yourselves are supporters of the scientific *Weltanschauung* which is attacked in these words, you will not be too profoundly shaken by this criticism. And here I should like to recall to you a remark that once went the rounds in Imperial Austria. The old gentleman once shouted at the Committee of a parliamentary party that was troublesome to him: "This isn't ordinary opposition any more! It's *factious* opposition!" Similarly, as you will recognize, the reproaches against science for not having yet solved the problems of the universe are exaggerated in an unjust and malicious manner; it has truly not had time enough yet for these great achievements. Science is very young—a human activity which developed late. Let us bear in mind, to select only a few dates, that only some three hundred years have passed since Kepler discovered the laws of planetary movement, that the life of Newton, who analysed light into the colours of the spectrum and laid down the theory of gravitation ended in 1727—that is to say, little more than two hundred years ago—and that Lavoisier discovered oxygen shortly before the French Revolution. The life of an individual is very short in comparison with the duration of human evolution; I may be a very old man to-day, but nevertheless I was already alive when Darwin published his book on the orgin of species. In the same year as that, 1859, Pierre Curie, the discoverer of radium, was born. And if you go further back, to the beginnings of exact science among the Greeks, to Archimedes, to Aristarchus of Samos (about 250 B.C.) who was the fore-runner of Copernicus, or even to the first beginnings of astronomy among the Babylonians, you will only have covered a small fraction of the length of time which anthropologists require for the evolution of man from an ape-like ancestral form, and which certainly comprises more than a hundred thousand years. And we must not forget that the last century has brought such a wealth of new discoveries, such a great acceleration of scientific advance that we have every reason to view the future of science with confidence.

We must admit to some extent the correctness of the other criticisms. The path of science is indeed slow, hesitating, laborious. This fact cannot be denied or altered. No wonder the gentlemen in the other camp are dissatisfied. They are spoilt: revelation gave them an easier time. Progress in scientific work is just as it is in an analysis. We bring expecta-tions with us into the work, but they must be forcibly held back. By observation, now at one point and now at another, we come upon some-thing new; but to begin with the pieces do not fit together. We put forward conjectures, we construct hypotheses, which we withdraw if they are not confirmed, we need much patience and readiness for any eventu-ality, we renounce early convictions so as not to be led by them into overlooking unexpected factors, and in the end our whole expenditure of effort is rewarded, the scattered findings fit themselves together, we get an insight into a whole section of mental events, we have completed our task and now we are free for the next one. In analysis, however, we have to do without the assistance afforded to research by experiment.

Moreover, there is a good deal of exaggeration in this criticism of science. It is not true that it staggers blindly from one experiment to another, that it replaces one error by another. It works as a rule like a sculptor at his clay model, who tirelessly alters his rough sketch, adds to it and takes away from it, till he has arrived at what he feels is a satisfactory degree of resemblance to the object he sees or imagines. Besides, at least in the older and more mature sciences, there is even to-day a solid ground-work which is only modified and improved but no longer demol-ished. Things are not looking so bad in the business of science.

And what, finally, is the aim of these passionate disparagements of science? In spite of its present incompleteness and of the difficulties attaching to it, it remains indispensable to us and nothing can take its place. It is capable of undreamt-of improvements, whereas the religious *Weltanschauung* is not. This is complete in all essential respects; if it was a mistake, it must remain one for ever. No belittlement of science can in any way alter the fact that it is attempting to take account of our dependence on the real external world, while religion is an illusion and it derives its strength from its readiness to fit in with our instinctual wishful impulses.

. . .

Paul Tillich
RELIGION AS A DIMENSION IN MAN'S SPIRITUAL LIFE

Paul Tillich (1886–1965) was one of the foremost theologians and philosophers of our time. Rooted in the tradition of religious existentialism, Tillich attempted to radically recast and transform Christian thought into a meaningful philosophy for our present age. In the article reprinted below, Tillich challenges the theist/atheist dichotomy on the grounds that it is necessary to reformulate the idea of God. This idea cannot refer to something whose existence or nonexistence can be debated, for that would make God merely one being among others. (In some of his other writings, Tillich identifies God with the ground of all being, with Being-itself, with the infinite, with ultimate concern.) For Tillich, then, religion is not about the relation of human beings to another (divine) being, but rather, it is an aspect of the human spirit; it is the dimension of depth; it is the ultimate concern manifested in all spheres of our spiritual life (moral, aesthetic, cognitive). But why, then, does religion present itself as one sphere among others? Tillich's answer that it is a reflection of our estrangement from the depth of our spiritual life points in a direction that Tillich does not himself address. What are the historical and social causes of human self-alienation? How can we create a social order in which the split between the religious and the secular can be overcome?

As soon as one says anything about religion, one is questioned from two sides. Some Christian theologians will ask whether religion is here considered as a creative element of the human spirit rather than as a gift of divine revelation. If one replies that religion is an aspect of man's spiritual life, they will turn away. Then some secular scientists will ask whether religion is to be considered a lasting quality of the human spirit instead of an effect of changing psychological and sociological conditions. And if one answers that religion is a necessary aspect of man's spiritual life, they turn away like the theologians, but in an opposite direction.

This situation shows an almost schizophrenic split in our collective conciousness, a split which threatens our spiritual freedom by driving the contemporary mind into irrational compulsive affirmations or negations of religion. And there is as much compulsive reaction to religion on the scientific side as there is on the religious side.

Those theologians who deny that religion is an element of man's spiritual life have a real point. According to them, the meaning of religion is that man received something which does not come *from* him, but which is given *to* him and may stand against him. They insist that the relation to God is not a human possibility and that God must first relate Himself to man. One could summarize the intention of these theologians in the sentence that religion is not a creation of the human spirit (spirit with a small s) but a gift of the divine Spirit (Spirit with a capital S). Man's spirit, they would continue, is creative with respect to itself and its world, but not with respect to God. With respect to God, man is receptive and only receptive. He has no freedom to relate himself to God. This, they would add, is the meaning of the classical doctrine of the Bondage of the Will as developed by Paul, Augustine, Thomas, Luther, and Calvin. In the face of these witnesses, we certainly ask: Is it then justified to speak of religion as an aspect of the human spirit?

The opposite criticism also has its valid point. It comes from the side of the sciences of man: psychology, sociology, anthropology, and history. They emphasize the infinite diversity of religious ideas and practices, the mythological character of all religious concepts, the existence of many forms of non-religion in individuals and groups. Religion, they say (with the philosopher Comte), is characteristic of a special stage of human development (the mythological stage), but it has no place in the scientific stage in which we are living. Religion, according to this attitude, is a transitory creation of the human spirit but certainly not an essential quality of it.

If we analyze carefully these two groups of arguments, we discover the surprising fact that although they come from opposite directions, they have something definite in common. Both the theological and the scientific critics of the belief that religion is an aspect of the human spirit define religion as man's relation to divine beings, whose existence the theological critics assert and the scientific critics deny. But it is just this idea of religion which makes any understanding of religion impossible. If you start with the question whether God does or does not exist, you can never reach Him; and if you assert that He does exist, you can reach Him even less that if you assert that He does not exist. A God about whose existence or non-existence you can argue is a thing beside others within the universe of existing things. And the question is quite justified whether such a thing does exist, and the answer is equally justified that it does not exist. It is regrettable that scientists believe that they have refuted religion when they rightly have shown that there is no evidence whatsoever for the assumption that such a being exists. Actually, they have not only not refuted religion, but they have done it a considerable service. They have forced it to reconsider and to restate the meaning of the tremendous word *God*. Unfortunately, many theologians make the same mistake. They begin their message with the assertion that there is a highest being called God, whose authoritative revelations they have received. They are more dangerous for religion that the so-called atheistic scientists. They take the first step on the road which inescapably leads to what is called atheism. Theologians who make of God a highest being who has given some people information about Himself, provoke inescapably the resistance of those who are told they must subject themselves to the authority of this information.

Against both groups of critics we affirm the validity of our subject: religion as an aspect of the human spirit. But, in doing so, we take into consideration the criticisms from both sides and the elements of truth in each of them.

When we say that religion is an aspect of the human spirit, we are saying that if we look at the human spirit from a special point of view, it presents itself to us as religious. What is this view? It is the point of view from which we can look into the depth of man's spiritual life. Religion is not a special function of man's spiritual life, but it is the dimension of depth in all of its functions. The assertion has far-reaching consequences for the interpretation of religion, and it needs comment on each of the terms used in it.

Religion is not a special function of the human spirit! History tells us the story of how religion goes from one spiritual function to the other to find a home, and is either rejected or swallowed by them. Religion comes to the moral function and knocks at its door, certain that it will be received. Is not the ethical the nearest relative of the religious? How could it be rejected? Indeed, it is not rejected; it is taken in. But it is taken in as a "poor relation" and asked to earn its place in the moral realm by serving morality. It is admitted as long as it helps to create good citizens, good husbands and children, good employees, officials, and soldiers. But the moment in which religion makes claims of its own, it is either silenced or thrown out as superfluous or dangerous for morals.

So religion must look around for another function of man's spiritual life, and it is attracted by the cognitive function. Religion as a special way of knowledge, as mythological imagination or as mystical intuition—this seems to give a home to religion. Again religion is admitted, but as subordinate to pure knowledge, and only for a brief time. Pure knowledge, strengthened by the tremendous success of its scientific work, soon recants its half-hearted acceptance of religion and declares that religion has nothing whatsoever to do with knowledge.

Once more religion is without a home within man's spiritual life. It looks around for another spiritual function to join. And it finds one, namely, the aesthetic function. Why not try to find a place within the artistic creativity of man? religion asks itself, through the mouths of the philosophers of religion. And the artistic realm answers, through the mouths of many artists, past and present, with an enthusiastic affirmative, and invites religion not only to join with it but also to acknowledge that art *is* religion. But now religion hesitates. Does not art express reality, while religion transforms reality? Is there not an element of unreality even in the greatest work of art? Religion remembers that it has old relations to the moral and the cognitive realms, to the good and to the true, and it resists the temptation to dissolve itself into art.

But now where shall religion turn? The whole field of man's spiritual life is taken, and no section of it is ready to give religion an adequate place. So religion turns to something that accompanies every activity of man and every function of man's spiritual life. We call it feeling. Religion is a feeling: this seems to be the end of the wanderings of religion, and this end is strongly acclaimed by all those who want to have the realms of knowledge and morals free from any religious interference. Religion, if banished to the realm of mere feeling, has ceased to be dangerous for any rational and practical human enterprise. But, we must add, it also has lost its seriousness, its truth, and its ultimate meaning. In the atmosphere of mere subjectivity of feeling without a definite object of emotion, without an ultimate content, religion dies. This also is not the answer to the question of religion as an aspect of the human spirit.

In this situation, without a home, without a place in which to dwell, religion suddenly realizes that it does not need such a place, that it does not need to seek for a home. It is at home everywhere, namely, in the depth of all functions of man's spiritual life. Religion is the dimension of depth in all of them. Religion is the aspect of depth in the totality of the human spirit.

What does the metaphor *depth* mean? It means that the religious aspect points to that which is ultimate, infinite, unconditional in man's spiritual life. Religion, in the largest and most basic sense of the word, is ultimate concern. And ultimate concern is manifest in all creative functions of the human spirit. It is manifest in the moral sphere as the unconditional seriousness of the moral demand. Therefore, if someone rejects religion in the name of the moral function of the human spirit, he rejects religion in the name of religion. Ultimate concern is manifest in the realm of knowledge as the passionate longing for ultimate reality. Therefore, if anyone rejects religion in the name of the cognitive function of the human spirit, he rejects religion in the name of religion. Ultimate concern is manifest in the aesthetic function of the human spirit, as the infinite desire to express ultimate meaning. Therefore, if anyone rejects religion in the name of the aesthetic function of the human spirit, he rejects religion in the name of religion. You cannot reject religion with ultimate seriousness, because ultimate seriousness, or the state of being ultimately concerned, is itself religion. Religion is the substance, the ground, and the depth of man's spiritual life. This is the religious aspect of the human spirit.

But now the question arises, what about religion in the narrower and customary sense of the word, be it institutional religion or the religion of personal piety? If religion is present in all functions of the spiritual life, why has mankind developed religion as a special sphere among others, in myth, cult, devotion, and ecclesiastical institutions? The answer is, because of the tragic estrangement of man's spiritual life from its own ground and depth. According to the visionary who has written the last book of the Bible, there will be no temple in the heavenly Jerusalem, for God will be all in all. There will be no secular realm, and for this very reason there will be no religious realm. Religion will be again what it is essentially, the all-determining ground and substance of man's spiritual life.

Religion opens up the depth of man's spiritual life which is usually covered by the dust of our daily life and the noise of our secular work. It gives us the experience of the Holy, of something which is untouchable, awe-inspiring, an ultimate meaning, the source of ultimate courage. This is the glory of what we call religion. But beside its glory lies its shame. It makes itself the ultimate and despises the secular realm. It makes its myths and doctrines, its rites and laws into ultimates and persecutes those who do not subject themselves to it. It forgets that its own existence is a result of man's tragic estrangement from his true being. It forgets its own emergency character.

This is the reason for the passionate reaction of the secular world against religion, a reaction which has tragic consequences for the secular realm itself. For the religious and the secular realm are in the same predicament. Neither of them should be in separation from the other, and both should realize that their very existence as separated is an emergency, that both of them are rooted in religion in the larger sense of the word, in the experience of ultimate concern. To the degree in which this is realized the conflicts between the religious and the secular are overcome, and religion has rediscovered its true place in man's spiritual life, namely, in its depth, out of which it gives substance, ultimate meaning, judgment, and creative courage to all functions of the human spirit.

Harvey Cox
FEASIBILITY AND FANTASY: TWO SOURCES OF SOCIAL TRANSCENDENCE

Harvey Cox is a professor of Church and Society at Harvard Divinity School and an author of several books that focus on the role of religion in social change. Like Tillich, Cox is concerned with de-mythologizing religion and reinterpreting its meaning in a way that speaks to the concerns of today. The essay that follows was written for a symposium on "Transcendence in Contemporary Culture." In it, Cox argues that religion needs to return to its visionary stance, by which it posits images of the future that transcend the limits of what our culture defines as "feasible." Thus, while acknowledging that religion has often acted as a deterrent to social change, Cox insists that it can also act as a catalyst for sociocultural transcendence.

In one of his essays Michael Harrington asserts that our society has lost the capacity for utopian fantasy. Our images of the future tend to be drawn as extensions of the present. Our imagination has atrophied. Unlike previous generations whose visions of the society transcended their means of accomplishing them, we suffer from a surplus of means and a shortage of visions. In this sense we have lost the capacity for transcending the present.

I think the evidence bears out Harrington's point. The many-colored maps of urban planners rarely include any ideas which are not quantitative extrapolations from existing cities. Planning institutes project futures which look woefully similar to the present in most of their characteristics. Even in that bedlam of future speculation, science fiction, the asteroid ages depicted seem to be marked mainly by vastly expanded and refined technologies. Space travel, telecommunication, robotry, and weapons systems have all been "improved," but nothing really new has entered the picture. In "Star Trek" the military mentality and the atmosphere of conflict have reached out to encompass the whole solar system and beyond. In *Walden Two* conflict has been eliminated, but people live in a world of controls imposed upon them from without. In *2001* man has still not solved the crises of his relation to his own tools. The problem is that when we run out of images of the future which are radically at variance with what we have now we limit the possible range of changes. We initiate a self-fulfilling prophecy mechanism resulting in more of the same. This process eventually produces social and cultural stagnation, leading to an inert society.

In his historical survey of Western man's way of thinking about the future, *The Image of the Future,* Fred L. Polak argues that the main dynamic in Western history has been contributed by images of the future. He suggests, like Harrington, that our failure to create new future images can result in what he calls "timeless time," a steady state situation in which innovation applies only to means and no longer to ends.[1]

Why has this happened? Why have we lost this particular capacity for self-transcendence? What part can religion play in restoring the capacity for imaginative self-transcendence?

Let me begin my response to these questions by focusing on the relationship between *feasibility* and *fantasy*. Feasibility has become a very important term in our current lexicon. Before we do anything or launch any program someone must do a "feasibility study." Those responsible for feasibility studies occupy in our time the place once held by the seers and oracles. We consult their data banks, computers, and extrapolation techniques; they no longer rely on the gizzards of birds or the patterns of bones dropped from a bag. Only the foolhardy set out on an enterprise which has not been pronounced feasible by an appropriately trained consultant.

But what does feasible really mean? It means possible of accomplishment in view of the social material and personal resources now at hand or foreseeable. Feasibility thus assumes a future which must grow out of

[1]Fred L. Polak, *The Image of the Future* (Dobbs Ferry, N.Y.: Oceana Publications, 1961).

the facts of the present. It discourages our hoping or aspiring toward something which flunks the feasibility test. This limits the sweep of human planning, political action, and cultural innovation.

One unorthodox systems analyst, Hasan Ozbekhan, says it should be the other way around:

> Desirable outcomes, however, should by definition arise from larger sets of ends than the set that is determined by feasibility alone. The range of choice is therefore bigger . . . which . . . is an important consideration. Furthermore the direction of the process—or better, its vector—becomes altered when the choice of ends is given primacy over the logical evolution of the means. A desirable outcome can be imagined and structured in detail as an independent conception of the future—independent, that is, from the powerful restrictions that the present imposes.[2]

How can we reignite the capacity for socio-cultural transcendence, or at least the gift for imagining radically alternative futures, futures which are neither mere extensions of existing conditions nor choices among options which have been found feasible in the light of existing or expected means?

In the past the spinning of visions was one of the functions performed by religion, or at least one type of religion. Of course religion performed and still does perform many other functions. It often simply legitimates existing institutions, personal styles, and patterns of power distribution. This is religion as "the opiate of the masses." But as Marx rightly saw, religion is not only an expression of injustice and suffering, it is also a form of protest against it. Often this protest expresses itself in the vision of a new epoch. The idea of a "messianic era," a new age in the relations of men with each other and with nature, arose quite early in the history of Israel. There are parallels though not equivalents in other religious traditions.

In Christianity this vision of the Kingdom of God or the New Jerusalem has had a rich and stormy career. Sometimes it has acted as a catalyst stimulating the culture to transcend itself and its current values; at other times it has acted as a deterrent to change. What are the conditions under which religion functions in these different ways?

In general there are three ways in which the catalytic power of a social vision of a new world to spark change and innovation is undercut. One way is to *postpone* it entirely to an epoch beyond time and history. One merely waits for it, with patience becoming the primary virtue. Another way is to identify it with a particular desired social institution or set of institutions such that when these are either attained or lost the tension is relaxed. A third way is to declare the religious institution itself the Kingdom of God and to spiritualize or individualize the radical hope until it becomes trivial.

[2]Hasan Ozbekhan,"Technology and Man's Future" (paper presented at the Symposium on the Technological Society, The Center for the Study of Democratic Institutions, Santa Barbara, California, December 19–23, 1965), p. 14.

Under the first condition the church becomes a small conventicle patiently enduring the travails of the present and awaiting the coming of the new order. Although it was once believed that early Christianity exemplified this model, recent research on the relation between Jesus and the zealots and the work of Ernst Benz on early Christianity raises some doubts. The Essene community which produced the Qumram library (the "Dead Sea Scrolls") is a better example. The second pattern has been followed by utopian groups and those who identify Christianity with a particular religio-political ideology for centuries. And the third approach is typical of the Constantinian-Catholic model which was instituted in a modified way in North America.

All three approaches undermine religiously inspired social transcendence. If the new epoch is found only in heaven, in a specially blueprinted state, or in the church, social transcendence—at least that which can be inspired by religion—is lost.

RELIGION AND TRANSCENDENT VISION

How does religion contribute to a society's capacity for social transcendence? It does so by symbolizing an ideal toward which to strive and by doing so with sufficient affective power that the ideal provides a real source of motivation. In order to do this a religion must be able to *change* such that its symbols inspire a society, but remain in *continuity* with the past so that the symbols have credibility. Let us look first at the problem of change in religion.

Since the middle of the nineteenth century theologians in both Catholic and Protestant churches and leading thinkers in Judaism have recognized that religions are not static but do develop historically and do change. It is not surprising that this recognition should have come so late, since the recognition that societies develop and change is also a relatively new realization of Western man. Since societies tend to change more rapidly than the value structures and belief patterns which guide them, it is understandable that religious thinkers should have recognized the changing and developing character of religion rather late. However, even though theologians have recognized religion as a developmental phenomenon, the next crucial step has not been taken: recognizing the need for conscious and planned change in religious systems and patterns of belief.

One of the most significant contributions of Pierre Teilhard de Chardin to recent religious and ethical thinking is his insistence that evolution has now reached a point where man is responsible for the next stage. He registers several stages in cosmic and animal evolution in which certain nodal points such as the emergence of life, of consciousness, and later of self-consciousness are the main ones. His central thesis is that, although the evolutionary process has moved from "within" so far, we have now arrived at a point where "The stuff of the universe has begun to think."[3] The fact that man must now take charge of the next stage of human and even of cosmic evolution naturally makes Teilhard de Chardin uncomfortable with certain inherited formulations of original sin. In fact, at one point he calls original sin "the iron collar around the neck of man." His ideas, although roundly condemned in recent years by the Vatican, have nonetheless become one of the most important ingredients in contemporary Catholic theology. They also have played an important role in Protestant theology. It is interesting, however, that although he insisted that man must take conscious measures in the next step in the evolution of the species, he nowhere suggests that man must be equally conscious about the next step in the evolution of religion.

The problem is that there is insufficient theological ground for legitimating religious innovation and the conscious development of symbols and belief systems. We do recognize that religions have developed and changed in the past, but generally the conscious innovation in religion has been condemned. The word for such innovation is "heresy." The first major task that theology must undertake in the next decades, therefore, is to work out how conscious innovation and symbol reformulation, even symbol creation, can occur. How are new symbols evaluated? How is their validity to be judged? All of these are questions to which theologians must now address themselves. In all of this it is clear that since experimentation must be encouraged rather than thwarted, the whole concept of heresy has outlived its usefulness.

Innovation also requires a *variety* of experiments going on, a "hundred flowers blooming." Here the picture seems fairly bright. Predictions about the future of religion in the technologized and industrialized world of the twenty-first century vary widely. Some futurologists predict the total disappearance of religion; others say that a single world religion will emerge synthesizing the major elements of existing religions; and others believe that a new religion only marginally similar to existing religious systems but shorn of any mythical or symbolic component will emerge. On the basis of existing trends, however, it seems most likely to me that we will have in the future world a variety of different religious belief systems. It is interesting to point out that in the twenty-three years since the end of the Second World War, the rapid economic and industrial development of Japan has *not* resulted in the disappearance of religion, but has, on the contrary, provided the setting in which an enormous variety of new religious movements has emerged.

Closely related to the problem of the creation of new values is the definition of who man is and what his appropriate task in history should be. Discussions about technology often use such phrases as "dehumanization" and "depersonalization." Obviously these terms cannot be used unless there is an underlying assumption about what it means to be human or to be a person. Close to the heart of the various world religious

[3]Pierre Teilhard de Chardin, *The Appearance of Man,* translated by J. M. Cohen (New York: Harper & Row, 1965).

systems is an understanding of who man is and what his essential relationship to history and the cosmos should be. One of the reasons why it is
unlikely that biblical religion can be merged or synthesized with Hindu
religion is that these two religious systems project highly divergent notions of man's place in the cosmos and in history. For biblical religion the
importance of terrestrial history is far more central than it is for Hinduism. In Christianity God actually "becomes flesh," and therefore earthly
realities have a significance which they do not have in the "nonhistorical"
religions such as Hinduism. It should be added immediately that this is
a simplification of two extremely elaborate symbol systems, and that the
recent history of Hinduism suggests a much more serious attitude toward
historical realities. Nonetheless there remains a marked contrast between
the answers these two religions would give to the question, "What is it
that is essential about the human?"

In Christian theology three main answers have been given to that
question. Roman Catholic theology, drawing on St. Thomas Aquinas and
through him on Aristotle, has tended to emphasize man's reason. Protestant theology, drawing more on St. Augustine, has tended to emphasize
man's freedom. The Greek and Russian Orthodox traditions, although
their emphasis has been less clear, have leaned more toward the concept
of "creativity" as man's distinguishing characteristic.[4]

It would seem that without sacrificing the notions of reason and
freedom, Western theology needs to develop far more explicitly the idea
of creativity as a distinguishing characteristic of human existence. This
means that man does not live in a world which is already finished but
rather in an open universe where he has the privilege and responsibility
of continuing the process of creation. In fact, the refusal to continue the
process of innovation and creation might very well be considered the
major form of sin in the contemporary world.

Christianity came into the world as a movement which expected a
radically different future and which legitimized a form of behavior which
was future-oriented. Certainly the early Christians and the Jews from
whom they inherited their messianic posture did not expect the kind of
future we expect; nonetheless they were basically a future-oriented people in the midst of a civilization which was by and large oriented toward
the past. With the emergence of the Constantinian compromise and the
substitution of Christianity for the emperor cultus as the *sacra publica* of
the empire, this future-oriented posture of Christianity disappeared.
Christianity became the sacral legitimation for the existing institutional
structure of the empire, and from the fourth century until relatively
recently Christianity has continued to provide the sacral legitimation for
the institutions of Western civilization.

From about the sixteenth century until the present another tendency
has been at work in Western civilization that has undercut the capacity

[4]See Nicholai Berdyaev, *The Destiny of Man* (London: G. Bles, 1937).

of Christianity to legitimate cultural values and social institutions. This phenomenon is called secularization. Although it has been feared and criticized by church leaders, secularization really frees biblical religion to assume its original posture of radical expectation and of criticism of the existing institutions in the society. The Roman Catholic theologian Johannes Metz suggests that the church must now become a "meta-critical institution." Certainly secularization means that Christianity will include a smaller minority of persons in the society. It provides, however, the possibility for a reappropriation of the critical, prophetic, and perhaps catalytic function which Christianity once played. Since the institutions of the society no longer need the kind of monolithic sacral legitimation once provided by Christianity, the church is now freed to play a more critical role in the social process.

Here and there throughout the history of Western Christianity movements have appeared which historians have labeled "visionary" or "utopian." Although they have sometimes become heretical, it is possible that these movements now provide a more adequate model for the role of the church in society than the model provided by the Constantinian church. In order to transcend itself society needs a goal which is symbolically powerful but resistant to complete actualization. Only with such a vision will society remain mobile, flexible, and changing. This suggests that the role of religion in society today might become that of the visionary. Drawing on its tradition in the Hebrew scriptures, the early history of Christianity, and the sectarian movements on the edges of the Western church, contemporary Christianity might provide those images and metaphors of a society of the future which would at once stimulate and induce social change without being so specific in their details as to choke off its possibility.

FANTASY AND MADNESS

So far I have discussed the role of religion in helping society achieve self-transcendence mainly in institutional terms. When I turn to look at the individual person, it seems clear that if we wish to regain the kind of radical vision which once inspired men to try to change quality instead of just quantity, we must discard most of what we now believe about "normalcy," "mental illness," and "mental health." If the concept of heresy prevents the church from exercising originality, current notions about mental hygiene operate even more powerfully in a society which is anxiously committed to mental health.

As Dr. Thomas Szasz has made clear in many of his writings, our culture now labors under a constrictive and ideologically narrow conception of what it means to be mentally healthy. Most of our standards of mental hygiene derive from the value assumptions of a late puritan, work-oriented, repressive historical period. We judge psychological deviancy on the basis of a person's relative capacity to operate in this society successfully. We reward people whose personalities lean toward competition, upward mobility, toughness, or even an obsessive need to accumulate material goods. We punish people who experiment with novel living styles, who cultivate esoteric interests or idiosyncratic beliefs. The person whose life ambition is to make a million dollars is lionized; the person who wants to meet God is tolerated: the person who wants to experience a trance is institutionalized.

There can be little doubt that many people need psychiatric care today. It is also true, however, that many people are subjected to incarceration and treatment mainly because their behavior, language, life styles, or beliefs do not comport with the conventional practices of the society. The use of mental health techniques, psychiatric screening, and long periods of "observation" in public institutions to control "deviancy" not only endangers our freedom as citizens; it also snuffs out the sparks of novelty and creativity any society needs in order to remain flexible and innovative.

In his dialogue *Phaedrus,* Plato has Socrates say, "The greatest blessings come by the way of *mania*, insofar as *mania* is heaven-sent" (244-a-6). Ever since there has been a lively discussion in Western thought about what *mania* is, how to tell whether it is "heaven-sent," and how it relates to what we call madness. By and large the notion that "mad" people have something to tell us has been retained by religious people while the medical profession, with some exceptions, has looked upon mania as a sickness to be cured. For Socrates himself the answer was clear. Later on in the *Phaedrus* he speaks of a man possessed by *mania* and says of him, "The multitude regard him as being out of his wits, for they know not that he is full of a god" (249-d-2).

The same problem existed in early Hebrew prophecy. Visionaries and ecstatics might well be simply mad or they might have a word from God, so it was wise to pay attention to them. Until just recently we thought we had solved the problem by deciding that all mania is madness: "deviants" are sick and must be returned to normalcy. I say "until recently" because in the past few years some psychiatrists have begun to suggest not only that the "rantings" of madmen make their own kind of sense, but that society may have much to learn from them. Their experience may not only reveal with poignant vividness the contradictions of the society focused in one person. They may also provide inputs and ideas, styles and aspirations not yet weazened by the heavy hand of feasibility.

Without surrendering to a romanticism of madness we need to develop ways to "test the spirits and see if they be of God." We need to recognize that "normalcy," "health," "feasibility," and even "reality" are historically and socially conditioned constructs. We must listen to the deviants of our society before pronouncing them all kooks. Some of them are. Some may be full of god, that is, full of feelings, hopes, and insights which still seem insane to our time but just may open fissures toward the future. The Greeks knew this when they relied on the oracles at Delphi and the Sibyl, usually in a state of transport (*theia mania*), to help them think about the future. The Hebrews knew it when they listened to prophets who often had periods of ecstasy. Tribal peoples have had shamans. Other cultures have had saints, poets, and holy men. We tend to see them all as a little odd or to tolerate them on the margins of society. We must now learn to appreciate them more as those without whom we literally have no real future.

CONCLUSION

Our capacity to transcend the limits of some arbitrary definition of "feasibility" in our hopes and aspirations for society may require us to take a closer look at two phenomena we have tended to regard as remnants of a prerational era, visionary religion and "holy" madness. For the health of the whole society some of us may have to become again "fools for Christ."

SECTION SIX

DEATH
AND
HUMAN
EXISTENCE

The emphasis placed on the fact of death in understanding human existence has differed widely among philosophers. Some, like the Epicureans and Stoics, have argued that because death is beyond human experience and because it is inevitable, the only reasonable attitude toward it is resignation without fear or regret. According to these philosophers, a preoccupation with death has no place in human life; simply in terms of its nature, death can have no real importance for us. On the other hand, there are those, particularly the existentialist thinkers, such as Martin Heidegger, who have argued that living with a conscious awareness that we will die, a condition uniquely human, is perhaps the single most important determinant of what it means to be a human being. According to this view, "the meaning I give to human existence rests upon my ability to come to terms with death as an immanent possibility for my own being."

The essays that follow are all concerned with analyzing the relation between death and human existence, with special emphasis on death in contemporary society. It is generally agreed that through an understanding of a culture's attitude toward death we can understand a great deal about that culture's attitude toward human beings and human values.

We can focus on death in either of two ways: as a possibility confronting each individual with which he or she must deal in a very personal way; and as an aspect of the human reality of any society with which that society must come to terms. In the essays that follow, we shall consider death from both these points of view.

Elisabeth Kübler-Ross
ON THE FEAR OF DEATH

Elisabeth Kübler-Ross, a psychiatrist, was one of the first doctors to focus seriously on the problems of death and dying in American society. Until she began a seminar at Billings Hospital in Chicago, where interviews were done with terminally ill patients to give them a chance to talk openly about their fears and to provide doctors with an opportunity to learn about the particular problems of the terminal patient, dying was virtually a taboo subject in hospitals and among patients' families. Even professionals in the health field found it difficult to confront patients with their impending death.

The essay that follows is the first chapter of Kübler-Ross's book On Death and Dying. *In it she suggests that death was for the ancients and remains for us a fundamentally frightening prospect. Fear of death is universal, and the rituals each culture designs to surround death are attempts to work through this fear, along with the guilt and rage that often accompany death for those who live on. In contemporary society we have attempted to mute the awareness of impending death for the patient and the fact of death for others. This flight from death is portrayed by Kübler-Ross as an impoverished way of coping with this universal fear.*

> Let me not pray to be sheltered from
> dangers but to be fearless in facing
> them.
> Let me not beg for the stilling of
> my pain but for the heart to conquer it.
> Let me not look for allies in life's
> battlefield but to my own strength.
> Let me not crave in anxious fear to
> be saved but hope for the patience to
> win my freedom.
> Grant me that I may not be a
> coward, feeling your mercy in my
> success alone; but let me find the grasp
> of your hand in my failure.

> *Rabindranath Tagore*
> FRUIT-GATHERING

Epidemics have taken a great toll of lives in past generations. Death in infancy and early childhood was frequent and there were few families who didn't lose a member of the family at an early age. Medicine has changed greatly in the last decades. Widespread vaccinations have practically eradicated many illnesses, at least in western Europe and the United States. The use of chemotherapy, especially the antibiotics, has contributed to an ever decreasing number of fatalities in infectious diseases. Better child care and education has effected a low morbidity and mortality among children. The many diseases that have taken an impressive toll among the young and middle-aged have been conquered. The number of old people is on the rise, and with this fact come the number of people with malignancies and chronic diseases associated more with old age.

Pediatricians have less work with acute and life-threatening situations as they have an ever increasing number of patients with psychosomatic disturbances and adjustment and behavior problems. Physicians have more people in their waiting rooms with emotional problems than they have ever had before, but they also have more elderly patients who not only try to live with their decreased physical abilities and limitations but who also face loneliness and isolation with all its pains and anguish. The majority of these people are not seen by a psychiatrist. Their needs have to be elicited and gratified by other professional people, for instance, chaplains and social workers. It is for them that I am trying to outline the changes that have taken place in the last few decades, changes that are ultimately responsible for the increased fear of death, the rising number of emotional problems, and the greater need for understanding of and coping with the problems of death and dying.

When we look back in time and study old cultures and people, we are impressed that death has always been distasteful to man and will probably always be. From a psychiatrist's point of view this is very understandable and can perhaps best be explained by our basic knowledge that, in our unconscious, death is never possible in regard to ourselves. It is inconceivable for our unconscious to imagine an actual ending of our own life here on earth, and if this life of ours has to end, the ending is always attributed to a malicious intervention from the outside by someone else. In simple terms, in our unconscious mind we can only be killed; it is inconceivable to die of a natural cause or of old age. Therefore death in itself is associated with a bad act, a frightening happening, something that in itself calls for retribution and punishment.

One is wise to remember these fundamental facts as they are essential in understanding some of the most important, otherwise unintelligible communications of our patients.

The second fact that we have to comprehend is that in our unconscious mind we cannot distinguish between a wish and a deed. We are all aware of some of our illogical dreams in which two completely opposite statements can exist side by side—very acceptable in our dreams but unthinkable and illogical in our wakening state. Just as our unconscious mind cannot differentiate between the wish to kill somebody in anger and the act of having done so, the young child is unable to make this distinction. The child who angrily wishes his mother to drop dead for not having gratified his needs will be traumatized greatly by the actual death of his mother—even if this event is not linked closely in time with his destructive wishes. He will always take part or the whole blame for the loss of his mother. He will always say to himself—rarely to others—"I did it, I am responsible, I was bad, therefore Mommy left me." It is well to remember that the child will react in the same manner if he loses a parent by divorce, separation, or desertion. Death is often seen by a child as an impermanent thing and has therefore little distinction from a divorce in which he may have an opportunity to see a parent again.

Many a parent will remember remarks of their children such as, "I will bury my doggy now and next spring when the flowers come up again, he will get up." Maybe it was the same wish that motivated the ancient Egyptians to supply their dead with food and goods to keep them happy and the old American Indians to bury their relatives with their belongings.

When we grow older and begin to realize that our omnipotence is really not so omnipotent, that our strongest wishes are not powerful enough to make the impossible possible, the fear that we have contributed to the death of a loved one diminishes—and with it the guilt. The fear remains diminished, however, only so long as it is not challenged too strongly. Its vestiges can be seen daily in hospital corridors and in people associated with the bereaved.

A husband and wife may have been fighting for years, but when the partner dies, the survivor will pull his hair, whine and cry louder and beat his chest in regret, fear and anguish, and will hence fear his own death more than before, still believing in the law of talion—an eye for an eye, a tooth for a tooth—"I am responsible for her death, I will have to die a pitiful death in retribution."

Maybe this knowledge will help us understand many of the old customs and rituals which have lasted over the centuries and whose purpose is to diminish the anger of the gods or the people as the case may be, thus decreasing the anticipated punishment. I am thinking of the ashes, the torn clothes, the veil, the *Klage Weiber* of the old days—they are all means to ask you to take pity on them, the mourners, and are expressions of sorrow, grief, and shame. If someone grieves, beats his chest, tears his hair, or refuses to eat, it is an attempt at self-punishment to avoid or reduce the anticipated punishment for the blame that he takes on the death of a loved one.

This grief, shame, and guilt are not very far removed from feelings of anger and rage. The process of grief always includes some qualities of anger. Since none of us likes to admit anger at a deceased person, these emotions are often disguised or repressed and prolong the period of grief or show up in other ways. It is well to remember that it is not up to us to judge such feelings as bad or shameful but to understand their true meaning and origin as something very human. In order to illustrate this I will again use the example of the child—and the child in us. The five-year-old who loses his mother is both blaming himself for her disappearance and being angry at her for having deserted him and for no longer gratifying his needs. The dead person then turns into something the child loves and wants very much but also hates with equal intensity for this severe deprivation.

The ancient Hebrews regarded the body of a dead person as something unclean and not to be touched. The early American Indians talked about the evil spirits and shot arrows in the air to drive the spirits away.

Many other cultures have rituals to take care of the "bad" dead person, and they all originate in this feeling of anger which still exists in all of us, though we dislike admitting it. The tradition of the tombstone may originate in this wish to keep the bad spirits deep down in the ground, and the pebbles that many mourners put on the grave are left-over symbols of the same wish. Though we call the firing of guns at military funerals a last salute, it is the same symbolic ritual as the Indian used when he shot his spears and arrows in the skies.

I give these examples to emphasize that man has not basically changed. Death is still a fearful, frightening happening, and the fear of death is a universal fear even if we think we have mastered it on many levels.

What has changed is our way of coping and dealing with death and dying and our dying patients.

Having been raised in a country in Europe where science is not so advanced, where modern techniques have just started to find their way into medicine, and where people still live as they did in this country half a century ago, I may have had an opportunity to study a part of the evolution of mankind in a shorter period.

I remember as a child the death of a farmer. He fell from a tree and was not expected to live. He asked simply to die at home, a wish that was granted without questioning. He called his daughters into the bedroom and spoke with each one of them alone for a few moments. He arranged his affairs quietly, though he was in great pain, and distributed his belongings and his land, none of which was to be split until his wife should follow him in death. He also asked each of his children to share in the work, duties, and tasks that he had carried on until the time of the accident. He asked his friends to visit him once more, to bid good-bye to them. Although I was a small child at the time, he did not exclude me or my siblings. We were allowed to share in the preparations of the family just as we were permitted to grieve with them until he died. When he did die, he was left at home, in his own beloved home which he had built, and among his friends and neighbors who went to take a last look at him where he lay in the midst of flowers in the place he had lived in and loved so much. In that country today there is still no make-believe slumber room, no embalming, no false makeup to pretend sleep. Only the signs of very disfiguring illnesses are covered up with bandages and only infectious cases are removed from the home prior to the burial.

Why do I describe such "old-fashioned" customs? I think they are an indication of our acceptance of a fatal outcome, and they help the dying patient as well as his family to accept the loss of a loved one. If a patient is allowed to terminate his life in the familiar and beloved environment, it requires less adjustment for him. His own family knows him well enough to replace a sedative with a glass of his favorite wine; or the smell of a home-cooked soup may give him the appetite to sip a few spoons of fluid which, I think, is still more enjoyable than an infusion. I will not minimize the need for sedatives and infusions and realize full well from my own experience as a country doctor that they are sometimes life-saving and often unavoidable. But I also know that patience and familiar people and foods could replace many a bottle of intravenous fluids given for the simple reason that it fulfills the physiological need without involving too many people and/or individual nursing care.

The fact that children are allowed to stay at home where a fatality has stricken and are included in the talk, discussions, and fears gives them the feeling that they are not alone in the grief and gives them the comfort of shared responsibility and shared mourning. It prepares them gradually and helps them view death as part of life, an experience which may help them grow and mature.

This is in great contrast to a society in which death is viewed as taboo, discussion of it is regarded as morbid, and children are excluded with the presumption and pretext that it would be "too much" for them. They are then sent off to relatives, often accompanied with some unconvincing lies of "Mother has gone on a long trip" or other unbelievable stories. The child senses that something is wrong, and his distrust in adults will only multiply if other relatives add new variations of the story, avoid his questions or suspicions, shower him with gifts as a meager substitute for a loss he is not permitted to deal with. Sooner or later the child will become aware of the changed family situation and, depending on the age and personality of the child, will have an unresolved grief and regard this incident as a frightening, mysterious, in any case very traumatic experience with untrustworthy grownups, which he has no way to cope with.

It is equally unwise to tell a little child who lost her brother that God loved little boys so much that he took little Johnny to heaven. When this little girl grew up to be a woman she never solved her anger at God, which resulted in a psychotic depression when she lost her own little son three decades later.

We would think that our great emancipation, our knowledge of science and of man, has given us better ways and means to prepare ourselves and our families for this inevitable happening. Instead the days are gone when a man was allowed to die in peace and dignity in his own home.

The more we are making advancements in science, the more we seem to fear and deny the reality of death. How is this possible?

We use euphemisms, we make the dead look as if they were asleep, we ship the children off to protect them from the anxiety and turmoil around the house if the patient is fortunate enough to die at home, we don't allow children to visit their dying parents in the hospitals, we have long and controversial discussions about whether patients should be told the truth—a question that rarely arises when the dying person is tended by the family physician who has known him from delivery to death and who knows the weaknesses and strengths of each member of the family.

I think there are many reasons for this flight away from facing death calmly. One of the most important facts is that dying nowadays is more gruesome in many ways, namely, more lonely, mechanical, and dehuman-ized; at times it is even difficult to determine technically when the time of death has occurred.

Dying becomes lonely and impersonal because the patient is often taken out of his familiar environment and rushed to an emergency room. Whoever has been very sick and has required rest and comfort especially may recall his experience of being put on a stretcher and enduring the noise of the ambulance siren and hectic rush until the hospital gates open. Only those who have lived through this may appreciate the discom-fort and cold necessity of such transportation which is only the beginning of a long ordeal—hard to endure when you are well, difficult to express in words when noise, light, bumps, and voices are all too much to put up with. It may well be that we might consider more the patient under the sheets and blankets and perhaps stop our well-meant efficiency and rush in order to hold the patient's hand, to smile, or to listen to a question. I include the trip to the hospital as the first episode in dying, as it is for many. I am putting it exaggeratedly in contrast to the sick man who is left at home—not to say that lives should not be saved if they can be saved by a hospitalization but to keep the focus on the patient's experience, his needs and his reactions.

When a patient is severely ill, he is often treated like a person with no right to an opinion. It is often someone else who makes the decision if and when and where a patient should be hospitalized. It would take so little to remember that the sick person too has feelings, has wishes and opinions, and has—most important of all—the right to be heard.

Well, our presumed patient has now reached the emergency room. He will be surrounded by busy nurses, orderlies, interns, residents, a lab technician perhaps who will take some blood, an electrocardiogram tech-nician who takes the cardiogram. He may be moved to X-ray and he will overhear opinions of his condition and discussions and questions to members of the family. He slowly but surely is beginning to be treated like a thing. He is no longer a person. Decisions are made often without his opinion. If he tries to rebel he will be sedated and after hours of waiting and wondering whether he has the strength, he will be wheeled into the operating room or intensive treatment unit and become an object of great concern and great financial investment.

He may cry for rest, peace, and dignity, but he will get infusions, transfusions, a heart machine, or tracheostomy if necessary. He may want one single person to stop for one single minute so that he can ask one single question—but he will get a dozen people around the clock, all busily preoccupied with his heart rate, pulse, electrocardiogram or pul-monary functions, his secretions or excretions but not with him as a human being. He may wish to fight it all but it is going to be a useless fight since all this is done in the fight for his life, and if they can save his life they can consider the person afterwards. Those who consider the person first may lose precious time to save his life! At least this seems to be the rationale or justification behind all this—or is it? Is the reason for this increasingly mechanical, depersonalized approach our own defensiveness? Is this approach our own way to cope with and repress the anxieties that a terminally or critically ill patient evokes in us? Is our concentration on equipment, on blood pressure our desperate attempt to deny the impending death which is so frightening and discomforting to us that we displace all our knowledge onto machines, since they are less close to us than the suffering face of another human being which would remind us once more of our lack of omnipotence, our own limits and failures, and last but not least perhaps our own mortality?

Maybe the question has to be raised: Are we becoming less human or more human? Though this book is in no way meant to be judgmental, it is clear that whatever the answer may be, the patient is suffering more —not physically, perhaps, but emotionally. And his needs have not changed over the centuries, only our ability to gratify them.

J. Glenn Gray
THE PROBLEM OF DEATH IN MODERN PHILOSOPHY

After several centuries of neglect, death has emerged as a problem for twentieth-century philosophy. J. Glenn Gray refers to it as a rediscovery, one prompted by the existentialist movement that arose on the Continent. In sharp contrast to other schools of thought, existentialism treats the inevitability of our death as a primary datum of human experience. Heidegger used the term "Being-toward-death" to capture the intimate relation between human existence and death, for death is not to be understood as something that awaits us at the end of our life; rather, it must be recognized as a permanent possibility of our existence. To be finite is to carry with us the immanent possibility that we will die, not in forty or sixty years, but at any moment. This feature of our existence brings with it anxiety—the realization that we, too, must die. In our efforts to cope with this anxiety we attempt to transform death into a public event, we surround it with trappings, we render it more and more impersonal, as Kübler-Ross has pointed out. But all these techniques are ultimately inadequate. The only way to deal with the fear is to meet it head on, to live our life with a conscious awareness of the inevitability of our death. According to existentialism, the best way to live life is as if we might die at any moment. If we keep this possibility in view, we shall be forced to render our existence meaningful, and in this way, to give our lives value.

"A free man thinks of nothing less than of death, and his wisdom is not a meditation upon death but upon life." This sentence, Proposition 67, Part IV, of Spinoza's *Ethics,* is a remarkable proposition, I think, and is predicated upon a no less remarkable metaphysics. In Spinoza's eyes, our universe is a vast mechanical order, marked by perfection of function and fullness of being. There are no abysses in it, nothing unintelligible or impenetrable by reason. God or Nature is an all-upholding, necessary power which prevents any loss of anything ever possessing real existence. If we could ask Spinoza: "Why should we not upon occasion meditate upon death?" he would no doubt answer: "Because death has no reality and you should meditate only upon essentials, upon eternal things. For by so doing you will become like the eternal: calm, self-sufficient, happy, indestructible, free. You will be directed in everything by reason, which can not pass away. Thus death is of no consequence to the free man and no fit problem for philosophical meditation!"

Spinoza, who is notable for having lived his philosophy, accordingly dismissed the subject, and, apart from the quoted proposition and a short demonstration under it, there is hardly a mention of death in his considerable writings. Though Spinoza and Spinozism met great opposition in the seventeenth, eighteenth, and nineteenth centuries, this particular proposition seems to have enjoyed nearly universal assent among thinkers. For the question of death has occupied modern thought astonishingly little. Socrates once defined philosophy as "the pursuit of death" and he became immortal by his teaching and example of how a philosopher should conduct himself in the face of death. In many Greek and Roman thinkers, Socrates' definition of philosophy met with intellectual approval as complete as the moral fervor stimulated by his death. The writers of the Renaissance were also largely preoccupied with the awareness of death and the problems posed by this awareness. But the theme largely disappeared in the post-Renaissance epochs from both philosophy and art, and I think that its disappearance has not been enough noticed. The ground swell of the Enlightenment with its hope for human improvement, its anti-historical bias, and its trust in mathematical science may have contributed something toward eclipsing the concern with human mortality. Other problems claimed attention. Though death, as an unpleasant occurrence, could not be denied, it did not lend itself easily to scientific analysis. Morally it harmonized ill with faith in progress, perfectibility, and the concept of rationality of the world order.

In the twentieth century, death has been rediscovered as a philosophical idea and problem. It is in fact with the contemporary German existentialists, Karl Jaspers and Martin Heidegger, near the center of their interpretation of reality and human existence. They assert emphatically that a proper understanding of, and right attitude toward, death, one's own death, is not only a *sine qua non* of genuine experience, but also of gaining any illumination about the nature of the world. They could not be further removed from the precept of Spinoza which we have already quoted, nor more out of line with dominant emphases of modern thought. I want to examine this present-day formulation of the idea of death and attempt to evaluate it. In what follows I shall be dealing chiefly with the two German existentialists because they have emphasized this theme much more than have Kierkegaard, Sartre, and the minor figures of this school of thought. Something of what is said in general on this topic will be applicable, to be sure, to all the existentialists, but for the more specific analysis Jaspers and Heidegger are necessarily the major sources.

What meaning and significance can be attached to the fact that man must die? How should I regard my own death as a future event? What values are to be derived from regarding it at all as contrasted with forgetting about it and living as though death were not real? If we are to find intelligible the answers existentialists give to these questions, we must first gain some appreciation of what I shall call the philosophic mood of existentialism, and review a little of the metaphysics. Existentialism consists chiefly, I think, of a pervasive mood and a metaphysics and the two are, curiously enough, related to the point where they mutually determine each other.

The mood can perhaps best be identified as a feeling of the homelessness of man. This world into which we come or are thrown as human creatures is radically insufficient to the claims and the requirements of the spirit. Our natural and social environment oppresses us with its foreignness, its unsuitability as a home for all that is specifically human about us as individuals. If we are genuine persons, sensitive to the human situation, we can gain no hold or support in nature or society. They are not our element. We are *in* the world, as Christians are wont to say, but not *of* it. All attempts to find a home for the spirit in this temporal, spatial realm are foredoomed. And this because the course of events is essentially unintelligible, not above reason as the Romantics thought, nor hidden from reason as in the Kantian philosophy. No, man's reason, like his soul, is a stranger in a world, impenetrable and unknowable, which cares not for him. Any order and meaning, if there are to be any, must be created by individual effort and resolve, and created anew by each individual all the time.

This deep-rooted conviction of homelessness places the existentialists at once in sharp contrast to idealistic and naturalistic philosophies in the Western heritage. The great idealists have always stressed coming to be at home in the world as the goal of all striving. Since Hegel particularly, idealism has been imbued with a sense of the intimate relationships existing between the individual and society, the individual and Nature, the individual and God or the Absolute. The true individual, for idealism, is not isolated but implicated in the whole world, in all its variegated relationships. Existential homelessness is, on the other hand, in equal contrast with the mood of the various naturalistic philosophies of our day. Naturalists always find the locus of human values and the source of social and individual aspirations in the world of material nature. Nature is always maternal and any estrangement from her is an arbitrary, irrational, even sinful act on the part of the individual. But the existentialists take no joy in Nature, and derive no metaphysical principles from her.

It is, in truth, difficult to find any good analogies in the Western tradition with the existentialist mood. It is tempting, but unprofitable, to liken this mood with Romanticism, particularly the pessimistic Romanticism of Schopenhauer and his followers. There are, of course, affinities, but the existentialists can hardly be said to share the hopelessness, the cynical detachment, and the consolatory aestheticism of Romantic pessimism. They vigorously protest against the critical charges of nihilism and despair as the outcome of their point of view, and on the whole, I think, rightly so. Bertrand Russell's famous little essay "A Free Man's Worship" voices an attitude toward Nature somewhat similar to existentialism, and the consolation Russell offers of comradeship with the few like-minded in "the long march through the night of life" is not unlike Jaspers' conviction that communication between single individuals is of timeless validity. Yet there is, on closer glance, a great difference. For Russell's mood, short-lived as most of his are, was evidently derived from his acquaintance with natural science and represented a heroic attitude of revolt against the facts which science teaches. Like that of so many Englishmen of the nineteenth century, his pathos derives from reaction to a science whose truths are no longer disputable but are at the same time an offense to the human spirit. Existentialism's mood is not so defiant and heroic. With Jaspers and Heidegger, at least, this "disenchantment of the world" brought about by science is assumed as a matter of course, and is not a cause for heroics. The sense of strangeness and estrangement between the individual and his world in existentialism is engendered, I think, though hardly explained by, the experiences of everyday living in a radically unstable social world. Not the revelations of science, but the applied technology of science is a chief source of existentialist sadness, in contrast to that of Russell. If spaced permitted, one might more profitably search for analogues to the existential mood among ancient writers in Greco-Roman or Jewish history.

For this philosophical mood is involved in a metaphysics which has not been at all prevalent in Western thought, and is in fact in sharp contradiction to the great systems. The German term *unheimlich*, which literally translates as "un-home-like," has in fact the denotation of the "uncanny." When you feel in German *unheimlich zu Mute*, you are seized with a nameless fear. You are out of your element, but more than that you have an intuition of abysses hidden from normal moods. These rare experiences of the uncanny, the existentialists hold, are revelatory of the innermost nature of reality. At such times we feel a sense of deep unease; we are threatened and oppressed by everything in general and nothing in particular. We are filled with dread or anguish, a psychological state which has for the existentialists metaphysical origins.[1] If someone asks us what is troubling us when we are oppressed with this feeling of the uncanny, we are likely to answer: "It is nothing." These words are truer than we know. For what has oppressed us is the primary intuition that we are not sustained by infinite power and plenitude of being, as so many philosophers have taught. On the contrary, we, human creatures, per-

---

[1] All the existentialists have treated this concept at length, but the best critical treatment of it I find in Otto Friedrich Bollnow's *Existenz Philosophie,* Kohlmann Verlag, Stuttgart. I am indebted to this brief, excellent treatise at several points in this essay.

ceive dimly in the experience of the uncanny that the world rests on nothing. It has no basis or ground. Human existence, as one form of Being, is suspended over the abyss of Non-being. As Heidegger puts it: "To exist as a human being means to be exposed to Nothingness."[2] The concept of Non-being or Nothingness is not merely a legitimate category of this metaphysics, it becomes the one which determines all other categories. Nothingness precedes, envelopes, and conditions all Being. In the experience of Dread we are confronted with the hidden truth that there is no ultimate consolation, that the end of all striving is shipwreck, the abyss of Non-being. It is hard to discover this truth, harder still to face it and live by it. Weak natures never know this mood of Dread at all, Kierkegaard insisted. And the German existentialists hold that even the strongest of us know it rarely, because we are chiefly creatures of comfort, not seekers of truth. Nevertheless, the experience of Dread is not something genuine persons want to avoid; it is, on the contrary, something to be sought and endured. These men believe strongly in the conviction of Goethe that *"Das Schaudern ist der Menschheit bestes Teil"* (The chill of dread is man's best quality). Only through the convulsion of our normal state of being can we reach the salvation of *Existenz* and overcome the original sin of merely vegetating in the everyday world. Of course, for Kierkegaard and the religious branch of existentialism, the experience of Dread is only preliminary to salvation in a fundamental sense: it precedes the leap of faith. And faith is defined as absolute trust in the Christian God of love, in whom eternal life is possible for man. To Jaspers, Heidegger, and Sartre, on the other hand, the salvation that can come by way of Dread is this-worldly; it lies in the quality of experience that issues from living in the truth. Dread does not precede anything; it reveals the truth of Nothingness and conditions our perception of all other truths. As Jaspers puts it: "The bottomless character of the world must become revealed to us, if we are to win through to the truth of the world."[3]

There is, say the existentialists, a true and a false way of evaluating the human situation. Of primary importance for the true way is the denudation of the spirit, the stripping away of all subterfuges, comforts and evasions. Our true condition is one of *exposure:* in reality, we are defenseless, naked to the winds of chance and blind accident. There is an expressive German participle, *geborgen,* which translates into English as "secure" or "safe," but connotes the delightful feeling of protectedness, the comfort of being hidden away or concealed from lurking dangers. The little bird is *geborgen* in the nest, the infant in the womb, the beloved in the arms of a strong and tender lover. By exposure is meant just the opposite of this. Though the desire for protection and security, for *Geborgenheit,* is a characteristic and primary impulse of human creatures, it is also a profound illusion. Spiritually, we are all exposed to the yawning abyss, the primal night which originates all and to which we all

[2]Martin Heidegger, *Was ist Metaphysik?,* p. 32.
[3]Karl Jaspers, *Philosophie,* p. 469.

278 DEATH AND HUMAN EXISTENCE

return. Only a small fraction of mankind ever recognizes this to be their real state, but it is no less true because of that.

Perhaps Karl Jaspers has made clearest the meaning of exposure in his description of the so-called "boundary situations." Every individual lives at every moment in a situation, one that is, to be sure, constantly changing and never totally grasped or understood. Boundary situations are situations involving a limit or an end, and, unlike the ordinary ones, they do not change in essence. These situations which reveal the limits of our being to us, and which are inescapable and constitutive of genuine life, are experiences of guilt, of suffering, conflict, chance, and death. Such experiences are not to be understood in conceptual terms; their implications are hidden from our ordinary logic. But by entering open-eyed into these boundary experiences, resolved to know them by direct acquaintance, we expose ourselves to that kind of vital experience which existentialists call truth.

The most extreme spiritual exposure is the exposure to death, and it is the most impenetrable of the boundary situations. It is the one which makes shipwreck of all human life inevitable. Death belongs to the human situation as such and to the situation of each individual. "Shipwreck is the ultimate," writes Jaspers, meaning thereby that hopes for immortality are vain. Our frail crafts are afloat on an unending sea around which there are no ports. To recognize this fact, the painful fact of human finitude, the inevitability of death, can alone make living meaningful and significant. This way is the path of liberation through truth. For "the deepest intimacy with actuality is at the same time the readiness to true shipwreck."[4]

What, then, is the fruitful way to regard death? How can we make of our own death an event of great import? Jaspers and Heidegger answer in effect: You must gain a vivid realization of death as a constitutive part of life, not as a mere end of life. Death is a phenomenon within life. If it is taken into life in a personal way, it will effect a revolution in our behavior. The fact of our mortality can properly be regarded as a fountain of possibility and potentiality. Indeed, in Heidegger's terms, death is at once "the most personal, the most detached, unrelated, and unsurpassable potentiality."[5] Once we learn to grasp the reality of death as life's greatest possibility, we shall not simply await it passively as a passing away of a biological sort, nor brood over it, nor desire to hasten its coming. Death will be regarded neither as a friend nor as a stranger.

The first requirement in becoming aware of death as a possibility of increase of Being is to recognize that death is always and ever my own, something that belongs to my very essence, as Nothingness belongs to Being. No one can take my place in death, nor can I, in this sense, ever die for another. I always die alone and the very meaning of death to me,

[4]Karl Jaspers, *Von der Wahrheit*, p. 529.
[5]Martin Heidegger, *Sein und Zeit*, p. 250.

according to Heidegger, is attained only in contemplation of my own death.

It is true that Jaspers makes a significant distinction between the death of a dearest friend and one's own death. The death of a friend can be "the deepest wound" in life. The friend dies alone, as everyone must, and seemingly the separation is absolute and forever. Yet for the one who remains behind, continuation of the communication the two friends have enjoyed is in a real, if mystical, sense possible. Communication, being nonphysical and not really confined in language, does not necessarily require the actual presence of the communicants. But to expound what Jaspers understands by communication and by the closely related concept of transcendence would require a separate essay. As far as I can see these ideas stand in rather sharp contradiction with his teachings on death and inevitable shipwreck, and place him religiously somewhere between the fervent Protestantism of Kierkegaard and the atheism of Sartre. In this respect his philosophy as a whole is to the last degree equivocal and ambivalent.

Nevertheless, for Jaspers as for Heidegger the decisive fact about death is that each person must regard his own death as the paramount reality. It is unsharable, the most isolated, separate, unrelated of life's possibilities, and for that reason the most significant. The individual who has achieved genuineness welcomes an event and a situation where everything depends on himself, unaided and unconsoled. Such an individual will also face the realization that, though our death is certain, the hour of its coming is indefinite and indeterminable. We must be certain *that* we shall die, and we can never know when we shall die. As a consequence of this seemingly commonplace truth, we must learn to live always in the face of death.

Before following out the implications of this conclusion, we must explain what Jaspers and Heidegger regard as the ordinary, which are, in their view, the perverse and false, ways of regarding death. The all but universal practice, they hold, is to refuse to accept the reality of death. For Jaspers the usual ways of escape are those of "positivism" and "mysticism." The positivist commonly follows the dubious wisdom of Epicurus, and repeats the formula: "While I am, death is not, and when death is, I am not. Therefore, death is of no concern to me." Now, it is true enough that I can not actually experience my death, and the consolation the positivists offer would be real enough if it were the fear of physical death that troubled us. But, as Jaspers rightly insists, I think, the thing about death which we fear is chiefly the prospect of no longer being, of vanishing into nullity. It is an "existential dread" at the prospect which grips the thoughtful person, and this feeling has little biological import. Against this dread, this shudder at Non-being, the positivist has no weapons. He knows only "helpless despair." No better is the other classic escape which Jaspers calls "worldless mysticism." Mystics, of whatever sort, refuse to believe in the reality of death because they do not accept the world of our experience as being real. They set up an unbridgeable dualism between an alleged real world and the experienced world of phenomena. Their faith is in immortality or metempsychosis, and death is only a moment of transition, a physical change, often an object of longing. It loses for the mystics, illegitimately, its true character as boundary situation. The mystics commit the opposite error from that of positivism in not accepting the organic aspect of all human existence, the union of spirit and flesh.

Heidegger's analysis of the common way of escape from facing death is perhaps more subtle. We rob ourselves, he maintains, of the sense of death's reality by making of it a public event, something that happens to everybody indiscriminately, and hence to no one in particular. We strive to make death just another event, among many, happening every day to somebody, and presumably someday to me, but it doesn't concern me at this time. Death is certain, we are wont to say, but hasn't happened to me yet. By our very manner of speaking we betray our desire to evade this most private, isolated, and unsurpassable possibility. In the end there comes to be a tacit agreement not to speak of death. The subject is tactless; the event itself an impertinence. Undue concern about it is a certain mark of cowardice. Heidegger's analysis of the impersonal pronoun in German, *das Man* (the one), as expressive of the fallen state of mankind in general and of the unwillingness to face death in particular, has become well known. In English we use, more commonly, the third person plural in an impersonal sense: "*they* say," "*they* do it," etc. When the pronoun is used thus impersonally we exclude this person and that person, and ourselves, of course, and frequently designate no one at all. Like our use of words such as "the public" or "the masses" as large categories with no individual members, so we speak of "one," "they," "the others," and mean really no one in particular. This escape into impersonality is for existentialism the original sin. It signifies a blunting of all intense feeling, an escape from personal responsibility, a refusal to regard death as something of profoundest concern to the individual personality. For I unconsciously identify myself with the impersonal "one." So we live in everyday banality, fallen creatures who shield ourselves from that which could make us genuine persons. We prefer forgetfulness to awareness and death overtakes us, as it overtook Ilya Ilitch in Tolstoi's famous short story, horrible to the last degree because life was vacuous and without authenticity.

To overcome this inveterate drive to unreality—this fallen, lost state —it is imperative to recognize that we live hourly in the face of death and to learn to act on that awareness. I must take as literally true and applicable to me the fact that my death is certain and can take place any instant. I have no claim on any but the present moment. On it, however, I have an absolute claim. It can be wholly mine. And mine is the responsibility of making the moment intense and full. I have the responsibility of separating at every moment in my life the essential from the inessential, the genuine from the false. Such responsibility can only really be assumed if one has learned to live in The face of death. "What in the face of death remains essential is done existentially; what falls away is mere *Dasein*"[6] (literally, "being there").

What does this mean practically to anyone who is concerned about becoming a wholly genuine person? The answer of the existentialists is that it means, for one thing, that we can not plan our lives as a whole or even as a significant part of a whole. We can not think of genuineness in terms of fulfillment. Life has nothing whatever to do with fulfillment. Some people fulfill themselves, at least in a superficial sense, and live on; many more die with potentialities unrealized; the majority, indeed, die after wasted lives which have been merely used up, having never really "come to themselves." Jaspers writes:

> In life everything attained is like death. Nothing completed can live. In so far as we strive for completeness, we are striving toward the finished, the dead. . . . As a drama for others a life can appear to be complete; in reality it does not possess this character. Life is tension and goal, inadequacy and unfulfillment.[7]

Living in the face of death then means living in such fashion that life can be broken off at any moment and not be rendered meaningless by such accident. We do not as genuine persons put the goals of our life somewhere in the future and make their attainment the measure of life's meaning. Meaningful living, for the existentialists, requires to be conceived not in terms of completion or in terms of duration, but rather in terms of an intensification and clarification of life's possibilities from moment to moment.

Heidegger's analysis of the nature of time helps to clarify and deepen this central doctrine of existentialism. Though his treatment in *Sein und Zeit* is complex and involved, it may be possible to suggest briefly the part relevant to our theme. For us as human creatures, says Heidegger, time is not truly conceived as a smooth passage from a past to a future through a present, just as death is not rightly conceived as a mere snipping of life spun out on a thread. Time does not flow, does not carry us along; it is not at all what Bergson held it to be. We must consider that the present moment is all we ever experience and inhabit. The present moment contains the whole richness of the world and the whole potentiality of experience. The past and the future are contained in our consciousness in the present, and, in a real sense, only there. The past, the "has been," acts as a restraining weight on our present; the future, the "not yet," as a liberating, releasing force. That is, the future can be liberating if it is conceived as part of the present, as experienced time and not as external calendar or clock time. Heidegger does not deny the reality of objective time, as some of his American critics seem to think. But he does hold that to gain genuine experience we must internalize time, learn to regard it as personal and private, *our* time as opposed to that of clocks and calen-

[6]Karl Jaspers,*Philosophie*, p. 486.
[7]*Ibid.*, p. 490.

dars. If we so regard it, time as linear progression will disappear from our thinking, and the future will be seen to belong to the present in a fundamental way. Though more is involved, Heidegger's chief emphasis in his treatment of time is that the future must be regarded in a new way, as part of the existential moment. As he sums it up in a sentence, difficult to translate:

> "Future" means, in the sense used here, not a Now that has not yet really become present, some time that will be, but on the contrary the coming [*Kunft*] in which existence in its most personal potentiality of Being approaches itself. The "running ahead" [*Vorlaufen*] in the present makes existence genuinely future.[8]

The future is thus for experienced, inner time always a realm of present possibility. The "not yet" is experienced as a "running forward" in thought into what might or can be. As genuine human beings we are open, uncompleted, "unfulfillable"; Heidegger seems at times to think that our potentiality, the "not yet," is all that genuinely *is*. The external future can bring us nothing we do not already possess, provided we are genuine persons. Potentiality is thus unconnected with teleology of an organic sort. Though life is always directed toward the future, as existentialists say, this expression is likely to be misleading unless we understand the term "future" as a dimension of the present.

How then is death related to this "not yet" which forms so great a part of our inner present? Heidegger proposes two interesting analogies, only to reject them. First, of the moon, when we say it is not yet full we mean that we do not perceive, say, the quarter that is not visible. But this is only a matter of perception, not of being. The invisible quarter is there all the time. The reverse is true of the human "not yet." With us it is a question of actual growth of being, not so with the moon. Secondly, of fruit, we say that it is becoming ripe but is not yet ripe. This analogy is much more adequate than the moon analogy because we are dealing with an actual change of being here, not with mere perception. Moreover, the condition of ripeness toward which the unripe fruit grows is not something external, brought about by others, or merely added as a sum, but is a constitutive part of the fruit. The "not yet" in this case belongs, as in human life, to the internal being of the fruit.

Nevertheless, the analogy is radically imperfect, as all analogies drawn from the organic world will be for the existentialists. Existentialism is emphatically not a "process philosophy" of either a naturalistic or idealistic sort. The ripeness of the fruit signifies its perfection or completion, its *telos*, whereas death can not be so conceived. Death is not the fulfillment of the "not yet," as ripeness is of the fruit requiring a definite time. On the contrary it is a *Bevorstand*, an imminence, something always directly before you. Being unto death, a phrase Heidegger borrows from Kierkegaard, is a way of life that looks at the possibility of death as an

[8]Martin Heidegger, *Sein und Zeit*, p. 325.

intimate part of life; it isolates man, it throws him back upon himself, it offers him the possibility of becoming a personality. As a way of life, this being unto death recognizes that life is delivered up to death at every instant—"a man is old enough to die as soon as he is born"—and at the same time affirms this fact as a great privilege and the most difficult challenge.

Once the full reality of personal death is accepted, the moment is informed with a sense of urgency and mission. The individual is liberated from the banality of existence in society, the fallen state of the mass of mankind. Genuine personality, painful and even tragic, will be achieved by the exceptional person through resoluteness, a key Heideggerian term. The genuine person gains resoluteness in realizing that existence must be given meaning; it does not as such possess it. He will be committed to an exploration of the dimensions of the present moment, to make his life in some way distinctive and unique. He will no longer avoid exposure nor the shudder of dread before Nothingness. On the contrary these will be his meat and drink.

Moreover, exposure to the most intimate and extreme experience of all, that of death, will develop a love of openness, or overt behavior, which is what Jaspers and Heidegger call truth. Like other philosophers, they lay claim to the discovery of important truth as the *raison d'être* of their philosophy. Truth for them is not something caught in the bonds of logic or concepts. It is a way of behaving or being. To be existentially is to be *in* the truth. Human existence is in the truth when Being is unveiled, opened, bared to the light. But concealment, obscurity, hiddenness, are in the very nature of things. Truth as an act is the uncovering of Being; it is a clarification, the lightening of Being, *Erhellung des Seins*. The clarified, enlightened individual portrays Being as it is to the extent that he exposes himself to the most extreme openness there is: the openness toward death. Here the existentialists' ultimate claim is plainly that the individual who lives in the face of death will not only gain insight into the truth of Being, but he will *be* that truth, at least a substantial part of it. And he will have gained freedom, which is identified in Heidegger with truth, and which has, with Sartre, become a theme of greater import than the theme of death. But the furthur analysis of truth and of freedom, as the existentialists see them, belongs to another paper. Let us turn to a brief evaluation of this idea of death and ask ourselves how much of the reasoning we can accept.

As Americans we are nearly certain to find something perverse in this European point of view. As a philosophy it is too bleak, too extreme, above all, too individualistic for us. Our normal response to this claim that life can gain authenticity only if pointed toward death is to assert that there are other and better ways. If you want your life to be genuine, meaningful, and intense, we rejoin, why not devote yourself wholeheartedly to social ideals? This means for us, I think, getting ourselves involved in important and urgent projects to the extent that our yearning for love and devotion is effectively satisfied. We realize our true selves by submerging them in such suprapersonal goals as world peace, racial equality, political and economic democracy, and the like. Personal life can be rescued from emptiness and futility, we think, only by recourse to the social or the political. My help is not in me. If I do not catch the vision of service in a great social cause I am lost. Salvation, like almost everything else, has for us become social salvation.

This overwhelming emphasis on the social is, of course, not simply an American phenomenon. It forms a large part of the current spirit of our Western civilization, and as such it is so intimately part of us that any deepgoing criticism is likely to sound quixotic in the extreme. Like all of the critics of existentialism I have read, I think that this philosophy is one-sided and unbalanced in its neglect, not to say repudiation, of the social dimensions of existence. At the same time, I am convinced that our very preoccupation with the social in this century has generated a deep dissatisfaction which makes existentialism darkly appealing. One need not renounce his faith in democracy in order to feel in his marrow that, expand the concept how he will, it is still insufficient spiritual nourishment. The same is surely true of communism, and our other purely social and secular religions. They are not enough to live by, and the suspicion grows that we all use these social faiths at times to escape the discipline of self-examination and self-knowledge. It is, in one sense, so easy to give oneself to a social and socially-approved goal, and, conversely, so difficult, as Kierkegaard knew, to attain to true selfhood or, as he put it, "subjectivity." We have today a great many convinced democrats and we have many communists who stake their all on communism as a way of life, but we have far fewer individuals with real depth and range to their personality. Whatever strictures we can and must bring against existentialism as a whole, it is hard to resist the point of Heidegger's analysis of the flight into impersonality, hard to deny that we have too often sought mere warmth in the crowd, preferring the protection and bliss of social anonymity to the opportunity for genuine personal growth. The hard tasks of self-examination and self-evaluation are certainly as vital in this age as in any preceding, and it may be existentialism's mission to make this evident. Few things are calculated, I think, to aid that task more than the courageous recognition that we are as individuals subject at every moment to death and that no one can spare us from it. If that recognition does not shake us into honesty and into seriousness, it can confidently be affirmed that nothing else will.

Nevertheless, an insistent question arises to challenge the existentialist doctrine at this point. Can we really conduct our lives in such fashion that an untimely death will not destroy the meaning and the purpose we have built into our existence? Or put more pointedly: Can a meaningful life be constructed out of existential moments? It seems to me to be highly doubtful, without modifying severely some of their premises. The existentialist analysis of time, involving as it does a sweeping denial of objective process and development, is hard to accept. Spiritual living, like organic life in this at least, seems to require time of the more conventional sort to realize values and to create meanings. It is doubtless illusory to think that a life can be a whole, an artistic unit, whatever ripeness and maturity we attain. But, clearly, there are varying degrees of wholeness and these are to some extent dependent on the number of calendar years attained. The achievement of genuine selfhood appears to me to be almost as much a process in time as, let us say, is the gaining of adequate understanding of a philosophical proposition about genuine selfhood. Authenticity is not attained at once by any of us and is probably never entirely pure, and unalloyed with its opposite. Inner, private time is, to be sure, more relevant as a measure of this growth than is chronological age. But, first, it is a growth, not an instantaneous state of being, and, second, this inner, private time is not to be disassociated, save in thought, from objective, public time.

The difficulty here is that the existentialists do not go far enough. They are not so much wrong as they are inadequate. The future is what Heidegger recognizes it to be—and more. If I am to achieve the resoluteness Heidegger desires, the calmness *(Gefasst sein)* Jaspers cherishes, I require goals not only future in present thought, but cumulative progress in calendar time toward their attainment. I know that they like to speak of resoluteness as such and commitment without an object, but their critics have pointed out with great unanimity the difficulty of being resolute about resoluteness and committed to commitment. It is hard to escape the conviction that spiritual growth and relative fulfillment make up a large part of whatever point our human lives possess.

If this be granted against the existentialists, we are left, of course, with the problem of the unrealized, the undeveloped life which is cut off by an untimely end. Recognizing untimeliness, as the existentialists do not, we seem to leave the fact of death as uninterpreted and irrational as it is in other philosophies. Death seems to make a mockery of all human potentialities and dreams. In so far as it is more than a biological end, it stands before us as blind, irreconcilable, absurd. On the one hand, we find it impossible to resist the existentialists' warning that we should be ready to die at any moment and hence should try to make sense of life, independent of duration. Yet, on the other hand, it is next to impossible to do this, so arbitrary and ambivalent is the end of life in full career. The awareness of death may well be, for many of us, a deep fountain of possibility, stirring us into full realization of the preciousness of living. But as an untimely occurrence, it can be also an unmitigated calamity, defying all efforts at understanding. I can only conclude that the yearning for rationality must here make place for religious faith in larger meanings. Though belief in immortality should not tempt us, as it did Spinoza, to deny the reality of death or to avoid facing its great threat, still there must be some deep-seated faith that we are not suspended over an abyss. We can grant the existentialists that awareness of personal death brings greater intensity and clarification to life, but at the same time we need not renounce our conviction that death as an occurrence holds, also, the promise of a greater fullness of Being.

Friedrich Nietzsche
ON FREE DEATH

Friedrich Nietzsche, who was born in 1844, had, by the time of his death in 1900, gone insane, probably as the result of syphilis. His thought and writing are characterized by a driving and passionate exultation of life, and this is nowhere more evident than in his attitude toward death.

According to Nietzsche, a proper life requires a proper death. He enjoins us to die at the right time and in the right manner. Thus, he treats death not so much as something that happens to us beyond our control as something we have the power to choose freely and to define for ourselves.

Some view Nietzsche as a precursor of existentialism, and there seems to be some basis for this in his treatment of death. For both Nietzsche and the existentialists, we are the sum total of our choices and our acts, and the way we die is as important for defining who and what we are as the way we live. From this point of view, death need not be seen as a final defeat; potentially, it is ultimate victory.

Many die too late, and a few die too early. The doctrine still sounds strange: "Die at the right time!"

Die at the right time—thus teaches Zarathustra. Of course, how could those who never live at the right time die at the right time? Would that they had never been born! Thus I counsel the superfluous. But even the superfluous still make a fuss about their dying; and even the hollowest nut still wants to be cracked. Everybody considers dying important; but as yet death is no festival. As yet men have not learned how one hallows the most beautiful festivals.

I show you the death that consummates—a spur and a promise to the survivors. He that consummates his life dies his death victoriously, surrounded by those who hope and promise. Thus should one learn to die; and there should be no festival where one dying thus does not hallow the oaths of the living.

To die thus is best; second to this, however, is to die fighting and to squander a great soul. But equally hateful to the fighter and the victor is your grinning death, which creeps up like a thief—and yet comes as the master.

My death I praise to you, the free death which comes to me because *I* want it. And when shall I want it? He who has a goal and an heir will want death at the right time for his goal and heir. And from reverence for his goal and heir he will hang no more dry wreaths in the sanctuary of life. Verily, I do not want to be like the ropemakers: they drag out their threads and always walk backwards

Some become too old even for their truths and victories: a toothless mouth no longer has the right to every truth. And everybody who wants fame must take leave of honor betimes and practice the difficult art of leaving at the right time.

One must cease letting oneself be eaten when one tastes best: that is known to those who want to be loved long. There are sour apples, to be sure, whose lot requires that they wait till the last day of autumn: and they become ripe, yellow, and wrinkled all at once. In some, the heart grows old first; in others, the spirit. And some are old in their youth: but late youth preserves long youth.

For some, life turns out badly: a poisonous worm eats its way to their heart. Let them see to it that their dying turns out that much better. Some never become sweet; they rot already in the summer. It is cowardice that keeps them on their branch.

All-too-many live, and all-too-long they hang on their branches. Would that a storm came to shake all this worm-eaten rot from the tree!

Would that there came preachers of *quick* death! I would like them as the true storms and shakers of the trees of life. But I hear only slow death preached, and patience with everything "earthly."

Alas, do you preach patience with the earthly? It is the earthly that has too much patience with you, blasphemers!

Verily, that Hebrew died too early whom the preachers of slow death honor; and for many it has become a calamity that he died too early. As yet he knew only tears and the melancholy of the Hebrew, and hatred of the good and the just—the Hebrew Jesus: then the longing for death overcame him. Would that he had remained in the wilderness and far from the good and the just! Perhaps he would have learned to live and to love the earth—and laughter too.

Believe me, my brothers! He died too early; he himself would have recanted his teaching, had he reached my age. Noble enough was he to recant. But he was not yet mature. Immature is the love of the youth, and immature his hatred of man and earth. His mind and the wings of his spirit are still tied down and heavy.

But in the man there is more of the child than in the youth, and less melancholy: he knows better how to die and to live. Free to die and free in death, able to say a holy No when the time for Yes has passed: thus he knows how to die and to live.

That your dying be no blasphemy against man and earth, my friends, that I ask of the honey of your soul. In your dying, your spirit and virtue should still glow like a sunset around the earth: else your dying has turned out badly.

Thus I want to die myself that you, my friends, may love the earth more for my sake; and to earth I want to return that I may find rest in her who gave birth to me.

Verily, Zarathustra had a goal; he threw his ball: now you, my friends, are the heirs of my goal; to you I throw my golden ball. More than anything, I like to see you, my friends, throwing the golden ball. And so I still linger a little on the earth: forgive me for that.

Thus spoke Zarathustra.

Joseph Fletcher
ELECTIVE DEATH

Joseph Fletcher, at one time Dean of St. Paul's Cathedral in Cincinnati, teaches philosophy and writes extensively on social issues. He is best known for his formulation of situation ethics, *which defines moral choice in terms of the specific circumstances of a given decision. Here he grapples with the issues raised by medical science's ability to prolong the biological condition of life long after the patient is healthy enough to enjoy living. Fletcher argues that in some situations a human being should have the right to choose to die.*

> Vex not his ghost: O, let him pass! He
> hates him
> That would upon the wrack of this
> tough world
> Stretch him out longer.
>
> *Shakespeare*

Since we shoulder our responsibility for birth control, a feature of every civilized culture, can death control be far behind? If we have a right to initiate a life deliberately, may we not terminate one? Depending, of course, upon the circumstances?

There are really two questions here, one factual and one moral. In what follows, the thrust is toward answering both of them in the affirmative. To a certain extent these questions are mutually penetrating. In actual fact the practice of death control is increasing, due to medical pressures and human needs so great that they provide their own moral justification. And as the practice is further justified by the situation, it is more easily and sensibly encouraged and disinhibited. It is exactly in this sense that I use the term *right*—as something justified pragmatically by the situation. Those who entertain any notion that there are some rights which are simply given in the very nature of things, above and beyond circumstances or human needs, will not be happy about everything I am about to say, and they ought to be alerted.

What is to be said to a nurse who is upset and suffers an acute anxiety reaction, unable to carry out her duty, because an intern, on instructions from a staff surgeon and a resident, has told her that a patient in the recovery room is to be "let go," and that she is to turn off the intravenous fluids and the oxygen? (Often only the slower strategy of starvation is used, without suffocation.) What is a man to do whose father has been lying virtually unconscious for four years in a hospital bed, following a massive cerebral hemorrhage? The patient cannot eat or speak, is incontinent, shows no neurological evidence of interpersonal communication and is kept going with tube feeding by around-the-clock private nurses. The patient's son would feel guilt about suggesting that the doctors bring it to a close, yet he also feels guilty about the expense ($40,000 a year), the wasted resources that other things and people need, and his father's distressingly subhuman status. After all, is the patient anymore his father?

Years ago, in 1954, I wrote that there is a logical contradiction in the Hippocratic Oath, subscribed to by the medical profession. As I saw it then, the Oath illogically promises two incompatible things, both to relieve suffering and, as I put it, to "prolong and protect life" [3]. But I was mistaken. Actually, there is not a word in that pious old apprenticeship agreement about either relieving suffering or prolonging life. Instead, the promise is to seek the "benefit of the sick," leaving the meaning of "benefit" unstipulated. The vitalistic idea that preserving life is the *summum bonum* of medicine appears nowhere in the Oath, except eisegetically (i.e., when read into it). On the contrary, making life sacrosanct was more likely a Pythagorean taboo, different from the empirical temper of Hippocrates and his case-minded approach. In place of such moral metaphysics, he said, in a famous maxim, "Life is short and art is long, the occasion fleeting, experience fallacious and judgment difficult." He knew the relativity of ethical decision. In fact, some of his disciples engaged in direct euthanasia on the same grounds that Plato, Socrates, Epicurus, and the Stoics approved it[16].

In any case, what appeared to be ethical to whomever it was who wrote the Oath is not an eternal verity. Almost certainly it was not Hippocrates, as Edelstein has now made abundantly clear [2]. There is no reason to take that unknown moralist's understanding of right and wrong or good and evil as a permanent model of conscience for all times and all conditions. What is right or good does not transcend changing circumstances; it arises out of them.

When biologists predict that by, let us say the year 2100, men will be free of hunger and infectious diseases, able to enjoy physical and mental life to the age of 90 or 100, replacing defective parts of the body as need develops, cyborg fashion, we can hope that the frequency of treatment situations posing the question of elective death will be cut down. But sooner or later it will arise for many patients, no matter what the longevity norm may become. Paradoxically, modern medicine's success in prolonging life has itself directly increased the incidence of death control decisions in the chronic and terminal ills of the American people. Those over 65 are expected to increase from 18.5 million in 1966 to 24.5 million in 1980—something in the order of one out of every eight persons.

Novels in the classic tradition have drawn a picture of the deathbed scene where the elderly "pass on," surrounded by their families and friends, making their farewell speeches and *meeting* death instead of being overtaken or snatched by it. This model of death has become almost archaic. Nowadays, most of the time, death comes to people (even the young and middle aged) in a sedated and comatose state; betubed nasally, abdominally, and intravenously; and far more like manipulated objects than like moral subjects. A whole fascinating array of devices—

surgical, pharmacological, and mechanical—are brought into play to stave death off clinically and biologically. Yet ironically, by their dehumanizing effects these things actually hasten personal death, i.e., loss of self-possession and conscious integrity. They raise in a new form the whole question of "life" itself, of how we are to understand it and whether the mere minimum presence of vital functions is what we mean by it.

For many people contemplating modern medicine's ability to prolong life (or, perhaps, to prolong death), death itself is welcome compared to the terrors of senility and protracted terminal treatment. Patients actually look for doctors who will promise not to allow them to "go through what mother did" or "lie there as Uncle John was made to." They are beginning to ponder ways of *escaping* medical ministrations; the white coats of our doctors and their paramedical attendants are taking on a grimmer hue, a new and less benign image. This is bound to increase as medicine's victories continue. It is a success problem, not a failure problem! The predominant illnesses become degenerative and chronic, not acute or infectious. Disorders in the metabolic group, cardiovascular ills, renal problems, and malignancies—these fill our hospital beds.

DEATH: ENEMY AND FRIEND

In all talk of elective death—that is, chosen or moral dying rather than fatal or amoral dying (*moral* always means the voluntary as against the involuntary or helpless)—the basic issue is whether human beings are always to regard death as an enemy, never as a friend. Is death never to be welcomed? May we never choose to go out to meet it? Dr. Logan Clendenning [1] years ago, in his popularizing effort to make knowledge a part of the public's weaponry against illness, thought of it as being sometimes a friend. He wrote:

> As I think it over death seems to me one of the few evidences in nature of the operation of a creative intelligence exhibiting qualities which I recognize as mind stuff. To have blundered onto the form of energy called life showed a sort of malignant power. After having blundered on life to have conceived of death was a real stroke of genius.

The logic of this is to either fight off or make an ally of *mortis,* as it happens to suit human needs. This is exactly what all medicine does; it either uses or outwits all biological forces for the sake of humanly chosen ends. Medicine is, at bottom, an interference with blind, brute nature. Three hundred years ago Thomas Sydenham called it "the support of enfeebled and the coercion of outrageous nature." Medicine refuses to "leave in God's (nature's) hands what must be" in everything else but death. Why should it stop there? Maurice Maeterlinck was sure that "there will come a day when science will protest its errors and will shorten our sufferings."[8] And that day is at hand, precisely because of the achievements of medical science and the pressures such achievements create to rethink our values and our view of man.

Medicine's primary *raison d'être* is, in Albert Schweitzer's phrase, "reverence for life." Life is its business. This, however, is very far from absolutizing the vital spark regardless of human personality and its claims. To subordinate every other consideration to bare sentience is to make biological life, as such, an idol. It is the vitalistic error. Respiration, circulation, reflexes, and the like, are not ends in themselves. Can it not be that life in its fullest meaning includes death, and that, since death is certain to come whether it does so constructively or willy-nilly, the only real question open to us is how it comes, as a good death ("euthanasia") or a bad death ("dysthanasia")?

Dr. David Karnofsky, who did so much for the Sloan-Kettering Institute, put the point of view of radical vitalism very clearly, at a meeting of the American Cancer Society in 1961. He opposed letting the patient go under any circumstances, arguing that the practice of keeping the patient alive is endorsed by "state planners, efficiency experts, social workers, philosophers, theologians, economists and humanitarians." Apart from this being a pretty wild *omnium gatherum* (practically everybody in the helping professions), the accusation is symptomatic of the embattled, almost paranoid mentality of many physicians. Karnofsky's main professed reason for preserving life by any and all means as long as possible was the old statistical absurdity about "something might turn up at the last minute, some new discovery or an inexplicable remission." But what is more irresponsible than to hide from decision making behind a logical possibility that is without antecedent probability?

As an example of "ethical" medicine, Dr. Karnofsky cited a patient with cancer of the large bowel. After a colostomy followed by recurrence, x-ray treatment was used; radioactive phosphorus checked abdominal fluids, and an antibiotic stopped broncho-pneumonia. Metastases ended liver function in spite of innumerable delaying actions, stupifying or traumatic, until the end "came." The patient was kept alive for 10 months, but might otherwise have died in a matter of days or weeks. Was it right or wrong to add 10 months? Was it more life or more death that was added? Who was benefited? What were the benefits? For Dr. Karnofsky, the obligation to maintain biological function or "life" was not a question of weighing benefits and forfeits. For him what is right or good was intrinsic; and life as such, per se, was precious—of greater value than anything else. This is the fundamental question in all cases of ethical concern, not only in life and death. Is the worth or desirability of thing or action inherent and intrinsic, regardless of the situation; or do right and good depend contingently and extrinsically upon the situation? If you take the intrinsic position, then some if not all obligations are absolute and universal; if you take the extrinsic view, all are relative. Karnofsky, like many others, was an absolutist. I am not. On the absolutist view some things are never open to responsible decision and choice; in "situation ethics" everything is.

IMPORTANT DISTINCTIONS

It is at this point that we need to pause to make distinctions of some practical importance. In the management of terminal illness there are two distinct moral problems, closely related but by no means the same. One is the classic issue over *euthanasia;* the other, and by far the more pressing in its frequency, is "letting the patient go" or, as I have called it, *antidysthanasia* [4]. The classic debate was about "mercy killing," i.e., doing something directly to end a life graciously when it would otherwise go on (active euthanasia, it is sometimes called). The more pressing and more common issue is whether one may graciously refrain from procedures, not *doing* something but *omitting* to do something, so that death will come (in some circles this is called *passive euthanasia*). This second problem is the one that our success with prolongation and resuscitation forces upon us daily in hospitals all around the world. Possibly the best way to put the distinction with its various sides is to speak of euthanasia in four forms:

1. *Direct voluntary,* as when a patient consciously chooses to end it all, with or without medical intervention. Such is the case of the patient who sneaks an overdose or is left one within reach, or who swallows a Kleenex or pulls out a tube. It is deliberately done and consciously willed by the patient.

2. *Indirect voluntary,* as when a patient before reaching an unconscious or comatose state (while still competent and with a *mens sana* even if not *in corpore sano*) gives leave to his medical servants to use discretion about letting death come. This, too, the patient has willed, yet his death is not directly done but indirectly by ceasing opposition to it. Such is the case of those who, after consultation, "pull the plug" at some point of diminishing returns.

3. *Indirect involuntary,* as when a patient's wishes are not known and yet doctors and/or family and friends *choose for him* to stop fighting off death. Such is the case when the pain, subhuman condition, irreversibility, cost, injustice to others, and the like, combine to outweigh the benefits of keeping him alive. This third form is far and away the most typical and frequent situation—indirect euthanasia, without the patient's past or present opinion in the account, except as it might be presumed.

4. *Direct involuntary,* as when a patient's wishes are not known, yet in the judgment of physicians, family, or friends it seems better to them to end his life by a "mercy killing" than to let it go on, as it will. Such a case would be a decerebrated person, perhaps one whose cerebral cortex has been shattered in an auto accident, in "excellent health" biophysically, fed by indwelling nasal tubes, unable to move a muscle, suffers no pain but only reacts by reflex to a needle prick. I know one such, a young man (who now looks like a little child), and his mother says, "My son is dead." Another case would be an obstetrician's

decision not to respirate a monster at birth, or a "blue baby" deoxygenated beyond tolerable limits of cyanosis or brain suffocation.

Some moralists have tended to put great store by the distinction between "direct" and "indirect" actions, Roman Catholics, for example. They argue that it is one thing morally to *do* an act such as ending a life by "bare bodkin" (as Shakespeare put it), and another thing altogether to *permit* a life to end by starvation, as when an intravenous therapy is discontinued. To others this seems a cloudy and tenuous distinction. Either way the intention is the same, the same end is willed and sought. And the means used do not justify the end in one case if not the other, nor are the means used anything that *can* be justified or "made sense of" except in relation to the gracious purpose in view. Kant said, as part of his practical reason, that if we will the end we will the means. Whether euthanasia is direct or indirect, voluntary or involuntary, is ethically something that *depends upon the facts in the situation,* not upon some intrinsic principle regardless of the realities. This is the shape of the tension between empirical and metaphysical moralities.

Curiously enough, in view of the religious and philosophical differences which divide moralists and ethicists, this matter of an alleged obligation to make the maintenance of a patient's life the supreme obligation is one around which moralists are pretty well united against the publicly professed opinion of the medical profession. (Note, I say "publicly.") That is, we find that Catholic, Protestant, Jewish, and humanist teachings all have a place for euthanasia in one form or another. Archbishop Temple [14], the Anglican theologian, once said of pacifism what can be said of Karnofsky's radical vitalism, that it

> . . . can only rest upon a belief that life, physiological life, is sacrosanct. That is not a Christian idea at all; for, if it were, the martyrs would be wrong. If the sanctity is *in* life, it must be wrong to give your life in a noble cause as well as to take another's . . . Of course, this implies that, *as compared to some things,* the loss of life is a small evil; and, if so, then, *as compared to some other things,* the taking of life is a small injury.

Catholic moralists, and most orthodox Jews and most orthodox Protestants, are opposed to euthanasia in forms #1 and #4 (see previous list); i.e., they rule out as immoral any direct methods of ending a life in order to end suffering and waste. But they allow forms #2 and #3, the indirect strategies. Catholic theologians refuse to call the indirect forms "euthanasia," and they add a further *caveat* or limitation. Pius XII [11] and his interpreters have restricted even the indirect forms (both of which they justify) to permission to cease and desist from the use of "extraordinary" treatments only, where there is no reasonable hope of benefit. All ordinary treatments must continue without letup. Usually, *extraordinary* procedures are taken to be those that are expensive, painful, or inconvenient [9].

The difficulty with this is, like so much else, due to the rapid advance of medical science and of the medical arts. Ordinary and extraordinary are very relative terms as the weaponry of health and control of nature's pathologies sweeps on. Look at how quickly penicillin ceased to be extraordinary, and also sulpha drugs and electronic cardiac devices such as the pacemakers. In no time prosthetic implants will be old hat. There is no way to establish a consensus (even if desirable) as to the defining features of an extraordinary treatment. Is it mortality rate, pain, inconvenience, expense, effectiveness, competence, subject's life expectancy (a lung removed in a child is not the same as in an old person), frequency, or what? And so it goes.

Those who live by situation ethics, and this includes many liberal Jews and Protestants and humanists (this writer being one), are ethically prepared to employ euthanasia in all four forms, depending in every actual case upon the circumstances. Nevertheless, no matter what rhetoric and doctrine are used at the theoretical level, there can be no doubt that in practice there is an increase of responsible situational decision making in proportion to the increase of the problem's occurrence in our hospitals. By now, due to greater longevity and medical know-how, it is an everyday, almost routine thing. Considerations of income and experience, especially in teaching hospitals, may tend to soft-pedal the issue and discourage it, but profit, training, and research are only brakes; they do not stop the trend to elective death. The frightening pressures of population only add to it. Sooner or later we shall be forced back on "statistical" morality. Speaking of a situation not unlike ours in America, the British medical journal Lancet[15] says: "If the average length of a patient's stay in a hospital is two weeks, a bed in that hospital occupied for a year could have been used by 26 other patients . . . In a country without a surplus of hospital beds, an irrevocably unconscious patient may sometimes be kept alive at the cost of other people's lives."

OBJECTIONS

In Morals and Medicine I have identified and thoroughly discussed 10 different objections to euthanasia [3]. I will not attempt to retrace all of that ground but there are some elements in the traditional opposition to euthanasia (we can call it elective death, if we prefer) that keep cropping up. The objection that it is suicide is only an epithet which is not really in question. The objection that it is murder only begs the question, since the problem is precisely whether a felo de se for medical cause is to be held an unlawful killing or not. When people cite the Ten Commandments they often fail to note that the decalogue prohibits murder, not killing as such, and this too ties in with the whole question of licit and illicit dying and killing. Obviously the Jews, as well as their Christian cousins, have not been in any significant numbers vegetarians or pacifists or opposed to capital punishment.

Once a bishop castigated me for saying that by wanting to release those caught in a painful and incurable condition I was ignoring the theologically alleged benefit spiritually ("the redemptive effect") of suffering, as in Jesus' crucifixion. The bishop himself ignored the fact that sacrificial suffering is voluntary and chosen and conscious. There is nothing redemptive going on *in most instances* of terminal misery and loss of human functions. And when it is said that given the right to choose death too many would do it impulsively or connive and encourage it in others for selfish reasons (e.g., "to get the deed to the old home place"), what reply is needed other than *abusus non tollit usum*, the abuse of a thing does not rule out its use? Otherwise we should always have to repress any research, innovation, and development which enlarges our human control over the conditions of life, since all such power can be used for ill as for good.

Some say that if our society and culture tolerated suicide in such cases as we have mentioned the result would be a cheapening of life and weakening of our moral fiber [13]. They seem to think that all interest would be lost, for example, in intensive care units, and nobody would respond to emergency Code 90 calls! If there is danger of becoming hardened by the practice of death control, by the same token there is danger of becoming hardened by the constant practice of prolonging life beyond any personal or human state. Pope's lines on vice cut two ways: "Yet seen too oft, familiar with her face, We first endure, then pity, then embrace." It is at least possible that euthanasia could not have half the demoralizing influence of stockpiling and planning to use weapons of mass extermination, even "tactical" bombs, and the total war of modern military technology. Besides, not every human being cries, *Timor Mortis conturbat me* (the fear of death confounds me); there are the pure in heart who fear not. "It is safe," said C. S. Lewis, "to tell the pure in heart that they shall see God, for only the pure in heart want to" [12]. The fear of the hereafter, among religious believers and skeptics alike, is nearly gone except for primitives and a few doctrinaire incorrigibles.

Perhaps the most anomalous stance in the whole developing discussion is the official or formal position of the medical fraternity, as taken in the American Medical Association and similar groups, that what they are opposed to only is making euthanasia *legal*. That is, they want to use their own discretion, as they are already doing, but they do not want any public acknowledgement that they have any such discretion or ever use it. The fact is, of course, that even in the case of euthanasia in form #3, doctors are vulnerable to malpractice suits ("failure to do what is of average competence and practice"). Hence the essentially scared and "phony" discussion in medical circles, and a tightly bound fraternal refusal to testify in court adversely to a fellow physician no matter what the charge or the facts. In this matter as in so many others, the law, and the conventional wisdom, are hopelessly antediluvian when seen in the light of medicine's progress. But the day is coming when doctors will recognize that just as they are slowly accepting the morality of terminating some

296 DEATH AND HUMAN EXISTENCE

lives at the beginning (abortion) for therapeutic reasons of mental, emotional, and social well-being, so they should be terminating for these reasons some lives at the ending, i.e., therapeutic euthanasia.

It would be unfair to the morally muscle-bound and false to the facts to urge the case for euthanasia in any of its forms as if there were no difficulties. The finest diagnosticians and prognosticians are sometimes baffled. At best the safest way to describe a professional person, whatever his field, is as an educated guesser. We cannot be "sure" that the "hopeless" case is really hopeless. Resuscitation procedures now have greatly increased our chances of reviving drowned people or frozen people who not long ago were beyond help. So also with cardiac arrests, anoxia, some cerebral vascular lesions, spontaneous hypoglycemia, and the like. The exciting thing about medicine is that even though it magnifies the problem of medical initiative in death for the aged and the chronic, it reduces it for the young and the acute. Yet there is no escape from the necessity of decision, case by case. This is as true for "ending it all" or "letting him go" as for whether to operate or not. Nothing is certain but death itself, on its own terms or ours. But if in the face of man's finite knowledge and understanding of health, life, and death, even our physicians cannot make good *"guesstimates,"* then we are indeed trapped in a merely fatalistic web. But if they have a truly creative competence, as I believe they have, then why refuse them the initiative late and not early? What does it mean to "have" a doctor?

WHAT IS DEATH AND WHEN?

Back and behind this very human and crucial question of when death is to be accepted lies the question, "When is death?" And, in a way, *what* is death? Even the most pragmatic value problems presuppose profound philosophical or theological commitments. The outmoded legal definition of death nearly completely misses the mark in these days of biochemistry and death control, and of genetic control. Almost certainly the heart-and-lungs definition, by which life is supposed to be present if there is clinically detectable breathing or heartbeat, will have to go. We cannot use mad Lear's test of Cordelia's corpse: "Lend me a looking glass; If that her breath will mist or stain the stone, Why then, she lives."

The philosophy of elective death turns its advocates in the direction of determining death as present, or life gone, when a patient's EEG (electroencephalographic tracing) has remained flat for say 24 hours, regardless of other criteria such as respiration or heartbeat [5]. This is certainly a long enough anoxia or cessation of the bioelectric activity of the brain to establish cerebral death, *and cerebral death is death.* This is reported to have been adopted by the French Academy of Medicine, and neurologists everywhere (e.g., Clarence Carfoord of Sweden) advocate it.

The point to note is that modern medical thinking, using a conceptual apparatus drawn from scientific method, no longer regards life and death as *events.* They are seen and understood now as points along a biological continuum. This makes nonsense of much of the old-fashioned abortion debate about when conception occurs, at insemination or fertilization or development of the embryo to certain stages, and so on along the pregnancy line. In the same way it undercuts the argument about when death "occurs," because death is a *process,* not an event. And the core of it is not sentience of the body or some arbitrary minimum of vital functions; *it is the person, and mental function.* When mind is gone, in the degenerative process, and with it the homeostasis of the organism, then life is gone: death has come. Then, at least, if not before, let the battle stop.

It is this problematic character of both life and death, medically regarded, that lends so much interest to a suggestion from Dr. Charles K. Hofling [7] of the College of Medicine in the University of Cincinnati: "Hospitals of the future may well have 'death boards.' Applications for permission to discontinue the artificial measures by which life is being maintained might be made to such boards either by the patient who is in possession of his mental faculties or by his next-of-kin." Such review boards could well have an ombudsman, an intelligent lay participant. Dr. Hofling is using a model from the "TA" boards of hospitals, those that make decisions in cases of therapeutic abortion.

Bernard Shaw has Sir Patrick say, in *The Doctor's Dilemma,* "All professions are conspiracies against the laity." The old gambit of writing prescriptions in Latin to keep patients from knowing what they say will not work any longer. Medicine is not a "mystery" any more, and its practitioners no longer have a craft of which everybody else is totally ignorant. This is the age of science, and that means a unity of knowledge and freedom of exchange. Repressed knowledge does not stay repressed, as the growing membership of the Nuclear Nations Club attests. Among other things this means that the doctors are no longer alone or isolated in their decision making. In situation problems about terminal cases the physician does not have to cast his own vote alone and uncounted with others. Nor, given medicine's great gains, is the range of decisions as narrow as it once was. When we have to reckon with death, we need not always only glimpse it over our shoulder as we run. Indeed, if we run we are lost.

FATALITY OR INTEGRITY

There are deep-rooted psychic inhibitions which prevent us from seeing our problem in a rational and responsible perspective. There is, or has been, too much *mystique* and superstitious metaphysics about it. But now it presents itself as a challenge to human control, as distinguished from supernatural or natural and fatalistic control. It is a question of responsible control of life, not merely of health and well-being but of being itself. It is time we confronted theology's blanket denunciation of suicide and medicine's uncritical opposition to death [6].

In the final analysis there are three postures we can assume. The one with the most tradition is absolutist. In its theological form it has been expressed in terms of a divine monopoly theory of life and death. It says that God is the creator of each person ("soul") and reserves to himself the right to decide when life shall come (as against birth control) and when death shall come (as against euthanasia). A much studied treatise in this old tradition says death control is "a violation of the property rights of Jesus Christ" [10]. If the absolutist posture takes a nontheological shape it becomes radical vitalism or a sort of naturalistic mystique about life as the highest good and death the worst evil, regardless of the situation. It is the first posture, the absolutist one, which lends itself to accusations of "playing God" when elective death is discussed.

The second posture is the one of stoic indifference or anomie. Because it finds no meaning in existence, it assigns no real value to it and can as easily embrace endurance of life at its worst as repudiation of life at its best.

In between these two extremes of absolutism and adiaphorism lies the pragmatic situation ethic. It finds life good sometimes, and death good sometimes, depending upon the case, the circumstances, the total context. In this view, life, no more than any other good thing or value, is good in itself but only by reason of the situation; and death, no more than any other evil, is evil in itself but only by reason of the situation. This is the method by which medicine makes decisions, and there is every reason why it should do so from first to last.

REFERENCES

1. Clendenning, L. *The Human Body* (3rd ed.). New York: Alfred A. Knopf, 1941.
2. Edelstein, L. *The Hippocratic Oath.* Baltimore: Johns Hopkins University Press, 1943.
3. Fletcher, J. *Morals and Medicine.* Princeton: Princeton University Press, 1954.
4. Fletcher, J. Death and medical initiative. *Folia Medica* (Tufts Univ.) 7:30, 1962.
5. Hamlin, H. Life or death by EEG. *J.A.M.A.* 190:112, 1964.
6. Hillman, J. *Suicide of the Soul.* New York: Harper & Row, 1964.
7. Hofling, C. K. Terminal decisions. *Medical Opinion and Review* 2:1, 1966.
8. Jacoby, G. W. *Physician, Pastor and Patient.* New York: Paul B. Hoeber, 1936.
9. Kelly, G. *Medico-Moral Problems.* St. Louis: Catholic Hospital Assoc., 1958.
10. Koch, A., and Preuss, A. *Handbook of Moral Theology.* St. Louis: Herder, 1924.
11. Pope Pius XII. *Acta Apostolicae Sedis* 49:1027, 1957.
12. Rhoads, P. S. Management of the patient with terminal illness. *J.A.M.A.* 192:661, 1965.
13. Shils, E. The sanctity of life. *Encounter* 28:39, 1967.
14. Temple, W. *Thoughts in War Time.* London: Macmillan & Co., 1940.
15. The prolongation of dying. Editorial. *Lancet* 2:1205, December 8, 1962.
16. Williams, G. *The Sanctity of Life and the Criminal Law.* New York: Alfred A. Knopf, 1957.

PART TWO

THE
SOCIAL DIMENSION

SECTION SEVEN

INDIVIDUALISM AND COMMUNITY

Each of us is an individual in the sense that we have our own feeling of personal identity, and we locate our experiences and our choices within ourselves. Yet, we are also fundamentally social, not only in the sense that our experiences and choices often refer to other people, but also in the sense that our idea of self and our self-identity are developed through social interaction (see G. H. Mead's and Erik Erikson's analyses in Section 2. Thus, as a number of social thinkers have pointed out, the individual and society can never, in reality, be separated from each other (see the analysis in this section by John Dewey and James H. Tufts).

Nonetheless, there is a tendency within this society to emphasize the development of the individual, independent of society. This is generally thought to require an area of personal freedom in which each individual can develop without interference from others: so long as an individual does not infringe on the freedom of others, he or she ought to be free to determine and pursue his or her personal goals. This position is what, in this section, we shall understand by the term "individualism." It is the main tenet of the liberal tradition.

In contrast, both the conservative tradition and the socialist tradition have emphasized the social nature of the individual. For those within these traditions, the primary concern is not personal freedom but the quality of our associative relations with one another. All these thinkers tend to reject individualism as a philosophy that exalts human selfishness and substitute for it a philosophy of community, in which individuals are bonded together by traditional ties (the conservative emphasis) or by the concern for collective self-development, work, and rationality (the socialist tradition). Conversely, the proponents of individualism tend to view this emphasis on community as a call for a totalitarian state to which all traces of individuality would fall victim.

The purpose of this section is twofold. First, we need to clarify precisely what is at issue. What are the implications of the concept of individualism? What kinds of human communities can there be? Are individualism and the value of community ultimately incompatible? Can there be a sense of community that respects and fosters the development of individuality? Second, we need to place the problem in historical perspective. Liberal individualism reflected the thinking of the emerging bourgeoisie of the seventeenth, eighteenth, and nineteenth centuries. It may need to be vastly transformed if it is to address the problems of the twentieth and twenty-first centuries. Similarly, the possibilities for associative life are far more numerous today than they were in the past. At the same time, it seems clear that we cannot return to many of the traditional communities of the past. We may need to create a wholly new sense of community, or we may need to discover that a historically new community ethic is already beginning to emerge, as the oppressed people of the world struggle to achieve liberation.

John Stuart Mill
INDIVIDUALISM

John Stuart Mill was a brilliant philosopher and social thinker of the nineteenth century. He is said to have had one of the highest IQs in all of recorded history. Mill is perhaps best known for his refinement of utilitarianism as it was developed by his father, James Mill, and by Jeremy Bentham, whose formulation appears on pp. 211–217 of this book. Mill's On Liberty, *from which the following selection is taken, is his classic defense of individual liberty and freedom of expression. In the first chapter of that book (see Section 8), Mill proclaims as the basic principle of liberty "that the only purpose for which power can be rightfully exercised over any member of a civilized community, against his will, is to prevent harm to others. His own good, either physical or moral, is not a sufficient warrant. He cannot rightfully be compelled to do or forbear because it will be better for him to do so, because it will make him happier, because in the opinion of others, to do so would be wise, or even right."*

The present selection begins with the third chapter of his book, whose title, "Of Individuality, As One of the Elements of Well-Being," makes it clear that it is Mill's intention to place the principle of liberty on a utilitarian foundation. The connection between the two rests on Mill's appraisal of the value of individuality, both for the individual and for the society at large. For the individual to develop his or her potentialities requires "different experiments of living," for what is conducive to the development of one person may hinder the development of another. This diversity, says Mill, not only is good in itself but also develops such traits as strength of character and originality, which contribute to the social good.

OF INDIVIDUALITY, AS ONE OF THE ELEMENTS OF WELL-BEING

. . . No one pretends that actions should be as free as opinions. On the contrary, even opinions lose their immunity when the circumstances in which they are expressed are such as to constitute their expression a positive instigation to some mischievous act. An opinion that corn dealers are starvers of the poor, or that private property is robbery, ought to be unmolested when simply circulated through the press, but may justly incur punishment when delivered orally to an excited mob assembled before the house of a corn dealer, or when handed about among the same mob in the form of a placard. Acts, of whatever kind, which without justifiable cause do harm to others may be, and in the more important cases absolutely require to be, controlled by the unfavorable sentiments, and, when needful, by the active interference of mankind. The liberty of the individual must be thus far limited; he must not make himself a nuisance to other people. But if he refrains from molesting others in what concerns them, and merely acts according to his own inclination and judgment in things which concern himself, the same reasons which show that opinion should be free prove also that he should be allowed, without molestation, to carry his opinions into practice at his own cost. That mankind are not infallible; that their truths, for the most part, are only half-truths; that unity of opinion, unless resulting from the fullest and freest comparison of opposite opinions, is not desirable, and diversity not an evil, but a good, until mankind are much more capable than at present of recognizing all sides of the truth, are principles applicable to men's modes of action not less than to their opinions. As it is useful that while mankind are imperfect there should be different opinions, so it is that there should be different experiments of living; that free scope should be given to varieties of character, short of injury to others; and that the worth of different modes of life should be proved practically, when anyone thinks fit to try them. It is desirable, in short, that in things which do not primarily concern others individuality should assert itself. Where not the person's own character but the traditions or customs of other people are the rule of conduct, there is wanting one of the principal ingredients of human happiness, and quite the chief ingredient of individual and social progress.

In maintaining this principle, the greatest difficulty to be encountered does not lie in the appreciation of means toward an acknowledged end, but in the indifference of persons in general to the end itself. If it were felt that the free development of individuality is one of the leading essentials of well-being; that it is not only a co-ordinate element with all that is designated by the terms civilization, instruction, education, culture, but is itself a necessary part and condition of all those things, there would be no danger that liberty should be undervalued, and the adjustment of the boundaries between it and social control would present no extraordinary difficulty. But the evil is that individual spontaneity is hardly recognized by the common modes of thinking as having any intrinsic worth, or deserving any regard on its own account. The majority, being satisfied with the ways of mankind as they now are (for it is they who make them what they are), cannot comprehend why those ways should not be good enough for everybody; and what is more, spontaneity forms no part of the ideal of the majority of moral and social reformers, but is rather looked on with jealousy, as a troublesome and perhaps rebellious obstruction to the general acceptance of what these reformers, in their own judgment, think would be best for mankind. Few persons, out of Germany, even comprehend the meaning of the doctrine which Wilhelm von Humboldt, so eminent both as a *savant* and as a politician, made the text of a treatise—that "the end of man, or that which is prescribed by the eternal or immutable dictates of reason, and not suggested by vague and transient desires, is the highest and most harmonious development of his powers to a complete and consistent whole"; that, therefore, the object "toward which every human being must ceaselessly direct his efforts, and on which especially those who design to influence their fellow men must ever keep their eyes, is the individuality of power and development"; that for this there are two requisites, "freedom, and variety of situations"; and that from the union of these arise "individual vigor and manifold diversity," which combine themselves in "originality."[1]

Little, however, as people are accustomed to a doctrine like that of von Humboldt, and surprising as it may be to them to find so high a value attached to individuality, the question, one must nevertheless think, can only be one of degree. No one's idea of excellence in conduct is that people should do absolutely nothing but copy one another. No one would assert that people ought not to put into their mode of life, and into the conduct of their concerns, any impress whatever of their own judgment or of their own individual character. On the other hand, it would be absurd to pretend that people ought to live as if nothing whatever had been known in the world before they came into it; as if experience had as yet done nothing toward showing that one mode of existence, or of conduct, is preferable to another. Nobody denies that people should be so taught and trained in youth as to know and benefit by the ascertained results of human experience. But it is the privilege and proper condition of a human being, arrived at the maturity of his faculties, to use and interpret experience in his own way. It is for him to find out what part of recorded experience is properly applicable to his own circumstances and character. The traditions and customs of other people are, to a certain extent, evidence of what their experience has taught *them*—presumptive evidence, and as such, have a claim to his deference: but, in the first place, their experience may be too narrow, or they may have not

[1] *The Sphere and Duties of Government,* from the German of Baron Wilhelm von Humboldt, pp. 11–13.

interpreted it rightly. Secondly, their interpretation of experience may be correct, but unsuitable to him. Customs are made for customary circumstances and customary characters; and his circumstances or his character may be uncustomary. Thirdly, though the customs be both good as customs and suitable to him, yet to conform to custom merely *as* custom does not educate or develop in him any of the qualities which are the distinctive endowment of a human being. The human faculties of perception, judgment, discriminative feeling, mental activity, and even moral preference are exercised only in making a choice. He who does anything because it is the custom makes no choice. He gains no practice either in discerning or in desiring what is best. The mental and moral, like the muscular, powers are improved only by being used. The faculties are called into no exercise by doing a thing merely because others do it, no more than by believing a thing only because others believe it. If the grounds of an opinion are not conclusive to the person's own reason, his reason cannot be strengthened, but is likely to be weakened, by his adopting it: and if the inducements to an act are not such as are consentaneous to his own feelings and character (where affection, or the rights of others, are not concerned), it is so much done toward rendering his feelings and character inert and torpid instead of active and energetic.

He who lets the world, or his own portion of it, choose his plan of life for him has no need of any other faculty than the ape-like one of imitation. He who chooses his plan for himself employs all his faculties. He must use observation to see, reasoning and judgment to foresee, activity to gather materials for decision, discrimination to decide, and when he has decided, firmness and self-control to hold to his deliberate decision. And these qualities he requires and exercises exactly in proportion as the part of his conduct which he determines according to his own judgment and feelings is a large one. It is possible that he might be guided in some good path, and kept out of harm's way, without any of these things. But what will be his comparative worth as a human being? It really is of importance, not only what men do, but also what manner of men they are that do it. Among the works of man which human life is rightly employed in perfecting and beautifying, the first in importance surely is man himself. Supposing it were possible to get houses built, corn grown, battles fought, causes tried, and even churches erected and prayers said by machinery—by automatons in human form—it would be a considerable loss to exchange for these automatons even the men and women who at present inhabit the more civilized parts of the world, and who assuredly are but starved specimens of what nature can and will produce. Human nature is not a machine to be built after a model, and set to do exactly the work prescribed for it, but a tree, which requires to grow and develop itself on all sides, according to the tendency of the inward forces which make it a living thing.

It will probably be conceded that it is desirable people should exercise their understandings, and that an intelligent following of custom, or even occasionally an intelligent deviation from custom, is better than a blind and simply mechanical adhesion to it. To a certain extent it is admitted that our understanding should be our own; but there is not the same willingness to admit that our desires and impulses should be our own likewise, or that to possess impulses of our own, and of any strength, is anything but a peril and a snare. Yet desires and impulses are as much a part of a perfect human being as beliefs and restraints; and strong impulses are only perilous when not properly balanced, when one set of aims and inclinations is developed into strength, while others, which ought to coexist with them, remain weak and inactive. It is not because men's desires are strong that they act ill; it is because their consciences are weak. There is no natural connection between strong impulses and a weak conscience. The natural connection is the other way. To say that one person's desires and feelings are stronger and more various than those of another is merely to say that he has more of the raw material of human nature and is therefore capable, perhaps of more evil, but certainly of more good. Strong impulses are but another name for energy. Energy may be turned to bad uses; but more good may always be made of an energetic nature than of an indolent and impassive one. Those who have most natural feeling are always those whose cultivated feelings may be made the strongest. The same strong susceptibilities which make the personal impulses vivid and powerful are also the source from whence are generated the most passionate love of virtue and the sternest self-control. It is through the cultivation of these that society both does its duty and protects its interests, not by rejecting the stuff of which heroes are made, because it knows not how to make them. A person whose desires and impulses are his own—are the expression of his own nature, as it has been developed and modified by his own culture—is said to have a character. One whose desires and impulses are not his own has no character, no more than a steam engine has a character. If, in addition to being his own, his impulses are strong and are under the government of a strong will, he has an energetic character. Whoever thinks that individuality of desires and impulses should not be encouraged to unfold itself must maintain that society has no need of strong natures—is not the better for containing many persons who have much character—and that a high general average of energy is not desirable.

In some early states of society, these forces might be, and were, too much ahead of the power which society then possessed of disciplining and controlling them. There has been a time when the element of spontaneity and individuality was in excess, and the social principle had a hard struggle with it. The difficulty then was to induce men of strong bodies or minds to pay obedience to any rules which required them to control their impulses. To overcome this difficulty, law and discipline, like the Popes struggling against the Emperors, asserted a power over the whole man, claiming to control all his life in order to control his character—which society had not found any other sufficient means of binding. But society has now fairly got the better of individuality; and the danger which threatens human nature is not the excess, but the deficiency, of personal impulses and preferences. Things are vastly changed since the passions of those who were strong by station or by personal endowment were in a state of habitual rebellion against laws and ordinances, and required to be rigorously chained up to enable the persons within their reach to enjoy any particle of security. In our times, from the highest class of society down to the lowest, everyone lives as under the eye of a hostile and dreaded censorship. Not only in what concerns others, but in what concerns only themselves, the individual or the family do not ask themselves, what do I prefer? or, what would suit my character and disposition? or, what would allow the best and highest in me to have fair play and enable it to grow and thrive? They ask themselves, what is suitable to my position? what is usually done by persons of my station and pecuniary circumstances? or (worse still) what is usually done by persons of a station and circumstances superior to mine? I do not mean that they choose what is customary in preference to what suits their own inclination. It does not occur to them to have any inclination except for what is customary. Thus the mind itself is bowed to the yoke: even in what people do for pleasure, conformity is the first thing thought of; they like in crowds; they exercise choice only among things commonly done; peculiarity of taste, eccentricity of conduct are shunned equally with crimes, until by dint of not following their own nature they have no nature to follow: their human capacities are withered and starved; they become incapable of any strong wishes or native pleasures, and are generally without either opinions or feelings of home growth, or properly their own. Now is this, or is it not, the desirable condition of human nature?

.   .   .

It is not by wearing down into uniformity all that is individual in themselves, but by cultivating it and calling it forth, within the limits imposed by the rights and interests of others, that human beings become a noble and beautiful object of contemplation; and as the works partake the character of those who do them, by the same process human life also becomes rich, diversified, and animating, furnishing more abundant aliment to high thoughts and elevating feelings, and strengthening the tie which binds every individual to the race, by making the race infinitely better worth belonging to. In proportion to the development of his individuality, each person becomes more valuable to himself, and is, therefore, capable of being more valuable to others. There is a greater fullness of life about his own existence, and when there is more life in the units there is more in the mass which is composed of them. As much compression as is necessary to prevent the stronger specimens of human nature from encroaching on the rights of others cannot be dispensed with; but for this there is ample compensation even in the point of view of human development. The means of development which the individual loses by being prevented from gratifying his inclinations to the injury of others are chiefly obtained at the expense of the development of other people. And even to himself there is a full equivalent in the better development of the social part of his nature, rendered possible by the restraint put upon the selfish part. To be held to rigid rules of justice for the sake of others develops the feelings and capacities which have the good of others for their object. But to be restrained in things not affecting their good, by their mere displeasure, develops nothing valuable except such force of character as may unfold itself in resisting the restraint. If acquiesced in, it dulls and blunts the whole nature. To give any fair play to the nature of each, it is essential that different persons should be allowed to lead different lives. In proportion as this latitude has been exercised in any age has that age been noteworthy to posterity. Even despotism does not produce its worst effects so long as individuality exists under it; and whatever crushes individuality is despotism, by whatever name it may be called and whether it professes to be enforcing the will of God or the injunctions of men.

Having said that the individuality is the same thing with development, and that it is only the cultivation of individuality which produces, or can produce, well-developed human beings, I might here close the argument; for what more or better can be said of any condition of human affairs than that it brings human beings themselves nearer to the best thing they can be? Or what worse can be said of any obstruction to good than that it prevents this? Doubtless, however, these considerations will not suffice to convince those who most need convincing; and it is necessary further to show that these developed human beings are of some use to the undeveloped—to point out to those who do not desire liberty, and would not avail themselves of it, that they may be in some intelligible manner rewarded for allowing other people to make use of it without hindrance.

In the first place, then, I would suggest that they might possibly learn something from them. It will not be denied by anybody that originality is a valuable element in human affairs. There is always need of persons not only to discover new truths and point out when what were once truths are true no longer, but also to commence new practices and set the example of more enlightened conduct and better taste and sense in human life. This cannot well be gainsaid by anybody who does not believe that the world has already attained perfection in all its ways and practices. It is true that this benefit is not capable of being rendered by everybody alike; there are but few persons, in comparison with the whole of mankind, whose experiments, if adopted by others, would be likely to be any improvement on established practice. But these few are the salt of the earth; without them, human life would become a stagnant pool. Not only is it they who introduce good things which did not before exist; it is they who keep the life in those which already exist. If there were nothing new to be done, would human intellect cease to be necessary? Would it be a reason why those who do the old things should forget why they are done, and do them like cattle, not like human beings? There is only too great a tendency in the best beliefs and practices to degenerate into the mechanical; and unless there were a succession of persons whose ever-recurring originality prevents the grounds of those beliefs and practices from becoming merely traditional, such dead matter would not resist the smallest shock from anything really alive, and there would be no reason why civilization should not die out, as in the Byzantine Empire. Persons of genius, it is true, are, and are always likely to be, a small minority; but in order to have them, it is necessary to preserve the soil in which they grow. Genius can only breathe freely in an *atmosphere* of freedom. Persons of genius are, *ex vi termini,* more individual than any other people—less capable, consequently, of fitting themselves, without hurtful compression, into any of the small number of molds which society provides in order to save its members the trouble of forming their own character. If from timidity they consent to be forced into one of these molds, and to let all that part of themselves which cannot expand under the pressure remain unexpanded, society will be little the better for their genius. If they are of a strong character and break their fetters, they become a mark for the society which has not succeeded in reducing them to commonplace, to point out with solemn warning as "wild," "erratic," and the like —much as if one should complain of the Niagara river for not flowing smoothly between its banks like a Dutch canal.

I insist thus emphatically on the importance of genius and the necessity of allowing it to unfold itself freely both in thought and in practice, being well aware that no one will deny the position in theory, but knowing also that almost everyone, in reality, is totally indifferent to it. People think genius a fine thing if it enables a man to write an exciting poem or paint a picture. But in its true sense, that of originality in thought and action, though no one says that it is not a thing to be admired, nearly all, at heart, think that they can do very well without it. Unhappily this is too natural to be wondered at. Originality is the one thing which unoriginal minds cannot feel the use of. They cannot see what it is to do for them: how should they? If they could see what it would do for them, it would not be originality. The first service which originality has to render them is that of opening their eyes: which being once fully done, they would have a chance of being themselves original. Meanwhile, recollecting that nothing was ever done which someone was not the first to do, and that all good things which exist are the fruits of originality, let them be modest enough to believe that there is something still left for it to accomplish, and assure themselves that they are more in need of originality, the less they are conscious of the want.

. . .

I have said that it is important to give the freest scope possible to uncustomary things, in order that it may in time appear which of these are fit to be converted into customs. But independence of action and disregard of custom are not solely deserving of encouragement for the chance they afford that better modes of action, and customs more worthy of general adoption, may be struck out; nor is it only persons of decided mental superiority who have a just claim to carry on their lives in their own way. There is no reason that all human existence should be constructed on some one or some small number of patterns. If a person possesses any tolerable amount of common sense and experience, his own mode of laying out his existence is the best, not because it is the best in itself, but because it is his own mode. Human beings are not like sheep; and even sheep are not undistinguishably alike. A man cannot get a coat or a pair of boots to fit him unless they are either made to his measure or he has a whole warehouseful to choose from; and is it easier to fit him with a life than with a coat, or are human beings more like one another in their whole physical and spiritual conformation than in the shape of their feet? If it were only that people have diversities of taste, that is reason enough for not attempting to shape them all after one model. But different persons also require different conditions for their spiritual development; and can no more exist healthily in the same moral than all the variety of plants can in the same physical, atmosphere and climate. The same things which are helps to one person toward the cultivation of his higher nature are hindrances to another. The same mode of life is a healthy excitement to one, keeping all his faculties of action and enjoyment in their best order, while to another it is a distracting burden which suspends or crushes all internal life.

. . .

OF THE LIMITS TO THE AUTHORITY OF SOCIETY OVER THE INDIVIDUAL

What, then, is the rightful limit to the sovereignty of the individual over himself? Where does the authority of society begin? How much of human life should be assigned to individuality, and how much to society?

Each will receive its proper share if each has that which more particularly concerns it. To individuality should belong the part of life in which it is chiefly the individual that is interested; to society, the part which chiefly interests society.

Though society is not founded on a contract, and though no good purpose is answered by inventing a contract in order to deduce social obligations from it, everyone who receives the protection of society owes a return for the benefit, and the fact of living in society renders it indispensable that each should be bound to observe a certain line of conduct toward the rest. This conduct consists, first, in not injuring the interests of one another, or rather certain interests which, either by express legal provision or by tacit understanding, ought to be considered as rights; and secondly, in each person's bearing his share (to be fixed on some equitable principle) of the labors and sacrifices incurred for defending the society or its members from injury and molestation. These conditions society is justified in enforcing at all costs to those who endeavor to withhold fulfillment. Nor is this all that society may do. The acts of an individual may be hurtful to others or wanting in due consideration for their welfare, without going to the length of violating any of their consti-tuted rights. The offender may then be justly punished by opinion, though not by law. As soon as any part of a person's conduct affects prejudicially the interests of others, society has jurisdiction over it, and the question whether the general welfare will or will not be promoted by interfering with it becomes open to discussion. But there is no room for entertaining any such question when a person's conduct affects the inter-ests of no persons besides himself, or needs not affect them unless they like (all the persons concerned being of full age and the ordinary amount of understanding). In all such cases, there should be perfect freedom, legal and social, to do the action and stand the consequences.

It would be a great misunderstanding of this doctrine to suppose that it is one of selfish indifference which pretends that human beings have no business with each other's conduct in life, and that they should not concern themselves about the well-doing or well-being of one another, unless their own interest is involved. Instead of any diminution, there is need of a great increase of disinterested exertion to promote the good of others. But disinterested benevolence can find other instruments to persuade people to their good than whips and scourges, either of the literal or the metaphorical sort. I am the last person to undervalue the self-regarding virtues; they are only second in importance, if even sec-ond, to the social. It is equally the business of education to cultivate both. But even education works by conviction and persuasion as well as by compulsion, and it is by the former only that, when the period of educa-tion is passed, the self-regarding virtues should be inculcated. Human beings owe to each other help to distinguish the better from the worse, and encouragement to choose the former and avoid the latter. They should be forever stimulating each other to increased exercise of their higher faculties and increased direction of their feelings and aims toward wise instead of foolish, elevating instead of degrading, objects and con-templations. But neither one person, nor any number of persons, is warranted in saying to another human creature of ripe years that he shall not do with his life for his own benefit what he chooses to do with it. He is the person most interested in his own well-being: the interest which any other person, except in cases of strong personal attachment, can have in it is trifling compared with that which he himself has; the interest which society has in him individually (except as to his conduct to others) is fractional and altogether indirect, while with respect to his own feelings and circumstances the most ordinary man or woman has means of knowl-edge immeasurably surpassing those that can be possessed by anyone else. The interference of society to overrule his judgment and purposes in what only regards himself must be grounded on general presumptions which may be altogether wrong and, even if right, are as likely as not to be misapplied to individual cases, by persons no better acquainted with the circumstances of such cases than those are who look at them merely from without. In this department, therefore, of human affairs, individuality has its proper field of action. In the conduct of human beings toward one another it is necessary that general rules should for the most part be observed in order that people may know what they have to expect; but in each person's own concerns his individual spontaneity is entitled to free exercise. Considerations to aid his judgment, exhortations to strengthen his will may be offered to him, even obtruded on him, by others; but he himself is the final judge. All errors which he is likely to commit against advice and warning are far outweighed by the evil of allowing others to constrain him to what they deem his good.

.   .   .

John Dewey and James H. Tufts
THE INDIVIDUAL AND THE SOCIAL

Historically, the principle of individualism was the weapon of the emerging bourgeois class in its struggle with the feudal aristocracy. Against feudal restrictions in the political and economic sphere, the principle argued for freedom of trade and industrial development and for the right of each individual to pursue his or her interests, so long as this did not interfere with the same right of others. Exponents of individualism believed that the problems of society would automatically be solved so long as government was limited to basic police powers.

The historical reality, however, failed to conform to the theory. Although the establishment of liberal democratic states did provide a greater degree of individual liberty than had hitherto been the case, it soon found itself confronted by other pressing social problems. As industry grew, wealth became concentrated in fewer and fewer hands. Those who controlled the wealth of the nation also controlled the political process to a degree vastly disproportional to their numbers. For the masses of people who hired themselves out for a wage, the liberal society did not offer the free development of individual potential that social thinkers like John Stuart Mill had hoped it would. What became clear was that various kinds of social legislation would be required beyond the scope of individualism as it was originally understood. Most of us now take for granted such things as public education, a progressive tax structure, social security, disability insurance, poverty programs, a welfare system, and a variety of regulatory agencies.

Part of the difficulty with historical individualism has been the tendency to see the main problem as a conflict between the individual and society, and to view individualism as necessarily opposed to any form of collectivism. In the selection that follows, John Dewey and James Tufts argue that this is a pseudo-opposition and that the separation of the individual from the social is a

*pure fiction. The real conflict is always between certain groups of individuals and
certain social institutions.*

*Nonetheless, while rejecting individualism in its historical form, Dewey and
Tufts attempt to give it a new content. The ethical ideal is still the greatest
possible freedom to develop one's potentials compatible with the same freedom for
others. But because the old-style individualism is now understood, in practice, to
favor those already powerful with the freedom to pursue their own advantage,
the new individualism must develop a material instead of a purely formal
analysis. It must seek to understand concretely the ways in which our social
institutions perpetuate an inequality of opportunity, and it must provide the basis
for developing public controls by which an equality of conditions can be
established. For a further consideration of this problem, the reader should consult
Section 9.*

The tendency to split into opposed camps concerning the respective
moral claims of unrestrained individuality and of social control affects all
phases of life, education, politics, economics, art, religion. It also determines the attitude taken toward more imponderable things. On one side,
it is asserted that collective action tends toward regimentation into mechanical uniformity; toward a mass production of people turned out in
a common mold, with individual differences wiped out; that social influence is leveling, that it obliterates distinction and tends toward an average which spells mediocrity. Democracy, as compared with aristocracy, is
condemned for its alleged tendencies in this direction. Organized society,
it is contended, favors censorship; it tends to meddle constantly with
private affairs; to interfere with what the individual thinks, eats, and
drinks; by its nature it is hostile, so it is said, to freedom of inquiry,
discussion, criticism, since such freedom almost certainly produces variation of judgment and action. Thinking is sure to bring some phase of the
established social order under adverse criticism and hence is suppressed
by those who have more concern for society than for individuals.

Thus there develops a definite school of thought which holds that the
action of society in its collective and organized capacity should be limited
to a minimum; that its action should be mainly negative, restricting privately initiated action only when it operates to harm others. All, except
the most extreme, of this school, admit the necessity of occasional interference of this negative sort, but urge that is should be confined to what
men do externally and should never be extended to the essentials of
individuality, to desire, emotion, thought, belief. And they support themselves by pointing to a long and disastrous historical persecution of
variation in belief; to the fanaticism and intolerance which have been bred
in desire for social conformity.

On the other side stands the collectivist school. Some of its members
assume that individuals left to themselves are actuated only by "self-
love," which is so powerful as to produce, when it is left to itself, a "war
of all against all." Others point to the influence of social connection in

the culture of individuals who left to themselves are at best raw and crude. They point to the fact that, from the standpoint of original nature, individuals hardly rise above the animal level; that what they possess in the way of civilization comes to them through nurture and not from nature; that culture is transmitted not by means of biological heredity, but by tradition, transmission of education, books, art products, and the influence of enduring institutions. Maintenance and strengthening of these collective social forces is, therefore, the primary duty of all those who are interested in the moralization of individuals. At the present time, the point more emphasized is a practical one. It is claimed that only organized social action can remake the old social institutions which persist because of mere inertia and the self-interest of a privileged few. Hence they are unfitted to serve the needs of the present day, a reconstruction especially of economic and industrial conditions being imperatively demanded. Such a change is obviously upon a large scale and of vast extent. It can be effected, therefore, only by collective organized action.

THREE ASPECTS OF THE CONFLICT

While persons incline in one direction or another, only confusion results from lumping together all issues as so many species of a more general issue of individual *versus* social. In fact, there are a number of questions which are distinct, each of which must be met and dealt with on its own merits, and in which the individual and the social are not opposed terms. Indeed, in the strict sense of the terms, *no* question can be reduced to the individual on one side and the social on the other. As is frequently pointed out, society consists of individuals, and the term "social" designates only the fact that individuals are in fact linked together, related to one another in intimate ways. "Society" cannot conflict, it is pointed out, with its own constituents; one might as well put number in general in opposition to integers taken severally. On the other hand, individuals cannot be opposed to the relations which they themselves maintain. Only an unreal and impossible being, one completely isolated, disconnected, can be put in opposition to society.

It is surely a fact that there is nothing called society over and above John Smith, Susan Jones, and other individual persons. Society as something apart from individuals is a pure fiction. On the other hand, nothing in the universe, not even physical things, exists apart from some form of association; there is nothing from the atom to man which is not involved in conjoint action. Planets exist and act in solar systems, and these systems in galaxies. Plants and animals exist and act in conditions of much more intimate and complete interaction and interdependence. Human beings are generated only by union of individuals; the human infant is so feeble in his powers as to be dependent upon the care and protection of others; he cannot grow up without the help given by others; his mind is nourished by contact with others and by intercommunication; as soon as the individual graduates from family life he finds himself taken into other associations, neighborhood, school, village, professional, or business associates. Apart from the ties which bind him to others, he is nothing. Even the hermit and Robinson Crusoe, as far as they live on a plane higher than that of the brutes, continue even in physical isolation to be what they are, to think the thoughts which go through their minds, to entertain their characteristic aspirations, because of social connections which existed in the past and which still persist in their imagination and emotions.

The facts urged are all of them true. They bear *upon false statements of the nature of the problems at issue; they do not in any way resolve the actual and important conflicts which exist.* It is important to bear them in mind because they protect us from misconceiving the nature of the problem. For reasons just stated, there can be no conflict between *the* individual and *the* social. For both of these terms refer to pure abstractions. What do exist are conflicts between *some* individuals and *some* arrangements in social life; between groups and classes of individuals; between nations and races; between old traditions imbedded in institutions and new ways of thinking and acting which spring from those few individuals who depart from and who attack what is socially accepted. There is also a genuine difference of convictions as to the way in which, at any given time, these conflicts should be met and managed. There are reasons for holding that they are best settled by private and voluntary action and also for holding that they are best settled by means of combined organized action. No general theory about the individual and the social can settle conflicts or even point out the way in which they should be resolved.

But conflicts nevertheless do exist; they are not got rid of by asserting, what is perfectly true, that there can be no wholesale opposition between society and individuals. How are they to be explained, and to what general kinds can they be reduced? In the first place, there is no single thing denominated "society"; there are many societies, many forms of association. These different groups and classes struggle in many ways against one another and have very diverse values. Men associate in friendship and in antagonism; for recreation and for crime; they unite in clubs and fraternities, in cliques and sects, in churches and armies; to promote science and art and to prey upon others; they unite in business partnerships and corporations. Then these social units compete vigorously against one another. They unite in nations and the nations war with one another; workers combine in trade unions and employers in trade associations and association intensifies struggle between opposite interests. Political life is carried on by parties which oppose each other, and within each party there are contending factions or "wings." Struggle within an organization is indeed a common phenomenon; in trade unions the central organization and the local units often pull different ways, just as in politics there is usually a struggle between forces making for centralization and for local autonomy. Economically, individuals form into groups, and the union accentuates struggle between producer, distributor, and consumer. Church has vied with State for supremacy; the scientific group has at times had to contend with both. Different groups try to get hold of the machinery of government. Officials tend to combine to protect their special interests and these interests are contrary to those of private individuals; it is a recurrent phenomenon for rulers to use power to oppress and harass their subjects. Indeed, so common is it that the whole struggle for political liberty has been represented as a struggle of subjects to emancipate themselves from the tyranny of rulers.

There are then a multitude of conflicts not between individuals and society but between groups and other groups, between some individuals and other individuals. Analysis shows that they tend to fall into classes marked by similar traits, and these traits help explain why there arose the idea that the conflict is between individual and society.

1. There is the struggle between the *dominant* group and the group of groups, occupying, at the time, an *inferior* position of power and economic wealth. The superior group under such circumstances always thinks of itself as representing the social interest, and represents other groups which challenge its power as rebels against constituted authority, as seeking for the satisfaction of their personal appetites against the demands of law and order. A somewhat striking example of this phase of the matter is seen at the present time in the split between those who hold up the political state as the supreme social form, the culminating manifestation of the supreme common moral will, the ultimate source and sole guarantor of all social values, and those who regard the state as simply one of many forms of association, and as one which by undue extension of its claims into virtual monopoly has brought evils in its train. The conflict is not, as was believed earlier, between the state and individual but between the state as the dominant group and other groups seeking greater liberty of action. It is similar in principle, though often opposite in point of material constituents, to the earlier struggle of political groups to get free from the dominant authority of the church.

2. At a certain stage of such conflicts, the inferior but growing group is not organized; it is loosely knit; its members often do not speak for a group which has achieved recognition, much less for social organization as a whole. The dominant group on the other hand is not only well established, but it is *accepted*, acknowledged; it is supported by the bulk of opinion and sentiment of that time. A government which at a later period is regarded as thoroughly despotic cannot always have been so regarded. In that case it would have been easily overthrown.

To remain in power a dominant class must at least seem to the mass to represent and to sustain interests which they themselves prize. There is thus added to the conflict of the old and established class with the inferior but developing group, the conflict of values that are generally accepted with those which are coming into being. This for a time takes the form of a struggle between a majority *conserving* the old, and a minority interested in the generation of something new, in *progress*. Since it takes time for an idea to gain recognition and for a value to become appreciated and shared, the new and relatively unorganized, although it may represent a genuinely important social value, is felt to be that of dissenting individuals. The values of a past society which are to be conserved are recognized as social, while those of a future society which has yet to be brought into being are taken to be those of individuals only.

In these two instances, the conflict is commonly thought to be between those interested in order and those concerned in progress, where maintenance of order is interpreted as "social" and the initiation of progress as the function of individuals. Even those whose activity in the end establishes a new social order often feel at the time that the enemy is social organization itself. Moreover, every social order has many defects, and these defects are taken to be signs of evils inhering in every kind of social organization. The latter is felt to be nothing but a system of chains holding individuals in bondage. This feeling grows up particularly when old institutions are decaying and corrupt. As in France in the latter eighteenth century and Russia in the later nineteenth, they then call out an intense moral individualism like that of Rousseau and that of Tolstoi respectively. When organization needs to be changed all organization is likely to be felt oppressive. The temporary phenomenon is taken as an illustration of an eternal truth, and the needs of a particular situation frozen into a universal principle.

3. There are also cases in which the troubles of the present are associated with the breakdown of a past order, while existing evils are capable of being remedied only by organized social action. Then the alignment of so-called individual and social is altered, indeed, is virtually reversed. Those who profit by the existing régime and who wish to have it retained are now the "individualists," and those who wish to see great changes brought about by combined action are the "collectivists." These latter feel that institutions as they exist are a repressive shell preventing social growth. They find disintegration, instability, inner competition to be so great that existing society is such only in outward appearance, being in reality what Carlyle called the "society" of his day, namely, "anarchy plus the constable." On the other hand stand those who are at a special advantage in the situation. They extol it as the product of individual energy, initiative, industry, and freedom; these precious qualities will be imperiled by adoption of a plan of conjoint collective activity. They represent the social order desired by others to be one of servility which crushes out the incentives to individual effort, and which creates dependence upon an impersonal whole, putting a vicious paternalism in place of self-reliance. "Collectivism" in their mouths is a term of reproach. In short, those who are on the side of keeping the *status quo* intact are now the "individualists," those who want great social changes are the "collectivists," since the changes desired are on so large a scale that they can be effected only through collective action.

We shall accordingly substitute the consideration of definite conflicts, at particular times and places, for a general opposition between social and individual. Neither "social" nor "individual," in general, has any fixed meaning. All morality (including immorality) is both individual and social—individual in its immediate inception and execution, in the desires, choices, dispositions from which conduct proceeds; social in its occasions, material, and consequences. That which is regarded as anti-social and immoral at one time is hailed later on as the beginning of great and beneficent social reform—as is seen in the fate of those moral prophets who were condemned as criminals only to be honored later as benefactors of the race. Organizations that were punished as conspiracies by despotic governments have been regarded as the authors of a glorious liberty after their work has succeeded. These facts do not signify that there is no enduring criterion for judgment but that this criterion is to be found in consequences, and not in some general conception of individual and social.

The points just made suggest three angles from which a social problem may be analyzed in detail in order to decide upon the moral values involved. First, the struggle between a dominant class and a rising class or group; secondly, between old and new forms and modes of association and organization; thirdly, between accomplishing results by voluntary private effort, and by organized action involving the use of public agencies. In historic terms, there is the struggle between class and mass; between conservative and liberal (or radical); and between the use of private and public agencies, extension or limitation of public action.

An illustration of the first issue is seen in the origin of states organized on a popular instead of upon an autocratic dynastic basis. This origin involved the overthrow of the established institutions which for a long time had regulated social affairs; it emancipated many individuals. But at the same time, it generated new types of social institutions and organizations. It was not in other words a movement toward mere individualism. The second mentioned struggle, that between conservative (or, as his opponents term him, reactionary) and liberal, between those who want to preserve intact what has been already attained and who fear and oppose all social change, and those who aim at social modifications more or less profound, is seen in all phases of life; in religious organizations, with the cleavage into fundamentalist and modernist; in education, with the traditionalist and the "progressive"; in politics, with its divisions into right and left; in industrial society, between capitalism and communism as extreme illustrations. The controversy between believers in private and in public action is manifested in every issue which concerns the extent and area of governmental action. At one extreme, are anarchists shading off into those who believe in *laissez faire* and hold that government is best which governs least, through those who believe in enlargement of governmental functions to serve the general interest, over to state socialists who would have government assume control of all means of production and distribution that are of any great size.

.   .   .

HISTORIC INDIVIDUALISM

... We shall here attempt to illustrate what has been said by a reference to the movement termed "individualism" in a particular sense determined by historical causes.

1. In economics, it is the notion that individuals left free to pursue their own advantage in industry and trade will not only best further their own private interests but will also best promote social progress and contribute most effectively to the satisfaction of the needs of others and hence to the general happiness.

2. Since the "left free" in this statement signifies in point of practice freedom from regulation by legislation and governmental administration, the doctrine has its political side. It signifies that the activities of government shall be restricted as closely as possible to policing society; that is, to keeping order, to preventing encroachments by one person upon the lawful rights of others, and to securing redress when such interference with the rights of others has occurred. In current phrases, it signifies "keep government out of business"; at least keep it out as much as possible.

3. Since the doctrine has an "ideological" support, it also signifies a certain general philosophy, which may be called that of the "natural" *versus* "artificial." Economic activities on this view are natural and governed by natural laws. Men naturally seek to satisfy their wants; labor or the expenditure of energy is naturally economized so that there will be the utmost return for the minimum outgo; to make the future secure men naturally abstain from consuming all they produce, thus laying by capital to increase their future productivity. Since the output of work is greatest when there is the skill which comes with restriction of effort to one field, division of labor is inherent in the development and this division brings about exchange and trade. There results a general interdependence in which each is forced to find the line of work in which he is most productive and to do the things which, in order to bring the most return to himself, will best serve the needs of others. In contrast with the "natural laws" of this economic process, political laws are artificial; the first are implanted by nature (often conceived of as vice-regent of God) in the human frame. The second are man-made. The presumption is always in favor of natural laws and their workings and against human "interference."

4. To this idea of natural laws, identical with economic laws, was joined an idea of natural *rights*. According to this view, certain rightful claims belong inherently to individuals apart from civil society and the state. The right to life, to property which one has personally produced, to contract or make agreements with others, are such rights; they contrast with civil and political rights which are dependent upon the civil and political organization of society. Being innate and inalienable, they set fixed limits to the activity of government. Government exists in order to protect them, if it infringes on them, it violates its own function so that

citizens are released from an obligation to obedience. At the least, courts must pronounce such action invalid because in violation of natural rights.

5. There was often, although not always, associated with the above mentioned four points, the doctrine of self-interest, taken as a scientific support based on psychology. According to this view, human nature is so constituted as to be averse to all activity involving the sacrifice of abstinence and toil except when an incentive of the prospect of a greater advantage or profit is offered. All individuals are supposed to be on the alert for their own interest and to be skilled in calculating where it lies —provided at least that they are not paralyzed or confused by oppressive laws and artificial social institutions.

These various considerations taken as a whole constitute the doctrine of "individualism" in its narrower historic sense. It was formulated during the eighteenth century. It had immense influence—far from extinct as yet—in shaping legal and political institutions throughout the nineteenth century. There were definite causes for its appearance and its growth. Newly invented machines, run by steam power instead of by hand, were creating a new industrial development, while existing laws and customs expressed an agrarian culture and contained many feudal survivals. They were filled with regulations which obstructed commerce, foreign and domestic, which hampered the development of the new type of industry, and which favored landlords at the expense of the manufacturing and mercantile class. European governments regulated (in fact obstructed) international trade in the interest of accumulation of specie in the governmental treasury, at the expense of industry and commerce. The doctrine of economic *laissez faire* then presented itself as an unshackling of human initiative, energy, and inventive skill, as opening a definite road of progress. Established organization on the other hand represented inertia, sloth, and repression. This temporary historic conflict was generalized into an inherent and absolute opposition between the "individual" and the "social," the "natural" and the "artificial."

The period coincided with the beginnings of what we now term popular and democratic government. Governments in general were either corrupt or oppressive or both. They were felt—and at the time with good reason—to mark arbitrary limitations on the legitimate freedom of individuals. In the United States, this feeling was reenforced by the struggle between the colonists and the home government in Great Britain. It was an easy step from the restrictions imposed on the colonies by Great Britain to the idea that all government by its very nature tends to be repressive, and that the great aim in political life is to limit the encroachments of governments in order to make secure the liberty of citizens. The United States was born in the atmosphere of jealousy and fear of state action; the tradition has persisted; it forms a large part of the present power of individualistic philosophy. This feeling, combined with the personal initiative, independence, and self-help that were so indispensable under pioneer conditions in a country of small population and having seemingly unbounded natural resources, operated to create a moral background for the doctrine of individualism. Although the idea of democracy was that of self-rule, the traditions and emotions generated under conditions of alien rule persisted to such an extent that any conception that the people could use their own instrument, government, as a constructive agency for furthering their own well-being, was confined at most to the administration of local communities. The doctrine of the superiority of "natural laws" to man-made law led to an abdication of effort at intelligent control; economic processes were supposed to work of themselves and to a beneficent end. The idea of natural rights was interpreted by courts to forbid legislation which in any way disturbed the *status quo* in the distribution of property, or which, in the interest of workers, limited the power of free contract—the legal fiction being that all parties to an industrial arrangement were equally free to enter or not into the arrangement.

Meantime the original circumstances, economic and political, under which the philosophy of so-called individualism grew up and had had, upon the whole, a useful effect, changed completely. Industrialism supplanted agrarianism as the ruling force. The machine became the regular instead of the novel and exceptional means of production. Impersonal corporations, instead of individual employers in personal contact with workmen, became the rule. Accumulations of capital grew large, and then merged into larger units. The doctrine of liberty and contract and of non-interference with the customary rules of industry inured to the benefit of the employer and investor, and to the detriment of the workers— that of the mass of people. Protective legislation began to make its way and was followed by the development of a "collectivist" point of view in opposition to the older "individualism." The rôles were reversed. The accepted, the established, social order came to include the things which earlier had had to be striven for by a minority. The social order was now itself "individualistic" in the sense defined above, and the doctrines and slogans which had been used earlier by dissidents and reformers were now used to defend the *status quo.* "Liberty" meant *in effect* the legally unrestrained action of those advantageously placed in the existing distribution of power, through possession of capital and ownership of the means of production.

The ethical formula of the individualistic philosophy was and still remains: The greatest possible freedom of individuals as long as that freedom is not used to the detriment of equal or *similar* liberty on the part of other individuals. The formula has had great vogue; as already intimated, it once did a useful service in getting rid of laws and institutions that had outlived their value. But there is, as an intellectual statement, a flaw in it, a "catch." What is meant by *like* or *equal* freedom? If it signified materially alike, equal in actual power, it would be difficult to take objection to it. The formula would be compatible with the efforts of organized society to *equalize conditions.* It would, for example, justify public action to secure to all an education which would effect a complete development of their capacities, so that they might meet one another on a plane of knowledge and trained intelligence as nearly even as possible. It would justify legislation to equalize the standing of those now at a disadvantage because of inequality in physical power, in wealth, in command of the machinery of employment. It would justify, in other words, a vast amount of so-called social legislation which the individualistic theory as usually held condemns.

But the interpretation given to the ideal of equality was formal, not material; it was legalistic not realistic. Individuals were said to be equal provided they were equal *before the law.* In legal theory, the individual who has a starving family to support is equal in making a bargain about hours and conditions of labor and wages, with an employer who has large accumulated wealth to fall back on, and who finds that many other workers near the subsistence line are clamoring for an opportunity to earn something with which to support their families.

Morally speaking, individuals cannot be split up into a number of isolated and independent powers, all of which can be compared, one by one, with like powers of others so as to determine their equality. The individual person is a whole: what he labors at and the reward he gets are things which affect all his capacities, desires, and satisfactions—and not only his own but those of the members of his family. Just as we cannot tell what is "due" a man until we have taken his whole self into account, so we cannot tell whether a man's freedom is furthered or is interfered with until we have taken into account not just some single point, formally and legally defined, but the bearing of the factor in question (for example, "freedom" of contract) upon his whole plane of living, his opportunities for development, and his relations to others.

The purpose of this historical survey is not to indicate that some anti-"individualistic" principle is correct, so that we should supplant it by a collectivistic formula and program in order to meet the moral requirements of society. It is, first, to suggest the *relativism* of social formulae in their ethical aspect. No single formula signifies the same thing, in its consequences, or in practical meaning under different social conditions. That which was on the side of moral progress in the eighteenth and early nineteenth centuries may be a morally reactionary doctrine in the twentieth century; that which is serviceable now may prove injurious at a later time. This fact is but a statement in more definite form of the impossibility of deriving concrete directions for moral action from the general concepts of individual and social.

From this fact follows the second point. We have to consider the probable consequences of any proposed measure with reference to the situation, as it exists at some defined time and place in which it is to apply. There cannot be any universal rule laid down, for example, regarding the respective scopes of private and public action. All but the most extreme "individualists" stop short of the logical conclusion that there should be no public schools supported by taxation. They are aware of how many children might, under a purely voluntary system, fail to get any education, and they know what inequalities in society would thereby be fostered. Yet, it does not follow that public education is always and only good. A ruling class and the government may use the schools to inculcate particular doctrines in plastic minds; to suppress freedom of inquiry; to turn out minds in a common mold, and a mold favorable to their own special interest. Under such conditions, there is justification for upholding, on moral grounds, the claims of other schools than those supported by the state.

Every question for the extension or restriction of public action should, then, be considered on its merits. There was a time when religion and religious worship were public functions. Almost all peoples are now convinced that it is better that they should be a private, a voluntary, affair. There was a time in English history when the courts of law were not indeed exactly private, but were attached to the domain of feudal lords; there are few today who would question the value of the transfer of the judicial function to the state. But even this transfer is not inconsistent with the growth, under the jurisdiction of government, of private arbitration as a method of settling commercial disputes. If we go further back in history we find the administration of justice in savage tribes a matter of "self-help." There may have been those who opposed its transfer to the public on the ground that it would weaken individual initiative and responsibility and create a servile dependence on state paternalism. In general, we can say that many interests have shifted from public to private and *vice versa* in connection with changes in science, industry, and public sentiment. Every proposed measure of public policy should, therefore, be considered on the ground of its own effects on the welfare of the members of a community, and not be disposed of on the basis of some abstract theory of either the individual or the social.

. . . .

K. T. Fann
CHINA AND THE ETHICS OF LIBERATION

The Chinese revolution has served as an important example for liberation movements throughout the world. This is not only because China has succeeded in creating a socialist economy in which the illiteracy and starvation of the recent past have been virtually eliminated. More important, Chinese socialism has opted for a fundamentally different moral order, in which the value of community takes precedence over individual self-interest.

In the following article, K. T. Fann analyzes the ethical impact of the Chinese revolution as a fundamental challenge to bourgeois individualism. According to Fann, the ideology of individualism helps perpetuate a state of affairs in which human beings act almost entirely from selfish, egotistical motives and in which they are alienated from one another. In other words, individualism's emphasis on a private sphere of personal development is an attempt to rationalize a sense of isolation. Individualism, Fann asserts, prevents us from acting in concert with one another to confront our mutual problems, and thus serves the interests of the capitalist class, which continues to dominate us. In contrast, the ethics of liberation emphasizes the value of community, in which "everybody thinks everything is their business." The alternative to privacy is not the manipulation or domination of others but a genuine mutuality of concern. This requires that we overcome the acquisitiveness and selfishness of capitalist ideology, that we replace "I" by "we," and that our main motive for doing something become, in Mao's words, "to serve the people."

What is the relationship between ethics and liberation? This is a question of central importance to any liberation movement. Living in bourgeois society, we are justified in viewing the moralizing of politicians and the preachings of ministers with extreme cynicism. And when we encounter a similar moral tone of voice in the pronouncements of liberation movements and their leaders we instinctively react with suspicion. But the apparent similarity is deceptive and we should try to be clear about their essential difference if we are to understand the meaning of liberation.

"Liberation" said Marx, "is a historical not a mental act."[1] It is a real, historical movement of the oppressed to gain freedom. Revolution is the politics of liberation. Its goal is freedom. Counter-revolution is the politics of oppression. Its goal is exploitation. For a revolution to occur, the oppressed must be dissatisfied with the status quo, with what is the case; and must desire something "better," something that should be the case but is not. The objective condition of misery in itself does not give rise to a revolutionary situation. If the oppressed are brainwashed into accepting their fate as a natural state of affairs they will not rebel. Perception of the "better" and belief in the possibility of change are prerequisites of any revolution. Consequently, liberation implies movement toward a goal, an ideal. Every true revolution is inspired and guided by an ideal of a better society. Traditionally, ethics deals with the goals, or the *telos* of human life. It deals with what ought to be the case as opposed to what is the case. It should be remembered that Aristotle wrote a treatise on *politics,* and what we call his *Ethics* was just the first part of his treatise on *politics,* the part that defined the goals, the most inclusive concepts and methods. For him it would be impossible to talk about how to organize a society without first settling the question of "what for?" Politics and economics deal with the "how" of society and ethics deals with the "what for" of society. It's obvious that any liberation movement must not only criticize the status quo but must also have a fairly clear idea of the new social order it wishes to bring about. Politics and ethics must be intimately connected in a revolution. To provide a real example, I shall describe the essential role of the new socialist ethics in shaping the Chinese Revolution. However, before I do that, I would like to analyze

[1]Marx and Engels, *The German Ideology* (Moscow: Progress Publishers, 1964), p. 56.

the separation of ethics from politics in bourgeois society and outline the main features of the bourgeois value system as an object for comparison.

In bourgeois society, since the goal of the economic system is the exploitation of the majority, it is best for the ruling class if people do not question the status quo—if the people do not ask how things ought to be. Since the whole economic system is unethical, it is best that none ask ethical questions. Under capitalism, alienated human individuals are bound to each other and to society by an invisible umbilical cord: the economic law of value. As Marx and Engels wrote in the *Communist Manifesto*:

> [The bourgeois] has left remaining no other bond between man and man than naked self-interest, than callous "cash payment." It has drowned the most heavenly ecstasies of religious fervor, of chivalrous enthusiasm, of philistine sentimentalism, in the icy water of egotistical calculation. It has resolved personal worth into exchange value, and in place of the numberless indefensible chartered freedoms, has set up that single, unconscionable freedom, free trade. In one word, for exploitation, veiled by religious and political illusions, it has established naked, shameless, direct, brutal exploitation. The bourgeoisie has stripped of its halo every occupation hitherto honored and looked up to with reverent awe. It has converted the physician, the lawyer, the priest, the poet, the man of science, into its paid wage-laborers.

The motivation for every activity and every profession is self-interest, profit. Money becomes the bond of all bonds. It acts upon all facets of our lives, shaping our needs and our destinies. We no longer ask the question "what for?" The profit motive becomes the dominant force in our lives and is reflected in our thinking. People became physicians not because they want to help the sick, but because they want to make money. The worth of things and persons is measured mainly in terms of money. The capitalist way of looking at things is so ingrained in our thoughts that we cannot even recognize that there are legitimate reasons for doing things other than making money. There is no human activity that cannot be turned into a business enterprise. Even a hobby such as stamp collecting has become a multi-million-dollar business. People cannot appreciate the value of an object of art in itself unless a price tag is attached to it. In their bourgeois way of thinking, everything has a price; otherwise it is worthless.

The capitalist mode of thought is applied not only to things but also to persons. A person's worth is calculated according to the amount of money he possesses. Marx described this succinctly in his early manuscript:

> The extent of the power of money is the extent of my power. Money's properties are my properties and essential powers—the properties and powers of its possessor. Thus, what *I am* and *am capable of* is by no means determined by my individuality. I *am* ugly, but I can buy for myself the most *beautiful* of women. Therefore I am not *ugly*, for the effect of *ugliness*—its

deterrent power is nullified by money. . . . I am bad, dishonest, unscrupulous, stupid; but money is honored, and hence its possessor. Money is the supreme good, therefore its possessor is good. . . . I am *stupid,* but money is the *real mind* of all things and how then should its possessor be stupid? Besides, he can buy talented people for himself, and is he who has power over the talented not more talented than the talented? Do not I, who thanks to money am capable of *all* that the human heart longs for, possess all human capacities? . . . If *money* is the bond binding me to *human* life, binding society to me, binding me and nature and man, is not money the bond of all *bonds?* Can it not dissolve and bind all ties? Is it not, therefore, the universal *agent of separation?* It is the true *agent of separation* as well as the true *binding agent.*[2]

Money binds us all together as selfish, egotistical, atomized, and alienated economic animals. It separates us from each other, from the community, from our human needs over and above our animal needs. We no longer know how to relate to each other on a human level. We treat others and ourselves as commodities, products. Professors speak of their own marketability and regard their students as products. At his inauguration a university president recently said, "We ought to think about the quality as well as the quantity of our products." At the back of his mind he sees the university as a factory producing certain products to be sold on the market. Unfortunately, this inhuman view of the educational system is an accurate description of reality. And how often do we make friends not because we like them, but because we want something from them? Persons are treated as objects, as use values. Alienated, egotistical individuals are incapable of relating to each other even on a man-and-woman basis. The perverse obsession with sex in the bourgeois world is not a sign of sexual liberation but a symptom of final alienation in a decaying society. The increase of pornographic literature and movies and the general liberalization of sexual behavior is not an indication of sexual fulfillment but an expression of sexual frustration. The individual in this decaying society is isolated, each pursuing a chimera called self-fulfillment, or individuality. Loneliness becomes epidemic. In bourgeois ideology this state of affairs is sanctified as individualism.

Recently I received a letter from a white friend of mine who is working in a community project in the South. She said: "In living with a black family I see and am beginning to accept a communal type environment, in which everybody helps everybody to their well being or worse being. Everybody thinks everything is their business. I haven't accepted that yet; it goes against the very grain of my nature." What constitutes a community is precisely the fact that everybody thinks everything is their business. This goes against the very grain of our "bourgeois" nature. We are taught from an early age "not to talk to strangers." But in a community no one is a stranger. We are always told to mind our own business, to do our own thing, etc. All this culminates in the alienation of individu-

[2]Marx, *The Economic and Philosophic Manuscripts of 1844* (New York: International Publishers, 1968), p. 167.

als from each other, in the loss of community. The result is that in the bourgeois society each person looks out for his or her own interests without regard for the common good, and consequently becomes easy prey for the capitalists.

There is another aspect of this matter. In bourgeois society any time someone else minds your business the purpose is "domination." But in a community the motivation is "concern." It is ironic that in the world today "community" exists only among the poorest, most oppressed sectors of the world—in the ghetto, the jungle, the rice paddies, and so on. The reconstruction of human society will, above all, depend on these people. Bourgeois individualism, with the attendant loss of community, serves the class interest of the capitalists. The atomized individual family, cut off from a community, seeking only its self-interest, provides a mobile work force and prevents the formation of a sense of community or class consciousness which could question and challenge the status quo. Bourgeois individualism is the old imperialist trick of divide-and-rule pushed to its logical extreme.

This same divide-and-rule strategy is even more successfully applied to the ideological sphere. The separation of ethics from politics, economics, sociology, and the natural sciences has become a dogma in the bourgeois educational system. Science (natural or social), we are told from our first day in college, is value free. The first chapter of many textbooks in social science starts with a distinction between "fact" and "value," between "is" and "ought," and then makes it clear that it is the job of science to deal with facts and not values. To be a scientist, to be objective, one is supposed only to describe the functioning of a system but never to evaluate it as good or bad. Marx was most forceful in his critique of political economy:

> If I ask the political economist: Do I obey economic laws if I extract money by offering my body for sale, by surrendering it to another's lust? . . . Then the political economist replies to me: You do not transgress my laws; but see what Cousin Ethics and Cousin Religion have to say about it. My *political economic* ethics and religion have nothing to reproach you with, but whom am I now to believe, political economy or ethics? The ethics of political economy is *acquisition*. . . . The political economy of ethics is the opulence of a good conscience, of virtue, etc.; but how can I live virtuously if I do not live? And how can I have a good conscience if I am not conscious of anything? It stems from the very nature of estrangement that each sphere applies to me a different and opposite yardstick—ethics one and political economy another. . . . [3]

Let us see what Cousin Ethics and Cousin Religion have to say about values and morals. The first lesson in any ethics course is that Ethics does not teach moral values, it only talks about ethics—it analyzes the meaning of words such as "good," "right," etc., and it argues about whether you

[3]*Ibid.,* pp. 151–152.

can derive an "ought" from an "is." Cousin Ethics has nothing to say, and when you ask him about a real moral issue he will recommend that you see Cousin Religion. But Cousin Religion only works on Sundays and he sells the "opiate of the people." He sells you an entrance ticket to a place you can go only after you are dead and for which you have to pay cash now. Besides, he runs his business according to the same capitalist principle as political economy. You deposit your good deeds now, and cash in later, in Heaven. What has this to do with Morality? Nothing. So where do we go to learn moral values? Absolutely nowhere. And this is exactly the way the ruling class wants it to be—a thoroughly unethical society where acquisition and exploitation rule supreme.

Liberation from this oppressive system requires, first of all, the reintroduction of ethics as a motivating force of the revolution. Commitment to a new ethical order is the first prerequisite of a revolutionary. This implies that the revolution must not only change the economic structure of the society, but also change man himself in the process. Marx himself always emphasized that "to work out their own emancipation . . . [the working class] will have to pass through long struggles, through a series of historical processes, transforming circumstances and men."[4] To over-emphasize the role of circumstances over man is mechanical materialism. Marx explains: "The materialist doctrine that men are products of circumstances and upbringing, and that, therefore, changed men are products of other circumstances and changed upbringing, forgets that it is man that changes circumstances and that the educator himself needs educating."[5] To over-emphasize the role of man over circumstances is philosophical idealism. Marx says, "Men make their own history, but they do not make it just as they please, they do not make it under circumstances chosen by themselves, but under circumstances directly encountered, given and transmitted from the past."[6] Liberation is a long historical process whereby both men and circumstances are transformed. Initially, a vanguard group of revolutionaries form a political party to effect changes in the society and in the process change themselves. Marx was most impressed by this process in his youth when he participated in workers' organizations in Paris. He observed: "When Communist artisans associate with one another, theory, propaganda, etc., is their first end. But, at the same time, as a result of this association, they acquire a new need—the need for society—and what appears as a means becomes an end. . . . Such things as smoking, drinking, eating, etc., are no longer means of contact or means that bring together. Company, association, and conversation, which again has society as its end, are enough for them; the brotherhood of man is no mere phrase with them but a fact of life. . . ."[7] The new human relationships, the new moral order practiced

[4]Marx and Engels, *Selected Works* (Moscow: Progress Publishers, 1969), volume 2, p. 224.

[5]*Ibid.*, volume 1, p. 13.

[6]*Ibid.*, p. 398.

[7]Marx, *The Economic and Philosophic Manuscripts*, pp. 154–155

by the vanguard of the revolution are then transformed into the new moral order for the whole restructured society.

Unless and until man is transformed into the antithesis of the selfish, egotistical, and aggressive capitalist man, capitalism will be restored. Changed circumstances alone do not change man. This is the important message of the Chinese Cultural Revolution. Orthodox Marxists assumed that after the means of production were socialized the new socialist man would naturally emerge; so they concentrated on the building of a social- ist economy and neglected to change man actively. Learning from the experience of Soviet Russia, Mao observed that even under a socialist regime there is a "selfish spontaneous tendency towards capitalism."[8] Why is this so? Because, as Marx said: "The tradition of all the dead generations weighs like a nightmare on the brain of the living. And just when they seem engaged in revolutionizing themselves and things, in creating something that has never yet existed, precisely in such periods of revolutionary crisis they anxiously conjure up the spirit of the past to their service. . . ."[9] Thus, in an attempt to increase productivity and to catch up with the West, Russia resorted to using capitalist means of stimulating workers by material incentives among other measures. But as Che Guevara emphasized—you can't bribe a man to become an un- bribable new socialist man. A new incentive for work must be introduced —the moral incentive.

The lesson the Chinese Revolution learned from what they call revi- sionism is that it is not enough to replace a capitalist economy with a socialist one, you must replace the selfish, acquisitive ethics of capitalism with a new socialist ethics. Thus, the slogan for the Cultural Revolution was: "criticize revisionism, fight selfishness." Bourgeois individualism was the main target of this revolution. Unlike the violent revolution of 1949 which aimed at socializing the economic base, the Cultural Revolu- tion aimed at changing the consciousness or the soul of people. The people's consciousness cannot be changed by force. As Mao puts it, "ideological struggle is not like other forms of struggle. The only method to be used in this struggle is that of painstaking reasoning and not crude coercion."[10] This requires a long educational process to replace the "I" as the center of reference with the "we," and to replace the profit motive with serving the people as the motive. Edgar Snow, who visited Mao in the 1930s while the Liberation Army was hiding out in the caves of Yenan, noticed that in giving an account of his life Mao unconsciously started to use the pronoun "we" instead of "I" when he talked about his activities after joining the revolution. Instead of saying "what I did" and "what I thought" he began to talk about "what we did" and "what we thought." Edgar Snow noticed the same transformation among other leaders he talked to.[11] This transformation constitutes the essence of the transfor-

[8]Mao Tse-tung, *Selected Readings* (Peking: Foreign Languages Press, 1967), p. 347.
[9]Marx and Engels, *Selected Works,* volume 1, p. 398.
[10]Mao, *op. cit.,* p. 376.
[11]Edgar Snow, *Red Star Over China* (New York: Grove Press, 1961), p. 175.

mation from bourgeois ethics to the new socialist ethics. During my
recent visit to China, I noticed the same type of transformation in talking
to old intellectuals and listening to their accounts of their experience
during the Cultural Revolution. There can be no liberation movement
until the isolated individuals in the bourgeois society purge themselves
of the bourgeois hang-ups of individualism through a revolutionary
transformation from "I" to "we." Too many so-called radical movements
have disintegrated because of the failure of the individual members to
make this transformation. The old imperialist trick of divide-and-rule has
proven to be especially effective in this ideological form.

The Cultural Revolution in China aimed at instilling in the whole
population the spirit of Yenan, the new morality which inspired and
guided the vanguard party. The main features of this new ethics are
embodied in what is called "three constantly read articles of Mao," written in the 1930s while he was living in the caves of Yenan. They are:
"Serve the People," "In Memory of Norman Bethune," and "The Foolish
Old Man Who Removed Mountains." "Serve the People" needs no explanation. Instead of the profit making of the capitalist society, "serving
the people" is the primary motive for every activity and profession. A
student wants to become a doctor because he wants to serve the people
and not because he wants to make money. This is as it should be. Only
those who are not perverted by bourgeois values can understand that. "In
Memory of Norman Bethune" was written to commemorate a Canadian
doctor who went to help the Red Army in 1938 in their war of resistance
against Japan, and who died while performing his duty. Mao says, "What
kind of spirit is this that makes a foreigner selflessly adopt the cause of
the Chinese people's liberation as his own? It is the spirit of internationalism, the spirit of Communism, from which every Chinese Communist
must learn. . . . We must all learn the spirit of absolute selflessness from
him. With this spirit everyone can be very useful to the people. A man's
ability may be great or small, but if he has this spirit, he is already
noble-minded and pure, a man of moral integrity and above vulgar interests, a man who is of value to the people."[12] The emphasis here is
selflessness and internationalism. Service to the people means service not
only to the Chinese people but to the oppressed people of the whole
world. Thus, peasants in the remotest village of China will tell you, with
all sincerity, that they are working hard to support the world revolution.
They consider it their duty to donate the fruits of their labor to the
Vietnamese people, as they are doing. The bourgeoisie fosters chauvi-
nism and racism as a part of their divide-and-rule strategy of oppression.
The new socialist ethics must foster internationalism to counteract that
strategy.

"The Foolish Old Man" is an ancient Chinese fable about a man in
front of whose house were two great mountains, blocking the way to the
city. He decided to lead his sons to dig them away. Another old man

[12]Mao, *op. cit.*, p. 146.

known as the Wise Old Man saw them and laughed, "How silly of you! It's impossible for a few of you to dig up these two huge mountains!" The Foolish Old Man replied, "When I die, my children will carry on; when they die, there will be my grandchildren, and so on. High as they are, the mountains cannot grow any higher and with every bit we dig they will be that much lower. Why can't we clear them away?" Mao used this fable to instill in the people a sense of perseverance. Not only should we serve the people in China and widen that service to the peoples of the world, but we must also serve the people of the future.

A revolutionary must take the long view of history. Liberation is a long historical process which requires a cooperative effort of many generations of individuals. The bourgeois notion of quick return for an investment is ingrained in our consciousness. We ask ourselves, "Will there be a revolution in my lifetime?" "What's in it for me?" "If I don't get to enjoy the fruits of the revolution, why should I waste my energy?" We are still thinking in terms of capitalist logic when we ask these questions.

The new ethics of liberation is the negation, the opposite, of bourgeois ethics or, more accurately, non-ethics. However, it must be pointed out that socialist ethics is a *transitional* ethics. A socialist society is a society in transition from capitalism to communism. Because there is conflict between individual and collective interest in the present world, the socialist ethics gives primacy to the collective interest. In the communist society of the future where "the free development of each is the pre-condition for the free development of all,"[13] where there is no longer a conflict between individual and collective interest, the socialist values of sacrifice, selflessness, etc., will be transcended. China is not yet a communist society but it is consciously moving in that direction. It may take generations before the new socialist ethical order is realized, not to mention the as yet undefined communist ethical order. As Mao emphasized, "The present Cultural Revolution is only the first; there will inevitably be many more in the future."[14]

Thomas B. Colwell, Jr.
THE ECOLOGICAL BASIS OF HUMAN COMMUNITY*

In the preceding articles in this section, both the problem of individualism and the problem of community have been analyzed in social terms. The problem of individualism may be seen, on the one hand, as the problem of the limits of

[13]Marx and Engels, *The Communist Manifesto.*
[14]Mao, quoted in *Peking Review* (September 26, 1969), p. 9.
*Paper read before the Fall Meeting of the Middle Atlantic States Philosophy of Education Society, Nov. 15, 1969, at the Belmont Plaza Hotel, New York City.

*social restrictions on the individual's attempt to develop his or her own
potentialities and, on the other hand, as the problem of developing social forms
that enhance the growth of individual potentials. The problem of community is
taken to be the problem of reconstructing the social environment and that of
creating a nonegoistic social consciousness. In either case, nature is left in the
background.*

*In the article that follows, Thomas B. Colwell, Jr., who is a professor of
educational philosophy, argues for a reconstruction of the problem of community
from an ecological perspective. Community, he insists, is both social and physical.
The relation between human beings and nature must no longer be one in which
nature is an adversary, an object of control and exploitation; but rather, it must
be a relation between equals. The problem of community, then, is no longer
simply the problem of reconstructing the human environment but of developing
social and industrial forms that conform to the values inherent in the system of
nature as a whole.*

There can be little doubt that the notion of community has enjoyed one
of the most influential histories of any word employed in educational
thought and practice in this century. From Dewey's early way of posing
the relationship between school and community, through the progressive
era, particularly in the community school movement, to our own involvement with school decentralization and community control, community
has been extolled and befriended, lost and rejected, or, more often, used
in an uncritical common-sense way to connote not much more than
"neighborhood," "city," or "state." But in its various meanings, and
from its various authors, talk of community has poured forth over the
waves of thought, writing and discussion during the past seventy years or
so in a profusion that has surely reached a peak today. The fascinating
thing about all of this is that "community" remains one of the most
confused, jumbled messes of a word in the English language. We have
gone through the better part of a century dominated by the search for
linguistic meaning without having seriously bothered to understand the
concept of community.[1]

Whatever the reasons for this philosophic neglect, I want to argue
that now more than ever, the issue of community needs the attention of
philosophers. Education today, and the collective institutional life of the
civilized world, is floundering and in various stages of crisis because it has
failed to devise a conception of human community appropriate to the
staggering demands placed upon it by the development of technological
society. In short, lasting solutions to educational and social problems rest
upon a solution to the problem of community.

[1]While no philosophical camp can claim to have paid much attention to "community,"
I am aware of but a single article by an exponent of analytic philosophy: John Ladd, "The
Concept of Community," in Carl J. Friedrich, ed., *Community* (New York: Liberal Arts Press,
1959), pp. 269–293.

While I am not going to offer a fully articulated theory of human community at this time, I do want to recommend an approach to one which I believe offers promise of moving the present languishing discussion of the subject to a new vantage point more conducive to theoretical construction. This approach I will call ecological—that is, a way of considering the problem that is drawn largely from the findings and procedures of the science of ecology.

The first thing that becomes apparent when we set out to apply the ecological outlook to the problem of community, is that it affects the way in which the problem is conceived and formulated. This, indeed, is perhaps one of ecology's most helpful contributions. Ecology enables us to see that the problem of community is not quite what we had thought it to be, and that the first step toward a new theory of community is a reconstruction of the problem. For trying to apply the ecological perspective to our already current understanding of community, would be much like trying to apply evolutionary theory to conceptions of natural processes set in the assumptions of the classical theory of fixed species.

Still it is with current views of the problem of community that we must begin if we are to appreciate the difference ecology makes in its formulation.

In spite of the many different ways in which community has been conceived, I think all of these share in the belief that the problem of community is a social problem. By "social problem" I do not mean that community has been thought to be of the same order as, say, poverty, unemployment or drug addiction. Rather, community has been regarded as a much more general social problem, one having to do, not with specific dysfunctional aspects of social relations, but with the pattern or way in which a total interconnecting body or network of institutional arrangements organizes the activities of its members at various levels of complexity, and also, though not necessarily, does so at or in a particular geographical place. Thus, whether we speak of the community of scholars, the scientific or academic community, the Bedford-Stuyvesant community, or Royce's blessed community—all of which have different place references—we have nevertheless had in mind in each case some mode of association or organization—some way of life, if you wish—according to which individuals and groups conduct the institutional work of the larger society. The community has been thought of as a set of enabling conditions, conditions which manifest and channel a larger set of institutional conventions, quite often with strong "local" overtones, and in so doing direct the social intercourse of humans.

But community has been thought of in still another way which might at first seem to lie outside the social perimeter just sketched. Community has often been held to consist of a kind of aura or atmosphere, a feeling of well-being, organic unity or mystical oneness that one feels or shares in by virtue of the intense participation or face-to-face contact which a particular community affords. We see this view in evidence whenever we say: "I feel a strong sense of community when I go to a Quaker meeting"; or, negatively: "There is no community at Bigtown University." But this way of thinking of community is not significantly different from the broadly social and institutional conception already described. It is really a conception of community that calls for certain kinds of social arrangements, those, namely, that will promote the special feelings and sentiments its proponents believe to be normatively desirable.

Both these views, then, merely serve to emphasize the strong social character that has been attributed to the nature of community. The community has been conceived of largely as a social environment, rather than a physical one. When we have talked of Bedford-Stuyvesant, Podunk, or the American community as a whole, we have had in mind in each case their way of life, their social identity much more than the plot of ground and the other aspects of the physical setting they have occupied and contained. The problem of community has been the problem of constructing, regulating, and if needs be, altering the social environment, of finding the optimum arrangement of its institutional activities. If I am correct, the physical environment, no matter how difficult a time we may have had taming it, or simply living in its midst, has been a secondary concern in securing the conditions of community. What has been of first importance is securing the right content of social-institutional relations.

What I have been trying to describe thus far is a way of considering the problem of community that has been common to nearly all who have thought about community, no matter what their differences. It might be thought, however, that regarding community as a social object and a social problem does not enable us to account for the widely divergent theories of community philosophers have arrived at. But what philosophers of community have tried to do is account for the social nature of community in different ways, rather than offer conflicting interpretations of the problem of community itself. Thus, there have been many conflicting versions of the nature of community, but relatively little disagreement over the conceptions of the problem of community these conflicting theories were designed to meet.

.   .   .

Stressing the social element in the problem of community, as I have been doing, might appear to be laboring an obvious point. For what else is community if not a social object, a social problem? The answer ecologically is that community is indeed social in nature. But it is something more too. In addition, it is physical, it is a matter of the natural environment. Community is both social *and* physical, both a function of human beings and social groups, *and* the non-human environment. It is the physical, non-human dimension that ecology adds to the obvious social dimension of community, and it is this addition that transforms a nominally social problem into an ecological problem. The problem of community, conceived ecologically, is, therefore, the problem of working out the conditions of human social organization *in relation to* and *in conjunction with* the resources and limitations of the non-human environment.

But, we might say, isn't this also obvious? Doesn't it go without saying that human life takes place in a physical, non-human setting; and hasn't man always taken this into account? Hasn't he always developed human communities "in relation to" and "in conjunction with" physical environments?

It is certainly true that human communities have always had to contend with physical elements, and indeed because these elements have often played decisive roles in the development of human history, men have obviously been aware of natural environment as a necessary context of their activities. But this awareness has not been extended to Nature as an equal. Nature has been regarded as an object of control, alteration, and exploitation,[2] and only secondarily as an object of aesthetic admiration. Man's relationship to Nature has been that of adversary, and the precarious and fickle ways of the natural world have quite understandably led him to regard his own designs as superior to Hers. Man was to be Nature's master, and Her fascinatingly complex but essentially dumb movements should be brought to follow his own will. This view of man's position in the world has been deeply embedded in all modern science, industry and technology, and is responsible for much that none would deny constitutes the finest achievements of the human mind. No one put it better than Mill, who argued with great confidence that "all human action whatever consists in altering, and all useful action in improving the spontaneous course of nature." In fact, Mill said, man's *duty* lies in "perpetually striving to amend the course of nature—and bringing that part of it over which we can exercise control, more nearly into conformity with a high standard of justice and goodness."[3]

[2]A fascinating historical discussion of Western man's relationship to Nature is provided by Lynn White, Jr., "The Historical Roots of Our Ecologic Crisis," *Science*, Vol. 155, No. 3767 (March 10, 1967), pp. 1203–1207, and reprinted in Shepard and McKinley, *The Subversive Science*, [*Essays Toward an Ecology of Man*. (Boston: Houghton Mifflin, 1969)] pp. 341-351. *Cf.* also Shepard's Introduction to *The Subversive Science, ibid.*, pp. 1-10.

[3]J. S. Mill, "Nature," in J. H. Randell, Jr., Justus Buchler, Evelyn Shirk, eds., *Readings in Philosophy* (New York: Barnes and Noble, Inc., 1950), p. 70. It is interesting to contrast Spinoza's view of man's relation to Nature with Mill's. Spinoza counselled that we should study and follow Nature with the aim of achieving a "union . . . between the mind and the whole nature." *Cf.* his *Improvement of the Understanding*, in *ibid.*, p. 258.

Our view of the relationship between man and Nature has been, to put it briefly, man-centered. Nature has been a kind of commodity, to be used and appropriated to satisfy our wishes in subservience to our own "high standard of justice and goodness," to use Mill's telling phrase. And it is just this view which has supported the social conception of the problem of community. For the preponderant concern with the community as a human, social invention has mirrored man's conceit that his values and institutions are sufficient unto themselves as ground of the human community.

But it is just this conceit that ecology challenges. As a result, the ecological insistence that the problem of community be viewed as a relationship between social and non-human environments is removed from the realm of the merely obvious or trivial. For the ecological approach does far more than recommend that Nature is a stage-setting for the great human drama. That indeed is obvious. Ecologically, Nature is also one of the actors in the drama—or rather, the life of Nature is the drama itself, and man is only one of a cast of thousands. But from the human perspective, Nature is more than a setting; it also contains conditions, sanctions and limitations which constitute a normative framework —a natural basis of human morality, if you will—which is the ultimate ground of all that man does or can do. The very success of our Baconian science of control[4] and our Enlightenment faith in unlimited progress has reinforced in us a narrow humanism which only feeds the delusion that man is the measure of all things. But now some of the alarming consequences of our extensive environmental interventions are beginning to humble our pretensions. These consequences are warnings that the limits of Nature have been transgressed, and suggest that what we want to do must be tempered in accordance with what other systems in Nature are doing—for their own good and ours.

Thus, it is imperative to see that formulating the problem of community as an ecological problem, instead of a merely social one, makes a profound difference to its solution. For making the problem of community turn on the issue of what is good for the system Nature as a whole, rather than man and *then* Nature, opens doors to ways of conceiving of community life, its organization and its values, that differ radically from present community designs.

The fundamental ecological requirement of all human communities is that they must be so designed that they successfully re-cycle resources and waste. Man can no longer take from the environment without putting back. Procedures for accomplishing this are already being contrived and implemented. But it is not generally realized that for the requirement to be accomplished there must be radical alterations in industrial econo-

[4] *Cf.* Lynn White, Jr., *op. cit., passim.*

mies. These economies, please recall, are predicated on the myth of perpetual growth, on an endless and ever greater taking from the natural environment. Thus, the seemingly simple ecological energy requirement involves revolutionary social and economic consequences. If the human economy, to be ecologically stable and sound, must achieve what Sears calls an open steady state,[5] it must do more than pursue the impossible dream of cleaning up our environment while simultaneously continuing to practice the economics of endless growth—a dream which, by the way, is being sold a gullible public today as "conservation" by corporate bodies whose very survival depends on endless growth.[6] The human economy, must, quite the contrary, begin to level off and cut back its giant productive and consumptive efforts. When you contemplate the staggering implications of growth reduction for *all* industrial economies, you can see why ecology has been called "the subversive science."

The structure and functions of human communities, then, must clearly reflect an ecological conception of growth—growth as an open steady state—rather than the man-centered values of endless proliferation. This applies as much to the production of human populations as to material goods and services. The population problem is only one of many ways of illustrating the folly of our obsession with perpetual growth.[7]

The limitation of production and consumption and the control of population would enable us to reconsider other ecological variables—size, density and noise, for example—and their role in the determination of community design. It seems clear that size is crucial. In elementary biology we learn that the growth of plants requires proper spacing or they will not grow. Yet in our pursuit of the values of endless growth, we have herded ourselves into extremely tight quarters in those places we call cities, without very much concern with the effect of urban environmental variables on us. Most of the research on the urban problem is not ecologically oriented—it does not deal critically with the adequacy of the various environmental effects of urban life; it rather notes them, and then curiously assumes their inevitability, as though the *fact* of urban crowding,

[5]Paul B. Sears, "Utopia and the Living Landscape,"[*Daedalus*, Vol. 94, No. 2(Spring, 1965)] Cf. also his "The Steady State: Physical Law and Moral Choice," in *The Subversive Science, op. cit.,* pp. 394–401.

[6]*Cf.,* for example, Warren T. Lindquist, "Development and Conservation—Natural Enemies?" *The New York Times* (May 11, 1969), Sec. 12, p. 12.

[7]On the population problem, *cf.:* Walter E. Howard, "The Population Crisis is Here Now," *Bio-Science,* Vol. 19, No. 9 (Sept., 1969), pp. 779–784; Paul Ehrlich, *The Population Bomb* (New York: Ballantine Books, 1968); Durward Allen, "Too Many Strangers," *National Parks Magazine,* Vol. 43, No. 263 (August, 1969), pp. 12–17; Jean Mayer, "Toward a Non-Malthusian Population Policy," *Columbia Forum,* Vol. XII, No. 2 (Summer, 1969), pp. 5–13; Samuel Brody, "Facts, Fables and Fallacies on Feeding the World Population," in *The Subversive Science, op. cit.,* pp. 55–76.

noise, filth and inefficiency somehow implied their *value,* and constituted the ineluctable conditions around which we must necessarily live our lives.[8] This tragically dumb acceptance of *de facto* urban arrangements as the only possible mode of city living, reveals not only our ecological ignorance, but even more, the extent to which our lives are dominated by the dogma of endless growth, since our great cities are primary expressions of this dogma.

But if we could surrender the idea of endless growth in the interests of ecological sanity, there would be nothing to prevent today's giant cities from being decentralized on a regional basis,[9] and a long overdue effort made to redress the rural-urban imbalance. The decentralization of cities would involve, of course, not simply the dispersion of populations, but the relocation of industries.[10] In short, there is no reason why the local community—in the traditional sense of small community—could not again be emphasized and become the basis of the greater personalization of social relations advocates of small community have always cared for. Many industries and services would have to remain centralized; but many formerly centralized could be decentralized. The aim would be to strike a balance.

The foregoing are some of the imaginative possibilities for practical community reconstruction which suggest themselves when the problem of community is looked at ecologically instead of socially. They are examples only, and it should not be thought that they represent any kind of agreed upon social program among ecologists. Nevertheless, ecologists are fast losing any timidity they may have had to include man within the networks of organism-environment interrelationships which are their chief concern.

[8]I have discussed the confusion of fact and value in present day urbanism more fully in my paper "The Urban Bias in American Education," *The Journal of Educational Thought,* forthcoming.

[9]For imaginative proposals for regional decentralization, *cf.* the late E. A. Gutkind's *The Twilight of Cities* (New York: The Free Press of Glencoe, Inc., 1962); and *Community and Environment* (London: Watts and Co., 1953). Particularly impressive is Gutkind's "Introduction" to the *International History of City Development:* Vol. 1—*Urban Development in Central Europe* (New York: The Free Press of Glencoe, Inc., 1964), pp. 3–51. *Cf.* also his "Education and the Good Life in the Urban Setting," *Teachers College Record,* Vol. 67, No. 3 (Dec., 1965), pp. 163–174. Baker Brownell has also written extensively on decentralization. *Cf.* his *The Human Community* (New York: Harper and Brothers Publishers, 1950), and *The College and the Community* (New York: Harper and Brothers Publishers, 1952).

Most recently, ecological decentralism has been associated with anarchism, in Murray Brookchin, "Ecology and Revolutionary Thought," *Anarchos,* No. 2 (Winter, 1968), pp. 3–22; "Towards a Liberatory Technology," *Anarchos,* No. 3 (Spring, 1969), pp. 49–67.

[10]Of particular interest for the problems of industrial decentralization, not without its shortcomings as far as the utilization of nuclear power is concerned, is Jacob Bronowski, " '1984' Could Be A Good Year," *The New York Times Magazine* (July 15, 1962), pp. 12 *passim.* *Cf.* also Baker Brownell, *The Human Community, op. cit.*

Human behavior, when viewed ecosystemically[11] —i.e., as a function of delicately balanced and enormously complex interwoven systems of biota which support all life—is seen to be intermeshed with all other natural phenomena. Man has learned much about this intermeshing through his physical knowledge. But he has regarded knowledge of himself, as a moral being, as somehow separated from the ecosystemic intermeshing he physically inhabits. Ecologically, the separation of human values from their physical matrix is unthinkable. What man *ought* to do is a question that can only be superficially distinguished from the forces of the physical environment which surrounds him. Human moral sentiments are the expression of individual and social strivings to sustain life in relation to various earth environments through specific institutional practices. They commit men to certain kinds of standing relationships to other men and to the goods and resources of the earth. The propriety and worth of these sentiments can therefore never be settled by reference to still other human moral sentiments—Mill's high standards of justice and goodness, for example. The manner in which human purposes are worthy is a question to be settled by reference to ecosystemic interrelations— i. e., by the way in which human activities affect and are affected by a system of sustaining natural phenomena.[12]

[11]*Cf.* S. Dillon Ripley, Helmut K. Buechner, "Ecosystem Science as a Point of Synthesis," *Daedalus,* Vol. 96, No. 4 (Fall, 1967), pp. 1192–1199. *Cf.* also Paul Shepard's Introduction to *The Subversive Science, op. cit.,* pp. 1–10.

[12]On the problem of the derivation of human norms from Nature, *cf.* my "Some Implications of the Ecological Revolution for the Construction of Value," forthcoming in Ervin Laszlo, James B. Wilbur, eds., *Human Values and Natural Science:* Proceedings of the Third Conference on Value Inquiry (New York: Gordon and Breach Publishers, 1970). *Cf.* also Ch. 16 of Marston Bates, *The Forest and The Sea* (New York: New American Library, 1960); and P. A. Jordan, "Ecology, Conservation and Human Behavior," *Bio-Science,* Vol. 18, No. 11 (Nov., 1968), pp. 1023–1029.

SECTION EIGHT

FREEDOM AND SOCIAL CONTROL

Historically, *freedom has meant different things to different interest groups. Like all social or political values, its content has evolved over the years in response to the needs and interests of different segments of society. For example, during the early period of the American Republic, its primary emphasis was on the right to practice certain narrowly defined religious beliefs, and the very same religious groups who demanded the freedom to worship as they chose thought nothing of persecuting other religious groups for holding views that diverged from their own. During the latter portion of the nineteenth century, freedom was defined in terms of the absence of governmental intrusion into the life of the individual. As the new industrial middle class took control from the landed aristocracy in the course of a bourgeois revolution designed to extend so-called democratic rights to many previously disenfranchised, freedom meant the protection of individual prerogative against the tyranny of the newly created majority. During much of the twentieth century, many have argued that genuine freedom for the individual required positive intervention by government, not its neutrality. According to this view, government must see to it that all individuals receive certain basic necessities and opportunities, such as a minimum wage, education, health care, and so on, in order to place all people in a position to be able to develop their own particular potential freely.*

During the most recent period, the concept of freedom has undergone still further modification. As Jeffrey Schrank, one of the authors in this section, suggests, American society has gradually come to define freedom as a feeling rather than, as was once the case, a state of affairs. The problem with this is that there is, of course, a great difference between feeling *free and* being *free, and the former cannot be taken as sufficient evidence of the latter. The feeling can be induced in us by the existence of trivial diversity and the presence of broad opportunities for false or meaningless choices. Perhaps we are so busy choosing among different-colored breakfast cereals and different-flavored toothpastes that we are in danger of losing entirely any real grasp on the meaning of freedom as a state of affairs that permits the individual to maximize her or his growth. If that is the case, we will have come to define ourselves primarily as consumers rather than as workers or thinkers or activists. We will seek the feeling of freedom in the supermarket or the sprawling suburban shopping mall and fail to work towards a society that values political and intellectual freedom.*

John Stuart Mill
ON LIBERTY

The son of James Mill, John Stuart Mill was born in 1806 and died in 1873. He was a social thinker of considerable renown, well known for his refinement of utilitarianism as it was developed by his father and by Jeremy Bentham, for his championship of women's rights, and for his stand on civil liberties. The following section is taken from On Liberty, *his classic defense of individual liberty and freedom of expression.*

The subject of this Essay is not the so-called Liberty of the Will, so unfortunately opposed to the misnamed doctrine of Philosophical Necessity; but Civil, or Social Liberty: the nature and limits of the power which can be legitimately exercised by society over the individual. A question seldom stated, and hardly ever discussed, in general terms, but which profoundly influences the practical controversies of the age by its latent presence, and is likely soon to make itself recognized as the vital question of the future. It is so far from being new, that, in a certain sense, it has divided mankind, almost from the remotest ages, but in the stage of progress into which the more civilized portions of the species have now entered, it presents itself under new conditions, and requires a different and more fundamental treatment.

The struggle between Liberty and Authority is the most conspicuous feature in the portions of history with which we are earliest familiar, particularly in that of Greece, Rome, and England. But in old times this contest was between subjects, or some classes of subjects, and the government. By liberty, was meant protection against tyranny of the political rulers. The rulers were conceived (except in some of the popular governments of Greece) as in a necessarily antagonistic position to the people whom they ruled. They consisted of a governing One, or a governing tribe or caste, who derived their authority from inheritance or conquest; who, at all events, did not hold it at the pleasure of the governed, and whose supremacy men did not venture, perhaps did not desire, to contest, whatever precautions might be taken against its oppressive exercise. Their power was regarded as necessary, but also as highly dangerous; as a weapon which they would attempt to use against their subjects, no less than against external enemies. To prevent the weaker members of the community from being preyed upon by innumerable vultures, it was needful that there should be an animal of prey stronger than the rest, commissioned to keep them down. But as the king of the vultures would be no less bent upon preying on the flock than any of the minor harpies, it was indispensable to be in a perpetual attitude of defence against his beak and claws. The aim, therefore, of patriots, was to set limits to the power which the ruler should be suffered to exercise over the community; and this limitation was what they meant by liberty. It was attempted in two ways. First, by obtaining a recognition of certain immunities, called political liberties or rights, which it was to be regarded as a breach of duty in the ruler to infringe, and which, if he did infringe, specific resistance, or general rebellion, was held to be justifiable. A second, and generally a later expedient, was the establishment of constitutional checks; by which the consent of the community, or of a body of some sort supposed to represent its interests, was made a necessary condition to some of the more important acts of the governing power. To the first of these modes of limitation, the ruling power, in most European countries, was compelled, more or less, to submit. It was not so with the second; and to attain this, or when already in some degree possessed, to attain it more completely, became everywhere the principal object of the lovers of liberty. And so long as mankind were content to combat one enemy by another, and to be ruled by a master, on condition of being guaranteed more or less efficaciously against his tyranny, they did not carry their aspirations beyond this point.

A time, however, came, in the progress of human affairs, when men ceased to think it a necessity of nature that their governors should be an independent power, opposed in interest to themselves. It appeared to them much better that the various magistrates of the State should be their tenants or delegates, revocable at their pleasure. In that way alone, it seemed, could they have complete security that the powers of government would never be abused to their disadvantage. By degrees, this new demand for elective and temporary rulers became the prominent object of the exertions of the popular party, wherever any such party existed; and superseded, to a considerable extent, the previous efforts to limit the power of rulers. As the struggle proceeded for making the ruling power emanate from the periodical choice of the ruled, some persons began to think that too much importance had been attached to the limitation of the power itself. *That* (it might seem) was a resource against rulers whose interests were habitually opposed to those of the people. What was now wanted was, that the rulers should be identified with the people; that their interest and will should be the interest and will of the nation. The nation did not need to be protected against its own will. There was no fear of its tyrannizing over itself. Let the rulers be effectually responsible to it, promptly removable by it, and it could afford to trust them with power of which it could itself dictate the use to be made. Their power was but the nation's own power, concentrated, and in a form convenient for exercise. This mode of thought, or rather perhaps of feeling, was common among the last generation of European liberalism, in the Continental section of which, it still apparently predominates. Those who admit any limit to what a government may do, except in the case of such governments as they think ought not to exist, stand out as brilliant exceptions among the political thinkers of the Continent. A similar tone of sentiment might by this time have been prevalent in our own country, if the circumstances which for a time encouraged it had continued unaltered.

But, in political and philosophical theories, as well as in persons, success discloses faults and infirmities which failure might have concealed from observation. The notion, that the people have no need to limit their power over themselves, might seem axiomatic, when popular government was a thing only dreamed about, or read of as having existed at some distant period of the past. Neither was that notion necessarily disturbed by such temporary aberrations as those of the French Revolution, the worst of which were the work of an usurping few, and which, in any case, belonged, not to the permanent working of popular institutions, but to a sudden and convulsive outbreak against monarchical and aristocratic despotism. In time, however, a democratic republic came to occupy a large portion of the earth's surface, and made itself felt as one of the most powerful members of the community of nations; and elective and responsible government became subject to the observations and criticisms which wait upon a great existing fact. It was now perceived that such phrases as "self-government," and "the power of the people over themselves," do not express the true state of the case. The "people" who exercise the power, are not always the same people with those over whom it is exercised, and the "self-government" spoken of, is not the government of each by himself, but of each by all the rest. The will of the most numerous or the most active *part* of the people; the majority, or those who succeed in making themselves accepted as the majority: the people, consequently, *may* desire to oppress a part of their number: and precautions are as much needed against this, as against any other abuse of power. The limitation, therefore, of the power of government over individuals, loses none of its importance when the holders of power are regularly accountable to the community, that is, to the strongest party therein. This view of things, recommending itself equally to the intelligence of thinkers and to the inclination of those important classes in European society to whose real or supposed interests democracy is adverse, has had no difficulty in establishing itself; and in political speculations "the tyranny of the majority" is now generally included among the evils against which society requires to be on its guard.

Like other tyrannies, the tyranny of the majority was at first, and is still vulgarly, held in dread, chiefly as operating through the acts of the public authorities. But reflecting persons perceived that when society is itself the tyrant—society collectively, over the separate individuals who compose it—its means of tyrannizing are not restricted to the acts which it may do by the hands of its political functionaries. Society can and does execute its own mandates: and if it issues wrong mandates instead of right, or any mandates at all in things with which it ought not to meddle, it practises a social tyranny more formidable than many kinds of political oppression, since, though not usually upheld by such extreme penalties, it leaves fewer means of escape, penetrating much more deeply into the details of life, and enslaving the soul itself. Protection, therefore, against the tyranny of the magistrate is not enough; there needs protection also against the tyranny of the prevailing opinion and feeling; against the tendency of society to impose, by other means than civil penalties, its own ideas and practices as rules of conduct on those who dissent from them; to fetter the development, and, if possible, prevent the formation, of any individuality not in harmony with its ways, and compel all characters to fashion themselves upon the model of its own. There is a limit to the legitimate interference of collective opinion with individual independence; and to find that limit, and maintain it against encroachment, is as indispensable to a good condition of human affairs, as protection against political despotism.

But though this proposition is not likely to be contested in general terms, the practical question, where to place the limit—how to make the fitting adjustment between individual independence and social control—is a subject on which nearly everything remains to be done. All that makes existence valuable to any one, depends on the enforcement of restraints upon the actions of other people. Some rules of conduct, therefore, must be imposed, by law in the first place, and by opinion on many things which are not fit subjects for the operation of law. What these rules should be, is the principal question in human affairs; but if we expect a few of the most obvious cases, it is one of those which least progress has been made in resolving. No two ages, and scarcely any two countries, have decided it alike; and the decision of one age or country is a wonder to another. Yet the people of any given age and country no more suspect any difficulty in it, than if it were a subject on which mankind had always been agreed. The rules which obtain among themselves appear to them self-evident and self-justifying. This all but universal illusion is one of the examples of the magical influence of custom, which is not only, as the proverb says, a second nature, but is continually mistaken for the first. The effect of custom, in preventing any misgiving respecting the rules of conduct which mankind impose on one another, is all the more complete because the subject is one on which it is not generally considered necessary that reasons should be given, either by one person to others, or by each to himself. People are accustomed to believe, and have been encouraged in the belief by some who aspire to the character of philosophers, that their feelings, on subjects of this nature, are better than reasons, and render reasons unnecessary. The practical principle which guides them to their opinions on the regulation of human conduct, is the feeling in each person's mind that everybody should be required to act as he, and those with whom he sympathizes, would like them to act. No one, indeed, acknowledges to himself that his standard of judgment is his own liking; but an opinion on a point of conduct, not supported by reasons, can only count as one person's preference; and if the reasons, when given, are a mere appeal to a similar preference felt by other people, it is still only many people's liking instead of one. To an ordinary man, however, his own preference, thus supported, is not only a perfectly satisfactory reason, but the only one he generally has for any of his notions of morality, taste, or propriety, which are not expressly written in his religious creed; and his chief guide in the interpretation even of that. Men's opinions, accordingly, on what is laudable or blameable, are affected by all the multifarious causes which influence their wishes in regard to the conduct of others, and which are as numerous as those which determine their wishes on any other subject. Sometimes their reason—at other times their prejudices or superstitions: often their social affections, not seldom their antisocial ones, their envy or jealousy, their arrogance or contemptuousness: but most commonly, their desires or fears for themselves—their legitimate or illegitimate self-interest. Wherever there is an ascendant class, a large portion of the morality of the country emanates from its class interests, and its feelings of class superiority. The morality between Spartans and Helots, between planters and negroes, between princes and subjects, between nobles and roturiers, between men and women, has been for the most part the creation of these class interests and feelings: and the sentiments thus generated, react in turn upon the moral feelings of the members of the ascendant class, in their relations among themselves. Where, on the other hand, a class, formerly ascendant, has lost its ascendancy, or where its ascendancy is unpopular, the prevailing moral sentiments frequently bear the impress of an impatient dislike of superiority. Another grand determining principle of the rules of conduct, both in act and forbearance which have been enforced by law or opinion, has been the servility of mankind towards the supposed preferences or aversions of their temporal masters, or of their gods. This servility, though essentially selfish, is not hypocrisy; it gives rise to perfectly genuine sentiments of abhorrence; it made men burn magicians and heretics. Among so many baser influences, the general and obvious interests of society have of course had a share, and a large one, in the direction of the moral sentiments: less, however, as a matter of reason, and on their own account, than as a consequence of the sympathies and antipathies which grew out of them: and sympathies and antipathies which had little or nothing to do with the interests of society, have made themselves felt in the establishment of moralities with quite as great force.

The likings and dislikings of society, or of some powerful portion of it, are thus the main thing which has practically determined the rules laid down for general observance, under the penalties of law or opinion. And in general, those who have been in advance of society in thought and feeling, have left this condition of things unassailed in principle, however they may have come into conflict with it in some of its details. They have occupied themselves rather in inquiring what things society ought to like or dislike, than in questioning whether its likings or dislikings should be a law to individuals. They preferred endeavoring to alter the feelings of mankind on the particular points on which they were themselves heretical, rather than make common cause in defence of freedom, with heretics generally. The only case in which the higher ground has been taken on principle and maintained with consistency, by any but an individual here and there, is that of religious belief: a case instructive in many ways, and not least so as forming a most striking instance of the fallibility of what is called the moral sense: for the *odium theologicum,* in a sincere bigot, is one of the most unequivocal cases of moral feeling. Those who first broke the yoke of what called itself the Universal Church, were in general as little willing to permit difference of religious opinion as that church itself. But when the heat of the conflict was over, without giving a complete victory to any party, and each church or sect was reduced to limit its hopes to retaining possession of the ground it already occupied; minorities, seeing that they had no chance of becoming majorities, were under the necessity of pleading to those whom they could not convert, for permission to differ. It is accordingly on this battle-field, almost solely, that the rights of the individual against society have been asserted on broad grounds of principle, and the claim of society to exercise authority over dissentients openly controverted. The great writers to whom the world owes what religious liberty it possesses, have mostly asserted freedom of conscience as an indefeasible right, and denied absolutely that a human being is accountable to others for his religious belief. Yet so natural to mankind is intolerance in whatever they really care about, that religious freedom has hardly anywhere been practically realized, except where religious indifference, which dislikes to have its peace disturbed by theological quarrels, has added its weight to the scale. In the minds of almost all religious persons, even in the most tolerant countries, the duty of toleration is admitted with tacit reserves. One person will bear with dissent in matters of church government, but not of dogma; another can tolerate everybody, short of a Papist or an Unitarian; another, every one who believes in revealed religion; a few extend their charity a little further, but stop at the belief in a God and in a future state. Wherever the sentiment of the majority is still genuine and intense, it is found to have abated little of its claim to be obeyed.

In England, from the peculiar circumstances of our political history, though the yoke of opinion is perhaps heavier, that of law is lighter, than in most other countries of Europe; and there is considerable jealousy of direct interference, by the legislative or the executive power with private conduct; not so much from any just regard for the independence of the individual, as from the still subsisting habit of looking on the government as representing an opposite interest to the public. The majority have not yet learnt to feel the power of the government their power, or its opinions their opinions. When they do so, individual liberty will probably be as much exposed to invasion from the government, as it already is from public opinion. But, as yet, there is a considerable amount of feeling ready to be called forth against any attempt of the law to control individuals in things in which they have not hitherto been accustomed to be controlled by it; and this with very little discrimination as to whether the matter is, or is not, within the legitimate sphere of legal control; insomuch that the feeling, highly salutary on the whole, is perhaps quite as often misplaced as well grounded in the particular instances of its application. There is, in fact, no recognized principle by which the propriety or impropriety of government interference is customarily tested. People decide according to their personal preferences. Some, whenever they see any good to be done, or evil to be remedied, would willingly instigate the government to undertake the business; while others prefer to bear almost any amount of social evil, rather than add one to the departments of human interests amenable to governmental control. And men range themselves on one or the other side in any particular case, according to this general direction of their sentiments; or according to the degree of interest which they feel in the particular thing which it is proposed that the government should do; or according to the belief they entertain that the government would, or would not, do it in the manner they prefer; but very rarely on account of any opinion to which they consistently adhere, as to what things are fit to be done by a government. And it seems to me that, in consequence of this absence of rule or principle, one side is at present as often wrong as the other; the interference of government is, with about equal frequency, improperly invoked and improperly condemned.

The object of this Essay is to assert one very simple principle, as entitled to govern absolutely the dealings of society with the individual in the way of compulsion and control, whether the means used be physical force in the form of legal penalties, or the moral coercion of public opinion. That principle is, that the sole end for which mankind are warranted, individually or collectively, in interfering with the liberty of action of any of their number, is self-protection. That the only purpose for which power can be rightfully exercised over any member of a civilized community, against his will, is to prevent harm to others. His own good, either physical or moral, is not a sufficient warrant. He cannot rightfully be compelled to do or forbear because it will be better for him to do so, because it will make him happier, because, in the opinions of others, to do so would be wise, or even right. There are good reasons for remonstrating with him, or reasoning with him, or persuading him, or entreating him, but not for compelling him, or visiting him with any evil, in case he do otherwise. To justify that, the conduct from which it is desired to deter him must be calculated to produce evil to some one else. The only part of the conduct of any one, for which he is amenable to society, is that which concerns others. In the part which merely concerns himself, his independence is, of right, absolute. Over himself, over his own body and mind, the individual is sovereign.

It is, perhaps, hardly necessary to say that this doctrine is meant to apply only to human beings in the maturity of their faculties. We are not speaking of children, or of young persons below the age which the law may fix as that of manhood or womanhood. Those who are still in a state to require being taken care of by others, must be protected against their own actions as well as against external injury. For the same reason, we may leave out of consideration those backward states of society in which the race itself may be considered as in its nonage. The early difficulties in the way of spontaneous progress are so great, that there is seldom any choice of means for overcoming them; and a ruler full of the spirit of improvement is warranted in the use of any expedients that will attain an end, perhaps otherwise unattainable. Despotism is a legitimate mode of government in dealing with barbarians, provided the end be their improvement, and the means justified by actually effecting that end. Liberty, as a principle, has no application to any state of things anterior to the time when mankind have become capable of being improved by free and equal discussion. Until then, there is nothing for them but implicit obedience to an Akbar or a Charlemagne, if they are so fortunate as to find one. But as soon as mankind have attained the capacity of being guided to their own improvement by conviction or persuasion (a period long since reached in all nations with whom we need here concern ourselves), compulsion, either in the direct form or in that of pains and penalties for non-compliance, is no longer admissible as a means to their own good, and justifiable only for the security of others.

It is proper to state that I forego any advantage which could be derived to my argument from the idea of abstract right, as a thing independent of utility. I regard utility as the ultimate appeal on all ethical questions; but it must be utility in the largest sense, grounded on the permanent interests of man as a progressive being. Those interests, I contend, authorize the subjection of individual spontaneity to external control, only in respect to those actions of each, which concern the interest of other people. If any one does an act hurtful to others, there is a *primâ facie* case for punishing him, by law, or, where legal penalties are not safely applicable, by general disapprobation. There are also many positive acts for the benefit of others, which he may rightfully be compelled to perform; such as, to give evidence in a court of justice; to bear his fair share in the common defence, or in any other joint work necessary to the interest of the society of which he enjoys the protection; and to perform certain acts of individual beneficence, such as saving a fellow creature's life, or interposing to protect the defenceless against ill-usage, things which whenever it is obviously a man's duty to do, he may rightfully be made responsible to society for not doing. A person may cause evil to others not only by his actions but by his inaction, and in either case he is justly accountable to them for the injury. The latter case, it is true, requires a much more cautious exercise of compulsion than the former. To make any one answerable for doing evil to others, is the rule; to make him answerable for not preventing evil, is, comparatively speaking, the exception. Yet there are many cases clear enough and grave enough to justify that exception. In all things which regard the external relations of the individual, he is *de jure* amenable to those whose interests are concerned, and if need be, to society as their protector. There are often good reasons for not holding him to the responsibility; but these reasons must arise from the special expediencies of the case: either because it is a kind of case in which he is on the whole likely to act better, when left to his own discretion, than when controlled in any way in which society have it in their power to control him; or because the attempt to exercise control would produce other evils, greater than those which it would prevent. When such reasons as these preclude the enforcement of responsibility, the conscience of the agent himself should step into the vacant judgment-seat, and protect those interests of others which have no external protection; judging himself all the more rigidly, because the case does not admit of his being made accountable to the judgment of his fellow-creatures.

But there is a sphere of action in which society, as distinguished from the individual, has, if any, only an indirect interest; comprehending all that portion of a person's life and conduct which affects only himself, or, if it also affects others, only with their free, voluntary, and undeceived consent and participation. When I say only himself, I mean directly, and in the first instance: for whatever affects himself, may affect others *through* himself; and the objection which may be grounded on this contingency, will receive consideration in the sequel. This, then, is the appropriate region of human liberty. It comprises, first, the inward domain of consciousness; demanding liberty of conscience, in the most comprehensive sense; liberty of thought and feeling; absolute freedom of opinion and sentiment on all subjects, practical or speculative, scientific, moral, or theological. The liberty of expressing and publishing opinions may seem to fall under a different principle, since it belongs to that part of the conduct of an individual which concerns other people; but, being almost of as much importance as the liberty of thought itself, and resting in great part on the same reasons, is practically inseparable from it. Secondly, the principle requires liberty of tastes and pursuits; of framing the plan of our life to suit our own character; of doing as we like, subject to such consequences as may follow; without impediment from our fellow-creatures, so long as what we do does not harm them, even though they should think our conduct foolish, perverse, or wrong. Thirdly, from this liberty of each individual, follows the liberty, within the same limits, of combination among individuals; freedom to unite, for any purpose not involving harm to others: the persons combining being supposed to be of full age, and not forced or deceived.

No society in which these liberties are not, on the whole, respected, is free, whatever may be its form of government; and none is completely free in which they do not exist absolute and unqualified. The only freedom which deserves the name, is that of pursuing our own good in our own way, so long as we do not attempt to deprive others of theirs, or impede their efforts to obtain it. Each is the proper guardian of his own health, whether bodily, or mental and spiritual. Mankind are greater gainers by suffering each other to live as seems good to themselves, than by compelling each to live as seems good to the rest.

.   .   .

OF THE LIBERTY OF THOUGHT AND DISCUSSION

The time, it is to be hoped, is gone by when any defence would be necessary of the "liberty of the press" as one of the securities against corrupt or tyrannical government. No argument, we may suppose, can now be needed, against permitting a legislature or an executive, not identified in interest with the people, to prescribe opinions to them, and determine what doctrines or what arguments they shall be allowed to hear. This aspect of the question, besides, has been so often and so triumphantly enforced by preceding writers, that it needs not be specially insisted on in this place. Though the law of England, on the subject of the press, is as servile to this day as it was in the time of the Tudors, there is little danger of its being actually put in force against political discussion, except during some temporary panic, when fear of insurrection drives ministers and judges from their propriety; and, speaking generally, it is not, in constitutional countries, to be apprehended, that the government, whether completely responsible to the people or not, will often attempt to control the expression of opinion, except when in doing so it makes itself the organ of the general intolerance of the public. Let us suppose, therefore, that the government is entirely at one with the people, and never thinks of exerting any power of coercion unless in agreement with what it conceives to be their voice. But I deny the right of the people to exercise such coercion, either by themselves or by their government. The power itself is illegitimate. The best government has no more title to it than the worst. It is as noxious, or more noxious, when exerted in accordance with public opinion, than when in opposition to it. If all mankind minus one, were of one opinion, and only one person were of the contrary opinion, mankind would be no more justified in silencing that one person, than he, if he had the power, would be justified in silencing mankind. Were an opinion a personal possession of no value except to the owner; if to be obstructed in the enjoyment of it were simply a private injury, it would make some difference whether the injury was inflicted only on a few persons or on many. But the peculiar evil of silencing the expression of an opinion is, that it is robbing the human race; posterity as well as the existing generation; those who dissent from the opinion, still more than those who hold it. If the opinion is right, they are deprived of the opportunity of exchanging error for truth: if wrong, they lose, what is almost as great a benefit, the clearer perception and livelier impression of truth, produced by its collision with error.

. . .

There is the greatest difference between presuming an opinion to be true, because, with every opportunity for contesting it, it has not been refuted, and assuming its truth for the purpose of not permitting its refutation. Complete liberty of contradicting and disproving our opinion, is the very condition which justifies us in assuming its truth for purposes of action; and on no other terms can a being with human faculties have any rational assurance of being right.

. . .

Arnold S. Kaufman
WANTS, NEEDS, AND LIBERALISM*

In this article, Arnold Kaufman examines a contemporary version of the problem raised by John Stuart Mill in On Liberty. *The question that confronts us today is not whether people are somehow unfree to do what they should do but whether the development of false needs keeps them from wanting to do what they should do. Kaufman's approach to the problem distinguishes between human needs and human rights. Like Mill, he emphasizes autonomy as a basic prerequisite for human growth.*

I. INTRODUCTION

Many regard democracy as better than other forms of government primarily because it more efficiently enables more people to get more of what they happen to want.** Democracy accomplishes this, so it is claimed, through majority rule and political equality (in the sense of one-person, one-equal-vote). Such democrats rarely suppose that majority rule and political equality are all-important. Individuals have rights

*A revised version of a paper presented, together with ensuing comment, at the Conference on Rights and Political Action held by the Ripon College Philosophy Department and sponsored by the American Council of Learned Societies and the Council for Philosophical Studies, October 1970. The present version was read at a meeting of the Society for Philosophy and Public Affairs, May 1970.
**I will throughout, unless otherwise indicated, use 'want' to cover all manner of different conative dispositions: conditions that are, in ordinary discourse, denoted by different terms; for example, desire, preference, unconscious want, intention, choice, etc. The differences among these are not relevant to the theoretical issues I discuss.

that ought to be constitutionally protected no matter what majorities decide. But this qualification apart, a political system's ability to satisfy peoples' wants is thought, on this view, to be enough to make it good, even just.

No doubt democracies like the United States and Great Britain, though far from being perfectly majoritarian or politically equal, have progressed toward the ideal over time. And as they have, the system's power to discover and satisfy people's wants has improved. Yet, recently the version of the democratic creed I have just sketched has been heavily criticized, and the satisfaction of peoples' actual wants as a morally adequate basis for evaluating political systems resolutely denied. For, it is argued, existing desires are too often morally and prudentially defective; especially so in advanced industrial societies. Majority rule as it presently functions is therefore an instrument of oppression; even of self-oppression.

That protection of civil liberties should be regarded as a basis for making exceptions to majority rule is dismissed as bourgeois formalism, signifying little in relation to the true nature and dimensions of existing social evils. It is not primarily that people are unfree to do what they should. It is that they generally do not want to do or to be what they should. This gap between what people actually want and what they should want is often expressed in terms of a distinction between wants and needs.

The same critics often blame the unhappy state of things that concerns them on liberals and liberalism. Latter day liberals, it is maintained, merely exhibit the morally shallow, want-satisfying utilitarianism of such architects of liberal doctrine as Jeremy Bentham and John Stuart Mill. By contrast it is claimed that Karl Marx had a more sensitive, more adequate moral aim—achievement of a *truly human existence* through satisfaction of *genuinely human needs.*

But neither Marx's discussion of human needs nor those of any of his followers help much to clarify this alleged basic distinction between wants and needs. And more analytical philosophical discussion, although achieving greater clarity, lacks an understanding of the factor which has disturbed thinkers like Marx.

My main purpose here is to clarify and develop what is sound in the thought of those who appeal so centrally to the distinction between wants and needs. I will argue that, in its most defensible form, the distinction builds on a view essential to John Stuart Mill's liberalism. Because Mill is the architect of one widely held version of liberalism, this claim implies that the Marxist tradition, to the extent that it relies heavily on the distinction between wants and needs in its defensible form, converges on what is soundest in current liberal doctrine.

I aim to defend a certain version of liberalism against its detractors; to counter the venomous liberal-baiting so fashionable among the *enragés.* So I will, perforce, discuss certain historically important texts.

But my ultimate purpose is political, not scholarly; to guide change in the world by a better understanding of what drives so many to want to transform it.

II. A THEORY OF HUMAN NEEDS

Uninterested in commonplace needs, our critics usually preface their use of 'need' with terms like 'basic', 'true', or, as in the case of Marx, 'human', sometimes intended descriptively (for example, 'Stalin had a basic need to wield power'), sometimes normatively (clearly Charles Reich intends a normative point when he complains that 'neither the work that people do nor the goods and services that are produced are judged by human needs . . .'). I am here interested in the latter. For the sake of simplicity I will use 'human need' wherever others might employ one of the other phrases.

To claim that someone's human need for x has not been met suggests that though he wants x, his desire remains unsatisfied. But sometimes another idea is conveyed: that somehow the person's *wanting x* has been prevented. In any event, corresponding to every human need is a want. Such wants will be called 'corresponding wants'. That a human need is unmet may be due principally or entirely to the fact that people do not generally have the corresponding want. It is, from the point of view of our critics, desirable *both* that individuals have corresponding wants and that they be satisfied.

Their complaints sometimes go deeper. They claim not only that the wants people actually happen to have are not corresponding wants, but that they actually interfere with the acquisition of corresponding wants. Such wants are sometimes called, 'false needs', and I will follow that usage. Unless false needs are eliminated, a person will not even be able to glimpse the possibility of a truly human existence. Slaves who acquire 'slavish' wants will not even be able to grasp the possibility, let alone the advantages, of freedom.

It is clear that the concepts of human and false needs are tied to prospects for living a good life. Satisfaction of a person's human needs are at least generally indispensable for, and his having false needs generally incompatible with, his living a good life. It follows that different theories of the good life will generate different catalogues of human and false needs.

As human needs are at least *generally* essential to a person's good life, claims about the presence or absence, satisfaction or non-satisfaction of human needs are typically guides to political action. Similarly in the case of false needs; for politics is the activity whereby people seek power to implement social policies, and the generality of human and false needs make them criteria for determining the desirability of social policies.

Social *policies* are the sorts of prescriptions that have such *general* bearing on human affairs.

Human needs are general in another way. They typically connote types of want sufficiently general to call for variation according to taste in mode of fulfilment. Everyone has a human need for food; and all have the corresponding want. But some like or dislike one specific sort of food, others like or dislike another. This makes for an emphasis on *variety* of need fulfilment. But it is not variety for variety's sake that is necessarily cherished. Rather it is the inevitable diversity of taste in fulfilling the same general wants that is often recognized and stressed.

Human needs are related to another important idea of political theory: namely human rights. For to claim that someone has an unmet human need at least entails that he is *entitled* to satisfaction of its corresponding want. That is, claims about human needs imply corresponding claims about human rights.

The important difference between someone's theory of human rights and his theory of human needs is this: whereas rights focus exclusively on satisfaction of wants which a person does or might have, implying nothing about which wants one ought to have, theories of human needs are centrally concerned with establishing criteria for the desirability of wants. Human needs imply an ideal conative pattern for those said to have the needs, whereas human rights do not. This shift in emphasis from doing what we happen to want to doing what we *should* want is, I shall argue, the most important factor in the shift in political preoccupation from rights to needs.

.   .   .

What are a person's interests? At least anything conducive to his living a good life. Such a life has two interdependent characteristics—autonomy and a 'fair share of happiness'.[1] Autonomy (which Mill calls 'individuality') is required for individuals to 'grow up to the mental, moral, and aesthetic stature of which their nature is capable'.[2] It is the 'same thing' with human development.[3] And 'what more or better can be said of any condition of human affairs than that it brings human beings themselves to the best thing they can be? Or what worse can be said of any obstruction to good than that it prevents this?'[4] Autonomy, or human freedom *in that sense,* is not only good in itself, it is an important condition of happiness for people generally—increasingly so as their mental, spiritual, and bodily conditions are raised to higher levels of development. That is to say, autonomy becomes an increasingly important condition of human happiness as individuals become more and more

[1] *On Liberty,* p. 69 (Bobbs-Merrill ed.).
[2] Ibid., p. 68.
[3] Ibid., p. 77.
[4] Ibid., p. 77.

autonomous. The individual's interest in personal freedom feeds on itself, so to speak. But even if one is miserable, it is still better to be, like Socrates, autonomous than to be a happy pig. (Mill's reference to Socrates is not accidental. For who, in the history of philosophy, is a greater symbol of the autonomous, examined life than Socrates?)

Some interests are more important than others. For they are much more basic conditions of an autonomous life. They are, so to speak, a person's *vital* interests. Among these vital interests none is more important once people have reached a certain level of 'maturity'[5] than liberty of thought and discussion. A free marketplace of ideas is not only an essential condition for producing autonomous human beings, the liberties involved are also constitutive of an autonomous life. Indeed, they, along with other vital interests, are those to which all persons have a human right.[6] It is in virtue of the status of these interests as human rights that others have specific duties of protection and non-interference with respect to them. Moreover, it is not enough that these rights should, above all things, be guaranteed. Individuals ought to be trained from earliest childhood—sometimes coercively—to *want* them. That is, they should be trained to cherish autonomy, to despise slavish subordination to custom and hierarchical authority, and to loathe ignorance and irrationality. It would be acceptable to *command* them to be autonomous, were it not that such commands are notoriously counterproductive. In any event they should somehow be brought to cherish a life in which 'great energies [are] guided by vigorous reason and strong feelings [are] controlled by a conscientious will', and to despise 'weak feelings and weak energies, which therefore can be kept in outward conformity to rule without any strength either of will or of reason'.[7] To the extent that one can justifiably be compelled to become autonomous, one may speak of forcing him to be free.

Only when our very 'desires and impulses' are shaped in ways that make for commitment to an autonomous existence, can we be reasonably sure that our lives are lived in accordance with our own natures. Only then can we be confident that our 'human capacities' will not be so 'withered and starved' that we come to 'have no nature to follow'.[8]

You will by now recognize that what I have been calling *vital interests* might just as well have been called *human needs*. That is, for people generally, satisfaction of these interests is the principal condition of living the best life of which individuals are capable. It is only this life which is specified in terms of autonomy and happiness, these thereby taking on a more concrete form than before. It is this same mix of utilitarian and non-utilitarian considerations that provides the basis for a theory of human rights.

[5]Ibid., p. 13.
[6]Ibid., p. 75.
[7]Ibid., p. 185.
[8]Ibid., pp. 59, 60, and 61.

The absurdity of regarding commitment to a theory of human needs (or vital interests) as logically and politically identical with the theories of Robespierre and Lenin should by now be clear. For commitment to the autonomous life as the basic, usually overriding, goal to be pursued through social and political effort, requires that we promote extensive liberty of action in two crucial respects. The freedom to experiment with our own lives is a crucial condition of becoming autonomous. And once having become autonomous, the most extensive freedom of action compatible with the like freedom of others is required for us to live the best and, when social circumstances are ideal, happiest life of which we are, in justice, capable.

What is this autonomy that is so valuable? I cannot here more than sketch an elucidation. Autonomy is a fusion of three interdependent and overlapping virtues; of rationality, authenticity, and strength of will in action. Reason is not, however, always desirable. There are spheres of life in which the habit of reason destroys valuable spontaneity. Inauthenticity is not only a more or less deliberate determination to act in conflict with one's own core nature; much more pervasive and pernicious are the modes of life by which we act in a way that is out of harmony with that nature because of self-ignorance. Sometimes we remain unaware of who and what we are at the core because we are manipulated by others. Sometimes we are self-deceived. And of all the causes of weakness of will in action, nothing is more pernicious than a false, though comfortable, tendency to do the prudential thing, thereby precluding the possibility of achieving deeper, more permanent levels of well-being. These few remarks must suffice to indicate the lines along which, given the space, I would develop a fuller, more detailed account of autonomy.

Though forcing people to be free may be justified, it should be clear that it is not necessarily or usually so. For liberty of action is itself *the most important means* of promoting autonomous lives. Equally important, the mere fact that someone engages in actions harmful to other peoples' satisfaction of human needs is not, in itself, enough to justify coercive restraint. It only opens the matter to discussion and debate. Mill is very clear about this.[9] As he says, inducing people to respect the conditions that support a good life for themselves or others normally requires better and more effective instruments than 'whips and scourges, either of the literal or metaphorical sort'.[10]

One presupposition of this theory of human needs is that individuals are capable of creating a society, of recreating themselves, so that personal and social harmony are achieved.

.   .   .

[9]See *On Liberty,* p. 92. 'As soon as any part of a person's conduct affects prejudicially the interests of others, society has jurisdiction over it, and the question whether the general welfare will or will not be promoted by interfering with it *becomes open to discussion.*' (Author's emphasis.)
[10]Ibid., p. 92.

Of course, the theoretical possibility that some individuals will tyrannize, abuse, and manipulate others in the effort to make them autonomous exists. But it is a remote possibility, not a probability. Those who cherish autonomy, not only for its useful consequences but for itself, will be least likely to betray it in order to achieve it. Policies and practices based on explicit commitment to the ideal jeopardize autonomy or diminish liberty less than any alternative course of action. In particular, unreflective acceptance of those modes of socialization that happen to prevail at a given stage in the development of any given society is not a better alternative.

. . .

Nevertheless, Mill was paradoxically much more aware than Marx of the dangers of bureaucracy. Marx casually assumed that the worst consequences of division of labor would naturally disappear once capitalism was overthrown, while Mill prophetically warned that bureaucratism would pose a continual threat to liberty and autonomy in any social system.

. . .

Jeffrey Schrank
PSEUDO-CHOICE AND THE ILLUSION OF FREEDOM

In his book Snap, Crackle, and Popular Taste, *from which this selection is taken, Jeffrey Schrank confronts the question of false, or pseudo-, needs head on. He contends that in contemporary American society, "feeling free" has replaced "being free" and that people have been encouraged to mistake the choosing among a seeming variety of products for real freedom. According to Schrank, in spite of this seeming variety, most of our choices are fast becoming pseudo-choices. In this selection, he illustrates his claim with reference to food and eating.*

This book is about the seemingly insignificant decisions in daily life. It is about watching television, shopping, reading ads, playing sports and other everyday activities that fill so much of a life span. *Snap, Crackle, and Popular Taste* is concerned more with what you might choose for breakfast tomorrow morning or with how you travel to work each day than with carefully constructed decisions to adopt a career, get married or join a commune. The book examines some of the hidden factors that shape everyday decisions and our experience of freedom.

Freedom exists only in the presence of choices, but it does not follow that the presence of choices creates freedom. Some choices contribute only to the illusion of freedom; these we will call pseudo-choices. A pseudo-choice should not be confused with the absence of choice. A pseudo-choice is a real choice exercised by a person using what is commonly recognized as free will, but the choice has carefully controlled boundaries that often exclude what the person choosing really wants.

For example, I might develop a sudden craving for a lemon cream pie. Thanks to modern technology I am able to race down to the local supermarket, pick out my pie and have it ready to eat as soon as it thaws a bit. What I wanted was a lemon cream pie such as my memory told me Mother used to make. What I bought was a box showing a picture of a lemon cream pie and containing a collection of water and chemicals utterly devoid of lemons or cream. But I eat the pie with a certain degree of enjoyment because I have learned to be satisfied with what is offered instead of with what I wanted. This is pseudo-choice.

While I was at the supermarket I picked up a box of Screaming Yellow Zonkers, a new kind of double-edged razor blade and my first package of chewing gum in six years. I'm not sure why I bought these things, but they're small and I'll use them. This, too, is pseudo-choice. It is pseudo-choice not because I acted on impulse but because I was unaware of the carefully constructed decision/environment that encouraged me to add these purchases.

Pseudo-choice is a selection guided by invisible limitations and structures. It is the invisibility of the decision-shaping factors that contributes to pseudo-choice. It is tempting to believe that choosing among the dazzling array of options offered is freedom. In pseudo-choice, the world is a multiple-choice test. We are free to answer questions only in terms of the options presented. A real-choice test would have only blank space for our answers which would be unshaped by the test maker. A multiple-choice test offers real choices but only the illusion of freedom.

A strong case can be made for the fact that the illusion of freedom is all we really desire. The case has been best presented by Erich Fromm in *Escape from Freedom.* Real freedom, Fromm observes, is a heavy burden, loaded with responsibility and far too painful for the average person to bear. Pseudo-choice services nicely to create the illusion of freedom and preserve us from the introspection needed to determine what we really want.

One reason freedom has become increasingly susceptible to control is that it has changed its meaning in the popular mind. Freedom has increasingly become associated with a feeling rather than a state of being. The noun "freedom" has become a verb. Freedom is no longer a fragile state of being or a goal to pursue with lifelong struggle and desire, it is a feeling that can come and go like fear, sadness or boredom. To "feel free" has replaced to "be free" both in common vocabulary and in the list of goals worth attaining. Ads and mass media reinforce this situation by associating products ranging from bras to cigars, from motorcycles to carpet cleaners, with the feeling of freedom. Feelings are relatively easy to manipulate compared to a state of being, living conditions or social structures. If freedom is a feeling, a rush of exhilaration, it can be briefly satisfied by consumer products and packaged entertainments. Pseudo-choice can contribute to the illusion of freedom while obscuring the lack of true freedom.

Pseudo-choices can be characterized in the following ways:

1. They are presented to the individual as a part of a mass—an audience, a consumer or potential customer. In the marketplace, objects of potential pseudo-choice are made for "anyone," and not for someone in particular.
2. They often consist of a set of carefully controlled options. Almost everyone who shops at a supermarket comes out with bags of food, half of which was produced by the ten leading food companies.
3. The factors shaping the choices are invisible to most people.
4. They tend to obscure (but not necessarily obliterate) real choices. In purchasing an automobile, there are so many options offered that real choices in safety and ease of maintenance are rarely considered.
5. Pseudo-choices are often supported by advertising or public relations efforts which invariably attempt to make them appear far more significant than they are.
6. They are preselected, controlled choices that tend to prevent people from asking the basic question: "What do I really want?" By so doing, they contribute to the state of general detachment and help create large numbers of people who simply don't know what they want. And those who don't know what they want are the most easily satisfied with pseudo-choice.

.   .   .

The everyday decision of what to eat shows increasing signs of becoming a pseudo-choice. This is true even though no people in history have had so overwhelming a variety of food from which to choose as do twentieth-century Americans. Pseudo-choice has entered the diet because of the change in food from a totally agricultural product to one that is a result of technology. Each year the percentage of food that reaches American tables unchanged by factory processing decreases. As food becomes increasingly equated with the manufacturing process, the consumer becomes more and more dependent on corporate food providers. And it is the food controllers who have the ability to offer eaters their daily pseudo-choice.

If consumers are habituated to food that can be manufactured only in multimillion-dollar factories and prepared by Ph.D.s in chemistry and food technology, a virtual monopoly of the food supply is possible. Any cook can prepare dozens of breakfast foods from corn (the corn can even be grown in a home garden), but only a sophisticated factory can make pink, sugar-coated, corn toaster tarts ready to eat with a free spaceman inside each foil package.

The change in food source from farm to factory is far from complete but has already reached a seemingly irreversible status. The change is as significant as that in transportation from nature (the horse) to machine (the automobile). Both changes are the result of apparently free choices on the part of consumers, both are corporately controlled and both leave a situation that is accepted as normal yet degrades the quality of life in many ways.

If we can believe the evidence of current trends in the food industry and the prophecies of its leaders, future food will resemble the ultimate both in convenience and pseudo-choice—the food pill. The major obstacle is the engineering of consumer acceptance of what at first appears a rather bleak diet. But the public accepted the idea of being sealed in a metal capsule called an automobile for at least a few years of a lifetime and pay dearly for the dubious privilege.

Most readers will find the idea of a food pill revolting and will firmly resolve never to surrender the sensual joy of eating real food. The food pill, they say, is certainly no more than a science fiction fantasy or a nightmare confined to B-grade movies like *Soylent Green.* But some of these same readers, their appetites no doubt stimulated by such fearful considerations, will put down this book and raid the kitchen for a snack that is little more than a prototype of the food pill cleverly disguised to look like a potato chip, cherry pie or even beef Stroganoff. Future food is not something that will arrive with great fanfare on 1–1–84; it is with us now in embryonic form. Astronauts, passengers on airline dinner flights and snack-food addicts stand as signs of future food-consumption patterns. If you enjoyed your food in 1976, you will certainly love the pseudo-choice menu of 1984.

Although the synthetic food chip available in twelve flavors and sixteen shapes is not yet a supermarket reality (and, hopefully, never will be), there are trends that indicate pseudo-choice in food is increasing. These trends are: (1) the normal situation of eater's alienation, (2) corporate control of various foods and grocery outlets, (3) atrophy of the taste buds and the attraction of synthetic foods and (4) the restaurant as a purveyor of glorified TV dinners.

EATER'S ALIENATION

For all of human history the source of food was very evident. One day's harvesting was next morning's breakfast, and Sunday dinner scratched around the front yard during the week. The battle against hunger united the family unit and consumed the vast majority of each member's time. But the Industrial Revolution took work, education and food-gathering out of the family and placed it into the hands of specialists. Food appeared in stores and was meant to take a minimum of time to prepare and "gather." Today, the normal meal should take as little time as possible to prepare and even less to eat. Exceptions to this norm are reserved for special occasions. The long-term result of this change is a loss of contact with the source of food, a phenomenon we shall call eater's alienation.

The alienated eater accepts food as something that comes from a grocery store rather than a farm. A common assumption it that only a few chemists know what is in all those packages so neatly arranged in supermarket rows and bathed all day in Muzak and fluorescent light. Alienated eaters have only minor problems telling their children where babies come from, but few have mustered the courage (or even see the need) to tell about eating cow meat and pigs. To measure the ascendancy of eater's alienation, try telling a four-year-old he or she is about to have cow meat for supper. The child of past ages not only knew where food originated, he probably helped in the slaughter or harvesting.

Few adults have been inside a food-processing factory and just as few know what is in the cellophane and four-color boxes at the supermarket. The average eater does not know what he or she is eating, how it is made, what it contains or even its long-term effects. With this ignorance of food established, the way is open for corporate control and pseudo-choice. To test your own degree of eater's alienation, see how many food products you can identify from the following list of ingredients. Admittedly this is far from a highly valid test of eater's alienation, but it does serve to illustrate the situation.

YOU ARE WHAT YOU EAT?
A FOOD TEST

Below are ingredient lists for six common foods. Each list is arranged in order of quantity. The first ingredient listed is the one that the food contains the most of, last listed is that ingredient the food contains least of. See how many of the six you can identify.

1. Corn syrup solids, vegetable fat, sodium caseinate, dipotassium phosphate, emulsifier, sodium silico-aluminate, artificial flavor and color.
2. Sugar, gelatin, adinic acid, sodium citrate, fumaric acid, artificial flavor and color.
3. Sugar, bleached flour, shortening with mono- and diglycerides and freshness preserver, dried apples preserved with sulfur dioxide, leavening, corn sugar, soy flour, nonfat dry milk, salt, propylene slycol monoesters, sorbitan and monostearate, spices, polysorbate 60 and artificial coloring.
4. Salt, hydrolized vegetable protein, sugar, autolyzed yeast, beef fat, malto-dextrin, onion, beef extract, celery, caramel, disodium inosinate, disodium guanylate.
5. Corn oil, soybean and cottonseed oils, skim milk, salt, lecithin, monoglyceride, isopropyl citrate (.01 percent), calcium disodium EDTA (.007 percent) added to protect flavor, 3.75 units vitamin A, artificially colored with carotene, artificial flavor.
6. Water, hydrogenated vegetable oil, dextrose, sugar, sodium caseinate, polysorbate 60, sorbitan monostearate, propylene glycol

monostearate, glyceryl monostearate, artificial flavor, salt, guar gum, algin, artificial color, propellants: nitrous oxide, chloropentafluoro-ethene.

Answers to You Are What You Eat? test:

1. Nondairy creamer (or cremer or kremer)
2. Wild raspberry Jell-O
3. Pillsbury applesauce batter cake mix
4. Instant beef-style bouillon
5. Margarine
6. Whipped dessert topping

Eater's alienation leads to consequences far more serious than a mere failure to complete successfully a food ingredients test. Ignorance of what is eaten leads to pseudo-choice susceptibility and possibly to poor nutrition. The U.S. Department of Agriculture's annual survey of family eating habits shows that nearly half the families sampled (and these were not poverty families) had what the USDA calls "inadequate diets." In 1955, the figure was only 15 percent, and in 1965 fully 20 percent had inadequate diets. Inadequate means that the diet contains less than two-thirds of one or more of the needed proteins, minerals and vitamins considered vital by the National Academy of Sciences.

A family shopper who complains about the high cost of meat and produce and who knows little about processed food will often forsake true nutrition for the illusion of convenience and economy. On this shopper's list might be Kool-Aid, a powdered drink mix that sells for $7 a pound; a breakfast powder with nonfat dry milk as the main ingredient for $2 per pound; a stuffing mix with flour as the main ingredient for $1.85 a pound; a "hamburger helper" type food that is basically noodles and shortening for $1.69 a pound; prepopped popcorn for $1.80 per pound and a cooking sauce with the main ingredients of skim milk and water for $4.15 a gallon. When such purchases become a standard part of the family diet, there is little doubt that eater's alienation is at work.

Eater's alienation renders a shopper vulnerable to the magic of food technology. Unfortunately, the magicians are working to duplicate the dream of the ancient alchemists. Instead of turning baser metals into gold, they work to turn simple substances such as air, water and basic foodstuffs into "convenience" foods that can be sold for prices higher than steak or any other unprocessed food. To illustrate the progress of the food technology revolution (or "conspiracy," if you prefer), let us take a brief stroll through a typical supermarket.

As we wander through the aisles squinting at fine print on package labels, we begin to learn some of the favorite ploys of the food manufac-turers. Just past the coffee display we find a creation of the alchemists at General Foods. They are selling a small tin of "Cafe Vienna" as a gourmet coffee for $3 per pound. A close look at the ingredients reveals that the delicacy is basically a mixture of nondairy creamer and instant coffee. None of the ingredients sold separately cost anywhere near $3 per pound. General Foods must believe that shoppers are willing to pay dearly to have an assembly line mix the two powders. If the new product succeeds, and first reports are encouraging to GF, pseudo-choice will have again asserted its strength.

Moving quickly to more substantial food, we arrive at the small section devoted to canned chili. There are four brands rather reasonably priced around 60¢–80¢ a pound. But three of the beef chilis with beans brands have water as the main ingredient (one of the favorite magic substances of the food alchemists). Only one of the four brands has beans listed as the main ingredient and only one has more beef than water. Perhaps the three should be called chili soup. At least the shopper still can select chili instead of bean soup with beef after a careful study of the labels.

Our experience with chili suggests a game we can play called the "Tell-It-Like-It-Is, Honesty-in-the-Supermarket Game." The object of the game is to find misnamed food items on the shelves and supply honest names based on the real contents of the package.

Over in the large frozen-food section we score our first points for Polynesian Style Dinner. A careful reading of the contents shows that the main ingredient is rehydrated potato flakes. So we wonder at the eating habits of the Polynesians but rename the dish a "Rehydrated Potato Flake Dinner." Farther down the aisle we score again as a frozen Spinach Soufflé becomes "Skim Milk Soufflé with Spinach." The shopper in the frozen-food section still can choose nutritious and convenient items, but the bulk of display space and advertising dollar goes to the increasing number of highly processed mixtures of questionable value. The value of freezing to preserve nutrition and choice year round is rapidly losing ground to freezing as another tool of the food alchemists used to increase corporate profits and offer only pseudo-choice.

In the meat department we find soybeans posing as bacon, sausage and lunch meat. Since soybeans can be grown about ten times faster than cows and since they are high in protein, their use as a food makes sense. But the food technologists are not content to offer a choice between traditional and expensive sources of protein (meat) and tasteful but inexpensive sources of protein provided by soybean products. Instead, they process the soybeans to imitate meat and vegetable products and sell them for prices only slightly lower than the product being imitated. General Mills combines spun soy protein with oil, dried egg whites, artificial colors and flavors and sells it as Bac*Os for $4 per pound—more than the cost of a good cut of steak. Other food companies use soy protein as a meat substitute to cut costs in the manufacture of pizza rolls or beef Stroganoff and similar frozen foods. The cost saving is passed on to the corporation rather than the consumer who is usually unaware the substitution has been made.

General Mills has already tested a line of simulated meats called Country Cuts as part of the Betty Crocker line of food. The Country Cuts are frozen, precooked chunks of texturized soy protein disguised to look, taste and feel like chicken and ham. Swift and Company is experimenting with a combination of soy and real meat to capture what it estimates to be a $200-million-a-year soy substitute market. Its contribution to pseudo-choice is to offer All American Fun Links—a hot-dog substitute already tested in several small markets.

A further tour of the supermarket confirms the suspicion that the shopper is almost forced to choose among an increasing number of highly processed food combinations and must exert extra effort to purchase simple, natural foods. One sign of the strength of pseudo-choice in food is the current interest in natural or organic foods. The food "revolution" has already progressed to the point where the highly processed, additive-laden food is considered normal. Natural or unprocessed food is the exception available at higher prices only to those with a firm resolve to avoid pseudo-choice.

The only ads for natural foods are the price lists in the daily paper for meat and produce, and these often serve only to discourage the less affluent and to draw shoppers to the store. Once in the store, marketing skills and packaging psychology takes over. The sheer volume of space given to processed as compared to natural food is the most powerful form of persuasion. More space is allocated processed foods because they offer higher potential profits to the grocer. A spokesperson for one of the largest food manufacturers says quite candidly that manufactured food will "totally absorb the food industry's energies in the future." *Food Engineering,* a prophetically named trade journal, notes "the more additives, the higher the potential profit margin."

But even with the temptation of high profits, food technology does not necessarily lead to pseudo-choice unless it is coupled with the ability to control the food market. Unfortunately, there are signs that our food sources are becoming increasingly controlled by a few large corporations.

CORPORATE CONTROL OF FOOD

Once people have only the vaguest idea of what they are eating, the way is open for the corporate control of food. The alienated eater will not eat what is nutritious but what is presented as most convenient, what is advertised as the most elegant or what is packaged in the most seductive box. And the supplier best able to present such pseudo-choices is not the local farmer but the corporate food company. The thousands of products that line the maze of aisles in the supermarket present much less variety than seems apparent.

In *Market Power and Economic Welfare,* Dr. William Shepherd observes that the average market share of the four leading firms in any given food-product line is 55 percent. In other words, an average of four companies share most of the market for any given food item. This average places the food industry as more monopolistic than the rubber and plastics industry, fabricated metals, textiles and most other industries. According to the FTC's Russell Parker, fifty food-processing companies take in over 60 percent of food-processing profits, and the trend toward concentration is increasing.

In areas such as beer and soft drinks, baby food, canned goods, cereal and meat-packing, three to five large firms already thoroughly dominate the field. Ninety percent of the soup Americans buy is Campbell's, and the company has been able to shape the national concept of what soup is. Ninety percent of our breakfast cereal comes from Kellogg, General Mills, Quaker Oats or General Foods; it is they who have decided that breakfast cereal and sugar are almost inseparable. General Foods sells over 40 percent of the nation's coffee under the brand names of Brim, Max-Pax, Maxim, Maxwell House, Sanka and Yuban. In beer, local breweries numbered in the thousands in the 1930s, but today Anheuser-Busch, Jos. Schlitz, Pabst and Coors account for nearly 55 percent of all beer sales, and the control increases slightly each year. In beer, as in automobiles protection against complete pseudo-choice is offered only by imported brands.

In testimony before the House Subcommittee on Monopolies, Ralph Nader presented data culled from unpublished doctoral studies showing near monopoly control by the four leading producers of baby food (95 percent of all sales), baking powder and yeast (86 percent), instant coffee (81 percent), dessert mixes (86 percent), refrigerated dough (87 percent) and catsup (81 percent). Dr. Shepherd places control by the four leading firms as 50 percent for butter, 85 percent for chocolate, 88 percent for chewing gum, 75 percent for blended and prepared flour and 70 percent for ice cream.

Hiding behind the overchoice of brand names in any supermarket is the fact that fifty corporations effectively control much of the food we eat. Although brand names are household words even to toddlers old enough to watch television, the corporations behind the brands are relatively unknown. Some of the largest food companies and the brands they produce include:

Kraftco Corporation (annual sales of about $3.8 billion)
>Stay'n Shape and Temp-Tee dairy products, American cheese, Butter Mints, Cheez Whiz, Chefs Surprise, Cracker Barrel cheese, Golden Caesar salad dressing, Great Beginnings, Koogle peanut butter, Kraft brand barbecue sauce, cake mix, mayonnaise, packaged dinners and salad dressings, Manor House coffee, Miracle margarine and Miracle Whip, Parkay margarine, Philadelphia cream cheese, Roka salad dressing, Velveeta cheese, Toffee candy, Sealtest ice cream and other foods, Breyers ice cream, Checkerboard ice cream and Twin Pop.

Beatrice Foods ($3.3 billion in sales yearly)

Clark bars, Holloway candy, Dannon yogurt, Meadow Gold, Sanalac, Swiss Miss, Viva yogurt, Burney Brothers bakery, Butter Krust, La Choy, Sexton Foods (suppliers to restaurants and institutions), Samsonite luggage, Eckrich meats, Lowrey meat, Airstream travel trailers, Charmglow gas grills, Miracle White laundry products, Spiegel industries, Taylor ice-cream dispensers ("soft" ice cream) and many other brands.

Ralston Purina Co. (annual sales of about $3.1 billion)

Chex cereals, Chicken of the Sea tuna, RyKrisp, Purina Chow pet foods, Van Camp Sea Foods. Restaurants under the names of Bear's Head, Boat House, The Dock, Hungry Hunter, The Jolly Ox, Stag and Jack-in-the-Box.

General Foods Corporation ($2.8 billion in sales annually)

Awake orange drink, Start, Tang, Birds Eye frozen foods, Cool'n Creamy, Cool Whip, Great Shakes, Iceflow slush, Orange Plus, Thick and Frosty shakes, Burger Chef, Burpee Seeds, Jell-O, Calumet, Certo, D-Zerta, Dream Whip, Minute Rice, Kool-Aid, Good Seasons, Batter'n Bake, Open Pit, Shake'n Bake, Swans Down, Toast'em, Maxwell House coffee, Max-Pax, Maxim, Sanka, Yuban, Post cereals, Log Cabin syrup, Gaines pet foods and Vivianne Woodard cosmetics.

Borden, Inc. (sales of about $2.7 billion yearly)

Aunt Jane's foods, Bama Foods, Calo pet foods, Campfire marshmallows, Colonial sugar, Cracker Jack, Cremora, Eagle brand condensed milk, Flavor House nuts, Kava coffee, Melba toast, Old London foods, ReaLemon, Wyler foods, Borden dairy products, Rich's cake mix, Mystik tapes, Elmer's glue, Wall-Text wall coverings and many others.

General Mills, Inc. (sales of $2.3 billion annually)

Bac*Os, Betty Crocker products, Bisquick, Breakfast Squares, Buc Wheats, Bugles, Cheerios, Chipos, Cocoa Puffs, Crispy Taters, Fruit Helper, Gold Medal, Hamburger Helper, Kix, Lucky Charms, Pepr-O's, Potato Crisps, Saus-O's, Sugar Jets, Total, Trix, Wheat Chips, Wheaties, Good Mark sausages, Gorton seafoods, Kenner toys, Lionel electric trains and Parker Brothers games, including Monopoly.

Norton Simon, Inc. ($1.4 billion in sales yearly)

Canada Dry beverages, Wink, Hunt's Foods, Reddi-Whip, Wesson oil, Max Factor cosmetics, McCall Publishing Co., Ohio Match Company, Crawford's scotch, John Begg scotch, Johnnie Walker scotch, Old Fitzgerald bourbon, Tanqueray gin, Weller bourbons, Gulf Kist fish, United Can Company and Wampole Laboratories.

CPC International (sales of about $1.3 billion)

Best Foods, Hellmann's mayonnaise, Golden Griddle syrup, Karo syrup, Mazola oil, Niagara starch, Nu Soft, Skippy peanut butter, Thomas frozen foods.

Standard Brands, Inc. ($1.3 billion yearly in sales)

Egg Beaters, Fleischmann's margarine, Chase and Sanborn Coffee, Royal gelatin and pudding, Blue Bonnet margarine, Tender Leaf tea, Baby Ruth candy bars, Butterfinger candies, Planters nuts, Canadian LTD whisky, Fleischmann's gin, Old Medley bourbon, White Tavern gin, B&B liqueur, Benedictine, Lloyd's English gin and a wide variety of other wines and spirits.

Procter & Gamble (sales of $6 billion yearly)

Food items include Big Top and Jif peanut butter, Crisco and Fluffo shortening, Duncan Hines, Pringles and Folgers Coffee. Nonfood items include Biz, Bold, Bonus, Cheer, Comet, Duz, Ivory, Joy, Mr. Clean, Oxydol, Spic and Span, Top Job and Zest soaps. Also Crest, Gleam, Head & Shoulders, Lilt, Prell, Scope, Secret and Sure anti-perspirant.

The advertising of these companies all carries a hidden message. No matter if the ads are for Tang, Pringles, Coffee-mate or Kool-Aid they say "eat manufactured food." Contrary to Alvin Toffler, overchoice is not the problem in supermarkets—at least not to the aware shopper. The problem is a limited range in which choice can be made. The pseudo-choice offered is between the products of one corporation or the nearly identical products from another—General Mills or General Foods, take your choice.

The lowly potato chip offers an interesting case study of the development both of corporate control and pseudo-choice. The state of the potato chip market in the early 1970s was one of healthy competition and numerous local producers. Potato chips remained relatively free of corporate control largely because they have a short shelf life and are too expensive to transport over large distances. But since Americans consume about a billion dollars a year worth of the salty chips, the market was eminently worthy of corporate attention.

In late 1973, Procter & Gamble introduced Pringles as a new kind of potato chip advertised as a great new advance in food and a superior chip. The "newfangled chip" was heavily advertised in print and television. P & G makes Pringles from dehydrated potatoes; adds water, mono- and diglycerides, sodium phosphate, sodium bisulfite, BHA, sugar and vitamin C and salt. The mushlike mixture moves along a conveyer belt and is solidified into "perfectly shaped" potato cookies. The "chips" are neatly stacked in a container strongly resembling a tennis ball can and sold for 70 percent more than ordinary potato chips. P & G sold close to $100 million worth of Pringles in 1973 with distribution to only 60 percent of the country. This already represents 10 percent of the potato chip market. In 1976, other corporate giants were tooling up assembly lines to turn out similar dehydrated potato chips and establish what will most likely be a shared monopoly by 1980.

The success of the corporate pseudo-chip will very likely force many of the local manufacturers of the real potato chips out of business. With

Procter & Gamble backing Pringles with national advertising, the smaller companies have little hope to compete effectively. Grocers will find that the new chips take up less valuable shelf space and have a higher profit margin than real chips. Consumers will find that the BHA will keep the chips tasting like instant potatoes for years without spoilage. The potato chip aficionado of the future will be offered a pseudo-choice among various brands of dehydrated chips. Perhaps real potato chips will be offered in the gourmet (or "organic foods") department for $10 a pound.

Even the decision on where to shop is tinged with elements of pseudo-choice. A significant percentage of the time that decision leads to one of three or four of the largest supermarket chains in the nation. Safeway, A & P, Kroger and ACME (American Stores) account for over one-fifth of all grocery sales in the United States in dollar volume. Add to the big four other chains such as Lucky, Jewel, Winn-Dixie, Food Fair, Grand Union and Supermarkets General, and the total jumps to nearly one-third of all food purchases. Twenty corporations own the retail outlets at which 40 percent of all food sales are made.

But the true level of oligopoly control is understated by these figures. A study in 1973 sponsored by the grocery industry and conducted by Metro Market Studies, Inc., found that in many cities the four largest chains (not necessarily the four largest in the country) have a near monopoly on grocery sales. In Akron, Ohio, the big four control 64.5 percent of sales; in Denver, Colorado, 74.3 percent; in Little Rock, Arkansas, 86.1 percent; in Seattle, Washington, 88.2 percent; in Washington, D.C., 71.8 percent. In these cities the food shopper is consistently restricted to a narrow range of choices.

The large food chains are not necessarily the most efficient or the best stores: they simply have the most money muscle. Between 1955–65 the top twenty supermarket chains purchased 272 stores and smaller chains, adding a total of 2600 more outlets and $3 billion in sales to their corporate coffers. The stores bought out were not near failing; rather, they were efficient competitors. The National Commission on Food Marketing, which supplied these statistics, concluded that many of the mergers "probably hurt potential competition."

Pseudo-choice in the decision where to shop has the potential for leading to artificially high food prices and all the other disadvantages of a lack of healthy competition. It also limits the chances for small food producers to obtain sales space in the local supermarkets to increase the shopper's real choice.

.   .   .

FUTURE FOOD

A decline in food taste and corporate control of the food supply seem to be related. No one has seriously accused Wonder Bread, Hostess Twinkies, Rice Krispies or TV dinners of being overflavored. Corporate control offers eaters a choice among a variety of blandness. Bland food is acceptable because it is now considered normal and atrophy of the sense of taste has set in. Taste bud atrophy need not be a physical process observable under a microscope; it need only be psychological. There is some evidence to suggest that our sense of taste is declining.

Psychologist Dr. Susan Schiffman fed a variety of foods to subjects and asked them to identify the food by taste alone. Sight clues were eliminated by a blindfold and texture clues erased by putting the foods through a blender until they all resembled baby food. In a group of normal-weight subjects only 41 percent were able to identify the taste of bananas correctly. The number jumped to 69 percent for a group of obese people and dropped to 24 percent among elderly people.

Reports in the *Journal of Marketing Research* undertaken to study consumer preference give further hints that taste buds are wearing thin. In a test of over three hundred confirmed beer drinkers, one study found that the prime consideration in taste ratings was the label. Drinking from a six-pack without labels, the beer lovers decided the quality of the beer was not very good and showed no particular preference for one bottle over another—even though their favorite brand was included as one of the unlabeled bottles. Later, given the same six-packs, this time with the proper brand labels, the taste ratings improved measurably and drinkers showed a definite preference for their own brand.

Another study tested forty-two shoppers tasting four loaves of identical bread labeled only as brands L, M, P and H. Each person tried each "brand" and within twelve trials half of those tested settled upon one particular brand preference.

In an experiment at the University of California's Davis Campus, visitors to an open house were given miscolored food. Orange sherbet with green coloring or lime sherbet colored red confused 75 percent of the tasters. The same experimenters found that drinkers could not tell the difference between red wine and white wine colored to look like red wine.

Not only is the discriminating taster becoming the exception, but the standards for judging tastes are changing. The age of pseudo-choice is also the age of imitation imitation. Food technologists at first strove to imitate natural flavors. But eaters have become so accustomed to artificial flavors that they have in turn become the standard by which natural flavors are judged.

The era of imitation imitation is best illustrated by the story of a major food processor who attempted to market a better catsup. The processor spent money for research and finally developed a catsup that preserved the smell and taste of real tomatoes. In spite of a superior product and promotion the tasty catsup flopped. The company had succeeded in eliminating from catsup the taste of overcooked, somewhat scorched tomatoes that is imparted in the normal processing. But it is precisely this overdone flavor that eaters associate with "real catsup." So the company made a few scorching adjustments to alter the catsup's taste and sales again turned profitable.

Charles Grimm, director of flavor creation at International Flavors and Fragrances, Inc., says that "more than ever before manufacturers request the taste of a product as it is usually found in the marketplace— processed, concentrated, freeze-dried, powdered or canned." The processed has become the norm. Food "flavorists" call this phenomenon the pineapple-juice bias. The taste that people associate with pineapple juice is invariably that of an artificial flavor. Part of that artificial flavor is the metallic taste the juice gains from the can, and part is the main ingredient of the pineapple flavoring agent—ethyl butyrate, ethyl acetate and butyric acid. Pineapple juice straight from a pineapple would be rejected as undrinkable, and few would even be able to identify the taste in a blindfold taste test.

Millions of kids raised on powdered orange drinks find real orange juice tastes "funny." Their wrinkled noses mean that the real thing is not sweet enough for palates accustomed to General Foods astronaut powder. There is a children's storybook that has its young readers solve a mystery with clues presented as scratch and sniff papers, or "microfragrances" as 3M calls them. These printed smells are excellent training for children growing up in a world of manufactured food. Each of the smells is genuine imitation imitation. The odor encapsulated to resemble chocolate smells no more like chocolate than the brown-colored coatings used on most ice-cream bars.

It is among children that one can find the signs of future food acceptance. Psychologists who have studied food preferences among adults find that people tend to prefer the food that they become accustomed to as children. An experiment at Miami of Ohio University shows that rats raised on water spiked with garlic later preferred garlic water to plain water. The yearning for food the way Mother used to make it is no mere figure of speech, it is a recognition of a partially conditioned response. If Mother serves cardboard bread and TV dinners regularly, chances are that each bite is an advance toward complete pseudo-choice in the future of food.

.   .   .

PSEUDO-CHOICE AND THE FROZEN-FOOD MENU

Americans currently eat one out of three meals away from home, and industry analysts expect to see that figure increase to one out of every two meals. The restaurant business is far less monopolistic than the grocery-store or food-processing industries, and any large city offers true choice in eating out. But pseudo-choice is invading even the realm of the dinner menu.

Because of rising costs of food and labor and heavy advertising on the part of the frozen-food industry, restaurant owners are increasingly filling the menu with frozen, precooked, ready-made items from large food processors. Many restaurants do a high-volume business acting as a dispenser of glorified TV dinners. From its status as lifeboat food for a shipwrecked dinner schedule, the frozen meal has moved into gourmet restaurants. Sam Martin, editor of *Quick Frozen Foods* magazine, claims that 80 percent of the better restaurants (not counting fast-food franchises) use some frozen entrees.

Armour Foods sells ready-made entrees such as Coq au Vin, Lumache, Empanadas and Veal Cordon-Bleu to restaurants for as little as 50 cents a serving. How much the restaurant can charge for the frozen dinner depends on the skill of the menu writer and the atrophy of the customer's taste buds. Another company offers frozen steaks with grill marks crisscrossing the bottom so customers will never suspect a microwave oven.

That restaurants serve frozen food does not in itself contribute to pseudo-choice, nor does it inevitably lead to poor taste or nutrition. But to the extent that restaurants become dependent on preprocessed, ready-to-serve foods, they become dependent on the leading processors. The question to ask a waiter is no longer who is your chef but do you order from General Mills, Sara Lee or Armour?

. . .

CONCLUSION

Pseudo-choice in food will be complete when shoppers and restaurant customers cease to choose from knowledge and instead succumb to the lures of marketing and advertising. It is still possible to purchase simple, nutritious food at fair prices and it is possible to dine where the food is carefully prepared and consistently fresh.

Knowledge of food ingredients, especially of "new foods" offered by the leading food producers, can help the shopper avoid pseudo-food. Books such as Michael Jacobson's *The Eater's Digest,* William Robbins' *The American Food Scandal,* James Hightower's *Eat Your Heart Out* and Beatrice Trum Hunter's *Consumer Beware!* can help immensely in shaping pseudo-choice resistance. Food co-ops help counter pseudo-choice and corporate control of grocery outlets as does participation in growing or raising one's own food supply. Convenience foods certainly have some place in the eating hierarchy, but one reserved for those emergencies when time is of the essence.

Home economics or consumer education teachers should make students aware of the corporate control of the food supply as well as the nature of the most common processing ingredients. The nature and uses of food would seem to be high on the list of important knowledge for both personal and social survival. School cafeterias and lunchrooms with vending machines often counteract any classroom teaching by serving pseudo-food delights and dispensing only sweets and soft drinks for snacks.

If the best food as we know it today does not exist for the citizen of the future, it will be because of the victory of pseudo-choice. Just as with automobiles and television, we will be offered a pseudo-choice and will pretend it is an expression of free will and a monument to our freedom as a nation.

Alan Wolfe
DEFINING REPRESSION

In this selection, Alan Wolfe, a contemporary political scientist, turns his attention to defining repression in general and to the understanding of the conditions under which it is in the interest of one group to carry out repression against another. He argues that one group in society, namely, the ruling class, consistently benefits from repression. According to this view, the ruling class in this country is the group that owns the means of production and uses its economic power to exert control over the media and various other political and social institutions, so that they, in turn, reinforce the capitalist system upon which its privilege rests. Production under capitalism is not organized around the principle of production for use (to produce what people need and see that products are built well and can last a long time) but around the desire for profit. The system must, therefore, convince people to work hard to produce products, many of which would be useless in a rational society, and most of which have a built-in obsolescence. And then, of course, it must convince people to buy things that they might otherwise have no desire to buy. It must, in fact, create artificial needs, so that the cycles of ever-increasing production and ever-increasing consumption can continue.

.   .   .

Our first task is to know what we are talking about, which in this case is not easy. The problem stems from the fact that repression is a value-laden word. Few people wish to be called repressive, and even fewer societies would admit to engaging periodically in repression. Most social scientists have traditionally regarded repression as something that took place somewhere else. After World War II, for example, American social scientists developed the concept of totalitarianism, which they applied to Germany, Italy, and Russia.[1] Numerous studies appeared documenting the

[1]The classic example of this work is Carl J. Friedrich and Zbigniew Brzezinski, *Totalitarian Dictatorship and Autocracy* (New York: Praeger, 1963). It is a fascinating exercise to read the book now, substituting "America" for "Germany" to see what one comes to. For an effective critique of this kind of book, see Herbert J. Spiro and Benjamin Barber, "Totalitarianism as Counter-Ideology," *Politics and Society* 1 (November 1970): 3–21.

role that the governments of those countries played in quashing dissent, and various theories were developed to explain why events happened as they did. Meanwhile, in the country where these books were being written, the government was also attempting to remove dissidents forcibly, but these incidents were often ignored. Few wrote about domestic repression, with the exception of some who were being repressed.[2] In addition, most books which did deal with it were either exposés or case studies;[3] few serious analyses of the nature of repression have yet been put forward.

A look at all these attempts to handle dissent by suppressing it brings us to a first element in a definition of repression: it is an act performed by people who have political power, that is, people who control the means of repression. In most countries this will mean that repression is governmental activity, a responsibility of the state. But this need not always be the case. In the United States, for example, nineteenth-century repression was often carried out by private detective agencies that were hired by corporation leaders to break strikes and infiltrate labor organizations. Although the government was not performing these acts of repression, people in power were, for the emerging corporate leaders of the time constituted a ruling class that determined the nature of the political system.

As those in power were the acting agents of the repression, a second element in the definition can be added: repression is practiced against those who challenge the existing power holders. Since anyone who does not hold power may at any time by his mere existence constitute a threat to those who do, the number of people who could potentially be repressed is very high, and it includes nearly all the people who live in a given society. When any of these people set themselves up in an organization that threatens the government, or when they develop a set of ideas contrary to the ruling ideas of the society, they face the threat of repression. In the United States, the repressive mechanisms of the state have been used most heavily against such groups as the Industrial Workers of the World (IWW), the Communist party, and the Black Panther party, groups with both an ideological and an organizational opposition to the way things were being run in the country at the time they existed.

We can now advance a formal definition of repression, and then go on to examine its weaknesses. *Repression is a process by which those in power try to keep themselves in power by consciously attempting to destroy or render harmless*

---

[2]An example of this phenomenon is Tom Hayden, *Rebellion and Repression* (New York: Meridian Books, 1969). But each repressed group has put out its own materials, from the IWW to books on the Red scare and Herbert Aptheker's book on the McCarthy Period.

[3]The best case studies are Robert K. Murray, *Red Scare* (New York: McGraw-Hill, 1964); William Preston, Jr., *Aliens and Dissenters* (Cambridge, Mass.: Harvard University Press, 1963); Earl Latham, *The Communist Controversy in Washington* (Cambridge, Mass.: Harvard University Press, 1966); Audrie Ginder and Anne Goftis, *The Great Betrayal* (New York: Macmillan, 1969). A recent attempt to deal theoretically with repression was published after this book was written: Murray Levin, *Political Hysteria in America* (New York: Basic Books, 1971).

organizations and ideologies that threaten their power. Repression can best be understood as a reproductive mechanism. In order to continue to exist, a society needs certain methods of ensuring that existing power relationships will be reproduced from generation to generation, as well as from day to day.[4] Repression is a process, one among many, that serves this function in the United States.

The concept of reproductive mechanisms focuses on the question of why those in power are allowed to remain in power, which is also a way of asking why those who are powerless accept that state of affairs. The powerless may do so because they believe that society can exist in no other way; they may wish to challenge their powerlessness but are afraid to do so because of possible reprisals; or they may actually have tried to change things but failed. In each case, what happens is that a situation in which some have power at the expense of others is reproduced continually. The means by which this process of reproduction takes place are the means of repression.

The process of repression can be illustrated by an example. In 1919, in the United States, dissatisfaction with the way things were taking place was concentrated in three organizations: the IWW, the Socialist party, and a group that was eventually to form the Communist party (actually, two Communist parties were formed at first).[5] The resulting structure contained a ruling group, organized in the presidency and other institutions of power, and containing an ideology that justified its rule; and a series of challenging groups, each with its own organization, and each containing its ideology challenging that rule. Diagrammatically, such a situation might look like [the chart on page 375].

In this example, the process of repression would constitute the various attempts by the group at the top to contain the influence of the group at the bottom. For example, leaders of the IWW were continually being arrested and brought to trial on the basis of vague and unsubstantiated charges. Offices of the organization were periodically raided. . . . Members of the Socialist party, duly elected to legislatures, were refused seats. Infiltrators were sent to join the Communist parties, and a secret unity meeting of the various groups was raided by the Justice Department. All these attempts to destroy the organizations that were seen as a threat were directly repressive.

But repression is not practiced solely against organizations. Once the dissidents existed, the government tried to destroy them by using force in the form of raids, trials, and infiltrators. From a point of view of the government, however, a better procedure existed, and that was to repress the ideology of the dissenting organizations. If the government could

---

[4]The concept of reproductive mechanisms is contained in Karl Marx, *Pre-Capitalist Economic Formations* (New York: International Publishers, 1965). For an example of how the term has been applied to repression, see Louis Althusser, "Ideology and Ideological State Apparatuses," in *Lenin and Philosophy* (London: New Left Books, 1971), pp. 121–73.

[5]See Murray, *Red Scare,* pp. 18–56.

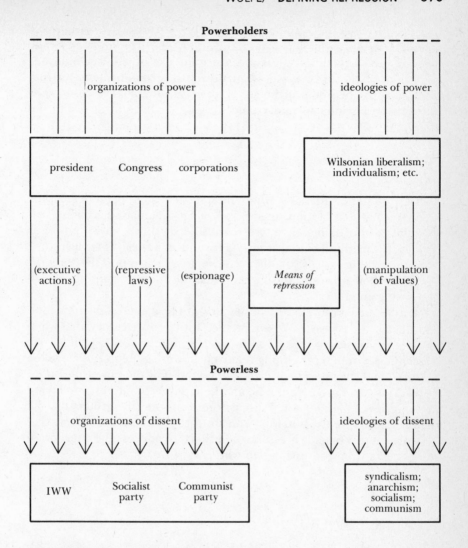

convince the overwhelming majority of the people in the United States that left-wing ideologies were evil, then the dissenting groups could gain no adherents and would die out. The result was the creation of a Committee on Public Information, which set out systematically to discredit the dissenters, not by destroying their organization, but by using propaganda to discredit their ideas. Few can see which of the government tactics, proceeding against the organization or discrediting the ideology, was more successful in repressing these groups. Certainly both tactics played a major role.

This example illustrates the fact that repression in America takes two broad forms. One is the use of *state violence,* the attempt to destroy an *organization* by using the means that the state has at its disposal. The other is *ideological repression,* the attempt to manipulate people's *consciousness* so that they accept the ruling ideology, and distrust and refuse to be moved by competing ideologies. The two forms proceed together; it is really impossible to talk about one without the other. Those in power generally prefer to use ideological repression, since the use of violence indicates political instability and may win sympathy for the group being destroyed. But violent repression will be used when the ideological form does not work, so in order to understand the one we have to deal with the other.

.   .   .

Despite some variations, when the state acts in a liberal democratic society such as that of the United States, it acts in a biased fashion . . . It is partial to the dominant interests, hostile to those whose power is minimal. By nearly all of its actions, it reproduces a society in which some have power at the expense of others, and it moves to support the "others" only when their protests are so strong that the "some" stand to lose all they have gained.

It follows that repression will similarly not be a neutral phenomenon but will have a class basis. We can predict, with good accuracy, that when the state intervenes to repress an organization or an ideology, it will be a dissenting group, representing relatively powerless people, that will be repressed and the interests upheld will be those of the powerful. But to say that is not to say enough. Who are these powerful interests? Who are the powerless? Without some discussion of the specific groups that fill these categories, repression will be an abstract phenomenon unrelated to this world at this time. It is essential, in short, to address the question of who benefits from repression and who is hurt by it.

LOCATING POWER

Many have realized the importance of making statements about who holds power in democratic societies, so a lack of literature on the subject is not the problem. The opposite of that is more likely to raise difficulties, for no clear consensus arises out of reading what exists on this subject. There are instead a series of mini-consensuses. One of these holds that power in America is no problem. The country is ruled by a series of minorities, each of these balancing out the potential power of others, thus making it impossible for any one group to dominate.[6] This pluralistic

[6]Daniel Bell, "Is There a Ruling Class in America?" in *The End of Ideology* (New York: Free Press, 1960), pp. 43–67; Robert A. Dahl, "A Critique of the Ruling Elite Model," *American Political Science Review* 52 (June 1958): 463–69; David B. Truman, *The Governmental Process* (New York: Knopf, 1951); John Kenneth Galbraith, *American Capitalism* (Boston: Houghton Mifflin, 1956); Arnold Rose, *The Power Structure* (New York: Oxford University Press, 1967).

vision has been subjected to fairly severe criticism, so much so that there is no need to accept it here.[7] More insightful are two other approaches. One holds that there is a power elite which runs things. It is composed of the occupants of some key positions in American society, organized into rings of influence.[8] A similar view argues that it is not a power elite that is in command, but a ruling class centered not in the important political positions, but in key economic areas.[9] Viewing these claims, one is left with the impression that little clarity and much confusion exist on a theoretical problem of first importance.

In attempting to sort through the confusion, two positive steps might help. One is to accept neither side in the debate between those who advocate a ruling class model and those who prefer a power elite. Rather, following the example of sociologist Wldozimierz Wesolowski,[10] it is best to recognize the existence of both concepts. Power in a society such as the United States exists at both the economic and political levels. The point is not to subsume arbitrarily one under the other but to recognize the different kinds of power associated with each and to examine the conditions under which one is more important than the other; we will try to do so [here].

Another step is to recognize that a bipolar model of power, in whch one group is seen to have it all and the other is seen to have none, distorts reality to such a great extent that it becomes useless. Power is at all times a relational phenomenon. One only has a certain amount of power in relation to something else. It is quite possible for A to exercise power over B, but it is also possible that B in turn will be more powerful when compared to C. Does that make B powerful or powerless? The answer is neither. It means that B has power in some situations and not in others. He would be at a middle level of power, a level that cannot be ignored in any meaningful discussion of who holds power in America.

These caveats leave us in the following situation. On a vertical dimension, power exists on a variety of levels, ranging from the most powerful institutions and people to the least. For the sake of convenience, we can begin to make sense out of these levels by calling them upper, middle, and lower, recognizing that each subdivision has gradations within itself. Horizontally, on the other hand, we have claimed that power has both an economic and a political dimension and that both are important. There are differences, however, in what they do. Because America

---

[7]C. Wright Mills, *The Power Elite* (New York: Oxford University Press, 1956); G. William Domhoff, *Who Rules America?* (Englewood Cliffs, N.J.: Prentice-Hall, 1967); Paul Sweezy, "Power Elite or Ruling Class?," in *C. Wright Mills and the Power Elite*, ed. G. William Domhoff and Hoyt Ballard (Boston: Beacon Press, 1968), pp. 115–32. See also the essays by Robert Lynd and Herbert Aptheker in that volume.

[8]Mills' *The Power Elite* is the most famous of this genre.

[9]See, for example, Sweezy, "Power Elite or Ruling Class?"

[10]Wlodzimierz Wesolowski, "Ruling Class and Power Elite," *Polish Sociological Bulletin* 11 (January 1965): 22–37.

is a capitalist society whose structure has continually evolved to accommodate changes in the nature of capitalism, those who are economically powerful, by their actions, shape the nature of the society in its most basic form. Within that form, the political leaders and political institutions decide on and implement policy matters. It makes a good deal of difference whether one policy or another is adopted, but in nearly all cases, *the range of available policy options are all perceived to be within the basic structure of a capitalist society.* In this sense, *the economic positions have a primary importance to which the political positions are secondary. . . .*

If we now combine all these levels together and attempt to represent them schematically, the result would look something like [Table 1].

All diagrams simplify reality, and this one is no exception. It helps to use it only if it eventually leads to a clarification of complexity, not to its obfuscation. Whether this one accomplishes that goal or not should become clearer as we proceed through each category. The attempt here will be to differentiate the kinds of power that exist in America, and to isolate the kinds of institutions that possess different levels of power.

Table 1   *Schematic Representation of Power in America*

Levels	Economic Elite (Ruling Class)	Political Elite (Power Elite)
Upper levels of power	corporation executives foundation heads, etc. *(function: shape the polity)*	president and state functionaries in executive branch, military, diplomats, etc. *(function: decide and implement policies)*
	Transmission belts	
Middle levels of power	corporate managers, high-level administrators, ex-military officers, national interest groups, local aristocrats	congressmen, judges, governors, lower level executive branch
	middle management, middle administrators, local interest groups, larger small businessmen, labor leaders	mayors, state legislators, other judicial, city, and state officials
	average small businessmen, professionals, highly paid workers	town and village officials
Lower levels of power	office workers, blue-collar workers unskilled workers youth, "deviant" groups, housewives unemployed, stigmatized, lumpen proletariat	

THE UPPER LEVELS OF POWER

The distinction between shaping the polity and deciding on policy within that shape is best seen at the highest levels of power. This is a point that pluralists such as David Truman or John Kenneth Galbraith often miss. Since their focus is on the relative influence of a group over specific policy outcomes, they may well be right in noting that various groups, ranging from corporations to labor unions, all have some say. But the question they never ask, the most important question to be asked, concerns the system in which the decision is being made. Pluralists accept liberal capitalism as inevitable, a given framework, and this leads to their uncon-cern with what brought it into being. But American capitalism did not mysteriously appear. It was brought into being by some very powerful people. It is continually reproduced by others who spend most of their time trying to ensure its reproduction. *In order, then, to speak of the ruling class, we would be mistaken to look at political decision making but must focus instead on those whose activities define the parameters of the system and reproduce those parameters on a day-to-day basis.*

America is defined by its consensus, by those political values that are alleged to be the only truly legitimate ones. Liberalism is the ideology of the consensus, and at the moment its most important aspects are three. One is that democracy of a representative sort, such as that enunciated in the Constitution, is the best form of government imaginable, which should be tampered with as little as possible. (Americans pride them-selves that they have changed their Constitution so little, which from another point of view simply indicates the inflexibility of the system.) A second significant aspect to the concensus is a commitment to the para-doxical notion that private enterprise capitalism is the only legitimate economic structure, but that it does create problems which require sub-stantial roles for the state to play: watching the "public" interest; inter-vening to ensure stability; and providing benefits to those displaced by the free market system. Finally, America is also united around the idea of America itself, i.e., the notion that the previous two things have been best accomplished in America and thus a preservation of this country against its foreign enemies is essential. Anticommunism, in other words, is part of the consensus as well.[11]

---

[11]For examples of attempts to portray the consensus, see the Rockefeller Brothers Fund, *Prospects for America* (Garden City, N. Y.: Doubleday, 1961). This volume contains six separate studies whose titles and (more importantly) whose order of publication are signifi-cant to this discussion of consensus: the mid-century challenge to U.S. foreign policy; international security: the military aspect; foreign economic policy for the twentieth cen-tury; the challenge to America: its economic and social aspects; the pursuit of excellence: education and the future of America; the power of the democratic idea. Also relevant in this connection is the President's Commission on National Goals, *Goals of Americans* (Englewood Cliffs, N.J.: Prentice-Hall, 1960). This is concerned basically with economic and social policy. Other examples of consensus-shaping are the Godkin lectures, given each year at Harvard. A typical one is McGeorge Bundy, *The Strength of Government* (Cambridge, Mass.: Harvard University Press, 1968).

The important point to realize about the nature of consensus, and one that many theorists of democracy seem to forget, is that it is not received but made.[12] It does not arise through magic, but is the work of real people in real situations. It is not inevitable, but could take quite a different form under different circumstances. *The consensus that does exist does so because it fulfills the needs of those who rule the democratic state.* For example, the commitment to modern corporate liberalism came into being in the years 1900–20, when a group of men associated with the National Civic Federation rejected both Social Darwinism on the Right and socialism on the Left, combining elements of both into a new ideology that has essentially governed the United States since that time. As James Weinstein has shown, the change in American liberalism from one of free market capitalism to one of state intervention was the work of a group of strong-minded and intelligent men who, through their diligence, brought it into being.[13]   It didn't just happen.

Those who created the modern American state in those years could be considered the ruling class of their time. (Interestingly enough, those same men were also instrumental in creating the modern system of repression.) *Today we would define the ruling class as those who play the greatest role in reproducing this ideology and the structure that services it.* Who they are may become clearer if we first show who they are not.

The members of the ruling class are not necessarily "America's sixty families,"[14] that is, the richest people in the United States, for many a Howard Hughes is concerned more with making money than with shaping the nature of a system. Nor are they necessarily the entire social aristocracy, the people who go only to certain schools, join certain clubs, work in certain firms, die of certain diseases, and are buried in certain sacred resting places.[15] These people constitute an upper class in the social sense, but not in the economic (for not all of them are wealthy and many with wealth are not among them) or political (for not all of them have political power) sphere. Chances are good that a member of the ruling class will be a member of the social aristocracy, but an aristocrat need not necessarily be a ruler. In addition, the ruling class is not composed of all heads of corporations which do X number of dollars worth of business or more. Some corporations are much more concerned with

[12]Neither Louis Hartz nor Daniel Boorstin concern themselves with the beneficiaries of the traditions they so much glorify. See Louis Hartz, *The Liberal Tradition in America* (New York: Harcourt Brace, 1955); and Daniel Boorstin, *The Genius of American Politics* (Chicago: University of Chicago Press, 1953).

[13]James Weinstein, *The Corporate Ideal in the Welfare State* (Boston: Beacon Press, 1968).

[14]Ferdinand Lundberg, *America's Sixty Families* (New York: Halcyon House, 1937). For a more recent and just as simplistic account by the same writer see *The Rich and the Super Rich* (New York: Lyle Stuart, 1968).

[15]E. Digby Baltzell, *An American Business Aristocracy* (New York: Collier Books, 1962); E. Digby Baltzell, *The Protestant Establishment* (New York: Random House, 1964); Stephen Birmingham, *The Right People* (Boston: Little, Brown, 1968). There are, of course, many other books on the subject too numerous to mention.

rulership than others, the difference between First National City Bank and Texas Instruments. Finally, all members of the ruling class do not possess last names of distinguished family lines.[16] Many of them do (Harriman, Rockefeller, Bundy), but this is neither a necessary nor a sufficient condition for membership.

Instead, *the ruling class contains what could be called the politicized members of the upper class*, those who, from training, innate desire, upbringing, decide that they will rule and accomplish their objective. Therefore, position and social class are important, vitally important. A member of the ruling class will most likely spring from an aristocratic and rich family. He could easily head a corporation, be on numerous boards, and possess a distinguished last name. Similarly, he would undoubtedly occupy some crucial positions. It would not be surprising if he ran the Ford Foundation, chaired the Chase Manhattan Bank, edited *Foreign Affairs*, partnered in Dillon Read or Sullivan and Cromwell, or directed NBC.

John McCloy, former high commissioner to Germany, is a trustee of the Ford Foundation, a director of the Council on Foreign Relations, a former chairman of the board of the Chase Manhattan Bank, a member of the National Advertising Council, an entry in the Social Register (New York), and a partner in a powerful law firm. McGeorge Bundy was a Harvard dean, key presidential adviser on defense, and is now president of the Ford Foundation. He is the son of a Lowell. His brother William, also a high-level policy maker, married Dean Acheson's daughter, while his sister married an Auchincloss closely related to Jacqueline Kennedy's stepfather.[17] If the objection is raised that those men are atypical because of their public visibility, consider the case of W. T. Moore of Centre Island, N.Y.[18] His name may be unfamiliar, but aside from running Moore-McCormick Shipping and serving on the Council of Foreign Relations, he serves both his business and his country through the influential role he plays in the following three international organizations: the Pan American Association, the Argentine American Chamber of Commerce, the American Brazilian Society.

The impact of this definition is that the ruling class is small in number, composed of no more than a few thousand individuals, nearly all of them living in the Boston-New York- Philadelphia-Washington axis. They are all rich. Nearly all are white Anglo-Saxon Protestants or German Jews. They are all either businessmen or descendants of businessmen. They are born to power and grow up in an atmosphere that cultivates power. They recognize each other, and each of them is fully conscious that he belongs

[16]Stephen Hess, *America's Political Dynasties* (Garden City, N.Y.: Doubleday, 1966), contains information on some such last names.

[17]On McCloy, see Domhoff, *Who Rules America?*, pp. 67, 76–79; on Bundy see Patrick Anderson, *The President's Men* (Garden City, N.Y.: Doubleday, 1968), pp. 260–62.

[18]Deborah Leavy, "Where the Ruling Class Lives: A Study of Centre Island, N.Y." (unpublished paper, Old Westbury College, State University of New York, n.d.).

to the ruling class. They are chairmen, directors, trustees, vice-presidents, consultants, partners, secretaries, advisers, presidents, members and relatives. They, in other words, are the "they" that people (with acute perception) blame for their troubles. And the blame is deserved, for they have taken the responsibility of shaping the society in their interest. They are conscious of that responsibility, and they want to be thanked when popular and shunned when unpopular. For amusement, they read books (often written with support from their foundations) which "prove" that no ruling class exists in the United States.

.   .   .

The members of the ruling class often seem to be above politics, and in a sense they are. Their enormous power comes not from political positions (though they have held them), or from direct corporate links. It comes from their role, often euphemistically described, as "public servants." America needs a group of leaders who at all times consider the interests of the whole society over the interests of any given segment of that society. But since the whole society is a capitalist one, the resulting "public interest" will in most cases be the interest of the capitalist class, rather than the interest of any one particular capitalist. It is because these men (and they are all men, or so it seems) shape a system based on the power of a few that they can be considered to be at the highest levels of power in that society. When affairs are running smoothly, one hardly notices them.

The political governing class, which also exists at the upper levels of power on our diagram but which has less power than the ruling class, is more likely to be composed of individuals sensitive to the interests of the ruling class than it is of individuals who are members of the ruling class. There is no need for the ruling class to dominate all the political positions. If it did, the class nature of the democratic state would be all the more apparent, and claims about its openness would be harder to make. Furthermore, a distinct political governing class means that positions can be opened up for talented men from other classes. This has two advantages: (1) preventing stagnation, which was perceived by E. Digby Baltzell when he suggested that the only way to preserve aristocratic authority (to him a vital need) was for the aristocrats to be receptive to ambitious men from outside their ranks;[19] and (2) providing the illusion of social mobility (anybody can grow up to be president). Given these advantages, so long as the ruling class finds little opposition to its interests in a distinct political elite (it may even be willing to lose a little, if necessary), it has a reason to maintain the political elite's autonomy. There is little danger that such a strategy will backfire, and if it does (nomination of a populist, for example), control over the transmission belts can be used to win over the "public" to personalities and policies more in keeping with the pur-

[19]Baltzell, *Protestant Establishment*, p. 382.

view of the ruling class. As moderate as he was George McGovern's defeat in 1972 is an example of the treatment given to one who challenges, even a little bit, the fundamental aspects of the consensus.

.   .   .

One implication is clear: *one class of people consistently benefits from repression, another carries out the policies of repression and feels benefits therefrom but is repressed in a sense as well, and a third is the object of repression.* In addition, each group is composed of fairly well-defined institutions, which enables the observer to rank any person reasonably accurately on a scale of repression, given certain socioeconomic information. In short, just as the state has a very definite bias in the way it operates, repression, as a policy of the state, is biased as well. The "who" that benefits from repression is not randomly decided, some days one group, other days, another. The objects of repression do not continually vary throughout the social structure. Instead, *repression is an aspect of class society,* a method in the class struggle. Repression is a way by which those at the top keep themselves there. . . .

SECTION NINE

EQUALITY

The Declaration of Independence states that "all men are created equal," and we are told that American democracy is founded on this belief. Yet, if taken literally, the statement is patently false. People are obviously born with different potentials and physical characteristics. Thus, the statement, to be meaningful, must be taken as an expression of moral conviction. All people ought *to be treated equally, at least with respect to certain basic opportunities. But even if equality is understood in this minimal way, practice has rarely conformed to this requirement. Despite those lofty words in the Declaration of Independence, the men who founded the American Republic excluded a large percentage of the population—women, indentured servants, slaves, and the entire indigenous population of American Indians—from the status of legal citizenship.*

In this section, we consider the concept of equality in general; the situation of two groups, women and blacks, who have been denied equality; and the question of how to remedy such inequities. Lying behind these concerns is a broader one. What, in fact, makes one thing equal to another in the first place? How can such calculations be made with respect to human beings? Is there an objective value inherent in things (and people) that gives them a value that can be calculated? Some people have alleged that this is the case. Some thinkers have claimed that both winners and losers are born as such. The only problem with this conclusion is that it rests on circular reasoning. If, for example, you succeed in the world, then your success is proof that you are meant for success; in the same fashion, your failure is proof that you are bound to fail. As stated, this position never misses its mark, but the price it pays for its "accuracy" is that it makes a circular and trivial claim. If being born a success means only that one does succeed, the doctrine does not tell us much—it simply offers a definition.

Thus, we are back at the beginning. How do we place a value on things, or more important, on people? What does it mean to demand to be recognized and

*treated as an equal? How are we to understand the situation of those who have
been denied equality? What kinds of equality do we want to exist, and how
ought we to go about achieving them?*

The Alva Myrdal Report to the Swedish Social Democratic Party
THE NEED FOR EQUALITY

*The selection that follows is excerpted from the Alva Myrdal Report to the
Swedish Democratic party. The Work Group on Equality, which rendered the
report, was established by the Party Congress in 1968. The report itself was
later accepted, and its principles were used as guidelines for formulating Social
Democratic party policy in Sweden. You will note that in place of a narrow
definition of equality, in terms of exclusively formal conditions (i.e., equal
treatment before the law), the report depicts equality as a state of affairs that
must be reflected and furthered by every aspect of social existence.*

The standard of living in industrialized countries is rising steadily. Nevertheless, all such countries—no matter what their social system—are characterized by inequalities between individuals and groups. The differences
in conditions of living are admittedly smaller in some societies than in
others, but no industrial nation has yet achieved a society in which citizens behave and value each other as equals. At the same time the gap is
widening between the rich nations and the poor peoples of the third
world. Economic growth and technological development are not automatically promoting an equal distribution of well-being and opportunities for making the most of life.

　This is a fundamental issue for the Swedish labour movement as it
enters the seventies. Greater equality has always been one of the strongest driving forces in political and trade-union work. While important
advances have been achieved, we are nevertheless forced to acknowledge
that great inequalities still exist. Prosperity has increased but is still unequally distributed.

　Considering the *increased opportunities* made available by technical and
economic development, the challenge is just as great today as it was at
the beginning of the century to create a society whose outstanding characteristics are concern for fellowmen and solidarity, where the abilities of
each citizen are made good use of. This task has two aspects. It is a
question of opposing the concentration of privileges and power in the
hands of traditionally-favoured groups. At the same time, special efforts
must be made to achieve a lasting improvement and equalization of
conditions in favour of individuals and groups which have been left
behind in various ways, the weakest members of society.

BACKGROUND

The demand for equality and recognition of human worth drew its strength from the material deprivation and lack of rights experienced by the working class during the breakthrough period of industrialism. Every day the worker found that equality had no real meaning under unbridled capitalism. As a result the labour movement became the standard-bearer of a policy demanding definite changes in industrial society.

This policy represented a clear alternative to the bourgeois-liberal approach and a sharpening and deepening of the striving for equality. Previously this aim, under the influence of the Age of Enlightenment, the French Revolution, and the ideas of liberalism, had limited itself chiefly to the elimination of political and legal bases of feudal or other upper-class privilege. It was for equality in this latter sense that the new middle-class really took up the cudgels. But as these demands became linked up with an economic system—free competition and an unrestrained market economy—they gradually cancelled themselves out. The political and economic structure of the liberal society resulted in new class distinctions and new privileges. The economically successful, who did not want to accept any limitation of their actions or opportunities to accumulate wealth, also accumulated economic and political power and, along with this, property and the means for achieving a completely different standard of living from that of the masses. These advantages were then inherited by their descendants. Opportunities were never equally distributed. The equal rights avowedly sought never became reality.

WHAT DO WE MEAN BY EQUALITY?

Equality in Conditions of Living

The Demand for Justice.   The principle that all men have equal worth has been defined by the Social Democrats to mean that *all men have the same right to live a full and satisfying life.* These rights, for example the right to education, the right to equality before the law, and the right to political and economic influence, are not enough. Nor can we accept the conservative method of preserving a society of privilege by asserting that those who live in deprived conditions are just as "satisfied with their lot" as the more favoured. The Social Democratic Party interpretation of equal rights to a full life is that each citizen should have equal *freedom of choice* to shape his own future. Thus a clear relationship exists between the desire for freedom of choice and the struggle for equality.

Human and Social Relationships.   Greater equality in conditions of living is not merely a goal in itself. Great disparities in standards and influence complicate and poison relationships and communication between individuals and groups. Socialism should be seen as a freedom movement, in which freedom from the pressure of external circumstances, class

divisions and insecurity is considered a *prerequisite* for new human relationships marked more by cooperation and community and less by self-
assertion, competition and conflict among various groups in society.
Equalizing conditions of life then become a means of changing human
relationships, of creating a better social climate. The cooperation which
the Social Democrats aim at should take place on equal terms and between equals.

An Efficient Society.   The traditional middle-class criticism of the equality policy of the Social Democratic Party is that greater equality must be
bought at the price of reduced efficiency, slower economic growth, etc.
It may be replied, however, that even in terms of efficiency it is gross
mismanagement to allow only the better-situated to develop their inherent talents and fully express themselves in society. Groups which are
lagging behind, with unused resources to contribute to the common
good, are a hindrance both to efficiency and to desirable social change.
     We are thinking not only of equality in the *utilization* of all of society's
facilities and resources. The concept of equality concerns just as much
the possibility of *influencing* the choice of what goods, services, cultural
experiences, environmental qualities will be available in society.
     This applies to:
     Economic democracy on the parliamentary level; that is to say, the
citizens' right to express themselves as voters on guidelines for production and economic life in general, and consequently about future consumption possibilities and environmental conditions. The disputes of the
fifties and the sixties in Sweden regarding the public sector should be
considered in this context.
     Democratic conditions at the grassroot level, that is to say, the op-
portunity for the individual, in cooperation with others, to influence his
own immediate life situation, in working life, in schools and institutions,
in his living environment.

Arguments Against Equality

One argument frequently advanced against the equality policy is that it
would involve the risk of sameness and uniformity—that everyone would
be cast in the same mould, it would eliminate distinctiveness. The Party
maintains that this is neither the objective nor will it be the result of the
equality policy. Greater equality in economic, social and cultural conditions does not prevent people from developing their own unique character, cultivating their personal interests, their particular way of life and
generally creating variation and diversity in society. On the contrary it is
inequality, class distinctions, which pigeonhole people and limit their
opportunities to shape their lives freely. A more equal distribution of
resources, influence and opportunities for choice increases variety in
society and in the life of the individual. There is strong reason to believe
that promoting equality of opportunity gives more scope to human indi-

viduality, for each person to shape his life according to his own ability and not along lines dictated by class.

Another objection concerns the feasibility and sometimes the justice of attempting to create equality, when human beings *are* so obviously different in physical, intellectual and mental capacity. Here also the arguments for equality are simple and well supported by experience. First, when individuals' aptitudes *are* similar, say for education, certain occupations, influence,—the possibilities open to them should also be similar regardless of birth, place of residence, parental income, etc.

Secondly, the Social Democrats' view of equality means that, where Nature has created great and fundamental differences in abilities, these must *not* be allowed to determine the individual's chances in life, but rather that society should intervene to "restore the balance." These differences, in the form of physical or intellectual handicaps, can never be eliminated, but they can be reduced in a generous social climate, and one can work against their leading to social discrimination. Disadvantages inflicted by Nature should not be accepted as something we can do nothing about.

Affluent Societies—But Still Poverty

The goal of equality is interpreted differently according to political conviction. The *liberal* view of equality, which is also held by large groups of conservatives, has had a tenacious vitality in the public debate in many countries. The objective is primarily to give individuals equal initial opportunities in life, by breaking down economic, educational and other barriers. The kind of society in which men subsequently work is much less important from the equality point of view. Instead the predominant factor is an economic doctrine which considers competition and rivalry to be the most important forces for improving economic growth and the standard of living. As a result, the liberal conception of equality becomes mainly a right to compete on equal terms. This view fails to see that the competitive orientation itself means that the less aggressive risk being elbowed out and isolated from the mainstream of society. Misfortune is built into the mechanism of such a society. Nor has it been understood that the effort to achieve more equal initial opportunities in an economic sense requires radical changes in the distribution of power and in the possibilities for large groups of wage-earners to exert influence.

Class distinctions and inequalities have instead been seen both in conservative and liberal circles as the price that has to be paid for a high degree of efficiency in production and a rapid rise in prosperity with a higher standard for all, even though it may be unequally distributed. Increasing numbers of people have become aware of the breakdown of this efficiency myth during the past decade. The experience of other countries has shown that policies based upon such premises involve the risk of social stagnation. Contact and communications between the different social classes decrease or become hostile. Broad strata of the population consider they have no reason to remain loyal to a social system and economic power groups, which neglect elementary demands for a socially dignified existence. Societies split up; the different social groups isolated behind obdurate barriers. The result is stalemate, which promotes neither the goal of economic efficiency nor the kind of social change where the great majority can develop their abilities and contribute to society.

A policy which aims to use the diverse resources of each individual and leads to the gradual reduction of differences in conditions of life is, in the opinion of the Social Democrats, justified by obvious principles of justice. More than this, it is a precondition for stable social development and for the preservation of social solidarity.

Equality requires a society in which a man's working conditions are more attuned to his abilities and preferences, where the residential environment makes possible contacts between generations and groups and counteracts the categorization of people, and where finally the individual has greater chances to participate in the decision-making processes, which affect his immediate life situation, at work, in the neighbourhood, etc. Such a social climate is necessary to modify those circumstances which exclude individuals and groups from the mainstream of society. It is also a crucial issue for the great majority of people.

In their working life most people are subordinate and have decisions thrust upon them from above because of a traditional structure of organization. Their freedom of action and of movement are limited by a narrow system of rules. Working environment has not improved at the same pace as the general improvement in standards. Eighty percent of wage-earners affiliated to the Confederation of Trade Unions are still subject to health risks in their work places.

Many of us live in modern and spacious housing; half of all Swedish dwellings have been built since World War II. But few of us have an environment around our housing accommodation which provides meaningful leisure activities, and all too few can influence the planning of that environment.

The distance between the leaders and the led increases rather than diminishes, in the public sector as well as in private industry. In the wake of technological development comes increased specialization and some centralization of decision-making. But it is not indisputable that all decisions ought to be centralized. A major task of the labour movement is to find ways to increase citizen participation and responsibility in an increasingly complex and to some extent entirely new industrial society.

The Demand for Equality Must Apply Throughout Life

Giving young people equal initial opportunities is an inadequate goal for one more reason: Social democracy maintains that society's responsibility for providing the individual with equal opportunities for development applies *throughout* his life.

This concept of equality leads to specific demands for social policy and at the same time spotlights serious difficulties. Individuals develop in different ways and under varying circumstances even from similar beginnings. We know that people who, early in life, become accustomed to success and rapid improvement in their standard of living later increase their *demands* on life. On the other hand, persons who meet unfavourable circumstances expect less and less of life. The initial differences are strengthened, to the good or to the worse, as life goes on.

The questions which now emerge as essential are:

In what respects do large groups in our society still make too modest demands on life?

What subgroups are especially subject to the escalation of adverse circumstances and should therefore receive special attention in the equality policy?

How should society design its measures to further the rights of weak groups and create real equality in those areas where modest demands and various types of environmental hindrances have made general measures insufficient?

Gaps Are Changing

Growth itself always involves risks of *new* distinctions. Efforts to create equality must comprise preventive measures to diminish new gaps or to keep them from developing.

Concentration of Power, Technological Development.   International concentration of private capital has resulted in increasingly expanding markets, more and more employees are dependent on giant multinational corporations, international combines, which lack any form of internal democratic representation and are also not directly affected by the limitations national governments can enforce on private corporations. These new concentrations of power are growing up around us in the world where we have to find employment.

The technological development promoting this process of concentration is a two-edged sword. Although it contributes to freeing us from many physical hardships of earlier times, it also leads to stress and monotony in working life and increases the distance between the decision-making expert and the worker. It is more difficult for the layman to exert political influence.

The programme we outline in the following pages expresses the fundamental belief that with determination we can pursue a policy of equality, in spite of the forces at home and abroad, which tend to safeguard and even widen class divisions. But this requires that the concept of solidarity which is the backbone of the labour movement finds expression in *all* areas of social life, constantly opposing the consolidation of the interests of the few and emphasizing the rights of the underprivileged.

In order to avoid development towards a tough and disintegrated society it is necessary that equality be supported by a *popular movement* which can fight hard against the interests of power groups, against elitist scales of value which dominate large areas in the world where we have to live and work.

. . . .

Samuel Bowles
UNEQUAL EDUCATION*

Samuel Bowles teaches economics at the University of Massachusetts in Amherst. In the following selection, Bowles challenges the view that education in a modern capitalist society serves as a great equalizer, making it equally possible for individuals from all sectors of the society to pursue and achieve "success." Bowles argues that instead of being the door to new and unlimited possibilities for the daughters and sons of the working class, education serves to replicate existing inequalities of wealth, power, and opportunity.

The ideological defense of modern capitalist society rests heavily on the assertion that the equalizing effects of education can counter the disequalizing forces inherent in the free-market system. That educational systems in capitalist societies have been highly unequal is generally admitted and widely condemned. Yet educational inequalities are taken as passing phenomena, holdovers from an earlier, less enlightened era, which are rapidly being eliminated.

The record of educational history in the United States, and scrutiny of the present state of our colleges and schools, lend little support to this comforting optimism. Rather, the available data suggest an alternative interpretation. In what follows I argue (1) that schools have evolved in the United States not as part of a pursuit of equality, but rather to meet the needs of capitalist employers for a disciplined and skilled labor force, and to provide a mechanism for social control in the interests of political stability; (2) that as the economic importance of skilled and well-educated labor has grown, inequalities in the school system have become increasingly important in reproducing the class structure from one generation to the next; (3) that the U.S. school system is pervaded by class inequalities, which have shown little sign of diminishing over the last half century; . . . Although the unequal distribution of political power serves to maintain inequalities in education, the origins of these inequalities are to be found outside the political sphere, in the class structure itself and in the

*Many of the ideas in this essay have been worked out jointly with Herbert Gintis and other members of the Harvard seminar of the Union for Radical Political Economics. I am grateful to them and to Janice Weiss and Christopher Jencks for their help.

class subcultures typical of capitalist societies. Thus, unequal education has its roots in the very class structure which it serves to legitimize and reproduce. Inequalities in education are part of the web of capitalist society, and are likely to persist as long as capitalism survives.

THE EVOLUTION OF CAPITALISM AND THE RISE OF MASS EDUCATION

In colonial America, and in most pre-capitalist societies of the past, the basic productive unit was the family. For the vast majority of male adults, work was self-directed, and was performed without direct supervision. Though constrained by poverty, ill health, the low level of technological development, and occasional interferences by the political authorities, a man had considerable leeway in choosing his working hours, what to produce, and how to produce it. While great inequalities in wealth, political power, and other aspects of status normally existed, differences in the degree of autonomy in work were relatively minor, particularly when compared with what was to come.

Transmitting the necessary productive skills to the children as they grew up proved to be a simple task, not because the work was devoid of skill, but because the quite substantial skills required were virtually unchanging from generation to generation, and because the transition to the world of work did not require that the child adapt to a wholly new set of social relationships. The child learned the concrete skills and adapted to the social relations of production through learning by doing within the family. Preparation for life in the larger community was facilitated by the child's experience with the extended family, which shaded off without distinct boundaries, through uncles and fourth cousins, into the community. Children learned early how to deal with complex relationships among adults other than their parents, and children other than their brothers and sisters.[1]

Children were not required to learn a complex set of political principles or ideologies, as political participation was limited and political authority unchallenged, at least in normal times. The only major socializing institution outside the family was the church, which sought to inculcate the accepted spiritual values and attitudes. In addition, a small number of children learned craft skills outside the family, as apprentices. The role of schools tended to be narrowly vocational, restricted to preparation of children for a career in the church or the still inconsequential state bureaucracy. The curriculum of the few universities reflected the aristocratic penchant for conspicuous intellectual consumption.

[1]This account draws upon two important historical studies: P. Aries, *Centuries of Childhood* (New York: Vintage, 1965); and B. Bailyn, *Education in the Forming of American Society* (Chapel Hill: University of North Carolina Press, 1960). Also illuminating are anthropological studies of education in contemporary pre-capitalist societies. See, for example, J. Kenyatta, *Facing Mount Kenya* (New York: Vintage Books, 1962) pp. 95–124.

The extension of capitalist production, and particularly the factory system, undermined the role of the family as the major unit of both socialization and production. Small peasant farmers were driven off the land or competed out of business. Cottage industry was destroyed. Ownership of the means of production became heavily concentrated in the hands of landlords and capitalists. Workers relinquished control over their labor in return for wages or salaries. Increasingly, production was carried on in large organizations in which a small management group directed the work activities of the entire labor force. The social relations of production—the authority structure, the prescribed types of behavior and response characteristic of the work place—became increasingly distinct from those of the family.

The divorce of the worker from control over production—from control over his own labor—is particularly important in understanding the role of schooling in capitalist societies. The resulting social division of labor—between controllers and controlled—is a crucial aspect of the class structure of capitalist societies, and will be seen to be an important barrier to the achievement of social-class equality in schooling.

Rapid economic change in the capitalist period led to frequent shifts of the occupational distribution of the labor force, and constant changes in the skill requirements for jobs. The productive skills of the father were no longer adequate for the needs of the son during his lifetime. Skill training within the family became increasingly inappropriate.

And the family itself was changing. Increased geographic mobility of labor and the necessity for children to work outside the family spelled the demise of the extended family and greatly weakened even the nuclear family. Meanwhile, the authority of the church was questioned by the spread of secular rationalist thinking and the rise of powerful competing groups.

While undermining the main institutions of socialization, the development of the capitalist system created at the same time an environment —both social and intellectual—which would ultimately challenge the political order. Workers were thrown together in oppressive factories, and the isolation which had helped to maintain quiescence in earlier, widely dispersed peasant populations was broken down. With an increasing number of families uprooted from the land, the workers' search for a living resulted in large-scale labor migrations. Transient, even foreign, elements came to constitute a major segment of the population, and began to pose seemingly insurmountable problems of assimilation, integration, and control. Inequalities of wealth became more apparent, and were less easily justified and less readily accepted. The simple legitimizing ideologies of the earlier period—the divine right of kings and the divine origin of social rank, for example—fell under the capitalist attack on the royalty and the traditional landed interests. The general broadening of the electorate—first sought by the capitalist class in the struggle against the entrenched interests of the pre-capitalist period—threatened soon to become an instrument for the growing power of the working class. Having risen to political power, the capitalist class sought a mechanism to ensure social control and political stability.

An institutional crisis was at hand. The outcome, in virtually all capitalist countries, was the rise of mass education. In the United States, the many advantages of schooling as a socialization process were quickly perceived. The early proponents of the rapid expansion of schooling argued that education could perform many of the socialization functions that earlier had been centered in the family and, to a lesser extent, in the church. An ideal preparation for factory work was found in the social relations of the school: specifically, in its emphasis on discipline, punctuality, acceptance of authority outside the family, and individual accountability for one's work.[2] The social relations of the school would replicate the social relations of the work place, and thus help young people adapt to the social division of labor. Schools would further lead people to accept the authority of the state and its agents—the teachers—at a young age, in part by fostering the illusion of the benevolence of the government in its relations with citizens. Moreover, because schooling would ostensibly be open to all, one's position in the social division of labor could be portrayed as the result not of birth, but of one's own efforts and talents. And if the children's everyday experiences with the structure of schooling were insufficient to inculcate the correct views and attitudes, the curriculum itself would be made to embody the bourgeois ideology. Where pre-capitalist social institutions, particularly the church, remained strong or threatened the capitalist hegemony, schools sometimes served as a modernizing counter-institution.

The movement for public elementary and secondary education in the United States originated in the nineteenth century in states dominated by the burgeoning industrial capitalist class, most notably in Massachusetts. It spread rapidly to all parts of the country except the South. In Massachusetts the extension of elementary education was in large measure a response to industrialization, and to the need for social control of the Irish and other non-Yankee workers recruited to work in the mills. The fact that some working people's movements had demanded free instruction should not obscure the basically coercive nature of the extension of schooling. In many parts of the country, schools were literally imposed upon the workers.

[2]A manufacturer, writing to the Massachusetts State Board of Education from Lowell in 1841 commented:
> I have never considered mere knowledge . . . as the only advantage derived from a good Common School education. . . . (Workers with more education possess) a higher and better state of morals, are more orderly and respectful in their deportment, and more ready to comply with the wholesome and necessary regulations of an establishment. . . . In times of agitation, on account of some change in regulations or wages, I have always looked to the most intelligent, best educated and the most moral for support. The ignorant and uneducated I have generally found the most turbulent and troublesome, acting under the impulse of excited passion and jealousy.

Quoted in Michael B. Katz, *The Irony of Early School Reform* (Cambridge, Mass.: Harvard University Press, 1968), p. 88.

The evolution of the economy in the nineteenth century gave rise to new socialization needs and continued to spur the growth of education. Agriculture continued to lose ground to manufacturing; simple manufacturing gave way to production involving complex interrelated processes; an increasing fraction of the labor force was employed in producing services rather than goods. Employers in the most rapidly growing sectors of the economy began to require more than obedience and punctuality in their workers; a change in motivational outlook was required. The new structure of production provided little built-in motivation. There were fewer jobs such as farming and piece-rate work in manufacturing in which material reward was tied directly to effort. As work roles became more complicated and interrelated, the evaluation of the individual worker's performance became increasingly difficult. Employers began to look for workers who had internalized the production-related values of the firm's managers.

The continued expansion of education was pressed by many who saw schooling as a means of producing these new forms of motivation and discipline. Others, frightened by the growing labor militancy after the Civil War, found new urgency in the social-control arguments popular among the proponents of education in the antebellum period.

A system of class stratification developed within this rapidly expanding educational system. Children of the social elite normally attended private schools. Because working-class children tended to leave school early, the class composition of the public high schools was distinctly more elite than the public primary schools. And as a university education ceased to be merely training for teaching or the divinity and became important in gaining access to the pinnacles of the business world, upper-class families used their money and influence to get their children into the best universities, often at the expense of the children of less elite families.

Around the turn of the present century, large numbers of working-class and particularly immigrant children began attending high schools. At the same time, a system of class stratification developed within secondary education. The older democratic ideology of the common school—that the same curriculum should be offered to all children—gave way to the "progressive" insistence that education should be tailored to the "needs of the child." In the interests of providing an education relevant to the later life of the students, vocational schools and tracks were developed for the children of working families. The academic curriculum was preserved for those who would later have the opportunity to make use of book learning, either in college or in white-collar employment. This and other educational reforms of the progressive education movement reflected an implicit assumption of the immutability of the class structure.

The frankness with which students were channeled into curriculum tracks, on the basis of their social-class background, raised serious doubts concerning the "openness" of the social-class structure. The relation between social class and a child's chances of promotion or tracking assignments was disguised—though not mitigated much—by another "progressive" reform: "objective" educational testing. Particularly after World War I, the capitulation of the schools to business values and concepts of efficiency led to the increased use of intelligence and scholastic achievement testing as an ostensibly unbiased means of measuring the product of schooling and classifying students. The complementary growth of the guidance counseling profession allowed much of the channeling to proceed from the students' own well-counseled choices, thus adding an apparent element of voluntarism to the system.

.   .   .

The class stratification of education during this period had proceeded hand in hand with the stratification of the labor force. As large bureaucratic corporations and public agencies employed an increasing fraction of all workers, a complicated segmentation of the labor force evolved, reflecting the hierarchical structure of the social relations of production. . . . The social division of labor had become a finely articulated system of work relations dominated at the top by a small group with control over work processes and a high degree of personal autonomy in their work activities, and proceeding by finely differentiated stages down the chain of bureaucratic command to workers who labored more as extensions of the machinery than as autonomous human beings.

One's status, income, and personal autonomy came to depend in great measure on one's place in work hierarchy. And in turn, positions in the social division of labor came to be associated with educational credentials reflecting the number of years of schooling and the quality of education received. The increasing importance of schooling as a mechanism for allocating children to positions in the class structure played a major part in legitimizing the structure itself. But at the same time, it undermined the simple processes which in the past had preserved the position and privilege of the upper-class families from generation to generation. In short, it undermined the processes serving to reproduce the social division of labor.

.   .   .

CLASS INEQUALITIES IN U.S. SCHOOLS

Unequal schooling reproduces the social division of labor. Children whose parents occupy positions at the top of the occupational hierarchy receive more years of schooling than working-class children. Both the amount and the content of their education greatly facilitates their movement into positions similar to those of their parents.

Because of the relative ease of measurement, inequalities in years of schooling are particularly evident. If we define social-class standing by the income, occupation, and educational level of the parents, a child from the 90th percentile in the class distribution may expect on the average to achieve over four and a half more years of schooling than a child from the 10th percentile.[3] As can be seen in Table 2.1, social-class inequalities in the number of years of schooling received arise in part because a disproportionate number of children from poorer families do not complete high school.[4] Table 2.2 indicates that these inequalities are exacerbated by social-class inequalities in college attendance among those children who did graduate from high school: even among those who had graduated from high school, children of families earning less than $3,000 per year were over six times as likely *not* to attend college as were the children of families earning over $15,000.

Table 2.1. *Percentage of Male Children Aged 16–17 Enrolled in Public School, and Percentage at Less than the Modal Grade Level, by Parent's Education and Income, 1960*[a]

Parent's Education	Enrolled in Public School	Below Modal Level
Less than 8 years		
Family income:		
less than $3,000	66.1	47.4
$3,000–4,999	71.3	35.7
$5,000–6,999	75.5	28.3
$7,000 and over	77.1	21.8
8–11 years		
Family income:		
less than $3,000	78.6	25.0
$3,000–4,999	82.9	20.9
$5,000–6,999	84.9	16.9
$7,000 and over	86.1	13.0
12 years or more		
Family income:		
less than $3,000	89.5	13.4
$3,000–4,999	90.7	12.4
$5,000–6,999	92.1	9.7
$7,000 and over	94.2	6.9

SOURCE: U.S. Bureau of the Census, *Census of Population, 1960*, vol. PC–(2)5a, Table 5.
[a] According to Census definitions, for 16-year-olds 9th grade or less and for 17-year-olds 10th grade or less define as below the modal level. Father's education is indicated if father is present; otherwise mother's education is indicated.

[3] The data for this calculation refer to white males who were aged 25–34 in 1962. See S. Bowles, "Schooling and Inequality from Generation to Generation" (Paper presented at the Far Eastern Meetings of the Econometric Society, Tokyo, 1970).
[4] Table 2.1 understates the degree of social-class inequality in school attendance because a substantial portion of upper-income children not enrolled in public schools attend private schools. Private schools provide a parallel educational system for the upper class. I have not given much attention to these institutions as they are not quantitatively very significant in the total picture. Moreover, to deal extensively with them might detract attention from the task of explaining class inequalities in the ostensibly egalitarian portion of our school system.

Because schooling, especially at the college level, is heavily subsidized by the general taxpayer, those children who attend school longer have access for this reason alone to a far larger amount of public resources than those who are forced out of school or who drop out early. . . .

Inequalities in schooling are not simply a matter of differences in years of schooling attained or in resources devoted to each student per year of schooling. Differences in the internal structure of schools themselves and in the content of schooling reflect the differences in the social-class compositions of the student bodies. The social relations of the educational process ordinarily mirror the social relations of the work roles into which most students are likely to move. Differences in rules, expected modes of behavior, and opportunities for choice are most glaring when we compare levels of schooling. Note the wide range of choice over curriculum, life style, and allocation of time afforded to college students, compared with the obedience and respect for authority expected in high school. Differentiation occurs also within each level of schooling. One needs only to compare the social relations of a junior college with those of an elite four-year college, or those of a working-class high school with those of a wealthy suburban high school, for verification of this point.

The various socialization patterns in schools attended by students of different social classes do not arise by accident. Rather, they stem from the fact that the educational objectives and expectations of both parents and teachers, and the responsiveness of students to various patterns of teaching and control, differ for students of different social classes.[5] Fur-

Table 2.2. *College Attendance in 1967 among High School Graduates, by Family Income*[a]

Family Income[b]	Percent Who Did Not Attend College
less than $3,000	80.2
$3,000–3,999	67.7
$4,000–5,999	63.7
$6,000–7,499	58.9
$7,500–9,999	49.0
$10,000–14,999	38.7
$15,000 and over	13.3

SOURCE: U.S. Bureau of the Census, *Current Population Report*, Series P–20, no. 185, 11 July 1969, p. 6. College attendance refers to both two- and four-year institutions.

[a]Refers to individuals who were high school seniors in October 1965 and who subsequently graduated from high school. 53.1 percent of all such students did not attend college.

[b]Family income for 12 months preceding October 1965.

[5]That working-class parents seem to favor more authoritarian educational methods is perhaps a reflection of their own work experiences which have demonstrated that submission to authority is an essential ingredient in one's ability to get and hold a steady, well-paying job.

ther, class inequalities in school socialization patterns are reinforced by the inequalities in financial resources documented above. The paucity of financial support for the education of children from working-class families not only leaves more resources to be devoted to the children of those with commanding roles in the economy; it forces upon the teachers and school administrators in the working-class schools a type of social relations which fairly closely mirrors that of the factory. Thus, financial considerations in poorly supported working-class schools militate against small intimate classes, against a multiplicity of elective courses and specialized teachers (except disciplinary personnel), and preclude the amounts of free time for the teachers and free space required for a more open, flexible educational environment. The lack of financial support all but requires that students be treated as raw materials on a production line; it places a high premium on obedience and punctuality; there are few opportunities for independent, creative work or individualized attention by teachers. The well-financed schools attended by the children of the rich can offer much greater opportunities for the development of the capacity for sustained independent work and the other characteristics required for adequate job performance in the upper levels of the occupational hierarchy.

Much of the inequality in American education exists between schools, but even within a given school different children receive different educations. Class stratification within schools is achieved through tracking, differential participation in extracurricular activities, and in the attitudes of teachers and guidance personnel who expect working-class children to do poorly, to terminate schooling early, and to end up in jobs similar to those of their parents.

.   .   .

The social-class inequalities in our school system and the role they play in the reproduction of the social division of labor are too evident to be denied. Defenders of the educational system are forced back on the assertion that things are getting better, that inequalities of the past were far worse. And, indeed, some of the inequalities of the past have undoubtedly been mitigated. Yet, new inequalities have apparently developed to take their place, for the available historical evidence lends little support to the idea that our schools are on the road to equality of educational opportunity. For example, data from a recent U.S. Census survey reported in Table 2.3 indicate that graduation from college has become increasingly dependent on one's class background. This is true despite the fact that the probability of high school graduation is becoming increasingly equal across social classes. On balance, the available data suggest that the number of years of schooling attained by a child depends upon the social-class standing of his father at least as much in the recent period as it did fifty years ago.

Table 2.3. Among Sons Who Had Reached High School, Percentage Who Graduated from College, by Son's Age and Father's Level of Education

Son's Age in 1962	Likely Dates of College Graduation[a]	Father's Education						
		Less than 8 Years	Some High School		High School Graduate		Some College or More	
			Percent Graduating	Ratio to <8	Percent Graduating	Ratio to <8	Percent Graduating	Ratio to <8
25–34	1950–59	7.6	17.4	2.29	25.6	3.37	51.9	6.83
35–44	1940–49	8.6	11.9	1.38	25.3	2.94	53.9	6.27
45–54	1930–39	7.7	9.8	1.27	15.1	1.96	36.9	4.79
55–64	1920–29	8.9	9.8	1.10	19.2	2.16	29.8	3.35

SOURCE: Based on U.S. Census data as reported in William G. Spady, "Educational Mobility and Access: Growth and Paradoxes," *American Journal of Sociology* 73, no. 3 (November 1967): 273–86.
[a] Assuming college graduation at age 22.

The argument that our "egalitarian" education compensates for in-equalities generated elsewhere in the capitalist system is so patently falla-cious that few persist in maintaining it. But the discrepancy between the ideology and the reality of the U.S. school system is far greater than would appear from a passing glance at the above data. In the first place, if education is to compensate for the social-class immobility caused by the inheritance of wealth and privilege, education must be structured so as to yield a negative correlation between social-class background of the child and the quantity and quality of his schooling. Thus the assertion that education compensates for inequalities in inherited wealth and privi-lege is falsified not so much by the extent of the social-class inequalities in the school system as by their very existence, or, more correctly, by the absence of compensatory inequalities.

. . .

Louis Knowles and Kenneth Prewitt
INSTITUTIONAL AND IDEOLOGICAL ROOTS OF RACISM

1969

Racism can be manifested in numerous ways—in the treatment of people, in attitudes and feelings toward them, in the literature of a culture, in the laws of a nation, in the practices of a business enterprise, and so on. In the following essay, the authors focus their attention on institutional racism in America, and in so doing, they help us understand the extent to which racist attitudes, a commitment toward the inequality of blacks and other groups, is a fundamental part of the theory and practice of our society.

. . .

TOWARD A DEFINITION

The murder by KKK members and law enforcement officials of three civil rights workers in Mississippi was an act of individual racism. That the sovereign state of Mississippi refused to indict the killers was institutional racism. The individual act by racist bigots went unpunished in Mississippi because of policies, precedents, and practices that are an integral part of that state's legal institutions. A store clerk who suspects that black chil-dren in his store are there to steal candy but white children are there to purchase candy, and who treats the children differently, the blacks as probable delinquents and the whites as probable customers, also illus-trates individual racism. Unlike the Mississippi murderers, the store clerk is not a bigot and may not even consider himself prejudiced, but his behavior is shaped by racial stereotypes which have been part of his unconscious since childhood. A university admissions policy which provides for entrance only to students who score high on tests designed primarily for white suburban high schools necessarily excludes black ghetto-educated students. Unlike the legal policies of Mississippi, the university admission criteria are not intended to be racist, but the university is pursuing a course which perpetuates institutional racism. The difference, then, between individual and institutional racism is not a difference in intent or of visibility. Both the individual act of racism and the racist institutional policy may occur without the presence of conscious bigotry, and both may be masked intentionally or innocently.

In an attempt to understand "institutional racism" it is best to consider first what institutions are and what they do in a society. Institutions are fairly stable social arrangements and practices through which collective actions are taken. Medical institutions, for instance, marshal talents and resources of society so that health care can be provided. Medical institutions include hospitals, research labs, and clinics, as well as organizations of medical people such as doctors and nurses. The health of all of us is affected by general medical policies and by established practices and ethics. Business and labor, for example, determine what is to be produced, how it is to be produced, and by whom and on whose behalf products will be created. Public and private schools determine what is considered knowledge, how it is to be transmitted to new generations, and who will do the teaching. Legal and political institutions determine what laws regulate our lives, how and by whom they are enforced, and who will be prosecuted for which violations.

Institutions have great power to reward and penalize. They reward by providing career opportunities for some people and foreclosing them for others. They reward as well by the way social goods and services are distributed—by deciding who receives training and skills, medical care, formal education, political influence, moral support and self-respect, productive employment, fair treatment by the law, decent housing, self-confidence, and the promise of a secure future for self and children. No society will distribute social benefits in a perfectly equitable way. But no society need use race as a criterion to determine who will be rewarded and who punished. Any nation that permits race to affect the distribution of benefits from social policies is racist.

It is our thesis that institutional racism is deeply embedded in American society. Slavery was only the earliest and most blatant practice. Political, economic, educational, and religious policies cooperated with slaveholders to "keep the nigger in his place." Emancipation changed little. Jim Crow laws as well as residential and employment discrimination guaranteed that black citizens remained under the control of white citizens. Second-class citizenship quickly became a social fact as well as a legal status. Overt institutional racism was widely practiced throughout American society at least until World War II.

With desegregation in the armed forces and the passage of various civil rights bills, institutional racism no longer has the status of law. It is perpetuated nonetheless, sometimes by frightened and bigoted individuals, sometimes by good citizens merely carrying on "business as usual," and sometimes by well-intentioned but naive reformers. An attack on institutional racism is clearly the next task for Americans, white and black, who hope to obtain for their children a society less tense and more just than the one of the mid-1960's. It is no easy task. Individual, overt racist acts, such as the shotgun slaying of civil rights workers, are visible. Techniques of crime detection can be used to apprehend guilty parties, and, in theory, due process of law will punish them. To detect institutional racism, especially when it is unintentional or when it is disguised, is a very different task. And even when institutional racism is detected, it is seldom clear who is at fault. How can we say who is responsible for residential segregation, for poor education in ghetto schools, for extraordinarily high unemployment among black men, for racial stereotypes in history textbooks, for the concentration of political power in white society?

Our analysis begins with attention to ideological patterns in American society which historically and presently sustain practices appropriately labeled "institutionally racist." We then turn attention to the procedures of dominant American institutions: educational, economic, political, legal, and medical. It is as a result of practices within these institutions that black citizens in America are consistently penalized for reasons of color.

Quite obviously the social arrangements which fix unequal opportunities for black and white citizens can be traced back through American history—farther back, as a matter of fact, than even the beginning of slavery. Our purpose is not to rewrite American history, although that needs to be done. Rather our purpose is to point out the historical roots of institutional racism by examining the ideology used to justify it. In understanding how deeply racist practices are embedded in the American experience and values, we can come to a fuller understanding of how contemporary social institutions have adapted to their heritage.

HISTORY AND IDEOLOGY

Some form of white supremacy, both as ideology and institutional arrangement, existed from the first day English immigrants, seeking freedom from religious intolerance, arrived on the North American continent. From the beginning, the early colonizers apparently considered themselves culturally superior to the natives they encountered. This sense of superiority over the Indians, which was fostered by the religious ideology they carried to the new land, found its expression in the self-proclaimed mission to civilize and Christianize—a mission which was to find its ultimate expression in ideas of a "manifest destiny" and a "white man's burden."

The early colonists were a deeply religious people. The church was the dominant social institution of their time, and the religious doctrines brought from England strongly influenced their contacts with the native Indians. The goals of the colonists were stated clearly:

> *Principal and Maine Ends* [of the Virginia colony] . . . first to preach and baptize into *Christian Religion* and by propogation of the *Gospell,* to recover out of the arms of the *Divell,* a number of poore and miserable soules, wrapt up unto death, in almost invincible ignorance . . . and to add our myte to the Treasury of Heaven.[1]

Ignorance about the white man's God was sufficient proof in itself of the inferiority of the Indian and, consequently, of the superiority of the white civilization.

The mission impulse was doomed to failure. A shortage of missionaries and an unexpected resistance on the part of the Indian (who was less sure that the white man's ways were inherently superior) led to the dismantling of the few programs aimed at Christianization. It became clear that conquering was, on balance, less expensive and more efficient than "civilizing."

Thus began an extended process of genocide, giving rise to such aphorisms as "The only good Indian is a dead Indian." It was at this time that the ideology of white supremacy on the North American continent took hold. Since Indians were capable of reaching only the stage of "savage," they should not be allowed to impede the forward (westward, to be exact) progress of white civilization. The Church quickly acquiesced in this redefinition of the situation. The disappearance of the nonwhite race in the path of expansionist policies was widely interpreted as God's will. As one student of America's history has written, "It apparently never seriously occurred to [spokesmen for Christianity] that where they saw the mysterious law of God in the disappearance of the nonwhite races before the advancing Anglo-Saxon, a disappearance which apparently occurred without anyone's willing it or doing anything to bring it about, the actual process was a brutal one of oppression, dispossession, and even extermination."[2]

In short, what began as a movement to "civilize and Christianize" the indigenous native population was converted into a racist force, accompanied, as always, by a justificatory ideology. In retrospect, the result is hardly surprising. The English colonists operated from a premise which has continued to have a strong impact on American thought: the Anglo-Saxon race is culturally and religiously superior; neither the validity nor the integrity of alien cultures can be recognized. (The Indian culture, though native to the land, was considered the alien one.) When it became clear that Indians could not be "saved," the settlers concluded that the race itself was inferior. This belief was strengthened by such racist theo-

[1]Quoted in Thomas F. Gossett, *Race: The History of an Idea in America* (Dallas: SMU Press, 1963), p. 18.

[2]*Ibid.,* p. 196.

ries as the Teutonic Theory of Origins, which pointed out the superiority of the Anglo-Saxons. The institution of slavery and its accompanying justification would seem to have been products of the same mentality.

It has, of course, been the white man's relationship with the black man which has led to the most powerful expressions of institutional racism in the society. This is a history which hardly needs retelling, although it might be instructive to consider how closely related was the justification of Indian extermination to that of black slavery. It was the heathenism or savagery, so-called, of the African, just as of the Indian, which became the early rationale for enslavement. A particularly ingenious version of the rationale is best known under the popular label "Social Darwinism."

The Social Darwinian theory of evolution greatly influenced social thought, hence social institutions, in nineteenth-century America. Social Darwinists extended the concept of biological evolution in the development of man to a concept of evolution in development of societies and civilizations. The nature of a society or nation or race was presumed to be the product of natural evolutionary forces. The evolutionary process was characterized by struggle and conflict in which the "stronger, more advanced, and more civilized" would naturally triumph over the "inferior, weaker, backward, and uncivilized" peoples.

> The idea of natural selection was translated to a struggle between individual members of a society, between members of classes of society, between different nations, and between different races. This conflict, far from being an evil thing, was nature's indispensable method of producing superior men, superior nations, and superior races.[3]

Such phrases as "the struggle for existence" and "the survival of the fittest" became *lingua franca,* and white Americans had a full-blown ideology to explain their treatment of the "inferior race."

The contemporary expression of Social Darwinian thinking is less blatant but essentially the same as the arguments used in the nineteenth century. The poverty and degradation of the nonwhite races in the United States are thought to be the result of an innate lack of ability rather than anything white society has done. Thus a long line of argument reaches its most recent expression in the now famous "Moynihan Report": the focal point of the race problem is to be found in the pathology of black society.

Social Darwinism was buttressed with two other ideas widely accepted in nineteenth-century America: manifest destiny and white man's burden. Briefly stated, manifest destiny was simply the idea that white Americans were destined, either by natural forces or by Divine Right, to control at least the North American continent and, in many versions of the theory, a much greater share of the earth's surface. Many churchmen

[3] *Ibid.,* p. 145.

supported the idea that such expansion was the will of God. The impact of this belief with respect to the Indians has already been noted. Let it suffice to say that manifest destiny helped provide the moral and theological justification for genocide. The belief that American expansion was a natural process was rooted in Social Darwinism. Expansionism was simply the natural growth process of a superior nation. This deterministic argument enjoyed wide popularity. Even those who were not comfortable with the overt racism of the expansionist argument were able to cooperate in policies of "liberation" in Cuba and the Philippines by emphasizing the evils of Spanish control. Many, however, felt no need to camouflage their racism. Albert J. Beveridge, Senator from Indiana, stated his position clearly:

> The American Republic is a part of the movement of a race—the most masterful race of history—and race movements are not to be stayed by the hand of man. They are mighty answers to Divine commands. Their leaders are not only statesmen of peoples—they are prophets of God. The inherent tendencies of a race are its highest law. They precede and survive all statutes, all constitutions. . . . The sovereign tendencies of our race are organization and government.[4]

In any case, if racism was not invoked as a justification for imperialist expansion in the first place, it subsequently became a justification for continued American control of the newly "acquired" territories. This was particularly true in the Philippines. "The control of one country by another and the denial of rights or citizenship to the Filipinos were difficult ideas to reconcile with the Declaration of Independence and with American institutions. In order to make these opposing ideas of government compatible at all, the proponents of the acquisition of the Philippines were forced to rely heavily on race theories."[5]

An argument commonly expressed was that the Filipinos were simply incapable of self-government. " 'The Declaration of Independence,' stated Beveridge, 'applies only to peoples capable of self-government. Otherwise, how dared we administer the affairs of the Indians? How dare we continue to govern them today?' "[6] The decision, therefore, as to who was capable of self-government and who was not so capable was left to the United States Government. The criteria were usually explicitly racist, as it was simply assumed that whites, at least Anglo-Saxons, had the "gift" of being able to govern themselves while the inferior nonwhite peoples were not so endowed.

The ideology of imperialist expansion had an easily foreseeable impact on the domestic race situation. As Ronald Segal points out in *The Race War,*

[4]*Ibid.,* p. 318.
[5]*Ibid.,* p. 328.
[6]*Ibid.,* p. 329.

Both North and South saw and accepted the implications. What was sauce for the Philippines, for Hawaii and Cuba, was sauce for the Southern Negro. If the stronger and cleverer race is free to impose its will upon "new-caught sullen peoples" on the other side of the globe, why not in South Carolina and Mississippi? asked the *Atlantic Monthly*. "No Republican leader," proclaimed Senator Tillman of South Carolina, ". . . will now dare to wave the bloody shirt and preach a crusade against the South's treatment of the Negro. The North has a bloody shirt of its own. Many thousands of them have been made into shrouds for murdered Filipinos, done to death because they were fighting for liberty." Throughout the United States doctrines of racial superiority received the assent of influential politicians and noted academics. The very rationalizations that had eased the conscience of the slave trade now provided the sanction for imperial expansion.[7]

Another component of the ideology which has nurtured racist policies is that of "the white man's burden." This phrase comes from the title of a poem by Rudyard Kipling, which appeared in the United States in 1899. Whatever Kipling himself may have wished to convey, Americans soon popularized and adopted the concept as an encouragement for accepting the responsibility of looking after the affairs of the darker races. This notion of the "white man's burden" was that the white race, particularly Anglo-Saxons of Britain and America, should accept the (Christian) responsibility for helping the poor colored masses to find a better way of life.

It should be clear that this notion is no less racist than others previously mentioned. Behind the attitude lies the assumption of white supremacy. In exhorting Americans to follow British policy in this regard, the philosopher Josiah Royce stated the assumption clearly.

. . . The Englishman, in his official and governmental dealings with backward peoples, has a great way of being superior without very often publicly saying that he is superior. You well know that in dealing, as an individual, with other individuals, trouble is seldom made by the fact that you are actually superior to another man in any respect. The trouble comes when you tell the other man, too stridently, that you are his superior. Be my superior, quietly, simply showing your superiority in your deeds, and very likely I shall love you for the very fact of your superiority. For we all love our leaders. But tell me I am your inferior, and then perhaps I may grow boyish, and may throw stones. Well, it is so with the races. Grant then that yours is the superior race. Then you can say little about the subject in your public dealings with the backward race. Superiority is best shown by good deeds and by few boasts.[8]

Both manifest destiny and the idea of a white man's burden, in disguised forms, continue to shape white America's values and policies.

[7]Ronald Segal, *The Race War* (Baltimore: Penguin Books, 1967), p. 219.
[8]Gossett, p. 334.

Manifest destiny has done much to stimulate the modern-day myth that colored peoples are generally incapable of self-government. There are whites who continue to believe that black Afro-Americans are not ready to govern themselves. At best, blacks must first be "properly trained." Of course, this belief influences our relations with nonwhites in other areas of the world as well.

The authors have found the concept of manifest destiny helpful in analyzing white response to "black power." Black power is based on the belief that black people in America are capable of governing and controlling their own communities. White rejection of black power reflects, in part, the widely accepted white myth that blacks are incapable of self-government and must be controlled and governed by whites. Many whites apparently still share with Albert Beveridge the belief that "organization and government" are among the "sovereign tendencies of our race."

The belief in a "white man's burden" also has its modern-day counterpart, particularly in the attitudes and practices of so-called "white liberals" busily trying to solve "the Negro problem." The liberal often bears a strong sense of responsibility for helping the Negro find a better life. He generally characterizes the Negro as "disadvantaged," "unfortunate," or "culturally deprived." The liberal generally feels superior to the black man, although he is less likely to publicly state his sense of superiority. He may not even recognize his own racist sentiments. In any case, much like Josiah Royce, he senses that "superiority is best shown by good deeds and by few boasts." Liberal paternalism is reflected not only in individual attitudes but in the procedures and policies of institutions such as the welfare system and most "war on poverty" efforts.

It is obvious that recent reports and action plans carry on a traditional, if diversionary, view that has long been acceptable to most white Americans: that it is not white institutions but a few bigots plus the deprived status of Negroes that cause racial tension. Such a view is mythical. . . . We are not content with "explanations" of white-black relations that are apolitical, that would reduce the causes of racial tension to the level of psychological and personal factors. Three hundred years of American history cannot be encapsulated so easily. To ignore the network of institutional controls through which social benefits are allocated may be reassuring, but it is also bad social history. America is and has long been a racist nation, because it has and has long had a racist policy. This policy is not to be understood by listening to the proclamations of intent by leading citizens and government officials; nor is it to be understood by reading off a list of compensatory programs in business, education, and welfare. The policy can be understood only when we are willing to take a hard look at the continuing and irrefutable racist consequences of the major institutions in American life. The policy will be changed when we are willing to start the difficult task of remaking our institutions.

Alice Rossi
SEX EQUALITY: THE BEGINNINGS OF IDEOLOGY

Alice Rossi is a professor of sociology. In this selection, she discusses the ways in which women in America receive unequal treatment throughout their lives. She then goes on to consider alternative models of equality toward which we might strive. In the course of her discussion, Rossi distinguishes the ways in which sexism differs from other forms of discrimination, including racism.

> It should not prejudice my voice that I'm not born a man
> If I say something advantageous to the present situation.
> For I'm taxed too, and as a toll provide men for the nation
>   While, miserable graybeards, you,
>   It is true
> Contribute nothing of any importance whatever to our needs;
>   But the treasure raised against the Medes,
> You've squandered, and do nothing in return, save that you
>   make
> Our lives and persons hazardous by some imbecile mistake.
> What can you answer? Now be careful, don't arouse my spite,
> Or with my slipper I'll take you napping
>   faces slapping
>   Left and right.

> *Aristophanes*
> LYSISTRATA, 413 B.C.

It is 2400 years since Lysistrata organized a sex strike among Athenian women in a play that masked a serious anti-war opposition beneath a thin veneer of bawdy hilarity. The play is unique in drama as a theme of women power and sex solidarity, and takes on a fresh relevance when read in the tumultuous 1960's. Women in our day are active as students, as blacks, as workers, as war protesters, but far less often as women qua women pressing for equality with men, or actively engaging in a dialogue of what such equality should mean. Until the last few years, women power has meant only womanpower, a "resource to be tapped," as the manpower specialists put it.

It has been exactly one hundred years since John Stuart Mill published his classic essay on "The Subjection of Women" in England, and the Seneca Falls Conference in New York State gave public recognition to the presence of women critical of the political and economic restrictions that barred their participation in the major institutions of American society. 1969 is, thus, a propitious year in which to examine what we mean by a goal of equality between the sexes, rather than to persist in the American penchant for tinkering with short-run "improvements in the status of women."

The major objective of this article is to examine three possible goals of equality between the sexes, while a secondary objective is to pinpoint the ways in which inequality on sex grounds differs from racial, ethnic, or religious inequality.

MEANING OF INEQUALITY

A group may be said to suffer from inequality if its members are restricted in access to legitimate valued positions or rewards in a society for which their ascribed status is not a relevant consideration. In our day, this is perhaps least ambiguous where the status of citizen is concerned: We do not consider race, sex, religion, or national background relevant criteria for the right to vote or to run for public office. Here we are dealing with a particular *form* of inequality—codified law—and a particular *type* of inequality—civil and political rights of an individual as a citizen. There are several other forms of inequality in addition to legal statute: corporate or organizational policies and regulations, and most importantly, those covert social pressures which restrict the aspirations or depress the motivation of individuals on the ascribed grounds of their membership in certain categories. Thus, a teacher who scoffs at a black boy or white girl who aspires to become an engineer, or a society which uniformly applies pressure on girls to avoid occupational choices in medicine and law are examples of covert pressures which bolster racial and sexual inequality. *Forms* of inequality therefore range from explicit legal statute to informal social pressure.

Type of inequality adds a second dimension: the area of life in which the inequality is evidenced. There are inequalities in the *public* sector, as citizens, employees, consumers, or students; and there are inequalities in the *private* sector, as family, organization, or club members. Throughout American history, the gains made for greater racial and sexual equality have been based on constitutional protection of individual rights in the public area of inequality, as citizens, students, and workers. But precisely because of constitutional protection of privacy of home, family, and person, it is more difficult to remove inequalities rooted in the private sphere of life. Attempts to compensate for emotional and nutritional deprivation of preschool, inner-city children are through three-hour Headstart exposure to verbal stimulation and nutritious food from caring adults. We have yet to devise a means to compensate for the influences of parents who depress a daughter's aspiration to become a physician, while urging a son to aspire beyond his capacity or preference. In both instances, the tactics used tend to be compensatory devices in the public sphere (counseling and teaching in the schools, for example) to make up for or undo the effects of inequalities that persist in the family.

There is, thus, a continuum of increasing difficulty in effecting social and political change along both dimensions of inequality: by *form,* from legal statute to corporate regulation to covert and deeply imbedded social mores; by *type,* from citizenship to schooling and employment, to the private sector of family. Hence, the easiest target in removing inequality involves legal statute change or judicial interpretation of rights in the public sector, and the most difficult area involves changes in the covert social mores in family and social life. It is far easier to change laws which presently penalize women as workers, students, or citizens than it will be to effect social changes in family life and higher education which depress the aspirations and motivations of women.

An example of this last point can be seen in higher education. Few graduate schools discriminate against women applicants, but there are widespread subtle pressures once women are registered as students in graduate departments—from both faculty and male peers. In one graduate department of sociology, women represent a full third of the students, and, hence, the faculty cannot be charged with discriminatory practices toward the admission of women students. On the other hand, it was not uncommon in that department to hear faculty members characterize a woman graduate student who showed strong commitment and independence as an "unfeminine bitch," and others who were quiet and unassertive as "lacking ambition"—women who will "never amount to much." Since it is difficult to be simultaneously independent and ambitious, but conventionally feminine and dependent, it would appear that the informal rules prevent many women from winning the game, although they are accepted as players.

Discrimination against women in hiring or promotion may be barred by statute and corporate policy, but this does not magically stimulate any great movement of women up the occupational status ladder. Progress on the legal front must be accompanied by compensatory tactics to free girls and women from the covert depression of their motivations and aspirations through ridicule and double-bind pressures to be contradictory things.

UNIQUE CHARACTERISTICS OF SEX INEQUALITY

Many women find an easy empathy with the plight of the poor, the black, and minority religious groups—not from any innate feminine intuition, but simply because a subordinate group is sensitive to both unintended and intentional debasement or discrimination where another subordinate group is concerned. Women know from personal experience what it is like to be "put down" by men, and can therefore understand what it is to be "put down" as a black by whites. But there are also fundamental differences between sex as a category of social inequality and the categories of race, religion, or ethnicity. I shall discuss three of the most important differences.

(1) Category Size and Residence:

In the case of race, religion, and ethnicity, we are literally dealing with minority groups in the American population, whether Mexican, Indian, Jewish, Catholic, or black. This is not the case for sex, since women are actually a numerical majority in the population.

While the potential is present for numerical strength to press for the removal of inequalities, this is counterbalanced by other ways in which women are prevented from effectively utilizing their numerical strength. The Irish, the Italians, and the Jews in an earlier period, and blacks in more recent history, have been able to exert political pressure for representation and legislative change because residential concentration gave them voter strength in large urban centers. By contrast, women are for the most part *evenly distributed throughout the population.* Women can exert political pressure in segmental roles as consumers, workers, New Yorkers, or the aged; but not as a cohesive political group based on sex solidarity. It is inconceivable that a political organization of blacks would avoid the "race" issue, yet the League of Women Voters does precisely this when it takes pride in avoiding "women's" issues.

(2) Early Sex-Role Socialization:

Age and sex are the earliest social categories an individual learns. The differentiation between mother and father, or parent and child, is learned at a tender, formative stage of life; and consequently, we carry into adulthood a set of age and sex role expectations that are extremely resistant to change. Not only do girls learn to accept authority from the older generation and from men, but they learn this lesson in intense, intimate relations. By the time they reach adulthood, women are well socialized to seek and to find gratification in an intimate dependence on men, and in responsible authority over children. They may be dominant and affirmative mothers with their own children, or as teachers in classrooms, but pliant and submissive as wives.

Sex role expectations tend to remain a stubborn part of our impulse lives. This is often not visible among young men and women until they become parents. Many young people are egalitarian peers in school, courtship, and early marriage. With the birth of a child, deeper layers of their personalities come into play. Since there is little or no formal education for parenthood in our society, only a thin veneer of Spock-reading hides the acting out of old parental models that have been observed and internalized in childhood, triggering a regression to traditional sex roles that gradually spreads from the parental role to the marriage and self-definition of both sexes.

As a result of early sex-role socialization, there is bound to be a lag between political and economic emancipation of women and the inner adjustment to equality of both men and women. Even in radical political movements, women have often had to caucus and fight for their acceptance as equal peers to men. Without such efforts on their own behalf, women are as likely to be "girl-Friday" assistants in a radical movement espousing class and racial equality as they are in a business corporation, a labor union, or a conservative political party.

(3) Pressures Against Sex Solidarity:

Racial, ethnic, and religious conflict can reach an acute stage of political strife in the movement for equality, without affecting the solidarity of the families of blacks, whites, Jews, or gentiles. Such strife may, in fact, increase the solidarity of these family units. A "we versus them" dichotomy does not cut into family units in the case of race, religion, or ethnicity as it does in the case of sex. Since women typically live in greater intimacy with men than they do with other women, there is potential conflict within family units when women press hard for sex equality. Their demands are on predominantly male legislators and employers in the public domain—husbands and fathers in the private sector. A married black woman can affiliate with an activist civil rights group with no implicit threat to her marriage. For a married woman to affiliate with an activist women's rights group might very well trigger tension in her marriage. While there is probably no limit to the proportion of blacks who might actively fight racial discrimination, a large proportion of married women have not combated sex discrimination. Many of them fear conflict with men, or benefit in terms of a comfortable high status in exchange for economic dependence upon their husbands. There are many more women in the middle class who benefit from sex inequality than there are blacks in the middle class who benefit from racial inequality.

The size of a women's rights movement has, therefore, been responsive to the proportion of "unattached" women in a population. An excess of females over males, a late age at marriage, postponement of childbearing, a high divorce rate, a low remarriage rate, and greater longevity for women, all increase the number of unattached women in a society, and therefore, increase the potential for sex equality activism. The hard core of activists in past suffrage and feminist movements were women without marital and family ties: Ex-wives, nonwives, or childless wives, whose need to support themselves triggered their concern for equal rights to vote, to work, and to advance in their work. The lull in the women's rights movement in the 1950's was related to the fact that this same decade saw the lowest age at marriage and the highest proportion of the population married in all of our history.

Since 1960, the age at marriage has moved up; the birth rate is down to what it was in the late 1930's; the divorce rate is up among couples married a long time, and more married women are in the labor force than ever before. These are all relevant contributors to the renascence of women's rights activism in the mid-1960's. The presence of older and

EQUALITY

married women in women's rights organizations (like the National Organization for Women) is also responsible for a broadening of the range of issues that concern women activists—from the civil, political, and economic concerns they share with feminists of an earlier day, to a host of changes affecting family roles: repeal of abortion laws, revision of divorce laws, community provision of child-care facilities, equal treatment under Social Security in old age, and a debunking of the clinging-vine or tempting-Eve image of married women that pervades the American mass media.

The point remains, however, that movement toward sex equality is restricted by the fact that our most intimate human relation is the heterosexual one of marriage. This places a major brake on the development of sex solidarity among women, a brake that is not present in other social inequalities, since marriage tends to be endogamous with respect to class, race, and religion.

MODELS OF EQUALITY

Courses in social stratification, minority groups, prejudice, and discrimination have been traditional fare in sociological curriculum for a long time. Many sociologists studied immigrants and their children and puzzled about the eventual shape of a society that underwent so massive an injection of diverse cultures. From these writings, we can extract three potential models that will be useful in sketching the alternate goals not only for the relations between ethnic groups, but for those of race and sex as well.

Three such models may be briefly defined, and then each in turn explored in somewhat greater detail:

(1) *Pluralist Model:* This model anticipates a society in which marked racial, religious, and ethnic differences are retained and valued for their diversity, yielding a heterogeneous society in which it is hoped cultural strength is increased by the diverse strands making up the whole society.

(2) *Assimilation Model:* This model anticipates a society in which the minority groups are gradually absorbed into the mainstream by losing their distinguishing characteristics and acquiring the language, occupational skills, and life style of the majority of the host culture.

(3) *Hybrid Model:* This model anticipates a society in which there is change in both the ascendant group and the minority groups—a "melting-pot" hybrid requiring changes not only in blacks and Jews and women, but white male Protestants as well.

PLURALIST MODEL OF EQUALITY

It is dubious whether any society has ever been truly pluralist in the sense that all groups which comprise it are on an equal footing of status, power, or rewards. Pluralism often disguises a social system in which one group dominates the upper classes (white Anglo-Saxon Protestants) and minor- ity ethnic, religious, or racial groups are confined to the lower classes. The upper classes may ceremonially invoke the country's cultural heterogeneity, and delight in ethnic food, art, and music, but exclude the ethnic members themselves from their professions, country clubs, and neighborhoods. Bagels and lox for breakfast, soul food for lunch, and lasagna for dinner; but no Jews, blacks, or Italians on the professional and neighborhood turf! Pluralism has been a congenial model for the race segregationist as well, rationalizing the confinement of blacks to unskilled labor, segregated schools, and neighborhoods.

In the case of sex, the pluralist model posits the necessity of tradi- tional sex role differentiation between the sexes on the grounds of funda- mental physiological and hence social differences between the sexes. This is the perspective subscribed to by most behavioral scientists, clinical psychologists, and psychoanalysts, despite the fact that the women they have studied and analyzed are the products of a society that systematically *produces* such sex differences through childrearing and schooling prac- tices. There is no way of allocating observed sex differences to innate physiology or to socio-cultural conditioning.

Freudian theory has contributed to the assumption of innate sex differences on which recent scholars in psychology and sociology have built their case for the necessity of social role and status differentiation between the sexes. Freud codified the belief that men get more pleasure than women from sex in his theory of the sexual development of the female: the transition from an early stage in which girls experience the clitoris as the leading erogenous zone of their bodies to a mature stage in which vaginal orgasm provides the woman with her major sexual plea- sure. Women who did not make this transition were then viewed as sexually "anaesthetic" and "psychosexually immature." Psychological theory often seems sterner and more resistant to change than the people to which it is applied. It is incredible that the Freudian theory of female sexuality was retained for decades despite thousands of hours of intimate therapeutic data from women, only recently showing signs of weakening under the impact of research conducted by Masters and Johnson and reported in their *Human Sexual Response*, that there is no anatomical differ- ence between clitoral and vaginal orgasm.

Implicit in both psychological theory of sex differences and the Freudian, vaginal-orgasm theory was a basic assumption that women should be exclusively dependent on men for their sexual pleasure, hiding from view the realization that masturbation may be different from, but not necessarily less gratifying sexually than sexual intercourse. Much the same function has been served by the strong pressures to disassociate sex from maternity. Physicians have long known that nursing is associated with uterine contractions and have noted that male babies often have erections while nursing, but no one has suggested that the starry-eyed contentment of a nursing mother is a blend of genital as well as maternal pleasure. The cultural insistence upon separating sex from maternity, as the insistence that vaginal orgasm is the only "normal satisfaction" of a mature woman, serves the function of preventing women from seeing that they can find pleasure and fulfillment from themselves, other women, and their children and do not have to depend exclusively upon men for such gratification.

Coupled with this is the further assumption, peculiar to American society, that childrearing is the exclusive responsibility of the parents themselves, and not a community responsibility to assure every child a healthy physical and social development (as it is, for example, in East European countries, Israel, and Sweden). This belief keeps women tied closely to the home for the most vigorous years of their adulthood. The "new" look to a woman's life span, now institutionalized by over 100 centers for continuing education for women in the United States, does nothing to alter this basic assumption, but merely adapts to our lengthened life span. Women are urged to withdraw from outside obligations during the childbearing and rearing years and to return for further training and participation in the labor force when children reach an appropriate mature age. The consequences of such late return to active work away from the home are lower incomes, work at levels below the ability of the women, and withdrawal for the very years all studies show to be the peaks of creativity in work, their 20's and 30's.

Why does American society persist in maintaining erroneous myths concerning female sexuality, contrary to research evidence, as it does in urging women to believe their children's development requires their daily attendance upon them, again contrary to research evidence? I believe the answer lies in the economic demand that men work at persistent levels of high efficiency and creativity. To free men to do this requires a social arrangement in which the family system serves as the shock-absorbing handmaiden of the occupational system. The stimulation of women's desires for an affluent style of life and a bountiful maternity—to be eager and persistent consumers of goods and producers of babies—serves the function of adding continual pressure on men to be high earners. The combination of pronatalist values and aspirations for a high standard of living has the effect of both releasing and requiring men to give heavy psychic and time investment to their jobs, and requiring women to devote their primary efforts and commitments to homemaking. As a result, the broad sweep of many an American woman's life span is caught by the transitions from Bill's daughter to John's wife to Johnny's mother and Billy's grandmother.

Behind the veneer of modern emancipation is a woman isolated in an apartment or suburban home, exclusively responsible for the care of young children, dependent on her husband for income, misled to believe that sex gratification is only possible via a vaginal orgasm simultaneous with male ejaculation, and urged to buy more and more clothes and household possessions, which she then takes more time but little pleasure in maintaining. Complementing the life of the woman in the pluralist model of sex roles, the American male is prodded to seek success and achievement in a competitive job world at the emotional cost of limited time or psychic energy for his marriage or his children, tempted by the same consumption-stimulating media and promises of easy credit, expected to uproot his family if a move is "good for his career," and ridiculed if he seeks to participate more extensively in home and child care as "unmanly."

The odds are heavily stacked against the pluralist model of society as a goal in terms of which racial, ethnic, or sex equality can be achieved.

ASSIMILATION MODEL OF EQUALITY

This model anticipates that with time, the minority groups will be gradually absorbed into the mainstream of society by losing their distinguishing characteristics, acquiring the language, educational attainment, and occupational skills of the majority host culture. Concern for inequality along ethnic or racial lines is concentrated on the political, educational, and economic institutions of society. Little sociological interest or political concern is shown once men in the minority group are distributed throughout the occupational system in roughly the same proportion as mainstream males.

Feminist ideology is but one variant of the assimilation model, calling upon women to seek their place with men in the political and occupational world in sufficient numbers to eventually show a 50–50 distribution by sex in the prestigious occupations and political organizations of the society. The federal government has served as a pacesetter for the economy in urging the appointment and promotion of competent women to the highest civil service posts and encouraging private employers to follow the federal example by facilitating the movement of women into executive posts.

The feminist-assimilation model has an implicit fallacy, however. No amount of entreaty will yield an equitable distribution of women and men in the top strata of business and professional occupations, for the simple reason that the life men have led in these strata has been possible only because their own wives were leading traditional lives as homemakers, doing double parent and household duty, and carrying the major burden of civic responsibilities. If it were not for their wives in the background, successful men in American society would have to be single or childless. This is why so many professional women complain privately that what they most need in life is a "wife"!

The assimilation model also makes an assumption that the institutional structure of American society developed over decades by predominantly white Protestant males, constitutes the best of all possible worlds. Whether the call is to blacks or to women to join white men in the mainstream of American society, both racial integration and a feminist ideology accept the structure of American society as it now exists. The assimilation model rejects the psychological theses of innate racial or sex differences implicit in most versions of the pluralist model, but it accepts the social institutions formed by the ascendant group. This is precisely the assumption numerous blacks, women, and members of the younger generation have recently been questioning and rejecting.

HYBRID MODEL OF EQUALITY

The hybrid model of equality rejects both traditional psychological assumptions and the institutional structure we have inherited. It anticipates a society in which the lives of men and of whites will be different, not only women and blacks. In fact, it might be that this hybrid model would involve greater change in the role of men than of women, because institutional changes it would require involve a restructuring to bring the world of jobs and politics closer to the fulfillment of individual human needs for both creativity and fellowship. From this point of view, the values many young men and women subscribe to today are congenial to the hybrid model of equality: the desire for a more meaningful sense of community and a greater depth to personal relations across class, sex, and racial lines; a stress on human fellowship and individual scope for creativity rather than merely rationality and efficiency in our bureaucracies; heightened interest in the humanities and the social sciences from an articulated value base; and a social responsibility commitment to medicine and law rather than a thirst for status and high income. These are all demands for social change by the younger generation in our time that are closer to the values and interests women have held than they are to the values and interests of men. They represent an ardent "no" to the image of society projected by the new crop of male technitronic futurists —a machine and consumption oriented society that rewards technological prowess in a "plasticWasp-9–5america."

Because women have tended to play the passive, adaptive role in the past, they have not been prominent as social and political critics of American institutions. In fact, the traditional roles of women confined them to the most conservative institutions of the society: the family, the public schools, and the church. Women deviant enough to seek greater equality with men in professional, business, and academic life have tended to share the values of their masculine colleagues, while professional women who did not share these values have been quiet, either because they distrusted their own critical bent as a vestige of unwanted "womanliness," or because they feared exclusion from the masculine turf they have precariously established themselves on.

But there is a new ground swell in American society, which is a hopeful sign of a movement toward the hybrid model briefly sketched here. One finds it in women's liberation groups across the country, particularly on the university campus. I would predict, for example, that these young women, unlike their professional older sisters, will not bemoan the fact that academic women have been less "productive" than men, but will be critical of the criteria used to assess academic productivity. Up to now these criteria have been such things as "number of publications," "number of professional organization memberships," and "number of offices held in professional organizations." The new breed of women will ask, as many young students are now demanding, that the quality of teaching, the degree of colleagueship with students, the extent of service to both an academic institution and its surrounding community, become part of the criteria on which the productivity of an academic man or woman is evaluated. No one has conducted research on academic productivity with this enlarged net of criteria, and it is a moot point whether men would show greater productivity than women if such criteria were applied. Though it will be a difficult road, with all the money and prestige pulling in the opposite direction, this thrust on the part of the young, together with like-minded older humanist scholars and critics, creative artists, and natural and behavioral scientists, has the potential of developing oases of health and sanity in many educational, welfare, and cultural institutions of American society.

CONCLUSION

A *pluralist* model of social equality is implicitly a conservative goal, a descriptive model that accepts what exists at a given point in time as desirable and good. The *assimilation* model is implicitly a liberal goal, a Horatio Alger model that accepts the present structure of society as stable and desirable, and urges minority groups to accept the values and goals of the dominant group within that system as their own. The *hybrid* model is a radical goal which rejects the present structure of society and seeks instead a new breed of men and women and a new vision of the future. Applied to the role of women, these models may be illustrated in a summary fashion as follows: The pluralist model says the woman's nurturance finds its best expression in maternity; the assimilation model says women must be motivated to seek professional careers in medicine similar to those pursued now by men; the hybrid model says, rather, that the structure of medicine can be changed so that more women will be attracted to medical careers, and male physicians will be able to live more balanced, less difficult and status-dominated lives.

An analysis of sex equality goals may start with the reality of contemporary life, but soon requires an imaginative leap to a new conception of what a future good society should be. With the hybrid model of equality one envisages a future in which family, community, and play are valued on a par with politics and work for both sexes, for all the races, and for all social classes and nations which comprise the human family. We are on the brink not of the "end" of ideology, but its "beginning."

SECTION TEN

SEXUALITY

The essays in this section focus on the problem of sexual liberation. But, is sexual liberation simply a matter of "anything goes"? There is a hotel in New York City that, for a small fee, admits couples for an evening of orgy and whirlpool bath. Have these couples found true freedom?

We need to place the problem of sexuality in a historical perspective. This century has witnessed a revolution in our sexual mores that has significantly challenged the puritanical restrictions of the past. But the sexual revolution has not taken place in a vacuum. Rather, it is occurring within a society in which the values of bourgeois culture are disintegrating; in which people feel increasingly rootless; and in which we are increasingly alienated from ourselves, from our bodies, and from other people. It should not be surprising, then, that the mere lifting of puritanical restrictions does not solve the problem of sexual alienation, which is the reverse side of the problem of sexual liberation. In other words, sexual liberation is not merely the absence of sexual restrictions but is, in our times, the overcoming of sexual alienation. And, this will require more than a reorganization of our sexual life in the narrow sense. It will require that we redefine our sexual social roles and, indeed, all of our social relations.

Alan Watts
SPIRITUALITY AND SEXUALITY

Alan Watts's death touched many people who had come to look upon his person and writings as important sources for understanding their own reality. Watts, who held a Doctor of Divinity degree, is perhaps best known as an authority on Eastern thought, particularly Zen Buddhism. In the selection that follows, taken from his book Nature, Man, and Woman, Watts describes the Christian West *as a culture caught between a view of human beings as, on the one hand, earthly and evil, and on the other, spiritual and good. The existence of this dualism reveals to us our own ambivalence about our sexual natures and the spontaneity we have come to associate with our sexuality. Watts argues that an adequate portrayal of human sexuality must transcend this dualism. Toward the end of the selection he offers an account of what satisfying sexual relations might be like when they are integrated into one's life instead of being emphasized out of proportion through abstinence or through overpreoccupation.*

The division of life into the higher and lower categories of spirit and nature usually goes hand in hand with a symbolism in which spirit is male and nature female. The resemblace was perhaps suggested by the rains falling from heaven to fertilize the earth, the planting of seed in the ground, and the ripening of the fruit by the warmth of the sun. To a considerable extent ancient man reasoned in terms of such correspondences, and made sense of his world by seeing analogies which were understood to be actual relationships. The art of astrology, for example, is the most complete monument to this way of reasoning, based as it is upon the correspondences between the macrocosm and the microcosm, the order of the stars and the order of terrestrial affairs. In the words of the Hermetic *Emerald Tablet:*

> Heaven above, heaven below;
> Stars above, stars below.
> All that is over, under shall show.
> Happy who the riddle readeth!

Unfortunately for those who search for consistent systems in ancient cosmology, it was always possible to read the correspondences as well as the very orders of heaven and earth in different ways. Heaven might be male and earth female, but then it was equally possible to think of space and the sky as an all-embracing womb in which the universe had been brought to birth, for such is apparently the sense of the Egyptian sky goddess Nut. It is easy, however, for us to dismiss such ways of thinking as mere projection, as a confusion of objective nature with fantasies which it evokes from the human mind. Yet after all our own science is likewise a projection, though what it reads into nature is not a loosely knit system of poetic images but the highly exact and consistent structure of mathematics. Both are products of the human mind, and mathematics in particular may be developed indefinitely in the abstract as a pure creation of thought without reference to any external experience. But mathematics works because of its immense inner consistency and precision, serving thus as an admirable tool for measuring nature to suit the purposes which *we* have in mind. However, not all cultures have the same purposes, so that other ways of "reading" the world may serve equally well for ends which are as legitimate as ours, for there are no laws by which these ends may be judged apart from the very readings of the world which serve them.

Indeed, the world is not unlike a vast, shapeless Rorschach blot which we read according to our inner disposition, in such a way that our interpretations say far more about ourselves than about the blot. But whereas the psychologist has tried to develop a science to judge and compare the various interpretations of the Rorschach Test, there is as yet no supracultural science, no "metascience," whereby we can assess our differing interpretations of the cosmic Rorschach blot. Cultural anthropology, the nearest thing to this, suffers the defect of being thoroughly embedded in the conventions of Western science, of one particular way of interpreting the blot.

The importance of the correspondence between spirit and man and nature and woman is that it projects upon the world a disposition in which the members of several cultures, including our own, are still involved. It is a disposition in which the split between man and nature is related to a problematic attitude to sex, though like egg and hen it is doubtful which came first. It is perhaps best to treat them as arising mutually, each being symptomatic of the other.

The historical reasons for our problematic attitude to sexuality are so obscure that there are numerous contradictory theories to explain it. It seems useless, therefore, to try to decide between them in the present state of our knowledge. The problem may be discussed more profitably just by taking the attitude as given, and by considering its consequences and alternatives. The fact is that in some unknown way the female sex has become associated with sexuality as such. The male sex could conceivably have been put in the same position, and there is no conclusive evidence that women are more desirous and provocative of sexual activity than men, or *vice versa*. These are almost certainly matters of cultural conditioning which do not explain how the culture itself came to be as it is. It seems plausible that the association of women with sexuality as such is a male point of view arising in cultures where the male is dominant, but this in turn may be not so much a cause of the attitude as one of its concurrent symptoms. It is, however, very possible that the attitude to women is rather more accidental than the attitude to sexuality, for we know that the male and the female alike can feel the sexual relationship to be a seduction, a danger, and a problem. But *why* they do so at any time may no longer be the reason for their having first done so, so that knowledge of historical causes may not of itself provide any solution to the problem.

Thus to say that man's relation to nature is in some sense parallel to his relation to woman is to speak symbolically. The real parallel is the relation of the human being, male or female, to the sexual division of the species and to all that it involves. When, therefore, we shall speak loosely of the *reasons* for certain sexual attitudes, we shall not be speaking of fundamental historical causes, for these are, strictly speaking, prehistoric —not necessarily so much in point of time as in extent of knowledge. We shall be speaking of the reasons as they exist today, either as matters of open knowledge or as forms of unconscious conditioning. There is no clear evidence that we are unconsciously conditioned by events from the remote historical past, and we must therefore be most cautious in using the insights of psychoanalysis for reconstructing the history of cultures. Certainly we can trace the historical effects of Christian, Buddhist, or Hindu doctrines upon our sexual attitudes, but what lies behind these doctrines and the attitudes from which they arose remains conjectural and dim. Furthermore, it is always possible to argue not that we are conditioned *by* the past, but that we use the past to condition ourselves in the present, and for reasons which are not historical but deeply inward and unknown. For example, a physiologist does not need to call upon the whole history of living creatures to explain why a person is hungry. He explains it from the present state of the organism.[1]

Let us then say that in the Christian and post-Christian West we simply find ourselves in a culture where nature is called Mother Nature, where God is exclusively male, and where one of the common meanings of Woman or Women with the Capital W is simply sex, whereas Man with the capital M means humanity in general. As part and parcel of this situation, as distinct from its historical explanation, we find that in the Indo-European language system the words *matter, materia,* and *meter* as well as *mother,* and its Latin and Greek forms *mater* and μήτηρ, are derived alike from the Sanskrit root *mā-* (*mātr-*), from which, in Sanskrit itself, come both *mātā* (mother) and *māyā* (the phenomenal world of nature). The meaning of the common root *mā-* is "to measure," thus giving *māyā* the sense of the world-as-measured, that is, as divided up into things, events, and categories. In contrast stands the world unmeasured, the infinite and undivided *(advaita)* Brahman, the supreme spiritual reality. While it can be pointed out that the Devil is *also* male, since as the angel Lucifer he is a pure spirit, it must be noted that his popular form is simply that of the god Pan—the lusty spirit of earth and fertility, the genius of natural beauty. Hell, his domian, lies downward in the heart of the earth, where all is dark, inward, and unconscious as distinct from the bright heavens above. The catalogue of popular images, figures of speech, and customs which associate spirit with the divine, the good, and the male and nature with the material, evil, sexual, and female could go on indefinitely.

But the heart of the matter begins to reveal itself when, considering nature in the Chinese sense of spontaneity *(tzu-jan),* we begin to realize that the opposition of spirit to both nature and sexuality is the opposition of the conscious will, of the ego, to that which it cannot control. If sexual abstinence is, as in so many spiritual traditions, the condition of enhanced

---

[1] It is of interest that in the academic world only the more or less "effete" disciplines are studied by the historical method. Beginning courses in religion, philosophy, or "culture" are usually historical, but the history of mathematics, chemistry, or medicine is the concern of a few specialists only. The ordinary student begins at once to learn them from their *present* rudiments.

consciousness, it is because consciousness as we know it is an act of restraint. The point comes out clearly in St. Augustine's discussion of the spontaneity of the sexual member:

> Justly, too, these members themselves, being moved and restrained not at our will, but by a certain independent autocracy, so to speak are called "shameful." Their condition was different before sin . . . because not yet did lust move those members without the will's consent. . . . But when [our first parents] were stripped of grace, that their disobedience might be punished by fit retribution, there began to be in the movement of their bodily members a shameless novelty which made nakedness indecent.[2]

This is clearly the reaction of one for whom the soul, the will, the spiritual part of man, is identified with that form of consciousness which we have seen to be a partial and exclusive mode of attention. It is the mode of attention which grasps and orders the world by seeing it as one-at-a-time things, excluding and ignoring the rest. For it is this which involves that straining of the mind which is also the sensation of willing and of being a separate, exclusive ego.

Shame is thus the accompaniment of the failure of concentrated attention and will which manifests itself not only in the spontaneity of sexual excitement, but also in crying, trembling, blushing, blanching, and so many other socially "shameful" reactions.[3] These reactions are ordinarily avoided by concentrating the attention elsewhere and so avoiding the shameful response, and thus the ascetic disciplinarian will overcome lust, not by pitting the will against it directly, but by attending resolutely to other matters.

Obviously, the sexual function is one of the most powerful manifestations of biological spontaneity, and thus more especially difficult for the will to control. The immediate reasons for controlling it vary from the belief that it saps virility, through proprietary rights upon women, to its association with a complex love relationship with one woman alone, to mention only a few. But these seem to be secondary to the fact that sexual restraint is a principal test of the strength of the ego, along with resistance to pain and regulation of the wanderings of thought and feeling. Such restraints are the very substance of individual consciousness, of the sensation that feeling and action are directed from within a limited center of the organism, and that consciousness is not the mere witness of activity but the responsible agent. Yet this is something quite different from the spontaneous self-control of, say, the circulation of blood, where the control is carried out by the organism as a whole, unconsciously. For willed control brings about a sense of duality within the organism, of consciousness in conflict with appetite.

[2] *De Civitate Dei*, xiv, 17. Tr. Dods (1), vol. 2, p. 33.
[3] Note the "double bind" involved in blushing. One blushes because of shame and is in turn ashamed to blush, and is thus left no alternative but to be "covered with confusion." This is a mild example of the way in which, as Gregory Bateson has shown, double-bind situations lead to the more serious "confusion" of insanity, and especially schizophrenia.

But this mode of control is a peculiar example of the proverb that nothing fails like success. For the more consciousness is individualized by the success of the will, the more everything outside the individual seems to be a threat—including not only the external world but also the "external" and uncontrolled spontaneity of one's own body, which, for example, continues to age, die, and corrupt against one's desire. Every success in control therefore demands a further success, so that the process cannot stop short of omnipotence. But this, save perhaps in some inconceivably distant future, is impossible. Hence there arises the desire to protect the ego from alien spontaneity by withdrawal from the natural world into a realm of pure consciousness or spirit.

Now withdrawal requires the inner detachment of consciousness, which is felt to be bound to nature so long as it desires it, or rather, so long as it identifies itself with the bodily organism's natural appetites. Thus it must not only control them but also cease to enjoy them. It makes little difference whether the realm of spirit be pure and formless, as in many types of mysticism, or whether it be a world of transfigured and spiritualized matter, as in Christianity. The point is that in either case will and consciousness triumph, attaining omnipotence either in their own right or by the grace of union with an omnipotent God whose whole nature is that of a self- and all-controlling will.[4]

On some such lines as these we must explain the ancient and widely prevalent conflict between spirituality and sexuality, the belief, found in East and West alike that sexual abstinence and freedom from lust are essential prerequisites for man's proper ultimate development. Presumably, we are free to define man's ultimate goal as we will, even if what we desire is the stimulus of eternal conflict or the repose of bodily insensitivity. But if we think of spirituality less in terms of what it avoids and more in terms of what it is positively, and if we may think of it as including an intense awareness of the inner identity of subject and object, man and the universe, there is no reason whatsoever why it should require the rejection of sexuality. On the contrary, this most intimate of relationships

[4]Yet it is curious that both nature mysticism and supernatural mysticism can arrive at experiences which are almost indistinguishable. For it would seem that the latter, in struggling not only with external nature but also with its own wayward will and desire, reaches a point of *impasse* where it discovers the perversion or selfishness of the will in the very will to struggle. It is then forced to "give itself up" to a higher power which has been conceived as the supernatural will of God. But in fact the power to which it surrenders may be the very different "omnipotence" of natural spontaneity. Thus, even when trained in a tradition of supernaturalism, the mystic may return after his experience into the world bereft of all disgust for nature. On the contrary, he is often endowed with a completely artless and childlike love for every kind of creature. In his eyes the same old world is already transfigured with the "glory of God," though to his less fortunate coreligionists it is as sinful and corrupt as ever. Cf. Dame Julian's *Revelations of the Divine Love:* "See! I am God: see! I am in all thing; see! I do all thing: see! I lift never mine hands off my works, nor ever shall, without end: see! I lead all thing to the end I ordained it to from without beginning, by the same Might, Wisdom and Love whereby I made it. How should anything be amiss?" (xi). "Sin is behovable [i.e., permissible], but all shall be well, and all shall be well, and all manner of thing shall be well" (xxvii).

of the self with another would naturally become one of the chief spheres of spiritual insight and growth.

This is in no way to say that the monastic and celibate life is an aberration, for man is not absolutely obliged to have sexual relations, nor even to eat or to live. As under certain circumstances a voluntary death or fast is perfectly justifiable, so also is sexual abstinence—in order, for example, that the force of the libido may be expended in other directions. The common mistake of the religious celibate has been to suppose that the highest spiritual life absolutely demands the renunciation of sexuality, as if the knowledge of God were an alternative to the knowledge of woman, or to any other form of experience.

Indeed, the life of total chastity is often undertaken as a monogamous marriage of the soul with God, as an all-consuming love of creature for Creator in which love for a mortal woman would be a fatal distraction. In this context sexuality is often renounced, not because it is evil, but because it is a precious and beautiful possession *offered* to God in sacrifice. But this raises the question as to whether renunciation as such is sacrifice in the proper sence of an act which "makes holy" *(sacer-facere)* the thing offered. For if sexuality is a relationship and an activity, can it be offered when neither the relationship nor the activity exists? Does a dancer offer her dancing to God by ceasing to dance? An offering can cease to exist, for its original owner, if given away to another for his use. But sacrifice is only accidentally associated with the cessation, death, or mutilation of the offering because it was once supposed that, say, burning bulls on an altar was the only way of transporting them to heaven.

The offering of sexuality to God is in all probability a survival of the idea that a woman's body, and its sexual enjoyment, is the property of her husband, to whom she is bound to reserve herself even if he does not actually lie with her. By analogy, the body of the celibate becomes the property of God, dedicated to him alone. But this is not only a confusion of God with what is after all only his symbol, the tribal father, but also the likening of the Creator-creature relationship to a strictly barbarous conception of marriage. Obviously, the possession of a body is not a relationship to a person; one is related to the person only in being related to the organism of another in its total functioning. For the human being is not a thing but a process, not an object but a life.

The offering may be defended by saying that God uses the sexual energy of his human spouses in other ways, diverting them into prayer or into acts of charity. With this there can be no quarrel—provided that it does not exclude the possibility that God may use them for sexual activity itself as an aspect of life no whit less holy than prayer or feeding the poor. Historically, the supernaturalists have admitted this only with great reluctance—outside the Semitic-Islamic traditions, which have largely escaped sexual squeamishness. But the literature of the spiritual life is overwhelmingly preoccupied with the sinful aspects of sex. It has almost nothing to say, positively, about what holy sex might be, save that it must be reserved to a single life partner and consummated for the purpose of procreation in one particular physical attitude alone!

That matrimony may be an estate as holy as virginity is something which the Christian tradition admits theoretically, as a consequence of its Hebrew background.[5] But the force of Hebraic insistence on the goodness of things physical has had little effect on the actual feeling and practice of the Church. For from the earliest times the Church Fathers virtually equated sex with sin by identifying all sexual feeling and desire with the evil of lust. At the same time they could maintain, as against the Gnostics and Manichaeans, that the mere physical apparatus and mechanics of sex were, as God's creation, inherently pure. Speaking, then, of "ideal" sexuality as it might have been before the Fall, St. Augustine wrote:

> Those members, like the rest, would be moved by the command of his will, and the husband would be mingled with the loins of the wife without the seductive stimulus of passion, with calmness of mind and with no corruption of the innocence of the body. . . . Because the wild heat of passion would not activate those parts of the body, but as would be proper, a voluntary control would employ them. Thus it would then have been possible to inject the semen into the womb through the female genitalia as innocently as the menstrual flow is now ejected.[6]

The general tenor and attitude of supernaturalism to sexuality is unmistakable: it is overwhelmingly negative, and to all intents and purposes the attitude is not the least modified by separating sexual mechanics from sexual feelings, a separation which in any case destroys the integrity of mind and body. Practically, if not theoretically, the basis of this attitude is the feeling that God and nature are simply incompatible. They may not have been so originally, but then nature was nothing like the nature we experience today. If we are to believe St. Augustine, it was something as lacking in spontaneity as artificial insemination.

Now the practical effect of a philosophy in which God and nature are incompatible is somewhat unexpected. For when the knowledge and love of God is considered to exclude other goals and other creatures, God is actually put on a par with his creatures. The knowledge of God and the knowledge of creatures can exclude one another only if they are of the same kind. One must choose between yellow and blue, as two of the kind color, but there is no need to choose between yellow and round, since what is round can also be yellow. If God is universal, the knowledge of God should include all other knowledge as the sense of sight includes all the differing objects of vision. But if the eye should attempt to see sight, it will turn in upon itself and see nothing.

[5]Protestantism, with its greater interest in Biblical Christianity, is therefore more Hebraic in its attitude to sexuality than Catholicism, as witness Luther and Milton. But if it has to some extent liberalized sexual restraints, it has had as little notion as Catholicism of a positive sexual holiness.

[6]*De Civitate Dei*, xiv, 26.

Indeed, the celibate life is more appropriate to "worldly" vocations than spiritual, for while it is possible to be both a sage and a physician or artist, the exigencies of a professional or creative vocation so often suggest the Latin tag, *Aut libri aut liberi*—either books or children. But the vocation to sanctity should hardly be a specialization on the same level as writing, medicine, or mathematics, for God himself—the "object" of sanctity—is no specialist. Were he so, the universe would consist of nothing but formally religious creations—clergymen, bibles, churches, monasteries, rosaries, prayer-books, and angels.

Sanctity or sagehood as an exclusive vocation is, once again, symptomatic of an exclusive mode of consciousness in general and of the spiritual consciousness in particular. Its basic assumption is that God and nature are in competition and that man must choose between them. Its standpoint is radically dualistic, and thus it is strange indeed to find it in traditions which otherwise abjure dualism. This is a basic inconsistency, and its appearance is strangest of all in the nondualistic traditions of Indian Vedanta and Buddhism. But the confusion out of which it arises is highly instructive.

As we have seen, the relegation of sexuality and nature to the forces of evil grows out of the belief that strength and clarity of consciousness depend upon cultivating a one-pointed and exclusive mode of attention. This is, in other words, a type of attention which *ignores* the background in fastening upon the figure, and which grasps the world serially, one thing at a time. Yet this is exactly the meaning of the Hindu-Buddhist term *avidya*, ignorance, or "ignoreance," the basic *unconsciousness* as a result of which it appears that the universe is a collection of *separate* things and events. A Buddha or "awakened one" is precisely the man who has overcome this unconsciousness and is no more bewitched by *sakaya-drishti*, the "vision of separateness." In other words, he sees each "part" of nature without ignoring its relation to the whole, without being deceived by the illusion of *māyā* which, as we also saw, is based on the idea of "measurement" (*mā-, mātr-*), the dividing of the world into classes, into countable things and events. So divided, the world appears to be dual (*dvaita*), but to the unobstructed vision of the sage it is in truth undivided or nondual (*advaita*) and in this state identical with Brahman, the immeasurable and infinite reality.

Considered as a collection of separate things, the world is thus a creation of thought. *Maya,* or measuring and classifying, is an operation of the mind, and as such is the "mother" (*mata*) of a strictly abstract conception of nature, illusory in the sense that nature is so divided only in one's mind. *Maya* is illusory in an evil sense only when the vision of the world as divided is not subordinate to the vision of the world as undivided, when, in other words, the cleverness of the measuring mind does not become too much of a good thing and is "unable to see the forest for the trees."

But the general trend of Indian thought was to fall into the very trap which it should have avoided: it confused the abstract world of *maya* with the concrete world of nature, of direct experience, and then sought liberation from nature in terms of a state of consciousness bereft of all sense experience. It interpreted *maya* an an illusion of the senses rather than of thought projecting itself through the senses. In various forms of *yoga* it cultivated prolonged exclusive concentration upon a single point —*avidya!*—in order to exclude sense experience from consciousness, regarding it as the supreme obstacle to spiritual insight. Above all, sense experience implied "woman," not only as a highly attractive experience, but also as the "source" of birth into the natural world, and thus the very incarnation of *maya,* the Cosmic Seductress.

Thus the identification of *maya* with nature and with woman is the classic example of deception by *maya,* of confusing the world projected by the mind with the real world. Yet although *maya* is figuratively the "mother" of the projected world, projection is rather a male function than a female. As usual, however, man projects his seed into the woman and then accuses her of seducing him. As Adam said, "This woman who thou gavest me, she tempted me and I did eat."

It was in this way that much of Indian philosophy became in practice the archetype of all world-denying dualisms, and in seeking liberation from sense experience became twice over the victim of *maya.* For in struggling for release from *maya* as the concrete world of nature, it confirmed itself more and more deeply in the very illusion that what our minds project upon the world is what we actually see. It forgot that the senses are innocent and that self-deception is the work of thought and imagination.

Confusions of this kind obscure the ways in which both sexuality and sensuality may become *maya* in its proper sense, that is, when the mind seeks more from nature than she can offer, when isolated aspects of nature are pursued in the attempt to force from them a life of joy without sorrow, or pleasure without pain. Thus the desire for sexual experience is *maya* when it is "on the brain," when it is a purely willful and imaginative craving to which the organism responds reluctantly, or not at all. Idealized and fashionable conceptions of feminine beauty are *maya* when, as is often the case, they have little relation to the actual conformations of women. Love, as de Rougemont points out, is *maya* when it is being in love with being in love, rather than a relationship with a particular woman. *Maya* is indeed Woman in the abstract.

Now sexuality is in this sense abstract whenever it is exploited or forced, when it is a deliberate, self-conscious, and yet compulsive pursuit of ecstasy, making up for the stark absence of ecstasy in all other spheres of life. Ecstasy, or transcending oneself, is the natural accompaniment of a full relationship in which we experience the "inner identity" between ourselves and the world. But when that relationship is hidden and the individual feels himself to be a restricted island of consciousness, his emotional experience is largely one of restriction, and it is as arid as the abstract *persona* which he believes himself to be. But the sexual act remains the one easy outlet from his predicament, the one brief interval in which he transcends himself and yields consciously by the spontaneity of his organism. More and more, then, this act is expected to compensate for defective spontaneity in all other directions, and is therefore abstracted or set apart from other experiences as *the* great delight.

Such abstract sexuality is thus the certain result of a forced and studied style of personality, and of confusing spirituality with mere will power—a confusion which remains even when one is *willing* one's will over to God. The individual ascetic may indeed succeed in sublimating his desire for sexual ecstasy into some other form, but he remains part of a society, a culture, upon which his attitude to *sex* has a powerful influence. By associating sex with evil he makes *the* great delight an even greater fascination for the other members of his society, and thereby unknowingly assists the growth of all the refinements of civilized lust. Considered from the standpoint of society as a whole, puritanism is as much a method of exploiting sex by titillation as black underwear, since it promotes the same shocking and exciting contrast between the naked flesh and the black of clerical propriety. It would not be unreasonable to regard puritanism, like masochism, as an extreme form of sexual "decadence."

The culture of Victorian England offers a striking example of this religious prurience, since it was by no means so sexless and staid as has often been supposed, but was, on the contrary, a culture of the most elegant lasciviousness. Extreme modesty and prudishness in the home so heightened the fascination of sex that prostitution, even for the upper classes, flourished on a far greater scale than in our own relatively liberal times. Fashionable and respectable boarding schools combined a total repression of overt sexuality with a proportionably flagrant indulgence in flagellomania. Fashions in clothing did everything to reveal and accentuate the feminine outline in the very act of covering it from neck to toe in veritable strait jackets of tweed, flannel, and boned corsetry. Even the chairs, tables, and household ornaments were suggestively bulged and curved—the chairs wide-shouldered and then waisted at the back, the seat broad, and the legs so obviously thighs or calves that squeamish housewives made the resemblance all the stronger by fitting them with skirts. For when sexuality is repressed it its direct manifestation, it irradiates other spheres of life to scatter on every side symbols and suggestions of its all the more urgent presence.

From the standpoint of cultural anthropology this backhanded manner of embellishing sexuality may be just one of many legitimate variants of the art of sex. For so sensitive a creature as man, art is natural. He does not care to masticate raw beef with hands and teeth, nor to make love with the same "natural" unconcern as that with which he sneezes, nor to live in homes thrown together anyhow to keep out the wet and cold. Therefore there is almost always an art of love, whether it be as directly concerned with the sexual act as the Indian *Kamasutra,* or a preoccupation with the long preliminaries of wooing to which the sexual act itself is merely the final swift climax. Puritanism is simply one of these variants

—that is, if we look at it as a natural phenomenon and do not take it at its own valuation of itself. It is another case of serving nature in trying to work against her, of an extreme of human artifice being no less natural than the supposedly freakish creatures of the wild. It is simply damming a stream to increase its force, but doing so unintentionally or unconsciously. Thus it has often been noted that periods of license and periods of puritanism alternate, the latter creating an excitement that can no longer be contained, and the former a lassitude that requires reinvigoration. The more normal means of keeping the stream at an even strength is modesty rather than prudery, the heightening of sexual fascination by aesthetic concealment as distinct from moral condemnation.[7]

But if puritanism and cultivated licentiousness are not fundamental deviations from nature, they are simply the opposite poles of one and the same attitude—that, right or wrong, sexual pleasure is *the* great delight.[8] This attitude, like the cultivation of the ego, is indeed one of the innumerable possibilities of the freedom of our nature, but because it abstracts sexuality from the rest of life (or *attempts* to do so), it hardly begins to realize its possibilities. Abstract sexuality is partial—a function of dissociated brains instead of total organisms—and for this reason is a singular confusion of the natural world with the *maya* of intellectual divisions and categories. For when sexuality is set apart as a specially good or specially evil compartment of life, it no longer works in full relation to everything else. In other words, it loses universality. It becomes a part doing duty for the whole—the idolatry of a creature worshipped in place of God, and an idolatry committed as much by the ascetic as the libertine.

So long, then, as sexuality remains this abstract *maya* it remains a "demonic" and unspiritualized force, unspiritual in the sense that it is divorced from the universal and concrete reality of nature. For we are trying to wrest it from subordination to the total pattern of organism-environment relationship which, in Chinese philosophy, is *li*—the ordering principle of the Tao. But the universalization of sex involves far more than Freud's recognition that art, religion, and politics are expressions of sublimated libido. We must also see that sexual relations are religious, social, metaphysical, and artistic. Thus the "sexual problem" cannot be

---

[7]Thus the Chinese and Japanese, who do not suffer from sexual guilt, have a strong sense of sexual shame, and have difficulty in appreciating our ready representation of the nude in art. Writing from Europe in 1900, a mandarin said, "The pictures in the palace set apart for them would not please the cultured mind of my venerable brother. The female form is represented nude or half nude. This would obtain fault from our propriety. . . . They have statues of plaster, and some of marble, in the public gardens and in this palace, most of them naked. In the winter's ice it makes me want to cover them. The artists do not know the attraction of rich flowing drapery." Hwuy-ung, *A Chinaman's Opinion of Us and His Own Country*. London, 1927.

[8]Thus a recent summary of the compendia of Catholic moral theology, Jone's *Moral Theology* (Newman Press, 1952), devotes 44 pages to a discussion of the various categories of sin, of which 32, in fine print, are occupied with sexual sins—showing their relative importance with respect to murder, greed, cruelty, lying, and self-righteousness.

solved simply at the sexual level, for which reason our whole discussion makes it subordinate to the problem of man and nature. Sexuality will remain a problem so long as it continues to be the isolated area in which the individual transcends himself and experiences spontaneity. He must first allow himself to be spontaneous in the whole play of inner feeling and of sensory response to the everyday world. Only as the senses in general can learn to accept without grasping, or to be conscious without straining, can the special sensations of sex be free from the grasping of abstract lust and its inseparable twin, the inhibition of abstract or "spiritual" disgust.

It is in this way alone that the problem can be taken out of the fruitlessly alternating dualism in which we have set it. In this dualism sexuality is now good and now bad, now lustful and now prudish, now compellingly grasped and now guiltily inhibited. For when sexual activity is sought in the abstract its disappointments are proportionate to its exaggerated expectations, associating themselves with the swift transition from extreme excitement to lassitude which accompanies detumescence. The aftermath of intercourse, which should be a state of fulfilled tranquillity, is for the prude the depression of guilt and for the libertine the depression of ennui. The reason is that both are grasping at the sensation of intense lust which immediately precedes the orgasm, making it a goal rather than a gift, and so experienced it is an elation which swings over to depression, its opposite *maya*. But when the mounting excitement is accepted rather than grasped, it becomes a full realization of spontaneity, and the resulting orgasm is not its sudden end but the bursting in upon us of peace.

It will by now be clear that a truly natural sexuality is by no means a spontaneity in the sense of promiscuity breaking loose from restraint. No more is it the colorlessly "healthy" sexuality of mere animal release from biological tension. To the degree that we do not yet know what man is, we do not yet know what human sexuality is. We do not know what man is so long as we know him piecemeal, categorically, as the separate individual, the agglomeration of blocklike instincts and passions and sensations regarded one by one under the fixed stare of an exclusive consciousness. What man is, and what human sexuality is, will come to be known only as we lay ourselves open to experience with the full sensitivity of feeling which does not grasp.

The experience of sexual love is therefore no longer to be sought as the repetition of a familiar ecstasy, prejudiced by the expectation of what we already know. It will be the exploration of our relationship with an everchanging, ever unknown partner, unknown because he or she is not in truth the abstract role or person, the set of conditioned reflexes which society has imposed, the stereotyped male or female which education has led us to expect. All these are *maya*, and the love of these is the endlessly frustrating love of fantasy. What is not *maya* is mystery, what cannot be described or measured, and it is in this sense—symbolized by the veil of modesty—that woman is always a mystery to man, and man to woman.

It is in this sense that we must understand van der Leeuw's remarkable saying that "the mystery of life is not a problem to be solved, but a reality to be experienced."

Rollo May
SEX AGAINST EROS

Heralded as a form of enlightenment, the twentieth-century revolution in our sexual mores has significantly altered our attitudes, our emotions, our ways of relating to one another, and even our language. Yet, it is not at all certain that we have achieved genuine sexual liberation. In the selection that follows, Rollo May, a practicing existential psychoanalyst and author of numerous books, notes that this so-called sexual enlightenment has by no means solved our sexual problems. Rather, it has tended, he argues, to become a new form of puritanism in which we feel guilty if we refrain from sex, in which emphasis is placed on technique and not on the emotional quality of the experience, in which feelings are limited and emotions impoverished, and in which sex itself is made banal. The root of the problem is, he claims, the separation of sex from Eros.

. . . .

In Victorian times, when the denial of sexual impulses, feelings, and drives was the mode and one would not talk about sex in polite company, an aura of sanctifying repulsiveness surrounded the whole topic. Males and females dealt with each other as though neither possessed sexual organs. William James, that redoubtable crusader who was far ahead of his time on every other topic, treated sex with the polite aversion characteristic of the turn of the century. In the whole two volumes of his epoch-making *Principles of Psychology,* only one page is devoted to sex, at the end of which he adds, "These details are a little unpleasant to discuss. . . ."[1] But William Blake's warning a century before Victorianism, that "He who desires but acts not, breeds pestilence," was amply demonstrated by the later psychotherapists. Freud, a Victorian who did look at sex, was right in his description of the morass of neurotic symptoms which resulted from cutting off so vital a part of the human body and the self.

Then, in the 1920's, a radical change occurred almost overnight. The belief became a militant dogma in liberal circles that the opposite of repression—namely, sex education, freedom of talking, feeling, and expression—would have healthy effects, and obviously constituted the only

---

[1] William James, *Principles of Psychology* (New York, Dover Publications, 1950; originally published by Henry Holt, 1890), II, p. 439.

stand for the enlightened person. In an amazingly short period following World War I, we shifted from acting as though sex did not exist at all to being obsessed with it. We now placed more emphasis on sex than any society since that of ancient Rome, and some scholars believe we are more preoccupied with sex than any other people in all of history. Today, far from not talking about sex, we might well seem, to a visitor from Mars dropping into Times Square, to have no other topic of communication.

.   .   .

Partly as a result of this radical shift, many therapists today rarely see patients who exhibit repression of sex in the manner of Freud's pre-World War I hysterical patients. In fact, we find in the people who come for help just the opposite: a great deal of talk about sex, a great deal of sexual activity, practically no one complaining of cultural prohibitions over going to bed as often or with as many partners as one wishes. But what our patients do complain of is lack of feeling and passion. "The curious thing about this ferment of discussion is how little anyone seems to be *enjoying* emancipation."[2] So much sex and so little meaning or even fun in it!

Where the Victorian didn't want anyone to know that he or she had sexual feelings, we are ashamed if we do not. Before 1910, if you called a lady "sexy" she would be insulted; nowadays, she prizes the compliment and rewards you by turning her charms in your direction. Our patients often have the problems of frigidity and impotence, but the strange and poignant thing we observe is how desperately they struggle not to let anyone find out they don't feel sexually. The Victorian nice man or woman was guilty if he or she did experience sex; now we are guilty if we *don't*.

One paradox, therefore, is that enlightenment has not solved the sexual problems in our culture. To be sure, there are important positive results of the new enlightenment, chiefly in increased freedom for the individual. Most external problems are eased: sexual knowledge can be bought in any bookstore, contraception is available everywhere except in Boston where it is still believed, as the English countess averred on her wedding night, that sex is "too good for the common people." Couples can, without guilt and generally without squeamishness, discuss their sexual relationship and undertake to make it more mutually gratifying and meaningful. Let these gains not be underestimated. External social anxiety and guilt have lessened; dull would be the man who did not rejoice in this.

But *internal* anxiety and guilt have increased. And in some ways these are more morbid, harder to handle, and impose a heavier burden upon the individual than external anxiety and guilt.

[2][*Atlas* (November, 1965), p. 302. Reprinted from *Times Literary Supplement*, London.]

The challenge a woman used to face from men was simple and direct —would she or would she not go to bed?—a direct issue of how she stood vis-à-vis cultural mores. But the question men ask now is no longer, "Will she or won't she?" but "Can she or can't she?" The challenge is shifted to the woman's personal adequacy, namely, her own capacity to have the vaunted orgasm—which should resemble a *grand mal* seizure. Though we might agree that the second question places the problem of sexual decision more where it should be, we cannot overlook the fact that the first question is much easier for the person to handle. In my practice, one woman was afraid to go to bed for fear that the man "won't find me very good at making love." Another was afraid because "I don't even know how to do it," assuming that her lover would hold this against her. Another was scared to death of the second marriage for fear that she wouldn't be able to have the orgasm as she had not in her first. Often the woman's hesitation is formulated as, "He won't like me well enough to come back again."

.   .   .

A second paradox is that *the new emphasis on technique in sex and love-making backfires.* It often occurs to me that there is an inverse relationship between the number of how-to-do-it books perused by a person or rolling off the presses in a society and the amount of sexual passion or even pleasure experienced by the persons involved. Certainly nothing is wrong with technique as such, in playing golf or acting or making love. But the emphasis beyond a certain point on technique in sex makes for a mechanistic attitude toward love-making, and goes along with alienation, feelings of loneliness, and depersonalization.

One aspect of the alienation is that the lover, with his age-old art, tends to be superseded by the computer operator with his modern efficiency. Couples place great emphasis on bookkeeping and timetables in their love-making—a practice confirmed and standardized by Kinsey. If they fall behind schedule they become anxious and feel impelled to go to bed whether they want to or not. My colleague, Dr. John Schimel, observes, "My patients have endured stoically, or without noticing, remarkably destructive treatment at the hands of their spouses, but they have experienced falling behind in the sexual time-table as a loss of love."[3] The man feels he is somehow losing his masculine status if he does not perform up to schedule, and the woman that she has lost her feminine attractiveness if too long a period goes by without the man at least making a pass at her. The phrase "between men," which women use about their affairs, similarly suggests a gap in time like the *entr'acte.* Elaborate accounting and ledger-book lists—how often this week have we

[3]John L. Schimel, "Ideology and Sexual Practices," *Sexual Behavior and the Law,* ed. Ralph Slovenko (Springfield, Ill., Charles C. Thomas, 1965), pp. 195, 197.

made love? did he (or she) pay the right amount of attention to me during the evening? was the foreplay long enough?—make one wonder how the spontaneity of this most spontaneous act can possibly survive. The computer hovers in the stage wings of the drama of love-making the way Freud said one's parents used to.

It is not surprising then, in this preoccupation with techniques, that the questions typically asked about an act of love-making are not, Was there passion or meaning or pleasure in the act? but, How well did I perform? Take, for example, what Cyril Connolly calls "the tyranny of the orgasm," and the preoccupation with achieving a simultaneous orgasm, which is another aspect of the alienation. I confess that when people talk about the "apocalyptic orgasm," I find myself wondering, Why do they have to try so hard? What abyss of self-doubt, what inner void of loneliness, are they trying to cover up by this great concern with grandiose effects?

.   .   .

It is a strange thing in our society that what goes into building a relationship—the sharing of tastes, fantasies, dreams, hopes for the future, and fears from the past—seems to make people more shy and vulnerable than going to bed with each other. They are more wary of the tenderness that goes with psychological and spiritual nakedness than they are of the physical nakedness in sexual intimacy.

The third paradox is that our highly-vaunted sexual freedom has turned out to be a new form of puritanism. I spell it with a small "p" because I do not wish to confuse this with the original Puritanism. That, as in the passion of Hester and Dimmesdale in Hawthorne's *The Scarlet Letter,* was a very different thing. I refer to puritanism as it came down via our Victorian grandparents and became allied with industrialism and emotional and moral compartmentalization.

I define this puritanism as consisting of three elements. First, *a state of alienation from the body.* Second, *the separation of emotion from reason.* And third, *the use of the body as a machine.*

In our new puritanism, bad health is equated with sin. Sin used to mean giving in to one's sexual desires; it now means not having full sexual expression. Our contemporary puritan holds that it is immoral *not* to express your libido. Apparently this is true on both sides of the ocean: "There are few more depressing sights," the London *Times Literary Supplement* writes, "than a progressive intellectual determined to end up in bed with someone from a sense of moral duty. . . . There is no more high-minded puritan in the world than your modern advocate of salvation through properly directed passion. . . ."[4] A woman used to be guilty if she went to bed with a man; now she feels vaguely guilty if after a certain number of dates she still refrains; her sin is "morbid repression," refusing to "give." And the partner, who is always completely enlightened (or at least pretends to be) refuses to allay her guilt by getting overtly angry at her (if she could fight him on the issue, the conflict would be a lot easier for her). But he stands broadmindedly by, ready at the end of every date to undertake a crusade to assist her out of her fallen state. And this, of course, makes her "no" all the more guilt-producing for her.

This all means, of course, that people not only have to learn to perform sexually but have to make sure, at the same time, that they can do so without letting themselves go in passion or unseemly commitment —the latter of which may be interpreted as exerting an unhealthy demand upon the partner. *The Victorian person sought to have love without falling into sex; the modern person seeks to have sex without falling into love.*

. . .

The new puritanism brings with it a depersonalization of our whole language. Instead of making love, we "have sex"; in contrast to intercourse, we "screw"; instead of going to bed, we "lay" someone or (heaven help the English language as well as ourselves!) we "are laid." This alienation has become so much the order of the day that in some psychotherapeutic training schools, young psychiatrists are taught that it is "therapeutic" to use solely the four-letter words in sessions; the patient is probably masking some repression if he talks about making love; so it becomes our righteous duty—the new puritanism incarnate!—to let him know he only fucks. Everyone seems so intent on sweeping away the last vestiges of Victorian prudishness that we entirely forget that these different words refer to different kinds of human experience. Probably most people have experienced the different forms of sexual relationship described by the different terms and don't have much difficulty distinguishing among them. I am not making a value judgment among these different experiences; they are all appropriate to their own kinds of relationship. Every woman wants at some time to be "laid"—transported, carried away, "made" to have passion when at first she has none, as in the famous scene between Rhett Butler and Scarlett O'Hara in *Gone with the Wind.* But if being "laid" is all that ever happens in her sexual life, then her experience of personal alienation and rejection of sex are just around the corner. If the therapist does not appreciate these diverse kinds of experience, he will be presiding at the shrinking and truncating of the patient's consciousness, and will be confirming the narrowing of the patient's bodily awareness as well as his or her capacity for relationship. This is the chief criticism of the new puritanism: it grossly limits feelings, it blocks the infinite variety and richness of the act, and it makes for emotional impoverishment.

It is not surprising that the new puritanism develops smoldering hostility among the members of our society. And that hostility, in turn, comes out frequently in references to the sexual act itself. We say "go fuck yourself" or "fuck you" as a term of contempt to show that the other is of no value whatever beyond being used and tossed aside. The biological lust is here in its *reductio ad absurdum*. Indeed, the word fuck is the most common expletive in our contemporary language to express violent hostility. I do not think this is by accident.

.   .   .

... [T]he contemporary paradoxes in sex and love have one thing in common, namely *the banalization of sex and love*. By anesthetizing feeling in order to perform better, by employing sex as a tool to prove prowess and identity, by using sensuality to hide sensitivity, we have emasculated sex and left it vapid and empty. The banalization of sex is well-aided and abetted by our mass communication. For the plethora of books on sex and love which flood the market have one thing in common—they oversimplify love and sex, treating the topic like a combination of learning to play tennis and buying life insurance. In this process, we have robbed sex of its power by sidestepping eros; and we have ended by dehumanizing both.

My thesis ... is that what underlies our emasculation of sex is the *separation of sex from eros*. Indeed, we have set sex over *against* eros, used sex precisely to avoid the anxiety-creating involvements of eros. In ostensibly enlightened discussions of sex, particularly those about freedom from censorship, it is often argued that all our society needs is full freedom for the expression of eros. But what is revealed beneath the surface in our society, as shown not only in patients in therapy but in our literature and drama and even in the nature of our scientific research, is just the opposite. We are in a flight from eros—and we use sex as the vehicle for the flight.

Sex is the handiest drug to blot out our awareness of the anxiety-creating aspects of eros. To accomplish this, we have had to define sex ever more narrowly: the more we became preoccupied with sex, the more truncated and shrunken became the human experience to which it referred. We fly to *the sensation of sex in order to avoid the passion of eros*.

.   .   .

Sex can be defined fairly adequately in physiological terms as consisting of the building up of bodily tensions and their release. Eros, in contrast, is the experiencing of the personal intentions and meaning of the act. Whereas sex is a rhythm of stimulus and response, eros is a state of being. The pleasure in sex is described by Freud and others as the reduction of tension; in eros, on the contrary, we wish not to be released from the excitement but rather to hang on to it, to bask in it, and even to increase it. The end toward which sex points is gratification and relaxation, whereas eros is a desiring, longing, a forever reaching out, seeking to expand.

.   .   .

Sex is thus a zoological term and is rightly applied to all animals as well as human beings. Kinsey was a zoologist, and appropriately to his profession, he studied human sexual behavior from a zoological point of view. Masters is a gynecologist and studies sex from the viewpoint of sexual organs and how you manage and manipulate them: sex, then, is a pattern of neurophysiological functions and the sexual problem consists of what you do with organs.

Eros, on the other hand, takes wings from human imagination and is forever transcending all techniques, giving the laugh to all the "how to" books by gaily swinging into orbit above our mechanical rules, making love rather than manipulating organs.

For eros is the power which *attracts* us. The essence of eros is that it draws us from ahead, whereas sex pushes us from behind. This is revealed in our day-to-day language when I say a person "allures" me or "entices" me, or the possibilities of a new job "invite" me. Something in me responds to the other person, or the job, and pulls me toward him or it. I participate in forms, possibilities, higher levels of meaning, on neurophysiological dimensions but also on aesthetic and ethical dimensions as well. As the Greeks believed, knowledge and even ethical goodness exercise such a pull. Eros is the drive toward union with what we belong to—union with our own possibilities, union with significant other persons in our world in relation to whom we discover our own self-fulfillment. Eros is the yearning in man which leads him to dedicate himself to seeking *arête,* the noble and good life.

Sex, in short, is the mode of relating characterized by tumescence of the organs (for which we seek the pleasurable relief) and filled gonads (for which we seek satisfying release). But eros is the mode of relating in which we do not seek release but rather to cultivate, procreate, and form the world. *In eros, we seek increase of stimulation.* Sex is a need, but eros is a desire; and it is this admixture of desire which complicates love. In regard to our preoccupation with the orgasm in American discussions of sex, it can be agreed that the aim of the sex act in its zoological and physiological sense is indeed the orgasm. But the aim of eros is not: eros seeks union with the other person in delight and passion, and the pro-creating of new dimensions of experience which broaden and deepen the being of both persons. It is common experience, backed up by folklore as well as the testimony of Freud and others, that after sexual release we tend to go to sleep—or, as the joke puts it, to get dressed, go home, and *then* go to sleep. But in eros, we want just the opposite: to stay awake thinking of the beloved, remembering, savoring, discovering ever-new facets of the prism of what the Chinese call the "many-splendored" experience.

It is this urge for union with the partner that is the occasion for human tenderness. For eros—not sex as such—is the source of tenderness. Eros is the longing to establish union, full relationship. This may be, first, a union with abstract forms. The philosopher Charles S. Peirce sat alone in his house in Milford, Connecticut working out his mathematical logic, but this did not prevent his experiencing eros; the thinker must be "animated by a true eros," he wrote, "for the task of scientific investigation." Or it may be a union with aesthetic or philosophical forms, or a union with new ethical forms. But it is most obvious as the pull toward the union of two individuals sexually. The two persons, longing, as all individuals do, to overcome the separateness and isolation to which we all are heir as individuals, can participate in a relationship that, for the moment, is not made up of two isolated, individual experiences, but a genuine union. A sharing takes place which is a new *Gestalt,* a new being, a new field of magnetic force.

We have been led astray by our economic and biological models to think that the aim of the love act is the orgasm. The French have a saying which, referring to eros, carries more truth: "The aim of desire is not its satisfaction but its prolongation." André Maurois, speaking of his preference for love-making to which the orgasm is not the goal but an incidental conclusion, quotes another French saying, "Every beginning is lovely."

The moment of greatest significance in love-making, as judged by what people remember in the experience and what patients dream about, is not the moment of orgasm. It is rather the moment of entrance, the moment of penetration of the erection of the man into the vagina of the woman. This is the moment that shakes us, that has within it the great wonder, tremendous and tremulous as it may be—or disappointing and despairing, which says the same thing from the opposite point of view. This is the moment when the persons' reactions to the love-making experience are most original, most individual, most truly their own. This, and not the orgasm, is the moment of union and the realization that we have won the other.

The ancients made Eros a "god," or more specifically, a daimon. This is a symbolic way of communicating a basic truth of human experience, that eros always drives us to transcend ourselves. When Goethe wrote, "Woman draws us upward," his line may be more accurately read, "Eros, in relation with a woman, draws us upward." Such a truth is both inner, personal, and *subjective* on one hand, and external, social, and *objective* on the other—that is, it is a truth which obtains in our relationships in the objective world. The ancients, taking sex for granted simply as a natural bodily function, saw no need to make it into a god. Antony presumably had all his sexual needs taken care of by the concubines accompanying the Roman army; it was only when he met Cleopatra that *eros* entered the picture and he became transported into a whole new world, ecstatic and destructive at the same time.

. . .

Linda Phelps
FEMALE SEXUAL ALIENATION

In the article that follows, Linda Phelps, who is active in the women's liberation movement, discusses the socialization of female sexuality and analyzes how it leads to a "sexually schizophrenic" existence, in which women are alienated from themselves as sexually self-directed persons and from their own sexual experiences. Women, she argues, are socialized to relate to a false world of erotic fantasies and images that are defined and controlled by men.

In the last few years, the so-called sexual revolution has turned sour. The end of inhibition and the release of sexual energies which have so often been documented as the innovation of the revolutionary culture are now beginning to be seen as just another fraud. After the gang-rapes at Altamont and Seattle, after the demands raised at People's Park for "Free Land, Free Dope, Free Women," after the analyses of (male) rock culture, women are beginning to realize that nothing new has happened at all. What we have is simply a new, more sophisticated (and thus more insidious) version of male sexual culture. Sexual freedom has meant more opportunity for men, not a new kind of experience for women. And it has been precisely our own experience as women which has been decisive in developing the Women's Liberation critique of the sexual revolution. I am concerned here with only one aspect of female sexuality—that between women and men. The generation of women who only a few years ago saw themselves as the vanguard of a sexual revolution between women and men suddenly find themselves plagued with all the problems of their grandmothers—loss of interest in sex, hatred of sex, disgust with self. This turn-about happened very fast for some of us and I think it happened because we opened ourselves up in consciousness-raising and a lot of bad feeling we thought we'd gotten rid of floated to the top. It has been good to get these feelings out and look at them. But can we *explain* them, can we understand what has happened to us in the last five years?

I would like to suggest that we can understand the destruction of female sexuality if we conceptualize it as a special case of alienation, understood as a political phenomenon. If alienation is the destruction of self which ultimately leads to schizophrenia, the widespread alienation of females from their own sexuality is a kind of rampant mental illness at the base of our experience which we must recognize for what it is.

Alienation is a much used and little explained term. Put simply, it refers to the disintegration of our very selves and personalities which occurs when we are powerless. The opposite of powerlessness is self-actualization; and the healthy, self-actualizing human being is one who moves through the world as an autonomous source of action. As Ernest Becker put it in an important essay on alienation:[1]

> People break down when they aren't 'doing'—when the world around them does not reflect the active involvement of their own creative powers.... Alienated man is man separated from involvement with and responsibility for the effective use of his *self-powers*.

What is more difficult to understand is precisely *how* alienation comes about in certain individuals. Becker suggests three ways: (1) Alienation occurs along the dimension of time. As children we learn certain patterns of behavior which bring us approval. As we grow older, however, we must constantly adapt to new situations. If our early childhood training has been too rigid, we are unable to make the necessary adjustments and become increasingly unable to handle our experiences. (2) Alienation also occurs in terms of the roles we play. This problem affects both men and women, but we are particularly familiar with the female version. Not only are females confined to a few narrow roles, but they are also subject to contradictory messages about the roles they play. Motherhood, for example, is viewed as a sacred task, but mothers are not taken seriously when they act outside their kitchens and homes. (3) The third dimension of alienation is more complex: breakdown of self occurs when the gap between thought and action, theory and practice, mind and body becomes too great. The classic and extreme example of this form of alienation is the schizophrenic, living totally in a thought world of her/his own creation with no relation to reality.

This three-dimensional model of alienation is complex but I think it can help us understand our own experience of sex between women and men. What I am about to say about female sexuality as schizophrenic will make more sense, however, if I digress for a moment to describe some attributes of schizophrenia. This extreme form of alienation, you will recall, is produced by a split between mind and body. Such an odd condition is possible in human beings as opposed to animals because we are self-conscious beings. We have an 'inner self' of reflection and thought but our body is part of the world 'out there' of experience and material objects. This mind-body dualism is at the base of human power —our ability to reflect upon and then act upon the material world. Such power becomes destructive—as in schizophrenia—when the mind turns in on itself and never tests its perceptions in concrete reality.

[1] Ernest Becker, "Mills' Social Psychology and the Great Historical Convergence on the Problem of Alienation," in Irving Horowitz, *The New Sociology, Essays in Social Science and Social Theory in Honor of C. Wright Mills* (New York, Oxford University Press, 1964), pp. 108–133.

In this reverse process, the schizophrenic fails to develop the necessary unity between mind and body, takes refuge in a world of *symbols*, and thereby forfeits *experience*. In other words, a schizophrenic is someone who becomes accustomed to relating to symbol-objects rather than person-objects and in doing so loses all self-powers.

I would argue that as females we are sexually schizophrenic, relating not to ouselves as self-directed persons, not to our partners as sexual objects of our desire, but to a false world of symbols and fantasy. This fantasy world of sex which veils our experience is the world of sex as seen through male eyes. It is a world whose eroticism is defined in terms of female powerlessness, dependency, and submission. It is the world of sado-masochistic sex. If you don't know what I mean by sado-masochism, think of the erotic themes of all the novels, comic books, movies, jokes, cartoons, and songs you've ever experienced. The major sexual theme which appears over and over again is the drama of conquest and submission: the male takes the initiative and the female waits, waits in a thousand variations on a single theme—eagerly, coyly, shyly, angrily, and at the outer edge of pornography and fantasy, is taken against her will. Usually it is more subtle. The female stands in awe of the hero's abilities, his powers; she is willing when he takes the initiative, guides her by the elbow, puts his arm around her waist, manoevres her into the bedroom. What is it that makes such descriptions arousing? Not a mere run-down of anatomy but the tension in the social situation as male advances on female, whether she is willing or not.

Such submission is acceptable in our culture if the man is superior, and this leads to the search for the man who is smarter, taller, more self-confident—someone to look up to and thus worthy of giving in to.

> In each of our lives, there was a first man for whom we were prepared like lambs for the slaughter. My fantasy of him was a composite of Prince Valiant, Gary Cooper, and my father. Trained in submission, in silence, I awaited him through a series of *adolescent boyfriends who were not masterful enough to fit the dream* . . . because I would not really graduate to the estate of womanhood until I had been taken by a strong man.[2]

Trained in submission, women instinctively look for the strong men who will continue the loving benevolence of the father. That this pattern of sexual relations is our society's model is confirmed by psychologist Abraham Maslow. In a study of sexual behavior, Maslow reported that women who find a partner more dominant than they usually make the best sexual adjustment. On the other hand, a very sexually active woman in his study failed to reach orgasm with several male partners because she

[2] Motherlode, Vol. 1, no. 1, p. 1.

considered them weaker than herself and thus could not "give in to them."[3] Thus, 'normal' sexual adjustment occurs in our society when the male plays the dominant role.

If we come to view male-dominated sexual relations as by definition healthy sex, the mechanism of this learning process is the bombardment of sexual fantasy that we experience long before we experience sex itself. Sexual images of conquest and submission pervade our imagination from an early age and lay the basis for how we will later look upon and experience sex. Through the television set and the storybook, we live out in imagination society's definition of sex and love. Rapunzel waits in her tower for years in hopes of the young prince who will free her body from its imprisonment. Sleeping Beauty's desires slumber until they are awakened and fulfilled by the kiss of the young prince. These fairy tale princesses are not unusual. There are few women, no matter how intelligent, no matter how dedicated to the pursuit of a goal, who will not finally be conquered—and like it. And if they are not conquered, it is understood that no man desired them anyway.

By experiencing such sexual fantasies at an early age, we become alienated along Becker's first dimension of time. Locked early into a set of fantasy images which define female sexual roles as passive, women are constantly denying feelings which don't fit the cultural definitions. And so all pervasive is the male bias of our culture that we seldom notice that the fantasies we take in, the images that describe to us how to act, are *male* fantasies about females. In a male world, female sex is from the beginning unable to get a clear picture of itself.

And from the beginning, women experience Becker's second dimension of alienation: the role of woman as sexual being is subject to contradictory evaluations by society. Young girls quickly become attuned to society's ambivalent view of their sexuality. Women come to see themselves as synonymous with sex, yet female sexuality is seen as valid only under certain conditions such as marriage. Even as such narrow restrictions break down in more permissive ages like our own and the limits of female sexuality expand, we still run up against those limits at the point where a female can be labelled promiscuous. And women who initiate and direct sexual activity on a regular basis find that they have gone beyond the limits of the possible and are termed castrating. Male sexual desires, on the other hand, are affirmed throughout and are associated with prowess, power, and man(self)hood.

As females, then, we relate to symbol-objects rather than person-objects. Like the schizophrenic, we are alienated from our own experi-

[3] A.H. Maslow, "Self-Esteem (Dominance-Feeling) and Sexuality in Women," in Hendrik M. Ruttenbeck, *Psychoanalysis and Female Sexuality* (New Haven, Conn., College and University Press, 1966), pp. 161–197.

ence and from our own self-powers of initiation. This form of alienation has to do with sex in a very direct way because women do not often take the initiative in relation to men.

> Schizophrenic passivity is a direct reflex of the abrogation of one's powers in the face of the object ... If you relate to an object under your own initiatory powers, then it becomes an object which enriches your own nature. If you lack initiatory powers over the object, it takes on a different value, for it then becomes an individual which crowds your own nature ... A girl really comes to exist as a feminine sex object for the adolescent only as he learns to exercise active courtship powers in relation to her.[4]

If women become objects of sexual desire for men in the social process of male-initiated relationships, how does the male become an object of sexual desire for the female? It is not clear, in fact, that the male body *per se* is deemed erotic by women, certainly not in the same way that the female body is for men. In fact, since women are bombarded with the same sex stimuli of the female body as is a man, females often respond in a narcissistic way to their own body and what is being *done* to it rather than projecting sexual desire out onto the male. The female is taught to be the object of sexual desires rather than to be a self-directed sexual being oriented toward another; she is taught to be adored rather than adoring. Is it surprising then that so many women find the male body ugly, that so many women see the drama of sex in what is done *to* them?

Two things happen to women's sexual lives. Many women have no sexual fantasies at all (since there is little male sexual imagery available in this culture). Masters and Johnson found that many women who could not focus on sexual imagery had difficulty having orgasm. The good doctors have tried to encourage sexual fantasy (by reading arousing material!) to enable women to experience orgasm.

Females that do have fantasies often have the same sado-masochistic fantasies that men do. As Shulamith Firestone points out in *The Dialectic of Sex*,

> Cultural distortion of sexuality also explains how female sexuality gets twisted in narcissism: women make love to themselves vicariously through the man rather than directly making love to him.[5]

In these fantasy episodes, the female does not always play the masochistic role. The female who is focusing on sexual imagery can take the part either of the male, the female, or an onlooker, but in any case eroticism is still dealing in female powerlessness.

[4] Becker, op. cit., p. 125.
[5] Shulamith Firestone, *The Dialectic of Sex* (New York, William Morrow, 1970), p. 178.

How do women tolerate a situation in which men control and define the experience of sex? I believe we solve our problem in the same way the schizophrenic does. A woman's sexuality is experienced in symbolic terms at the expense of active physical involvment. Sex is re-presented to her by society in symbolic messages of passivity and conquest. Like the symbolic world of the schizophrenic, a woman's fantasy life—her desire to be taken, overpowered, mastered—allows her to play the passive role and perhaps even to enjoy it *if she fully accepts the world as defined by men.* Caught between the demands of a male-dominated society and the demands of our own self-definition, we survive by fully accepting the masochistic symbol-world given to us by male society at the expense of our own experience. In fact, our physical experience has been denied and distorted for so long that most of us aren't even aware of the sacrifice we have made. We are only uneasy that all is not well.

Yet ultimately in the lives of those women for whom fantasy and reality become too far apart, a crisis occurs. The mechanism of crisis in some cases may be merely the demystification of the male through years of marriage. It is hard to keep intact fantasies of male power when confronted with the reality of a pot-bellied, lethargic husband. Such a crisis may result either in a transfer of fantasy to a new male or in a loss of interest in sex altogether. For women in Women's Liberation the whole fragile structure of fantasy and power often falls along with the myth of male supremacy. Males are subject to the same fantasies of conquest, yet their fantasy life is an expression of their own active powers (albeit in a false way) and does not separate them from their own experience.

Women, then, are alienated from their sexuality along several dimensions. From an early age, we are alienated from ourselves as sexual beings by a male society's ambivalent definition of our sexuality: we are sexy but we are pure; we are insatiable but we are frigid; we have beautiful bodies but we must shave and anoint them. We are also alienated because we are separated from our own experience by the prevailing male cultural definition of sex—the male fantasy of active man and passive woman. From an early age, our sexual impulses are trained to turn back onto ourselves in the narcissistic counterpart of the male fantasy world. In social relations with men, we are alienated from ourselves as initiating, self-directed persons. Some women hold all these contradictory parts together; most women, I suspect, have given up on sex, whether or not they have informed their husbands and lovers.

Calling into question our traditional female role has meant calling into question more and more layers of our experience. With this questioning has come the discovery that there is not much left that is valid in male-female relations as we have known them. Kate Millet showed us in *Sexual Politics* that fascism—the relations of dominance and submission that begin with sex and extend throughout our society—is at the very core of our cultural experience. So it is with little joy and much sadness that we peel back the layers of our consciousness and see our sexual experience for what it really is. And it is also with much sadness that we admit that there is no easy answer. It is too easy to say that we have been merely the victims of male power plays. The sado-masochistic content of sex is in the heads of women too. As long as female powerlessness is the unspoken underlying reality of sexual relations, women will want to be conquered. As long as our cultural vision is the projection of solely male experience, women will not be able to understand even their own alienation.

To say this is to suggest some ways out of our cultural and sexual alienation. Yet it is also too easy to blithely assume, as we often do, that all this sexual distortion is going to be easily changed in some new culture in the future. We have pushed beyond the economic revolution and the cultural revolution to come face to face with the real sexual revolution and we are not sure what we have left in the way of hope and affirmation.

Perhaps the most courageous and in the long run the most positive statement we can make is to acknowledge the pain we feel now and the perhaps irreparable damage that we have sustained. But saying this is not totally to despair. Sometimes it is necessary to touch rock bottom before we can find the strength to push up for air.

Ann Ferguson
ANDROGYNY AS AN IDEAL FOR HUMAN DEVELOPMENT

In the previous article, the way in which female sexuality has been socialized was discussed. But males and females in this society are socialized in more ways than simply sexual ones; indeed, sexual socialization, in the narrow sense, is dependent on a more total sex-role socialization. In other words, "male" and "female" are general social roles, in which sexual behavior as such is only a part. Thus, the question of male and female sexuality must confront the broader question of the division of human behavior into male and female social roles.

In the essay reprinted here, Ann Ferguson, a socialist feminist who teaches philosophy at the University of Massachusetts in Amherst, argues for the elimination of social sex roles and the development of androgynous human beings. Among the many implications of her position is that bisexuality would probably become the norm, rather than the exception.

In this paper I shall defend androgyny as an ideal for human development. To do this I shall argue that male/female sex roles are neither inevitable results of "natural" biological differences between the sexes, nor socially desirable ways of socializing children in contemporary societies. In fact, the elimination of sex roles and the development of androgynous human beings is the most rational way to allow for the possibility of, on the one hand, love relations among equals, and on the other, development of the widest possible range of intense and satisfying social relationships between men and women.

I. ANDROGYNY: THE IDEAL DEFINED

The term "androgyny" has Greek roots: *andros* means man and *gynē*, woman. An androgynous person would combine some of each of the characteristic traits, skills, and interests that we now associate with the stereotypes of masculinity and femininity It is not accurate to say that the ideal androgynous person would be both masculine and feminine, for there are negative and distorted personality characteristics associated in our minds with these ideas.[1] Furthermore, as we presently understand these stereotypes, they exclude each other. A masculine person is active, independent, aggressive (demanding), more self-interested than altruistic, competent and interested in physical activities, rational, emotionally controlled, and self-disciplined. A feminine person, on the other hand, is passive, dependent, nonassertive, more altruistic than self-interested (supportive of others), neither physically competent nor interested in becoming so, intuitive but not rational, emotionally open, and impulsive rather than self-disciplined. Since our present conceptions of masculinity and femininity thus defined exclude each other, we must think of an ideal androgynous person as one to whom these categories do not apply—one who is neither masculine nor feminine, but human: who transcends those old categories in such a way as to be able to develop positive human potentialities denied or only realized in an alienated fashion in the current stereotypes.

The ideal androgynous being, because of his or her combination of general traits, skills, and interests, would have no internal blocks to attaining self-esteem. He or she would have the desire and ability to do socially meaningful productive activity (work), as well as the desire and ability to be autonomous and to relate lovingly to other human beings. Of course, whether or not such an individual would be able to *achieve* a sense of autonomy, self-worth, and group contribution will depend importantly on the way the society in which he/she lives is structured. For example, in a classist society characterized by commodity production, none of these goals is attainable by anyone, no matter how androgynous, who comes from a class lacking the material resources to acquire (relatively) nonalienating work. In a racist and sexist society there are social

[1]I owe these thoughts to Jean Elshtain and members of the Valley Women's Union in Northampton, Massachusetts, from discussions on androgyny.

roles and expectations placed upon the individual which present him/her with a conflict situation: either express this trait (skill, interest) and be considered a social deviant or outcast, or repress the trait and be socially accepted. The point, however, is that the androgynous person has the requisite skills and interests to be able to achieve these goals if only the society is organized appropriately.

II. LIMITS TO HUMAN DEVELOPMENT: THE NATURAL COMPLEMENT THEORY

There are two lines of objection that can be raised against the view that androgyny is an ideal for human development: first, that it is not possible, given the facts we know about human nature; and second, that even if it is possible, there is no reason to think it particularly desirable that people be socialized to develop the potential for androgyny. In this section I shall present and discuss Natural Complement theories of male/female human nature and the normative conclusions about sex roles.

There are two general facts about men and women and their roles in human societies that must be taken into account by any theory of what is possible in social organization of sex roles: first, the biological differences between men and women—in the biological reproduction of children, in relative physical strength, and in biological potential for aggressive (dominant, demanding) behavior; and second, the fact that all known human societies have had a sexual division of labor.

According to the Natural Complement theory, there are traits, capacities, and interests which inhere in men and women simply because of their biological differences, and which thus define what is normal "masculine" and normal "feminine" behavior. Since men are stronger than women, have bodies better adapted for running and throwing, and have higher amounts of the male hormone androgen, which is linked to aggressive behavior,[2] men have a greater capacity for heavy physical labor and for aggressive behavior (such as war). Thus it is natural that men are the breadwinners and play the active role in the production of commodities in society and in defending what the society sees as its interests in war. Since women bear children, it is natural that they have a maternal, nurturing instinct which enables them to be supportive of the needs of children, perceptive and sensitive to their needs, and intuitive in general in their understanding of the needs of people.

The Natural Complement theory about what men and women should do (their moral and spiritual duties, ideal love relations, etc.) is based on this conception of what are the fundamental biologically based differences between men and women. The universal human sexual division of labor is not only natural, but also desirable: men should work, provide

[2]See Roger Brown, *Social Psychology* (New York: Free Press, 1965).

for their families, and when necessary, make war; women should stay home, raise their children, and, with their greater emotionality and sensitivity, administer to the emotional needs of their men and children.

The ideal love relationship in the Natural Complement view is a heterosexual relationship in which man and woman complement each other. On this theory, woman needs man, and man, woman; they need each other essentially because together they form a whole being. Each of them is incomplete without the other; neither could meet all their survival and emotional needs alone. The woman needs the man as the active agent, rationally and bravely confronting nature and competitive social life; while the man needs the woman as his emotional guide, ministering to the needs he doesn't know he has himself, performing the same function for the children, and being the emotional nucleus of the family to harmonize all relationships. Love between man and woman is the attraction of complements, each being equally powerful and competent in his or her own sphere—man in the world, woman in the home—but each incompetent in the sphere of the other and therefore incomplete without the other.

The validity of the Natural Complement theory rests on the claim that there are some natural instincts (drives and abilities) inherent in men and women that are so powerful that they will determine the norm of masculine and feminine behavior for men and women under any conceivable cultural and economic conditions. That is, these natural instincts will determine not only what men and women can do well, but also what will be the most desirable (individually satisfying and socially productive) for them.

Even strong proponents of the Natural Complement theory have been uneasy with the evidence that in spite of "natural" differences between men and women, male and female sex roles are not inevitable. Not only are there always individual men and women whose abilities and inclinations make them exceptions to the sexual stereotypes in any particular society, but there is also a wide cross-cultural variation in just what work is considered masculine or feminine. Thus, although all known societies indeed do have a sexual division of labor, the evidence is that what behavior is considered masculine and what feminine is *learned* through socialization rather than mandated through biological instincts. So, for example, child care is said by the proponents of the Natural Complement theory to be women's work, supposedly on the grounds that women have a natural maternal instinct that men lack, due to women's biological role in reproduction. And it is true that in the vast majority of societies in the sexual division of labor women do bear a prime responsibility for child care. However, there are some societies where that is not so. The Arapesh have both mother and father play an equally strong nurturant role.[3] A case of sex-role reversal in child care would be the

3For information on the Arapesh and variations in male/female roles in primitive societies, see Margaret Mead, *Sex and Temperament* (New York: William Morrow, 1963).

fabled Amazons, in whose society those few men allowed to survive past infancy reared the children. In the case of the Amazons, whose historical existence may never be conclusively proved, what is important for the purposes of our argument is not the question of whether such a culture actually existed. Rather, insofar as it indicated that an alternative sexual division of labor was possible, the existence of the myth of the Amazon culture in early Western civilizations was an ongoing challenge to the Natural Complement theory.

It is not only the sexual division of labor in child care that varies from society to society, but also other social tasks. Natural Complement theorists are fond of arguing that because men are physically stronger than women and more aggressive, it is a natural division of labor for men to do the heavy physical work of society as well as that of defense and war. However, in practice, societies have varied immensely in the ways in which heavy physical work is parceled out. In some African societies, women do all the heavy work of carrying wood and water, and in most South American countries Indian men and women share these physical chores. In Russia, women do the heavy manual labor involved in construction jobs, while men do the comparatively light (but higher-status) jobs of running the machinery.[4] In predominantly agricultural societies, women's work overlaps men's. From early American colonial times, farm women had to be prepared to fight native American Indians and work the land in cooperation with men. Israeli women make as aggressive and dedicated soldiers as Israeli men. Furthermore, if we pick any *one* of the traits supposed to be primarily masculine (e.g., competitiveness, aggressiveness, egotism), we will find not only whole societies of both men *and* women who seem to lack these traits, but also whole societies that exhibit them.[5]

Further evidence that general sex-linked personality traits are learned social roles rather than inevitable biological developments is found in studies done on hermaphrodites.[6] When children who are biological girls, but because of vestigial penises are mistaken for boys, are trained into male sex roles, they develop the cultural traits associated with males in their society and seem to be well adjusted to their roles.

Faced with the variability of the sexual division of labor and the evidence that human beings as social animals develop their self-concept and their sense of values from imitating models in their community rather than from innate biological urges, the Natural Complement theorists fall back on the thesis that complementary roles for men and women, while not inevitable, are desirable. Two examples of this approach are found

[4]See "The Political Economy of Women," *Review of Radical Political Economics,* Summer 1973.

[5]Contrast the Stone Age tribe recently discovered in the Philippines, where competition is unknown, with the competitive male and female Dobus from Melanesia. See Ruth Benedict, *Patterns of Culture* (Boston: Houghton Mifflin, 1934).

[6]See Eleanor E. Maccoby, ed., *The Development of Sex Differences* (Stanford, Calif.: Stanford University Press, 1966).

in the writings of Jean-Jacques Rousseau (in *Émile*) and in the contemporary writer George Gilder (in *Sexual Suicide*).[7] Both of these men are clearly male supremacists in that they feel women ought to be taught to serve, nurture, and support men.[8] What is ironic about their arguments is their belief in the biological inferiority of men, stated explicitly in Gilder and implicitly in Rousseau. Rousseau's train of reasoning suggests that men can't be nurturant and emotionally sensitive the way women can, so if we train women to be capable of abstract reasoning, to be self-interested and assertive, women will be able to do both male and female roles, and what will be left, then, for men to excel at? Gilder feels that men need to be socialized to be the breadwinners for children and a nurturant wife, because otherwise men's aggressive and competitive tendencies would make it impossible for them to cooperate in productive social work.

The desirability of complementary sex roles is maintained from a somewhat different set of premises in Lionel Tiger's book *Men in Groups*.[9] Tiger argues that the earliest sexual division of labor in hunting and gathering societies required men to develop a cooperative division of tasks in order to achieve success in hunting. Therefore, men evolved a biological predisposition toward "male bonding" (banding together into all-male cohort groups) that women lack (presumably because activities like gathering and child care didn't require a cooperative division of tasks that would develop female bonding.) Because of this lack of bonding, women are doomed to subjection by men, for this biological asset of men is a trait necessary for achieving political and social power.

It is hard to take these arguments seriously. Obviously, they are biased toward what would promote male interests, and give little consideration to female interests. Also, they reject an androgynous ideal for human development, male and female, merely on the presumption that biological lacks in either men or women make it an unattainable ideal. It simply flies in the face of counter-evidence (for example, single fathers

[7]George Gilder, *Sexual Suicide* (New York: Bantam Books, 1973).

[8]Rousseau says, in a typical passage from *Émile*, "When once it is proved that men and women are and ought to be unlike in constitution and in temperament, it follows that their education should be different." And on a succeeding page he concludes, "A woman's education must therefore be planned in relation to man. To be pleasing in his sight, to win his respect and love, to train him in childhood, to tend him in manhood, to counsel and console, to make his life pleasant and happy, these are the duties of woman for all time, and this is what she should be taught while she is young. The further we depart from this principle, the further we shall be from our own good, and all our precepts will fail to secure her happiness or our own" (trans. Barbara Foxley [New York: E. P. Dutton, 1911] pp. 326, 328).

Gilder's conclusion is as follows: "But at a profounder level the women are tragically wrong. For they fail to understand their own sexual power; and they fail to perceive the sexual constitution of our society, or if they see it, they underestimate its importance to our civilization and to their own interest in order and stability. In general across the whole range of the society, marriage and careers—and thus social order—will be best served if most men have a position of economic superiority over the relevant women in his [*sic*] community and if in most jobs in which colleagues must work together, the sexes tend to be segregated either by level or function." *Sexual Suicide*, p. 108.

[9]Lionel Tiger, *Men in Groups* (New York: Random House, 1969).

in our society) to argue as Gilder does that men will not be providers and relate to family duties of socializing children unless women center their life around the nurturing of men. And to argue as Tiger does that women cannot bond ignores not only the present example of the autonomous women's movement, but also ethnographic examples of women acting as a solidarity group in opposing men. The women of the Ba-Ila in southern Africa may collectively refuse to work if one has a grievance against a man.[10] A more likely theory of bonding seems to be that it is not biologically based, but learned through the organization of productive and reproductive work.

III. HISTORICAL MATERIALIST EXPLANATIONS OF SEX ROLES

Even if we reject the Natural Complement theory's claims that sex roles are either inevitable or desirable, we still have to explain the persistence, through most known societies, of a sexual division of labor and related sexual stereotypes of masculine and feminine behavior. This is due, I shall maintain, to patriarchal power relations between men and women based initially on men's biological advantages in two areas: that women are the biological reproducers of children, and that men as a biological caste are, by and large, physically stronger than women. As Shulamith Firestone argues in *The Dialectic of Sex* and Simone de Beauvoir suggests in *The Second Sex*, the fact that women bear children from their bodies subjects them to the physical weaknesses and constraints that pregnancy and childbirth involve. Being incapacitated for periods of time makes them dependent on men (or at least the community) for physical survival in a way not reciprocated by men. Breast-feeding children, which in early societies continued until the children were five or six years old, meant that women could not hunt or engage in war. Men have both physical and social advantages over women because of their biological reproductive role and the fact that allocating child-rearing to women is the most socially efficient division of reproductive labor in societies with scarce material resources. Thus, in social situations in which men come to perceive their interests to lie in making women subservient to them, men have the edge in a power struggle based on sexual caste.

It is important to note at this point, however, that these biological differences between men and women are only *conditions* which may be *used* against women by men in certain economic and political organizations of society and in social roles. They are like *tools* rather than mandates. A tool is only justified if you agree with both the tool's efficiency and the worth of the task that it is being used for, given other available options in

---

[10]Edwin W. Smith and Andrew M. Dale, *The Ila-Speaking Peoples of Northern Rhodesia* (London: Macmillan, 1920).

achieving the task. In a society with few material resources and no available means of birth control, the most efficient way of ensuring the reproduction of the next generation may be the sexual division of labor in which women, constantly subject to pregnancies, do the reproductive work of breast-feeding and raising the children, while the men engage in hunting, trading, and defense. In a society like ours, on the other hand, where we have the technology and means to control births, feed babies on formula food, and combat physical strength with weapons, the continuation of the sexual division of labor can no longer be justified as the most efficient mode for organizing reproductive work.

It seems that we should look for a social explanation for the continued underdevelopment and unavailability of the material resources for easing women's reproductive burden. This lack is due, I maintain, to a social organization of the forces of reproduction that perpetuates the sexual division of labor at home and in the job market, and thus benefits the perceived interests of men, not women.

.   .   .

V. CONCLUSIONS ABOUT THE NATURAL COMPLEMENT THEORY

We have discussed several different views of the "natural" sex differences between men and women prevalent in different historical periods. When we observe the shift in ideology as to what constitutes "true" female and male nature, we note that the shift has nothing to do with the further scientific discovery of biological differences between men and women. It seems rather to correlate to changes in the relation between men's and women's roles in production and reproduction, and to what serves the interests of the dominant male economic class. Given this fact of its ideological role, the Natural Complement theory, and any other static universal theory of what the "natural relationship" of man to woman should be, loses credibility.

Instead, it seems more plausible to assume that human nature is plastic and moldable, and that women and men develop their sexual identities, their sense of self, and their motivations through responding to the social expectations placed upon them. They develop the skills and personality traits necessary to carry out the productive and reproductive roles available to them in their sociohistorical context, given their sex, race, ethnic identity, and class background.

If we wish to develop a realistic ideal for human development, then, we cannot take the existing traits that differentiate men from women in this society as norms for behavior. Neither can we expect to find an ideal in some biological male and female substratum, after we strip away all the socialization processes we go through to develop our egos. Rather, with the present-day women's movement, we should ask: what traits are desirable and possible to teach people in order for them to reach their full individual human potential? And how would our society have to restructure its productive and reproductive relations in order to allow people to develop in this way?

VI. AN IDEAL LOVE RELATIONSHIP

One argument for the development of androgynous personalities (and the accompanying destruction of the sexual division of labor in production and reproduction) is that without such a radical change in male and female roles an ideal love relationship between the sexes is not possible. The argument goes like this. An ideal love between two mature people would be love between equals. I assume that such an ideal is the only concept of love that is historically compatible with our other developed ideals of political and social equality. But, as Shulamith Firestone argues,[11] an equal love relationship requires the vulnerability of each partner to the other. There is today, however, an unequal balance of power in male-female relationships. Contrary to the claims of the Natural Complement theory, it is not possible for men and women to be equal while playing the complementary sex roles taught in our society. The feminine role makes a woman less equal, less powerful, and less free than the masculine role makes men. In fact, it is the emotional understanding of this lack of equality in love relations between men and women which increasingly influences feminists to choose lesbian love relationships.

Let us consider the vulnerabilities of women in a heterosexual love relationship under the four classifications Juliet Mitchell gives for women's roles:[12] production, reproduction, socialization of children, and sexuality.

1. Women's Role in Production.   In the United States today, 42 percent of women work, and about 33 percent of married women work in the wage-labor force. This is much higher than the 6 percent of women in the wage-labor force around the turn of the century, and higher than in other industrialized countries. Nonetheless, sex-role socialization affects women's power in two important ways. First, because of job segregation by sex into part-time and low-paying jobs, women, whether single or married, are at an economic disadvantage in comparison with men when it comes to supporting themselves. If they leave their husbands or lovers, they drop to a lower economic class, and many have to go on welfare. Second, women who have children and who also work in the wage-labor force have two jobs, not one: the responsibility for the major part of child-raising and housework, as well as the outside job. This keeps many

[11]Shulamith Firestone *The Dialectic of Sex* (New York: William Morrow, 1970), ch. 6.
[12]Juliet Mitchell, *Woman's Estate* (New York: Random House, 1971).

housewives from seeking outside jobs, and makes them economically dependent on their husbands. Those who do work outside the home expend twice as much energy as the man and are less secure. Many women who try to combine career and motherhood find that the demands of both undermine their egos because they don't feel that they can do both jobs adequately.

2. Women's Role in Reproduction.   Although women currently monopolize the means of biological reproduction, they are at a disadvantage because of the absence of free contraceptives, adequate health care, and free legal abortions. A man can enjoy sex without having to worry about the consequences the way a woman does if a mistake occurs and she becomes pregnant. Women have some compensation in the fact that in the United States today they are favored legally over the father in their right to control of the children in case of separation or divorce. But this legal advantage (a victory won by women in the early 20th century in the ongoing power struggle between the sexes for control of children, i.e. control over social reproduction) does not adequately compensate for the disadvantages to which motherhood subjects one in this society.

3. Women's Role in Socialization: As Wife and Mother.   The social status of women, and hence their self-esteem, is measured primarily in terms of how successful they are in their relationships as lovers, wives, and mothers. Unlike men, who learn that their major social definition is success in work, women are taught from childhood that their ultimate goal is love and marriage. Women thus have more invested in a love relationship than men, and more to lose if it fails. The "old maid" or the "divorcee" is still an inferior status to be pitied, while the "swinging bachelor" is rather envied.

The fact that men achieve self- and social definition from their work means that they can feel a lesser commitment to working out problems in a relationship. Furthermore, men have more options for new relationships than do women. The double standard in sexuality allows a man to have affairs more readily than his wife. Ageism is a further limitation on women: an older man is considered a possible lover by both younger and older women, but an older woman, because she is no longer the "ideal" sex object, is not usually considered a desirable lover by either male peers or by younger men.

A woman's role as mother places her in a more vulnerable position than the man. Taking care of children and being attentive to their emotional needs is very demanding work. Many times it involves conflicts between the woman's own needs and the needs of the child. Often it involves conflict and jealousy between husband and children for her attention and emotional energy. It is the woman's role to harmonize this conflict, which she often does at the expense of herself, sacrificing her private time and interests in order to provide support for the projects of her husband and children.

No matter how devoted a parent a father is, he tends to see his time with the children as play time, not as work time. His job interests and hobbies take precedence over directing his energy to children. Thus he is more independent than the woman, who sees her job as making husband and children happy. This is the sort of job that is never completed, for there are always more ways to make people happy. Because a woman sees her job to be supporting her husband and mothering her children, the woman sees the family as her main "product." This makes her dependent on their activities, lives, and successes for her own success, and she lives vicariously through their activities. But as her "product" is human beings, when the children leave, as they must, to live independent lives, middle age brings an end to her main social function. The woman who has a career has other problems, for she has had to support her husband's career over hers wherever there was a conflict, because she knows male egos are tied up with success and "making it" in this competitive society. Women's egos, on the other hand, are primed for failure. Successful women, especially successful women with unsuccessful husbands, are considered not "true" women, but rather as deviants, "castrating bitches," "ball-busters," and "masculine women." For all these reasons, a woman in a love relationship with a man is geared by the Natural Complement view of herself as a woman to put her interests last, to define herself in terms of husband and children, and therefore to be more dependent on them than they are on her.

A woman is also vulnerable in her role as mother because there are limited alternatives if, for example, she wishes to break off her relationship with the father of her children. As a mother, her social role in bringing up children is defined as more important, more essential for the well-being of the children than the man's. Therefore, she is expected to take the children to live with her, or else she is considered a failure as a mother. But the life of a divorced or single mother with children in a nuclear-family-oriented society is lonely and hard: she must now either do two jobs without the companionship of another adult, in a society where jobs for women are inadequate, or she must survive on welfare or alimony with a reduced standard of living. When this is the alternative, is it any wonder that mothers are more dependent on maintaining a relationship—even when it is not satisfying—than the man is?

4. Women's Role in Sexuality.   A woman's sexual role is one in which she is both elevated by erotic romanticism and deflated to being a mere "cunt"—good for release of male sexual passions but interchangeable with other women. Because women play a subordinate role in society and are not seen as equal agents or as equally productive, men must justify a relationship with a particular woman by making her something special, mystifying her, making her better than other women. In fact, this idealization doesn't deal with her as a real *individual*; it treats her as either a beautiful object or as a mothering, supportive figure.

This idealization of women which occurs in the first stages of infatuation wears off as the couple settles into a relationship of some duration. What is left is the idea of woman as passive sex object whom one possesses and whose job as wife is to give the husband pleasure in bed. Since the woman is not seen as (and doesn't usually see herself as) active in sex, she tends to see sex as a duty rather than as a pleasure. She is not socially expected to take the active kind of initiative (even to the extent of asking for a certain kind of sex play) that would give her a sense of control over her sex life. The idea of herself as a body to be dressed and clothed in the latest media-advertised fashions "to please men" keeps her a slave to fashion and forces her to change her ego-ideal with every change in fashion. She can't see herself as an individual.

VII. ANDROGYNY AS A PROGRESSIVE IDEAL

It is the sexual division of labor in the home and at work that perpetuates complementary sex roles for men and women. In underdeveloped societies with scarce material resources such an arrangement may indeed be the most rational way to allow for the most efficient raising of children and production of goods. But this is no longer true for developed societies. In this age of advanced technology, men's relative strength compared to women's is no longer important, either in war or in the production of goods. The gun and the spinning jenny have equalized the potential role of men and women in both repression and production. And the diaphragm, the pill, and other advances in the technology of reproduction have equalized the potential power of women and men to control their bodies and to reproduce themselves.[13] (The development of cloning would mean that men and women could reproduce without the participation of the opposite sex.)

We have seen how complementary sex roles and their extension to job segregation in wage labor make an ideal love relationship between equals impossible for men and women in our society. The questions that remain are: would the development of androgynous human beings through androgynous sex-role training be possible? If possible, would it allow for the development of equal love relationships? What other human potentials would androgyny allow to develop? And how would society have to be restructured in order to allow for androgynous human beings and equal love relationships?

There is good evidence that human babies are bisexual, and only *learn* a specific male or female identity by imitating and identifying with adult models. This evidence comes from the discovery that all human beings possess both male and female hormones (androgen and estrogen respectively), and also from concepts first developed at length by Freud. Freud argued that heterosexual identity is not achieved until the third

[13]Thanks to Sam Bowles for this point.

stage of the child's sexual development. Sex identity is developed through the resolution of the Oedipus complex, in which the child has to give up a primary attachment to the mother and learn either to identify with, or love, the father. But Shulamith Firestone suggests that this process is not an inevitable one, as Freud presents it to be. Rather, it is due to the power dynamics of the patriarchal nuclear family.[14] Note that on this analysis, if the sexual division of labor were destroyed, the mechanism that trains boys and girls to develop heterosexual sexual identities would also be destroyed. If fathers and mothers played equal nurturant roles in child-rearing and had equal social, economic, and political power outside the home, there would be no reason for the boy to have to reject his emotional side in order to gain the power associated with the male role. Neither would the girl have to assume a female role in rejecting her assertive, independent side in order to attain power indirectly through manipulation of males. As a sexual identity, bisexuality would then be the norm rather than the exception.

If bisexuality were the norm rather than the exception for the sexual identities that children develop,[15] androgynous sex roles would certainly be a consequence. For, as discussed above, the primary mechanism whereby complementary rather than androgynous sex roles are maintained is through heterosexual training, and through the socialization of

[14]Firestone, op. cit. The boy and girl both realize that the father has power in the relationship between him and the mother, and that his role, and not the mother's, represents the possibility of achieving economic and social power in the world and over one's life. The mother, in contrast, represents nurturing and emotionality. Both boy and girl, then, in order to get power for themselves, have to reject the mother as a love object—the boy, because he is afraid of the father as rival and potential castrator; and the girl, because the only way as a girl she can attain power is through manipulating the father. So she becomes a rival to her mother for her father's love. The girl comes to identify with her mother and to choose her father and, later, other men for love objects; while the boy identifies with his father, sublimates his sexual attraction to his mother into superego (will power), and chooses mother substitutes, other women, for his love objects.

[15]It should be understood here that no claim is being made that bisexuality is more desirable than homo- or heterosexuality. The point is that with the removal of the social mechanisms in the family that channel children into heterosexuality, there is no reason to suppose that most of them will develop in that direction. It would be more likely that humans with androgynous personalities would be bisexual, the assumption here being that there are no innate biological preferences in people for sexual objects of the same or opposite sex. Rather, this comes to be developed because of emotional connections of certain sorts of personality characteristics with the male and female body, characteristics which develop because of complementary sex-role training, and which would not be present without it.

The other mechanism which influences people to develop a heterosexual identity is the desire to reproduce. As long as the social institution for raising children is the heterosexual nuclear family, and as long as society continues to place social value on biological parenthood, most children will develop a heterosexual identity. Not, perhaps, in early childhood, but certainly after puberty, when the question of reproduction becomes viable. Radical socialization and collectivization of child-rearing would thus have to characterize a society before bisexuality would be the norm not only in early childhood, but in adulthood as well. For the purposes of developing androgynous individuals, however, full social bisexuality of this sort is not necessary. All that is needed is the restructuring of the sex roles of father and mother in the nuclear family so as to eliminate the sexual division of labor there.

needs for love and sexual gratification to the search for a love partner of the opposite sex. Such a partner is sought to complement one in the traits that one has repressed or not developed because in one's own sex such traits were not socially accepted.

VIII. THE ANDROGYNOUS MODEL

I believe that only androgynous people can attain the full human potential possible given our present level of material and social resources (and this only if society is radically restructured). Only such people can have ideal love relationships: and without such relationships, I maintain that none can develop to the fullest potential. Since human beings are social animals and develop through interaction and productive activity with others, such relationships are necessary.

Furthermore, recent studies have shown that the human brain has two distinct functions: one associated with analytic, logical, sequential thinking (the left brain), and the other associated with holistic, meta-phorical, intuitive thought (the right brain). Only a person capable of tapping both these sides of him/herself will have developed to full poten-tial. We might call this characteristic of the human brain "psychic bisexu-ality,"[16] since it has been shown that women in fact have developed skills which allow them to tap the abilities of the right side of the brain more than men, who on the contrary excel in the analytic, logical thought characteristic of the left side. The point is that men and women have the potential for using both these functions, and yet our socialization at present tends to cut off from one or the other of these parts of ourselves.

What would an androgynous personality be like? My model for the ideal androgynous person comes from the concept of human potential developed by Marx in *Economic and Philosophical Manuscripts.* Marx's idea is that human beings have a need (or a potential) for free, creative, productive activity which allows them to control their lives in a situation of cooperation with others. Both men and women need to be equally active and independent; with an equal sense of control over their lives; equal opportunity for creative, productive activity; and a sense of mean-ingful involvement in the community.

Androgynous women would be just as assertive as men about their own needs in a love relationship: productive activity outside the home, the right to private time, and the freedom to form other intimate personal and sexual relationships. I maintain that being active and assertive—traits now associated with being "masculine"—are positive traits that all people need to develop. Many feminists are suspicious of the idea of self-asser-tion because it is associated with the traits of aggression and competitive-ness. However, there is no inevitability to this connection: it results from

[16]Charlotte Painter, Afterword to C. Painter and M. J. Moffet, eds., *Revelations: Diaries of Women* (New York: Random House, 1975).

the structural features of competitive, hierarchical economic systems, of which our own (monopoly capitalism) is one example. In principle, given the appropriate social structure, there is no reason why a self-assertive person cannot also be nurturant and cooperative.

Androgynous men would be more sensitive and aware of emotions than sex-role stereotyped "masculine" men are today. They would be more concerned with the feelings of all people, including women and children, and aware of conflicts of interests. Being sensitive to human emotions is necessary to an effective care and concern for others. Such sensitivity is now thought of as a "motherly," "feminine," or "maternal" instinct, but in fact it is a role and skill learned by women, and it can equally well be learned by men. Men need to get in touch with their own feelings in order to empathize with others, and, indeed, to understand themselves better so as to be more in control of their actions.

We have already discussed the fact that women are more vulnerable in a love relationship than men because many men consider a concern with feelings and emotions to be part of the woman's role. Women, then, are required to be more aware of everyone's feelings (if children and third parties are involved) than men, and they are under more pressure to harmonize the conflicts by sacrificing their own interests.

Another important problem with a non-androgynous love relationship is that it limits the development of mutual understanding. In general, it seems true that the more levels people can relate on, the deeper and more intimate their relationship is. The more experiences and activities they share, the greater their companionship and meaning to each other. And this is true for emotional experiences. Without mutual understanding of the complex of emotions involved in an ongoing love relationship, communication and growth on that level are blocked for both people. This means that, for both people, self-development of the sort that could come from the shared activity of understanding and struggling to deal with conflicts will not be possible.

In our society as presently structured, there are few possibilities for men and women to develop themselves through shared activities. Men and women share more activities with members of their own sex than with each other. Most women can't get jobs in our sexist, job-segregated society which allow them to share productive work with men. Most men just don't have the skills (or the time, given the demands of their wage-labor jobs) to understand the emotional needs of children and to share the activity of child-rearing equally with their wives.

How must our society be restructured to allow for the development of androgynous personalities? How can it be made to provide for self-development through the shared activities of productive and reproductive work? I maintain that this will not be possible (except for a small privileged elite) without the development of a democratic socialist society. In such a society no one would benefit from cheap labor (presently provided to the capitalist class by a part-time reserve army of women). Nor would anyone benefit from hierarchical power relationships (which encourage competition among the working class and reinforce male sex-role stereotypes as necessary to "making it" in society).

As society is presently constituted, the patriarchal nuclear family and women's reproductive work therein serve several crucial roles in maintaining the capitalist system. In the family, women do the unpaid work of social reproduction of the labor force (child-rearing). They also pacify and support the male breadwinner in an alienating society where men who are not in the capitalist class have little control of their product or work conditions. Men even come to envy their wives' relatively non-alienated labor in child-rearing rather than dealing with those with the real privilege, the capitalist class. Since those in power relations never give them up without a struggle, it is utopian to think that the capitalist class will allow for the elimination of the sexual division of labor without a socialist revolution with feminist priorities. Furthermore, men in the professional and working classes must be challenged by women with both a class and feminist consciousness to begin the process of change.

In order to eliminate the subordination of women in the patriarchal nuclear family and the perpetuation of sex-role stereotypes therein, there will need to be a radical reorganization of child-rearing. Father and mother must have an equal commitment to raising children. More of the reproductive work must be socialized—for example, by community child care, perhaps with parent cooperatives. Communal living is one obvious alternative which would de-emphasize biological parenthood and allow homosexuals and bisexuals the opportunity to have an equal part in relating to children. The increased socialization of child care would allow parents who are incompatible the freedom to dissolve their relationships without denying their children the secure, permanent loving relationships they need with both men and women. A community responsibility for child-rearing would provide children with male and female models other than their biological parent—models that they would be able to see and relate to emotionally.

Not only would men and women feel an equal responsibility to do reproductive work, they would also expect to do rewarding, productive work in a situation where they had equal opportunity. Such a situation would of course require reduced work-weeks for parents, maternity and paternity leaves, and the development of a technology of reproduction which would allow women complete control over their bodies.

As for love relationships, with the elimination of sex roles and the disappearance, in an overpopulated world, of any biological need for sex to be associated with procreation, there would be no reason why such a society could not transcend sexual gender. It would no longer matter what biological sex individuals had. Love relationships, and the sexual relationships developing out of them, would be based on the individual meshing-together of androgynous human beings.

SECTION ELEVEN

SOCIAL RESPONSIBILITY AND MORALITY

When most people think of moral dilemmas, they tend to think in highly personal and immediate terms. "If I make a promise, do I have an obligation to keep it?" "Is it moral to have an abortion?" "Am I obligated to help a friend in need?" Such questions are difficult to answer, precisely because we usually recognize some degree of moral responsibility for persons and things in the immediate area of our concern. But, it often turns out that the same person who would feel morally bound to feed a starving child, if one turned up on her or his doorstep, would not feel the same obligation to help a poverty-ridden family living on the other side of town or to contribute to an organization that undertakes to feed children in Africa or Asia.

The unequal distribution of wealth and opportunity within American society, as well as the fact that the United States is responsible for fifty percent of the world's yearly consumption of raw materials, while constituting no more than six percent of the world's total population, raises all kinds of questions about the causes of suffering at home and abroad and about our responsibility to alleviate such suffering.

As difficult as it might be to determine to what extent individuals can be held responsible for such suffering, even more difficult is the question of whether or not we can blame collective entities, such as corporations or entire populations, for actions carried out by them, or in their name. The essays that follow represent attempts to raise and deal with such problems, problems thrust upon us due to both the relative abundance in America and its unequal distribution, and the growth of a worldwide media system, which makes it possible for people to stay at home in their living rooms but still share the plight of those who are suffering around the corner or halfway around the world.

William Ryan
BLAMING THE VICTIM

William Ryan teaches psychology and writes extensively on the fields of mental health and social problems. Concerned with the poverty and racial injustice that plague American society, Ryan argues that a serious obstacle to correctly defining and solving these problems lies in the prevailing ideology of placing the blame on the victim. This ideology so distorts our views and disorients our thinking that we often end up holding the victims of social ills responsible for their own misery, instead of seeking the social and economic causes of their plight.

I

Twenty years ago, Zero Mostel used to do a sketch in which he impersonated a Dixiecrat Senator conducting an investigation of the orgins of World War II. At the climax of the sketch, the Senator boomed out, in an excruciating mixture of triumph and suspicion, "What was Pearl Harbor *doing* in the Pacific?" This is an extreme example of Blaming the Victim.

Twenty years ago, we could laugh at Zero Mostel's caricature. In recent years, however, the same process has been going on every day in the arena of social problems, public health, anti-poverty programs, and social welfare. A philosopher might analyze this process and prove that, technically, it is comic. But it is hardly ever funny.

Consider some victims. One is the miseducated child in the slum school. He is blamed for his own miseducation. He is said to contain within himself the causes of his inability to read and write well. The shorthand phrase is "cultural deprivation," which, to those in the know, conveys what they allege to be inside information: that the poor child carries a scanty pack of cultural baggage as he enters school. He doesn't know about books and magazines and newspapers, they say. (No books in the home: the mother fails to subscribe to *Reader's Digest*.) They say that if he talks at all—an unlikely event since slum parents don't talk to their children—he certainly doesn't talk correctly. (Lower-class dialect spoken here, or even—God forbid!—Southern Negro. *Ici on parle nigra.*) If you can manage to get him to sit in a chair, they say, he squirms and looks out the window. (Impulse-ridden, these kids, motoric rather than verbal.) In a word he is "disadvantaged" and "socially deprived," they say, and this, of course, accounts for his failure (*his* failure, they say) to learn much in school.

Note the similarity to the logic of Zero Mostel's Dixiecrat Senator. What is the culturally deprived child *doing* in the school? What is wrong with the victim? In pursuing this logic, no one remembers to ask questions about the collapsing buildings and torn textbooks, the frightened, insensitive teachers, the six additional desks in the room, the blustering, frightened principals, the relentless segregation, the callous administrator, the irrelevant curriculum, the bigoted or cowardly members of the school board, the insulting history book, the stingy taxpayers, the fairy-tale readers, or the self-serving faculty of the local teachers' college. We are encouraged to confine our attention to the child and to dwell on all his alleged defects. Cultural deprivation becomes an omnibus explanation for the educational disaster area known as the inner-city school. This is Blaming the Victim.

Pointing to the supposedly deviant Negro family as the "fundamental weakness of the Negro community" is another way to blame the victim. Like "cultural deprivation," "Negro family" has become a shorthand phrase with stereotyped connotations of matriarchy, fatherlessness, and pervasive illegitimacy. Growing up in the "crumbling" Negro family is supposed to account for most of the racial evils in America. Insiders have the word, of course, and know that this phrase is supposed to evoke images of growing up with a long-absent or never-present father (replaced from time to time perhaps by a series of transient lovers) and with bossy women ruling the roost, so that the children are irreparably damaged. This refers particularly to the poor, bewildered male children, whose psyches are fatally wounded and who are never, alas, to learn the trick of becoming upright, downright, forthright all-American boys. Is it any wonder the Negroes cannot achieve equality? From such families! And, again, by focusing our attention on the Negro family as the apparent *cause* of racial inequality, our eye is diverted. Racism, discrimination, segregation, and the powerlessness of the ghetto are subtly, but thoroughly, downgraded in importance.

The generic process of Blaming the Victim is applied to almost every American problem. The miserable health care of the poor is explained away on the grounds that the victim has poor motivation and lacks health information. The problems of slum housing are traced to the characteristics of tenants who are labeled as "Southern rural migrants" not yet "acculturated" to life in the big city. The "multiproblem" poor, it is claimed, suffer the psychological effects of impoverishment, the "culture of poverty," and the deviant value system of the lower classes; consequently, though unwittingly, they cause their own troubles. From such a viewpoint, the obvious fact that poverty is primarily an absence of money is easily overlooked or set aside.

The growing number of families receiving welfare are fallaciously linked together with the increased number of illegitimate children as twin results of promiscuity and sexual abandon among members of the lower orders. Every important social problem—crime, mental illness, civil disorder, unemployment—has been analyzed within the framework of the victim-blaming ideology. In the following pages, I shall present in detail nine examples that relate to social problems and human services in urban areas.

It would be possible for me to venture into other areas—one finds a perfect example in literature about the underdeveloped countries of the Third World, in which the lack of prosperity and technological progress is attributed to some aspect of the national character of the people, such as lack of "achievement motivation"—but I plan to stay within the confines of my own personal and professional experience, which is, generally, with racial injustice, social welfare, and human services in the city.

I have been listening to the victim-blamers and pondering their thought processes for a number of years. That process is often very subtle. Victim-blaming is cloaked in kindness and concern, and bears all the trappings and statistical furbelows of scientism; it is obscured by a perfumed haze of humanitarianism. In observing the process of Blaming the Victim, one tends to be confused and disoriented because those who practice this art display a deep concern for the victims that is quite genuine. In this way, the new ideology is very different from the open prejudice and reactionary tactics of the old days. Its adherents include sympathetic social scientists with social consciences in good working order, and liberal politicians with a genuine commitment to reform. They are very careful to dissociate themselves from vulgar Calvinism or crude racism; they indignantly condemn any notions of innate wickedness or genetic defect. "The Negro is *not born* inferior," they shout apoplectically. "Force of circumstance," they explain in reasonable tones, "has *made* him inferior." And they dismiss with self-righteous contempt any claims that the poor man in America is plainly unworthy or shiftless or enamored of idleness. No, they say, he is "caught in the cycle of poverty." He is trained to be poor by his culture and his family life, endowed by his environment (perhaps by his ignorant mother's outdated style of toilet training) with those unfortunately unpleasant characteristics that make him ineligible for a passport into the affluent society.

Blaming the Victim is, of course, quite different from old-fashioned conservative ideologies. The latter simply dismissed victims as inferior, genetically defective, or morally unfit; the emphasis is on the intrinsic, even hereditary, defect. The former shifts its emphasis to the environmental causation. The old-fashioned conservative could hold firmly to the belief that the oppressed and the victimized were born that way—"that way" being defective or inadequate in character or ability. The new ideology attributes defect and inadequacy to the malignant nature of poverty, injustice, slum life, and racial difficulties. The stigma that marks the victim and accounts for his victimization is an acquired stigma, a stigma of social, rather than genetic, origin. But the stigma, the defect, the fatal difference—though derived in the past from environmental forces—is still located *within* the victim, inside his skin. With such an elegant formulation, the humanitarian can have it both ways. He can, all at the same time, concentrate his charitable interest on the defects of the victim, condemn the vague social and environmental stresses that produced the defect (some time ago), and ignore the continuing effect of victimizing social forces (right now). It is a brilliant ideology for justifying a perverse form of social action designed to change, not society, as one might expect, but rather society's victim.

As a result, there is a terrifying sameness in the programs that arise from this kind of analysis. In education, we have programs of "compensatory education" to build up the skills and attitudes of the ghetto child, rather than structural changes in the schools. In race relations, we have social engineers who think up ways of "strengthening" the Negro family, rather than methods of eradicating racism. In health care, we develop new programs to provide health information (to correct the supposed ignorance of the poor) and to reach out and discover cases of untreated illness and disability (to compensate for their supposed unwillingness to seek treatment). Meanwhile, the gross inequities of our medical care delivery systems are left completely unchanged. As we might expect, the logical outcome of analyzing social problems in terms of the deficiencies of the victim is the development of programs aimed at correcting those deficiencies. The formula for action becomes extraordinarily simple: change the victim.

All of this happens so smoothly that it seems downright rational. First, identify a social problem. Second, study those affected by the problem and discover in what ways they are different from the rest of us as a consequence of deprivation and injustice. Third, define the differences as the cause of the social problem itself. Finally, of course, assign a government bureaucrat to invent a humanitarian action program to correct the differences.

Now no one in his right mind would quarrel with the assertion that social problems are present in abundance and are readily identifiable. God knows it is true that when hundreds of thousands of poor children drop out of school—or even graduate from school—they are barely literate. After spending some ten thousand hours in the company of professional educators, these children appear to have learned very little. The fact of failure in their education is undisputed. And the racial situation in America is usually acknowledged to be a number one item on the nation's agenda. Despite years of marches, commissions, judicial decisions, and endless legislative remedies, we are confronted with unchanging or even widening racial differences in achievement. In addition, despite our assertions that Americans get the best health care in the world, the poor stubbornly remain unhealthy. They lose more work because of illness, have more carious teeth, lose more babies as a result of both miscarriage and infant death, and die considerably younger than the well-to-do.

The problems are there, and there in great quantities. They make us uneasy. Added together, these disturbing signs reflect inequality and a puzzlingly high level of unalleviated distress in America totally inconsistent with our proclaimed ideals and our enormous wealth. This thread —this rope—of inconsistency stands out so visibly in the fabric of American life, that it is jarring to the eye. And this must be explained, to the satisfaction of our conscience as well as our patriotism. Blaming the Victim is an ideal, almost painless, evasion.

The second step in applying this explanation is to look sympathetically at those who "have" the problem in question, to separate them out and define them in some way as a special group, a group that is *different* from the population in general. This is a crucial and essential step in the process, for that difference is in itself hampering and maladaptive. The Different Ones are seen as less competent, less skilled, less knowing—in short, less human. The ancient Greeks deduced from a single characteristic, a difference in language, that the barbarians—that is, the "babblers" who spoke a strange tongue—were wild, uncivilized, dangerous, rapacious, uneducated, lawless, and, indeed, scarcely more than animals. Automatically labeling strangers as savages, weird and inhuman creatures (thus explaining difference by exaggerating difference) not infrequently justifies mistreatment, enslavement, or even extermination of the Different Ones.

Blaming the Victim depends on a very similar process of identification (carried out, to be sure, in the most kindly, philanthropic, and intellectual manner) whereby the victim of social problems is identified as strange, different—in other words, as a barbarian, a savage. Discovering savages, then, is an essential component of, and prerequisite to, Blaming the Victim, and the art of Savage Discovery is a core skill that must be acquired by all aspiring Victim Blamers. They must learn how to demonstrate that the poor, the black, the ill, the jobless, the slum tenants, are different and strange. They must learn to conduct or interpret the research that shows how "these people" think in different forms, act in different patterns, cling to different values, seek different goals, and learn different truths. Which is to say that they are strangers, barbarians, savages. This is how the distressed and disinherited are redefined in order to make it possible for us to look at society's problems and to attribute their causation to the individuals affected.

II

Blaming the Victim is an ideological process, which is to say that it is a set of ideas and concepts deriving from systematically motivated, but *unintended,* distortions of reality. In the sense that Karl Mannheim[1] used the term, an ideology develops from the "collective unconscious" of a group or class and is rooted in a class-based interest in maintaining the *status quo* (as contrasted with what he calls a *utopia,* a set of ideas rooted

[1]Karl Mannheim, *Ideology and Utopia,* trans. Louis Wirth and Edward Shils (New York: Harcourt, Brace & World, Inc., A Harvest Book, 1936). First published in German in 1929.

in a class-based interest in *changing* the *status quo*). An ideology, then, has several components: First, there is the belief system itself, the way of looking at the world, the set of ideas and concepts. Second, there is the systematic distortion of reality reflected in those ideas. Third is the condition that distortion must not be a conscious, intentional process. Finally, though they are not intentional, the ideas must serve a specific function: maintaining the *status quo* in the interest of a specific group. Blaming the Victim fits this definition on all counts, as I will attempt to show in detail in the following chapters. Most particularly, it is important to realize that Blaming the Victim is not a process of *intentional* distortion although it does serve the class interests of those who practice it. And it has a rich ancestry in American thought about social problems and how to deal with them.

Thinking about social problems is especially susceptible to ideological influences since, as John Seeley has pointed out,[2] defining a social problem is not so simple. "What is a social problem?" may seem an ingenuous question until one turns to confront its opposite: "What human problem is *not* a social problem?" Since any problem in which people are involved is social, why do we reserve the label for some problems in which people are involved and withhold it from others? To use Seeley's example, why is crime called a social problem when university administration is not? The phenomena we look at are bounded by the act of definition. They become social problems only by being so considered. In Seeley's words, "*naming* it as a problem, after naming it as a *problem.*"

It is only recently, for example, that we have begun to *name* the rather large quantity of people on earth as the *problem* of overpopulation, or the population explosion. Such phenomena often become proper predicaments for certain solutions, certain treatments. Before the 1930's, the most anti-Semitic German was unaware that Germany had a "Jewish problem." It took the Nazis to *name* the simple existence of Jews in the Third Reich as a "social problem," and that act of definition helped to shape the final solution.

We have removed "immigration" from our list of social problems (after executing a solution—choking off the flow of immigrants) and have added "urbanization. Nowadays, we define the situation of men out of work as the social problem of "unemployment" rather than, as in Elizabethan times, that of "idleness." (The McCone Commission, investigating the Watts Riot of 1966, showed how hard old ideologies die; it specified both unemployment *and* idleness as causes of the disorder.) In the near future, if we are to credit the prophets of automation, the label "unemployment" will fade away and "idleness," now renamed the "leisure-time problem," will begin again to raise its lazy head. We have been

[2]John Seeley, "The Problems of Social Problems," *Indian Sociological Bulletin,* II, No. 3 (April, 1965). Reprinted as Chapter Ten in *The Americanization of the Unconscious* (New York: International Science Press, 1967), pp. 142–48.

comfortable for years with the "Negro problem," a term that clearly implies that the existence of Negroes is somehow a problematic fact. *Ebony* magazine turned the tables recently and renamed the phenomenon as "The White Problem in America," which may be a good deal more accurate.

We must particularly ask, "To whom are social problems a problem?" And usually, if truth were to be told, we would have to admit that we mean they are a problem to those of us who are outside the boundaries of what we have defined as the problem. Negroes are a problem to racist whites, welfare is a problem to stingy taxpayers, delinquency is a problem to nervous property owners.

Now, if this is the quality of our assumptions about social problems, we are led unerringly to certain beliefs about the causes of these problems. We cannot comfortably believe that *we* are the cause of that which is problematic to us; therefore, we are almost compelled to believe that *they*—the problematic ones—are the cause and this immediately prompts us to search for deviance. Identification of the deviance as the cause of the problem is a simple step that ordinarily does not even require evidence.

C. Wright Mills analyzed the ideology of those who write about social problems and demonstrated the relationship of their texts to class interest and to the preservation of the existent social order.[3] In sifting the material in thirty-one widely used textbooks in "social problems," "social pathology," and "social disorganization," Mills found a pervasive, coherent ideology with a number of common characteristics.

First, the textbooks present material about these problems, he says, in simple, descriptive terms, with each problem unrelated to the others and none related in any meaningful way to other aspects of the social environment. Second, the problems are selected and described largely according to predetermined norms. Poverty is a problem in that it deviates from the standard of economic self-sufficiency; divorce is a problem because the family is supposed to remain intact; crime and delinquency are problematic insofar as they depart from the accepted moral and legal standards of the community. The norms themselves are taken as givens, and no effort is made to examine them. Nor is there any thought given to the manner in which norms might themselves contribute to the development of the problems. (In a society in which everyone is assumed and expected to be economically self-sufficient, as an example, doesn't economic dependency almost automatically mean poverty? No attention is given to such issues.)

Within such a framework, then, deviation from norms and standards comes to be defined as failed or incomplete socialization—failure to learn the rules or the inability to learn how to keep to them. Those with social

[3]C. Wright Mills, "The Professional Ideology of Social Pathologists," *American Journal of Sociology*, XLIX, No. 2 (September, 1943), pp. 165–80.

problems are then viewed as unable or unwilling to adjust to society's standards, which are narrowly conceived by what Mills calls "independent middle class persons verbally living out Protestant ideas in small town America." This, obviously, is a precise description of the social origins and status of almost every one of the authors.

In defining social problems in this way, the social pathologists are, of course, ignoring a whole set of factors that ordinarily might be considered relevant—for instance, unequal distribution of income, social stratification, political struggle, ethnic and racial group conflict, and inequality of power. Their ideology concentrates almost exclusively on the failure of the deviant. To the extent that society plays any part in social problems, it is said to have somehow failed to socialize the individual, to teach him how to adjust to circumstances, which, though far from perfect, are gradually changing for the better. Mills' essay provides a solid foundation for understanding the concept of Blaming the Victim.

This way of thinking on the part of "social pathologists," which Mills identified as the predominant tool used in *analyzing* social problems, also saturates the majority of programs that have been developed to *solve* social problems in America. These programs are based on the assumption that *individuals* "have" social problems as a result of some kind of unusual circumstances—accident, illness, personal defect or handicap, character flaw or maladjustment—that exclude them from using the ordinary mechanisms for maintaining and advancing themselves. For example, the prevalent belief in America is that, under normal circumstances, everyone can obtain sufficient income for the necessities of life. Those who are unable to do so are special deviant cases, persons who for one reason or another are not able to adapt themselves to the generally satisfactory income-producing system. In times gone by these persons were further classified into the worthy poor—the lame, the blind, the young mother whose husband died in an accident, the aged man no longer able to work—and the unworthy poor—the lazy, the unwed mother and her illegitimate children, the malingerer. All were seen, however, as individuals who, for good reasons or bad, were personal failures, unable to adapt themselves to the system.

In America health care, too, has been predominantly a matter of particular remedial attention provided individually to the more or less random group of persons who have become ill, whose bodily functioning has become deviant and abnormal. In the field of mental health, the same approach has been, and continues to be, dominant. The social problem of mental disease has been viewed as a collection of individual cases of deviance, persons who—through unusual hereditary taint, or exceptional distortion of character—have become unfit for normal activities. The solution to these problems was to segregate the deviants, to protect them, to give them *asylum* from the life of the community for which they were no longer competent.

This has been the dominant style in American social welfare and health activities, then: to treat what we call social problems, such as poverty, disease, and mental illness, in terms of the individual deviance of the special, unusual groups of persons who had those problems. There has also been a competing style, however—much less common, not at all congruent with the prevalent ideology, but continually developing parallel to the dominant style.

Adherents of this approach tended to search for defects in the community and the environment rather than in the individual; to emphasize predictability and usualness rather than random deviance; they tried to think about preventing rather than merely repairing or treating—to see social problems, in a word, as social. In the field of disease, this approach was termed public health, and its practitioners sought the cause of disease in such things as the water supply, the sewage system, the density and quality of housing conditions. They set out to prevent disease, not in individuals, but in the total population, through improved sanitation, inoculation against communicable disease, and the policing of housing conditions. In the field of income maintenance, this secondary style of solving social problems focused on poverty as a predictable event, on the regularities of income deficiency. And it concentrated on the development of standard, generalized programs affecting total groups. Rather than trying to fit the aged worker ending his career into some kind of category of special cases, it assumed all sixty-five-year-old men should expect to retire from the world of work and have the security of an old age pension, to be arranged through public social activity. Unemployment insurance was developed as a method whereby all workers could be protected against the effects of the normal ups and downs of the business cycle. A man out of work could then count on an unemployment check rather than endure the agony of pauperizing himself, selling his tools or his car, and finding himself in the special category of those deserving of charity.

These two approaches to the solution of social problems have existed side by side, the former always dominant, but the latter gradually expanding, slowly becoming more and more prevalent.

Elsewhere[4] I have proposed the dimension of *exceptionalism-universalism* as the ideological underpinning for these two contrasting approaches to the analysis and solution of social problems. The *exceptionalist* viewpoint is reflected in arrangements that are private, voluntary, remedial, special, local, and exclusive. Such arrangements imply that problems occur to specially-defined categories of persons in an unpredictable man-

---

[4]William Ryan, "Community Care in Historical Perspective: Implications for Mental Health Services and Professionals," *Canada's Mental Health,* supplement No. 60, March–April, 1969. This formulation draws on, and is developed from, the *residential-institutional* dimension outlined in H. L. Wilensky and C. N. Lebeaux, *Industrial Society and Social Welfare* (paperback ed.; New York: The Free Press, 1965). Originally published by Russell Sage Foundation, 1958.

ner. The problems are unusual, even unique, they are exceptions to the rule, they occur as a result of individual defect, accident, or unfortunate circumstance and must be remedied by means that are particular and, as it were, tailored to the individual case.

The universalistic viewpoint, on the other hand, is reflected in arrangements that are public, legislated, promotive or preventive, general, national, and inclusive. Inherent in such a viewpoint is the idea that social problems are a function of the social arrangements of the community or the society and that, since these social arrangements are quite imperfect and inequitable, such problems are both predictable and, more important, preventable through public action. They are not unique to the individual, and the fact that they encompass individual persons does not imply that those persons are themselves defective or abnormal.

Consider these two contrasting approaches as they are applied to the problem of smallpox. The medical care approach is exceptionalistic; it is designed to provide remedial treatment to the special category of persons who are afflicted with the disease through a private, voluntary arrangement with a local doctor. The universalistic public health approach is designed to provide preventive inoculation to the total population, ordered by legislation and available through public means if no private arrangements can be made.

A similar contrast can be made between an exceptionalistic assistance program such as Aid to Families with Dependent Children and the proposed universalistic program of family allowances based simply on the number of children in a family. The latter assumes that the size of a family should automatically be a consideration in income supplementation, since it is in no way taken into account in the wage structure, and that it should be dealt with in a routine and universal fashion. The AFDC program, on the other hand, assumes that families need income assistance only as a result of special, impoverishing circumstances.

Fluoridation is universalistic; it is aimed at preventing caries in the total population; oral surgery is exceptionalistic, designed to remedy the special cases of infection or neglect that damage the teeth of an individual. Birth control is universalistic; abortion exceptionalistic. It has been said that navigational aids have saved far more lives than have rescue devices, no matter how refined they might be. The compass, then, is universalistic, while the lifeboat is exceptionalistic.

The similarity between exceptionalism and what Mills called the "ideology of social pathologists" is readily apparent. Indeed, the ideological potential of the exceptionalist viewpoint is unusually great. If one is inclined to explain all instances of deviance, all social problems, all occasions on which help is provided to others as the result of unusual circumstances, defect, or accident, one is unlikely to inquire about social inequalities.

This is not to devalue valid exceptionalistic services. Despite fluoridation, some instances of caries and gum disease will require attention; despite excellent prenatal care, handicapped children will occasionally be born; husbands will doubtless continue to die unexpectedly at early ages, leaving widows and orphans in need. And at any given moment, the end products of society's malfunctioning—the miseducated teenager, the unskilled adult laborer, the child brain-damaged as a result of prenatal neglect—will require service that is predominantly exceptionalistic in nature.

The danger in the exceptionalistic viewpoint is in its impact on social policy when it becomes the dominant component in social analysis. Blaming the Victim occurs exclusively within an exceptionalistic framework, and it consists of applying exceptionalistic explanations to universalistic problems. This represents an illogical departure from fact, a method, in Mannheim's words, of systematically distorting reality, of developing an ideology.

Blaming the Victim can take its place in a long series of American ideologies that have rationalized cruelty and injustice.

Slavery, for example, was justified—even praised—on the basis of a complex ideology that showed quite conclusively how useful slavery was to society and how uplifting it was for the slaves.[5] Eminent physicians could be relied upon to provide the biological justification for slavery since after all, they said, the slaves were a separate species—as, for example, cattle are a separate species. No one in his right mind would dream of freeing the cows and fighting to abolish the ownership of cattle. In the view of the average American of 1825, it was important to preserve slavery, not simply because it was in accord with his own group interests (he was not fully aware of that), but because reason and logic showed clearly to the reasonable and intelligent man that slavery was good. In order to persuade a good and moral man to *do* evil, then, it is not necessary first to persuade him to *become* evil. It is only necessary to teach him that he is doing good. No one, in the words of a legendary newspaperman, thinks of himself as a son of a bitch.

In late-nineteenth-century America there flowered another ideology of injustice that seemed rational and just to the decent, progressive person. But Richard Hofstadter's analysis of the phenomenon of Social Darwinism[6] shows clearly its functional role in the preservation of the *status quo.* One can scarcely imagine a better fit than the one between this ideology and the purpose and actions of the robber barons, who descended like piranha fish on the America of this era and picked its bones clean. Their extraordinarily unethical operations netted them not only hundreds of millions of dollars but also, perversely, the adoration of the nation. Behavior that would be, in any more rational land (including today's America), more than enough to have landed them all in jail, was praised as the very model of a captain of modern industry. And the

[5]For a good review of this general ideology, see I. A. Newby, *Jim Crow's Defense* (Baton Rouge: Louisiana State University Press, 1965).

[6]Richard Hofstadter, *Social Darwinism in American Thought* (revised ed.; Boston: Beacon Press, 1955).

philosophy that justified their thievery was such that John D. Rockefeller could actually stand up and preach it in church. Listen as he speaks in, of all places, Sunday school:

> The growth of a large business is merely a survival of the fittest. . . . The American Beauty rose can be produced in the splendor and fragrance which bring cheer to its beholder only by sacrificing the early buds which grow up around it. This is not an evil tendency in business. It is merely the working-out of a law of nature and a law of God.[7]

This was the core of the gospel, adapted analogically from Darwin's writings on evolution. Herbert Spencer and, later, William Graham Sumner and other beginners in the social sciences considered Darwin's work to be directly applicable to social processes: ultimately as a guarantee that life was progressing toward perfection but, in the short run, as a justification for an absolutely uncontrolled laissez-faire economic system. The central concepts of "survival of the fittest," "natural selection," and "gradualism" were exalted in Rockefeller's preaching to the status of laws of God and Nature. Not only did this ideology justify the criminal rapacity of those who rose to the top of the industrial heap, defining them automatically as naturally superior (this was bad enough), but at the same time it also required that those at the bottom of the heap be labeled as patently *unfit*—a label based solely on their position in society. According to the law of natural selection, they should be, in Spencer's judgment, eliminated. "The whole effort of nature is to get rid of such, to clear the world of them and make room for better."

For a generation, Social Darwinism was the orthodox doctrine in the social sciences, such as they were at that time. Opponents of this ideology were shut out of respectable intellectual life. The philosophy that enabled John D. Rockefeller to justify himself self-righteously in front of a class of Sunday school children was not the product of an academic quack or a marginal crackpot philosopher. It came directly from the lectures and books of leading intellectual figures of the time, occupants of professorial chairs at Harvard and Yale. Such is the power of an ideology that so neatly fits the needs of the dominant interests of society.

If one is to think about ideologies in America in 1970, one must be prepared to consider the possibility that a body of ideas that might seem almost self-evident is, in fact, highly distorted and highly selective; one must allow that the inclusion of a specific formulation in every freshman sociology text does not guarantee that the particular formulation represents abstract Truth rather than group interest. It is important not to delude ourselves into thinking that ideological monstrosities were constructed by monsters. They were not; they are not. They are developed through a process that shows every sign of being valid scholarship, com-

[7]William J. Ghent, *Our Benevolent Feudalism* (New York: The Macmillan Co., 1902), p. 29.

plete with tables of numbers, copious footnotes, and scientific terminology. Ideologies are quite often academically and socially respectable and in many instances hold positions of exclusive validity, so that disagreement is considered unrespectable or radical and risks being labeled as irresponsible, unenlightened, or trashy.

Blaming the Victim holds such a position. It is central in the mainstream of contemporary American social thought, and its ideas pervade our most crucial assumptions so thoroughly that they are hardly noticed. Moreover, the fruits of this ideology appear to be fraught with altruism and humanitarianism, so it is hard to believe that it has principally functioned to block social change.

III

A major pharmaceutical manufacturer, as an act of humanitarian concern, has distributed copies of a large poster warning "LEAD PAINT CAN KILL!" The poster, featuring a photograph of the face of a charming little girl, goes on to explain that if children *eat* lead paint, it can poison them, they can develop serious symptoms, suffer permanent brain damage, even die. The health department of a major American city has put out a coloring book that provides the same information. While the poster urges parents to prevent their children from eating paint, the coloring book is more vivid. It labels as neglectful and thoughtless the mother who does not keep her infant under constant surveillance to keep it from eating paint chips.

Now, no one would argue against the idea that it is important to spread knowledge about the danger of eating paint in order that parents might act to forestall their children from doing so. But to campaign against lead paint *only* in these terms is destructive and misleading and, in a sense, an effective way to support and agree with slum landlords— who define the problem of lead poisoning in precisely these terms.

This is an example of applying an exceptionalistic solution to a universalistic problem. It is not accurate to say that lead poisoning results from the actions of individual neglectful mothers. Rather, lead poisoning is a social phenomenon supported by a number of social mechanisms, one of the most tragic by-products of the systematic toleration of slum housing. In New Haven, which has the highest reported rate of lead poisoning in the country, several small children have died and many others have incurred irreparable brain damage as a result of eating peeling paint. In several cases, when the landlord failed to make repairs, poisonings have occurred time and again through a succession of tenancies. And the major reason for the landlord's neglect of this problem was that the city agency responsible for enforcing the housing code did nothing to make him correct this dangerous condition.

The cause of the poisoning is the lead in the paint on the walls of the apartment in which the children live. The presence of the lead is illegal. To use lead paint in a residence is illegal; to permit lead paint to be exposed in a residence is illegal. It is not only illegal, it is potentially criminal since the housing code does provide for criminal penalties. The general problem of lead poisoning, then, is more accurately analyzed as the result of a systematic program of lawbreaking by one interest group in the community, with the toleration and encouragement of the public authority charged with enforcing that law. To ignore these continued and repeated law violations, to ignore the fact that the supposed law enforcer actually cooperates in lawbreaking, and then to load a burden of guilt on the mother of a dead or dangerously-ill child is an egregious distortion of reality. And to do so under the guise of public-spirited and humanitarian service to the community is intolerable.

But this is how Blaming the Victim works. The righteous humanitarian concern displayed by the drug company, with its poster, and the health department, with its coloring book, is a genuine concern, and this is a typical feature of Blaming the Victim. Also typical is the swerving away from the central target that requires systematic change and, instead, focusing in on the individual affected. The ultimate effect is always to distract attention from the basic causes and to leave the primary social injustice untouched. And, most telling, the proposed remedy for the problem is, of course, to work on the victim himself. Prescriptions for cure, as written by the Savage Discovery set, are invariably conceived to revamp and revise the victim, never to change the surrounding circumstances. They want to change his attitudes, alter his values, fill up his cultural deficits, energize his apathetic soul, cure his character defects, train him and polish him and woo him from his savage ways.

Isn't all of this more subtle and sophisticated than such old-fashioned ideologies as Social Darwinism? Doesn't the change from brutal ideas about survival of the fit (and the expiration of the unfit) to kindly concern about characterological defects (brought about by stigmas of social origin) seem like a substantial step forward? Hardly. It is only a substitution of terms. The old, reactionary exceptionalistic formulations are replaced by new progressive, humanitarian exceptionalistic formulations. In education, the outmoded and unacceptable concept of racial or class differences in basic inherited intellectual ability simply gives way to the new notion of cultural deprivation: there is very little functional difference between these two ideas. In taking a look at the phenomenon of poverty, the old concept of unfitness or idleness or laziness is replaced by the newfangled theory of the culture of poverty. In race relations, plain Negro inferiority—which was good enough for old-fashioned conservatives—is pushed aside by fancy conceits about the crumbling Negro family. With regard to illegitimacy, we are not so crass as to concern ourselves with immorality and vice, as in the old days; we settle benignly on the explanation of the "lower-class pattern of sexual behavior," which no one condemns as evil, but which is, in fact, simply a variation of the old explanatory idea. Mental illness is no longer defined as the result of hereditary taint or congenital character flaw; now we have new causal hypotheses regarding the ego-damaging emotional experiences that are supposed to be the inevitable consequence of the deplorable child-rearing practices of the poor.

In each case, of course, we are persuaded to ignore the obvious: the continued blatant discrimination against the Negro, the gross deprivation of contraceptive and adoption services to the poor, the heavy stresses endemic in the life of the poor. And almost all our make-believe liberal programs aimed at correcting our urban problems are off target; they are designed either to change the poor man or to cool him out.

IV

We come finally to the question, Why? It is much easier to understand the process of Blaming the Victim as a way of thinking than it is to understand the motivation for it. Why do Victim Blamers, who are usually good people, blame the victim? The development and application of this ideology, and of all the mythologies associated with Savage Discovery, are readily exposed by careful analysis as hostile acts—one is almost tempted to say acts of war—directed against the disadvantaged, the distressed, the disinherited. It is class warfare in reverse. Yet those who are most fascinated and enchanted by this ideology tend to be progressive, humanitarian, and, in the best sense of the word, charitable persons. They would usually define themselves as moderates or liberals. Why do they pursue this dreadful war against the poor and the oppressed?

Put briefly, the answer can be formulated best in psychological terms —or, at least, I, as a psychologist, am more comfortable with such a formulation. The highly-charged psychological problem confronting this hypothetical progressive, charitable person I am talking about is that of reconciling his own self-interest with the promptings of his humanitarian impulses. This psychological process of reconciliation is not worked out in a logical, rational, conscious way; it is a process that takes place far below the level of sharp consciousness, and the solution—Blaming the Victim—is arrived at subconsciously as a compromise that apparently satisfies both his self-interest and his charitable concerns. Let me elaborate.

First, the question of self-interest or, more accurately, class interest. The typical Victim Blamer is a middle-class person who is doing reasonably well in a material way; he has a good job, a good income, a good house, a good car. Basically, he likes the social system pretty much the way it is, at least in broad outline. He likes the two-party political system, though he may be highly skilled in finding a thousand minor flaws in its functioning. He heartily approves of the profit motive as the propelling engine of the economic system despite his awareness that there are abuses of that system, negative side effects, and substantial residual inequalities.

On the other hand, he is acutely aware of poverty, racial discrimination, exploitation, and deprivation, and, moreover, he wants to do something concrete to ameliorate the condition of the poor, the black, and the disadvantaged. This is not an extraneous concern; it is central to his value system to insist on the worth of the individual, the equality of men, and the importance of justice.

What is to be done, then? What intellectual position can he take, and what line of action can he follow that will satisfy both of these important motivations? He quickly and self-consciously rejects two obvious alternatives, which he defines as "extremes." He cannot side with an openly reactionary, repressive position that accepts continued oppression and exploitation as the price of a privileged position for his own class. This is incompatible with his own morality and his basic political principles. He finds the extreme conservative position repugnant.

He is, if anything, more allergic to radicals, however, than he is to reactionaries. He rejects the "extreme" solution of radical social change, and this makes sense since such radical social change threatens his own well-being. A more equitable distribution of income might mean that he would have less—a smaller or older house, with fewer yews or no rhododendrons in the yard, a less enjoyable job, or, at the least, a somewhat smaller salary. If black children and poor children were, in fact, reasonably educated and began to get high S.A.T. scores, they would be competing with *his* children for the scarce places in the entering classes of Harvard, Columbia, Bennington, and Antioch.

So our potential Victim Blamers are in a dilemma. In the words of an old Yiddish proverb, they are trying to dance at two weddings. They are old friends of both brides and fond of both kinds of dancing, and they want to accept both invitations. They cannot bring themselves to attack the system that has been so good to them, but they want so badly to be helpful to the victims of racism and economic injustice.

Their solution is a brilliant compromise. They turn their attention to the victim in his post-victimized state. They want to bind up wounds, inject penicillin, administer morphine, and evacuate the wounded for rehabilitation. They explain what's wrong with the victim in terms of social experiences *in the past,* experiences that have left wounds, defects, paralysis, and disability. And they take the cure of these wounds and the reduction of these disabilities as the first order of business. They want to make the victims less vulnerable, send them back into battle with better weapons, thicker armor, a higher level of morale.

In order to do so effectively, of course, they must analyze the victims carefully, dispassionately, objectively, scientifically, empathetically, mathematically, and hardheadedly, to see what made them so vulnerable in the first place.

What weapons, now, might they have lacked when they went into battle? Job skills? Education?

What armor was lacking that might have warded off their wounds? Better values? Habits of thrift and foresight?

And what might have ravaged their morale? Apathy? Ignorance? Deviant lower-class cultural patterns?

This is the solution of the dilemma, the solution of Blaming the Victim. And those who buy this solution with a sigh of relief are inevitably blinding themselves to the basic causes of the problems being addressed. They are, most crucially, rejecting the possibility of blaming, not the victims, but themselves. They are all unconsciously passing judgments on themselves and bringing in a unanimous verdict of Not Guilty.

If one comes to believe that the culture of poverty produces persons *fated* to be poor, who can find any fault with our corporation-dominated economy? And if the Negro family produces young men *incapable* of achieving equality, let's deal with that first before we go on to the task of changing the pervasive racism that informs and shapes and distorts our every social institution. And if unsatisfactory resolution of one's Oedipus complex accounts for all emotional distress and mental disorder, then by all means let us attend to that and postpone worrying about the pounding day-to-day stresses of life on the bottom rungs that drive so many to drink, dope, and madness.

That is the ideology of Blaming the Victim, the cunning Art of Savage Discovery. The tragic, frightening truth is that it is a mythology that is winning over the best people of our time, the very people who must resist this ideological temptation if we are to achieve nonviolent change in America.

Peter Singer
FAMINE, AFFLUENCE, AND MORALITY

Peter Singer is an Australian philosopher best known for his defense of animal rights in general and his advocacy of vegetarianism in particular. In this essay, he provides a forceful argument for his view that we have an obligation to use what money we have left over, after providing for our own basic needs, to alleviate the starvation and suffering of others throughout the world. The use of our money in such a way is portrayed by Singer not as a praiseworthy act of charity but rather as a compelling moral obligation. Although Singer does not make the point explicitly, his article clearly revolves around refusing to distinguish between acts of commission and acts of omission. Traditionally, we tend to hold people responsible for things they actually do; increasingly, however, we hear the suggestion that people should also be held responsible for things they fail to do. According to such reasoning, if I have money beyond what I need to provide for my basic needs and fail to use that money to help alleviate starvation and suffering, I can be held morally responsible for that failure.

As I write this, in November 1971, people are dying in East Bengal from lack of food, shelter, and medical care. The suffering and death that are occurring there now are not inevitable, not unavoidable in any fatalistic sense of the term. Constant poverty, a cyclone, and a civil war have turned at least nine million people into destitute refugees; nevertheless, it is not beyond the capacity of the richer nations to give enough assistance to reduce any further suffering to very small proportions. The decisions and actions of human beings can prevent this kind of suffering. Unfortunately, human beings have not made the necessary decisions. At the individual level, people have, with very few exceptions, not responded to the situation in any significant way. Generally speaking, people have not given large sums to relief funds; they have not written to their parliamentary representatives demanding increased government assistance; they have not demonstrated in the streets, held symbolic fasts, or done anything else directed toward providing the refugees with the means to satisfy their essential needs. At the government level, no government has given the sort of massive aid that would enable the refugees to survive for more than a few days. Britain, for instance, has given rather more than most countries. It has, to date, given £14,750,000. For comparative purposes, Britain's share of the nonrecoverable development costs of the Anglo-French Concorde project is already in excess of £275,000,000, and on present estimates will reach £440,000,000. The implication is that the British government values a supersonic transport more than thirty times as highly as it values the lives of the nine million refugees. Australia is another country which, on a per capita basis, is well up in the "aid to Bengal" table. Australia's aid, however, amounts to less than one-twelfth of the cost of Sydney's new opera house. The total amount given, from all sources, now stands at about £65,000,000. The estimated cost of keeping the refugees alive for one year is £464,000,000. Most of the refugees have now been in the camps for more than six months. The World Bank has said that India needs a minimum of £300,000,000 in assistance from other countries before the end of the year. It seems obvious that assistance on this scale will not be forthcoming. India will be forced to choose between letting the refugees starve or diverting funds from her own development program, which will mean that more of her own people will starve in the future.[1]

These are the essential facts about the present situation in Bengal. So far as it concerns us here, there is nothing unique about this situation except its magnitude. The Bengal emergency is just the latest and most acute of a series of major emergencies in various parts of the world, arising both from natural and from man-made causes. There are also many parts of the world in which people die from malnutrition and lack of food independent of any special emergency. I take Bengal as my example only because it is the present concern, and because the size of the problem has ensured that it has been given adequate publicity. Nei-

[1]There was also a third possibility: that India would go to war to enable the refugees to return to their lands. Since I wrote this paper, India has taken this way out. The situation is no longer that described above, but this does not affect my argument, as the next paragraph indicates.

ther individuals nor governments can claim to be unaware of what is happening there.

What are the moral implications of a situation like this? In what follows, I shall argue that the way people in relatively affluent countries react to a situation like that in Bengal cannot be justified; indeed, the whole way we look at moral issues—our moral conceptual scheme—needs to be altered, and with it, the way of life that has come to be taken for granted in our society.

In arguing for this conclusion I will not, of course, claim to be morally neutral. I shall, however, try to argue for the moral position that I take, so that anyone who accepts certain assumptions, to be made explicit, will, I hope, accept my conclusion.

I begin with the assumption that suffering and death from lack of food, shelter, and medical care are bad. I think most people will agree about this, although one may reach the same view by different routes. I shall not argue for this view. People can hold all sorts of eccentric positions, and perhaps from some of them it would not follow that death by starvation is in itself bad. It is difficult, perhaps impossible, to refute such positions, and so for brevity I will henceforth take this assumption as accepted. Those who disagree need read no further.

My next point is this: if it is in our power to prevent something bad from happening, without thereby sacrificing anything of comparable moral importance, we ought, morally, to do it. By "without sacrificing anything of comparable moral importance" I mean without causing anything else comparably bad to happen, or doing something that is wrong in itself, or failing to promote some moral good, comparable in significance to the bad thing that we can prevent. This principle seems almost as uncontroversial as the last one. It requires us only to prevent what is bad, and not to promote what is good, and it requires this of us only when we can do it without sacrificing anything that is, from the moral point of view, comparably important. I could even, as far as the application of my argument to the Bengal emergency is concerned, qualify the point so as to make it: if it is in our power to prevent something very bad from happening, without thereby sacrificing anything morally significant, we ought, morally, to do it. An application of this principle would be as follows: if I am walking past a shallow pond and see a child drowning in it, I ought to wade in and pull the child out. This will mean getting my clothes muddy, but this is insignificant, while the death of the child would presumably be a very bad thing.

The uncontroversial appearance of the principle just stated is deceptive. If it were acted upon, even in its qualified form, our lives, our society, and our world would be fundamentally changed. For the principle takes, firstly, no account of proximity or distance. It makes no moral difference whether the person I can help is a neighbor's child ten yards from me or a Bengali whose name I shall never know, ten thousand miles away. Secondly, the principle makes no distinction between cases in which I am the only person who could possibly do anything and cases in which I am just one among millions in the same position.

I do not think I need to say much in defense of the refusal to take proximity and distance into account. The fact that a person is physically near to us, so that we have personal contact with him, may make it more likely that we *shall* assist him, but this does not show that we *ought* to help him rather than another who happens to be further away. If we accept any principle of impartiality, universalizability, equality, or whatever, we cannot discriminate against someone merely because he is far away from us (or we are far away from him). Admittedly, it is possible that we are in a better position to judge what needs to be done to help a person near to us than one far away, and perhaps also to provide the assistance we judge to be necessary. If this were the case, it would be a reason for helping those near to us first. This may once have been a justification for being more concerned with the poor in one's own town than with famine victims in India. Unfortunately for those who like to keep their moral responsibilities limited, instant communication and swift transportation have changed the situation. From the moral point of view, the development of the world into a "global village" has made an important, though still unrecognized, difference to our moral situation. Expert observers and supervisors, sent out by famine relief organizations or permanently stationed in famine-prone areas, can direct our aid to a refugee in Bengal almost as effectively as we could get it to someone in our own block. There would seem, therefore, to be no possible justification for discriminating on geographical grounds.

There may be a greater need to defend the second implication of my principle—that the fact that there are millions of other people in the same position, in respect to the Bengali refugees, as I am, does not make the situation significantly different from a situation in which I am the only person who can prevent something very bad from occurring. Again, of course, I admit that there is a psychological difference between the cases; one feels less guilty about doing nothing if one can point to others, similarly placed, who have also done nothing. Yet this can make no real difference to our moral obligations.[2] Should I consider that I am less obliged to pull the drowning child out of the pond if on looking around I see other people, no further away than I am, who have also noticed the child but are doing nothing? One has only to ask this question to see the absurdity of the view that numbers lessen obligation. It is a view that is an ideal excuse for inactivity; unfortunately most of the major evils—

[2]In view of the special sense philosophers often give to the term, I should say that I use "obligation" simply as the abstract noun derived from "ought," so that "I have an obligation to" means no more, and no less, than "I ought to." This usage is in accordance with the definition of "ought" given by the *Shorter Oxford English Dictionary:* "the general verb to express duty or obligation." I do not think any issue of substance hangs on the way the term is used; sentences in which I use "obligation" could all be rewritten, although somewhat clumsily, as sentences in which a clause containing "ought" replaces the term "obligation."

poverty, overpopulation, pollution—are problems in which everyone is almost equally involved.

The view that numbers do make a difference can be made plausible if stated in this way: if everyone in circumstances like mine gave £5 to the Bengal Relief Fund, there would be enough to provide food, shelter, and medical care for the refugees; there is no reason why I should give more than anyone else in the same circumstances as I am; therefore I have no obligation to give more than £5. Each premise in this argument is true, and the argument looks sound. It may convince us, unless we notice that it is based on a hypothetical premise, although the conclusion is not stated hypothetically. The argument would be sound if the conclusion were: if everyone in circumstances like mine were to give £5, I would have no obligation to give more than £5. If the conclusion were so stated, however, it would be obvious that the argument has no bearing on a situation in which it is not the case that everyone else gives £5. This, of course, is the actual situation. It is more or less certain that not everyone in circumstances like mine will give £5. So there will not be enough to provide the needed food, shelter, and medical care. Therefore by giving more than £5 I will prevent more suffering than I would if I gave just £5.

It might be thought that this argument has an absurd consequence. Since the situation appears to be that very few people are likely to give substantial amounts, it follows that I and everyone else in similar circumstances ought to give as much as possible, that is, at least up to the point at which by giving more one would begin to cause serious suffering for oneself and one's dependents—perhaps even beyond this point to the point of marginal utility, at which by giving more one would cause oneself and one's dependents as much suffering as one would prevent in Bengal. If everyone does this, however, there will be more than can be used for the benefit of the refugees, and some of the sacrifice will have been unnecessary. Thus, if everyone does what he ought to do, the result will not be as good as it would be if everyone did a little less than he ought to do, or if only some do all that they ought to do.

The paradox here arises only if we assume that the actions in question—sending money to the relief funds—are performed more or less simultaneously, and are also unexpected. For if it is to be expected that everyone is going to contribute something, then clearly each is not obliged to give as much as he would have been obliged to had others not been giving too. And if everyone is not acting more or less simultaneously, then those giving later will know how much more is needed, and will have no obligation to give more than is necessary to reach this amount. To say this is not to deny the principle that people in the same circumstances have the same obligations, but to point out that the fact that others have given, or may be expected to give, is a relevant circumstance: those giving after it has become known that many others are giving and those giving before are not in the same circumstances. So the seemingly absurd consequence of the principle I have put forward can occur only if people are in error about the actual circumstances—that is, if they think they are giving when others are not, but in fact they are giving when others are. The result of everyone doing what he really ought to do cannot be worse than the result of everyone doing less than he ought to do, although the result of everyone doing what he reasonably believes he ought to do could be.

If my argument so far has been sound, neither our distance from a preventable evil nor the number of other people who, in respect to that evil, are in the same situation as we are, lessens our obligation to mitigate or prevent that evil. I shall therefore take as established the principle I asserted earlier. As I have already said, I need to assert it only in its qualified form: if it is in our power to prevent something very bad from happening, without thereby sacrificing anything else morally significant, we ought, morally, to do it.

The outcome of this argument is that our traditional moral categories are upset. The traditional distinction between duty and charity cannot be drawn, or at least, not in the place we normally draw it. Giving money to the Bengal Relief Fund is regarded as an act of charity in our society. The bodies which collect money are known as "charities." These organizations see themselves in this way—if you send them a check, you will be thanked for your "generosity." Because giving money is regarded as an act of charity, it is not thought that there is anything wrong with not giving. The charitable man may be praised, but the man who is not charitable is not condemned. People do not feel in any way ashamed or guilty about spending money on new clothes or a new car instead of giving it to famine relief. (Indeed, the alternative does not occur to them.) This way of looking at the matter cannot be justified. When we buy new clothes not to keep ourselves warm but to look "well-dressed" we are not providing for any important need. We would not be sacrificing anything significant if we were to continue to wear our old clothes, and give the money to famine relief. By doing so, we would be preventing another person from starving. It follows from what I have said earlier that we ought to give money away, rather than spend it on clothes which we do not need to keep us warm. To do so is not charitable, or generous. Nor is it the kind of act which philosophers and theologians have called "supererogatory"—an act which it would be good to do, but not wrong not to do. On the contrary, we ought to give the money away, and it is wrong not to do so.

I am not maintaining that there are no acts which are charitable, or that there are no acts which it would be good to do but not wrong not to do. It may be possible to redraw the distinction between duty and charity in some other place. All I am arguing here is that the present way of drawing the distinction, which makes it an act of charity for a man living at the level of affluence which most people in the "developed nations" enjoy to give money to save someone else from starvation, cannot be supported. It is beyond the scope of my argument to consider whether the distinction should be redrawn or abolished altogether. There would be many other possible ways of drawing the distinction—for instance, one might decide that it is good to make other people as happy as possible, but not wrong not to do so.

Despite the limited nature of the revision in our moral conceptual scheme which I am proposing, the revision would, given the extent of both affluence and famine in the world today, have radical implications. These implications may lead to further objections, distinct from those I have already considered. I shall discuss two of these.

One objection to the position I have taken might be simply that it is too drastic a revision of our moral scheme. People do not ordinarily judge in the way I have suggested they should. Most people reserve their moral condemnation for those who violate some moral norm, such as the norm against taking another person's property. They do not condemn those who indulge in luxury instead of giving to famine relief. But given that I did not set out to present a morally neutral description of the way people make moral judgments, the way people do in fact judge has nothing to do with the validity of my conclusion. My conclusion follows from the principle which I advanced earlier, and unless that principle is rejected, or the arguments shown to be unsound, I think the conclusion must stand, however strange it appears.

It might, nevertheless, be interesting to consider why our society, and most other societies, do judge differently from the way I have suggested they should. In a well-known article, J. O. Urmson suggests that the imperatives of duty, which tell us what we must do, as distinct from what it would be good to do but not wrong not to do, function so as to prohibit behavior that is intolerable if men are to live together in society.[3] This may explain the origin and continued existence of the present division between acts of duty and acts of charity. Moral attitudes are shaped by the needs of society, and no doubt society needs people who will observe the rules that make social existence tolerable. From the point of view of a particular society, it is essential to prevent violations of norms against killing, stealing, and so on. It is quite inessential, however, to help people outside one's own society.

If this is an explanation of our common distinction between duty and supererogation, however, it is not a justification of it. The moral point of view requires us to look beyond the interests of our own society. Previously, as I have already mentioned, this may hardly have been feasible, but it is quite feasible now. From the moral point of view, the prevention of the starvation of millions of people outside our society must be considered at least as pressing as the upholding of property norms within our society.

---

[3]J. O. Urmson, "Saints and Heroes," in *Essays in Moral Philosophy*, ed. Abraham I. Melden (Seattle and London, 1958), p. 214. For a related but significantly different view see also Henry Sidgwick, *The Methods of Ethics*, 7th edn. (London, 1907), pp. 220–221, 492–493.

It has been argued by some writers, among them Sidgwick and Urmson, that we need to have a basic moral code which is not too far beyond the capacities of the ordinary man, for otherwise there will be a general breakdown of compliance with the moral code. Crudely stated, this argument suggests that if we tell people that they ought to refrain from murder and give everything they do not really need to famine relief, they will do neither, whereas if we tell them that they ought to refrain from murder and that it is good to give to famine relief but not wrong not to do so, they will at least refrain from murder. The issue here is: Where should we draw the line between conduct that is required and conduct that is good although not required, so as to get the best possible result? This would seem to be an empirical question, although a very difficult one. One objection to the Sidgwick-Urmson line of argument is that it takes insufficient account of the effect that moral standards can have on the decisions we make. Given a society in which a wealthy man who gives five percent of his income to famine relief is regarded as most generous, it is not surprising that a proposal that we all ought to give away half our incomes will be thought to be absurdly unrealistic. In a society which held that no man should have more than enough while others have less than they need, such a proposal might seem narrow-minded. What it is possible for a man to do and what he is likely to do are both, I think, very greatly influenced by what people around him are doing and expecting him to do. In any case, the possibility that by spreading the idea that we ought to be doing very much more than we are to relieve famine we shall bring about a general breakdown of moral behavior seems remote. If the stakes are an end to widespread starvation, it is worth the risk. Finally, it should be emphasized that these considerations are relevant only to the issue of what we should require from others, and not to what we ourselves ought to do.

The second objection to my attack on the present distinction between duty and charity is one which has from time to time been made against utilitarianism. It follows from some forms of utilitarian theory that we all ought, morally, to be working full time to increase the balance of happiness over misery. The position I have taken here would not lead to this conclusion in all circumstances, for if there were no bad occurrences that we could prevent without sacrificing something of comparable moral importance, my argument would have no application. Given the present conditions in many parts of the world, however, it does follow from my argument that we ought, morally, to be working full time to relieve great suffering of the sort that occurs as a result of famine or other disasters. Of course, mitigating circumstances can be adduced—for instance, that if we wear ourselves out through overwork, we shall be less effective than we would otherwise have been. Nevertheless, when all considerations of this sort have been taken into account, the conclusion remains: we ought to be preventing as much suffering as we can without sacrificing something else of comparable moral importance. This conclusion is one which we may be reluctant to face. I cannot see, though, why it should be regarded as a criticism of the position for which I have argued, rather than a criticism of our ordinary standards of behavior. Since most people are self-interested to some degree, very few of us are likely to do everything that we ought to do. It would, however, hardly be honest to take this as evidence that it is not the case that we ought to do it.

It may still be thought that my conclusions are so wildly out of line with what everyone else thinks and has always thought that there must be something wrong with the argument somewhere. In order to show that my conclusions, while certainly contrary to contemporary Western moral standards, would not have seemed so extraordinary at other times and in other places, I would like to quote a passage from a writer not normally thought of as a way-out radical, Thomas Aquinas.

> Now, according to the natural order instituted by divine providence, material goods are provided for the satisfaction of human needs. Therefore the division and appropriation of property, which proceeds from human law, must not hinder the satisfaction of man's necessity from such goods. Equally, whatever a man has in superabundance is owed, of natural right, to the poor for their sustenance. So Ambrosius says, and it is also to be found in the *Decretum Gratiani:* "The bread which you withhold belongs to the hungry; the clothing you shut away, to the naked; and the money you bury in the earth is the redemption and freedom of the penniless."[4]

I now want to consider a number of points, more practical than philosophical, which are relevant to the application of the moral conclusion we have reached. These points challenge not the idea that we ought to be doing all we can to prevent starvation, but the idea that giving away a great deal of money is the best means to this end.

It is sometimes said that overseas aid should be a government responsibility, and that therefore one ought not to give to privately run charities. Giving privately, it is said, allows the government and the non-contributing members of society to escape their responsibilities.

This argument seems to assume that the more people there are who give to privately organized famine relief funds, the less likely it is that the government will take over full responsibility for such aid. This assumption is unsupported, and does not strike me as at all plausible. The opposite view—that if no one gives voluntarily, a government will assume that its citizens are uninterested in famine relief and would not wish to be forced into giving aid—seems more plausible. In any case, unless there were a definite probability that by refusing to give one would be helping to bring about massive government assistance, people who do refuse to make voluntary contributions are refusing to prevent a certain amount of suffering without being able to point to any tangible beneficial conse-

[4] *Summa Theologica,* II–II, Question 66, Article 7, in *Aquinas, Selected Political Writings,* ed. A. P. d'Entreves, trans. J. G. Dawson (Oxford, 1948), p. 171.

quence of their refusal. So the onus of showing how their refusal will bring about government action is on those who refuse to give.

I do not, of course, want to dispute the contention that governments of affluent nations should be giving many times the amount of genuine, no-strings-attached aid that they are giving now. I agree, too, that giving privately is not enough, and that we ought to be campaigning actively for entirely new standards for both public and private contributions to famine relief. Indeed, I would sympathize with someone who thought that campaigning was more important than giving oneself, although I doubt whether preaching what one does not practice would be very effective. Unfortunately, for many people the idea that "it's the government's responsibility" is a reason for not giving which does not appear to entail any political action either.

Another, more serious reason for not giving to famine relief funds is that until there is effective population control, relieving famine merely postpones starvation. If we save the Bengal refugees now, others, perhaps the children of these refugees, will face starvation in a few years' time. In support of this, one may cite the now well-known facts about the population explosion and the relatively limited scope for expanded production.

This point, like the previous one, is an argument against relieving suffering that is happening now, because of a belief about what might happen in the future; it is unlike the previous point in that very good evidence can be adduced in support of this belief about the future. I will not go into the evidence here. I accept that the earth cannot support indefinitely a population rising at the present rate. This certainly poses a problem for anyone who thinks it important to prevent famine. Again, however, one could accept the argument without drawing the conclusion that it absolves one from any obligation to do anything to prevent famine. The conclusion that should be drawn is that the best means of preventing famine, in the long run, is population control. It would then follow from the position reached earlier that one ought to be doing all one can to promote population control (unless one held that all forms of population control were wrong in themselves, or would have significantly bad consequences). Since there are organizations working specifically for population control, one would then support them rather than more orthodox methods of preventing famine.

A third point raised by the conclusion reached earlier relates to the question of just how much we all ought to be giving away. One possibility, which has already been mentioned, is that we ought to give until we reach the level of marginal utility—that is, the level at which, by giving more, I would cause as much suffering to myself or my dependents as I would relieve by my gift. This would mean, of course, that one would reduce oneself to very near the material circumstances of a Bengali refugee. It will be recalled that earlier I put forward both a strong and a moderate version of the principle of preventing bad occurrences. The strong version, which required us to prevent bad things from happening unless in doing so we would be sacrificing something of comparable moral significance, does seem to require reducing ourselves to the level of marginal utility. I should also say that the strong version seems to me to be the correct one. I proposed the more moderate version—that we should prevent bad occurrences unless, to do so, we had to sacrifice something morally significant—only in order to show that even on this surely undeniable principle a great change in our way of life is required. On the more moderate principle, it may not follow that we ought to reduce ourselves to the level of marginal utility, for one might hold that to reduce oneself and one's family to this level is to cause something significantly bad to happen. Whether this is so I shall not discuss, since, as I have said, I can see no good reason for holding the moderate version of the principle rather than the strong version. Even if we accepted the principle only in its moderate form, however, it should be clear that we would have to give away enough to ensure that the consumer society, dependent as it is on people spending on trivia rather than giving to famine relief, would slow down and perhaps disappear entirely. There are several reasons why this would be desirable in itself. The value and necessity of economic growth are now being questioned not only by conservationists, but by economists as well.[5] There is no doubt, too, that the consumer society has had a distorting effect on the goals and purposes of its members. Yet looking at the matter purely from the point of view of overseas aid, there must be a limit to the extent to which we should deliberately slow down our economy; for it might be the case that if we gave away, say, forty percent of our Gross National Product, we would slow down the economy so much that in absolute terms we would be giving less than if we gave twenty-five percent of the much larger GNP that we would have if we limited our contribution to this smaller percentage.

I mention this only as an indication of the sort of factor that one would have to take into account in working out an ideal. Since Western societies generally consider one percent of the GNP an acceptable level for overseas aid, the matter is entirely academic. Nor does it affect the question of how much an individual should give in a society in which very few are giving substantial amounts.

It is sometimes said, though less often now than it used to be, that philosophers have no special role to play in public affairs, since most public issues depend primarily on an assessment of facts. On questions of fact, it is said, philosophers as such have no special expertise, and so it has been possible to engage in philosophy without committing oneself to any position on major public issues. No doubt there are some issues of social policy and foreign policy about which it can truly be said that a really expert assessment of the facts is required before taking sides or

---

[5]See, for instance, John Kenneth Galbraith, *The New Industrial State* (Boston, 1967); and E. J. Mishan, *The Costs of Economic Growth* (London, 1967).

acting, but the issue of famine is surely not one of these. The facts about the existence of suffering are beyond dispute. Nor, I think, is it disputed that we can do something about it, either through orthodox methods of famine relief or through population control or both. This is therefore an issue on which philosophers are competent to take a position. The issue is one which faces everyone who has more money than he needs to support himself and his dependents, or who is in a position to take some sort of political action. These categories must include practically every teacher and student of philosophy in the universities of the Western world. If philosophy is to deal with matters that are relevant to both teachers and students, this is an issue that philosophers should discuss.

Discussion, though, is not enough. What is the point of relating philosophy to public (and personal) affairs if we do not take our conclusions seriously? In this instance, taking our conclusion seriously means acting upon it. The philosopher will not find it any easier than anyone else to alter his attitudes and way of life to the extent that, if I am right, is involved in doing everything that we ought to be doing. At the very least, though, one can make a start. The philosopher who does so will have to sacrifice some of the benefits of the consumer society, but he can find compensation in the satisfaction of a way of life in which theory and practice, if not yet in harmony, are at least coming together.

Peter French
MORALLY BLAMING WHOLE POPULATIONS

Philosopher Peter French analyzes what it means to blame an individual for the consequences of his or her actions and then proceeds to argue that when certain conditions are fulfilled, it is perfectly meaningful and appropriate to blame collective entities, such as "the American people," for actions carried out in their name.

Whenever wartime atrocities are revealed to the general public issues of legal and moral responsibility arise. The legal questions are surely complex and important, especially when the plea of superior orders is involved. On the moral side, however, arise other questions which are often shrouded in confusions and yet, I think, they are at least as important as whether or not a specific number of soldiers and their officers are guilty of crimes against humanity or against peace. I am most concerned with the justification of ascriptions of moral blame to collectivities. I am particularly interested in ascriptions of blame to whole populations (or ethnic groups). We have been told by some writers that the American people are to blame for the Vietnam atrocities.[1] After the Second World War the collective "German people" or just "the Germans" were frequently blamed for the atrocities of the concentration camps. I shall attempt to expose the moral foundations which support such ascriptions of collective blame. If, as I hope to demonstrate, blame is in some cases justifiably placed on collectivities, many of our ethical standards may need reconsideration.

The etymological roots of 'to blame' lie in 'to blaspheme' ('to speak evil of'). Although there are numerous everyday occasions where the sole function of blaming seems to be identifying the cause of unhappy or untoward events (for example, "Blame the weather for ruining the vacation"), there is more to blaming than the determination of causes or faults. There are at least two major senses of 'blame.' In the first, to blame is to fix responsibility, to identify the cause or causes of an untoward or disvalued event: the weather is to blame for a ruined vacation, the dead battery is to blame for the flashlight's failure, etc. In the second sense, to blame is to hold responsible. It is a key to our various uses of 'blaming' that we cannot hold the weather responsible or the dead battery responsible for the unhappy events for which they are to blame. It is a fact in both our legal and moral institutions that some things and some people[2] may be *to blame* for certain unhappy events, though they are not *to be blamed* for them.

Where blaming is an expression of displeasure directed without distinction at animate and inanimate objects, persons and things, I shall call that type of blame "non-moral." Surely there are many distinguishing characteristics of such non-moral blame over and above the mere expression of displeasure at the untoward event and its alleged causes, though often non-moral blaming is just dispraising. Expressions of disapprobation are central to all blaming episodes. It is a characteristic of non-moral blaming that it is used in cases of accident, mistake, and often where the blamed party is not believed to be capable of helping what it does. My son, for example, is to blame for breaking his toy train, even though he is only four years old and it was surely an accident. To resurrect one of Austin's famous illustrations,[3] I am to blame for killing your donkey even though I shot it in the mistaken belief that it was my donkey. Non-moral blame does not necessarily occasion evaluations of intelligence, states of mind, intentions, or responsibilities. In the case of persons, we only need to know (some of us need only to suspect) that an individual did bring

---

[1]Even Lt. Calley has made such a claim. "The guilt: as Medina said, we all as American citizens share it. I agree . . . I say if there's guilt, we must suffer it." From "The Concluding Confessions of Lieutenant Calley," by First Lieutenant William L. Calley, Jr., interviewed by John Sack, *Esquire,* September 1971.

[2]See my "On Blaming Psychopaths" in D. E. Cooper, ed., *The Manson Murders: A Philosophical Inquiry* (Cambridge: Schenkman Publishing Co., 1973).

[3]J. L. Austin, "A Plea for Excuses," The Presidential Address to the Aristotelian Society, 1956, *Proceedings of the Aristotelian Society,* 1956–57, Vol. VII, 1957.

about the unpleasant or unwanted circumstances in order to blame him. As I have stressed, there is no difference in kind between blaming persons and blaming such things as inanimate objects and the weather, as long as blame is of a non-moral sort. A further characteristic of non-moral blaming (though I think this may be the case with blaming in general) would seem to be that occasions of its use are not necessarily directed at altering future behavior. This is most obvious in the example of blaming the weather.

We ascribe non-moral blame even when most people would admit that the person or thing blamed could not have affected the outcome of his (its) actions by intention. This type of blame does not involve us in issues of whether or not the blamed could have done something other than he did. We make no assumption that the blamed acted freely (that the blamed has free will) when we non-morally blame. It is entirely consistent with this type of blaming to blame sociopaths and psychopaths for their anti-social behavior and to blame children for breaking toys in so far as a causal relationship can be shown between the occurrence of the disapproved event and the thing blamed.

To non-morally blame is first to identify the cause of an untoward event. It is not so much to grade the cause as it is to single it out as having fallen below expected standards. It is like answering the question "Who (or what) is to blame for this (disvalued event)?" To blame the December weather in Minnesota for my automobile accident is not necessarily to grade the December weather. After all, it is standard for the weather in December in Minnesota to be violently snowy and icy, and many of the residents like it that way. It is to say that the weather conditions were a major contributory factor in the disvalued outcome, and it might be to say that the weather was the cause of substandard road conditions. The brakes are to blame for an auto accident if the brakes should have worked, if it would have been standard for them to work, but because they did not the accident occurred.

Non-moral blaming does, however, differ from just citing the causes of disapproved events in so far as it is not dispassionate. It is to use animadvertives in an objurgatory way toward the thing, event, or person blamed. Consider the following contrasting examples:

(A.) While driving at a legal speed down a residential street, Mr. X is shocked to see a young child dart in front of his car. The shock of what is about to occur is too much for Mr. X's heart. He suffers a massive attack. The car swerves directly at the child. She is dead on impact, but later Mr. X recovers.

(B.) While driving at a legal speed down a residential street, Mr. Y suddenly is shocked to see a young child dart in front of his vehicle. Mr. Y panics and instead of braking slams his foot on the accelerator. The child is killed instantly.

Surely both X and Y caused the deaths of children. But we would be inclined to blame Y for the child's death and reluctant to do the same in X's case, though we surely might blame X's heart for the accident. For that matter automobiles also caused those deaths. But in neither case are we likely to blame the car or its manufacturer. After all, the car operated as advertised, as cars are expected to operate. Had there been some mechanical fault in the construction of the car which made emergency stopping impossible, we would blame not only the car but its manufacturer or perhaps the most recent mechanic to have serviced it. Cars are expected to perform according to a certain automotive standard, and when accidents occur because of failure to meet that standard, we (and Ralph Nader) are entirely justified in blaming the car for the accident and often exonerating the driver. Notice, however, that where standards are harder to determine, as in the case of the weather being to blame for an accident, there is a reluctance to exonerate the driver completely. Unless the weather unexpectedly changed, we are likely to say that the driver is to blame for having ventured out at all, "He should have known better."

In regard to (A.) we might find ourselves blaming the child for her own death, but that likely would be contingent upon the age of the child. If she were only one or two years old, it would seem unlikely we would say she was to blame for her death, unless we were consoling Mr. X. If the child were somewhat older, say four or five, and of normal health, we might be more inclined to include her in the blame. Our reluctance to ascribe even non-moral blame to the very young child is due to our expectations and standards of performance. Seldom do we blame those persons who should not be expected to comprehend the possible disastrous consequences of performing certain acts. It makes no sense to say, "She should have known better," nor does it make sense to speak with objurgation toward or about her.

Returning to the drivers, I think that we would say that X is not to be blamed for the child's death. It makes little sense to talk of standards in regard to heart attacks. Perhaps we might say that X's heart was to blame for the child's death: in so far as it malfunctioned it tragically fell below the standards customarily applied to hearts. But, assuming X does not have a history of heart ailment, that he should not have been expecting an attack, X would seem to be blameless, even in the non-moral sense of blame, for the child's death.

Y, on the other hand, is to be blamed, non-morally, for the child's death. Y's performance behind the wheel was substandard. Panic is not sufficient exculpation for driving at top speed directly at the child. Most drivers do not do that; they are expected not to do so. Keeping the car under control is the first rule of the road. Y should have known which pedal was the brake, and he should have swerved to avoid the fatal accident. Y is more than just the cause of the child's death: he merits blame (in the non-moral sense) even if it is claimed that he was so gripped with panic that he could not have acted other than he did. It should by now be evident that primary in blaming is the notion of *should have,* not *could have.*

To begin with, we must distinguish between 'should have' and the rather more often discussed 'should have if I had chosen.' Although I agree with Austin that Moore is confused when he appears to hold that 'should have if I had chosen' may be substituted for 'could have if I had chosen,' I find a different distinction more important for the present purposes. Consider the following:

(C.) Teacher to pupil: "You should have written more on *natura naturans.* I'm afraid I can't give you a very good grade."

Two elements are worth noting: (1.) 'should have' refers to a standard (explicit or implicit) and (2.) 'should have' does not depend for its sense upon the capacities, dispositions, or abilities of its subjects. Suppose the pupil in (C.) has no capacity or ability to understand or comment on *natura naturans.* He could not have written more on it in his essay without producing gibberish. Would we then say that he should not have written more? I think not. It is appropriate then to blame the pupil for his poor grade although blame, it must be reminded, is surely not at this level of a moral sort. When one says of the pupil in (C.) that he "should have" written more on *natura naturans,* one is *not* prepared to say that "if (such and such) he would have." What has been said is simply that he failed to reach a certain expected standard, one which is involved when judgments are made within the type of activity in which he was engaged.

Our practices of blaming rest upon the existence of certain standards and expectations relevant to our various activities and the events of our lives. It is not here important to discuss the genesis of those standards and whether or not they stand in need of justification. Someone or something is to blame when the major criterion of our adverse judgment of him or it is of the "should have" variety. This might be only an attitude that it "should have" (what J. L. Austin called the behabitive sense of blaming). Hence to say the weather should have been better, i.e. to blame the weather for our ruined vacation, is to express the attitude that we disvalue the weather. We had counted on sunny days and it rained for a week. 'The weather should have been better' is then 'We had in mind a standard of acceptable weather which was not met when it rained for a week.' Obviously some types of non-moral blaming are like scolding or rebuking or chiding, while others are merely expressions of attitude.

In regard to justifying collective non-moral blame to whole populations let us consider the case of war crimes. The ascription of non-moral blame for war crimes in Vietnam to the American people can be justified, if the blamer can cite (1) reasons for treating that particular section of humanity as a collectivity, i.e. there is a solidarity (to use Feinberg's term) to the group; (2) evidence that the perpetrators of the war atrocities, those strictly liable for them, would not have had opportunity to perform them had not the collectivity acted in such a way as to have allowed themselves to be led or misled by political leaders, paid taxes without protest, failed to question governmental decision, etc.; (3) standards or behavioral norms by which the conduct of a people in relation to their government is judgable (the American people in relation to the American state); and (4) a demonstration that those acts (as in (2)) of the collectivity did fall short of the standards (as in (3)) regardless of whether or not anyone or all of the members of the population could have altered the whole population's pattern of behavior or their government's policies, even if they had had the mechanics for such alteration. By claiming in the non-moral sense that the American people are to blame for the Vietnam atrocities, events which aroused in him feelings of disapprobation, one is saying that he believes that the American people should have done x, y, and z, and of course, that they did not do x, y, and z. However, moral condemnation of the American people is quite another matter.

The types of judgments which signal the practice of moral blaming are first, "should have's" of a particular kind, i.e. moral judgments based on our moral standards, and secondly "could have's." It would not be profitable or justifiable in a paper of this length to compare and contrast the various positions taken in the discussion of whether responsibility may be reconciled with some form of determinism. I take it to be a fact of our ordinary language and everyday behavior that we do hold certain individuals morally blameworthy for some, though not all, of their actions. That is, we hold ourselves and others morally responsible for some of our behavior and its consequences. It is also a fact that we refrain from holding morally responsible some human beings no matter what they do: certain mental defectives and infants. And we never literally hold animals or mechanical devices morally responsible. What distinguishes those cases where we are inclined to hold people morally responsible (blameworthy) from those where we are reluctant to do so?

It should by now be clear that an essential element of all blaming is the existence of standards, either implicit or explicit. The standards in question where non-moral blaming is involved are standards of performance. When moral blaming is at issue, 'He should have done something other than he did when he fell below standard,' is a moral judgment and we are concerned with whether or not "he could have. . . . "

'Could have,' as many writers have pointed out, is problematic. Clearly though, if it is said of someone (Lt. Calley, for example) that "He could have prevented the atrocity," we are generally aware of what the speaker believes about Lt. Calley and the situation. In the first place, he believes that Calley did not prevent the atrocity. Secondly, he believes that Calley possessed a certain amount of power relative to the situation, that Calley had opportunity to alter the situation (he was in command of Charlie Company). Also he believes that Calley was in possession of his mental faculties and thereby capable of assessing the situation and drawing upon and acting upon those assessments. In brief, to say "He could have prevented the massacre at My Lai," is to make implicit reference to Calley's abilities and opportunities. I take 'could have done n' to mean

'There is something such that if he had tried to do that (and that was not what he did do) he would have done n'.[4] Calley is to be morally blamed for the My Lai atrocity because there were many conceivable alternative courses of action, which had he tried to do them he would not have led Charlie Company to massacre innocent villagers (which is not to say that the massacre would not have occurred had Calley tried to do something other than he did). Assuming that mitigating circumstances relative to Calley's mental health are not demonstrable, we have grounds for the belief that Calley "could have done something other than he did," and he is thereby blameworthy for the massacre.

There is an important sequential relationship to be drawn between "should have's" and "could have's" in the practice of blaming. "Should have's" are the primary grounds for judgments of blame for untoward or disvalued events. "Should have's" express our standards, moral or non-moral, usually by citing specific courses of action, that have not been met. A natural progression from the recognition of the event as substandard, the determination of the cause or causes and the expression of our disap-probation to the question of blameworthiness is indicated by the passage to consideration of "could have's." Hence the expressions 'I know he did it, but you can't blame him' or 'Well, yes, he is to blame for it, but how can we blame him?' indicate that mitigating circumstances have affected the secondary "could have" evaluation: where moral blame is not justi-fied some conditions must be believed to exist such that there is really nothing conceivable in his province that if he had tried to do that he could not have caused or participated in the production of the untoward (dis-valued) event. In effect, "could have" questions arise only in light of "should have" questions where blaming is concerned.

Simply then, moral blame is justifiable when no mitigation or excul-pation is demonstrable in the secondary "could have" evaluation of an individual already to blame for failure to meet a moral standard. We need not consider here what might be sufficient grounds for mitigation, though I think we should expect that most if not all examinations into mitigation would begin with the question, "Was he capable of doing anything that we would normally expect would have resulted in different (i.e. not unto-ward) consequences?" After that question might then follow, "Was he capable of appreciating alternative courses of action to the one he pur-sued?" The relationship which I am herein emphasizing is typified by a statement by Daniel Ellsberg in which he was blaming Robert McNamara for the Vietnam war. Ellsberg said, "It must occur to him that the things he did not know were things he should and could have discovered."

When the criteria above are applied to the driver in (A.) we see why no moral blame is due him. Also regarding (B.) we are not likly to morally blame the panic-stricken driver if only because there was nothing con-

[4] I owe much here to the work of Roderick Chisholm, "J. L. Austin's Philosophical Papers," *Mind*, 1964, especially pp. 20–25.

ceivable he could have tried to do which would have prevented the accident (assuming we understand his state of panic to be a mitigating circumstance—he did not "willfully panic"; perhaps anyone would have panicked in such a situation, although most people would have had better bodily reactions and hit the brake). If the pupil in (C.) simply lacks the ability or the capacity to succeed at his task, again he could not have learned more and thereby could not have written more and thereby he is not blameworthy for his failures. Contrary to "should have's," "could have's" are suppressed hypotheticals, though as Austin rightly points out,[5] they are not causal conditionals.

It is necessary, however, to make clear that where judgments of blameworthiness are concerned, the blamer is justified only if he is able to cite some specific action which if the blamed could have done that he would have acted differently. 'He could have done n,' if n stands for a normal verbal expression such as 'written more on *natura naturans*' or 'paid his debts,' needs to be supported by demonstrating the satisfaction of a number of conditions regarding his rather special abilities. 'He could have done n' is true then only if those conditions are satisfied and not true if conditions favorable to his doing n are only a matter of happenstance, chance, or luck. On the other hand, the broader statement 'He could have acted differently' is true just in so far as 'He would have acted differently if he had chosen' is true, and that might be true when his abilities and skills are not essentially involved in the act. 'He would have run the four-minute mile if he had chosen' leaves open whether his success would have been the result of his skills or of the luck of having a brisk wind at his back. Hence the expression 'done something other than he did' is not to be simply equated with 'acted differently'. This is, of course, to elaborate upon the relationship in blaming between 'should have' and 'could have'. 'He should have acted differently' is incomplete. It must be supplemented by reference to the standard of behavior, which is generally, as I have maintained, to cite a specific norm of action.

I have spoken at some length of the different senses of blame, and I have indicated how collective blame may be justified in the non-moral senses of blaming, i.e. if 'they should have done something other than they did' is not a moral judgment. In that sense, a whole population which aided, even by their acquiescence, the perpetration of the untoward events is to blame for those events. But when the "should have" judgment is a moral one and its subject is a collectivity such as the American people, a number of further problems arise. I shall examine some of those problems with reference to war crimes.

Three issues must be met head on: (a) Can one be morally to blame for the acts of another? (b) Can a collectivity such as "the American people" be the bearer of moral blame? and (c) Is "vicarious collective moral blame" reducible to individual vicarious liabilities? Many philosophers have rejected the whole idea of collective responsibility because

---

[5] J. L. Austin, "Ifs and Cans," [*Proceedings of the British Academy*, XLII, 1956].

they feel compelled to answer (a) in the negative. Common usage, however, suggests that there do exist cases in which not only persons *can* be held, but in which we *do* hold people morally responsible (blameworthy) for the acts of others. Possibly underlying the negative answer to (a) is a confusion of the concept of guilt with that of blame.

'Guilt' is generally applied in cases of willful breach of legal codes. If Mr. X is guilty of *y*, he is a perpetrator, inciter, abettor, or accomplice, etc. in the performance of the untoward or unpermitted *y*. (I am not here interested in the legalistic sense of guilt as 'having been found guilty.') No one, to be sure, can be guilty of the illegal acts of another, though as history has painfully shown, one can be found guilty of the acts of another.

If my child steals a car, he is guilty of stealing. I cannot be guilty of his stealing, but I may well be held to blame for his stealing. I may, of course, be guilty of raising my child to be a thief, but that is not to be guilty of his thievery. For me to be guilty of stealing the car it must be shown that I was an abettor, accomplice, inciter, etc. Even then, however, I am not guilty of his stealing. I am guilty myself of stealing. Considering such examples it should be evident that 'guilt' and 'blame' are not synonymous (cannot always be used interchangeably) and furthermore that blame can be vicarious (I am to blame for the child's thievery, even though I am not the thief). As I have argued, moral blame stresses the censure that is coincidental with one's being held liable for substandard behavior. As there are a number of things I might have tried to do which would normally be expected in order to raise a child with a greater respect for private property and as I do not qualify for any acceptable exemptions, others are justified in morally blaming me for my child's thievery. I might even blame myself. It is not simply that I should have raised him better than I did, I could have done so. It might be objected that I am really only morally to blame for being a poor parent and not vicariously to blame for my son's thefts. I think, however, such an objection misses the point of expressions such as 'The boy stole the car, but the parents are to blame.' When we are speaking of moral blame, guilt is not the major problem. I am inclined to the view that to be guilty is to have done the disapprobated deed, that the paradigmatic use of the word is its legalistic use. I assume then, that to be "morally guilty" is to have transgressed a moral code, but that is only the first step in determining moral blameworthiness. After all, psychopaths, mental defectives, young children, and idiots are constantly transgressing such codes. The notion that such persons cannot transgress moral codes because they cannot appreciate the moral nature of such codes begs the question. To argue that "moral guilt" is the willful transgression of such codes will not do either. Surely some of the above-mentioned transgress those codes not only willingly but with finesse.[6]

---

[6]Charles Manson might well be a case in point.

What the illustration of the thieving child shows is that moral blame is transferable. There is nothing out of the ordinary in the notion of vicarious liability. Another example may be made to bear more specifically on the issue of justifying the blaming of collectivities. We have all seen science fiction movies in which a scientist attempting to probe the limits of knowledge in search of the "secret of life" (and often for some humane reason) creates a human-looking monster which soon goes berserk and indiscriminately ravages the countryside. The scientist is beset with overwhelming pangs of self-blame, and the good people of the town also blame him for the monstrous evil deeds. Despite the fact that the scientist has no control over the monster, despite the fact that he had only good intentions at its creation, I think we are justified in holding him morally blameworthy for the monster's deeds. He should have expected dire consequences to occur when he created a super-human monster. But not only should he have refrained from creating the monster; he could have, in the relevant sense, so refrained, assuming, of course, that he was not a mental defective, psychopath, etc. The scientist I have in mind is not of the "mad" variety, though he may be obsessed with his theories. Obsessions of this sort do not alter what he "could have done"; after all, an obsession is not unalterable.

Now let us expand this science fiction example in order to examine the issues of collective moral blame. Suppose our scientist were not working in isolation, that he was one of a team of scientists. I think that we would not be reluctant to morally blame the team of scientists for the monster's deeds; we can make perfectly good sense of the expression 'The whole team of scientists is to blame.' First let us assume that the team of scientists was organized in such a way that they could make group decisions on the value and advisability of various avenues of research in their project, that as a team they were capable of making judgments including moral ones and of putting them into practice. Let us also assume that no one was forced to join the team and that they all knew that they were "searching for the secret of life." This would fulfill certain requirements for identifying them as a specific collectivity and not just a gathering of scientists. As a team they would then satisfy the criteria for moral blameworthiness in the case of the monster's acts. Not only should they have chosen a different avenue of research, they could have done so.

But once we have blamed the team, we have not necessarily blamed each scientist individually for the monstrous deeds. If X, Y, and Z form collectivity A, and if A can and does act as a collectivity, e.g. it has and makes use of its decision methods for action, then we may be justified in finding A morally blameworthy for its acts; though the sum of X, Y, and Z's liability is not equivalent to that we ascribe to A. 'Collectivity A is blameworthy for event n and A is composed of individuals X, Y, and Z' does not entail 'X is blameworthy for n, Y is blameworthy for n, and Z is blameworthy for n'. Herein, of course, lies one of the stickiest problems with the notion of blaming collectivities: how can a collectivity be held morally to blame for event n when not all of its members are held morally blameworthy for n? The approach I am suggesting for blaming collectivities appears to make the collectivity an entity capable of bearing moral blame over and above the sum of the blame due each individual member. I think that there are good reasons for holding such a view. Collectivities are, in fact, often organized in such a way that they may shoulder blame for the failure of their projects without reflecting on individuals. For example, the Honeywell corporation is said by many to be to blame for the damage done by its anti-personnel bombs in North Vietnam.[7] Most people, however, would recognize as unjust blaming every Honeywell worker individually for that destruction.

It should be noted, however, that from 'Collectivity A is blameworthy for event n and A is composed of X, Y, and Z' it would be presumptuous to conclude that X, Y, or Z do not warrant any blame for n or that either X, Y, or Z is not himself blameworthy in the case of n. My point is that such judgments assessed on members of the collectivity do not follow necessarily from judgments of collective blame. Indeed, we may expect that at least one of the scientists in the team merits individual blame for n, but the grounds for justifying such blaming are not those by which the collective blame is justified. It has been argued by Virginia Held[8] that the assessment of moral responsibility on a collectivity is not distributive but that it can be concluded from such an assessment that at least some members of the collectivity are responsible for the act in question. I shall argue that although such is often the case, it is not a defining characteristic of morally blaming collectivities that one is able to conclude from the ascription of collective responsibility that some member or members of the collectivity is/are liable for the act in question.

Three questions bear most significantly on the question of justifying morally blaming collectivities: (1) Can collectivities act in ways not simply reducible to the acts of their members? (2) Does it make sense to say that a collectivity should have done something other than it did do? (or Do standards of collective action exist?), and (3) Are collectivities capable of trying courses of action different from those they actually took? There are any number of things one can say about the actions of a collectivity which cannot be said of or cannot be reduced to statements about the acts of individuals, or at least such reductions destroy the sense of the original statement about the collectivity. In the case of the team of scientists, it might be said that they created a monster, though no individual scientist on the team could have done so alone. 'The X, Y, Z team of scientists made a monster' does not entail, 'X made a monster, Y made a monster, and Z made a monster.' If the point is not yet clear, compare the above to the statement, 'The team lost the big game,' which does not entail 'The quarterback lost the big game' or 'The middle linebacker lost the big

---

[7]Honeywell disputes this, however, by claiming that they only make the bombs for their government as a patriotic service. They do not drop them on Vietnamese citizens.
[8]Held, in my *Individual and Collective Responsibility*.

game,' etc. It does not even entail that any of the players played poorly as individuals. The team effort was just not up to the occasion, perchance a general spirit was lacking; or perhaps the team, through circumstances for which no individual could be cited, is so constituted that even when all members play as well as they possibly can, the total performance is dismal. The team simply lacks a certain complementarity.

Some have argued that although fault may be collective, group liability is always distributive. I think that in such a view is embedded a confusion. Let us take the example with which we are basically concerned:

(D.) "The American people are to blame for the Vietnam atrocities."

Assume that we are dealing with moral blame. How is (D.) to be justified? Anyone sincerely saying (D.) must be able to show (1) that there exists a recognizable or referable collectivity designated by the term 'the American people'; (2) that events describable as "atrocities" took place in Vietnam;[9] (3) that a causal relationship can be drawn from acts of the collectivity to the "atrocities" in question; (4) that the American people should have acted (collectively) in a manner different from the manner in which they did act; (5) that the American people were not completely unaware of the nature of their behavior (that is, the American people did not believe they were authorizing a cultural exchange of ballet troupes with the Vietnamese); and (6) that the collectivity could have acted (had the ability and opportunity of acting) in those alternative ways cited in (4), that is, there were conceivable alternative courses of collective action which had they been tried would have made less likely the perpetration of atrocities in Vietnam (the untoward events).

Now it might be argued that my position seems to ignore the fact that collectivities are collections of individuals, that "the American people" is a composition of all Americans (compared to "Mankind is a composition of all men"), and that it seems intuitively unjust to morally blame the American people (all Americans) when a goodly number evidence their lack of support for the war effort. But far from having ignored such a view, I have shown that it rests on a misunderstanding; collectivities are not *just* collections of individuals.

The terms 'the American people' and 'all Americans' are not equivalent. In 'all Americans' 'Americans' acts as a general term. What is true of all Americans is true of each and every American. If we were saying "All Americans are to blame for the Vietnam atrocities" then we would have to justify blaming each American, a task which would be most difficult in the case of some Americans. On the other hand 'the American people' is not a general term. It is a singular term which names or purports to name a collectivity. What is true of "the American people" need not be, and actually often is not true of each and every American. For example consider the statement 'The American people have the

[9]Clearly the word 'atrocity' is an implicit blaming expression.

highest standard of living in the world,' which certainly does not mean that each and every American has the highest standard of living in the world. Notice also that the statement 'The American people grew tired of hearing about the Vietnamese war' may be true when the statement 'American John Doe grew tired of hearing about the Vietnamese war' is false. There is therefore no question of justifying ascriptions of blame for the war to each and every American citizen.

Those who might seek to preserve the notion that responsibility is primarily an individual matter might propose we treat statements such as (D.) as a shorthand version of

(E.) "All American citizens who did not overtly behave in ways which manifested their non-membership in the subcollectivity 'American war supporters' are individually to blame (degrees of blame would probably be appropriate) for the Vietnam atrocities."

But (E.) as the above suggests, is not an acceptable substitute for (D.). They mean entirely different things. The membership of a blamed collectivity (like the American people) cannot be defined, *ad hoc,* in terms of individual participation (overt or covert) in the untoward events which were the occasion of the blaming episode. When someone blames "the American people" or "the Honeywell corporation" or the team of scientists or the football team he is not usually adding (softly under his breath so that he and a few methodological individualists can hear) some qualification to the effect "except those who did. . . ." The collectivity would soon die the death of "a thousand qualifications."[10] "The American people" is a collectivity of which action is predicable and to which blame (moral responsibility) is ascribable. If it were the case that the meaning of a statement about "the American people" were identical to the conjunction of a number of statements about the members of the collectivity "the American people," then had one of the individuals belonging to the American people (collectivity) not in fact been a member, the meaning of the original statement would have been different. It is a mistake thereby to seek grounds for exculpation for individual collectivity members, when (D.) is not individually blaming anyone (which is not to say that individuals are not morally to blame). The only issue of exculpation in regard to (D.) is that of whether or not in the relevant sense one is justified in saying that "the American people" could not have tried to do anything other than it did in the circumstances even if it should have.

Membership in "the American people" or "the Honeywell corporation" or "the football team" is not determined by whether one materially contributed to the particular untoward event for which the collectivity is being blamed, but instead whether one has the "credentials" of membership in the collectivity that can act in such a way as to be productive of

[10]This term is borrowed from Antony Flew.

such an untoward event. The credentials of membership in "the American people" would seem to include at least citizenship, perhaps maturity, common descent, language, or history, if you like. But the expression 'the American people' surely does not mean 'only those people of American citizenship who support program x or y or z of their government.' In fact, 'the American people' is used in ordinary discourse to name not only a collectivity of individuals but also the nation for which the President of the United States speaks and in whose name the armies of the United States march. It should not be forgotten that, theoretically at least, "the American people" are sovereign in the United States.

There remains another possible objection: it might be argued that we are not justified in morally blaming whole populations without blaming individuals because there is really no point in it; that there is no reason to expect our blaming to alter the future behavior of the collectivity. Certainly few national populations alter their actions because of a fear of blame or censure. Perhaps, however, such a statement as 'The German people are to blame for Dachau' has had some impact at least as a kind of warning (the plaque at Dachau reads, "For the past, honor, for the future a warning.") The confusion here, however, is in treating the efficacy of blaming as the grounds for blaming. Whether or not blaming X for *n* is or should be expected to be productive of desired results is not the same problem as whether or not X merits moral blame for *n*. It must be remembered that moral blaming is "to hold responsible," "to deem blameworthy." It is not "to punish." The only justifiable reason for morally blaming a whole population is that that population merits moral blame, and the determination of blameworthiness is first a question of standards and then one of abilities and opportunities.

To the question, "Why should we blame the American people?", the answer "Because it will make the American people act differently in the future" rests only on the vaguest of hopes and goes counter to most of what we know of history. But then history gives us little precedent for morally dealing with the powerful technological conglomerates and political machines which now proliferate at a blinding rate of speed. Standards for individual behavior and standards of collective behavior should not be thought *a priori* to be ineffably linked. What is needed is not a reversion to traditional theories of individualism but a realistic approach to the problem of standards of behavior for both individuals and collectivities.

SECTION TWELVE

SOCIAL CHANGE AND REVOLUTION

In the 18th Brumaire of Louis Bonaparte, *Karl Marx wrote: "Men make their own history but they do not make it just as they please; they do not make it under circumstances chosen by themselves, but under circumstances directly encountered, given and transmitted from the past." Here we have a formulation of the two aspects of social change. First, social change is the result of human action, and second, such action is itself a response to prevailing social conditions. Human beings make history, but they often do so unconsciously; that is, social change, while the result of human action, is perhaps most often an unreflective response to the social conditions that we confront.*

However, human beings have also attempted to understand the historical and social conditions in which they find themselves, and they have attempted consciously to change those conditions. In the sixteenth, seventeenth, and eighteenth centuries, revolutions were made in the name of individual liberty and equality, and the philosophy that emerged from them came to be known as liberalism. In the twentieth century, it is Marxism that exemplifies the philosophy of revolution; while liberalism has become the philosophy of peaceful, social reform. The problems posed in this section are those that have grown out of the historical confrontation between liberalism and Marxism.

Karl Marx and Friedrich Engels
THE COMMUNIST MANIFESTO

Only a century and a quarter has passed since the first publication of The Communist Manifesto, *but since that time, great social movements influenced by its thinking have arisen in almost every country of the world. At present, over half the world lives in countries whose leaders at least claim to be followers of Marx and Engels.*

The appeal of Marxism is too vast to be attributed to their often fiery rhetorical style or to the frustration of people who are oppressed. For Marxism is, above all, a tool for the analysis of social structure and historical change. It is not merely a call to arms but a theoretical guide to revolutionary practice.

In his preface to A Contribution to the Critique of Political Economy, *Marx writes: "The general result at which I arrived and which, once won, served as a guiding thread for my studies, can be briefly formulated as follows: In the social production of their life, men enter into definite relations that are indispensable and independent of their will, relations of production which correspond to a definite stage of the development of their material productive forces. The sum total of these relations of production constitutes the economic structure of society, the real foundation on which rises a legal and political superstructure and to which correspond definite forms of social consciousness. The mode of production of material life conditions the social, political and intellectual life processes in general. . . . At a certain stage of their development, the material productive forces of society come in conflict with the existing relations of production, or—what is but a legal expression for the same thing—with the property relations within which they have been at work hitherto. From forms of development of the productive forces these relations turn into their fetters. Then begins an epoch of social revolution."*

Historical change, then, is generated by conflict, tensions, and antagonisms (Marx and Engels often referred to them as "contradictions") at the economic level of society, which is the most basic level and the foundation upon which rest all other social and political institutions and intellectual life (social consciousness). Within the economic base, historical change is generated by the tensions between the growth of the productive forces (technology, raw materials, organization of labor within the work place) and the social relations of production, that is, between the development of the means of production, on the one hand, and property relations on the other. However, this antagonism does not erupt automatically but rather is expressed through class struggle, the struggle between the class (or classes) that would further develop the new means of production to its collective benefit and the class (or classes) whose privilege and rule depends upon maintaining the property relations, and with them, the whole social and political setup, which would hold back or, at least, retard that development. These class struggles, in turn, manifest themselves not only in the economic realm but at every other level of social activity (religion, family, politics, morality, art, philosophy). Thus, as the manufacturing industry developed and came into conflict with feudal property relations, the bourgeoisie assumed a revolutionary stance against the entire feudal social and political order. Similarly, as the development of modern industry strains against the limits of capitalist (bourgeois) economic organization, the proletariat (the working class), brought into existence by capitalism itself, emerges as the new agent of revolutionary change.

.   .   .

The history of all hitherto existing society is the history of class struggles.

Freeman and slave, patrician and plebeian, lord and serf, guild-master[1] and journeyman, in a word, oppressor and oppressed, stood in constant opposition to one another, carried on an uninterrupted, now hidden, now open fight, a fight that each time ended, either in a revolutionary re-constitution of society at large, or in the common ruin of the contending classes.

In the earlier epochs of history, we find almost everywhere a complicated arrangement of society into various orders, a manifold gradation of social rank. In ancient Rome we have patricians, knights, plebeians, slaves; in the Middle Ages, feudal lords, vassals, guild-masters, journeymen, apprentices, serfs; in almost all of these classes, again, subordinate gradations.

The modern bourgeois society that has sprouted from the ruins of feudal society has not done away with class antagonisms. It has but established new classes, new conditions of oppression, new forms of struggle in place of the old ones.

Our epoch, the epoch of the bourgeoisie, possesses, however, this distinctive feature: it has simplified the class antagonisms. Society as a whole is more and more splitting up into two great hostile camps, into two great classes directly facing each other: Bourgeoisie and Proletariat.

From the serfs of the Middle Ages sprang the chartered burghers of the earliest towns. From these burgesses the first elements of the bourgeoisie were developed.

The discovery of America, the rounding of the Cape, opened up fresh ground for the rising bourgeoisie. The East-Indian and Chinese markets, the colonisation of America, trade with the colonies, the increase in the means of exchange and in commodities generally, gave to commerce, to navigation, to industry, an impulse never before known, and thereby, to the revolutionary element in the tottering feudal society, a rapid development.

The feudal system of industry, under which industrial production was monopolised by closed guilds, now no longer sufficed for the growing wants of the new markets. The manufacturing system took its place. The guild-masters were pushed on one side by the manufacturing middle class; division of labour between the different corporate guilds vanished in the face of division of labour in each single workshop.

Meantime the markets kept ever growing, the demand ever rising. Even manufacture no longer sufficed. Thereupon, steam and machinery revolutionised industrial production. The place of manufacture was taken by the giant, Modern Industry, the place of the industrial middle class,

[1]Guild-master, that is, a full member of a guild, a master within, not a head of a guild. [*Note by Engels to the English edition of 1888.*]

by industrial millionaires, the leaders of whole industrial armies, the modern bourgeois.

Modern industry has established the world-market, for which the discovery of America paved the way. This market has given an immense development to commerce, to navigation, to communication by land. This development has, in its turn, reacted on the extension of industry; and in proportion as industry, commerce, navigation, railways extended, in the same proportion the bourgeoisie developed, increased its capital, and pushed into the background every class handed down from the Middle Ages.

We see, therefore, how the modern bourgeoisie is itself the product of a long course of development, of a series of revolutions in the modes of production and of exchange.

Each step in the development of the bourgeoisie was accompanied by a corresponding political advance of that class. An oppressed class under the sway of the feudal nobility, an armed and self-governing association in the mediaeval commune[2]; here independent urban republic (as in Italy and Germany), there taxable "third estate" of the monarchy (as in France), afterwards, in the period of manufacture proper, serving either the semi-feudal or the absolute monarchy as a counterpoise against the nobility, and, in fact, corner-stone of the great monarchies in general, the bourgeoisie has at last, since the establishment of Modern Industry and of the world-market, conquered for itself, in the modern representative State, exclusive political sway. The executive of the modern State is but a committee for managing the common affairs of the whole bourgeoisie.

The bourgeoisie, historically, has played a most revolutionary part.

The bourgeoisie, wherever it has got the upper hand, has put an end to all feudal, patriarchal, idyllic relations. It has pitilessly torn asunder the motley feudal ties that bound man to his "natural superiors," and has left remaining no other nexus between man and man than naked self-interest, than callous "cash payment." It has drowned the most heavenly ecstasies of religious fervour, of chivalrous enthusiasm, of philistine sentimentalism, in the icy water of egotistical calculation. It has resolved personal worth into exchange value, and in place of the numberless indefeasible chartered freedoms, has set up that single, unconscionable freedom— Free Trade. In one word, for exploitation, veiled by religious and political illusions, it has substituted naked, shameless, direct, brutal exploitation.

The bourgeoisie has stripped of its halo every occupation hitherto honoured and looked up to with reverent awe. It has converted the physician, the lawyer, the priest, the poet, the man of science, into its paid wage-labourers.

---

[2]This was the name given their urban communities by the townsmen of Italy and France, after they had purchased or wrested their initial rights of self-government from their feudal lords. [*Note by Engels to the German edition of 1890.*]

The bourgeoisie has torn away from the family its sentimental veil, and has reduced the family relation to a mere money relation.

The bourgeoisie has disclosed how it came to pass that the brutal display of vigour in the Middle Ages, which Reactionists so much admire, found its fitting complement in the most slothful indolence. It has been the first to show what man's activity can bring about. It has accomplished wonders far surpassing Egyptian pyramids, Roman aqueducts, and Gothic cathedrals; it has conducted expeditions that put in the shade all former Exoduses of nations and crusades.

The bourgeoisie cannot exist without constantly revolutionising the instruments of production, and thereby the relations of production, and with them the whole relations of society. Conservation of the old modes of production in unaltered form, was, on the contrary, the first condition of existence for all earlier industrial classes. Constant revolutionising of production, uninterrupted disturbance of all social conditions, everlasting uncertainty and agitation distinguish the bourgeois epoch from all earlier ones. All fixed, fast-frozen relations, with their train of ancient and venerable prejudices and opinions, are swept away, all new-formed ones become antiquated before they can ossify. All that is solid melts into air, all that is holy is profaned, and man is at last compelled to face with sober senses, his real conditions of life, and his relations with his kind.

The need of a constantly expanding market for its products chases the bourgeoisie over the whole surface of the globe. It must nestle everywhere, settle everywhere, establish connexions everywhere.

The bourgeoisie has through its exploitation of the world-market given a cosmopolitan character to production and consumption in every country. To the great chagrin of Reactionists, it has drawn from under the feet of industry the national ground on which it stood. All old-established national industries have been destroyed or are daily being destroyed. They are dislodged by new industries, whose introduction becomes a life and death question for all civilised nations, by industries that no longer work up indigenous raw material, but raw material drawn from the remotest zones; industries whose products are consumed, not only at home, but in every quarter of the globe. In place of the old wants, satisfied by the productions of the country, we find new wants, requiring for their satisfaction the products of distant lands and climes. In place of the old local and national seclusion and self-sufficiency, we have intercourse in every direction, universal inter-dependence of nations. And as in material, so also in intellectual production. The intellectual creations of individual nations become common property. National one-sidedness and narrow-mindedness become more and more impossible, and from the numerous national and local literatures, there arises a world literature.

The bourgeoisie, by the rapid improvement of all instruments of production, by the immensely facilitated means of communication, draws all, even the most barbarian, nations into civilisation. The cheap prices of its commodities are the heavy artillery with which it batters down all

Chinese walls, with which it forces the barbarians' intensely obstinate hatred of foreigners to capitulate. It compels all nations, on pain of extinction, to adopt the bourgeois mode of production; it compels them to introduce what it calls civilisation into their midst, *i.e.,* to become bourgeois themselves. In one word, it creates a world after its own image.

The bourgeoisie has subjected the country to the rule of the towns. It has created enormous cities, has greatly increased the urban population, as compared with the rural, and has thus rescued a considerable part of the population from the idiocy of rural life. Just as it has made the country dependent on the towns, so it has made barbarian and semi-barbarian countries dependent on the civilised ones, nations of peasants on nations of bourgeois, the East on the West.

The bourgeoisie keeps more and more doing away with the scattered state of the population, of the means of production, and of property. It has agglomerated population, centralised means of production, and has concentrated property in a few hands. The necessary consequence of this was political centralisation. Independent, or but loosely connected provinces, with separate interests, laws, governments and systems of taxation, became lumped together into one nation, with one government, one code of laws, one national class-interest, one frontier and one customs-tariff.

The bourgeoisie, during its rule of scarce one hundred years, has created more massive and more colossal productive forces than have all preceding generations together. Subjection of Nature's forces to man, machinery, application of chemistry to industry and agriculture, steam-navigation, railways, electric telegraphs, clearing of whole continents for cultivation, canalisation of rivers, whole populations conjured out of the ground—what earlier century had even a presentiment that such productive forces slumbered in the lap of social labour?

We see then: the means of production and of exchange, on whose foundation the bourgeoisie built itself up, were generated in feudal society. At a certain stage in the development of these means of production and of exchange, the conditions under which feudal society produced and exchanged, the feudal organisation of agriculture and manufacturing industry, in one word, the feudal relations of property became no longer compatible with the already developed productive forces; they became so many fetters. They had to be burst asunder; they were burst asunder.

Into their place stepped free competition, accompanied by a social and political constitution adapted to it, and by the economical and political sway of the bourgeois class.

A similar movement is going on before our own eyes. Modern bourgeois society with its relations of production, of exchange and of property, a society that has conjured up such gigantic means of production and of exchange, is like the sorcerer, who is no longer able to control the powers of the nether world whom he has called up by his spells. For many a decade past the history of industry and commerce is but the history of the revolt of modern productive forces against modern conditions of production, against the property relations that are the conditions for the existence of the bourgeoisie and of its rule. It is enough to mention the commercial crises that by their periodical return put on its trial, each time more threateningly, the existence of the entire bourgeois society. In these crises a great part not only of the existing products, but also of the previously created productive forces, are periodically destroyed. In these crises there breaks out an epidemic that, in all earlier epochs, would have seemed an absurdity—the epidemic of over-production. Society suddenly finds itself put back into a state of momentary barbarism; it appears as if a famine, a universal war of devastation had cut off the supply of every means of subsistence; industry and commerce seem to be destroyed; and why? Because there is too much industry, too much commerce. The productive forces at the disposal of society no longer tend to further the development of the conditions of bourgeois property; on the contrary, they have become too powerful for these conditions, by which they are fettered, and so soon as they overcome these fetters, they bring disorder into the whole of bourgeois society, endanger the existence of bourgeois property. The conditions of bourgeois society are too narrow to comprise the wealth created by them. And how does the bourgeoisie get over these crises? On the one hand by enforced destruction of a mass of productive forces; on the other, by the conquest of new markets, and by the more thorough exploitation of the old ones. That is to say, by paving the way for more extensive and more destructive crises, and by diminishing the means whereby crises are prevented.

The weapons with which the bourgeoisie felled feudalism to the ground are now turned against the bourgeoisie itself.

But not only has the bourgeoisie forged the weapons that bring death to itself; it has also called into existence the men who are to wield those weapons—the modern working class—the proletarians.

In proportion as the bourgeoisie, *i.e.,* capital, is developed, in the same proportion is the proletariat, the modern working class, developed —a class of labourers, who live only so long as they find work, and who find work only so long as their labour increases capital. These labourers, who must sell themselves piecemeal, are a commodity, like every other article of commerce, and are consequently exposed to all the vicissitudes of competition, to all the fluctuations of the market.

Owing to the extensive use of machinery and to division of labour, the work of the proletarians has lost all individual character, and, conse-quently, all charm for the workman. He becomes an appendage of the machine, and it is only the most simple, most monotonous, and most easily acquired knack, that is required of him. Hence, the cost of produc-tion of a workman is restricted, almost entirely, to the means of subsis-tence that he requires for his maintenance, and for the propagation of his race. But the price of a commodity, and therefore also of labour, is equal to its cost of production. In proportion, therefore, as the repulsiveness of the work increases, the wage decreases. Nay more, in proportion as the use of machinery and division of labour increases, in the same proportion the burden of toil also increases, whether by prolongation of the working hours, by increase of the work exacted in a given time or by increased speed of the machinery, etc.

Modern industry has converted the little workshop of the patriarchal master into the great factory of the industrial capitalist. Masses of labourers, crowded into the factory, are organised like soldiers. As privates of the industrial army they are placed under the command of a perfect hierarchy of officers and sergeants. Not only are they slaves of the bourgeois class, and of the bourgeois State; they are daily and hourly enslaved by the machine, by the overlooker, and, above all, by the individual bourgeois manufacturer himself. The more openly this despotism proclaims gain to be its end and aim, the more petty, the more hateful and the more embittering it is.

The less the skill and exertion of strength implied in manual labour, in other words, the more modern industry becomes developed, the more is the labour of men superseded by that of women. Differences of age and sex have no longer any distinctive social validity for the working class. All are instruments of labour, more or less expensive to use, according to their age and sex.

No sooner is the exploitation of the labourer by the manufacturer, so far, at an end, and he receives his wages in cash, than he is set upon by the other portions of the bourgeoisie, the landlord, the shopkeeper, the pawnbroker, etc.

The lower strata of the middle class—the small tradespeople, shopkeepers, and retired tradesmen generally, the handicraftsmen and peasants—all these sink gradually into the proletariat, partly because their diminutive capital does not suffice for the scale on which Modern Industry is carried on, and is swamped in the competition with the large capitalists, partly because their specialised skill is rendered worthless by new methods of production. Thus the proletariat is recruited from all classes of the population.

The proletariat goes through various stages of development. With its birth begins its struggle with the bourgeoisie. At first the contest is carried on by individual labourers, then by the workpeople of a factory, then by the operatives of one trade, in one locality, against the individual bourgeois who directly exploits them. They direct their attacks not against the bourgeois conditions of production, but against the instruments of production themselves; they destroy imported wares that compete with their labour, they smash to pieces machinery, they set factories ablaze, they seek to restore by force the vanished status of the workman of the Middle Ages.

At this stage the labourers still form an incoherent mass scattered over the whole country, and broken up by their mutual competition. If anywhere they unite to form more compact bodies, this is not yet the consequence of their own active union, but of the union of the bourgeoisie, which class, in order to attain its own political ends, is compelled to set the whole proletariat in motion, and is moreover yet, for a time, able to do so. At this stage, therefore, the proletarians do not fight their enemies, but the enemies of their enemies, the remnants of absolute monarchy, the landowners, the non-industrial bourgeois, the petty bourgeoisie. Thus the whole historical movement is concentrated in the hands of the bourgeoisie; every victory so obtained is a victory for the bourgeoisie.

But with the development of industry the proletariat not only increases in number; it becomes concentrated in greater masses, its strength grows, and it feels that strength more. The various interests and conditions of life within the ranks of the proletariat are more and more equalised, in proportion as machinery obliterates all distinctions of labour, and nearly everywhere reduces wages to the same low level. The growing competition among the bourgeois, and the resulting commercial crises, make the wages of the workers ever more fluctuating. The unceasing improvement of machinery, ever more rapidly developing, makes their livelihood more and more precarious: the collisions between individual workmen and individual bourgeois take more and more the character of collisions between two classes. Thereupon the workers begin to form combinations (Trades' Unions) against the bourgeois; they club together in order to keep up the rate of wages; they found permanent associations in order to make provision beforehand for these occasional revolts. Here and there the contest breaks out into riots.

Now and then the workers are victorious, but only for a time. The real fruit of their battles lies, not in the immediate result, but in the ever-expanding union of the workers. This union is helped on by the improved means of communication that are created by modern industry and that place the workers of different localities in contact with one another. It was just this contact that was needed to centralise the numerous local struggles, all of the same character, into one national struggle between classes. But every class struggle is a political struggle. And that union, to attain which the burghers of the Middle Ages, with their miserable highways, required centuries, the modern proletarians, thanks to railways, achieve in a few years.

This organisation of the proletarians into a class, and consequently into a political party, is continually being upset again by the competition between the workers themselves. But it ever rises up again, stronger, firmer, mightier. It compels legislative recognition of particular interests of the workers, by taking advantage of the divisions among the bourgeoisie itself. Thus the ten-hours' bill in England was carried.

Altogether collisions between the classes of the old society further, in many ways, the course of development of the proletariat. The bourgeoisie finds itself involved in a constant battle. At first with the aristocracy; later on, with those portions of the bourgeoisie itself, whose interests have become antagonistic to the progress of industry; at all times, with the bourgeoisie of foreign countries. In all these battles it sees itself compelled to appeal to the proletariat, to ask for its help, and thus, to drag it into the political arena. The bourgeoisie itself, therefore, supplies the proletariat with its own elements of political and general education, in other words, it furnishes the proletariat with weapons for fighting the bourgeoisie.

Further, as we have already seen, entire sections of the ruling classes are, by the advance of industry, precipitated into the proletariat, or are at least threatened in their conditions of existence. These also supply the proletariat with fresh elements of enlightenment and progress.

Finally, in times when the class struggle nears the decisive hour, the process of dissolution going on within the ruling class, in fact within the whole range of old society, assumes such a violent, glaring character, that a small section of the ruling class cuts itself adrift, and joins the revolutionary class, the class that holds the future in its hands. Just as, therefore, at an earlier period, a section of the nobility went over to the bourgeoisie, so now a portion of the bourgeoisie goes over to the proletariat, and in particular, a portion of the bourgeois ideologists, who have raised themselves to the level of comprehending theoretically the historical movement as a whole.

Of all the classes that stand face to face with the bourgeoisie today, the proletariat alone is a really revolutionary class. The other classes decay and finally disappear in the face of Modern Industry; the proletariat is its special and essential product.

The lower middle class, the small manufacturer, the shopkeeper, the artisan, the peasant, all these fight against the bourgeoisie, to save from extinction their existence as fractions of the middle class. They are therefore not revolutionary, but conservative. Nay more, they are reactionary, for they try to roll back the wheel of history. If by chance they are revolutionary, they are so only in view of their impending transfer into the proletariat, they thus defend not their present, but their future interests, they desert their own standpoint to place themselves at that of the proletariat.

The "dangerous class," the social scum, that passively rotting mass thrown off by the lowest layers of old society, may, here and there, be swept into the movement by a proletarian revolution, its conditions of life, however, prepare it far more for the part of a bribed tool of reactionary intrigue.

In the conditions of the proletariat, those of old society at large are already virtually swamped. The proletarian is without property; his relation to his wife and children has no longer anything in common with the bourgeois family-relations; modern industrial labour, modern subjection to capital, the same in England as in France, in America as in Germany, has stripped him of every trace of national character. Law, morality, religion, are to him so many bourgeois prejudices, behind which lurk in ambush just as many bourgeois interests.

All the preceding classes that got the upper hand, sought to fortify their already acquired status by subjecting society at large to their conditions of appropriation. The proletarians cannot become masters of the productive forces of society, except by abolishing their own previous mode of appropriation, and thereby also every other previous mode of appropriation. They have nothing of their own to secure and to fortify; their mission is to destroy all previous securities for, and insurances of, individual property.

All previous historical movements were movements of minorities, or in the interest of minorities. The proletarian movement is the self-conscious, independent movement of the immense majority, in the interests of the immense majority. The proletariat, the lowest stratum of our present society, cannot stir, cannot raise itself up, without the whole superincumbent strata of official society being sprung into the air.

Though not in substance, yet in form, the struggle of the proletariat with the bourgeoisie is at first a national struggle. The proletariat of each country must, of course, first of all settle matters with its own bourgeoisie.

In depicting the most general phases of the development of the proletariat, we traced the more or less veiled civil war, raging within existing society, up to the point where that war breaks out into open revolution, and where the violent overthrow of the bourgeoisie lays the foundation for the sway of the proletariat.

Hitherto, every form of society has been based, as we have already seen, on the antagonism of oppressing and oppressed classes. But in order to oppress a class, certain conditions must be assured to it under which it can, at least, continue its slavish existence. The serf, in the period of serfdom, raised himself to membership in the commune, just as the petty bourgeois, under the yoke of feudal absolutism, managed to develop into a bourgeois. The modern labourer, on the contrary, instead of rising with the progress of industry, sinks deeper and deeper below the conditions of existence of his own class. He becomes a pauper, and pauperism develops more rapidly than population and wealth. And here it becomes evident, that the bourgeoisie is unfit any longer to be the ruling class in society, and to impose its conditions of existence upon society as an over-riding law. It is unfit to rule because it is incompetent to assure an existence to its slave within his slavery, because it cannot help letting him sink into such a state, that it has to feed him, instead of being fed by him. Society can no longer live under this bourgeoisie, in other words, its existence is no longer compatible with society.

The essential condition for the existence, and for the sway of the bourgeois class, is the formation and augmentation of capital; the condition for capital is wage-labour. Wage-labour rests exclusively on competition between the labourers. The advance of industry, whose involuntary promoter is the bourgeoisie, replaces the isolation of the labourers, due to competition, by their revolutionary combination, due to association. The development of Modern Industry, therefore, cuts from under its feet the very foundation on which the bourgeoisie produces and appropriates products. What the bourgeoisie, therefore, produces, above all, is its own grave-diggers. Its fall and the victory of the proletariat are equally inevitable.

.   .   .

John Dewey
LIBERALISM AND SOCIAL ACTION

A major figure in the development of pragmatism, a philosophical method that emphasizes the relation of thought to action, John Dewey (1859–1952) is known also as a social psychologist, a political theorist, and a pioneer in the field of progressive education. In the selection that follows, Dewey argues that liberalism, while committed to "radical" social change, is opposed to class struggle and violence. Instead, liberalism insists on employing the method of organized intelligence, which Dewey equates politically with the method of democracy. With respect to the last, Dewey argues that it is contradictory to espouse democracy as an ideal end while using violence as a means.

.   .   .

When, then, I say that the first object of a renascent liberalism is education, I mean that its task is to aid in producing the habits of mind and character, the intellectual and moral patterns, that are somewhere near even with the actual movements of events. It is, I repeat, the split between the latter as they have externally occurred and the ways of desiring, thinking, and of putting emotion and purpose into execution that is the basic cause of present confusion in mind and paralysis in action. The educational task cannot be accomplished merely by working upon men's minds, without action that effects actual change in institutions. The idea that dispositions and attitudes can be altered by merely "moral" means conceived of as something that goes on wholly inside of persons is itself one of the old patterns that has to be changed. Thought, desire and purpose exist in a constant give and take of interaction with environing conditions. But resolute thought is the first step in that change of action that will itself carry further the needed change in patterns of mind and character.

In short, liberalism must now become radical, meaning by "radical" perception of the necessity of thorough-going changes in the set-up of institutions and corresponding activity to bring the changes to pass. For the gulf between what the actual situation makes possible and the actual state itself is so great that it cannot be bridged by piecemeal policies undertaken *ad hoc*. The process of producing the changes will be, in any case, a gradual one. But "reforms" that deal now with this abuse and now with that without having a social goal based upon an inclusive plan, differ entirely from effort at re-forming, in its literal sense, the institutional scheme of things. The liberals of more than a century ago were denounced in their time as subversive radicals, and only when the new economic order was established did they become apologists for the *status quo* or else content with social patchwork. If radicalism be defined as perception of need for radical change, then today any liberalism which is not also radicalism is irrelevant and doomed.

But radicalism also means, in the minds of many, both supporters and opponents, dependence upon use of violence as the main method of effecting drastic changes. Here the liberal parts company. For he is committed to the organization of intelligent action as the chief method.

. . .

The argument drawn from past history that radical change must be effected by means of class struggle, culminating in open war, fails to discriminate between the two forces, one active, the other resistant and deflecting, that have produced the social scene in which we live. The active force is, as I have said, scientific method and technological application. The opposite force is that of older institutions and the habits that have grown up around them. Instead of discrimination between forces and distribution of their consequences, we find the two things lumped together. The compound is labeled the capitalistic or the bourgeois class, and to this class as a class is imputed all the important features of present industrialized society—much as the defenders of the régime of economic liberty exercised for private property are accustomed to attribute every improvement made in the last century and a half to the same capitalistic régime. Thus in orthodox communist literature, from the Communist Manifesto of 1848 to the present day, we are told that the bourgeoisie, the name for a distinctive class, has done this and that. It has, so it is said, given a cosmopolitan character to production and consumption; has destroyed the national basis of industry; has agglomerated population in urban centers; has transferred power from the country to the city, in the process of creating colossal productive force, its chief achievement. In addition, it has created crises of ever renewed intensity; has created imperialism of a new type in frantic effort to control raw materials and markets. Finally, it has created a new class, the proletariat, and has created it as a class having a common interest opposed to that of the bourgeoisie, and is giving an irresistible stimulus to its organization, first as a class and then as a political power. According to the economic version of the Hegelian dialectic, the bourgeois class is thus creating its own complete and polar opposite, and this in time will end the old power and rule. The class struggle of veiled civil war will finally burst into open revolution and the result will be either the common ruin of the contending parties or a revolutionary reconstitution of society at large through a transfer of power from one class to another.

The position thus sketched unites vast sweep with great simplicity. I am concerned with it here only as far as it emphasizes the idea of a struggle between classes, culminating in open and violent warfare as being the method for production of radical social change. For, be it noted, the issue is not whether some amount of violence will accompany the effectuation of radical change of institutions. The question is whether force or intelligence is to be the method upon which we consistently rely and to whose promotion we devote our energies. Insistence that the use of violent force is *inevitable* limits the use of available intelligence, for wherever the inevitable reigns intelligence cannot be used. Commitment to inevitability is always the fruit of dogma; intelligence does not pretend to *know* save as a result of experimentation, the opposite of preconceived dogma. Moreover, acceptance in advance of the inevitability of violence tends to produce the use of violence in cases where peaceful methods might otherwise avail. The curious fact is that while it is generally admitted that this and that particular social problem, say of the family, or railroads or banking, must be solved, if at all, by the method of intelligence, yet there is supposed to be some one all-inclusive social problem which can be solved only by the use of violence. This fact would be inexplicable were it not a conclusion from dogma as its premise.

It is frequently asserted that the method of experimental intelligence can be applied to physical facts because physical nature does not present conflicts of class interests, while it is inapplicable to society because the latter is so deeply marked by incompatible interests. It is then assumed that the "experimentalist" is one who has chosen to ignore the uncomfortable fact of conflicting interests. Of course, there *are* conflicting interests; otherwise there would be no social problems. The problem under discussion is precisely *how* conflicting claims are to be settled in the interest of the widest possible contribution to the interests of all—or at least of the great majority. The method of democracy—inasfar as it is that of organized intelligence—is to bring these conflicts out into the open where their special claims can be seen and appraised, where they can be discussed and judged in the light of more inclusive interests than are represented by either of them separately. There is, for example, a clash of interests between munition manufacturers and most of the rest of the population. The more the respective claims of the two are publicly and scientifically weighed, the more likely it is that the public interest will be disclosed and be made effective. There is an undoubted objective clash of interests between finance-capitalism that controls the means of production and whose profit is served by maintaining relative scarcity, and idle workers and hungry consumers. But what generates violent strife is failure to bring the conflict into the light of intelligence where the conflicting interests can be adjudicated in behalf of the interests of the great majority. Those most committed to the dogma of inevitable force recognize the need for intelligently discovering and expressing the dominant social interest up to a certain point and then draw back. The "experimentalist" is one who would see to it that the method depended upon by all in some degree in every democratic community be followed through to completion.

In spite of the existence of class conflicts, amounting at times to veiled civil war, any one habituated to the use of the method of science will view with considerable suspicion the erection of actual human beings into fixed entities called classes, having no overlapping interests and so internally unified and externally separated that they are made the protagonists of history—itself hypothetical. Such an idea of classes is a survival of a rigid logic that once prevailed in the sciences of nature, but that no longer has any place there. This conversion of abstractions into entities smells more of a dialectic of concepts than of a realistic examination of facts, even though it makes more of an emotional appeal to many than do the results of the latter. To say that all past historic social progress has been the result of coöperation and not of conflict would be also an exaggeration. But exaggeration against exaggeration, it is the more reasonable of the two. And it is no exaggeration to say that the measure of civilization is the degree in which the method of coöperative intelligence replaces the method of brute conflict.

But the point I am especially concerned with just here is the indiscriminate lumping together as a single force of two different things—the results of scientific technology and of a legal system of property relations. It is science and technology that have had the revolutionary social effect while the legal system has been the relatively static element. According to the Marxians themselves, the economic foundations of society consist of two things, the forces of production on one side and, on the other side, the social relations of production, that is, the legal property system under which the former operates. The latter lags behind, and "revolutions" are produced by the power of the forces of production to change the system of institutional relations. But what are the modern forces of production save those of scientific technology? And what is scientific technology save a large-scale demonstration of organized intelligence in action?

It is quite true that what is happening socially is the result of the combination of the two factors, one dynamic, the other relatively static. If we choose to call the combination by the name of capitalism, then it is true, or a truism, that capitalism is the "cause" of all the important social changes that have occurred—an argument that the representatives of capitalism are eager to put forward whenever the increase of productivity is in question. But if we want to *understand,* and not just to paste labels, unfavorable or favorable as the case may be, we shall certainly begin and end with discrimination. Colossal increase in productivity, the bringing of men together in cities and large factories, the elimination of distance, the accumulation of capital, fixed and liquid—these things would have come about, at a certain stage, no matter what the established institutional system. They are the consequence of the new means of technological production. Certain other things have happened because of inherited institutions and the habits of belief and character that accompany and support them. If we begin at this point, we shall see that the release of productivity is the product of coöperatively organized intelligence, and shall also see that the institutional framework is precisely that which is not subjected as yet, in any considerable measure, to the impact of inventive and constructive intelligence. That coercion and oppression on a large scale exist, no honest person can deny. But these things are not the product of science and technology but of the perpetuation of old institutions and patterns untouched by scientific method. The inference to be drawn is clear.

The argument, drawn from history, that great social changes have been effected only by violent means, needs considerable qualification, in view of the vast scope of changes that are taking place without the use of violence. But even if it be admitted to hold of the past, the conclusion that violence is the method now to be depended upon does not follow —unless one is committed to a dogmatic philosophy of history. The radical who insists that the future method of change must be like that of the past has much in common with the hide-bound reactionary who holds to the past as an ultimate fact. Both overlook the *fact that history in being a process of change generates change not only in details but also in the method of directing social change.* I recur to what I said at the beginning of this chapter. It is true that the social order is largely conditioned by the use of coercive force, bursting at times into open violence. But what is also true is that mankind now has in its possession a new method, that of coöperative and experimental science which expresses the method of intelligence. I should be meeting dogmatism with dogmatism if I asserted that the existence of this historically new factor completely invalidates all arguments drawn from the effect of force in the past. But it is within the bounds of reason to assert that the presence of this social factor demands that the present situation be analyzed on its own terms, and not be rigidly subsumed under fixed conceptions drawn from the past.

.   .   .

The final argument in behalf of the use of intelligence is that as are the means used so are the actual ends achieved—that is, the consequences. I know of no greater fallacy than the claim of those who hold to the dogma of the necessity of brute force that this use will be the method of calling genuine democracy into existence—of which they profess themselves the simon-pure adherents. It requires an unusually credulous faith in the Hegelian dialectic of opposites to think that all of a sudden the use of force by a class will be transmuted into a democratic classless society. Force breeds counterforce; the Newtonian law of action and reaction still holds in physics, and violence is physical. To profess democracy as an ultimate ideal and the suppression of democracy as a means to the ideal may be possible in a country that has never known even rudimentary democracy, but when professed in a country that has anything of a genuine democratic spirit in its traditions, it signifies desire for possession and retention of power by a class, whether that class be called Fascist or Proletarian. In the light of what happens in nondemocratic countries, it is pertinent to ask whether the rule of a class signifies the dictatorship of the majority, or dictatorship over the chosen class by a minority party; whether dissenters are allowed even within the class the party claims to represent; and whether the development of literature and the other arts proceeds according to a formula prescribed by a party in conformity with a doctrinaire dogma of history and of infallible leadership, or whether artists are free from regimentation? Until these questions are satisfactorily answered, it is permissible to look with considerable suspicion upon those who assert that suppression of democracy is the road to the adequate establishment of genuine democracy. The one exception—and that apparent rather than real—to dependence upon organized intelligence as the method for directing social change is found when society through an authorized majority has entered upon the path of social experimentation leading to great social change, and a minority refuses by force to permit the method of intelligent action to go into effect. Then force may be intelligently employed to subdue and disarm the recalcitrant minority.

.   .   .

Howard Selsam
ENDS AND MEANS: WHICH JUSTIFIES WHICH?

The question of political violence is often posed as the question, "Do the ends justify the means?" In the selection that follows, Howard Selsam, a former professor of philosophy at Brooklyn College, Director of the Jefferson School of Social Science, and author of numerous works on Marxist philosophy, argues that the question needs to be posed more concretely. That is, given accepted ends, how can we determine what means are justified by them? Means and ends, he insists, are dialectically interconnected, so that we must, in a particular social context, determine which means are justified by which ends. The means to achieve socialism are determined not only by the nature of socialism but also by the nature of the capitalist society within which the struggle for socialism takes place.

.   .   .

In all history, those who worked for social change have been branded immoral by the defenders of the existing order. Although this is an old practice in recent times it has taken a new form. It is expressed in the accusation that those who oppose the *status quo* believe "the end justifies the means." Often they merely ask the question: "Do you believe the end justifies the means?" But the question is often asked with malice aforethought, with the implication that those asked would sacrifice all moral principles in pursuing their goal—that they are without principle, unscrupulous and "Machiavellian."

Nevertheless this is a serious question and a serious charge. If one professes to believe that the end justifies the means then it is assumed that he will stop at nothing to attain his ends. No crime would supposedly be too monstrous. Lies, betrayal of pledges, blackmail, frame-up, murder, torture, mass annihilation—all these would be taken in stride as mere incidents in the pursuit of the end. That there have been such fanatics in many historical movements no one can deny. On the other hand, that Roman slavery and European feudalism accepted no restraints in their desperate efforts to save their system is a recognized fact of history. One need only remember the methods used by Rome for the suppression of slave revolts and those of the epoch of the Inquisition to save feudalism. Has not all war been carried on by the principle, "the end justifies the means," or "everything for victory?" To be sure, poison gas was not used by agreement in World War II, but then atomic bombs were. Is there anyone in the world who believes that war has become less horrible today because of the moral progress of mankind; that nations would sacrifice victory to morality?

. . .

But does the end justify the means? The simplest answer is that the question is unanswerable in this form. Everybody believes that some ends justify some means. Nobody believes that any end justifies any means. And all agree that nothing but an end can justify a means. As we shall see each is defined only by its relation to the other.

There are many acts regarded as abhorrent by mankind generally, but there is scarcely one of these that some people somewhere, or all people everywhere, do not believe to be justified under some circumstances for some good end. We do not believe it right to take another's life, but our laws justify killing in self-defense; we use the electric chair and gas chamber to punish various crimes; and we still honor as heroes those who kill the greatest number of the enemy in battle. War is increasingly recognized as a terrible evil, but there is scarcely a people or a government on earth that would not resort to arms under some determinate circumstances for some end regarded as justifying war's horrors.

Official social doctrine holds it wrong to resist civil authority, but the Boston clergyman Jonathan Mayhew preached a sermon in 1750 commemorating the beheading of Charles I, saying that for a nation to rise and resist their prince when he tyrannizes over them "is making use of the means, and the only means, which God has put into their power for mutual and self-defense." And another American, Henry David Thoreau, defended civil disobedience in an essay that influenced Tolstoy in Russia, Gandhi in India and the Reverend Martin Luther King and other leaders in the struggle for Negro rights in the United States today.

No people or nation has ever abrogated its right to use every means in its power to achieve its liberation and there is no society which forbids itself the means necessary for its maintenance or perpetuation.

The question: "Does the end justify the means?" is too abstract to be intelligently discussed. As Corliss Lamont has well said, to ask it is like asking whether any object is worth its price. No sane person would dream of answering such a question. He would ask, rather, what objects are being talked about and what price is being asked for them. The very posing of the question in this universal and abstract form puts it into the class of such questions as "Is Life worth living?" This was once answered in a popular American magazine with the quip: "Not if that's the way you feel about it." The real question, of course, concerns the kind of life that is worth living and the circumstances under which it is lived. As Hegel once wrote: "Life has a value only when it has something valuable as its object," which is to say that the value of life can be found only in life itself. Asking the question in this generalized form already raises insoluble problems. The same is true of the question whether the end justifies the means. Means are good only when they have good as their end. But this brings us only to the threshold of the problem.

INTERRELATION OF MEANS AND ENDS

What is meant by "means" and "ends"? Both terms must be recognized as relative—as relative as up and down, right and left, inner and outer. "Means" are means to an end, ways of achieving something desired. As Joseph Dietzgen observed a century ago we eat to live, but inasmuch as one of the necessities and pleasures of living is eating, we live to eat too. "Means" can be defined only in relation to "ends" and vice versa. We domesticate animals for our food. Cows are raised to be slaughtered, not as an end in themselves. Yet for many Hindus cows are sacred and must not be killed for human use. But how they live is not considered important and the late Prime Minister Nehru often told his countrymen that Indian cows lead a much more miserable existence than those in countries where they are not so much revered.

Our ordinary understanding of the term "means" is of something not good in itself but necessary to achieve something else that is itself good. But what is good in and of itself, good as an end only? This is the central question that the classic moralists and philosophers have sought to answer for ages. Is it Plato's eternal and absolute justice (which comes close to everyone keeping in his place)? Or is it pleasure or the greatest total amount of happiness? Or is Kant's "good will" the only thing in the world that can be called good? For idealists it has always been conformity to some eternal principle far removed from the realities of actual life. For pre-Marxist materialists it was only too often the mere pleasure of the moment or a state of mind, from the tranquillity of Epicurus to the universal love of Feuerbach. For Marxists it can be nothing more nor less than people living well, living ever better materially and culturally, and ever freer to develop their own capacities or potentialities in harmony with the development of those of all other people.

The classic German philosopher, Immanuel Kant, taught that men should be treated as ends only, never as means. This would have been a revolutionary principle if applied to capitalist society, for as Marx pointed out in his *Theories of Surplus Value,* the central distinction between the capitalist and socialist conceptions of the relation of the worker to production is that in the first the worker appears as what he really is in capitalist production, "a mere means of production; not as an end in himself and the goal of production." But Kant never thought of applying his general principle so concretely. On the contrary, he inconsistently proceeded to sacrifice human life on the altar of his abstract moral law, rather than have morality serve to improve and enrich human life. This is the inevitable result of believing in any "good in itself" outside of the actual context of human life under specific conditions of its existence.

For any dynamic point of view, as opposed to the static positions of most classic philosophy and traditional religion, the only "good in itself" is movement in a defined direction. It is not something you have reached and enjoy forever after, but rather the striving after greater fulfillment of existent possibilities and the further extension of such. If the only "good in itself" is such movement in a determinate direction it follows that in real life means and ends are dialectically interrelated. Every good is not a final resting place but a state or stage in mankind's never ceasing struggle. As such it is a precondition, a starting point or a means towards a further good or end. John Dewey and American pragmatists have taken the same dialectical approach to means and ends. They have this dynamic conception of direction but strikingly fail to define it. As a result, any movement and process becomes good for them as movement *per se* rather than as movement towards a definite and rationally definable goal. Thus they glorify movement without direction as opposed to traditional idealism which was satisfied with end or goal without movement.

But progress, as movement in a good direction, must be defined. It is in the light of such definition that we must conceive and evaluate some of the great achievements of the early modern bourgeois world, from its extraordinary development of the forces of production to the achievement of political democracy. The parliamentary system, free and universal suffrage, the secret ballot, are ends for which immense historical struggles were waged. In the same category are such legal safeguards as *habeas corpus,* trial by jury, the right of non-self-incrimination, the independence of the judiciary, and many others. It is not at issue here whether these always work as they are supposed to, or how they are used in perverted forms to uphold the capitalist system. The point is that they are things for which people fought, and as protections of individual rights against arbitrary misuse of power they are good in themselves. But their essential virtue consists not simply in protecting the liberties of given individuals, as good as that is. They are good primarily as means by which people can safely and freely work for further goods by processes of democratic social change. They are good, in short, for the point to which they have brought us and are good again as means to a still better life.

Every progressive social movement reveals the dialectical insepara- bility of means and ends. In order to achieve their independence the American people had to assert themselves. They had to *exercise* their independence in order to fight for it. They had to organize *Committees of Correspondence, Sons of Liberty,* and so on. The organizing activities were means to the end they sought, but inasmuch as they were themselves expressions of the people's growing unity and strength they were an integral part of the end itself.

In the same way, Egypt's taking over the Suez Canal was a means to the strengthening of the Egyptian economy and became of assistance in building the Aswan Dam. With even greater certainty it was an end in itself with respect to the struggles of the colonial and semi-colonial world against imperialism, giving these countries new confidence, new solidarity, new allies. Castro's overthrow of the Batista government in Cuba and the establishment of the power of Cuba's workers and farmers was an even more striking example of means passing over into ends and of ends finding appropriate means. Means and ends are thus always inter-connected, each becoming transformed into the other as phases of the historic process.

This interrelation of means and ends in no way implies that any end justifies any means. It implies rather that means and ends are so inextrica- bly connected that the question cannot be answered by any simple "yes" or "no." The common opinion of mankind supports this. Just as it be- lieves that some actions are justified by the results they bring about, it equally insists that there are some things that should and must not be done for no matter what end. But this is precisely where the real difficulty arises. What is it that must not be done no matter how good the end? What is so bad in itself that it cannot be done for any cause, however noble, and under whatever conditions such a cause must be pursued? What are the criteria for determining what means are justified by what ends?

This is the real question before us, rather than the abstract one: "Does the end justify the means?" Its answer, furthermore, requires an analysis of the standards for judging the goodness or justification of means and of ends *equally.* Clearly there is no way by which we can ascertain whether a given end justifies a given means other than by standards or principles by which both means and ends can be weighed. Means A may be unacceptable for end X and justifiable for end Y, and so on round the alphabet. The beginning of the answer to the question of the relation of the two lies in the proposition that while nothing can justify a means but an end, it in no wise follows that any end justifies *any* means.

The only concrete form of the question, therefore, is: *Given accepted ends how can we determine what means are justified by them?*

This can be put in simpler terms. Suppose we all agree on a broad social goal as good. This means, of course, as Spinoza insisted, that we really want it. This qualification immediately eliminates any fradulent mouthing of phrases about how good something would be if only we didn't have to make any sacrifices to achieve it. The goal may be anything from desegregation to national independence, or from the elimination of illiteracy to socialism. Then it will be possible to discuss quite clearly and objectively the best way of reaching it. We could, of course, differ greatly on this, but still not make accusations of moral nihilism against one another in the process. On the other hand, conceivably we could agree on what are proper ways of going anywhere but be unable to come to any agreement as to where it is good to go. Each side could then say rightfully that the other has no moral objective.

Now suppose we should all agree that a given end was supremely good for mankind, but disagreed hopelessly on whether it was attainable without violating fundamental standards concerning means.

We would then be in a most serious dilemma from which we would have to escape either by (1) reevaluating the end as the highest good; (2) changing our standards of acceptable means; or (3) finding new means by which the agreed upon end can be achieved. Such is the position of many in the world today who "theoretically" accept the goal of socialism but have been shocked by many of the means employed in the Soviet Union and other socialist countries. Clearly we cannot rest on the horns of this dilemma [alternatives (1) and (2)] but must find means both appropriate to the end and in harmony with the deep-seated moral principles of the widest masses of people. Otherwise, we are left in one case with means without ends, and in the other with ends without means. Here we can paraphrase Kant's famous dictum on percepts and concepts, and say that means without ends are blind, and ends without means are empty.

To achieve any great and long-range historical goals, such as the bourgeois democratic societies of England, France and the United States, the ending of slavery in the United States, the military defeat of the Rome-Berlin-Tokyo Axis—a planned and comprehensive program of action is indispensable. Such a program itself reveals the unity of means and ends, inasmuch as it must, at one and the same time, present the goal sought and the measures required to reach it. We must ask two major questions of any such long-range program and the measures involved in the effort to achieve it.

THE ADEQUACY OF MEANS

The first question to be asked is: Are the means adequate to the given end and such as to achieve it most effectively? This of course can never be completely known. But we can and must demand that they be means which give the highest possible guarantee of adequacy in reaching the goal. Such adequacy and effectiveness, too, cannot be judged in the abstract but only in terms of the concrete circumstances of a given situation. They must be evaluated in relation to the range of possibilities allowed by existing conditions.

No morally sensitive or politically mature person would support terrorist methods when democratic processes allow for mass organization and struggle. But when there are no other possible means, as in the case of South Vietnam, South Africa and Algeria prior to independence from France, support comes from many who would otherwise oppose the means used. Such struggles for freedom and self-government, for land or nation, cannot be judged by fixed and immutable standards borrowed from other places and times under different circumstances and with different levels of the development of moral concepts and attitudes. Neither can they be judged apart from the methods of the oppressors.

While terrorism violates all normal codes of moral behavior, it was unconditionally supported by the most morally sensitive people when used against the Nazis by resistance forces in the occupied countries. At the same time, the brutal methods used by Ku-kluxers and other rabid Southern anti-integrationists strike all decent people with horror not merely because of the beatings and bombings and shootings but because their ends are so miserably evil. They have had all the forces of the law behind them but the moment the Negro people and federal law oppose special privileges these whites have "enjoyed" as a heritage of slavery, they defy law, order and the rights of all others, whether these constitute a minority or majority. If on the other hand the Negro people had no other recourse, no other method of struggle open to them, then the only course possible would be the armed defense of their rights. And the moral conscience of most of mankind would support them. The question here is clearly not "Does the end justify the means?" but another question altogether, "Which side are you on?"

The criteria of the effectiveness and adequacy of the means employed is more complex than first appears. The Boston Tea Party was scarcely an effective means of keeping tea out of the American Colonies but by dramatizing the issue of British-imposed import duties it became a powerful stimulus towards resistance. John Brown's raid on Harper's Ferry was of itself a most inadequate means towards the liberation of the slaves. It failed dismally to liberate anyone and brought increased repression and terror in its wake. Yet its impact on the moral conscience of millions made it play a great historical role in the movement which ultimately destroyed the slave power.

The second question to be asked of any proposed program is: Are its means such as not to corrupt or destroy the end desired by the very effort to achieve it? This question is really inseparable from the first, because if the means used are such as to pervert the very end sought then they are not means of reaching it. This has been a special accusation against Marxists and the whole Marxist revolutionary program, namely, that the means by which it proposes to achieve socialism are such as not to bring genuine socialism but some form of bureaucratic state with its attendant entrenched vested interests.

Marxists have tended to ignore this argument until recent years or to dismiss it much too lightly. The principle, however, is a sound one, inasmuch as it is certainly possible theoretically to defeat the very thing one is striving for in the process of striving for it. Every psychologist and psychiatrist knows that people often use methods to win the sympathy or love of others which are doomed by their nature to defeat themselves and to alienate those whose affection is sought. Early Christianity was certainly changed into something quite different from its original character by some of the means employed to win converts and to build the Church. Certain trade unions have been built by means which did not bring the desired benefits for the workers but became organizations run by a few officials for their own power and fortune. Only the active participation of the rank and file in the affairs of their union through democratic processes can guarantee the real ends for which unions are organized.

Such, too, was the great danger inherent in the Stalin regime with its violation of civil rights during twenty years or more. Fortunately, socialism proved too vigorous to be destroyed by these aberrant means used purportedly for defending and consolidating it. But the danger was there, fostered by means in contradiction to the end sought. The "tragedy of Stalin" was that his devotion to the cause of socialism became so intertwined with his love of power that he was led to employ means that threatened the very goal he thought he was seeking to achieve. Marxists throughout the world had believed that the theories of Marx and Lenin, coupled with the release of mass energy and increase of democracy for working people, provided a built-in guarantee against tyranny and one-man dictatorship in the building of socialism. The shortcoming of such thought lay not in the belief that the end justifies the means but rather in a too ready pragmatic acceptance of whatever was done so long as it appeared to "work."

These questions of the relations of means and ends are found everywhere in all religious, national or class struggles. The problems are inherent in any effort to move from one state of things to another. Those who seek no change have no such problems. They *do* whatever they do to maintain things as they are. Their means, too, are subject to the same examination as has just been made. But they never trouble to make such an examination. They may use effective or ineffective means to preserve, let us say, feudalism or capitalism. They themselves lose no sleep over such a theoretical question as whether "the end justifies the means."

.   .   .

Thus far, nothing or little has been said that is distinctively Marxist. These general principles have been shared by broad strata of people as well as by leading thinkers. All allegations and accusations notwithstanding, Marxists have no special position on this question of means and ends. More than most others, perhaps, Marxists recognize their dialectical interrelation, a recognition which arises both from the conscious use of the dialectical method and from a consistently historical approach to all social phenomena. Further, as materialists, Marxists are more down to earth than are other schools of thought and seek to analyze all social movements and forces in terms of their concrete material foundations. They do not make the mistake of accepting on face value the alleged motives or goals of any social group or class. Marx and Engels once expressed this succinctly with regard to traditional historians:

> Whilst in ordinary life every shopkeeper is very well able to distinguish between what somebody professes to be and what he really is, our historians have not yet won even this trivial insight. They take every epoch at its word and believe that everything it says and imagines about itself is true. (*German Ideology,* Pt. 1.)

Marxists thus do not accept on face value the claims of the ideologists of imperialism that they are for world freedom, that they seek to help the underdeveloped countries to achieve industrialization, or that they are enemies of colonialism. But no more than anyone else do Marxists believe and teach that "the end justifies the means." No less than anyone else, they believe that it is right and proper and necessary to do certain things, and not to do others, to protect and further certain fundamental human goods.

Marxists are more keenly aware than most people of the conflict of forces in social movement and the resultant fact that what are good ends for some are bad for others. This was also implied in Frederick Douglass' classic statement: "Without struggle there is no progress," for there is no struggle unless there are opposed sides with different and opposed ends. Abraham Lincoln, too, expressed this beautifully when he said in Baltimore in 1864:

> The shepherd drives the wolf from the sheep's throat, for which the sheep thanks the shepherd as his liberator, while the wolf denounces him for the same act, as the destroyer of liberty. . . . Hence we behold the process by which thousands are daily passing from under the yoke of bondage hailed by some as the advance of liberty and bewailed by others as the destruction of all liberty.

THE MEANS AND ENDS OF SOCIALISM

There is no theoretical difference between such a position and that of Marxists except that Marxism has made new applications of these ideas of progress through struggle and of the conflict in ethical judgments of opposed sides or classes. With regard to the transition from capitalism to socialism, Marxism makes two positive moral affirmations, based upon its whole analysis of political economy and human history:

(1) That the goal of socialism is a most worthy and noble goal, freeing mankind for the first time in recorded history of the evils of exploitation of man by man, and thereby establishing the basis for true human brotherhood and equality, universal peace, and opening up vast vistas of human progress.

(2) That the means by which socialism can be achieved are determined not only by the nature of socialism as the end but also by the nature of capitalist state power, the degree of democratic development, the relative strength of the opposing forces, specific situations, and so on.

This latter is the point at which all the arguments on the subject of means and ends arise today and around which they focus. If the means of achieving socialism were to be entirely determined by the nature of socialism, all would be easy. There would be no class struggle and no question of means and ends. But the fact is that it is also determined by the nature of capitalism with all its means of perpetuating itself—from its control of the whole apparatus of the state and the media of mass propaganda to the threat of fascism and nuclear war. The capitalist class will not be *persuaded* by reason or example that it is a hindrance to social progress and should therefore resign. It can only be replaced by a people which wants not only to supplant the existent capitalist class but to eliminate the whole capitalist system.

Capitalism cannot be defeated on its own terms by means determined by its historically evolved ideas and structure. By such means power can shift only from one group of capitalists to another. In the semi-colonial world this change occurs through putsches and palace revolutions. All the CIA operations and all the Tshombes in the world can never bring a new system of society. They can never bring more than a change in the rulers, not in the social-economic order.

An historic illustration of this principle is found in the American anti-slavery struggle. If the methods of the slaves, the free Negroes, and their white Abolitionist supporters had been entirely determined by and taken over from the nature of slave society, the method of struggle would have been one of unmitigated terror and the goal could not have been other than the physical annihilation of all slave owners or their enslavement. But, historically, this has rarely been the accepted aim of an oppressed people, any more than the means they employed were derived simply from existing conditions. Slaves otherwise, ancient or modern, would have sought only to be slave owners, serfs only to be feudal lords, and workers only to be capitalists with their present employers as *their* workers.

All such struggles, on the contrary, are movements towards another form of social organization involving the broadening of the base of power and greater freedom for a greater number. They must therefore employ methods which already represent essential features of the new order and involve the broadening of participation in various forms of political and economic life. Yet the means of achieving a new form of society are determined in part by the existing social structure, by the institutions that already stand condemned. This is the defense Thoreau made when he answered the attacks against the methods of the abolitionists by declaring in his famous essay, *Civil Disobedience,* that if the remedy was worse than the evil it was the fault of the government that supported slavery. *"It makes it worse,"* he said. Similarly, it is not only the nature of freedom from any form of oppression that determines the means required to achieve it, but also the nature of the oppressing society.

Such, for example, is the two-fold problem of the movement towards socialism. It has to be won and consolidated with means appropriate to its nature—the fullest development of democratic processes and the fullest participation of all working people and their supporters in the determination of all the conditions of life. On the other hand it must be recognized that this movement towards socialism takes place in a society ruled by a minority that is rapacious, ruthless and desperate in its efforts to maintain its economic, political and social domination. As C. Wright Mills said, the "Power Elite" rules by "the higher immorality." Yet it is only in such an immoral world that the moral goals of socialism can be achieved, and that world determines in large part the means that alone can achieve it.

.   .   .

Kai Nielsen
ON JUSTIFYING REVOLUTION

How and under what conditions can a violent revolution be justified? In the article reprinted here, Kai Nielsen, who teaches philosophy at the University of Calgary, argues that while socialists should not (on moral and strategic grounds) initiate violence, they should expect counterrevolutionary violence and be prepared to combat it. In other words, revolutionary violence is defensive violence; whether it should be employed depends upon the nature of the capitalist response. The proper strategy for socialist revolutionaries is, then, to proceed nonviolently, while preparing for the likelihood of an eventual armed struggle.

.   .   .

I shall, in this section, set out in general terms the conditions under which a socialist revolution is in my opinion justified, under what conditions it should be actively worked for and under what conditions it should actually be attempted.[1]

[1] I have said some further things about this in my "On the Ethics of Revolution," *Radical Philosophy 6* (Winter, 1973).

A socialist, to be a socialist, must believe that capitalism must come to an end—utterly disappear—to be replaced by a fundamentally different socioeconomic system. He need not, though he may, speak of the destruction of capitalism. But he must believe in its replacement.

A socialist, who accepts socialist revolution as a live option or as what is in all likelihood a dire necessity, will have as a central *empirical* belief, the belief that the capitalist system is not likely to be undermined and brought to an end by nonviolent means. Such a socialist will believe that if capitalism is to be replaced, it will likely have to be done by revolutionary activity. Notice that, right or wrong, justified or unjustified, such a brief is not an article of faith or a bit of ideology but a perfectly empirical belief open to evidential and rational assessment.

It should be noticed in passing that revolutionary socialists, like all humane and sane men, recognize that violence is an evil never to be engaged in lightly and to be reprobated under normal circumstances. If there is a nonviolent way of attaining an end, then it is, everything else being equal, to be used rather than the violent alternative. Indeed, to have an understanding of what morality is all about, is to see the moral necessity of using nonviolent means in such circumstances. But everything else may not be equal and it is also plainly the case that violence is not the only evil in the world or the greatest evil. And it is further evident that there are circumstances in which whatever is done violence will occur. Under such circumstances we must decide which stretch of violence is the lesser evil. To avoid such a decision is to relinquish moral responsibility. Such considerations should make it evident that under certain circumstances violence, which is always prima facie wrong, is sometimes justified.[2]

At this point, I want to state a crucial argument made by Brian Medlin in his important and powerfully argued "Strategy For The Revolution."[3] It is both bad tactics and bad morality, he argues, for socialists to *initiate* violence and indeed they must not only not initiate violence they must strive, in the face of counterrevolutionary propaganda, to be *seen* not to be the initiators of violence. Revolutionary violence, to be justified, must always be in response to counterrevolutionary violence. Moreover, there must be nothing, where counterrevolutionary violence has not been practiced, like a preemptive anticipatory strike against the bourgeoisie. In the bourgeois democracies, socialists should proceed by making perfectly reasonable and nonviolent attempts to transform society so that the means of production will be collectively owned and so that the working class—that is the vast mass of people—will control their own destinies, including the control of their own means and manner of work.

[2]See my general account of this in my "Against Moral Conservatism," *Ethics*, Vol. 82, No. 3 (April, 1972).

[3]Brian Medlin, "Strategy For The Revolution," *Dialectic*, Vol. 7 (1972). A similar position is held by Ernest Mandel. See Jean Amery's account of his conversation with Mandel. Jean Amery, "Revolutionar ohne Ungeduld," *Frankfurter Rundschau*, Nr. 126, 3 (June, 1972).

Such nonviolent measures, Medlin argues, when they come within a country mile of being successful, will in all likelihood be met by the violence of the counterrevolution. He claims that the violence of the revolution will, when justified, always be in response to that counterrevolutionary violence. Socialists must expect counterrevolutionary violence —anything else would be a lamentable departure from realism—and be thoroughly prepared to meet it and not offer themselves as sacrificial lambs. But we socialists must not initiate the violence ourselves and we must do what we can (and sometimes that is not very much) to make that perfectly evident to the world, knowing that our position will be distorted by the bourgeois press.

There is a network of interrelated moral, tactical, and empirical considerations involved in Medlin's claim. The core empirical ones—to put it crudely—center around the empirical belief that in the face of a serious socialist thrust to fundamentally redistribute power and wealth, the capitalists will not give up without a fight. They will never, for example, simply following the rules of parliamentary democracy, allow their power to be so eroded that capitalism and the capitalist class will become a thing of the past. (Their violent destruction of a socialist democracy in Chile is a dramatic and saddening, though hardly a surprising, example of this.) The bourgeoisie will make concessions when they have to 'cut their losses' but they will never surrender power out of humane considerations or because socialists have established their point morally or rationally.

The related tactical considerations are the following: (1) people lacking power, though oppressed, will not as a rule employ violence against an armed state unless they are first compelled to do so by the violence of the state, (2) effective revolutionary violence will only result when such brutal, direct, and palpable violent oppression obtains and (3) the initiation of violence by socialists will discredit socialism and strengthen, at least temporarily, the capitalist order.

The moral point is simply to keep quite steadfastly before our minds the recognition that the *initiation* of violence is wrong. With that recognition and with the recognition of the fallibility of empirical beliefs, such as the ones we subscribed to, socialists out of the revolutionary tradition in contexts like our own should proceed nonviolently in trying to achieve socialism, *hoping,* but *not believing,* that the Fabians and Bernsteinians are right about the chances of building socialism without resort to armed struggle. We may, after all, be mistaken in our belief that the transition from capitalism to socialism cannot be achieved nonviolently.

If peaceful attempts to achieve socialism, with the proper wariness about capitalist ruling class intransigence and retaliation, turn out, after all, to be successful, then we should be pleasantly surprised and grateful that our tough-minded assessment of the situation has turned out to be mistaken.

The other alternatives are that this attempt to achieve socialism nonviolently will be frustrated—as it was in Chile—or that the working class movement will develop effective forms of counterviolence—meeting fire with fire—to face the counterrevolutionary violence directed against their attempts to achieve socialism peacefully.

Where the movement is crushed—something to be avoided by not trying to institute a socialist order prematurely before there is a mass base —there still remains from this bashing something of a consciousness-raising lesson and the recognition of, and a partial justification for, socialists to prepare for, at a later date, when conditions are different, an armed struggle with the ruling classes. But there is neither moral justification for nor practical utility in *initiating* violence in trying to achieve a socialist transformation of society.

Medlin's claim that revolutionary socialists must never initiate violence will not go unchallenged by other socialists. It will be argued by some that this claim is both false and in effect harmful to the socialist cause—harmful by leading socialists to be more passive and manageable than they need be or indeed should be. Even where capitalist power is weakening and socialist movements are gaining in strength and where the ruling class is preparing to attempt to destroy the socialist movement, Medlin—so the argument would run—would never sanction preemptive violence on the socialist's part to break or try to break such an impending capitalist onslaught. But to hold back from preemptive violence in such a situation, where its use might be successful, is both foolish and immoral.

Surely Medlin's claim is not, or at least should not be, an a priori one. It should not be held, no matter what the circumstances. There are indeed *conceivable* circumstances in which it would be mistaken; the important consideration, for Medlin's argument, is whether, as things are, or are likely to be, it is a justified belief.

What I think can and should be said in response is that when a situation has so developed that Medlin's critic can plausibly speak of revolutionaries exercising the option of preemptive violence, that by then the capitalist ruling class will already, through arbitrary imprisonment, brutal exploitation, McCarthyite tactics and the like, have deployed so much violence that such a preemptive strike will not count as *initiating* violence but as a response to counterrevolutionary violence. In such situations, socialist revolutionaries will, of course, be labeled by the mass media as inhuman terrorists, irrational nihilists, etc. They will be said by the media to be 'the initiators of violence.' But this is ideology, not truth, and a central task for socialist intelligentsia is to do their best to counteract such propaganda by making it evident that the revolutionary violence is in response to ruling class violence and is resorted to in situations where the utilization of violence by the ruling class (through the holding of political prisoners, through police brutality at demonstrations, through interrogations, through strikebreaking and the like) is very high and nonviolent methods only strengthen the capitalist's repressive power.

The abstract moral point is indeed well taken that one may very well be justified in initiating violence if someone is threatening violence and probably will use violence unless he is forcefully stopped. Whether one would actually be justified in initiating violence in such a circumstance would depend on the exact circumstance. But in many circumstances there could be such a justification. I take it that Medlin is not denying that general moral point and I certainly am not. What I take it he is saying, and what I at least am claiming, is that because of the special circumstances described above, the socialist revolutionary is not justified in initiating violence.

In talking about revolution, I am, of course, talking about sociopolitical revolution. I am talking about a complete overthrow of a given state apparatus and the substitution for it of a radically different apparatus and the initiation of a development toward a radically changed social order.[4] We have with the sort of revolution I am talking about a seizure of power directed toward the destruction of the old social system and the setting in motion of the machinery leading to the attainment of a new order, though it may take years before the new order can take its anticipated and hoped for form. (What this order will be like in advance of actual practice will have to be stated rather generally.) Capitalist exploitation, as Marx realized, can under certain circumstances be ended by a few deft strokes, attendant on the seizure of power by determined revolutionaries with the massive backing of the proletariat, but for a long time afterwards capitalist mentality and certain customary capitalist ways of doing things will live on in the early stages of socialism. It will take time, determination, and imagination to change deeply rooted cultural patterns so that socialist persons and a fully developed socialist society can become a reality. Time must pass after the seizure of power before there can be a genuine transformation of society in which human liberation would be a reality: that is, where we would have a state of affairs where there are masses of people whose full human powers and creative capacities are developed in many directions such that they will find pleasure in genuinely creative work, manage their own affairs, help in the ordering and directing of society in the interests of everyone alike and be capable of a wide range of enjoyments and creative activities.

We intellectuals have been conditioned in such a way that such talk about liberation sounds platitudinous. Yet surely, if human liberation is at all possible, this is what in general terms it would come to. Many people of good will and generous sympathies who remain Burkean conservatives do so in large measure because they have reluctantly come to the conclusion that human liberation is a pipe dream. For socialism to be more than a heuristic ideal such a liberation must be a responsible possibility. I do not think that our knowledge of society is such that we can rightly say that we *know* that it is a realistic possibility. But we do know enough about the

---

[4] I discuss this in my "On the Choice Between Reform and Revolution," in *Philosophy and Political Action,* ed. by Virginia Held, Kai Nielsen, and Charles Parsons (New York: Oxford University Press, 1972). For some important remarks about revolution, including nonviolent forms, see Adam Schaff, "Marxist Theory on Revolution and Violence," *Journal of the History of Ideas,* Vol. XXXIV, No. 2 (April–June, 1973).

plasticity of human nature, human conditioning, and intelligence to realize that a cynical rejection of this possibility is not rooted in the authority of science or in some quite unassailable forms of common sense.

It may well be that such a world will never come into existence. But it is essential for us to realize two things. (1) That such a world will not automatically come into existence with the end of the capitalist order and that its attainment (if indeed it can be attained) will take time, thought, vigilance, and determination. (2) That what we do have good grounds for believing is that it cannot come into existence under capitalism. A necessary but *not sufficient* condition for its attainment is the ending of the capitalist order. And it is this which at present should be foremost among socialist strategic aims.

Paradigms of such revolutions are the French, Algerian, Chinese, and Cuban revolutions. We are not speaking of a mere coup d'état where one gang of tyrants or a ruling elite throws out and then replaces another gang of tyrants or a ruling elite. Rather we are speaking of seizures of state power which aim at a profound change in social structure.

Where revolutions have overwhelming popular support there can be, under optimum conditions, an almost bloodless seizure of power. But nonetheless even in the best of conditions there is likely to be some violence and some killing. Since violence and killing are plain evils, they require justification by showing that they, under the circumstances, are the lesser evil. What the revolutionary socialist should say in a very general and abstract way concerning revolutionary violence is (1) that revolutionary violence is only justified when, of the alternatives available, it will, everything considered, make for less misery and human degradation all around, (2) that *in fact* the continued existence of capitalism does cause, and will continue to cause, as long as it is allowed to exist, extensive misery and human degradation and that a socialist transformation of society (including a revolutionary seizure of power) will very probably, of the available alternatives (including the continued existence of capitalism), cause less misery and human degradation, everything considered, and (3) that socialists should be concerned to minimize the violence of change and not seek to bring about an immediate revolutionary change except where the revolution has the support of the overwhelming majority of the proletariat. This last consideration is important, for socialists, like militant liberals, prize liberty and a free society. Apart from, and in addition to, the intrinsic badness of the suffering and pain caused by violence, violence is also often instrumentally bad, for, if there is extensive violence in the revolution, it will be very hard to achieve a free society after the revolution and if the revolution is actually carried out without popular support, extensive repression is unavoidable in the period directly after the revolution.

The first consideration, recall, was that revolutionary violence is justified when it, of the alternatives available, will make for less suffering, everything considered, than the other alternatives when all the people involved are given equal consideration. This moral claim could hardly be *directly* objected to by anyone, except someone who would take the kind of absolutist position in ethics which claims that no matter what the consequences one must never kill or use violence. But this plainly has absurd consequences. It would mean that if some yahoo or group of yahoos, Dr. Strangelove-fashion, got a plane with a nuclear device such that their dropping that nuclear device would kill the entire population of New York, Peking, or Moscow, it would be wrong, if this was the only way of stopping them, to shoot their plane down.

Extensive rational resistance to a justification of socialist revolution will turn on the second consideration. It will be said by some that when we look at the history of sociopolitical revolutions, including the aftermath of these revolutions, we will come to see that it is very dubious whether the continued existence of capitalism will cause more misery and degradation all around than will its violent overthrow to establish a socialist order. Moreover, given modern weaponry, such a revolutionary socialist adventure is quite unthinkable. Surely, this is a question open to empirical assessment which cannot be settled in a philosopher's study. If such a critic of revolutionary socialism has in mind the causing of a nuclear war which will destroy human life or most human life or devastate whole continents, he is without doubt right. No violent response to counterrevolutionary violence is worth that. But there is violence and violence; violence, we must not forget, admits of degrees. When India started a war with Pakistan over what was then called East Pakistan, there were rough calculations made by the Indian government concerning the probable amounts of violence and the resulting suffering, death, and misery. Using these rough calculations and considering the effect on all the peoples on the Indian subcontinent, it is at least reasonable to believe that this war was justified in terms of lessening misery all around. Even if this judgment is mistaken, it would be shown to be mistaken by making just the rough consequentialist calculations I am claiming are relevant. A revolutionary socialist can make the same calculations and while he will not, if he is sensible, claim that in any circumstances revolutionary violence is justified, he will insist that there are circumstances in which it is indeed not only justified but morally mandatory to try to bring down capitalism by revolution.[5]

However, this does not yet touch the central consideration in such an objection. What we need to consider is what about socialist revolution now in our lives and in the forseeable future? The answer should be that presently in the western industrial countries—even France and Italy—there is not the working class movement with the support of a class-conscious working class to make any *present* attempt at revolution anything more than the infantile adventurism of which Marx accused Bakunin. Such adventurism—particularly when accompanied by terrorist

[5]See here Herbert Marcuse, "Ethics and Revolution," in *Ethics and Society,* ed. by Richard T. De George (Garden City, New York: Anchor Books, 1966). See also Andre Gorz, "Revolution in the Metropolis," *Canadian Dimension,* Vol. 10, No. 3 (July, 1974), pp. 42–49.

tactics—would only strengthen the hands of the most reactionary elements in the bourgeois democracies and would alienate large sections of the working class and keep left liberals from coming over to socialism. The present is a time to work toward building among the working class (and this on my count includes students, salaried technicians, and salaried professionals) a militant, class-conscious political base which will push for radical reforms which can be seen not only by such socialists, but also by concerned, morally sensitive liberals, to be legitimate and reasonable moral demands. I have in mind—as a beginning—such things as militant pressure to end the substandard conditions of life afforded Indian and métis people, genuine and not purely formal equality of educational opportunity, more equal distribution of wages, greater control by the workers over their own working conditions, and the like.

In the present situation, the strategy (and this is an open, morally defensible strategy) should be, with each such reformist victory, to up the ante in a genuinely socialist and egalitarian direction.[6] By so proceeding we can and should work with militant liberals and social democrats. If they are right and revolutionary socialists are wrong, by fighting for these quite legitimate moral demands, we can eventually topple capitalism; if we are right and they are wrong, our reformist demands, plainly reasonable and plainly morally legitimate, will be met, when they threaten the positions of power and prestige of the ruling class, with repression and violence. By proceeding in this way, we may eventually be able to produce a mass base. The militant liberals and members of the working class—I do not mean to suggest they are necessarily exclusive—who have come to see the rightness of our demands, will have had their consciousness raised and may well be prepared, after several such defeats, to work for revolution. They may instead fall into despair or cynicism and cop out of the struggle by taking to the hills or to religion or both. This is a possibility that cannot be discounted and, as we are seeing, will indeed happen with some. But it will by no means happen to everyone and (1) such 'dropouts' are no supporters of the capitalist system and (2) they are probably, when the circumstances are more favorable, potential if somewhat unreliable supporters of socialism. There can be no guarantees but what other alternatives are there, and is this not a reasonable strategy?

In defending socialist revolution at present in our situation, it is the above general policy that should be defended. We are saying to our social democratic friends: we do not believe that capitalists will ever give up their exploitation and positions of power and prestige peacefully and we do not believe they will assent to the conditions of egalitarian justice. Thus, if we are right about the facts, and if we are really serious about attaining egalitarian justice and a truly human society, we should prepare for class warfare and eventual revolution. We should add that we hope

[6] I have argued in my "On the Choice Between Reform and Revolution," a) that such a strategy is not to be identified with reformism and b) that in certain circumstances the choice between reform and revolution is an unreal one.

that we are wrong about the facts and we hope that our morally justified demands can be achieved by peaceful agitation and furthermore we proclaim that we should not be the first to use violence. But we also contend that we should prepare ourselves to meet counterrevolutionary violence with violence.

To this, it can be replied, that if the upshot of such a pressure for morally legitimate but radical social demands is going to be met with such counterrevolutionary violence, then we had better drop these demands. To this, we should again apply rough consequentialist calculations (nothing more accurate is possible). Where the forces of reaction are so strong that pressure for the achievement of these reforms will lead to such a bashing of socialist forces that the movement would be destroyed and all resistance would be hopeless, then the pressing of such demands in such a context would indeed be mistaken. One had better fight this issue on another day. But where working class strength, class consciousness, and movement organization are at least probably sufficient for a spontaneous and massive resistance to counterrevolutionary repression and violence, then resistance should be undertaken where it is likely to be successful either in the sense, on the one hand, of winning that particular battle or, on the other, of even losing that battle but affording a good chance of winning the war. There can, of course, be no certainty here. Such matters are always very chancy affairs. We need a good tactical sense, knowledge of the specific situation, and we need to make careful calculations with the understanding that they are very subject to error. But there are no good moral or empirical grounds for saying that we in the bourgeois democracies are never justified in pressing for radical moral demands, no matter how just, which will bring on the repressive force of the bourgeois state. It depends on the probable consequences. If, on the one hand, it is more likely that more misery and less human liberation all around for everyone involved will obtain by such presure under such circumstances, then the demands should not at that time be pressed; if, on the other hand, the reverse is the case, then the demands should be pressed. In principle this is simple; in practice it is difficult because of the difficulty in predicting or even making educated guesses concerning the probable consequences.

To be reasonable about a socialism with a revolutionary option in western capitalist countries is to be committed to such a revolutionary strategy on such moral grounds. Note that it is not, any more than was Marx, in principle committed to violent revolution. If socialism can be achieved by peaceful means, so much the better. Such a socialist strategy indeed has a kind of fail-safe device built into it, namely always start by proceeding peacefully. This means, where we are in a parliamentary system, that we should at least initially proceed by parliamentary means. There are, of course, in such a system perfectly nonviolent forms of extraparliamentary opposition such as civil disobedience and they will often have to be used. Indeed, if I am right, they are a stage on socialism's way. Here I am making the familiar tactical point that in a parliamentary system we should start by using parliamentary means and not rule out the possibility that they will be sufficient. The nice point is how long we should continue to use them where the ruling class repeatedly abuses them. (Indeed, we should expect where they have a chance the capitalist ruling class will try to play a 'Chile' on us.)

Only when those means are exhausted and the needs of working class people are being frustrated, should we proceed to extraparliamentary opposition.[7] The move to violent opposition—meeting violence with violence—should be resorted to only when peaceful extraparliamentary opposition is met by violent repression. And even here such an option should only be exercised when working class forces have a reasonable chance of winning and lessening the total misery and repression of freedom. It is such a strategy that is a reasonable revolutionary stance for socialists in the bourgeois democracies. I see nothing morally irresponsible or outrageous about it at all. Moreover, if contemporary corporate capitalism with its resultant imperialism, exploitation, degradation, and violent repressiveness is as socialists have taken capitalism to be, it is a moral and strategical stance that we ought to adopt.

[7]It is surely natural to respond that by now in bourgeois democracies the parliamentary means have been exhausted and human needs remain drastically frustrated. To continue to go through parliamentary procedures is pointless. To this, two points should be made in response: 1) this is where people in our circumstances are at politically and given the political consciousness of most people—including, of course, most workers—this is the only place where we can start and have their support, 2) it is not, as Rosa Luxemburg recognized, the formal apparatus of bourgeois democracies that are the prime sources of conservatism, but the utilization of them by the ruling class. We do not know that we could not successfully utilize parliamentary means to achieve a socialist order. The case of the crushed Allende government certainly makes for skepticism, on this score. But it is also important to remember that Chile's situation is not the only type of situation in which 'socialism via the ballot box' might become an issue. Even France's or Italy's situation is quite different from Chile's. See here Ernst Vollrath, "Rosa Luxemburg's Theory of Revolution," *Social Research*, Vol. 40, No. 1 (Spring, 1973), pp. 83–109.

SECTION THIRTEEN

FUTURE CHOICE

In recent years, a new science called futurology has gradually come into being, and today, there are thousands of individuals involved in futures research. Perhaps the main reason for the growth of the field lies in the incredible speed at which change is occurring in the world today. One example can make this point dramatically clear. In 1932, Aldous Huxley wrote Brave New World, his vision of the kind of dehumanized society that might await us some 600 years in the future if we did not alter our course. Fifteen years later, Huxley wrote a new foreword to that book, in which he predicted that his vision might be realized within a single century. Today, some 32 years later, some of the scientific techniques used in Brave New World have already been developed and put into practice.

Because things change so rapidly, and because new technologies make possible human experiments on an unheard-of scale, it becomes important for social scientists to raise questions about the kind of future society that would be most viable for human existence, and to make conscious decisions about the ways in which we will use the new technology. Underlying these questions are some fundamental philosophical issues, because in order to choose among possible futures, we must refine our conception of the human being and ask what kinds of social forms and practices will maximize human development.

As a result of the kind of fantasy science fiction has offered us through movies and television, some people have come to think of the future and the technology that will shape it as being out of control and beyond our reach. Contrary to this opinion, all three of the authors presented in this section argue that the future will be the result of conscious choices made by human beings. But, in order for this to be the case, we must understand how change comes about, and we must be able to anticipate the consequences for the future that flow from policies and practices in the present. Futurology is an attempt to develop these skills; and to the extent that we master them, we, too, can play a pivotal role in future choice.

Willis Harman
AN INCOMPLETE GUIDE TO THE FUTURE

*Willis W. Harman is Director of the Center for Study of Social Policy at the
Stanford Research Institute. In "An Incomplete Guide to the Future," which is
taken from his book of the same name, Harman sketches some of the principles
that underlie futures research and touches upon some of the conceptions of
possible futures that have been postulated by contemporary social scientists.
Perhaps most important, he reminds us that our vision of the future plays an
important role both in shaping our future and in determining our present
circumstances.*

We are all accustomed to thinking of the past as a cause of subsequent
events—a decision was made, a law was passed, an encounter took place,
and *as a result* various other events transpired. We reason this way every
day. Less obvious is the fact that our view of the future shapes the kind
of decisions we make in the present. Someone has a vision of the future
—of a great bridge, a new industrial process, or an utopian state—and
as a result certain events are taking place in the present. Our view of the
future affects the present as surely as do our impressions of the past or
the more tangible residues of past actions.

This book entreats you to think about the future and, more importantly, to explore how our vision of the future affects the crucial decisions
of today. Every action involves some view of the future—as we expect it
to be, or as we desire it to be, or as we fear it may be. If our image of
the future were different, the decision of today would be different. If our
expectations are inaccurate, our decisions are likely to be faulty. If our
vision is inspiring, it will impel us to action. If our collective vision
arouses no enthusiasm, or if there is no commonly held image of what
is worth striving for, our society will lack both motivation and direction.

We often assume (with considerable justification) that the most probable future is a direct continuation of past trends. Yet it is apparent today
that many long-standing trends cannot continue unaltered: World population cannot forever expand exponentially; world energy use cannot
increase endlessly; patterns of world mineral consumption must change.
In fact, it has been apparent for several decades that modern society has
broken with the past in a number of important respects. Peter Drucker
has called our time "the age of discontinuity." In his book of that name,
published in 1968, he described four important discontinuities with the
past:

1. Genuinely new technologies, such as computers and semiconduc-
tors, were creating new major industries and rendering existing industries obsolete. Future technologies were most likely to stem, not from
independent investors, but from new knowledge of atomic and nuclear
structure, biochemistry, psychology, and symbolic logic.

2. Major changes were taking place in the world's economy, moving it toward a worldwide economy and what Drucker calls "a global shopping center."

3. A new pluralist social and political organization was emerging in which all major tasks, from investment advising and care of the aging to dating and partygiving, were becoming institutionalized so that society was coming to be dominated by a web of overlapping, interdependent, special-purpose organizations.

4. Access to knowledge, rather than raw materials and transportation, had already become the crucial resource of modern economies. It was the major determinant of success in industries, represented the crucial capital, and was changing the character of work, the labor force, and education.

Drucker's book quickly became obsolete because new discontinuities have appeared that are at least as significant as the ones he had identified. It will suffice to mention five:

1. Individuals and governments alike began to recognize the serious threat from industrialized civilization to sufficiency of fossil fuels, minerals, and natural fresh water; of arable land and habitable space; of the waste-absorbing capacity of the environment; and of the resilience of the planet's life-support systems. This "new scarcity" was different in kind from the scarcities of food and shelter that have always been a part of human existence, being more fundamentally linked to approaching planetary limits.

2. Great masses of people were no longer content with the economic and political status quo. Rising levels of education and awareness, in part due to the impact of modern communications, had led to expectations of better living conditions and increased self-determination and had created dissatisfaction with the disparities and inequities of the old order.

3. Growing numbers of people in the industrialized nations had become disillusioned with the once-accepted belief that ever-increasing material growth and ever-expanding technology and industrialization would overcome world poverty and help mankind to achieve a more meaningful existence.

4. Nonindustrialized Third World nations began to exert new power. They became a moral force, influenced world economy by forming cartels of resource-producing nations, and demonstrated the disruptive capability of the discontented poor.

5. A "new transcendentalism" emerged, both in the general population and among a faction of scientists, which placed new emphasis on intuitive and spiritual experience. This new weight given to spiritual intuition reversed a long-standing trend toward empirical explanations and materialistic values.

Yet even this expanded list fails to capture the full spirit of our times. Significant as these discontinuities are, they appear to be manifestations of a far more fundamental change—a change involving all our social, political, and economic institutions; our social roles and expectations;

and even the basic premises underlying modern culture and values. This change is not just an evolutionary development from one phase of history to another. Rather, the evidence suggests that the technologically advanced nations of the world may be approaching one of the great transformations of human history.

From a broad historical perspective, the modern industrial era is a brief episode—a jump from a preindustrial society in which man made relatively low demands on natural resources and had little impact on the natural environment to a "transindustrial" society in which man has a high ability to manipulate and shape his physical environment. Whereas industrial society's emphasis has been on economic and material growth, the transindustrial society would place more emphasis on human growth and development. Whereas industrial society has been greatly concerned with the physical frontiers of geography and technology, in the transindustrial society concern would shift to the inner frontiers of mind and spirit. In the transindustrial society institutions would have to serve persons, not the reverse. Learning would be a prime concern at all phases of life and of all social institutions—not an activity of limited duration in preparation for the "real" business of fitting into the institutions of the industrial state.

We tend to view recent decades from the perspective of our own lifespan. Thus we are impressed with the technological accomplishment and the seemingly endless cornucopia of physical products of modern industry. But taking the longer perspective, we can see the nature of the brief historical interval—this "jump" from preindustrial to transindustrial society—that our industrial era comprises. Consider population growth for example. We have come to accept that the planet's population is increasing at about 2 percent per year, following an exponential growth curve. Yet in the longer historical perspective, from say 6000 B.C. to A.D. 6000, the plot of world population has to look something like the upper step curve of *Figure 1*. To grasp the significance of the metamorphosis to a transindustrial era, imagine a similar plot of the average demand that each individual makes on the environment through resources used and waste products discarded. Of necessity, this is an assumed arbitrary scale because appropriate data do not exist, but we can judge that the plot has to look something like the lower curve of *Figure 1*. Our present point in history is unique—illustrated both in terms of population growth and individual demands upon the environment: At no other time has such growth been so rapid. Because of planetary limitations, this exponential growth cannot continue; at some point it must once again level off.

Let me emphasize, however, that this future transformation to a transindustrial society is not predictable, automatic, or even necessarily probable. All one can say is that there does appear to be a tendency toward this metamorphosis. The forces that could produce such a transformation were set in motion long ago and in one way or another will play themselves out. In the same sense that a seedling seeks sunlight or

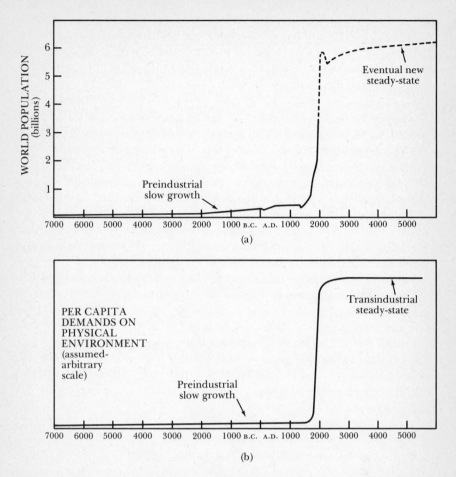

Figure 1. Two curves illustrating the uniqueness of the present point in history: (a) world population, and (b) per capita demands on the physical environment.

adolescents seek to establish their own identity (in ways that are often unconscious), so we may say that society shows signs of attempting a transformation—even though most of the participants are relatively oblivious to what impels them.

.   .   .

Among those who are future watchers, even those with impeccable credentials, there is considerable disagreement. Certainly not all scholars of the future find an imminent transformation of industrialized society in their crystal balls. For instance, Herman Kahn, director of the Hudson Institute and coauthor of *The Next 200 Years,* offers an impressive case for a "postindustrial perspective" in which, within the next century, "the more desperate and seemingly eternal problems of human poverty will have largely been solved or greatly alleviated" and "most misery will derive from the anxieties and ambiguities of wealth and luxury, not from physical suffering due to scarcities." Kahn believes that pollution, resource depletion, food and energy shortages, technological excesses, the gaping disparities between rich and poor nations, and the supposed deterioration of the qualify of life are not insurmountable problems—if appropriate technological and institutional approaches are used to resolve them. He postulates that "the postindustrial economy should be close to a humanistic utopia by most historical standards"—if we do not falter or lose our nerve by succumbing to the "limits-to-growth" argument that economic growth must be precipitately slowed down because we are approaching planetary limitations. Kahn concludes, "New technology and capital investment are necessary . . . to help protect and improve the environment, to keep resource costs down, and to provide an economic surplus for problems and crises. . . . If we are reasonably prudent and flexible we will not have to contend with any really serious shortages in the medium run, and the long run looks even better." In other words, as Kahn sees it, there is no systemic crisis— just a crisis of will.

Other technological optimists, such as Daniel Bell, agree that there is no need for or likelihood of systemic transformation. In *The Coming of Post-Industrial Society* Bell predicts that there will be sufficient growth in service occupations and knowledge-based industries to provide work for all, and he expects that advancing technology will bring societal problems under control.

Many other futures researchers, however, see a need for, and signs of, some sort of systemic transformation. In *An Inquiry Into the Human Prospect* Robert Heilbroner presents a strong argument attesting to the need for such a transformation but doubts that we will achieve it. He explains, "The long-term solution requires nothing less than the gradual abandonment of the lethal techniques, the uncongenial ways of life, and the dangerous mentality of industrial civilization itself. . . . The [nearer-term] outlook is for convulsive change—change forced upon us by external events rather than by conscious choice, by catastrophe rather than by calculation. . . . If we ask whether it is possible to meet the challenges of the future without the payment of a fearful price, the answer must be: There is no such hope."

Some humanistic optimists writing about the future see the need for system transformation (away from the emphasis on materialistic values and economic growth and toward a more humane and person-centered society) and believe it can be brought about without causing a serious disruption of society. Charles Reich, author of *The Greening of America,* and George Leonard, author of *The Transformation,* are examples. This group pays little regard to the powerful institutionalized forces that would resist such profound systemic change. Thus, their romantic vision lacks an element of realism.

   This diversity of forecasts raises the question as to whether we have any reliable basis for making forecasts of the future. In other words, is there anything to the esoteric art of futures research?

SIX PRINCIPLES UNDERLYING FUTURES RESEARCH

Every action decision implies some assumption about the future; it is the function of futures research to make those assumptions explicit. Since we cannot know the future precisely, we must delineate alternative possibilities so that choices can be tested against various future states that *could* occur. But which futures are feasible and which are not? That is the central question of futures research.

   If one presumes to say anything at all about the future of a social system, he must assume that there is something *dependable* about the behavior of that system. There are relatively few distinct ways in which social systems are dependable. The different methods of futures research are based essentially on various combinations of six principles that characterize complex, highly interconnected social systems.

One: Continuity.   First of all, societies exhibit continuity. Social systems change smoothly from one state to another; generally they do not change in discontinuous jumps. (Even during relatively disruptive and seemingly discontinuous periods, such as the American Civil War or the French Revolution, much of the culture, social roles, and institutional framework of a society persists without fundamental change.) Thus, in making forecasts we commonly and reasonably extrapolate from past experience. This principle of continuity is used in all sorts of projections of trends and cycles—for forecasting demographic trends, economic cycles, and annual energy consumption; for anticipating future attitudes from polling data; for estimating future financial performance—to mention only a few.

   Kahn and coauthor Anthony Wiener provide an interesting example of extrapolation from the past to forecast possible alternative futures in *The Year 2000: A Framework for Speculation.* They observe in the evolutionary development of Western society over many centuries a "basic long-term multifold trend." This trend consists of a number of basic tendencies—for example, Western culture has become increasingly manipulative, utilitarian, and based on rational thought and the senses rather than on intuition; technological change has become increasingly institutionalized; and industrialization and urbanization have expanded (see Table 1, p. 548). Extrapolating from these long-term tendencies, they postulate alternative future possibilities that involve relatively minor or slow variations from this central multifold trend. (Kahn has subsequently altered his view and sees some indication of eventual modification of the multifold trend, but expects any major shift to take a century or more.)

Table 1.   *The Long-Term Multifold Trend of Western Culture*

1. Increasingly sensate (empirical, this-worldly, secular, humanistic, pragmatic, manipulative, explicitly rational, utilitarian, contractual, epicurean, hedonistic, etc.) cultures.
2. Bourgeois, bureaucratic, and meritocratic elites.
3. Centralization and concentration of economic and political power.
4. Accumulation of scientific and technical knowledge.
5. Institutionalization of technological change, especially research, development, innovation, and diffusion.
6. Increasing military capability.
7. Westernization, modernization, and industrialization.
8. Increasing affluence and (recently) leisure.
9. Population growth.
10. Urbanization, recently suburbanization and "urban sprawl"—soon the growth of megalopoli.
11. Decreasing importance of primary and (recently) secondary occupations; increasing importance of tertiary and (recently) quaternary occupations.
12. Increasing literacy and education and (recently) the "knowledge industry" and increasing role of intellectuals.
13. Innovative and manipulative social engineering—i.e., rationality increasingly applied to social, political, cultural, and economic worlds as well as to shaping and exploiting the material world.
14. Increasing universality of the multifold trend.
15. Increasing tempo of change in all the above.

Additional components that seem more important than they did a few years ago:
16. Increasing scale of environmental impact of human activities.
17. Increasing rate of use of "nonrenewable" natural resources of minerals and fossil fuels.
18. Movement toward a single world economy with closely linked worldwide economic institutions.
19. Increasing gap between rich and poor populations.
20. Increasing subordination of the economic function to the political order (Bell).
21. Decreasing importance of private property (Bell).

SOURCE: The Hudson Institute (Herman Kahn and Bruce Briggs, 1972).

In *The Coming of Post-Industrial Society* Daniel Bell provides a scholarly case of extrapolative social forecasting. He contends that the technologically advanced society of the future will increasingly depend upon theoretical knowledge as the prime source of innovation and of policy formulation. To arrive at the characteristics of postindustrial society, he projects this tendency, along with other components of the multifold trend, including two elements not specifically identified by Kahn. Bell writes:

> The decisive social change taking place in our time—because of the interdependence of men and the aggregative character of economic actions, the rise of externalities and social costs, and the need to control the effects of technical change—is the subordination of the economic function of the political order.... The second major historical change is the sundering of social function [or place in society, primarily occupational] from property.

From this projection he derives his description of postindustrial society, distinguished by a high fraction of the working force in service and knowledge industries and by the commanding role of a technocratic elite.

It should be noted that the postindustrial society as described by Bell essentially involves a continuation of the long-term multifold trend. It seems reasonable enough that these central tendencies which have persisted for eight centuries or so would continue a while longer; yet, clearly these component trends are among the aspects of the old order that are currently being challenged. The social forecast of a transindustrial society postulates a future society that differs fundamentally from the postindustrial society discussed by both Bell and Kahn. Such a transformation to a transindustrial society presumes that a major departure from the long-term multifold trend will occur before the end of the present century.

Two: Self-consistency.   A second guiding principle underlying futures research is that societal systems tend to be internally self-consistent. That is, the behavior of one sector of society does not generally contradict that of another. For instance, basic research is not likely to be well supported and flourishing when the economy is depressed.

The principle of self-consistency underlies one of the popular, if less systematic, techniques for examining the future—namely, scenario writing. The purpose of writing scenarios about the future is to insure that the characteristics asserted, whether arrived at from trend projections or other methods, "hang together" and make a reasonable story. A plausible future has to feel like it might be lived in. Familiar examples of scenario writing include Edward Bellamy's *Looking Backward,* Aldous Huxley's *Brave New World,* and George Orwell's *1984.*

Three: Similarities among Social Systems.   Because the individuals making up varied social systems have fundamental characteristics in common, the systems themselves inevitably exhibit certain similarities. Accordingly, one group will tend to behave somewhat like another under similar circumstances. This observation of similarities across groups is used in anthropological approaches to the study of the future, in gaming methods where an individual assumes the role of a group or a nation, and in cross-cultural comparisons (e.g., of stages of economic development).

Historical analogies in particular, if not carried too far, can be useful in suggesting possible future scenarios. For example, studies of historical occurrences of revolutionary cultural and political transformations suggest possible parallels today.

Four: Cause-Effect Relationships.   Social systems exhibit apparent cause-effect connections or statistical correlations that imply cause and effect relationships. For instance, when making economic projections we assume that if scarcities occur, prices will rise; or that if the rate of inflation is lowered by manipulating the money supply, unemployment will increase. Such presumed cause-effect linkages underlie much economic and simulation modeling. They are the basis for the models in the Club of Rome's study *The Limits to Growth* which has generated much controversy since its publication in 1972. They form the basic principle in the widely used method of cross-impact analysis (in which aspects of the future are studied through the presumed interactions of contributing events on one another).

Five: Holistic Trending.   In their process of evolving and changing, social systems behave like integrated organic wholes. They have to be perceived in their entirety; thus there is no substitute for human observation and judgment about the future state of a system. To overcome the problem of bias of an individual observer, collective opinion can be sought in various ways. One of these is the so-called Delphi technique wherein the opinions of a number of judges are systematically processed and the results fed back to each of the judges as additional input, the object being to obtain refined judgments (but not necessarily consensus).

Six: Goal Seeking.   Societies have goals. They act with apparent intentionality, although the goals that might be inferred from observation are not necessarily declared ones. Just as individuals have aims of which they are but dimly aware, so do societies seek destinies that they have never explicitly proclaimed. In short, social change is not aimless, however obscured the goal. Modern industrialized society is confronted with a set of dilemmas that it seeks to resolve. Goals that once inspired commitment and loyalty no longer have the same power, and new priorities are being formed. The possible futures are distinguished, as much as anything, by the ways society seeks resolution of its dilemmas, and by the kinds of new goals that emerge.

LIMITATIONS OF FUTURES RESEARCH

Various systematic approaches have been devised utilizing these six principles. Some approaches are strongly holistic while others concentrate on particular aspects of the society; some deal primarily with quantitative information (economic indicators, age distribution, population statistics, migration patterns, etc.) and other hard data about technological developments and ecological shifts, while others place more emphasis on factors that are hard to quantify, such as social innovations and shifts in cultural values and attitudes. Regardless of the approach, future research inevitably remains more art than science, if only because of human unpredictability, perverseness, and creativity.

It is extremely difficult, whatever analysis or research method may be used, to achieve enough objectivity about the future to avoid being misled. We are not referring here to an idealized "value-free" position, which is sometimes mistakenly assumed to be characteristic of pure science. Rather, the aim is to achieve the kind of nonattachment and freedom from bias that a judge strives for in a court of law. Bias seems inevitable, especially with any single research approach. If the method deals primarily with numerical data, there is bias in favor of information that is easily quantifiable. If the method concentrates on theoretical issues and rational analysis, it may slight irrational and unconscious forces. The method may be biased by an implicit image of man—as free and rational or as unfree and controlled by his drives, habits, and social roles. It may be biased by a Malthusian pessimism or a technocratic optimism. Bias can be offset somewhat by deliberately employing several diverse approaches, synthesizing the results where they complement one another and carrying out further analyses when results conflict.

It is particularly difficult to overcome the bias that results from being immersed in a particular culture—from living in a particular area of the globe at a particular time in history. One is a product of his culture. Every culture has its blind spots, and there is no reason to suppose that ours is an exception. The anthropologist studying a primitive tribe, or the foreign traveler, sees things that the native misses; the historian is aware of characteristics of a particular period that were not apparent to the person living at that time. It is as difficult for a futures researcher to be objective today as it was for a scholar in the Middle Ages to comprehend what the post-Copernican world might be like.

GENERATING ALTERNATIVE FUTURES—SIMPLIFIED

We have identified six principles that can be used to test a described future (or trend) for plausibility. Still, much uncertainty about the future remains—because our knowledge of the present state of affairs and our comprehension of historical trends is imperfect, because unpredictable random events can affect the future, and because human choice is essentially unpredictable.

This uncertainty is to be recognized and honored. Consequently one cannot talk prudently about a single predicted future, but rather must describe several plausible futures. The six principles of futures research can be used, in a variety of ways, to delineate a set of alternative future paths that society might follow. The primary utility of generating alternative plausible futures is that contemplated action decisions can be tested against these different future contexts to determine under what conditions these projected decisions would appear to be appropriate and to alert the decision maker to future contexts in which these choices might be disastrous. Thus decision making becomes a dynamic process, in which the unfolding future prompts a continuing reexamination of available options and their probable consequences.

.   .   .

Kenneth Boulding
THE MEANING OF THE TWENTIETH CENTURY: THE GREAT TRANSITION

Kenneth Boulding is a professor of economics at the University of Michigan. In "The Meaning of the Twentieth Century: The Great Transition," which is taken from his book of the same name, Boulding argues that the period in which we are living marks the middle period of a great transition in the development of human civilization. He examines here the preconditions for change in society, focusing on the way in which economics, technology, and social inventions interact to bring about change, and he suggests ways in which the developments in this century raise questions about the form that the projected great transition from civilization to postcivilization will take.

The twentieth century marks the middle period of a great transition in the state of the human race. It may properly be called the second great transition in the history of mankind.

The first transition was that from precivilized to civilized society which began to take place about five (or ten) thousand years ago.[1] This is a transition that is still going on in some part of the world, although it can be regarded as almost complete. Precivilized society can now be found only in small and rapidly diminishing pockets in remote areas. It is doubtful whether more than 5 per cent of the world's population could now be classified as living in a genuinely precivilized society.

Even as the first great transition is approaching completion, however, a second great transition is treading on its heels. It may be called the transition from civilized to postcivilized society. We are so accustomed to giving the word civilization a favorable overtone that the words postcivilized or postcivilization may strike us as implying something unfavorable. If, therefore, the word technological or the term developed society is preferred I would have no objection. The word postcivilized, however, does bring out the fact that civilization is an intermediate state of man dividing the million or so years of precivilized society from an equally long or longer period which we may expect to extend into the future postcivilization. It is furthermore a rather disagreeable state for most people living in it, and its disappearance need occasion few tears.

The origins of the first great transition from precivilized society are lost in the mists of prehistory except in so far as they can be reconstructed with the aid of archeology. The more we know the further these origins seem to recede in time, and it now seems clear that the beginning of agriculture and the domestication of animals can be traced back at least

---

[1]The first transition falls into two parts, the transition from the paleolithic to the neolithic, following the invention of agriculture, and the subsequent transition from the neolithic village to urban civilization.

ten thousand years. Agriculture is a precondition of the development of civilization because it is not until man settles down and begins to cultivate crops and domesticate livestock that he is able to develop a surplus of food from the food producer above and beyond what the food producer and his family require themselves for their own maintenance. . . . There must be a continuous and reasonably stable excess of food production above the requirements of the food producer if civilization is to be established.

The mere existence of surplus food, while it is a prerequisite for the existence of civilization, does not necessarily produce it, for surplus may be "wasted" in leisure or unproductive activities. In order for towns and cities to exist there must be some machinery whereby the food surplus of the food producer is extracted from him and collected in one place so that the kings, priests, soldiers, builders, and artisans of civilization can subsist. I am assuming here that the prime mark of civilization is the city. This is indeed what the derivation of the word civilization suggests. In its earliest form the city seems to have been a product of some system of coercion. Agriculture provides the opportunity, but in the early stages at least it seems to take some form of coercion to take advantage of it. The earliest forms of coercion may well have been spiritual, for there is some evidence that the earliest cities were organized as theocracies. A priesthood arises which claims a monopoly on the supposedly supernatural forces which govern the affairs of man and the fertility of crops and livestock. The priest then is able to extract food from the food producer by threatening to deprive him of the assistance of these supernatural forces. The coercive system of the priest, however, is based to a large extent on bluff, for the priest does not really control the forces that make the crops grow. When the priest ceases to inspire belief in his imaginary powers the spiritual coercive system usually seems to be replaced by a more physical coercive system in the shape of a king and army. . . .

The origins of the second great transition are perhaps not so obscure as the origins of the first but there are many puzzling and unresolved questions connected with them. All through the history of civilization, indeed, one can detect a slowly rising stream of knowledge and organization that has a different quality from that of the civilized society around it. The astronomy of Babylonia, the geometry of the Greeks, and the algebra of the Arabs represent as it were foretastes of the great flood of knowledge and technological change to come. Some of the ancient empires, even the Roman Empire, seem to have been technologically stagnant and scientifically backward. If one is looking for the beginning of a continuous process of scientific and technological development this might be traced to the monastic movement in the West of the sixth century A.D., especially the Benedictines. Here for almost the first time in history we had intellectuals who worked with their hands, and who belonged to a religion which regarded the physical world as in some sense sacred and capable of enshrining goodness. It is not surprising therefore that an interest in the economizing of labor and in extending its productive powers began in the monasteries, however slowly. From the sixth century on we can trace a slowly expanding technology. The water wheel comes in the sixth century, the stirrup in the eighth, the horse collar and the rudder in the ninth, the windmill in the twelfth, and so on. For Europe the invention of printing in the fifteenth century represents an irreversible take-off, because from this point on the dissemination of information increased with great rapidity. The seventeenth century saw the beginning of science, the eighteenth century an acceleration of technological change so great that it has been called, perhaps rather misleadingly, the Industrial Revolution. The nineteenth century saw the development of science as an ongoing social organization, and the twentieth century has seen research and development heavily institutionalized with an enormous increase in the rate of change both of knowledge and of technology as a result. It must be emphasized that the rate of change still seems to be accelerating. We may not even have reached the middle of whatever process we are passing through, and there are certainly no signs that the rate of change is slowing down. It seems clear for instance that we are now on the edge of a biological revolution which may have results for mankind just as dramatic as the nuclear revolution of a generation ago.

A few symptoms will indicate the magnitude of the change through which we are now passing. Consider for instance the position of agriculture in the most developed societies today. In all societies of classical civilization, as we have seen, at least 75 per cent of the population, and often a larger percentage, were engaged in agriculture and would merely produce enough to support themselves and the remaining urban 25 per cent. Even in the United States at the time of the American Revolution, it has been estimated that about 90 per cent of the people were in agriculture. Today in the United States only about 10 per cent of the population are so engaged, and if present trends continue it will not be long before we can produce all the food that we need with 5 per cent, or even less, of the population. This is because with modern techniques, a single farmer and his family can produce enough food to feed ten, twenty, or even thirty families. This releases more than 90 per cent of the population to work on other things, and to produce automobiles, houses, clothing, all the luxuries and conveniences of life as well as missiles and nuclear weapons.

. . . Another startling fact is that about 25 per cent of the human beings who have ever lived are now alive, and what is even more astonishing, something like 90 per cent of all the scientists who have ever lived are now alive. My eight-year-old son asked me the other day, "Daddy, were you born in the olden days?" It is the sort of question that makes a parent feel suddenly middle-aged. There is perhaps more truth in his remark than he knew. In a very real sense the changes in the state of mankind since the date of my birth have been greater than the changes that took place in many thousands of years before this date.

Another indication of the magnitude of the transition is the extraordinary ability of modern societies to recover from disaster. In 1945, for instance, many of the cities of Germany and Japan lay in almost total ruin. Today it is hard to tell that they were ever destroyed, for they have been completely rebuilt in a space of less than twenty years. It took Western Europe almost three hundred years to recover from the fall of the Roman Empire, and it took Germany decades to recover from the Thirty Years War (1618–1648). It is perhaps an optimistic feature of the present time that as well as great powers of destruction, we also have greatly increased powers of recuperation and recovery.

The great transition is not only something that takes place in science, technology, the physical machinery of society, and in the utilization of physical energy. It is also a transition in social institutions. Changes in technology produce change in social institutions, and changes in institutions produce change in technology. In the enormously complex world of social interrelations we cannot say in any simple way that one change produces the other, only that they are enormously interrelated and both aspects of human life change together. For instance, it has been argued that the invention of the rudder and the improvement in the arts of navigation and shipbuilding which took place in Europe in the fifteenth century led inevitably to the discovery of America by Europeans. As a schoolboy is reported to have said, "How could Columbus miss it?" Once it was possible to navigate a course of three thousand miles in a straight line, the discovery of America by the Europeans was virtually inevitable, and of course this discovery enormously expanded the horizon and the opportunities of these European societies.

On the other hand, the societies which pioneered in the discovery of America did not ultimately profit very much from it. Spain and Portugal obtained a great empire and a sizable inflation but stagnated as a result, because of the failure of their social institutions to adapt.

.   .   .

The social invention of parliamentary democracy permitted societies to develop with much greater diversity and wider distribution of power than in the earlier absolute monarchies, and the rise of modern science is quite closely associated with the development of democratic and pluralistic institutions of this kind. It could not arise, for instance, in imperial China or feudal Japan. It is no accident that an acceleration in the growth of science took place in Western Europe following the French Revolution. It is clear that we must look at pure science, technological change, and social invention as parts of a single pattern of development in which each element supports the other. It may be argued indeed that social institutions play more of a negative than a positive role, in that they can inhibit scientific and technological change but cannot initiate it. Even this proposition, however, must now be called in question. Organized research and development is essentially a social invention which has resulted in an enormous increase in the pace of technological change.

.   .   .

Social inventions often take place so softly and imperceptibly that they are hardly noticed, and the history of social invention as a result still largely remains to be written. Who for instance invented the handshake? How did we change from a society in which almost every man went armed to a society in which we have achieved almost complete personal disarmament, and in which human relations are governed by conventions of politeness, by disarming methods of communication, and by largely nonviolent techniques of conflict? Most of all, how do changes take place in child rearing? These perhaps are the most fundamental social inventions of all, for the personality structure of one generation depends mainly on the way children were brought up in the previous generation.

As part of the ongoing process of social invention the great transition involves changes in moral, religious, and aesthetic aspects of life just as much as it involves changes in our knowledge and use of the physical world. It involves, for instance, changes in the nature of the family and in the patterns of child rearing. Civilized society on the whole is characterized by the extended family, and by strong loyalty to kinfolk and by methods of child rearing which generally involve a rough transition from an extremely permissive and protective early childhood to an authoritarian and unpleasant regime in later childhood. As we move to postcivilized society, we find an extension of loyalty from the kinship group to larger areas such as the national state, or even to the world as a whole. The family structure and living arrangement tend to shift from the extended family group and large household to the small nuclear family of parents and children, and we find that the child-rearing practices which may be well adapted to a society in which the threat systems are important and aggression pays off, have become poorly adapted to a society in which the subtler arts of personal manipulation replace the more violent forms of aggression. We therefore find a shift in the methods of child rearing from those which produce the authoritarian personalities which are characteristic of civilized societies to those which produce more flexible, adaptable, and manipulative persons.

Drastic changes in the nature and behavior of the family are also implied by the health revolution which is also a part of the transition. In civilized society, mortality is high and there is a necessity therefore for a high birth rate. Civilized society can be in equilibrium with birth and death rates between thirty and forty per thousand and a corresponding expectation of life between thirty-three and twenty-five. It is a matter of simple arithmetic that in an equilibrium population in which birth rate and death rate are equal, the level of the birth and death rates is the simple reciprocal of the average age at death. In the advanced societies today the average age at death is about seventy, and for such a population to be in equilibrium the birth and death rate must be about fourteen. To put the matter in somewhat different terms, if all children live to maturity and if the whole population marries, then the average number of children in one family cannot exceed two, if population is to be stable. This also implies no more than an average of two births per family. This involves an enormous shift in attitude toward children and even perhaps toward sex. Yet this is an essential part of the transition. If this part of the transition is not made, all the rest cannot be made either, except as a temporary and unstable condition.

.   .   .

Furthermore the rapid and easy transportation which postcivilization permits makes it much more difficult to maintain culture traits in isolation. Civilizations could flourish at the same time on the earth which had little or no contact one with another. The Mayan civilization certainly had no contact with Rome, and Rome had very little contact with China. The transition to civilization indeed may have been accomplished in at least three independent locations or perhaps even more, though these origins are so obscure that we cannot be sure of this. Now, however, it is as easy to go halfway around the world as it used to be to go to a neighboring town, and under these circumstances an enormous process of cultural mixture is taking place which can hardly help producing much greater uniformity even in a few hundred years. It is doubtful whether a single world language will emerge in the near future, but certainly in styles of clothing, housing, mass entertainment, and transportation it is becoming increasingly hard to distinguish one part of the world from another.

An important difference which is likely to be maintained for a considerable time is that between societies which are making the transition under democratic and capitalistic institutions and those which are making the transition under institutions of totalitarian socialism. It certainly seems possible to make the technological transition under both sets of institutions. Nevertheless the societies which will emerge as a result might be quite different not only in the political and social institutions but in the value systems and the nature and quality of human life which they support. In the short run this raises many problems and unquestionably increases the danger of war and the probability that the transition will not be made. In the long perspective of history, however, this may turn out to have been a fortunate accident, if indeed it is an accident. It might well be that one of the greatest problems of postcivilized society will be how to preserve enough differentiation of human culture and how to prevent the universal spread of a drab uniformity. Cultural change and development at all times has frequently come about as a result of the interaction of cultures which previously have developed in isolation. . . .

Perhaps the most difficult of all these problems involving diversity and uniformity is the problem of the future of different races. The different races of mankind have a sufficient sexual attraction for each other so that in the absence of any geographical or cultural obstacles to genetic mixture it is highly probable that in the course of a few thousand years the human race would become radically uniform, and the existing differences between races will be largely eliminated. From some points of view this may be very desirable, and it will certainly eliminate certain problems of interhuman conflict, most of which however are defined culturally rather than biologically. We know so little about human genetics, however, especially on the positive side of the forces which lead to genetic excellence, that it is impossible now to prophesy what may be regarded as eugenic in the future. The eugenic movement of the nineteenth century was based on inadequate knowledge of human genetics and hence could not get very far. If we develop as we may well do more accurate knowledge of the genetic factors which make for human excellence both of mind and body, the consequences for ethics, for almost all social relations, and for political behavior might be immense. But this is a bridge which we have not yet come to, and it may be well to postpone worrying about it until we do. In the meantime knowledge of human genetics, apart from a few factors making for certain defects, is not developed enough so that from it we can justify either racial purity or racial admixture. It might well be indeed that we will end by classifying mankind genetically along quite different lines from the way in which the races are now classified by strictly superficial characteristics, and we may then be able to warn against dangerous genetic combinations, as we do already with the Rh factor, and perhaps even encourage desirable combinations. Much of this, however, is in the future, though at the rate at which the biological sciences are now developing it may not be in the very distant future.

The great question as to whether the transition from civilization to postcivilization is a "good" change is one that cannot be answered completely until we know the nature and quality of different postcivilized societies. We might well argue in contemplating the first great transition from precivilized to civilized societies that in many cases this was a transition from a better state of man to a worse. As we contemplate the innumerable wars of civilized societies, as we contemplate the hideous religion of human sacrifice and the bloody backs of innumerable slaves on which the great monuments of civilization have been built, it is sometimes hard to refrain from a certain romantic nostalgia for the "noble savage." . . . Anthropologists have somewhat dispelled the romantic view of precivilized society, which was in many cases not only poor but cruel and disagreeable beyond even the excesses of civilization. Nevertheless it will not be difficult to contrast the best of precivilized societies and the worst of civilized societies and come out much in favor of the precivilized. Similarly a type of postcivilized society is possible as portrayed, for instance, in the anti-Utopias of George Orwell and Aldous Huxley in the middle of the twentieth century, in which the quality of human life and the dignity of man seem to be much inferior to that in the best of civilized societies.

There is clearly here a problem to be solved. We do not make men automatically good and virtuous by making them rich and powerful; indeed the truth frequently seems to be the opposite. Nevertheless we must not fall into the other trap of equating innocence with ignorance or thinking that impotence is the same thing as virtue. An increase in power increases the potential both for good and for evil. A postcivilized society of unshakable tyranny, resting upon all the knowledge which we are going to gain in social sciences, and of unspeakable corruption resting on man's enormous power over nature, especially biological nature, is by no means inconceivable. On the other hand the techniques of postcivilization also offer us the possibility of a society in which the major sources of human misery have been eliminated, a society in which there will be no war, poverty, or disease, and in which a large majority of human beings will be able to live out their lives in relative freedom from most of the ills which now oppress a major part of mankind. This is a prize worth driving for even at the risk of tyranny and corruption. There is no real virtue in impotence, and the virtue to strive for is surely the combination of power with goodness.

In any case there is probably no way back. The growth of knowledge is one of the most irreversible forces known to mankind. It takes a catastrophe of very large dimensions to diminish the total stock of knowledge in the possession of man. Even in the rise and fall of great civilizations surprisingly little has been permanently lost, and much that was lost for a short time was easily regained. Hence there is no hope for ignorance or for a morality based on it. Once we have tasted the fruit of the tree of knowledge, as the Biblical story illustrates so well, Eden is closed to us. We cannot go back to the childhood of our race any more than we can go back to our own childhood without disaster. Eden has been lost to us forever and an angel with a flaming sword stands guard at its gates. Therefore either we must wander hopelessly in the world or we must press forward to Zion. We must learn to master ourselves as we are learning to master nature. There is no reason in the nature of things which says that ethical development is impossible, and indeed one would expect that the process of development, whether economic, political, or social, will go hand in hand with a similar process of ethical development which will enable us to use wisely the power that we have gained. This ethical development may take forms which will seem strange to us now, but just as we can trace development in the values and ethical standards of mankind as his economic and physical powers increased from precivilized society, so it is reasonable that new ethical standards will arise appropriate to the new technology of postcivilization.

We must emphasize that there is no inevitability and no determinism in making this great transition. . . . [T]here are a number of traps which lie along the way and which may either prevent man and his planet earth from making the transition altogether or delay it for many generations or even thousands of years. The first most obvious and immediate trap is the war trap. It is now theoretically possible for man to build a device which will eliminate all life from the earth. Even if this extreme event is highly improbable, less extreme disasters are at least within a range of probability that makes them a matter of serious concern. A major nuclear war would unquestionably set back the transition to a postcivilized world by many generations, and it might indeed eliminate the possibility of making this transition altogether. The effect of such war on the whole ecological system of the planet is so unpredictable that we cannot tell how large a disaster it will be, although we know it will be very large. It is possible that such a disaster will be irretrievable. It is also possible that even if we had a retrievable disaster we might not learn enough from it to retrieve ourselves. It is clear that what is desperately needed at the present time is to diminish the probability of such a disaster to the vanishing point.

Another possible trap which might delay the attainment of the transition for a long time is the population trap. This is perhaps the main reason for believing that the impact of a few postcivilized techniques on existing civilized societies might easily be disastrous in the next hundred years or so. One of the first impacts of postcivilized medicine and medical knowledge on civilized society is a large and immediate reduction in the death rate, especially in infant mortality. This is seldom if ever accompanied by a similar decrease in birth rate, and hence the first impact of postcivilized techniques on a previously stable civilized society is a tremendous upsurge in the rate of population increase. This increase may be so large that the society is incapable of adapting itself to it, and incapable in particular of devoting sufficient resources to the education of its unusually large cohorts of young people. We therefore have the tragic situation that the alleviation of much human misery and suffering in the short run may result in enormous insoluble problems in a longer period.

A third possible trap is the technological trap itself: that we may not be able to develop a genuinely stable high-level technology which is independent of exhaustible resources. Technology at the present time, even the highest technology, is largely dependent for its sources of energy and materials on accumulations in the earth which date from its geological past. In a few centuries, or at most a few thousand years, these are likely to be exhausted, and either man will fall back on a more primitive technology or he will have to advance to knowledge well beyond what he has now. Fortunately there are signs that this transition to a stable high-level technology may be accomplished, but we certainly cannot claim that it has been accomplished up to date.

A fourth possible trap may lie in the very nature of man itself. If the dangers and difficulties which now beset man are eliminated in postcivilized society and if he has no longer anything to fear but death itself, will not his creativity be diminished and may he not dissipate his energies in a vast ennui and boredom? This is a question which cannot be answered. But it lurks uneasily at the back of all optimistic statements about the long-run future of man.

Leon R. Kass
THE NEW BIOLOGY: WHAT PRICE RELIEVING MAN'S ESTATE?

In the following thoughtful essay, Leon R. Kass, former executive secretary of the Committee on the Life Sciences and Social Policy, National Research Council, National Academy of Sciences, Washington, D.C., considers some of the awesome possibilities that new biomedical techniques carry with them and asks us to consider the social and ethical implications of those possibilities. The likelihood that science, in the near future, will be able to manipulate and perhaps to create human life according to its own design, means that we must rededicate ourselves to seeking answers to the age-old philosophical questions of what the good human being and the good life are.

Recent advances in biology and medicine suggest that we may be rapidly acquiring the power to modify and control the capacities and activities of men by direct intervention and manipulation of their bodies and minds. Certain means are already in use or at hand, others await the solution of relatively minor technical problems, while yet others, those offering perhaps the most precise kind of control, depend upon further basic research. Biologists who have considered these matters disagree on the question of how much how soon, but all agree that the power for "human engineering," to borrow from the jargon, is coming and that it will probably have profound social consequences.

These developments have been viewed both with enthusiasm and with alarm; they are only just beginning to receive serious attention. Several biologists have undertaken to inform the public about the technical possibilities, present and future. Practitioners of social science "futurology" are attempting to predict and describe the likely social consequences of and public responses to the new technologies. Lawyers and legislators are exploring institutional innovations for assessing new technologies. All of these activities are based upon the hope that we can harness the new technology of man for the betterment of mankind.

Yet this commendable aspiration points to another set of questions, which are, in my view, sorely neglected—questions that inquire into the meaning of phrases such as the "betterment of mankind." A *full* understanding of the new technology of man requires an exploration of ends, values, standards. What ends will or should the new techniques serve? What values should guide society's adjustments? By what standards should the assessment agencies assess? Behind these questions lie others: what is a good man, what is a good life for man, what is a good community? This article is an attempt to provoke discussion of these neglected and important questions.

While these questions about ends and ultimate ends are never unimportant or irrelevant, they have rarely been more important or more relevant. That this is so can be seen once we recognize that we are dealing here with a group of technologies that are in a decisive respect unique: the object upon which they operate is man himself. The technologies of energy or food production, of communication, of manufacture, and of motion greatly alter the implements available to man and the conditions in which he uses them. In contrast, the biomedical technology works to change the user himself. To be sure, the printing press, the automobile, the television, and the jet airplane have greatly altered the conditions under which and the way in which men live: but men as biological beings have remained largely unchanged. They have been, and remain, able to accept or reject, to use and abuse these technologies; they choose, whether wisely or foolishly, the ends to which these technologies are means. Biomedical technology may make it possible to change the inherent capacity for choice itself. Indeed, both those who welcome and those who fear the advent of "human engineering" ground their hopes and fears in the same prospect: *that man can for the first time recreate himself.*

Engineering the engineer seems to differ in kind from engineering his engine. Some have argued, however, that biomedical engineering does not differ qualitatively from toilet training, education, and moral teachings—all of which are forms of so-called "social engineering," which has man as its object, and is used by one generation to mold the next. In reply, it must at least be said that the techniques which have hitherto been employed are feeble and inefficient when compared to those on the horizon. This quantitative difference rests in part on a qualitative difference in the means of intervention. The traditional influences operate by speech or by symbolic deeds. They pay tribute to man as the animal who lives by speech and who understands the meanings of actions. Also, their effects are, in general, reversible, or at least subject to attempts at reversal. Each person has greater or lesser power to accept or reject or abandon them. In contrast, biomedical engineering circumvents the human context of speech and meaning, bypasses choice, and goes directly to work to modify the human material itself. Moreover, the changes wrought may be irreversible.

In addition, there is an important practical reason for considering the biomedical technology apart from other technologies. The advances we shall examine are fruits of a large, humane project dedicated to the conquest of disease and the relief of human suffering. The biologist and physician, regardless of their private motives, are seen, with justification, to be the well-wishers and benefactors of mankind. Thus, in a time in which technological advance is more carefully scrutinized and increasingly criticized, biomedical developments are still viewed by most people as benefits largely without qualification. The price we pay for these developments is thus more likely to go unrecognized. For this reason, I shall consider only the dangers and costs of biomedical advance. As the benefits are well known, there is no need to dwell upon them here. My discussion is deliberately partial.

I begin with a survey of the pertinent technologies. Next, I will consider some of the basic ethical and social problems in the use of these technologies. Then, I will briefly raise some fundamental questions to which these problems point. Finally, I shall offer some very general reflections on what is to be done.

THE BIOMEDICAL TECHNOLOGIES

The biomedical technologies can be usefully organized into three groups, according to their major purpose: (i) control of death and life, (ii) control of human potentialities, and (iii) control of human achievement. The corresponding technologies are (i) medicine, especially the arts of prolonging life and of controlling reproduction, (ii) genetic engineering, and (iii) neurological and psychological manipulation. I shall briefly summarize each group of techniques.

1) Control of Death and Life.   Previous medical triumphs have greatly increased average life expectancy. Yet other developments, such as organ transplantation or replacement and research into aging, hold forth the promise of increasing not just the average, but also the maximum life expectancy. Indeed, medicine seems to be sharpening its tools to do battle with death itself, as if death were just one more disease.

More immediately and concretely, available techniques of prolonging life—respirators, cardiac pacemakers, artificial kidneys—are already in the lists against death. Ironically, the success of these devices in forestalling death has introduced confusion in determining that death has, in fact, occurred. The traditional signs of life—heartbeat and respiration—can now be maintained entirely by machines. Some physicians are now busily trying to devise so-called "new definitions of death," while others maintain that the technical advances show that death is not a concrete event at all, but rather a gradual process, like twilight, incapable of precise temporal localization.

The real challenge to death will come from research into aging and senescence, a field just entering puberty. Recent studies suggest that aging is a genetically controlled process, distinct from disease, but one that can be manipulated and altered by diet or drugs. Extrapolating from animal studies, some scientists have suggested that a decrease in the rate of aging might also be achieved simply by effecting a very small decrease in human body temperature. According to some estimates, by the year 2000 it may be technically possible to add from 20 to 40 useful years to the period of middle life.

Medicine's success in extending life is already a major cause of excessive population growth: death control points to birth control. Although we are already technically competent, new techniques for lowering fertility and chemical agents for inducing abortion will greatly enhance our powers over conception and gestation. Problems of definition have been raised here as well. The need to determine when individuals acquire enforceable legal rights gives society an interest in the definition of human life and of the time when it begins. These matters are too familiar to need elaboration.

Technologies to conquer infertility proceed alongside those to promote it. The first successful laboratory fertilization of human egg by human sperm was reported in 1969 (1). In 1970, British scientists learned how to grow human embryos in the laboratory up to at least the blastocyst stage [that is, to the age of 1 week (2)]. We may soon hear about the next stage, the successful reimplantation of such an embryo into a woman previously infertile because of oviduct disease. The development of an artificial placenta, now under investigation, will make possible full laboratory control of fertilization and gestation. In addition, sophisticated biochemical and cytological techniques of monitoring the "quality" of the fetus have been and are being developed and used. These developments not only give us more power over the generation of human life, but make it possible to manipulate and to modify the quality of the human material.

2) Control of Human Potentialities.   Genetic engineering, when fully developed, will wield two powers not shared by ordinary medical practice. Medicine treats existing individuals and seeks to correct deviations from a norm of health. Genetic engineering, in contrast, will be able to make changes that can be transmitted to succeeding generations and will be able to create new capacities, and hence to establish new norms of health and fitness.

Nevertheless, one of the major interests in genetic manipulation is strictly medical: to develop treatments for individuals with inherited diseases. Genetic disease is prevalent and increasing, thanks partly to medical advances that enable those affected to survive and perpetuate their mutant genes. The hope is that normal copies of the appropriate gene, obtained biologically or synthesized chemically, can be introduced into defective individuals to correct their deficiencies. This *therapeutic* use of genetic technology appears to be far in the future. Moreover, there is some doubt that it will ever be practical, since the same end could be more easily achieved by transplanting cells or organs that could compensate for the missing or defective gene product.

Far less remote are technologies that could serve *eugenic* ends. Their development has been endorsed by those concerned about a general deterioration of the human gene pool and by others who believe that even an undeteriorated human gene pool needs upgrading. Artificial insemination with selected donors, the eugenic proposal of Herman Muller (3), has been possible for several years because of the perfection of methods for long-term storage of human spermatozoa. The successful maturation of human oocytes in the laboratory and their subsequent fertilization now make it possible to select donors of ova as well. But a far more suitable technique for eugenic purposes will soon be upon us —namely, nuclear transplantation, or cloning. Bypassing the lottery of sexual recombination, nuclear transplantation permits the asexual reproduction or copying of an already developed individual. The nucleus of a mature but unfertilized egg is replaced by a nucleus obtained from a specialized cell of an adult organism or embryo (for example, a cell from the intestines or the skin). The egg with its transplanted nucleus develops as if it had been fertilized and, barring complications, will give rise to a normal adult organism. Since almost all the hereditary material (DNA) of a cell is contained within its nucleus, the renucleated egg and the individual into which it develops are genetically identical to the adult organism that was the source of the donor nucleus. Cloning could be used to produce sets of unlimited numbers of genetically identical individuals, each set derived from a single parent. Cloning has been successful in amphibians and is now being tried in mice; its extension to man merely requires the solution of certain technical problems.

Production of man-animal chimeras by the introduction of selected nonhuman material into developing human embryos is also expected. Fusion of human and nonhuman cells in tissue culture has already been achieved.

Other, less direct means for influencing the gene pool are already available, thanks to our increasing ability to identify and diagnose genetic diseases. Genetic counselors can now detect biochemically and cytologically a variety of severe genetic defects (for example, Mongolism, Tay-Sachs disease) while the fetus is still in utero. Since treatments are at present largely unavailable, diagnosis is often followed by abortion of the affected fetus. In the future, more sensitive tests will also permit the detection of heterozygote carriers, the unaffected individuals who carry but a single dose of a given deleterious gene. The eradication of a given genetic disease might then be attempted by aborting all such carriers. In fact, it was recently suggested that the fairly common disease cystic fibrosis could be completely eliminated over the next 40 years by screening all pregnancies and aborting the 17,000,000 unaffected fetuses that will carry a single gene for this disease. Such zealots need to be reminded of the consequences should each geneticist be allowed an equal assault on his favorite genetic disorder, given that each human being is a carrier for some four to eight such recessive, lethal genetic diseases.

3) Control of Human Achievement.   Although human achievement depends at least in part upon genetic endowment, heredity determines only the material upon which experience and education impose the form. The limits of many capacities and powers of an individual are indeed genetically determined, but the nurturing and perfection of these capacities depend upon other influences. Neurological and psychological manipulation hold forth the promise of controlling the development of human capacities, particularly those long considered most distinctively human: speech, thought, choice, emotion, memory, and imagination.

These techniques are now in a rather primitive state because we understand so little about the brain and mind. Nevertheless, we have already seen the use of electrical stimulation of the human brain to produce sensations of intense pleasure and to control rage, the use of brain surgery (for example, frontal lobotomy) for the relief of severe anxiety, and the use of aversive conditioning with electric shock to treat sexual perversion. Operant-conditioning techniques are widely used, apparently with success, in schools and mental hospitals. The use of so-called consciousness-expanding and hallucinogenic drugs is widespread, to say nothing of tranquilizers and stimulants. We are promised drugs to modify memory, intelligence, libido, and aggressiveness.

The following passages from a recent book by Yale neurophysiologist José Delgado—a book instructively entitled *Physical Control of the Mind: Toward a Psychocivilized Society*—should serve to make this discussion more concrete. In the early 1950's, it was discovered that, with electrodes placed in certain discrete regions of their brains, animals would repeatedly and indefatigably press levers to stimulate their own brains, with obvious resultant enjoyment. Even starving animals preferred stimulating these so-called pleasure centers to eating. Delgado comments on the electrical stimulation of a similar center in a human subject (*4*, p. 185).

> [T]he patient reported a pleasant tingling sensation in the left side of her body 'from my face down to the bottom of my legs.' She started giggling and making funny comments, stating that she enjoyed the sensation 'very much.' Repetition of these stimulations made the patient more communicative and flirtatious, and she ended by openly expressing her desire to marry the therapist.

And one further quotation from Delgado (*4*, p. 88).

> Leaving wires inside of a thinking brain may appear unpleasant or dangerous, but actually the many patients who have undergone this experience have not been concerned about the fact of being wired, nor have they felt any discomfort due to the presence of conductors in their heads. Some women have shown their feminine adaptability to circumstances by wearing attractive hats or wigs to conceal their electrical headgear, and many people have been able to enjoy a normal life as outpatients, returning to the clinic periodically for examination and stimulation. In a few cases in which contacts were located in pleasurable areas, patients have had the opportunity to stimulate their own brains by pressing the button of a portable instrument, and this procedure is reported to have therapeutic benefits.

It bears repeating that the sciences of neurophysiology and psychopharmacology are in their infancy. The techniques that are now available are crude, imprecise, weak, and unpredictable, compared to those that may flow from a more mature neurobiology.

BASIC ETHICAL AND SOCIAL PROBLEMS IN THE USE OF BIOMEDICAL TECHNOLOGY

After this cursory review of the powers now and soon to be at our disposal, I turn to the questions concerning the use of these powers. First, we must recognize that questions of use of science and technology are always moral and political questions, never simply technical ones. All private or public decisions to develop or to use biomedical technology— and decisions *not* to do so—inevitably contain judgments about value. This is true even if the values guiding those decisions are not articulated or made clear, as indeed they often are not. Secondly, the value judgments cannot be derived from biomedical science. This is true even if scientists themselves make the decisions.

These important points are often overlooked for at least three reasons:

1) They are obscured by those who like to speak of "the control of nature by science." It is men who control, not that abstraction "science." Science may provide the means, but men choose the ends; the choice of ends comes from beyond science.

2) Introduction of new technologies often appears to be the result of no decision whatsoever, or of the culmination of decisions too small or unconscious to be recognized as such. What can be done is done. However, someone is deciding on the basis of some notions of desirability, no matter how self-serving or altruistic.

3) Desires to gain or keep money and power no doubt influence much of what happens, but these desires can also be formulated as reasons and then discussed and debated.

Insofar as our society has tried to deliberate about questions of use, how has it done so? Pragmatists that we are, we prefer a utilitarian calculus: we weigh "benefits" against "risks," and we weigh them for both the individual and "society." We often ignore the fact that the very definitions of "a benefit" and "a risk" are themselves based upon judgments about value. In the biomedical areas just reviewed, the benefits are considered to be self-evident: prolongation of life, control of fertility and of population size, treatment and prevention of genetic disease, the reduction of anxiety and aggressiveness, and the enhancement of memory, intelligence, and pleasure. The assessment of risk is, in general, simply pragmatic—will the technique work effectively and reliably, how much will it cost, will it do detectable bodily harm, and who will complain if we proceed with development? As these questions are familiar and congenial, there is no need to belabor them.

The very pragmatism that makes us sensitive to considerations of economic cost often blinds us to the larger social costs exacted by biomedical advances. For one thing, we seem to be unaware that we may not be able to maximize all the benefits, that several of the goals we are promoting conflict with each other. On the one hand, we seek to control population growth by lowering fertility; on the other hand, we develop techniques to enable every infertile woman to bear a child. On the one hand, we try to extend the lives of individuals with genetic disease; on the other, we wish to eliminate deleterious genes from the human population. I am not urging that we resolve these conflicts in favor of one side or the other, but simply that we recognize that such conflicts exist. Once we do, we are more likely to appreciate that most "progress" is heavily paid for in terms not generally included in the simple utilitarian calculus.

To become sensitive to the larger costs of biomedical progress, we must attend to several serious ethical and social questions. I will briefly discuss three of them: (i) questions of distributive justice, (ii) questions of the use and abuse of power, and (iii) questions of self-degradation and dehumanization.

DISTRIBUTIVE JUSTICE

The introduction of any biomedical technology presents a new instance of an old problem—how to distribute scarce resources justly. We should assume that demand will usually exceed supply. Which people should receive a kidney transplant or an artificial heart? Who should get the benefits of genetic therapy or of brain stimulation? Is "first-come, first-served" the fairest principle? Or are certain people "more worthy," and if so, on what grounds?

It is unlikely that we will arrive at answers to these questions in the form of deliberate decisions. More likely, the problem of distribution will continue to be decided ad hoc and locally. If so, the consequence will probably be a sharp increase in the already far too great inequality of medical care. The extreme case will be longevity, which will probably be, at first, obtainable only at great expense. Who is likely to be able to buy it? Do conscience and prudence permit us to enlarge the gap between rich and poor, especially with respect to something as fundamental as life itself?

Questions of distributive justice also arise in the earlier discussions to acquire new knowledge and to develop new techniques. Personnel and facilities for medical research and treatment are scarce resources. Is the development of a new technology the best use of the limited resources, given current circumstances? How should we balance efforts aimed at prevention against those aimed at cure, or either of these against efforts to redesign the species? How should we balance the delivery of available levels of care against further basic research? More fundamentally, how should we balance efforts in biology and medicine against efforts to eliminate poverty, pollution, urban decay, discrimination, and poor education? This last question about distribution is perhaps the most profound. We should reflect upon the social consequences of seducing many of our brightest young people to spend their lives locating the biochemical defects in rare genetic diseases, while our more serious problems go begging. The current squeeze on money for research provides us with an opportunity to rethink and reorder our priorities.

Problems of distributive justice are frequently mentioned and discussed, but they are hard to resolve in a rational manner. We find them especially difficult because of the enormous range of conflicting values and interests that characterizes our pluralistic society. We cannot agree —unfortunately, we often do not even try to agree—on standards for just distribution. Rather, decisions tend to be made largely out of a clash of competing interests. Thus, regrettably, the question of how to distribute justly often gets reduced to who shall decide how to distribute. The question about justice has led us to the question about power.

USE AND ABUSE OF POWER

We have difficulty recognizing the problems of the exercise of power in the biomedical enterprise because of our delight with the wondrous fruits it has yielded. This is ironic because the notion of power is absolutely central to the modern conception of science. The ancients conceived of science as the *understanding* of nature, pursued for its own sake. We moderns view science as power, as *control* over nature; the conquest of nature "for the relief of man's estate" was the charge issued by Francis Bacon, one of the leading architects of the modern scientific project (5).

Another source of difficulty is our fondness for speaking of the abstraction "Man." I suspect that we prefer to speak figuratively about "Man's power over Nature" because it obscures an unpleasant reality about human affairs. It is in fact particular men who wield power, not Man. What we really mean by "Man's power over Nature" is a power exercised by some men over other men, with a knowledge of nature as their instrument.

While applicable to technology in general, these reflections are especially pertinent to the technologies of human engineering, with which men deliberately exercise power over future generations. An excellent discussion of this question is found in *The Abolition of Man*, by C. S. Lewis (6).

> It is, of course, a commonplace to complain that men have hitherto used badly, and against their fellows, the powers that science has given them. But that is not the point I am trying to make. I am not speaking of particular corruptions and abuses which an increase of moral virtue would cure: I am considering what the thing called "Man's power over Nature" must always and essentially be. . . .
>
> In reality, of course, if any one age really attains, by eugenics and scientific education, the power to make its descendants what it pleases, all men who live after it are the patients of that power. They are weaker, not stronger: for though we may have put wonderful machines in their hands, we have pre-ordained how they are to use them. . . . The real picture is that of one dominant age . . . which resists all previous ages most successfully and domi-

nates all subsequent ages most irresistibly, and thus is the real master of the human species. But even within this master generation (itself an infinitesimal minority of the species) the power will be exercised by a minority smaller still. Man's conquest of Nature, if the dreams of some scientific planners are realized, means the rule of a few hundreds of men over billions upon billions of men. There neither is nor can be any simple increase of power on Man's side. Each new power won *by* man is a power *over* man as well. Each advance leaves him weaker as well as stronger. In every victory, besides being the general who triumphs, he is also the prisoner who follows the triumphal car.

Please note that I am not yet speaking about the problem of the misuse or abuse of power. The point is rather that the power which grows is unavoidably the power of only some men, and that the number of powerful men decreases as power increases.

Specific problems of abuse and misuse of specific powers must now, however, be overlooked. Some have voiced the fear that the technologies of genetic engineering and behavior control, though developed for good purposes, will be put to evil uses. These fears are perhaps somewhat exaggerated, if only because biomedical technologies would add very little to our highly developed arsenal for mischief, destruction, and stultification. Nevertheless, any proposal for large-scale human engineering should make us wary. Consider a program of positive eugenics based upon the widespread practice of asexual reproduction. Who shall decide what constitutes a superior individual worthy of replication? Who shall decide which individuals may or must reproduce, and by which method? These are questions easily answered only for a tyrannical regime.

Concern about the use of power is equally necessary in the selection of means for desirable or agreed-upon ends. Consider the desired end of limiting population growth. An effective program of fertility control is likely to be coercive. Who should decide the choice of means? Will the program penalize "conscientious objectors"?

Serious problems arise simply from obtaining and disseminating information, as in the mass screening programs now being proposed for detection of genetic disease. For what kinds of disorders is compulsory screening justified? Who shall have access to the data obtained, and for what purposes? To whom does information about a person's genotype belong? In ordinary medical practice, the patient's privacy is protected by the doctor's adherence to the principle of confidentiality. What will protect his privacy under conditions of mass screening?

More than privacy is at stake if screening is undertaken to detect psychological or behavioral abnormalities. A recent proposal, tendered and supported high in government, called for the psychological testing of all 6-year-olds to detect future criminals and misfits. The proposal was rejected; current tests lack the requisite predictive powers. But will such a proposal be rejected if reliable tests become available? What if certain genetic disorders, diagnosable in childhood, can be shown to correlate with subsequent antisocial behavior? For what degree of correlation and for what kinds of behavior can mandatory screening be justified? What use should be made of the data? Might not the dissemination of the information itself undermine the individual's chance for a worthy life and contribute to his so-called antisocial tendencies?

Consider the seemingly harmless effort to redefine clinical death. If the need for organs for transplantation is the stimulus for redefining death, might not this concern influence the definition at the expense of the dying? One physician, in fact, refers in writing to the revised criteria for declaring a patient dead as a "new definition of heart donor eligibility" (7, p. 526).

Problems of abuse of power arise even in the acquisition of basic knowledge. The securing of a voluntary and informed consent is an abiding problem in the use of human subjects in experimentation. Gross coercion and deception are now rarely a problem; the pressures are generally subtle, often related to an intrinsic power imbalance in favor of the experimentalist.

A special problem arises in experiments on or manipulations of the unborn. Here it is impossible to obtain the consent of the human subject. If the purpose of the intervention is therapeutic—to correct a known genetic abnormality, for example—consent can reasonably be implied. But can anyone ethically consent to nontherapeutic interventions in which parents or scientists work their wills or their eugenic visions on the child-to-be? Would not such manipulation represent in itself an abuse of power, independent of consequences?

There are many clinical situations which already permit, if not invite, the manipulative or arbitrary use of powers provided by biomedical technology: obtaining organs for transplantation, refusing to let a person die with dignity, giving genetic counselling to a frightened couple, recommending eugenic sterilization for a mental retardate, ordering electric shock for a homosexual. In each situation, there is an opportunity to violate the will of the patient or subject. Such opportunities have generally existed in medical practice, but the dangers are becoming increasingly serious. With the growing complexity of the technologies, the technician gains in authority, since he alone can understand what he is doing. The patient's lack of knowledge makes him deferential and often inhibits him from speaking up when he feels threatened. Physicians *are* sometimes troubled by their increasing power, yet they feel they cannot avoid its exercise. "Reluctantly," one commented to me, "we shall have to play God." With what guidance and to what ends I shall consider later. For the moment, I merely ask: 'By whose authority?"

While these questions about power are pertinent and important, they are in one sense misleading. They imply an inherent conflict of purpose between physician and patient, between scientist and citizen. The discussion conjures up images of master and slave, of oppressor and oppressed. Yet it must be remembered that conflict of purpose is largely absent, especially with regard to general goals. To be sure, the purposes of medical scientists are not always the same as those of the subjects experimented on. Nevertheless, basic sponsors and partisans of biomedical technology are precisely those upon whom the technology will operate. The will of the scientist and physician is happily married to (rather, is the offspring of) the desire of all of us for better health, longer life, and peace of mind.

Most future biomedical technologies will probably be welcomed, as have those of the past. Their use will require little or no coercion. Some developments, such as pills to improve memory, control mood, or induce pleasure, are likely to need no promotion. Thus, even if we should escape from the dangers of coercive manipulation, we shall still face large problems posed by the voluntary use of biomedical technology, problems to which I now turn.

VOLUNTARY SELF-DEGRADATION AND DEHUMANIZATION

Modern opinion is sensitive to problems of restriction of freedom and abuse of power. Indeed, many hold that a man can be injured only by violating his will. But this view is much too narrow. It fails to recognize the great dangers we shall face in the use of biomedical technology, dangers that stem from an excess of freedom, from the uninhibited exercises of will. In my view, our greatest problem will increasingly be one of voluntary self-degradation, or willing dehumanization.

Certain desired and perfected medical technologies have already had some dehumanizing consequences. Improved methods of resuscitation have made possible heroic efforts to "save" the severely ill and injured. Yet these efforts are sometimes only partly successful; they may succeed in salvaging individuals with severe brain damage, capable of only a less-than-human, vegetating existence. Such patients, increasingly found in the intensive care units of university hospitals, have been denied a death with dignity. Families are forced to suffer seeing their loved ones so reduced, and are made to bear the burdens of a protracted death watch.

Even the ordinary methods of treating disease and prolonging life have impoverished the context in which men die. Fewer and fewer people die in the familiar surroundings of home or in the company of family and friends. At that time of life when there is perhaps the greatest need for human warmth and comfort, the dying patient is kept company by cardiac pacemakers and defibrillators, respirators, aspirators, oxygenators, catheters, and his intravenous drip.

But the loneliness is not confined to the dying patient in the hospital bed. Consider the increasing number of old people who are still alive, thanks to medical progress. As a group, the elderly are the most alienated members of our society. Not yet ready for the world of the dead, not deemed fit for the world of the living, they are shunted aside. More and more of them spend the extra years medicine has given them in "homes for senior citizens," in chronic hospitals, in nursing homes—waiting for the end. We have learned how to increase their years, but we have not learned how to help them enjoy their days. And yet, we bravely and relentlessly push back the frontiers against death.

Paradoxically, even the young and vigorous may be suffering because of medicine's success in removing death from their personal experience. Those born since penicillin represent the first generation ever to grow up without the experience or fear of probable unexpected death at an early age. They look around and see that virtually all of their friends are alive. A thoughtful physician, Eric Cassell, has remarked on this in "Death and the physician" (*8,* p. 76):

> [W]hile the gift of time must surely be marked as a great blessing, the *perception* of time, as stretching out endlessly before us, is somewhat threatening. Many of us function best under deadlines, and tend to procrastinate when time limits are not set. . . . Thus, this unquestioned boon, the extension of life, and the removal of the threat of premature death, carries with it an unexpected anxiety: the anxiety of an unlimited future
>
> In the young, the sense of limitless time has apparently imparted not a feeling of limitless opportunity, but increased stress and anxiety, in addition to the anxiety which results from other modern freedoms: personal mobility, a wide range of occupational choice, and independence from the limitations of class and familial patterns of work. . . . A certain aimlessness (often ringed around with great social consciousness) characterizes discussions about their own aspirations. The future is endless, and their inner demands seem minimal. Although it may appear uncharitable to say so, they seem to be acting in a way best described as "childish"—particularly in their lack of a time sense. They behave as though there were no tomorrow, or as though the time limits imposed by the biological facts of life had become so vague for them as to be nonexistent.

Consider next the coming power over reproduction and genotype. We endorse the project that will enable us to control numbers and to treat individuals with genetic disease. But our desires outrun these defensible goals. Many would welcome the chance to become parents without the inconvenience of pregnancy; others would wish to know in advance the characteristics of their offspring (sex, height, eye color, intelligence); still others would wish to design these characteristics to suit their tastes. Some scientists have called for the use of the new technologies to assure the "quality" of all new babies (*8*). As one obstetrician put it: "The business of obstetrics is to produce *optimum* babies." But the price to be paid for the "optimum baby" is the transfer of procreation from the home to the laboratory and its coincident transformation into manufacture. Increasing control over the product is purchased by the increasing depersonalization of the process. The complete depersonalization of procreation (possible with the development of an artificial placenta) shall be, in itself, seriously dehumanizing, no matter how optimum the product. It should not be forgotten that human procreation not only issues new human beings, but is itself a human activity.

Procreation is not simply an activity of the rational will. It is a more complete human activity precisely because it engages us bodily and spiritually, as well as rationally. Is there perhaps some wisdom in that mystery of nature which joins the pleasure of sex, the communication of love, and the desire for children in the very activity by which we continue the chain of human existence? Is not biological parenthood a build-in "mechanism," selected because it fosters and supports in parents an adequate concern for and commitment to their children? Would not the laboratory production of human beings no longer be *human* procreation? Could it keep human parenthood human?

The dehumanizing consequences of programmed reproduction extend beyond the mere acts and processes of life-giving. Transfer of procreation to the laboratory will no doubt weaken what is presently for many people the best remaining justification and support for the existence of marriage and the family. Sex is now comfortably at home outside of marriage; child-rearing is progressively being given over to the state, the schools, the mass media, and the child-care centers. Some have argued that the family, long the nursery of humanity, has outlived its usefulness. To be sure, laboratory and governmental alternatives might be designed for procreation and child-rearing, but at what cost?

This is not the place to conduct a full evaluation of the biological family. Nevertheless, some of its important virtues are, nowadays, too often overlooked. The family is rapidly becoming the only institution in an increasingly impersonal world where each person is loved not for what he does or makes, but simply because he is. The family is also the institution where most of us, both as children and as parents, acquire a sense of continuity with the past and a sense of commitment to the future. Without the family, we would have little incentive to take an interest in anything after our own deaths. These observations suggest that the elimination of the family would weaken ties to past and future, and would throw us, even more than we are now, to the mercy of an impersonal, lonely present.

Neurobiology and psychobiology probe most directly into the distinctively human. The technological fruit of these sciences is likely to be both more tempting than Eve's apple and more "catastrophic" in its result. One need only consider contemporary drug use to see what people are willing to risk or sacrifice for novel experiences, heightened perceptions, or just "kicks." The possibility of drug-induced, instant, and effortless gratification will be welcomed. Recall the possibilities of voluntary self-stimulation of the brain to reduce anxiety, to heighten pleasure, or to create visual and auditory sensations unavailable through the peripheral sense organs. Once these techniques are perfected and safe, is there much doubt that they will be desired, demanded, and used?

What ends will these techniques serve? Most likely, only the most elemental, those most tied to the bodily pleasures. What will happen to thought, to love, to friendship, to art, to judgment, to public-spiritedness in a society with a perfected technology of pleasure? What kinds of creatures will we become if we obtain our pleasure by drug or electrical stimulation without the usual kind of human efforts and frustrations? What kind of society will we have?

We need only consult Aldous Huxley's prophetic novel *Brave New World* for a likely answer to these questions. There we encounter a society dedicated to homogeneity and stability, administered by means of instant gratifications and peopled by creatures of human shape but of stunted humanity. They consume, fornicate, take "soma," and operate the machinery that makes it all possible. They do not read, write, think, love, or govern themselves. Creativity and curiosity, reason and passion, exist only in a rudimentary and mutilated form. In short, they are not men at all.

True, our techniques, like theirs, may in fact enable us to treat schizophrenia, to alleviate anxiety, to curb aggressiveness. We, like they, may indeed be able to save mankind from itself, but probably only at the cost of its humanness. In the end, the price of relieving man's estate might well be the abolition of man (*11*).

There are, of course, many other routes leading to the abolition of man. There are many other and better known causes of dehumanization. Disease, starvation, mental retardation, slavery, and brutality—to name just a few—have long prevented many, if not most, people from living a fully human life. We should work to reduce and eventually to eliminate these evils. But the existence of these evils should not prevent us from appreciating that the use of the technology of man, uninformed by wisdom concerning proper human ends, and untempered by an appropriate humility and awe, can unwittingly render us all irreversibly less than human. For, unlike the man reduced by disease or slavery, the people dehumanized à la *Brave New World* are not miserable, do not know that they are dehumanized, and, what is worse, would not care if they knew. They are, indeed, happy slaves, with a slavish happiness.

SOME FUNDAMENTAL QUESTIONS

The practical problems of distributing scarce resources, of curbing the abuses of power, and of preventing voluntary dehumanization point beyond themselves to some large, enduring, and most difficult questions: the nature of justice and the good community, the nature of man and the good for man. My appreciation of the profundity of these questions and my own ignorance before them makes me hesitant to say any more about them. Nevertheless, previous failures to find a shortcut around them have led me to believe that these questions must be faced if we are to have any hope of understanding where biology is taking us. Therefore, I shall try to show in outline how I think some of the larger questions arise from my discussion of dehumanization and self-degradation.

My remarks on dehumanization can hardly fail to arouse argument. It might be said, correctly, that to speak about dehumanization presupposes a concept of "the distinctively human." It might also be said, correctly, that to speak about wisdom concerning proper human ends presupposes that such ends do in fact exist and that they may be more or less accessible to human understanding, or at least to rational inquiry. It is true that neither presupposition is at home in modern thought.

The notion of the "distinctively human" has been seriously challenged by modern scientists. Darwinists hold that man is, at least in origin, tied to the subhuman; his seeming distinctiveness is an illusion or, at most, not very important. Biochemists and molecular biologists extend the challenge by blurring the distinction between the living and the nonliving. The laws of physics and chemistry are found to be valid and are held to be sufficient for explaining biological systems. Man is a collection of molecules, an accident on the stage of evolution, endowed by chance with the power to change himself, but only along determined lines.

Psychoanalysts have also debunked the "distinctly human." The essence of man is seen to be located in those drives he shares with other animals—pursuit of pleasure and avoidance of pain. The so-called "higher functions" are understood to be servants of the more elementary, the more base. Any distinctiveness or "dignity" that man has consists of his superior capacity for gratifying his animal needs.

The idea of "human good" fares no better. In the social sciences, historicists and existentialists have helped drive this question underground. The former hold all notions of human good to be culturally and historically bound, and hence mutable. The latter hold that values are subjective: each man makes his own, and ethics becomes simply the cataloging of personal tastes.

Such appear to be the prevailing opinions. Yet there is nothing novel about reductionism, hedonism, and relativism; these are doctrines with which Socrates contended. What is new is that these doctrines seem to be vindicated by scientific advance. Not only do the scientific notions of nature and of man flower into verifiable predictions, but they yield marvelous fruit. The technological triumphs are held to validate their scientific foundations. Here, perhaps, is the most pernicious result of technological progress—more dehumanizing than any actual manipulation or technique, present or future. We are witnessing the erosion, perhaps the final erosion, of the idea of man as something splendid or divine, and its replacement with a view that sees man, no less than nature, as simply more raw material for manipulation and homogenization. Hence, our peculiar moral crisis. We are in turbulent seas without a landmark precisely because we adhere more and more to a view of nature and of man which both gives us enormous power and, at the same time, denies all possibility of standards to guide its use. Though well-equipped, we know not who we are nor where we are going. We are left to the accidents of our hasty, biased, and ephemeral judgments.

Let us not fail to note a painful irony: our conquest of nature has made us the slaves of blind chance. We triumph over nature's unpredictabilities only to subject ourselves to the still greater unpredictability of our capricious wills and our fickle opinions. That we have a method is no proof against our madness. Thus, engineering the engineer as well as the engine, we race our train we know not where.

While the disastrous consequences of ethical nihilism are insufficient to refute it, they invite and make urgent a reinvestigation of the ancient and enduring questions of what is a proper life for a human being, what is a good community, and how are they achieved. We must not be deterred from these questions simply because the best minds in human history have failed to settle them. Should we not rather be encouraged by the fact that they considered them to be the most important questions?

As I have hinted before, our ethical dilemma is caused by the victory of modern natural science with its nonteleological view of man. We ought therefore to reexamine with great care the modern notions of nature and of man, which undermine those earlier notions that provide a basis for ethics. If we consult our common experience, we are likely to discover some grounds for believing that the questions about man and human good are far from closed. Our common experience suggests many difficulties for the modern "scientific view of man." For example, this view fails to account for the concern for justice and freedom that appears to be characteristic of all human societies. It also fails to account for or to explain the fact that men have speech and not merely voice, that men can choose and act and not merely move or react. It fails to explain why men engage in moral discourse, or, for that matter, why they speak at all. Finally, the "scientific view of man" cannot account for scientific inquiry itself, for why men seek to know. Might there not be something the matter with a knowledge of man that does not explain or take account of his most distinctive activities, aspirations, and concerns?

Having gone this far, let me offer one suggestion as to where the difficulty might lie: in the modern understanding of knowledge. Since Bacon, as I have mentioned earlier, technology has increasingly come to be the basic justification for scientific inquiry. The end is power, not knowledge for its own sake. But power is not only the end. It is also an important *validation* of knowledge. One definitely knows that one knows only if one can make. Synthesis is held to be the ultimate proof of understanding. A more radical formulation holds that one knows only what one makes: knowing *equals* making.

Yet therein lies a difficulty. If truth be the power to change or to make the object studied, then of what do we have knowledge? If there are no fixed realities, but only material upon which we may work our wills, will not "science" be merely the "knowledge" of the transient and the manipulatable? We might indeed have knowledge of the laws by which things change and the rules for their manipulation, but no knowledge of the things themselves. Can such a view of "science" yield any knowledge about the nature of man, or indeed, about the nature of anything? Our questions appear to lead back to the most basic of questions: What does it mean to know? What is it that is knowable?

We have seen that the practical problems point toward and make urgent certain enduring, fundamental questions. Yet while pursuing these questions, we cannot afford to neglect the practical problems as such. Let us not forget Delgado and the "psychocivilized society." The philosophical inquiry could be rendered moot by our blind, confident efforts to dissect and redesign ourselves. While awaiting a reconstruction of theory, we must act as best we can.

WHAT IS TO BE DONE?

First, we sorely need to recover some humility in the face of our awesome powers. The arguments I have presented should make apparent the folly of arrogance, of the presumption that we are wise enough to remake ourselves. Because we lack wisdom, caution is our urgent need. Or to put it another way, in the absence of that "ultimate wisdom," we can be wise enough to know that we are not wise enough. When we lack sufficient wisdom to do, wisdom consists in not doing. Caution, restraint, delay, abstention are what this second-best (and, perhaps, only) wisdom dictates with respect to the technology for human engineering.

If we can recognize that biomedical advances carry significant social costs we may be willing to adopt a less permissive, more critical stance toward new developments. We need to reexamine our prejudice not only that all biomedical innovation is progress, but also that it is inevitable. Precedent certainly favors the view that what can be done will be done, but is this necessarily so? Ought we not to be suspicious when technologists speak of coming developments as automatic, not subject to human control? Is there not something contradictory in the notion that we have the power to control all the untoward consequences of a technology but lack the power to determine whether it should be developed in the first place?

What will be the likely consequences of the perpetuation of our permissive and fatalistic attitude toward human engineering? How will the large decisions be made? Technocratically and self-servingly, if our experience with previous technologies is any guide. Under conditions of laissez-faire, most technologists will pursue techniques, and most private industries will pursue profits. We are fortunate that, apart from the drug manufacturers, there are at present in the biomedical area few large industries that influence public policy. Once these appear, the voice of "the public interest" will have to shout very loudly to be heard above their whisperings in the halls of Congress. These reflections point to the need for institutional controls.

Scientists understandably balk at the notion of the regulation of science and technology. Censorship is ugly and often based upon ignorant fear; bureaucratic regulation is often stupid and inefficient. Yet there is something disingenuous about a scientist who professes concern about the social consequences of science, but who responds to every suggestion of regulation with one or both of the following: "No restrictions on scientific research," and "Technological progress should not be curtailed." Surely, to suggest that *certain* technologies ought to be regulated or forestalled is not to call for the halt of *all* technological progress (and says nothing at all about basic research). Each development should be considered on its own merits. Although the dangers of regulation cannot be dismissed, who, for example, would still object to efforts to obtain an effective, complete, global prohibition on the development, testing, and use of biological and nuclear weapons?

The proponents of laissez-faire ignore two fundamental points. They ignore the fact that not to regulate is as much a policy decision as the opposite, and that it merely postpones the time of regulation. Controls will eventually be called for—as they are now being demanded to end environmental pollution. If attempts are not made early to detect and diminish the social costs of biomedical advances by intelligent institutional regulation, the society is likely to react later with more sweeping, immoderate, and throttling controls.

The proponents of laissez-faire also ignore the fact that much of technology is already regulated. The federal government is already deep in research and development (for example, space, electronics, and weapons) and is the principal sponsor of biomedical research. One may well question the wisdom of the direction given, but one would be wrong in arguing that technology cannot survive social control. Clearly, the question is not control versus no control, but rather what kind of control, when, by whom, and for what purpose.

Means for achieving international regulation and control need to be devised. Biomedical technology can be no nation's monopoly. The need for international agreements and supervision can readily be understood if we consider the likely American response to the successful asexual reproduction of 10,000 Mao Tse-tungs.

To repeat, the basic short-term need is caution. Practically, this means that we should shift the burden of proof to the *proponents* of a new biomedical technology. Concepts of "risk" and "cost" need to be broadened to include some of the social and ethical consequences discussed earlier. The probable or possible harmful effects of the widespread use of a new technique should be anticipated and introduced as "costs" to be weighed in deciding about the *first* use. The regulatory institutions should be encouraged to exercise restraint and to formulate the grounds for saying "no." We must all get used to the idea that biomedical technology makes possible many things we should never do.

But caution is not enough. Nor are clever institutional arrangements. Institutions can be little better than the people who make them work. However worthy our intentions, we are deficient in understanding. In the *long* run, our hope can only lie in education: in a public educated about the meanings and limits of science and enlightened in its use of technology; in scientists better educated to understand the relationships between science and technology on the one hand, and ethics and politics on the other; in human beings who are as wise in the latter as they are clever in the former.

REFERENCES AND NOTES

1. R. G. Edwards, B. D. Bavister, P. C. Steptoe, *Nature* **221**, 632 (1969).
2. R. G. Edwards, P. C. Steptoe, J. M. Purdy, *ibid.* **227**, 1307 (1970).
3. H. J. Muller, *Science* **134**, 643 (1961).
4. J. M. R. Delgado, *Physical Control of the Mind: Toward a Psychocivilized Society* (Harper & Row, New York, 1969).
5. F. Bacon, *The Advancement of Learning. Book I,* H. G. Dick, Ed. (Random House, New York, 1955), p. 193.
6. C. S. Lewis, *The Abolition of Man* (Macmillan, New York, 1965), pp 69–71.
7. D. D. Rutstein, *Daedalus* (Spring 1960), p. 523.
8. E. J. Cassell, *Commentary,* (June 1969), p. 76.
9. B. Glass, *Science* **171**, 23 (1971).
10. It is, of course, a long-debated question as to whether the fall of Adam and Eve ought to be considered "catastrophic," or more precisely, whether the Hebrew tradition considered it so. I do not mean here to be taking sides in this quarrel by my use of the term "catistrophic," and, in fact, tend to line up on the negative side of the questions, as put above. Curiously, as Aldous Huxley's *Brave New World* [(New York: Harper & Row, 1969)] suggests, the implicit goal of the biomedical technology could well be said to be the reversal of the Fall and a return of man to the hedonic and immortal existence of the Garden of Eden. Yet I can point to at least two problems. First, the new Garden of Eden will probably have no gardens; the received, splendid world of nature will be buried beneath asphalt, concrete, and other human fabrications, a transformation that is already far along. (Recall that in *Brave New World* elaborate consumption-oriented, mechanical amusement parks—featuring, for example, centrifugal bumble-puppy—had supplanted wilderness and even ordinary gardens.) Second, the new inhabitant of the new "Garden" will have to be a creature for whom we have no precedent, a creature as difficult to imagine as to bring into existence. He will have to be simultaneously an innocent like Adam and a technological wizard who keeps the "Garden" running. (I am indebted to Dean Robert Goldwin, St. John's College, for this last insight.)
11. Some scientists naively believe that an engineered increase in human intelligence will steer us in the right direction. Surely we have learned by now that intelligence, whatever it is and however measured, is not synonymous with wisdom and that, if harnessed to the wrong ends, it can cleverly perpetrate great folly and evil. Given the activities in which many, if not most, of our best minds are now engaged, we should not simply rejoice in the prospect of enhancing IQ. On what would this increased intelligence operate? At best, the programming of further increases in IQ. It would design and operate techniques for prolonging life, for engineering reproduction, for delivering gratifications. With no gain in wisdom, our gain in intelligence can only enhance the rate of our dehumanization.

12. The philosopher Hans Jonas has made the identical point: "Thus the slow-working accidents of nature, which by the very patience of their small incre-ments, large numbers, and gradual decisions, may well cease to be 'accident' in outcome, are to be replaced by the fast-working accidents of man's hasty and biased decisions, not exposed to the long test of the ages. His uncertain ideas are to set the goals of generations, with a certainty borrowed from the presumptive certainty of the means. The latter presumption is doubtful enough, but this doubtfulness becomes secondary to the prime question that arises when man indeed undertakes to 'make himself': in what image of his own devising shall he do so, even granted that he can be sure of the means? In fact, of course, he can be sure of neither, not of the end, nor of the means, once he enters the realm where he plays with the roots of life. Of one thing only can he be sure: of his power to move the foundations and to cause incalculable and irreversible consequences. Never was so much power coupled with so little guidance for its use." [*J. Cent. Conf. Amer. Rabbis* (January 1968). p. 27.] These remarks demonstrate that, contrary to popu-lar belief, we are not even on the right road toward a rational understanding of and rational control over human nature and human life. It is indeed the height of irrationality triumphantly to pursue rationalized techique, while at the same time insisting that questions of ends, values, and purposes lie beyond rational discourse.

13. It is encouraging to note that these questions are seriously being raised in other quarters—for example, by persons concerned with the decay of cities or the pollution of nature. There is a growing dissatisfaction with ethical nihilism. In fact, its tenets are unwittingly abandoned, by even its staunchest adherents, in any discussion of "what to do." For example, in the biomedical area, everyone, including the most unreconstructed and technocratic reduc-tionist, finds himself speaking about the use of powers for "human better-ment." He has wandered unawares onto ethical ground. One cannot speak of "human betterment" without considering what is meant by *the human* and by the related notion of *the good for man.* These questions can be avoided only by asserting that practical matters reduce to tastes and power, and by confessing that the use of the phrase "human betterment" is a deceptiion to cloak one's own will to power. In other words, these questions can be avoided only by ceasing to discuss.

14. Consider, for example, the widespread acceptance, in the legal systems of very different societies and cultures, of the principle and the practice of third-party adjudication of disputes. And consider why, although many soci-eties have practiced slavery, no slave-holder has preferred his own enslave-ment to his own freedom. It would seem that some notions of justice and freedom, as well as right and truthfulness, are constitutive for any society, and that a concern for these values may be a fundamental characteristic of "human nature."

15. Scientists may, of course, continue to believe in righteousness or justice or truth, but these beliefs are not grounded in their "scientific knowledge" of man. They rest instead upon the receding wisdom of an earlier age.

16. This belief, silently shared by many contemporary biologists, has recently been given the following clear expression: "One of the acid tests of under-standing an object is the ability to put it together from its component parts. Ultimately, molecular biologists will attempt to subject their understanding of all structure and function to this sort of test by trying to synthesize a cell.

It is of some interest to see how close we are to this goal." [P. Handler, ed., *Biology and the Future of Man* (New York: Oxford Univ. Press, 1970), p. 55.]

17. When an earlier version of this article was presented publicly, it was criticized by one questioner as being "antiscientific." He suggested that my remarks "were the kind that gave science a bad name." He went on to argue that, far from being the enemy of morality, the pursuit of truth was itself a highly moral activity, perhaps the highest. The relation of science and morals is a long and difficult question with an illustrious history, and it deserves a more extensive discussion than space permits. However, because some readers may share the questioner's response, I offer a brief reply. First, on the matter of reputation, we should recall that the pursuit of truth may be in tension with keeping a good name (witness Oedipus, Socrates, Galileo, Spinoza, Solzhenitsyn). For most of human history, the pursuit of truth (including "science") was not a reputable activity among the many, and was, in fact, highly suspect. Even today, it is doubtful whether more than a few appreciate knowledge as an end in itself. Science has acquired a "good name" in recent times largely because of its technological fruit; it is therefore to be expected that a disenchantment with technology will reflect badly upon science. Second, my own attack has not been directed against science, but against the use of *some* technologies and, even more, against the unexamined belief—indeed, I would say, superstition—that all biomedical technology is an unmixed blessing. I share the questioner's belief that the pursuit of truth is a highly moral activity. In fact, I am inviting him and others to join in a pursuit of the truth about whether all these new technologies are really good for us. This is a question that merits and is susceptible of serious intellectual inquiry. Finally, we must ask whether what we call "science" has a monopoly on the pursuit of truth. What is "truth"? What is knowable, and what does it mean to know? Surely, these are also questions that can be examined. Unless we do so, we shall remain ignorant about what "science" is and about what it discovers. Yet "science"—that is, modern natural science—cannot begin to answer them; they are philosophical questions, the very ones I am trying to raise at this point in the text.